lonely p

D0174495

Discover
China

Contents

Throughout this book, we use these icons to highlight special recommendations:

 The Best...
Lists for everything from bars to wildlife – to make sure you don't miss out

 Don't Miss
A must-see – don't go home until you've been there

Local Knowledge Local experts reveal their top picks and secret highlights

 Detour
Special places a little off the beaten track

If you like...
Lesser-known alternatives to world-famous attractions

These icons help you quickly identify reviews in the text and on the map:

 Sights

 Eating

 Drinking

 Sleeping

 Information

This edition written and researched by

Damian Harper

Piera Chen, Chung Wah Chow, David Eimer, Daisy Harper, Robert Kelly, Michael Kohn, Shawn Low, Bradley Mayhew, Daniel McCrohan, Christopher Pitts

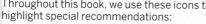

Běijīng & the Great Wall **p53**

Xī'ān & the North **p127**

Shànghǎi & the Yangzi Region **p185**

Hong Kong & the South **p255**

Běijīng & the Great Wall

Highlights 54

o Běijīng's Hútòng
o Explore the Forbidden City
o Wander Around the Summer Palace
o Gallivanting Along the Great Wall
o Marvel at the Temple of Heaven
o Gawp at the National Centre for the Performing Arts

Xī'ān & the North

Highlights 128

o Potter Around Píngyáo
o Marvel at the Terracotta Warriors
o Wonder at the Yúngāng Caves
o Explore Qūfù's Confucius Temple
o Watch the Sunrise from Tài Shān
o Temple Trekking in Wǔtái Shān

Shànghǎi & the Yangzi Region

Highlights 186

o The Bund
o Exploring Zhūjiājiǎo
o Savouring the French Concession
o Wandering Around West Lake
o Hiking up Huángshān
o Drifting through the Three Gorges

Contents

Plan Your Trip

This Is China	6
China Map	8
China's Top 25 Experiences	10
China's Top Itineraries	32
China Month by Month	42
Get Inspired	47
Need to Know	48

On the Road

● ● ●

Běijīng & the Great Wall 51

Highlights	54
Best...	58
Itineraries	60
Běijīng	62
798 Art District	*90*
Around Beijing	**109**
Ming Tombs	109
Chuāndǐxià (Cuàndǐxià)	*110*
Marco Polo Bridge	111
The Great Wall	**111**
Bādálǐng	113
Mùtiányù	114
Sīmǎtái	114
Jīnshānlǐng	115
Jiànkòu	116
Huánghuā	116
Chéngdé	119

● ● ●

Xī'ān & the North 125

Highlights	128
Best...	132
Itineraries	134
Xī'ān	**136**
Around Xī'ān	143
The North	**148**
Huà Shān	148

● Hong Kong & the South

Highlights	256

- Central, Hong Kong
- Ruins of the Church of St Paul
- Amble Around Gǔlàng Yǔ
- Explore Yángshuò
- Discover Fènghuáng
- Explore the Hakka Tǔlóu

Contents

On the Road

Luòyáng 150
Fǎmén Temple 150
Around Luòyáng 153
Píngyáo 155
Around Píngyáo 158
Wǔtái Shān 159
Around Wǔtái Shān ... 162
Dàtóng 163
Around Dàtóng 165
Tài'ān 166
Tài Shān 169
Qūfù 171
Tiānzhú Peak Route 171
Qīngdǎo 176

Shànghǎi & the Yangzi Region .. 183

Highlights 186
Best... 190
Itineraries 192
Shànghǎi 194
Around Shànghǎi 220
Yangzi Region 221
Sūzhōu 221
Around Sūzhōu 226
Hángzhōu 229
Around Hángzhōu 235
Túnxī 240
Huángshān 242
Wùyuán 247
Cruising the Yangzi ... 247
*Chóngqìng &
Yíchāng* 251

Hong Kong & the South 253

Highlights 256
Best... 260
Itineraries 262
Hong Kong 264
*Lamma & Cheung
Chau* 284
Macau 291
The South 304
Guǎngzhōu 304
Guìlín 305
Dragon's Backbone
Rice Terraces 308
Kāipíng 309
Yángshuò 311
Moon Hill 313
Around Yángshuò 314
*Great Guǎngxī Bike
Ride* 314
Déhāng 315
Fènghuáng 316
Xiàmén 320
Gǔlàng Yǔ 322
Hakka Tǔlóu 324

Best of the Rest 325

Yúnnán 326
Dàlǐ 326
Lìjiāng 328
Yùlóng Xuěshān 330
Tiger Leaping Gorge . 330
Tiger Leaping Gorge
to Báishuǐtái 333
Sìchuān 334
Giant Panda Breeding
Research Base 334
Éméi Shān 334
Lèshān 336
Jiǔzhàigōu Nature
Reserve 337
The Silk Road 338
Lánzhōu 338
Xiàhé 338
Jiāyùguān Fort 341
Mògāo Caves 341
Singing Sands
Mountain & Crescent
Moon Lake 341
Kashgar 342

In Focus

China Today 346

History 348

Family Travel 358

The People of China 360

Chinese Cuisine 366

Arts & Architecture .. 374

Religion & Beliefs 380

China's Landscapes .. 384

Survival Guide

Directory **390**

Accommodation........390

Activities 394

Business Hours 394

Customs Regulations 394

Discount Cards.......... 395

Gay & Lesbian Travellers................... 395

Health 395

Insurance 398

Internet Access 398

Legal Matters............. 398

Money........................ 399

Passports................... 400

Public Holidays.......... 400

Safe Travel 401

Telephone 402

Time........................... 402

Visas 402

Volunteering 404

Transport................... **404**

Getting There & Away...................... 404

Getting Around.......... 411

Language................... **419**

Mandarin.................... 419

Cantonese.................. 420

Behind the Scenes..... **421**

Index............................ **422**

How to Use This Book **430**

Our Writers................ **432**

This Is China

Antique here, up-to-the-minute there, familiar yet unrecognisable, outwardly urban but quintessentially rural, conservative yet path-breaking, space-age but old-fashioned, China is a mesmerising land of eye-opening contradictions.

China is modernising at a head-spinning pace.

But the slick skyscrapers, Lamborghini showrooms and Maglev trains are just gift-wrap. Let's face it: the world's oldest continuous civilisation can pull an artefact or two out of its hat. Travel selectively around China and tap into a rich seam of antiquity: ponder the legends of the Forbidden City, rediscover your sense of wonder on the Great Wall or try to fathom the timeless expressions of the Terracotta Warriors. Submit to the charms of Píngyáo or glimpse Nirvana at the serene Mógāo Caves outside Dūnhuáng. Meander among the historic villages of Wùyuán or wake in an ancient Hakka roundhouse.

Out-of-this-world flavours also come as standard.

China is fixated with food but you need to abandon your meagre local Chinatown menu for the lavish Middle Kingdom cookbook. Get to slippery grips with a Shànghǎi hairy crab, wolf down a Peking duck, experience the liquid fire of a Sìchuān hotpot and eat your way around China. Impress your friends as you *gānbēi* (down-in-one) the local firewater; alternatively chill out with a frozen daiquiri in a slick Běijīng bar. When all's said and done, you'll come back from China with highly stimulated taste buds and some seriously cherished culinary memories.

There's also some stupendous scenery out there.

So get outside: island-hop in Hong Kong, squint up at the peaks of Wǔtái Shān and the Himalaya, or gaze over Hángzhōu's West Lake. Cycle between the fairy tale karst pinnacles of Yángshuò or swoon at Huángshān's mists. Become entranced by Dragon's Backbone Rice Terraces, size up the awesome sand dunes near Dūnhuáng or hike your way around Déhāng. And if your energy fails you, plonk down in a riverside cafe in Fènghuáng and stay put.

> 66
> China is a mesmerising land of eye-opening contradictions
> 99

Zhuang girl walking through terraced rice paddies, Guǎngxī (p308)

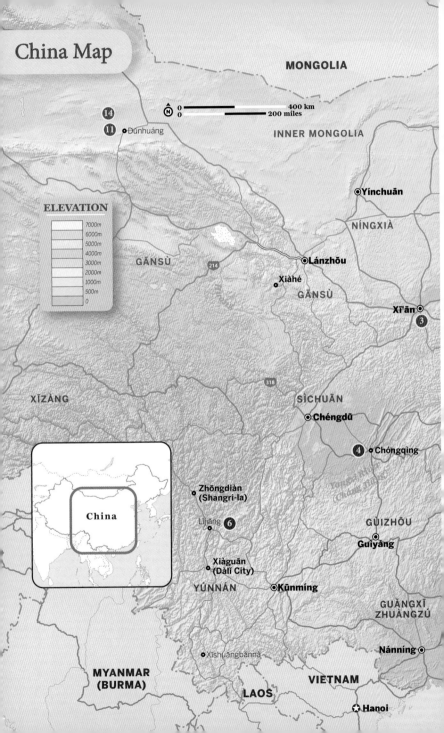

25
Top Experiences

1 The Great Wall
2 Forbidden City
3 Terracotta Warriors
4 Yangzi River Cruise
5 Cruising Up Victoria Harbour
6 Lìjiāng
7 French Concession, Shànghǎi
8 Chinese Cuisine
9 Huángshān
10 Dragon's Backbone Rice Terraces
11 Silk Road
12 Lí River
13 Hakka Roundhouses
14 Mògāo Caves
15 Píngyáo
16 Fènghuáng
17 Yángshuò
18 Wùyuán
19 Giant Panda Breeding Research Base
20 Běijīng's Hútòng
21 Gǔláng Yǔ
22 Canal Towns
23 Yúngāng Caves
24 Wǔtái Shān
25 West Lake, Hángzhōu

25 China's Top Experiences

Great Wall

Spotting it from space is both tough and pointless: the only place you can truly put the Great Wall (p111) under your feet is in China. Serve up the Great Wall according to taste: perfectly chiselled, dilapidated, stripped of its bricks, overrun with saplings, coiling splendidly into the hills or returning to dust. Offering an epic journey across north China, the fortification is a fitting symbol of those perennial Chinese traits: diligence, mass manpower, ambitious vision, engineering skill (and distrust of the neighbours).

1

Forbidden City

Not a city and no longer forbidden, Běijīng's enormous palace (p68) is the epitome of dynastic grandeur, with its vast halls, splendid gates and age-old relics. Nowhere else in China teems with so much history, legend and old-fashioned imperial intrigue. From imposing palace halls to dazzling imperial collections, it doesn't come much better. You may get totally lost here but you'll always find something to write about on the first postcard you can lay your hands on.

Terracotta Warriors

Standing silent guard over their emperor for more than 2000 years, the Terracotta Warriors (p143) are one of the most extraordinary archaeological discoveries ever made. It's not just that there are thousands of the life-sized figures lined up in battle formation; it's the fact that no two of them are alike, with every single one of them bearing a distinct expression. This is an army, but it's one made up of individuals. Gazing at these superbly sculpted faces brings the past alive in an utterly unique way.

The Best...
Places for Food

BĔIJĪNG

Ancestral home of Bĕijīng duck and a delicious smorgasbord of Chinese and international food. p93

SHÀNGHĂI

Where else for hairy crab and a cornucopia of cuisine. p210

HONG KONG

Dim sum devotees should go nowhere else. p281

MACAU

Enticing and unexpected blend of Chinese, Asian, Portuguese and African culinary traditions. p299

XĪ'ĀN

Make the Muslim Quarter your first port of call for China's scrumptious Silk Road cuisine. p139

The Best...
Modern Architecture

HONG KONG
A dramatic statement of modernity, even more spectacular at night. p264

PŮDŌNG, SHÀNGHĂI
MAINLAND
China's most iconic towerscape rises up on the far side of the Huángpǔ River. p203

BĚIJĪNG
Architecture addicts will love the CCTV Building and the National Centre for the Performing Arts. p89 and p74

PEOPLE'S SQUARE, SHÀNGHĂI
The aptly named Tomorrow Square rockets into the clouds above Pǔxī. p200

Yangzi River Cruise

4

Snowmelt from the world's third pole – the high-altitude Tibet-Qīnghǎi plateau – is the source of China's mighty Yangzi (Cháng Jiāng). The country's longest river surges dramatically west–east across the nation before pouring into the Pacific Ocean. The Yangzi reaches a dramatic crescendo with the Three Gorges, carved over millennia by the force of the powerful waters. The gorges are magnificent and a Yangzi River cruise (p247) is a rare chance to take a seat, relax and watch the drama unfold.

Cruising Up Victoria Harbour

5

A whistle blows, your boat chugs forward. Beyond the waves, one of the world's most famous views unfolds: Hong Kong's skyscrapers in their steel and neon splendour, against a backdrop of mountains. You're on the Star Ferry (p282), a legendary service that's been carrying passengers between Hong Kong Island and Kowloon Peninsula since the 19th century.

Líjiāng

The Naxi town of Líjiāng (p328), in Yúnnán province, is one of China's most rewarding destinations for the ancient textures of ethnic minority life in its old town and the breathtaking beauty of Yúlóng Xuěshān (Jade Dragon Snow Mountain) rising over town. While the old town itself can be crowded, an early rise is rewarded with quieter back alleys and, outside town, almost limitless exploration beckons.

Women in traditional dress, Líjiāng

French Concession, Shànghǎi

Shànghǎi is China's neonlit beacon of change, opportunity and sophistication. Its definitive landscape may be the towers of Pǔdōng, but the charisma, romance, fashion and charm are in the French concession (p201). Wander along leafy side streets, pop into delicatessens, admire outstanding villa architecture and art deco apartment blocks and dine at some of China's best restaurants. You'll find plenty to indulge in the French Concession.

Chinese Cuisine

Say *zàijiàn* to that Chinatown schlock and *nǐ hǎo* to a whole new world of food and flavour (p366). For sure you'll find dim sum, noodles and dumplings aplenty, but there's also the liquid fire of a Sìchuān hotpot, Tibetan cuisine or the adventurous flavours of Kāifēng's night market. You'll see things you've never seen before, eat things you've never heard of and drink things *(báijiǔ)* that could lift a rocket into space. And that's just for starters. Dim sum cart, Guǎngzhōu

The Best...
Nightlife

HONG KONG
Great music, dance, drinking, dining and general letting-down-of-hair. p284

MACAU
Romantic, elegant, European, charming, fun and a paradise for gamblers. p299

BĚIJĪNG
Běijīng's tirelessly updating universe of clubs, bars and live-music venues should satisfy all comers. p98

SHÀNGHǍI
The name alone is synonymous with excess, hedonism and entertainment. p213

Huángshān

Shrouded in mist and light rain for more than 200 days a year. Maddeningly crowded most of the time. Yet Huángshān (p242) has an appeal that attracts millions of annual visitors. Perhaps it's the barren landscape, an other-worldly vibe on the mountain. Mist – a fickle mistress – rolls in and out at will; spindly bent pines stick out like lone pins across sheer cragged granite faces. And not far from the base are the perfectly preserved Hui villages including Xīdì and Hóngcūn. Unesco, Ang Lee and Zhang Yimou were all captivated; you will be too.

⑨

The Best...
Places for Karma

WǓTÁI SHĀN
A confluence of Buddhist magic, mountain air and alpine scenery. p159

MAHAYANA HALL, PǓNÍNG TEMPLE, CHÉNGDÉ
Feel Lilliputian next to China's awesome Goddess of Mercy statue. p118

PO LIN MONASTERY, LANTAU, HONG KONG
The world's largest seated bronze Buddha statue. p274

PǓTUÓSHĀN
China's sacred island home of Guānyīn. p238

LAMA TEMPLE, BĚIJĪNG
The most important Tibetan temple outside of Tibet. p78

Dragon's Backbone Rice Terraces

After a bumpy bus ride to the highland in northern Guǎngxī, you'll be dazzled by one of China's most archetypal and photographed landscapes: the splendidly named Dragon's Backbone Rice Terraces (p308). The region is a beguiling patchwork of minority villages, with sparkling layers of waterlogged terraced fields climbing the hillsides tenaciously. You'll be enticed into a game of village-hopping. The most invigorating walk between Píng'ān and Dàzhài villages offers spine-tingling views. After the summer rains the fields glisten with reflections.

Silk Road

There are other Silk Road cities in countries such as Uzbekistan and Turkmenistan, but it's really in China where you get the feeling of stepping on the actual Silk Road (p338). Travel by bus and experience the route as ancient traders once did – mile-by-mile, town-by-town. Kashgar is the ultimate Silk Road town and today remains a unique melting pot of peoples, and Jiāyùguān Fort (p341) is a Great Wall fort, framed by snow-capped mountains.

KEREN SU/LONELY PLANET IMAGES ©

12

Lí River

It's hard to exaggerate the beauty of the Lí River (p314). It's one of the classic, legendary images travellers tend to have of China: with weeping willow trees leaning over bubbling streams, wallowing water buffaloes and farmers sowing the fields, all set against a backdrop of jagged limestone peaks. Take a bamboo-raft ride along the river and you'll understand why this stunning rural landscape has inspired painters and poets for centuries.

KEREN SU/LONELY PLANET IMAGES ©

13

Hakka Roundhouses

The vast, multistorey fortified earth villages (p324) of the Hakka people are scattered in profusion around a swath of rural China where the provinces of Fújiàn, Jiāngxī and Guǎngdōng meet. The *tǔlóu* are a mind-boggling sight: each colossal edifice could house hundreds of people. Thousands have managed to survive China's epic history of internecine strife. Try and spend the night in a *tǔlóu*: it's a very simple, but highly unique, experience.

Mógāo Caves

As China starts transforming into a lunar desertscape in the far west, the handsome oasis town of Dūnhuáng is a natural staging post for dusty Silk Road explorers. Mountainous sand dunes swell outside town while Great Wall fragments lie scoured by abrasive desert winds, but it is the magnificent caves at Mógāo (p341) that truly dazzle. The cream of China's crop of Buddhist caves, Mógāo's statues are ineffably sublime and perhaps the nation's most superlative cultural treasures.

The Best...
Getaways

YÁNGSHUÒ
China's most photographed natural landscape verges on the idyllic. p311

DÉHĀNG
Call time on urban smog and aerate your lungs in the splendid Húnán karst countryside. p315

COLOANE, MACAU
Gorgeous island retreat and one of Macau's most charming features. p294

LAMMA ISLAND, HONG KONG
Hong Kong: Gucci, sky-scrapers, fake Rolexes and high population density. Not here though. p284

PÍNGYÁO
No other town has ye olde China quite like this. p155

The Best...
Areas of the Great Wall

JIÀNKÒU
For the tumbledown, collapsing, wall-as-it-should-look, look. p116

HUÁNGHUĀ
Magnificent sections of wall far away from the madding crowd. p116

JIĀYÙGUĀN FORT
Out in China's far west, pounded and scoured by the Gobi winds. p341

JĪNSHĀNLĬNG
Quite an expedition from Běijīng but the starting point of an exceptional hike. p115

15

Píngyáo

Time-warped Píngyáo (p155)
is a true gem: an intact, walled
Chinese town with an unbroken
sense of continuity to its Qing
dynasty heyday. The town ticks
most of your China boxes with
a convincing flourish: imposing city walls, narrow alleys,
ancient shopfronts, traditional
architecture, a litter of excellent
hotels, a population of hospi-
table locals and a manageable
size. You can literally travel the
length and breadth of China
and never find another city
quite like it and it's so easy to
get to, you may never want to
leave. Left: Nan Dajie, Píngyáo; Above:
Shuānglín Temple, near Píngyáo

LEFT: MARTIN MOOS/LONELY PLANET IMAGES © RIGHT: KRZYSZTOF DYDYNSKI/LONELY PLANET IMAGES ©

Fènghuáng

With houses perched precariously on stilts, gate towers, ancestral halls and crumbling temples set amid a warren of back alleys full of shops selling mysterious eats and medicines – it's enough to make the ancient town of Fènghuáng (p316) an essential stop. Add the seductive setting on either side of the Tuó River, and the chance to stay in an inn right by the water, and you have one of the most evocative towns in China.

Hóng Bridge, Fènghuáng

Yángshuò

Embarking on a bike tour along Yùlóng River is one of the best ways to enjoy the incredible natural beauty around Yángshuò (p311). Pack your lunch and some water to enjoy a picnic along the banks but don't forget your camera. Whether it's just meandering along a small farmer's path between the paddy fields or sitting by the river indulging yourself in rural and karst landscape, you'll find yourself immersed in what is possibly China's most other-worldly beauty.

Wùyuán

When urban China has finally taken its toll on your lungs and the countryside insists on exploration, come to Wùyuán (p247). The rural Jiāngxī landscape is a picture, the air is pure and the little villages that dot the scenery around Wùyuán are truly delightful. Find yourself a base in a village such as Little Lǐkēng and set out to explore from village to village along the old postal roads. You may have been to Shànghǎi and Běijīng, but your memories of Wùyuán may be your best.

The Best...
History

BĚIJĪNG
China's leading city was capital to three imperial dynasties: the Yuan, Ming and Qing. p62

PÍNGYÁO
China's most sublime concentration of historic architecture. p155

XĪ'ĀN
Where traders came to rest at the end of the Silk Road and home of the Terracotta Warriors. p136

ZHŪJIĀJIĂO
Jiāngnán canal town on the outskirts of Shànghǎi with oodles of history. p220

FÈNGHUÁNG
Magnificent old Húnán architecture overlooking the Tuo River. p316

Giant Panda Breeding Research Base

Your chances of seeing a giant panda in the wilds of China are practically zilch, even if you're a motivated expert with acres of time. You can catch a couple of specimens at China's penitentiary-like zoos, but that's hardly the same. The Giant Panda Breeding Research Base (p334) in Chéngdū isn't the wilds but neither is it a zoo, and with a population of almost 50 pandas, it's an excellent opportunity to see the giant panda in a setting approximating its natural habitat.

The Best...
Places for Photography

YÁNGSHUÒ
You can't go wrong with the subject matter: stupendous karst and river scenery. p311

THE BUND, SHÀNGHĂI
For a perfect view of the skyscrapers of Lùjiāzuǐ across the river. p195

WEST LAKE, HÁNGZHŌU
Sunset on a clear day over the water is one of China's top sights. p230

CENTRAL DISTRICT, HONG KONG
Choose a night-time lookout on Tsim Sha Tsui and face due south for Hong Kong's most iconic vista. p267

Běijīng's Hútòng

20

To truly get under the skin of the capital, you need to get lost at least once in the city's ancient alleyways (p81). Peking's DNA can be found here: it's *hútòng* life that makes Běijīng people so warm and fun to be around. The city may be trying to sell itself as a 21st-century metropolis, but Běijīng's true charms – heavenly courtyard architecture, pinched lanes, one-storey higgledy-piggledy rooftops and a strong sense of community – were never high-rise. It's easy: check into a courtyard hotel, stay put for a few days and true Běijīng will be right on your doorstep.

Dōngchéng *hútòng*, Běijīng

Gǔlàng Yǔ

Linking Vietnam with North Korea, China's long coastline is dotted with the odd concession and the occasional colony where 19th-century foreign powers erected their buildings and embassy districts. Not the most famous, but perhaps the most charming of all, is Gǔlàng Yǔ (p322). A leisurely, car-free island of slowly decaying villa architecture and old churches, Gǔlàng Yǔ is an unexpected portrait of yestercentury European style and almost Mediterranean rhythms. Cable car, Gǔlàng Yǔ

AMANDA AHN/ALAMY ©

DIANA MAYFIELD/LONELY PLANET IMAGES ©

Canal Towns

Partly due to their small size, the lovely water towns of Zhéjiāng and Jiāngsū have preserved their Ming and Qing dynasty architecture despite being embedded in China's rapidly changing eastern seaboard. A tempting tableau of arched bridges, stone alleyways, ancient temples, canals and creaking architecture, the towns of Zhūjiājiǎo (p220), Wūzhén (p237) and Tónglǐ (p226) are all easily accessible, offering a glimpse of a vanishing way of life. Canal boats, Zhūjiājiǎo

Yúngāng Caves

Somehow sidestepping China's often destructive anti-Buddhist purges and doing their best to fend off the caustic atmospheric pollution emanating from nearby Dàtóng, the simply beautiful effigies and carvings of Shānxī province's Yúngāng Caves (p165) are enthralling. The most powerful message is perhaps not of the statues' incredible artistry and colour, but of the depth of faith that compelled their creation. If you don't have time to make Dūnhuáng, don't fret, these caves are almost equally sublime (and a lot closer to Běijīng).

23

The Best...
Shopping

HONG KONG
Retail hub and shoppers' paradise on the South China coast. p285

BĚIJĪNG
Great for clothes, arts and crafts, street markets and more. p101

SHÀNGHĂI
Shop your way around the French concession and see Shànghăi's best side. p215

FÈNGHUÁNG
Excellent for souvenirs, trinkets, knick-knacks and keepsakes. p316

PÍNGYÁO
All sorts, from paper cuts to embroidered shoes, sold from traditional-style shops. p155

Wǔtái Shān

Even though you've a chance of running headlong into snow as late as May, the mountain scenery and monastic disposition of Buddhist Wǔtái Shān (p159) is a fabulous north China experience. It's not the place for a quick in-and-out. Treat it as a spiritual retreat. Unwind, tune out completely from the chaos and noise of urban China and submit to some Buddhist mystery. After you've followed pilgrims and monks from temple to temple, set about exploring the rest of the vast mountain and turn up some of the oldest temple halls in China.

The Best...
Places for Ethnic Culture

LÌJIĀNG
Traditional Naxi village in the north of Yúnnán. p328

DÀLǏ
Excellent potential for exploration in the Bai heartland of Yúnnán. p326

DÉHĀNG
Miao village plonked in a sublime karst landscape in the west of Húnán province. p315

XIÀHÉ
In the ancestral Tibetan homelands of southwestern Gānsū, Xiàhé attracts a constant stream of pilgrims. p338

West Lake, Hángzhōu

China's most famous urban lake (p230) is one of the gems south of the mighty Yangzi River. In a charming vignette of traditional China, pagodas rise on hills above the lake, willow branches hang limply over the water and boats float unhurriedly across a liquid expanse. This may be one of China's most-visited panoramas, but the lake is so large you always find space to admire the scenery and drift into a reverie. Try to spend an evening in Hángzhōu if you can, as the lake saves its best side for nightfall.

China's Top Itineraries

Běijīng to Dàtóng Northern Tour

7 DAYS

You can get a lot done in a week. You'll need three to four days in Běijīng to see the main sights and walk on the Great Wall, followed by two days in Dàtóng before coming to a relaxing halt in China's most attractive walled town: Píngyáo

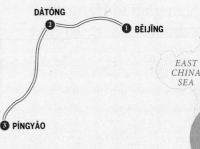

① Běijīng (p62)

To put China in instant perspective, zero in on the very centre of town and size up both **Tiān'ānmén Square** and the **Forbidden City**. You'll need half a day for the **Summer Palace**, but find time for the bars and restaurants of **Nanluogu Xiang** and some *hútòng* exploration. Also find yourself a room in a **courtyard hotel**, for doses of old Peking charm. Plan for a day for the **Great Wall** and half a day to appreciate the **Temple of Heaven,** but don't overlook the treasures of the **Poly Art Museum** or the Lama Temple.

BĚIJĪNG ◐ DÀTÓNG

🚊 **5½ hours** From Běijīng train station.
🚊 **4½ hours**

② Dàtóng (p163)

Firstly head to Dàtóng's recently restored **Old Quarter** at the centre of town, where you can find a crop of recently restored temples, the resplendent **Nine Dragon Screen** and the **Huáyán Temple**. Dàtóng's premier sight however is outside town: the magnificent **Yúngāng Caves**.

One of China's three major collections of Buddhist cave statuary, the caves are the nearest to Běijīng and constitute a priceless collection of China's artistic heritage. If you have time, make a journey to the gravity-defying **Hanging Monastery** which clings to a cliff side.

DÀTÓNG ◐ PÍNGYÁO
🚊 **Seven to 8½ hours**

③ Píngyáo (p155)

Try to have your Píngyáo accommodation booked in advance and someone should meet you at Píngyáo train station. Wander the streets and alleys, enjoying their ancient textures, then explore the **Rishengchang Financial House Museum**. The **City Walls** are among the best preserved in China and the lovely old **City Tower** is a gem at the heart of town. Píngyáo's **Confucian Temple** contains the town's oldest surviving building. But perhaps the town's most appealing aspect is staying in one of the lovely courtyard hotels and seeing an authentic Chinese old town refuse to modernise.

Hikers climbing the Great Wall, Bādálǐng (p113)

Shànghǎi to Hángzhōu
Eastern Highlights

Shànghǎi is a phenomenon, but three days is enough to get under its skin before the short journey to the famous canal town of Sūzhōu. After two days in Sūzhōu, hop on a bus to Hángzhōu for a few days' exploration of gorgeous West Lake.

1 Shànghǎi (p194)

Shànghǎi's most grandiose sight is the **Bund**, facing skyscraper-encrusted Lùjiāzuǐ in **Pǔdōng** over the Huángpǔ River. You'll want to stroll along East Nanjing Road all the way to **People's Square** and the standout **Shànghǎi Museum**; the **French Concession** is the place for boutique shopping, dining, drinking and slow ambling past European villa architecture along leafy side streets as well as the shikumen architecture of **Xīntiāndì** and **Tiánzǐfáng**. Save Pǔdōng till last and climb to the observation decks of the **Shànghǎi World Financial Center** for evening views of Shànghǎi before dinner and drinks on the **Bund**.

SHÀNGHǍI ➔ SŪZHŌU

🚆 30 minutes 🚌 90 minutes From the Shànghǎi South long-distance bus station.

2 Sūzhōu (p221)

Sūzhōu is minute compared to Shànghǎi. Start at the excellent **Sūzhōu Museum** before quietly exploring Sūzhōu's gardens, including the **Garden of the Master of the Nets** and the **Humble Administrator's Garden**. Sūzhōu's fascinating crop of temples includes the **North Temple Pagoda** and the **West Garden Temple**, and further historic charm can be explored on **evening boat tours** in the outer canal. It's only a short hop away by bus to **Tónglǐ**, for an escape to a traditional Jiāngsū water town.

SŪZHŌU ➔ HÁNGZHŌU

🚌 Two hours From the North long-distance bus station in Sūzhōu.

3 Hángzhōu (p229)

You won't have to stray too far from Hángzhōu's **West Lake** to fully enjoy the city so book your accommodation as close to the water as possible. Hire a bike to cycle round the lakeside and along its causeways, hop on a boat across the lake, seek divine inspiration at **Língyǐzn Temple** and **Jìngcí Temple** and pop down to **Qīnghéfāng Old Street** for some entertaining street stalls. Enjoy some Hángzhōu food for dinner and walk it off alongside the lake as night falls.

Outdoor diners at a restaurant on the Bund (p195), Shànghǎi

10 DAYS

Běijīng to Hángzhōu
The Capital Tour

After three days in Běijīng, chart your way southwest to Xī'ān and the Terracotta Warriors before recrossing China to Shànghǎi in the east via Luòyáng, with a detour to the Shàolín Temple, before concluding your journey next to West Lake in Hángzhōu.

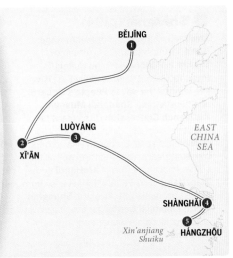

BĚIJĪNG ①

LUÒYÁNG ③

② XĪ'ĀN

EAST CHINA SEA

SHÀNGHǍI ④

Xīn'anjiang Shuiku

⑤ HÁNGZHŌU

① Běijīng (p62)

Běijīng is all about the **Forbidden City**, **Tiān'ānmén Square**, the **Temple of Heaven** and the **Great Wall**, but don't forget some outstanding temples. To get a feel for Běijīng, exploration of the ancient *hútòng* is essential, so find yourself a courtyard hotel room to maximise their charms. The **Summer Palace** is captivating but try to make a detour to the **798 Art District**.

BĚIJĪNG ⊙ XĪ'ĀN

✈110 minutes 🚆11½ hours Night train from Běijīng West train station.

② Xī'ān (p136)

The former Tang dynasty capital, today's Xī'ān is rapidly developing, but its venerable Ming dynasty **city walls** are famous across China. Most visitors are here to see the awe-inspiring **Terracotta Warriors** outside town, however. The **Great Mosque** and the **Muslim Quarter** are reminders that this city marked the start of the Silk Road; to the east of town rises the Taoist peak of **Huà Shān**, one of China's most sacred mountains.

XĪ'AN ⊙LUÒYÁNG

🚆Two hours From Xian station to Luòyáng Lóngmén station. 🚌Four hours

③ Luòyáng (p150)

Erstwhile capital of 13 dynasties, Luòyáng today has little history beyond its intriguing **old town**, but outside the city stand the **Lóngmén Caves**, one of China's most celebrated Buddhist grottoes. The **White Horse Temple** is China's oldest Buddhist temple, while a short bus trip from Luòyáng brings you to the **Shàolín**

Temple, birthplace of China's martial arts and **Sōng Shān**, the central mountain of Taoism's five sacred peaks.

LUÒYÁNG ⊙ SHÀNGHĂI

✈One hour 🚆13 hours

④ Shànghǎi (p194)

Journey from the Chinese ancestral heartland to Shànghǎi, the nation's financial capital. It's essential to spend time on the **Bund**, Shànghǎi's most august length of bombastic architecture. Try to book a terrace table at **M on the Bund** for lunch with a view. Take time to savour the **French Concession** and peruse the shops and traditional architecture of **Xīntiāndì** and **Tiānzǐfáng** before weighing up modern Chinese art at **M50**. Admire the **Yùyuán Gardens** and the **Shànghǎi Museum**.

SHÀNGHĂI ⊙ HÁNGZHŌU

🚆1½ hours From Shànghǎi South train station.
🚌2½ hours From the Shànghǎi South long-distance bus station.

⑤ Hángzhōu (p229)

You can head down to Hángzhōu – former capital of the Southern Song – as a day trip from Shànghǎi or spend the night. With its picture-postcard views and unhurried tempo, Hángzhōu's **West Lake** is perhaps the ideal conclusion to this itinerary: find yourself a lakeside bench.

Girl and bronze Buddha in Quīnghéfāng Old St (p232), Hángzhōu

PHOTOGRAPHER: GREG ELMS/LONELY PLANET IMAGES ©

10 DAYS

Hong Kong to Xī'ān
South to North Highlights

After a few days in Hong Kong, journey to Guìlín for the region's beautiful karst landscape before heading to Fènghuáng and on to Yíchāng and a Three Gorges trip to Chóngqìng. Come to a halt in Xī'ān, via the Sìchuān capital, Chéngdū.

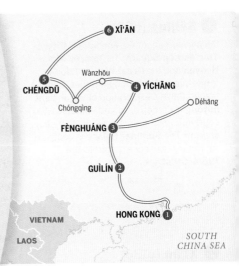

⑥ XĪ'ĀN
Wànzhōu
⑤ CHÉNGDŪ ④ YÍCHĀNG
Chóngqìng ○ Déhāng
FÈNGHUÁNG ③
GUÌLÍN ②
HONG KONG ①
VIETNAM
LAOS
SOUTH CHINA SEA

① Hong Kong (p264)

As well as being a major point of access to China, buzzing Hong Kong has a wealth of sights and experiences. Hop aboard the **Star Ferry** from Tsim Sha Tsui to Central and climb **Victoria Peak** aboard the **Peak Tram** for long views over the territory. A day trip to **Macau** for good food, gorgeous ecclesiastical architecture and Portuguese charms is essential.

HONG KONG ○ GUÌLÍN

✈ 2¼ hours From Hong Kong International Airport to Guìlín Liǎngjiāng International Airport. 🚃 15 hours Need to change trains in Guǎngzhōu.

② Guìlín (p305)

Guìlín is a useful base for more diverting excursions: take a boat down the Lí River to gorgeous **Yángshuò** and get out hiking or cycling into some splendid karst country-tryside. Also plan a trip north to the glittering **Dragon's Backbone Rice Terraces**; plan on four to five hours for the Dàzhài to Píng'ān village trek.

GUÌLÍN ○ FÈNGHUÁNG

🚌 12 hours From Guìlín to Huáihuà, then on by bus to Fènghuáng.

③ Fènghuáng (p316)

The funky ancient riverside town of **Fènghuáng** is one of China's most attractive walled towns after Píngyáo, and detours can be made to bucolic **Déhāng**, via the nearby town of Jíshǒu.

FÈNGHUÁNG ○ YÍCHĀNG

🚌🚃 Bus from Fènghuáng to Huáihuà then train to Yíchāng.

④ Yíchāng & the Three Gorges (p247)

On the Yangzi River – China's longest – Yíchāng has few sights, but it's the port of departure for hydrofoils and boats upstream through the **Three Gorges**.

YÍCHĀNG ○ CHÉNGDŪ

⛴🚌 Six hours Hydrofoil to Wànzhōu, then bus to Chóngqìng (three hours). ⛴ 38 hours Passenger boat to Chóngqìng; longer for tourist boats. 🚃 Two hours Chóngqìng to Chéngdū.

⑤ Giant Panda Breeding Research Base (p334)

From Chóngqìng, jump on a fast bullet train to reach Chéngdū in just two hours. Explore the city's sights, and make sure you make a morning visit to the **Giant Panda Breeding Research Base**, home to a population of both giant and red pandas.

CHÉNGDŪ ○ XĪ'ĀN

🚃 13 to 18 hours Sleeper train to Xī'ān. ✈ 70 minutes

⑥ Xī'ān (p136)

The ancient Tang capital of Cháng'ān may be hard to discern, but Xī'ān's Ming history survives in its robust **city walls**. The city's highlight, however, vastly predates even the Tang: the **Terracotta Warriors**.

Passengers on the Peak Tram (p268), Victoria Peak, Hong Kong
PHOTOGRAPHER: GREG ELMS/LONELY PLANET IMAGES ©

Shànghǎi to Hong Kong
The Big Loop

This epic adventure takes you on a Yangzi region loop from Shànghǎi to Hong Kong via Tài Shān, Běijīng, Píngyáo, Xī'ān and Guìlín, experiencing a roll call of the nation's most inimitable imperial sights, Buddhist treasures, most breathtaking landscapes and ancient towns.

① Shànghǎi (p194)

Where better to start this grand tour than in Shànghǎi – just south of the Yangzi River but roughly halfway around China's epic coastline. Stock up with a few days' sightseeing around the major sights: explore the **Bund**, the **French Concession** and the hallmark sights of **Pǔdōng**. Stock up on some excellent **food** and **entertainment**: Shànghǎi has some of the best restaurants and bars in the nation.

SHÀNGHǍI ◯ TÀI SHĀN

🚆 **Seven hours** Express train to Tài'ān train station.
🚌 **12 hours**

② Tài Shān (p169)

Explore the town of Tài'ān, visiting the **Dai Temple** before climbing the holy Taoist peak of **Tài Shān**. Try to spend the night on the mountain so you can catch the sunrise before descending the next day.

TÀI SHĀN ◯ BĚIJĪNG

🚆 **Four hours** 🚌 **Six hours**

③ Běijīng (p62)

China's 'northern capital' is a roll call of China's big sights: the **Forbidden City**, **Tiān'ānmén Square**, the **Great Wall** and the **Summer Palace**. Check into a courtyard hotel for a few nights to experience the city's adorable *hútòng* close up and make sure you explore the city's outstanding restaurant options.

BĚIJĪNG ◯ DÀTÓNG

🚌 **4½ hours** From Beijing's main station.
🚌 **5½ hours**

④ Dàtóng (p163)

Explore the city's recently restored **old town** but the top priority is the magnificent **Yúngāng Caves** outside town, one of China's most famous and colourful collections of Buddhist statuary and a stupendous chunk of artistic heritage.

DÀTÓNG ◯ PÍNGYÁO

🚆 **Seven to 8½ hours** 🚌 **Six hours** Via Tàiyuán where you change bus.

Fan dancing exercise on the Bund (p195), Shànghǎi
PHOTOGRAPHER: HUW JONES/LONELY PLANET IMAGES ©

XĪ'ĀN ● GUÌLÍN
🚆 27 hours

❼ Guìlín (p305)

On arrival in Guìlín, head immediately down to **Yángshuò** to explore the region's stunning karst landscape. Have a room booked at one of Yángshuò's hotels and spend a few days hiking and cycling around the region, journeying to nearby villages and settlements along the **Lí River**.

GUÌLÍN ● HONG KONG
✈ 2¼ hours 🚆 15 hours Need to change trains in Guǎngzhōu to Hung Hom from Guangzhou East station

❽ Hong Kong (p264)

The perfect conclusion to your China adventure – the ex-British colony of Hong Kong: renowned for its dim sum, lovely islands, colonial heritage, stunning modern architecture and proximity to **Macau**. Take the **Peak Tram** up to **Victoria Peak**, explore Hong Kong's Island's **Central district**, catch the **Star Ferry** over to **Tsim Sha Tsui** and gaze across Victoria Harbour for the illuminated night-time spectacle of Central.

❺ Píngyáo (p155)

Come to a leisurely halt in this marvellous **old walled Shānxī town** where China's best collection of preserved, traditional homesteads creates a virtually immaculate portrait of old China. Check into an old courtyard hotel and explore the sights, making a few diversions out of town to visit nearby attractions, including the **Shuānglín Temple** and the **Wang Family Courtyard**.

PÍNGYÁO ● XĪ'ĀN
🚌 Seven hours 🚆 8½ to 10½ hours

❻ Xī'ān (p136)

Fabled home of the **Terracotta Warriors** and start of the Silk Road, Xī'ān – like Píngyáo – is also enclosed by a Ming dynasty **city wall**. Explore the city's Muslim Quarter, sample some of the local Silk Road cuisine, peruse the Shaanxi History Museum and if you still have the energy, make a detour to the exhilarating Taoist mountain of **Huà Shān** east of town.

China Month by Month

Top Events

🎇 **Monlam Great Prayer Festival,** February or March

🎇 **Běijīng International Literary Festival,** March

🎇 **Luoyang Peony Festival,** April

🎇 **Rapeseed Fields around Wùyuán,** March

📅 January

North China is a deep freeze but the south is much better; Xīshuāngbǎnnà is balmy and south Hǎinán Island is positively warm. High-altitude destinations are shockingly cold. Full-scale commercial preparations for the Chinese New Year get underway well in advance of the festival, which arrives any time between late January and March.

🎇 Spring Festival

Arriving any time between late January and March, the Chinese New Year is family-focused, with dining on dumplings and gift-giving of *hóngbāo* (red envelopes stuffed with money). Most families feast together on the New Year's Eve, then China goes on a big week-long holiday. Expect fireworks, parades and temple fairs.

📅 February

North China remains shockingly cold and dry but things are warming up in Hong Kong and Macau. The Chinese New Year could well be firing on all cylinders – sort out your tickets well in advance.

🎇 Monlam Great Prayer Festival

Held over two weeks from the third day of the Tibetan New Year and celebrated with spectacular processions across the huge Tibetan world; huge silk *thangka* are unveiled and, on the last day, a statue of the Maitreya Buddha is conveyed around towns and monasteries; catch it in Xiàhé.

🎇 Lantern Festival

Held 15 days after the Spring Festival, the festival was traditionally a time when Chinese hung out highly decorated lanterns. Lantern-hung Píngyáo in Shānxī is an atmospheric place to enjoy the festival (sometimes held in March).

February Lantern Festival, Shànghǎi
PHOTOGRAPHER: KEREN SU/LONELY PLANET IMAGES ©

March

China comes back to life after a long winter, although high-altitude parts such as west Sìchuān and north Yúnnán of China remain glacial. The mercury climbs in Hong Kong and abrasive dust storms billow into Běijīng. Admission prices are still low-season.

🎊 Běijīng Book Bash

Curl up with a good book at the Bookworm Cafe (p97) for Běijīng's International Literary Festival, and lend an ear to lectures from international and domestic authors. Also earmark Shànghǎi for its International Literary Festival in the Bundside Glamour Bar (p212) or the Man Hong Kong International Literary Festival.

◉ Fields of Yellow

Delve into south Chinese countryside and be bowled over by a landscape saturated in bright yellow rapeseed. In some parts of China, such as lovely Wùyuán in Jiāngxī province, it's a real tourist draw.

April

Most of China is warm so it's a good time to be on the road, ahead of the May holiday period and before China's summer reaches its full power.

🎊 Paeon to Peonies

Wángchéng Park in Luòyáng bursts into full-coloured bloom with its Peony Festival: pop a flower garland on your head and join in the floral fun (but don't forget your camera).

🎊 Third Moon Festival

This Bai ethnic minority festival is an excellent reason to pitch up in the lovely north Yúnnán town of Dàlǐ. It's a week of horse racing, singing and merrymaking at the end of April and the beginning of May.

◉ Formula One

Petrol heads and aficionados of speed, burnt rubber and hairpin bends flock to Shànghǎi for some serious motor racing at the track near Anting. Get your hotel room booked early; it's one of the most glamorous events on the Shànghǎi calendar.

May

China is in full bloom in mountain regions such as Sìchuān's Wolong Nature Reserve, as azaleas and rhododendrons bring splashes of colour to the landscape. The first four days of May see China on holiday for one of the three big holiday periods, kicking off with Labour Day (1 May) so avoid going on the road...

🤸 Great Wall Marathon

Experience the true meaning of pain (but get your Great Wall sightseeing done and dusted at the same time). Not for the infirm or unfit (or the cable-car fraternity). See www.great-wall-marathon.com for more details.

June

Most of China is hot and getting hotter. Once-frozen areas, such as Jílín's Heaven Lake, are accessible – and nature springs instantly to life. The great peak season is cranking up.

🎊 Dragon Boat Festival

Find yourself the nearest large river and catch all the waterborne drama of Dragon Boat racers in this celebration of one of China's most famous poets. The Chinese traditionally eat *zòngzi* (triangular glutinous rice dumplings wrapped in reed leaves).

Rainstorms hit Běijīng, which is usually way over 40°C; so is Shànghǎi. So head uphill: Mògānshān, Huángshān or Tài Shān and other mountains are much cooler than the sweltering plains. Or elbow your way onto the beach.

✿ Qīngdǎo International Beer Festival

Slake that chronic summer thirst with a round of beers and devour a plate of mussels in Shāndōng's best-looking port town, home of the Tsingtao beer brand.

September

Come to Běijīng and stay put – September is part of the fleetingly lovely *tiāngāo qìshuǎng* ('the sky is high and the air is fresh') autumnal season with blue skies to die for and the heat of summer over – it's an event in itself.

✿ Mid-Autumn Festival

Also called the Moon Festival. Chinese celebrate by devouring daintily prepared moon cakes – stuffed with bean paste, egg yolk, walnuts and more. With a full moon, it's a romantic occasion for lovers and a special time for families. It's on the 15th day of the eighth lunar month.

July

Typhoons can wreak havoc with travel itineraries down south, lashing the Guǎngdōng and Fújiàn coastlines. Plenty of rain sweeps across China: the big 'plum rains' give Shànghǎi a serious soaking and the grasslands of Inner Mongolia turn green.

✿ Torch Festival, Dali Merrymaking

Held on the 24th day of the sixth lunar month (normally July), this is possibly the best photo op in the province. Flaming torches are paraded at night through homes and fields.

August

The temperature gauge of the 'three ovens' of Yangzi-region China – Chóngqìng, Wǔhàn and Nánjīng – gets set to blow.

October

The first week of October can be hellish if you're on the road: the National Day week-long holiday kicks off, so train and bus tickets can be hard to get, tourists sights are swamped and hotel room prices go through the roof (it's not called 'Golden Week' for nothing). Go mid-month instead.

✪ Kurban Bairam (Gu'erbang Jie)

Catch the four-day festivities of the Muslim Festival of Sacrifice in Muslim communities across China; the festival is at its liveliest and most colourful in Kashgar.

✕ Hairy Crabs in Shànghǎi

Now's the time to sample delicious hairy crabs in Shànghǎi. Male and female crabs are eaten together with shots of lukewarm Shàoxīng rice wine. They are at their best between October and December.

November

Most of China is getting pretty cold as tourist numbers drop and holidaygoers begin to flock south for sun and the last pockets of South China warmth.

◎ Macau Formula 3 Grand Prix

It's usually not hard to find a good reason to visit Macau any time of the year, but if you wait till November you can tie it in with this celebrated motor-racing event in the former Portuguese territory.

Far left: September Preparing moon cakes for the Píngyáo Moon Festival **Left: June** Dragon boat races, Hong Kong

Get Inspired

Books

○ When a Billion Chinese Jump (2010) Jonathan Watts' riveting account of China's environmental challenges.

○ The Classic of the Way and Its Power The seminal text of Taoism, penned by Laotzu and replete with ineffable insight.

○ A Madman's Diary (1918) Lu Xun's modernist horror story and powerfully influential piece of modern literature.

○ The Writing on the Wall: China and the West in the 21st Century (2007) Will Hutton's sharp analysis of the contradictions of the Chinese economy.

🎦 Films

○ Still Life (2006) Jia Zhangke's moving meditation on the impact of the Three Gorges Dam's construction on local lives.

○ Raise the Red Lantern (1991) Zhang Yimou's sumptuous and beautiful tragedy starring Gong Li.

○ Drunken Master II (1994) One of Jackie Chan's finest and funniest.

○ Chungking Express (1994) So good, Wong Kar Wai gets a second listing.

🎵 Music

○ Tibetan Plateau (2003) Tibetan singer Han Hong's musical high-water mark.

○ Yiwu Suoyou (1986) Cui Jian's gutsy rock milestone from a very different age.

○ Masterpieces of Chinese Traditional Music (1995) Exquisite collection of traditional Chinese tunes.

○ Lang Lang Live at Carnegie Hall (2004) Astonishing display of virtuoso skill from China's leading pianist.

🌐 Websites

○ Danwei (www.danwei. org) Resourceful reflections on Chinese media, advertising and urban life.

○ Guardian (www. guardian.co.uk) UK newspaper with excellent commentary on China news.

○ Hao Hao Report (www. haohaoreport.com) Resourceful variety of articles across a variety of themes on China with a great travel page.

Short on time?

This list will give you an instant insight into the country.

Read *Wolf Totem* (2008) by Jiang Rong charts the clash between Han Chinese and Inner Mongolian culture.

Watch *In the Mood for Love* (2000) is Wong Kar Wai's gorgeously filmed romance set in 1962 Hong Kong.

Listen *The 1st Complete Collection from Faye Wong* by Faye Wong is the Hong Kong diva's definitive collection.

Log on Lost Laowai Click (www.lostlaowai.com) for reams of riveting China info.

Left: Taichi in Shànghǎi; above right: Běijīng opera performer

Need to Know

Currency
The yuan (Y)

Languages
Mandarin and Cantonese

ATMs
In big cities and towns

Credit Cards
OK in big cities; elsewhere not generally accepted

Visas
Needed for visits to China except Hong Kong and Macau. Additional permit required for Tibet and a few other areas.

Mobile Phones
Pay-as-you-go SIM cards can be bought locally for most mobile phones

Wi-Fi
Common in top-end hotels, some midrange hotels and some cafes and bars; widespread in Hong Kong

Internet Access
In most towns, many 24 hours; Y2 to Y4 per hour

Driving
Cars can be hired with a temporary driving licence at airports, and in Hong Kong and Macau

Tipping
Small tip for hotel porters only

When to Go

Warm to hot summers, mild winters
Mild to hot summers, cold winters
Mild summers, very cold winters
Desert, dry climate
Cold climate

Beijing
GO Sep–Oct

Shànghǎi
GO Oct

Chéngdū
GO Mar–May

Guìlín
GO Apr–May

Hong Kong
GO Nov–Feb

High Season (May–Aug)
o Prepare for crowds at traveller hot spots, and summer downpours.

o Accommodation prices peak during the May holiday period.

Shoulder Season (Feb–Apr, Sep & Oct)
o Expect warmer days in spring, cooler days in autumn (the optimum season for north China).

o Accommodation prices peak during the October holiday period.

Low Season (Nov–Feb)
o Little domestic tourism, but busy and expensive at Chinese New Year.

o It's bitterly cold in the north; only warm in the far south.

o Expect to find far fewer tourist crowds at the top destinations.

Advance Planning

o **Three months before** Start shopping for your flight and in the high season, book your accommodation.

o **One month before** Get your visa arranged.

o **One week before** Book sleeper berths on trains

Your Daily Budget

BUDGET LESS THAN Y200

o Dorm beds: Y40 to Y50.

o Excellent, very cheap hole-in-the-wall restaurants and food markets.

o Affordable internet access and bike hire.

o Some free museums.

MIDRANGE Y200-1000

o Double room in a midrange hotel: Y200 to Y600.

o Lunch and dinner in decent local restaurants.

TOP END Y1000+

o Double room in a high-end hotel: Y600 or more.

o Lunch and dinner in excellent local or hotel restaurants.

o Shopping at high-end shops.

Exchange Rates		
Australia	A$1	Y6.32
Canada	C$1	Y6.70
Euro Zone	€1	Y10.36
Japan	¥100	Y6.50
New Zealand	NZ$1	Y5.58
UK	UK£1	Y15.22
USA	US$1	Y7.72

For current exchange rates see www.xe.com.

What to Bring

o **Passport** You'll need it to enter the country and to register at hotels and some internet cafes.

o **Money belt** Petty theft is a small but significant risk on buses and at train stations.

o **Travel insurance** Essential.

o **A good book** For those long-distance bus journeys.

o **Mandarin phrasebook** English won't get you far even on the beaten path.

o **Hiking, waterproof boots** You may not be able to find your shoe size in China.

Arriving in China

o Běijīng Capital Airport

Airport Express – To metro lines 2 and 10 every 15 minutes 6am to 10.30pm.

Express Buses – To centre of Běijīng every 10 to 20 minutes, 7am to 11pm.

Taxi – Y85; around 30 to 60 minutes into town.

o Pǔdōng International Airport

Maglev – To Longyang Rd station every 20 minutes, 6.45am to 9.40pm.

Metro Line 2 – 75 minutes to People's Sq, 1¾ hours to Hóngqiáo Airport.

Buses – Every 15 to 25 minutes, 5.30am to 9.30pm.

Taxi – Y160; one hour into Shànghǎi.

o Hong Kong International Airport

Airport Express – To Hong Kong station in Central every 12 minutes.

Buses – To many Hong Kong destinations.

Taxi – HK$300 to Central, luggage HK$5 per item.

Getting Around

o **Train** Extensive modern network covers the nation; high-speed trains connect many cities.

o **Bus** Extensive network; cheaper but slower than the train, but reaches some extra destinations.

o **Air** Numerous internal flights.

o **Car** Limited but growing options; roads chaotic.

o **Taxis** Cheap and plentiful in cities and big towns.

Accommodation

o **Hotels** Plentiful, ranging from two- to five-star.

o **Youth hostels** Decent budget accommodation.

o **Guesthouses** Spartan budget accommodation.

o **Courtyard hotels** Charming converted historic residences in Běijīng; usually midrange.

o **Homesteads** Cheap, rural accommodation.

Be Forewarned

o **First week of October** National holiday period sees sights swamped; hotel prices peak.

o **First three days of May** Same as above.

o **Spring Festival** A week any time from late January to early March; transport tickets scarce.

o **Health** Drink bottled water.

Běijīng &
the Great
Wall

Běijīng is China's supreme historic capital. Other Chinese towns may boast longer histories, but none offers as much tangible evidence of its dynastic past or fashions the same imperial grandeur. Yet Běijīng is also the up-to-the-minute capital of a nation undergoing the greatest transformation that China – and the world – has ever witnessed. You'll discover modernity and a switched-on, confident populace, but you'll also find enchanting alleyways, imperial palaces and incense-wreathed temples. Shedding bricks willy-nilly into gullies and ravines, the Great Wall is one of China's great ruins, sinuously careening across Běijīng's hilly north. Even though its remains can be explored across north China, the wall is largely synonymous with Běijīng, its principal access point. To the east, the Héběi town of Chéngdé is home to a magnificent imperial resort and a delightful sprinkling of Qing-dynasty temples.

Great Wall of China, Bādálǐng (p113)
RICHARD I'ANSON/LONELY PLANET IMAGES ©

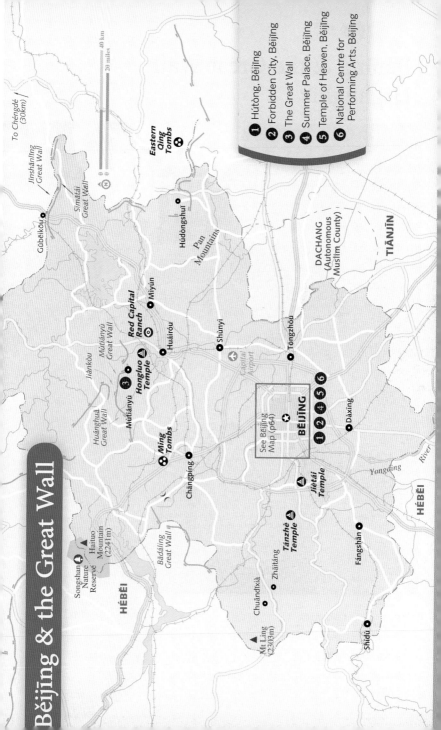

Běijīng & the Great Wall

1 Hútòng, Běijīng
2 Forbidden City, Běijīng
3 The Great Wall
4 Summer Palace, Běijīng
5 Temple of Heaven, Běijīng
6 National Centre for Performing Arts, Běijīng

40 km
20 miles

To Chéngdé (30km)

Jīnshānlǐng Great Wall

Gǔběikǒu

Sīmǎtái Great Wall

Eastern Qīng Tombs

Hǔdòngshuǐ

Pan Mountains

DACHANG (Autonomous Muslim County)

TIĀNJĪN

Jiànkòu

Mùtiányù Great Wall

Red Capital Ranch

Miyún

Huáiróu

Shùnyì

Tōngzhōu

Capital Airport

Hóngluó Temple

Huánghuā Great Wall

Mùtiányù

Ming Tombs

Chāngpíng

See Běijīng Map (p64)

BĚIJĪNG

1 2 4 5 6

Dàxīng

Yǒngdìng River

Jiètái Temple

Songshan Nature Reserve

Hǎituó Mountain (2241m)

Bādálǐng Great Wall

Tánzhè Temple

HÉBĚI

Zhǎitáng

Fángshān

Mt Ling (2303m)

Chuāndǐxià

Shídù

HÉBĚI

Běijīng & the Great Wall Highlights

① Běijīng's Hútòng

Hútòng lie at the very geographic and cultural heart of traditional Běijīng. To gauge the authentic Běijīng behind its dazzling modern guise, it's crucial to plumb this low-rise brick universe of charming courtyard houses, pinched alleyways and leafy lanes.

Need to Know

LOCATION Within second ring road, mainly Dōngchéng and Xīchéng. **GETTING ABOUT** Bicycle or on foot. **NAVIGATION** Most *hútòng* run east–west. **DINING** Restaurants abound. **For more, see p81.**

Běijīng's Hútòng Don't Miss List

LI MEI, 32, MEDIA AGENT/PLAYWRIGHT

1 NANLUOGU XIANG
Probably the best known tourist *hútòng* (alleyways), especially with young locals, this long north–south hub is a great blend of ancient and modern. Nanluogu Xiang's (p80) style stays close to the original low-rise grey brick, but each home has been converted to shops, snack stalls, cafes and bars. It's crazy on weekends during daytime, with window-shoppers galore. Around 18 smaller *hútòng* run off Nanluogu Xiang; each one is worth a peek.

2 MAO'ER HÚTÒNG
One of the streets off Nanluogu Xiang is this relatively undeveloped *hútòng* that provides a beautiful tree-lined walk to nearby Houhai Lake tourist area. Most of its houses are still residential or privately owned, so it's really serene at night.

3 WUDAOYING HÚTÒNG
A few years ago it was billed as the next place for *hútòng* hipsters but it never really reached its potential. There are a few diamonds in the rough, however, and it's definitely worth a slow walk down. Some of the restaurants are popular with expats and it's conveniently located directly west of the Lama Temple (p78).

4 FANGJIA HÚTÒNG
A few streets south of Wudaoying Hútòng, this is my pick for the next big thing, although who knows? There are already some reasonable bars, galleries and shops, and the No 46 courtyard art complex with a theatre and cafes draws a young crowd. Further down the street you might find a local bar serving beer on a wooden bench or a slightly bigger place cranking out live music next to old folk sitting around, chatting.

5 DASHILAN WEST STREET
Southwest of Qiánmén, there's a long *hútòng* with a diverse mix of shops, Peking-duck restaurants, guesthouses and pretty much anything else you can think of. It's a little touristy near the main strip, but the further west you go, the better it gets. Like many *hútòng*, it ends in a bit of a maze, but getting lost is half the fun!

Explore the Forbidden City

Home to two dynasties of emperors, the outstanding Forbidden City (p68) is Běijīng's other must-see sight after the Great Wall. No other collection of buildings in China has the same cachet or wall-to-wall sense of history. You can easily spend a day here and you'd still be turning up new discoveries after three. It's also money well spent: the entrance ticket is a bargain.

2

4 ## Wander Around the Summer Palace

Choose a sunny day for this magnificent regal encampment (p86) in the suburbs and pack your camera for mouthwatering sunset views over sparkling Kūnmíng Lake. Prepare also to hike – there are some fantastic walks. The Běijīng metro has done everyone a huge favour by plonking a station nearby so you can shuttle in at speed.

AMERENS HEDWICH/LONELY PLANET IMAGES ©

Gallivanting along the Great Wall ③

China's best-known wall (p111) is easily reached from Běijīng where most of China's remaining brick-clad sections survive. Tourists head to Bādálǐng, but travellers earmark Jiànkŏu for its sense of excitement and the chance to see the wall au naturel. Wherever you choose to explore, you'll need to put aside a day at least for your Great Wall trip and consider overnighting nearby for a multiday excursion.

GREG ELMS/LONELY PLANET IMAGES ©

⑤ Marvel at the Temple of Heaven

OK, so it's not really a temple but the Imperial architecture is simply astonishing and the surrounding park (p83) is huge enough to totally escape the hubbub of modern-day Běijīng. The Hall of Prayer for Good Harvests may be the centrepiece, but try to arrive early in the morning to catch practitioners of taichi and put aside half a day to fully explore the sights.

⑥ Gawp at the National Centre for the Performing Arts

To some it's a radical statement of modernity and a glittering addition to Běijīng's architectural firmament (p74); to others it's a blot on the landscape and a further kick in the teeth to old Peking. It's difficult not to have an opinion about this shimmering metallic entity west of Tiān'ānmén Sq. On the inside, it's Běijīng's premier venue for classical-music performances.

Běijīng & the Great Wall's Best...

Wining & Dining

○ **Běijīng Dàdǒng Roast Duck Restaurant** (p96) The roast duck restaurant for both novices and seasoned duck aficionados.

○ **Dàlǐ Courtyard** (p94) For exquisite Běijīng courtyard charms and delightful cuisine from Yúnnán.

○ **Crescent Moon Muslim Restaurant** (p94) Kebabs that are the talk of the town.

○ **Vineyard Cafe** (p94) Outstanding breakfasts, excellent service and a tip-top *hútòng* locale.

Architecture

○ **Forbidden City** (p68) China's largest and best-preserved collection of imperial buildings.

○ **CCTV Building** (p89) Totally audacious chunk of gravity-defying engineering prowess.

○ **National Centre for the Performing Arts** (p74) Ultramodern bauble and counterpoint to the monumental Great Hall of the People.

○ **Summer Palace** (p86) Landscaped imperial summer retreat in the northwest of town.

Views

○ **Tiān'ānmén Square** (p63) Climb up the Gate of Heavenly Peace for the longest views.

○ **Kūnmíng Lake, Summer Palace** (p86) The lake at sunset is gorgeous.

○ **Jǐngshān Park** (p82) Choice vistas right over the Forbidden City.

○ **Jiànkòu Great Wall** (p116) For panoramas of the crumbling bastion clinging to precarious mountain ridges.

○ **Pǔtuózōngchéng Temple, Chéngdé** (p120) Climb to the top for some delicious views of Chéngdé.

Need to Know

Shopping

o **Nanluogu Xiang** (p80) Get your *hútòng* shopping and exploration done at the same time.

o **Bookworm Café** (p97) One of Běijīng's great literary institutions – great for literature, and food.

o **Pānjiāyuán Market** (p103) Běijīng's ultimate emporium of knick-knacks and collectables.

o **Silk Street** (p102) Heaving multilevel bazaar of togs, silk and ceaseless haggling.

o **Shard Box Store** (p102) For a unique line in porcelain boxes.

ADVANCE PLANNING

o **One Month Before** Get your accommodation sorted and book your hotel room in Běijīng.

o **One Week Before** Book your train or air tickets out of Běijīng through your hotel or a local travel agent.

RESOURCES

o **The Beijinger** (www.thebeijinger.com) For restaurant, bar and club listings.

o **Time Out** (www.timeout.com/beijing) Up-to-date listings.

o **Beijing Boyce** (www.beijingboyce.com) Handy blog for the ins and outs of Běijīng's bar and club scene.

o **Beijingpage** (www.beijingpage.com) Informative online directory with reams of practical info on the city.

o **CTrip** (www.english.ctrip.com) Discounted hotels and ticketing; recommended.

GETTING AROUND

o **Train** From Capital Airport into town; high-speed trains from several stations to other points in China.

o **Metro** The best way to get around in town: fast, regular, dependable, extensive network.

o **Bus** To/from airport; extensive network around town (not user-friendly for Westerners); also long-distance.

o **Taxi** Ubiquitous, easy to hail, but Běijīng traffic is among the world's very worst.

o **Air** For long-distance flights.

BE FOREWARNED

o **Taxi Sharks** Avoid them at Capital Airport: join the taxi queue.

o **Crossing the Road** Cars can turn on red lights; traffic chaos reigns.

o **Scams** Avoid being taken to ultra-expensive teahouses and cafes by English-speaking girls along Wangfujing Dajie and other spots.

o **Pedicabs** Avoid as you may be ripped off.

o **Pollution** Still bad and sometimes shocking.

o **Language** English rarely used outside of tourist hotels and restaurants.

o **Hotels** Some cheap hotels don't take foreigners.Ullabor

Left: Street food in Běijīng; **Above:** Bicycles and pedestrians, Tiān'ānmén Sq

59

PHOTOGRAPHERS: (LEFT) LINDA CHING/LONELY PLANET IMAGES ©

Běijīng & the Great Wall Itineraries

These trips focus on Běijīng and the town's surrounding sights. You'll encounter the Great Wall, while the longer tour brings you to the temple town of Chéngdé and a traditional village on the cusp of Běijīng municipality.

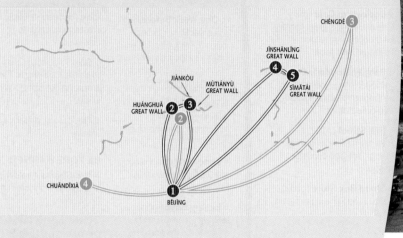

BĚIJĪNG TO THE GREAT WALL
Highlights Tour

The kicking-off point for this tour is **(1) Běijīng** which warrants some pretty energetic exploration for its unequalled collection of sights. There's enough right in the centre of town for a day's sightseeing, including the Forbidden City, the Gate of Heavenly Peace and Tiān'ānmén Sq. Try to have your accommodation sorted near Nanluogu Xiang so you can spend the night in a nearby *hútòng* courtyard hotel and dine locally. Rise early the next day for an expedition to the Great Wall. Putting aside an entire day is not unreasonable: you can hire a taxi with a driver to take you around two to three sections of

wall; this way you could compare the wall at **(2) Huánghuā** and **(3) Jiànkòu and Mùtiányù**. Alternatively embark on a day trip to **(4) Jīnshānlǐng Great Wall** for the hike towards **(5) Sīmǎtái**. Another option is to spend the night at a hotel near the Great Wall to maximise the sense of adventure and allow more time the next day for continued exploration.

On day three, return to Běijīng to resume your sightseeing in the capital. The Summer Palace is essential viewing: try to catch the sun setting over the hills west of Kūnmíng Lake.

5
DAYS

BĚIJĪNG TO CHUĀNDĬXIÀ
City to Country Tour

Begin your journey in similar fashion to the Highlights Tour in **(1) Běijīng**, but put aside a bit of extra time for sightseeing around town so you can fully explore other sights, including the displays at the Poly Art Museum and Capital Museum and perhaps make a detour to the 798 Art District to peruse modern Chinese art. Earmark the **(2) Great Wall** for a day's exploration of the top sections and consider hiring a taxi for a tour of the main areas. Take a train or a bus from Běijīng to **(3) Chéngdé** for its imperial heritage and superb collection of Buddhist temples. It's worth spending the night in Chéngdé to fully savour the

scenery and have time to properly explore the imperial resort of Bìshǔ Shānzhuāng. The standout temples, including Pǔníng Temple, home to a simply awesome statue of Guanyin, the Buddhist Goddess of Compassion, also need to be seen. Return to Běijīng and catch a bus or take a taxi to **(4) Chuāndǐxià**, the ancient village in the distant southwest of the municipality. There are several homesteads where you can spend the night, introducing you to the bucolic charms of China's rural side.

Tower section of the Great Wall, Sīmǎtái (p114)
PHOTOGRAPHER: GREG ELMS/LONELY PLANET IMAGES ©

61

Discover Běijīng & the Great Wall

At a Glance

o **Běijīng's hútòng** (p81) Get to the heart of traditional Běijīng.

o **Forbidden City** (p68) Stroll where only the privileged could for 500 years.

o **Summer Palace** (p86) Be enchanted by this fabulous regal encampment.

o **Great Wall** (p111) Explore one of mankind's greatest constructions.

o **Chéngdé** (p119) Take a visit to an emperor's summer resort.

War memorial, Tiān'ānmén Sq
PHOTOGRAPHER: TIM MAKINS/LONELY PLANET IMAGES ©

Běijīng

♫010 / POP 22 MILLION

Běijīng (北京) is one of China's true ancient capitals. It is also a confident and modern city that seems assured of its destiny to rule over China till the end of time. Its architecture traces every mood swing from Mongol times to the present, from neglected hútòng (alleyways) to bomb shelters scooped out during the 1970s to the shimmering baubles of contemporary architects.

The city's denizens chat in Běijīnghuà, the gold standard of Mandarin, and marvel at their good fortune for occupying the centre of the known world. And for all its gusto, Běijīng dispenses with the persistent pace of Shànghǎi or Hong Kong, and locals instead find time to sit out the front, play chess and watch the world go by.

History

Although seeming to have presided over China since time immemorial, Běijīng (Northern Capital) – positioned outside the central heartland of Chinese civilisation – only emerged as a cultural and political force that would shape the destiny of China with the 13th-century Mongol occupation of China.

Chinese historical sources identify the earliest settlements in these parts from 1045 BC. In later centuries Běijīng was successively occupied by foreign forces: it was established as an auxiliary capital under the Khitan Liao and later as the capital under the Jurchen Jin, when it was enclosed within fortified walls, accessed by eight gates.

In AD 1215 the army of the great Mongol warrior Genghis Khan razed Běijīng, an event that was paradoxically to mark Běijīng's transformation into a powerful national capital. The city came to be called Dàdū (大都; Great Capital), also assuming the Mongol name Khanbalik (the Khan's town). By 1279, under the rule of Kublai Khan, grandson of Genghis Khan, Dàdū was the capital of the largest empire the world has ever known.

The basic grid of present-day Běijīng was laid during the Ming dynasty, and Emperor Yongle (r 1403–24) is credited with being the true architect of the modern city. Much of Běijīng's grandest architecture, such as the Forbidden City and the Temple of Heaven, date from his reign.

The Manchus, who invaded China in the 17th century to establish the Qing dynasty, essentially preserved Běijīng's form. In the last 120 years of the Qing dynasty, Běijīng, and subsequently China, was subjected to power struggles and invasions and the ensuing chaos. The list is long: the Anglo-French troops who in 1860 burnt the Old Summer Palace to the ground; the corrupt regime of Empress Dowager Cixi; the catastrophic Boxer Rebellion; General Yuan Shikai; the warlords; the Japanese occupation of 1937; and the Kuomintang. Each and every period left its undeniable mark, although the shape and symmetry of Běijīng was maintained.

Like the emperors before them, the communists significantly altered the face of Běijīng. The *páilou* (decorative archways) were brought down and whole city blocks were pulverised to widen major boulevards. From 1950 to 1952, the city's magnificent outer walls were levelled in the interests of traffic circulation.

The past quarter of a century has transformed Běijīng into a modern city, with skyscrapers, slick shopping malls and heaving flyovers. The once flat skyline is now crenellated with vast apartment blocks and office buildings. Recent years have also seen a convincing beautification

of Běijīng: from a toneless and unkempt city to a greener, cleaner and more pleasant place.

The year 2008 was Běijīng's modern coming-of-age. The city spent three times the amount Athens spent on the 2004 Olympics to ensure the Běijīng Olympic Games was the most expensive in history.

As Běijīng continues to evolve, it is shredding its increasingly tenuous links with its ancient past one fibre at a time, with an estimated 40% of its downtown area being demolished since 1990.

◉ Sights

The lion's share of Běijīng's sights lie within the city proper. Notable exceptions are the Great Wall and the Ming Tombs.

Dōngchéng 东城区

FREE **TIĀN'ĀNMÉN SQUARE**　　Square
(天安门广场; Tiān'ānmén Guǎngchǎng; Map p66; Ⓜ Tiānānmén Xī, Tiānānmén Dōng or Qiánmén) Flanked by stern 1950s Soviet-style buildings and ringed by white peri meter fences, the world's largest public square (440,000 sq m) is an immense flatland of paving stones at the heart of Běijīng.

Height restrictions have kept surrounding buildings low, allowing largely uninterrupted views of the dome of the sky. Kites flit through the air, children stamp around on the paving slabs and Chinese out-of-towners huddle together for the obligatory photo opportunity with the great helmsman's portrait. On National Day (1 October), Tiān'ānmén Sq heaves with visitors.

In the square, one stands in the symbolic centre of the Chinese universe. The rectangular arrangement, flanked by halls to both east and west, to some extent echoes the layout of the Forbidden City: as such, the square employs a conventional plan that pays obeisance to traditional Chinese culture, but many of its ornaments and buildings are Soviet-inspired. Mao conceived the square to project the enormity of the Communist Party, so it's all a bit Kim Il-Sungish. During

Beijing City Overview

Anheqiao North 安河桥北地铁站

Blessing Lake

Back Lake

Xiyuan

Yuanmingyuan 圆明园地铁站

WŬDÀOKŎU

Badaling Expwy

Xueyuan Lu 学院路

Summer Palace

Kunming Lake

West Lake

Yiheyuan Lu

East Gate of Peking University 北京大学东门地铁站

Chengfu Lu

Wudaokou 五道口

YUQUAN MOUNTAIN

See Summer Palace Map (p88)

Zhongguancun 中关村地铁站

Bagou 巴沟

Haidian Huangzhuang 海淀黄庄地铁站

Suzhoujie 苏州街

Zhichunlu 知春路

Zhichunli 知春里

Zhichunlu

Xitucheng 西土城

Renmin University 人民大学地铁站

Dazhongsi 大钟寺铁站

Xitucheng Lu

Weigongcun 魏公村地铁站

XĪCHÉNG

HĂIDIÀN

Zizhuyuan Lu

Xisanhuan Beilu

National Library 国家图书馆地铁站

Beijing North Train Station 积水潭地铁站

Zizhuyuan Park

Zizhuyuan Park

Beijing Zoo 动物园

Xizhimen 西直门地铁站

Xisihuan Beilu (Fourth Ring Rd)

Wulu Train Station 五路火车站

Third Ring Rd

Chegongzhuang 车公庄地铁站

Fucheng Lu

Sanlihe Lu

Fuchengmen 阜城门地铁站

XĪDĀN

Yúyuán Tán

Yuquanlu 玉泉路地铁站

Wukesong 五棵松地铁站

Wanshoulu 万寿路地铁站

Gongzhufen 公主坟地铁站

Muxidi 木樨地地铁站

Fuxingmen 复兴门地铁站

Fuxing Lu 复兴路

Junshibowuguan 军事博物馆地铁站

Nanlishilu 南礼士路地铁站

Beijing West Train Station 北京西火车站

Changchunjie 长椿街地铁站

Xisihuan Nanlu

Guang'anmenwai Dajie

Niu Jie

Third Ring Rd

FĒNGTÁI

Guang'anmen Train Station 广安门火车站

Beijing-Shijiazhuang Gaosu Gonglu

XUĀNWŬ

Fengtai Beilu

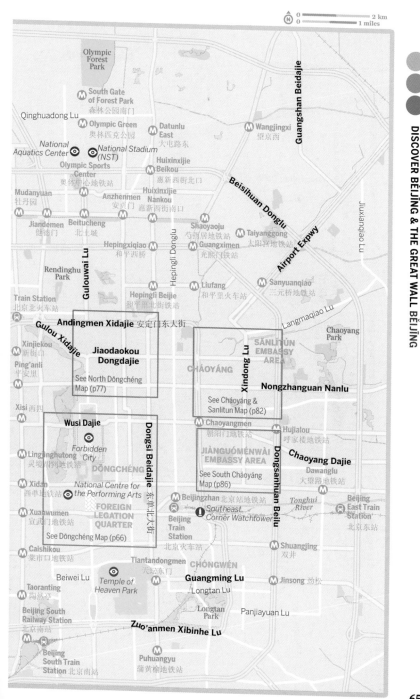

Olympic Forest Park

South Gate of Forest Park 森林公园南门

Qinghuadong Lu

Olympic Green 奥林匹克公园

Datunlu East 大屯路东

Wangjingxi 望京西

National Aquatics Center

National Stadium (NST)

Olympic Sports Center 奥体中心地铁站

Huixinxijie Beikou 惠新西街北口

Mudanyuan 牡丹园

Anzhenmen 安贞门

Huixinxijie Nankou 惠新西街南口

Beisihuan Donglu

Jiandemen 健德门

Beitucheng 北土城

Shaoyaoju 芍药居地铁站

Taiyanggong 太阳宫地铁站

Airport Expwy

Jiuxianqiao Lu

Hepingxiqiao 和平西桥

Guangximen 光熙门铁站

Gulouwai Lu

Hepingli Donglu

Sanyuanqiao 三元桥地铁站

Rendinghu Park

Hepingli Beijie 和平里北街铁站

Liufang 和平里火车站

Langmaqiao Lu

Chaoyang Park

Train Station 北京北火车站

Gulou Xidajie

Andingmen Xidajie 安定门东大街

SĀNLĬTÚN EMBASSY AREA

Xinjiekou 新街口

Jiaodaokou Dongdajie

Xindong Lu

Ping'anli 平安里

See North Dōngchéng Map (p77)

CHÁOYÁNG

Nongzhanguan Nanlu

Xisi 西四

See Cháoyáng & Sanlitun Map (p82)

Wusi Dajie

Chaoyangmen 朝阳门地铁站

Hujialou 呼家楼地铁站

Forbidden City

Dongsi Beidajie

JIÀNGUÓMÉNWÀI EMBASSY AREA

Chaoyang Dajie

Lingjinghutong 灵境胡同地铁站

DŌNGCHÉNG

Dawanglu 大望路地铁站

Dongsanhuan Beilu

Xidan 西单地铁站

National Centre for the Performing Arts

See South Cháoyáng Map (p86)

Tonghui River

Beijing East Train Station 北京东站

Xuanwumen 宣武门地铁站

FOREIGN LEGATION QUARTER

Beijingzhan 北京站地铁站

Shuangjing 双井

Caishikou 菜市口地铁站

See Dōngchéng Map (p66)

Southeast Corner Watchtower

Beijing Train Station 北京火车站

Tiantandongmen 天坛东门

CHÓNGWÉN

Jinsong 劲松

Beiwei Lu

Temple of Heaven Park

Guangming Lu

Taoranting 陶然亭

Longtan Lu

Panjiayuan Lu

Beijing South Railway Station 北京南站

Longtan Park

Zuo'anmen Xibinhe Lu

Beijing South Train Station 北京南站

Puhuangyu 蒲黄榆地铁站

65

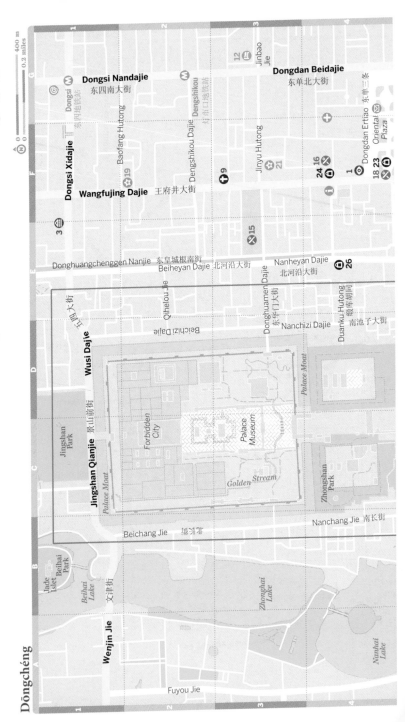

Dōngchéng

Dongsi Nandajie 东四南大街

Dongdan Beidajie 东单北大街

Dongsi 东四地铁站 M

Baofang Hutong

Dongsi Xidajie

Wangfujing Dajie 王府井大街

Dengshikou 灯市口地铁站 M

Dengshikou Dajie

Jinbao Jie

12

Dongdan Ertiao 东单三条
Oriental Plaza

Jinyu Hutong

21

9

24 16

1

18 23

15

3

Wusi Dajie
五四大街

Donghuangchenggen Nanjie 东皇城根南街

Beiheyan Dajie 北河沿大街

Nanheyan Dajie
北河沿大街

26

Qihelou Jie

Beichizi Dajie

Donghuamen Dajie
东华门大街

Nanchizi Dajie

Duankui Hutong
缎库胡同

Jingshan Qianjie 景山前街

Jingshan Park

Forbidden City

Palace Moat

Palace Museum

Golden Stream

Palace Moat

Zhongshan Park

Nanchang Jie 南长街

Beichang Jie 北长街

Wenjin Jie

Jade Islet
Beihai Park

Beihai Lake

文津街

Zhonghai Lake

Nanhai Lake

Fuyou Jie

400 m
0.2 miles

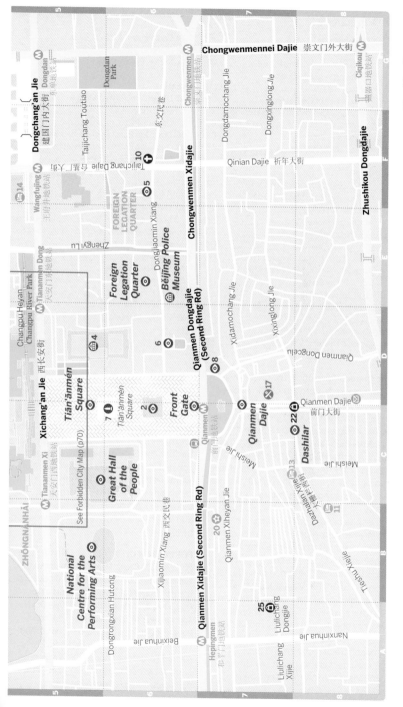

Dōngchéng

◎ Top Sights

Běijīng Police Museum..........................E6
Dashilar C8
Foreign Legation Quarter E6
Front Gate...C6
Great Hall of the People C5
National Centre for the Performing
   Arts B5
Qianmen Dajie......................................C7
Tiān'ānmén Square C5

◎ Sights

1 Arts and Crafts Mansion.........................F4
2 Chairman Mao Memorial Hall C6
3 China Art Gallery................................... E1
4 China National Museum D5
5 Former French Legation.........................F6
6 Legation Quarter.................................... D6
7 Monument to the People's Heroes.......C6
8 Old Station Building (Qián Mén
   Railway Station)................................... D7
9 St Joseph's Church F3
10 St Michael's Church F6

◎ Sleeping

11 Leo's Hostel B8

12 Park Plaza..G3
13 Qiánmén Hostel......................................C7
14 Raffles Běijīng Hotel.............................. F5

✕ Eating

15 Dōnghuámén Night Market E3
   Food Republic..................................(see 23)
   Oriental Plaza..................................(see 23)
16 Quánjùdé Roast Duck Restaurant F4
17 Quánjùdé Roast Duck Restaurant D7
18 Wangfujing Snack Street........................ F4

◉ Entertainment

19 Capital Theatre....................................... F2
20 Lǎo Shě Teahouse...................................B7
   Star Cinema City ....(see 23)
21 Sundongan Cinema City.......................... F3

◎ Shopping

22 Dashilar Entrance....................................C7
23 Oriental Plaza.. F4
24 Ten Fu's Tea... F4
25 Ten Fu's Tea.. A7
26 Zhāoyuán Gé..E4

the Cultural Revolution, the Chairman, wearing a Red Guard armband, reviewed parades of up to a million people here. The 'Tiananmen Incident' is the term given to the 1976 near-riot in the square that accompanied the death of Premier Zhou Enlai. Another million people jammed the square to pay their last respects to Mao in the same year. In 1989 the military forced prodemocracy demonstrators out of the plaza.

Despite being a public place, the square remains more in the hands of the government than the people; it is monitored by closed-circuit TV cameras, and plainclothes police can move faster than the Shànghǎi Maglev if anyone strips down to a Free Tibet T-shirt. The designated points of access, sporadic security checks and twitchy mood cleave Tiān'ānmén Sq from the city. A tangible atmosphere of restraint and authority reigns; in fact, some might say the square symbolises the 'harmonious' China of today.

If you get up early you can watch the flag-raising ceremony at sunrise, performed by a troop of People's Liberation Army (PLA) soldiers drilled to march at precisely 108 paces per minute, 75cm per pace. The soldiers emerge through the Gate of Heavenly Peace to goosestep impeccably across Chang'an Jie; all traffic is halted. The same ceremony in reverse is performed at sunset. Ask at your hotel for flag-raising and lowering times; rise early, crowds can be intense.

FORBIDDEN CITY   Historic Site
(紫禁城; Zǐjìn Chéng; Map p70; www.dpm.org.cn; admission high/low season Y60/40, Clock Exhibition Hall Y10, Hall of Jewellery Y10, audio tour Y40; ⏰8.30am-4.30pm, last tickets 3.30pm Oct-Mar, 4pm Apr-Sep; Ⓜ Tiānānmén Xī or Tiānānmén Dōng) Ringed by a 52m-wide moat at the very heart of Běijīng, the fantastically named Forbidden City is China's largest and best-preserved complex of ancient buildings. So called because it was

off-limits for 500 years, when it was steeped in stultifying ritual and Byzantine regal protocol, the other-worldly palace was the reclusive home to two dynasties of imperial rule until the Republic demoted the last Qing emperor to has-been.

Today, the Forbidden City is prosaically known as the Palace Museum (故宫博物馆; Gùgōng Bówùguǎn). In former ages the price for uninvited admission was instant execution; these days Y40 will do. Allow yourself a full day for exploration or several trips if you're an enthusiast.

Guides – many with mechanical English – mill about the entrance, but the automatically activated audio tours are cheaper (Y40; over 40 languages, including Esperanto) and reliable (and you can switch them off). Restaurants, a cafe, toilets and even a police station can be found within the palace grounds. Wheelchairs (Y500 deposit) are free to use, as are strollers (Y300 deposit).

Much of the Forbidden City is sadly out of bounds, including the now ruined Hall of Rectitude (Zhōngzhèng Diàn), destroyed by fire in 1923, which was once lavishly furnished with Buddhist figures and ornaments. The sound of ping pong may emerge from other closed-off halls.

The palace's ceremonial buildings lie on the north–south axis, from the **Meridian Gate** (午门; Wǔ Mén; Map p70) in the south to the **Divine Military Genius Gate** (神武门; Shénwǔ Mén; Map p70) to the north.

Restored in the 17th century, the Meridian Gate is a massive portal that in former times was reserved for the use of the emperor. Across the Golden Stream, which is shaped to resemble a Tartar bow and is spanned by five marble bridges, towers the **Gate of Supreme Harmony** (太和门; Tàihé Mén; Map p70), overlooking a colossal courtyard that could hold imperial audiences of up to 100,000 people.

Raised on a marble terrace with balustrades are the Three Great Halls (Sān Dàdiàn), which comprise the heart of the Forbidden City. The imposing **Hall of Supreme Harmony** (太和殿; Tàihé Diàn; Map p70) is the most important and the largest structure in the Forbidden

Běijīng In...

ONE DAY

The **Forbidden City** is Běijīng's obligatory sight, so devote at least a morning to the palace and the sights of nearby **Tiān'ānmén Square**. Hop on the subway from Tiananmen Xi to Wangfujing Dajie and lunch at **Wángfǔjǐng Snack Street**. Walk off your meal browsing shops along Wangfujing Dajie before taking the metro to the **Temple of Heaven Park** for a few hours' exploration. Spend the rest of the afternoon exploring the *hútòng* around **Nanluogu Xiang**, wining and dining the night away at its bars and restaurants, or walk west to the watering holes of the lakes.

THREE DAYS

If it's a Sunday, rise early to sift through the goods at **Pānjiāyuán Market**, then prepare for a day trip to the Great Wall; if you are pressed for time, skip the Ming Tombs. Back in Běijīng, pop into the **Poly Art Museum**, and have a table booked at **Dàlǐ Courtyard** or **Xiao Wang's Home Restaurant**. On day three, journey to the **Summer Palace** and find time for the **Lama Temple**, followed by shopping at **Silk Street**, the **Sānlǐtún Yashou Clothing Market** or **Dashilar**.

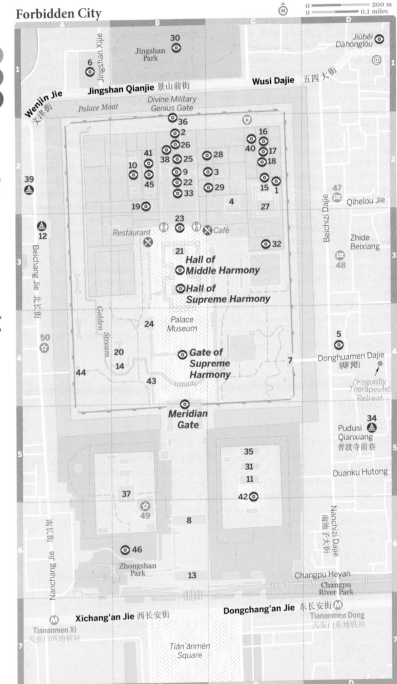

Forbidden City

City. Originally built in the 15th century, it was used for ceremonial occasions such as the emperor's birthday, the nomination of military leaders and coronations.

Inside the Hall of Supreme Harmony is the richly decorated **Dragon Throne** (Lóngyǐ) where the emperor would preside over trembling officials. Bronze *shuǐgāng* (vats) – once containing water for dousing fires – stand in front of the hall; in all, 308 *shuǐgāng* were dotted around the Forbidden City, with fires lit under them in winter to keep them from freezing over (hopefully the flames did not accidentally start larger conflagrations). Water for the Forbidden City was once provided by 72 wells, 30 of which have been preserved.

Behind the Hall of Supreme Harmony is the smaller **Hall of Middle Harmony** (中和殿; Zhōnghé Diàn; Map p70),

which served as a transit lounge for the emperor. Here he would make last-minute preparations, rehearse speeches and receive close ministers.

The third hall, which has no support pillars, is the **Hall of Preserving Harmony** (保和殿; Bǎohé Diàn; Map p70), used for banquets and later for imperial examinations. To the rear descends a 250-tonne marble imperial carriageway carved with dragons and clouds, dragged into Běijīng along an ice path. The emperor was conveyed over the carriageway in his sedan chair as he ascended or descended the terrace.

Note the fascinating exhibitions in the halls on the eastern flank of the Three Great Halls, with displays covering the gates and guards in the Forbidden City and an intriguing collection exploring the Emperor's Tibetan Buddhist beliefs.

Forbidden City

◉ Top Sights

Gate of Supreme Harmony.................. B4
Hall of Middle Harmony B3
Hall of Supreme Harmony B3
Meridian Gate B5

◉ Sights

1 Chàngyīn Pavilion C2
2 Chéngguāng Gate................................. B2
3 Chengqian Hall..................................... C2
4 Clock Exhibition Hall............................ C2
5 Courtyard Gallery D4
6 Dagaoxuan Temple A1
7 Donghua Gate....................................... C4
8 Duān Gate B6
9 Earthly Tranquillity Palace.................. B2
10 Eternal Spring Palace........................... B2
11 Front Hall.. C5
12 Fúyòu Temple A3
13 Gate of Heavenly Peace B6
14 Gate of Military Prowess...................... B4
15 Hall of Character Cultivation C2
16 Hall of Harmony................................... C2
17 Hall of Jewellery.................................. C2
18 Hall of Joyful Longevity....................... C2
19 Hall of Mental Cultivation.................... B2
20 Hall of Military Prowess B4
21 Hall of Preserving Harmony................. B3
22 Hall of Union... B2
23 Heavenly Purity Gate............................ B3
24 Hongyi Pavilion B4

25 Imperial Garden..................................... B2
26 Imperial Peace Hall B2
27 Imperial Supremacy Hall C2
28 Jadeware Exhibition.............................. C2
29 Jingren Hall... C2
30 Jingshan Park B1
31 Middle Hall C5
32 Nine Dragon Screen.............................. C3
33 Palace of Heavenly Purity.................... B2
34 Pudu Temple... D5
35 Rear Hall... C5
36 Shenwu Gate... B2
37 Square Altar.. B5
38 Thousand Autumns Pavilion B2
39 Wanshou Xinglong Temple A2
40 Well of Concubine Zhen....................... C2
41 Western Palaces B2
42 Workers Cultural Palace....................... C5
43 Xihe Gate B4
44 Xihua Gate A4
45 Yìkūn Palace B2
46 Zhongshan Park.................................... B6

🛏 Sleeping

47 Emperor... D2
48 Peking International Youth Hostel........ D3

🎭 Entertainment

49 Forbidden City Concert Hall................. B6
50 What Bar?.. A4

Halls to the west of the Three Great Halls exhibit treasures from the palace.

The basic configuration of the Three Great Halls is echoed by the next group of buildings, smaller in scale but more important in terms of real power, which in China traditionally lies in the northernmost part.

The first structure is the **Palace of Heavenly Purity** (乾清宫; Qiánqīng Gōng; Map p70), a residence of Ming and early Qing emperors, and later an audience hall for receiving foreign envoys and high officials.

Beyond the **Hall of Union** (交泰殿; Jiāotài Diàn; Map p70) and the **Earthly Tranquillity Palace** (坤宁宫; Kūnníng Gōng; Map p70) at the northern end of the Forbidden City ranges the much-needed 7000-sq-metre **Imperial Garden** (御花园; Yù Huāyuán; Map p70), a classical Chinese arrangement of fine landscaping, rockeries, walkways and pavilions among ancient and malformed cypresses propped up on stilts. Try to find the **lump tree**, the Elephant Man of the cypress

world. Kneeling in front of **Chéngguāng Gate** (承光门; Chéngguāng Mén; Map p70) as you approach the Shénwǔ Gate is a pair of bronze elephants, whose front legs bend in anatomically impossible fashion.

On the western and eastern sides of the Forbidden City range the palatial former living quarters, once containing libraries, temples, theatres, gardens and even the tennis court of the last emperor. Some of these now function as museums with a variety of free exhibitions on everything from imperial concubines to scientific instruments, weapons, paintings, jadeware and bronzes.

The mesmerising **Clock Exhibition Hall** (钟表馆; Zhōngbiǎo Guǎn; Map p70; admission Y10; ☺8.30am-4pm summer, to 3.30pm winter) is one of the highlights of the Forbidden City. Located in the Fèngxiàn Hall (Fèngxiàn Diàn), the exhibition contains a fascinating array of elaborate timepieces, many of which were gifts to the Qing emperors from overseas. Many of the 18th-century examples were imported

through Guǎngdōng from England; others are from Switzerland, America and Japan. Time your arrival for 11am or 2pm and treat yourself to the clock performance in which choice timepieces strike the hour and give a display to wide-eyed children and adults.

Also look out for the excellent **Hall of Jewellery** (珍宝馆; Zhēnbǎo Guǎn; Map p70; admission Y10; ⏰8.30am-4pm summer, to 3.30pm winter), tickets for which also entitle you to glimpse the **Well of Concubine Zhen** (珍妃井; Zhēnfēi Jǐng; Map p70), into which the namesake wretch was thrown on the orders of Cixi, and the glazed **Nine Dragon Screen** (九龙壁; Jiǔlóng Bì; Map p70). The treasures on view are fascinating: within the **Hall of Harmony** (颐和轩; Yíhé Xuān; Map p70) sparkle Buddhist statues fashioned from gold and inlaid with gems, and a gold pagoda glittering with precious stones, followed by jade, jadeite, lapis lazuli and crystal pieces displayed in the **Hall of Joyful Longevity**

(乐寿堂; Lèshòu Táng; Map p70). Further objects are displayed within the **Hall of Character Cultivation** (养性殿; Yǎngxìng Diàn; Map p70). The **Chàngyīn Pavilion** (畅音阁; Chàngyīn Gé; Map p70) to the east was formerly an imperial stage.

GATE OF HEAVENLY PEACE
Historic Site

(天安门; Tiān'ānmén; Map p70; admission Y15, bag storage Y1-6; ⏰8.30am-4.30pm; 🚇Tiān'ānmén Xī or Tiān'ānmén Dōng) Hung with a vast, beatific portrait of Mao and lending its name to the square immediately south, the Gate of Heavenly Peace is a potent national symbol. Built in the 15th century and restored in the 17th century, the double-eaved gate was formerly the largest of the four gates of the Imperial Wall that enveloped the imperial grounds.

The gate is divided into five doors and reached via seven bridges spanning a stream. Each of these bridges was

73

GREG ELMS/LONELY PLANET IMAGES ©

Don't Miss **National Centre for the Performing Arts**

Critics have compared the centre to an egg, but it's more like a massive mercury bead, an ultramodern missile silo or the futuristic lair of a James Bond villain. The unmistakable building rises – if that is the word for it – just west of the Great Hall of the People, its glass membrane perennially cleaned by squads of roped daredevil cleaners fending off the Běijīng dust.

Examine the bulbous interior, including the titanic steel ribbing of interior bolsters (each of the 148 bolsters weighs 8 tonnes). A fascinating exhibition inside displays failed competition conceptions and construction efforts that realised the final building; note how many of the failed entrants (eg the proposal from Obermeyer & Deilmann) incorporated echoes of the Great Hall of the People into their design, something that the winning design (from ADP Aeroports de Paris) avoided at all costs.

NEED TO KNOW

国家大剧院; Map p66; Guójiā Dàjùyuàn; Y30; ⊙1.30-5pm Tue-Fri, 9.30am-5pm Sat & Sun; Ⓜ Tiānānmén Xī

restricted in its use and only the emperor could use the central door and bridge.

Mao proclaimed the People's Republic on 1 October 1949 from here and his gigantic portrait is the dominating feature, with anachronistic slogans on either side.

Climb up for sweeping views of Tiān'ānmén Sq, and peek inside at the impressive beams and overdone paintwork; in all there are 60 gargantuan wooden pillars and 17 vast lamps suspended from the ceiling.

It's free to walk through the gate, but if you climb it you'll have to pay the admission fee and pay to store your bag at the kiosk (one hour max). Security at the gate is intense and locals are scrupulously frisked. The ticket office only sells tickets for the gate; to visit the Forbidden City, continue north until you can go no further.

FRONT GATE　　　　　　Historic Site
(前门; Qián Mén; Map p66; admission high/low season Y20/10, audio guide Y20; ⏱8.30am-4.30pm; Ⓜ Qiánmén) The Front Gate actually consists of two gates, originally linked by a semicircular enceinte, which was swept aside in the early 20th century. Without the city walls, the gate sits entirely out of context, like a door without a wall. The northerly gate, 40m-high **Zhèngyáng Gate** (正阳门; Zhèngyáng Mén) – literally 'Facing the Sun Gate' – dates from the Ming dynasty. The largest of the nine impressive gates of the inner city wall dividing the Inner or Tartar (Manchu) City from the Outer or Chinese City, the gate was partially destroyed during the Boxer Rebellion of 1900 and the temples that flanked it have vanished. Also torched during the Boxer Rebellion, the **Arrow Tower** (箭楼; Jiàn Lóu) to the south is of a similar age and looks down Qianmen Dajie. To the east is the former British-built **Old Station Building** (老车站; Lǎo Chēzhàn; Map p66; Qián Mén Railway Station), now housing the (unopened) Běijīng Railway Museum.

GREAT HALL OF THE PEOPLE
　　　　　　　　　　　　Historic Site
(人民大会堂; Rénmín Dàhuìtáng; Map p66; adult Y30, bag deposit Y2-5; ⏱8.30am-3pm; Ⓜ Tiānānmén Xī) The Great Hall of the People, on the western side of Tiān'ānmén Sq, is where the National People's Congress convenes. The 1959 architecture is monolithic and intimidating; the tour parades visitors past a choice of 29 of its lifeless rooms. Also on the billing is a 5000-seat banquet room and the 10,000-seat auditorium with the familiar red star embedded in a galaxy of lights in the ceiling. It's closed when the National People's

Běijīng City Walls

Had they been preserved – or even partially protected Nánjīng-style – rather than almost entirely obliterated in the ideological 1950s and '60s, Běijīng's mighty city walls and imposing gates would rank among China's top sights.

An epitaph for the city walls, the **Ming City Wall Ruins Park** (明城墙遗志公园; Míng Chéngqiáng Yízhǐ Gōngyuán; Chōngwénmén Dongdajie; admission free; ⏱24hr; Ⓜ Chōngwénmén) runs next to a section of the Ming inner-city wall along the entire length of the northern flank of Chongwenmen Dongdajie. The restored wall stretches for around 2km, rising to a height of around 15m and interrupted every 80m with *dūn tái* (buttresses), which extend south from the wall.

The park extends from the former site of Chōngwén Mén (one of the nine gates of the inner city wall) to the **Southeast Corner Watchtower** (东南角楼; Dōngnán Jiǎolóu; Dongbianmen; admission Y10; ⏱8am-5.30pm; Ⓜ Jiànguómén or Chōngwénmén). The highly impressive interior has some staggering carpentry: huge red pillars surge upwards, topped with solid beams. On the 1st floor is the superb **Red Gate Gallery** (红门画廊; Hóngmén Huàláng; www.redgategallery.com; admission free; ⏱10am-5pm); say you are visiting the Red Gate Gallery and the Y10 entry fee to the watchtower is waived. A fascinating exhibition on the 2nd floor within details the history of Běijīng's city gates.

Humble counterpart of the Southeast Corner Watchtower, the **Southwest Corner Watchtower** (Xībiànmén Jiǎolóu; Map p64) is not as impressive as its famous sibling, but you can climb up onto a section of the old city wall amid the roaring traffic.

Congress is in session. Bags must be checked in but cameras are admitted.

FREE CHAIRMAN MAO MEMORIAL HALL
Mausoleum

(毛主席纪念堂; Máo Zhǔxí Jìniàntáng; Map p66; bag storage Y2-10, camera storage Y2-5; ⏱8am-noon Tue-Sun; ⓜTiānānmén Xī, Tiānānmén Dōng or Qiánmén) Chairman Mao died in September 1976 and his Memorial Hall was constructed shortly thereafter on the former site of the Zhōnghuá Gate.

The Great Helmsman's mummified corpse lies in a crystal cabinet, draped in a red flag emblazoned with hammer and sickle while impatient guards in white gloves brusquely wave the hoi polloi on towards further rooms and Mao memorabilia. At certain times of the year the body requires maintenance and is not on view. Bags must be deposited at the building east of the memorial hall across the road (if you leave your camera in your bag you will be charged for it).

MONUMENT TO THE PEOPLE'S HEROES
Monument

(人民英雄纪念碑; Rénmín Yīngxióng Jìniànbēi; Map p66; ⓜTiānānmén Xī, Tiānānmén Dōng or Qiánmén) Completed in 1958, this 37.9m-high obelisk, made of Qīngdǎo granite, bears bas-relief carvings of key patriotic and revolutionary events (such as Lin Zexu destroying opium at Hǔmén in the 19th century, and Tàipíng rebels).

FOREIGN LEGATION QUARTER
Historic Site

(Map p66; ⓜQiánmén, Wǎngfǔjǐng or Chōngwénmén) For grand shades of Europe, the former Foreign Legation Quarter where the 19th-century foreign powers flung up embassies, schools, churches, post offices and banks is well worth a stroll.

Access the area walking up the steps east from Tiān'ānmén Sq into Dongjiaomin Xiang (东交民巷), once called Legation St and renamed 'Anti-Imperialism Road' during the iconoclastic Cultural Revolution. **Legation Quarter** (Map p66; 23 Qianmen Dongdajie) is a classy cluster of elegantly restored legation buildings towards the west end of Dongjiaomin Xiang. The attractive green-roofed, orange-brick building further east at No 40 is the stately former **Dutch Legation**.

The domed building at 4a Zhengyi Lu, on the corner of Zhengyi Lu (正义路) and Dongjiaomin Xiang, is the former **Yokahama Specie Bank**. The grey building at No 19 Dongjiaomin Xiang is the former **French post office**, now the Jingyuan Sichuan Restaurant, not far from the former **French Legation** (法国使馆旧址; Fǎguó Shǐguǎn Jiùzhǐ; Map p66) at No 15.

Backing onto a small school courtyard, the twin spires of the Gothic **St Michael's Church** (东交民巷天主教堂; Dōngjiàomínxiàng Catholic Church; Map p66) rises ahead at No 11, facing the green roofs and ornate red brickwork of the former **Belgian Legation**.

North along Taijichang Dajie is a brick street sign embedded in the northern wall of Táijīchǎng Tóutiáo (台基厂头条), carved with the old name of the road, Rue Hart.

BĚIJĪNG POLICE MUSEUM
Museum

(北京警察博物馆; Běijīng Jǐngchá Bówùguǎn; 36 Dongjiaomin Xiang; Map p66; admission Y5, through ticket Y20; ⏱9am-4pm Tue-Sun; ⓜQiánmén) Propaganda-infested maybe, but some mesmerising exhibits make this museum a fascinating peek into Běijīng's police force. Upstairs gets to grips with morbid crimes and their investigations; for police weapons, head to the 4th floor. The through ticket includes laser shooting practice and a souvenir.

CHINA NATIONAL MUSEUM
Museum

(中国国家博物馆; Zhōngguó Guójiā Bówùguǎn; Map p66; admission Y30, audio tour Y30; ⏱8.30am-4.30pm; ⓜTiānānmén Dōng) This Soviet-style building is due to reopen by 2011 after a massive expansion program that has seen it closed for an interminably long period.

WORKERS CULTURAL PALACE
Park

(劳动人民文化宫; Láodòng Rénmín Wénhuà Gōng; Map p70; admission Y2; ⏱6.30am-7.30pm; ⓜTiānānmén Dōng) Sounding like a social centre for Leninist labourers, this haven of peace was actually the

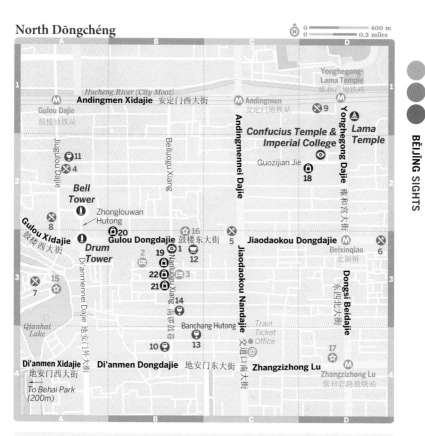

North Dōngchéng

◎ Top Sights

Bell Tower A2
Confucius Temple & Imperial
  College D2
Drum Tower A3
Lama Temple D1

◎ Sights

1 Nanluogu Xiang B3

⊜ Sleeping

2 Courtyard 7 .... B3
3 Gǔxiàng 20 .... B3

⊗ Eating

4 Café Sambal A2
5 Dàlǐ Courtyard C3
6 Ghost Street D3
7 Hútóng Pizza A3
8 Le Little Saigon A2
9 Vineyard Cafe D1

⊖ ⊜ Drinking

10 12sqm B4
11 Bed Bar A2
12 Cafe Zara B3
13 Mao Mao Chong Bar B4
14 Passby Bar B3

⊛ Entertainment

15 East Shore Bar A3
16 MAO Livehouse B3
17 Yúgōng Yíshān D4

⊖ Shopping

18 Bannerman Tang's Toys &
   Crafts D2
19 Clockwork Monkey B3
20 Mega Mega Vintage B3
21 Plastered T-Shirts B3
22 Pottery Workshop B3

PHIL WEYMOUTH/LONELY PLANET IMAGES ©

Don't Miss **Lama Temple**

If you only have time for one temple (and the Temple of Heaven isn't really a temple) make it this one, where riveting roofs, fabulous frescos, magnificent decorative arches, tapestries, eye-popping carpentry, Tibetan prayer wheels, tantric statues and a superb pair of Chinese lions mingle with dense clouds of incense.

The most renowned Tibetan Buddhist temple outside the historic lands of Tibet, the Lama Temple was converted to a lamasery in 1744 after serving as the former residence of Emperor Yong Zheng. Today the temple is an active place of worship, attracting pilgrims from afar, some of whom prostrate themselves in submission at full length within its halls.

Resplendent within the **Hall of the Wheel of the Law** (Fǎlún Diàn) is a substantial bronze statue of a benign and smiling Tsong Khapa (1357–1419), founder of the Gelukpa or Yellow Hat sect.

A magnificent 18m statue of the Maitreya Buddha in his Tibetan form, reputedly sculpted from a single block of sandalwood, rises up magnificently within the **Wànfú Pavilion** (Wànfú Gé). Behind the statue is the Vault of Avalokiteshvara, from where a diminutive and blue-faced statue of Guanyin peeks out. The Wànfú Pavilion is linked by an overhead walkway to the **Yánsuí Pavilion** (Yánsuí Gé), which encloses a huge lotus flower that revolves to reveal an effigy of the longevity Buddha.

Don't miss the collection of bronze Tibetan Buddhist statues within the **Jiètái Lóu**. Most effigies date from the Qing dynasty, from languorous renditions of Green Tara and White Tara to tantric pieces and figurines of the fierce-looking Mahakala. Also peruse the collection of Tibetan Buddhist ornaments within the **Bānchán Lóu**, with an array of *dorje* (Tibetan sceptres), mandalas, Tantric figures and an impressive selection of ceremonial robes in silk and satin.

NEED TO KNOW

雍和宫; Yōnghé Gōng; Map p77; 28 Yonghegong Dajie; admission Y25, English audio guide Y20; ⊙9am-4pm; Ⓜ Yōnghégōng-Lama Temple

emperor's premier place of worship, the **Supreme Temple** (太庙; Tài Miào). The often-overlooked temple halls, cloaked in imperial yellow tiles and hunched over expansive courtyards, suggest a mini version of the Forbidden City, sans crowds.

ST JOSEPH'S CHURCH
Church

(东堂; Dōng Táng; Map p66; 74 Wangfujing Dajie; ⏱6.30-7am Mon-Sat, to 8am Sun; ⓜDēngshìkǒu) Sublimely illuminated at night and called 'East Cathedral' in Chinese, St Joseph's Church was originally built in 1655, damaged by an earthquake in 1720 and rebuilt. The luckless church also caught fire in 1807, was destroyed again in 1900 during the Boxer Rebellion, and restored in 1904, only to be shut in 1966.

ANCIENT OBSERVATORY
Historic Site

(古观象台; Gǔ Guānxiàngtái; Map p86; admission Y10; ⏱9.30am-4.30pm Tue-Sun; ⓜJiànguómén) Stargazing is perhaps on the back foot in today's Běijīng – it could take a supernova to penetrate the haze that frequently blankets the nocturnal sky – but the Chinese capital has a sparkling history of astronomical observation. Běijīng's ancient observatory, mounted on the battlements of a watchtower lying along the line of the old Ming city wall, originally dates to Kublai Khan's days when it lay north of the present site.

Climb the steps to the roof and an array of Jesuit-designed astronomical instruments, embellished with sculptured bronze dragons and other Chinese flourishes – a unique alloy of East and West. The Jesuits, scholars as well as proselytisers, arrived in 1601 when Matteo Ricci and his associates were permitted to work alongside Chinese scientists, becoming the Chinese court's official advisers.

CONFUCIUS TEMPLE & IMPERIAL COLLEGE
Confucian Temple

An incense stick's toss away from the Lama Temple, the desiccated **Confucius Temple** (孔庙、国子监; Kǒng Miào; Map p77; 13 Guozijian Jie; admission Y20; ⏱8.30am-5pm; ⓜYonghegong-Lama Temple) had a pre-Olympics spruce up that failed to shift its indelible sense of other-worldly detachment. Some of Běijīng's last remaining *páilou* bravely survive in the *hútòng* outside (Guozijian Jie) while antediluvian *bìxì* (tortoiselike dragons) glare inscrutably from repainted pavilions. Lumpy and ossified ancient cypresses claw stiffly at the sky while at the rear a numbing forest of 190 stelae (stones or slabs etched with figures or inscriptions) records the 13 Confucian classics in 630,000 Chinese characters.

West of the Confucius Temple is the **Imperial College** (国子监; Guózǐjiàn; Map p77), where the emperor expounded the Confucian classics to an audience of thousands of kneeling students, professors and court officials – an annual rite. On the site is a marvellous glazed, three-gate, single-eaved decorative archway. The Bìyōng Hall beyond is a twin-roofed structure with yellow tiles surrounded by a moat and topped with a shimmering gold knob.

The surrounding streets and *hútòng* are ideal for browsing, harbouring a charming selection of cafes, restaurants and small shops.

DRUM TOWER & BELL TOWER
Historic Site

Repeatedly destroyed and restored, the **Drum Tower** (鼓楼; Gǔlóu; Map p77; Gulou Dongdajie; admission Y20, both towers through ticket Y30; ⏱9am-5pm, last tickets 4.40pm) originally marked the centre of the old Mongol capital. The drums of this later Ming-dynasty version were beaten to mark the hours of the day. Stagger up the incredibly steep steps for impressive views over Běijīng's *hútòng* rooftops. Drum performances are given hourly from 9.30am to 11.30am and from 1.30pm to 4.50pm.

Fronted by a stele from the Qing dynasty, the **Bell Tower** (钟楼; Zhōnglóu; Map p77; ☏6401 2674; Zhonglouwan Hutong; admission Y15, both towers through ticket Y30; ⏱9am-5pm, last tickets 4.40pm) originally dates from Ming times. The Ming structure went up in a sheet of flame

ALAMY/CHINA PHOTOS

Don't Miss **Nanluogu Xiang**

Once neglected and ramshackle, strewn with spent coal briquettes in winter and silent except for the hacking coughs of old-timers or the jangling of bicycle bells, the fun-filled north–south alleyway of Nanluogu Xiang (literally 'South Gong and Drum Alley') underwent accelerated evolution from around 2000 when the pioneering Passby Bar served its first customer. In the mid-noughties, money was tipped into a Nanluogu Xiang facelift: the alley is now the model for how an old *hútòng* haunt can be converted for those in need of decent breakfasts, diverse shopping, appetising lunches, *hútòng* sightseeing, a round of imported beers with dinner and funky courtyard accommodation (in that order). If you're looking to put a pillow under your head, a mushrooming array of fine courtyard hotels has sprung up.

Today you can hoover up a miscellany of food from German waffles to crepes, Mongolian, Tibetan or Qīnghǎi yoghurt, fish and chips and cheap alcohol, or fork out for toys, trendy T-shirts, ceramics and much more. The shop with the eternal queue is the Wēnyǔ Cheese Shop (No 49), flogging Mongolian cheese. Taxis occasionally cruise up the narrow alley, leaving camera-toting pedestrians pinned to the wall.

NEED TO KNOW

南锣鼓巷; **Map p77**

and the present structure is a Qing edifice dating from the 18th century. Augment visits with drinks at the Drum & Bell Bar.

Both the Drum and Bell Towers can be reached on bus 5, 58 or 107; get off at the namesake Gǔlóu stop.

CHINA ART GALLERY   Art Gallery
(中国美术馆; Zhōngguó Měishùguǎn; Map p66; 1 Wusi Dajie; admission Y20; ⏱9am-5pm, last entry 4pm; Ⓜ Dōngsī) The China Art Gallery has a range of modern paintings and hosts occasional photographic exhibitions. The subject matter of art on display

is frequently anodyne – especially from Chinese artists – so consider a trip to 798 Art District for something more electrifying. There's no permanent collection so all exhibits are temporary.

Xīchéng 西城区

BĚIHĂI PARK 北海公园   Park
(Běihǎi Gōngyuán; Map p64; admission Y5/10 high/low season, through ticket low/high season Y15/20; ⏱ 6.30am-8pm, buildings until 4pm; Ⓜ Tiānānmén Xī, then bus 5) Běihǎi Park, northwest of the Forbidden City, is largely occupied by the North Sea (*běihǎi*), a huge lake that freezes in winter and blooms with lotuses in summer. Old folk dance together outside temple halls and come twilight, young couples cuddle on benches.

The site is associated with Kublai Khan's palace, Běijīng's navel before the arrival of the Forbidden City. All that survives of the Khan's court is a large jar made of green jade in the Round City (团城; Tuánchéng), near the southern entrance. Attached to the North Sea, the South (Nánhǎi) and Middle Seas (Zhōnghǎi) to the south lend their name to the nerve centre of the Communist Party west of the Forbidden City, Zhōngnánhǎi (literally 'Middle and South Seas').

Topping **Jade Islet** (琼岛; Qióngdǎo) on the lake, the 36m-high Tibetan-style

Běijīng's Hútòng

Běijīng's medieval genotype is most discernible down the city's leafy *hútòng* (胡同; narrow alleyways). The spirit and soul of the city lives and breathes among these charming and ragged lanes where a warm sense of community and hospitality survives. Criss-crossing chunks of Běijīng within the Second Ring Rd, the *hútòng* link up into a huge and enchanting warren of one-storey dwellings and historic courtyard homes. Hundreds of *hútòng* survive but many have been swept aside in Běijīng's race to build a modern city.

After Genghis Khan's army reduced the city of Běijīng to rubble, the new city was redesigned with *hútòng*. By the Qing dynasty over 2000 such passageways riddled the city, leaping to around 6000 by the 1950s; now the figure has drastically dwindled. Today's *hútòng* universe is a hotchpotch of the old and the new: Qing-dynasty courtyards are scarred with socialist-era conversions and outhouses while others have been assiduously rebuilt, with a garage perhaps for the Mercedes.

Hútòng nearly all run east–west so that the main gate faces south, satisfying feng shui (wind/water) requirements. This south-facing aspect guarantees sunshine and protection from negative principles amassing in the north.

Old walled *sìhéyuàn* (courtyards) are the building blocks of this delightful universe. Many are still lived in and hum with activity. From spring to autumn, men collect outside their gates, drinking beer, playing chess, smoking and chewing the fat. Inside, scholar trees soar aloft, providing shade and a nesting ground for birds.

More venerable courtyards are fronted by large, thick red doors, outside of which perch either a pair of Chinese lions or drum stones. Tours are easy to find: *hútòng* trishaw drivers lurk in packs around Qiánhǎi Lake: if you are foreign and not walking with real intent, they pounce, waiving flimsy plastic-wrapped cards detailing their tours and repeating the words '*hútòng, hútòng*' (all too often the extent of their 'English').

White Dagoba (白塔; Báitǎ) was originally built in 1651 for a visit by the Dalai Lama, and was rebuilt in 1741. Climb up to the *dagoba* via the **Yǒng'ān Temple** (永安寺; Yǒng'ān Sì).

Xītiān Fànjīng (西天梵境; Western Paradise), situated on the northern shore of the lake, is a lovely temple (admission included in park ticket). The nearby **Nine Dragon Screen** (九龙壁; Jiǔlóng Bì), a 5m-high and 27m-long spirit wall, is a glimmering stretch of coloured glazed tiles depicting coiling dragons, similar to its counterpart in the Forbidden City (p68).

JĪNGSHĀN PARK 景山公园   Park
(Jīngshān Gōngyuán; Map p64; ☏6403 3225; admission Y5; ⌚6am-9.30pm; Ⓜ Tiānānmén Xī, then bus 5) A feng shui barrier shielding the Forbidden City from evil spirits (or dust

storms), Jīngshān Park was formed from the earth excavated to create the palace moat. Come here for classic panoramas over the Forbidden City's russet roofing to the south. On the eastern side of the park a locust tree stands in the place where the last of the Ming emperors, Chongzhen, hanged himself as rebels swarmed at the city walls.

PRINCE GONG'S RESIDENCE 恭王府
Historic Site
(Gōngwáng Fǔ; Map p64; ☏6616 8149, 6601 6132; 14 Liuyin Jie; admission Y40, guided tours incl tea & performance Y60; ⌚7.30am-4.30pm summer, 8am-4pm winter; Ⓜ Pinganli, then bus 118) Reputed to be the model for the mansion in Cao Xueqin's 18th-century classic *Dream of the Red Mansions*, this residence is one of Běijīng's largest private residential compounds. If you

Cháoyáng & Sanlitun

◉ Top Sights
Poly Art Museum A3

🛏 Sleeping
1 Hotel G B4
2 Opposite House Hotel C2

🍴 Eating
3 April Gourmet C2
4 Běijīng Dàdǒng Roast Duck
   Restaurant D3
5 Dōngběirén A2
6 Element Fresh C3
Hatsune .... (see 16)
7 Pure Lotus D3

🍷🍸 Drinking
8 Bookworm Café D4
9 Face B4
10 Tree C3

🎭 Entertainment
11 Destination B4
12 MixBěijīng B3
13 Poly Plaza International Theatre A3
14 Tiāndì Theatre A3

🛍 Shopping
Bookworm Café .... (see 8)
15 Sānlǐtún Yashou Clothing Market C3
16 The Village C3

can, get here ahead of the tour buses and admire the rockeries, plants, pools, pavilions, corridors and elaborately carved gateways. Arrive with the crowds and you won't want to stay. Performances of Běijīng opera are held regularly in the Qing-dynasty Grand Opera House in the east of the grounds.

MIÀOYĪNG TEMPLE WHITE DAGOBA
Buddhist Temple

(妙应寺白塔; Miàoyīng Sì Báitǎ; Map p64; ☎6616 0211; 171 Fuchengmennei Dajie; admission Y20; ◷9am-4pm; Ⓜ Fùchéngmén) Buried away down a ragged *hútòng*, the Miàoyīng Temple slumbers beneath its distinctive, pure-white Yuan dynasty dagoba. The **Hall of the Great Enlightened One** (大觉宝殿; Dàjué Bǎodiàn) glitters splendidly with hundreds of Tibetan Buddhist effigies, the highlight of any visit.

Take bus 13, 101, 102 or 103 to Báitǎ Sì bus stop (near Baitasi Lu) or take the subway to Fùchéngmén and walk east.

Chóngwén 崇文区

TEMPLE OF HEAVEN PARK
Park

(天坛公园; Tiāntán Gōngyuán; Map p64; Tiantan Donglu; admission park/through ticket high season Y15/35, low season Y10/30, audio tour available at each gate Y40; ◷park 6am-9pm, sights 8am-6pm; Ⓜ Tiāntándōngmén) A tranquil oasis of peace and methodical Confucian design in one of China's busiest urban landscapes, the 267-hectare Temple of Heaven Park is encompassed by a long

wall with a gate at each compass point. The temple – the Chinese actually means 'Altar of Heaven' so don't expect burning incense or worshippers – originally served as a vast stage for solemn rites performed by the Son of Heaven, who prayed here for good harvests, and sought divine clearance and atonement. Around 4000 ancient, knotted cypresses (some 800 years old, their branches propped up on poles) poke towards the Běijīng skies within the grounds.

Seen from above, the temple halls are round and the bases square, in accordance with the notion 'Tiānyuán Dìfāng' (天圆地方) – 'Heaven is round, Earth is square'. Also observe that the northern rim of the park is semicircular, while its southern end is square. The traditional approach to the temple was from the south, via **Zhāohēng Gate** (昭亨门; Zhāohēng Men); the north gate is an architectural afterthought.

The 5m-high **Round Altar** (圜丘; Yuánqiū; admission Y20) was constructed in 1530 and rebuilt in 1740. Consisting of white marble arrayed in three tiers, its geometry revolves around the imperial number nine. Odd numbers possess heavenly significance, with nine the largest single-digit odd number. Symbolising heaven, the top tier is a huge mosaic of nine rings, each composed of multiples of nine stones, so that the ninth ring equals 81 stones. The stairs and balustrades are similarly presented

in multiples of nine. Sounds generated from the centre of the upper terrace undergo amplification from the marble balustrades (the acoustics can get noisy when crowds join in).

The octagonal **Imperial Vault of Heaven** (皇穹宇; Huáng Qióngyǔ) was erected at the same time as the Round Altar, its shape echoing the lines of the Hall of Prayer for Good Harvests. The hall contained tablets of the emperor's ancestors, employed during winter solstice ceremonies.

Wrapped around the Imperial Vault of Heaven just north of the altar is the **Echo Wall** (回音壁; Huíyīnbì; admission Y20). A whisper can travel clearly from one end to your friend's ear at the other – unless a cacophonous tour group joins in (get here early for this one).

The dominant feature of the park is the **Hall of Prayer for Good Harvests** (祈年殿; Qínián Diàn; admission Y20), an astonishing structure with a triple-eaved purplish-blue umbrella roof mounted on a three-tiered marble terrace. The wooden pillars (made from Oregon fir) support the ceiling without nails or cement – for a building 38m high and 30m in diameter, that's quite an accomplishment. Embedded in the ceiling is a carved dragon, a symbol of the emperor. Built in 1420, the hall was reduced to carbon after being zapped by a lightning bolt during the reign of Guangxu in 1889; a faithful reproduction based on Ming architectural methods was erected the following year.

POLY ART MUSEUM   Museum
(保利艺术博物馆; Bǎolì Yìshù Bówùguǎn; Map p82; www.polymuseum.com; Poly Plaza, 14 Dongzhimen Nandajie; admission Y20; Ⓜ Dong sishitiao) Caressed with Chinese music, this excellent museum displays a glorious array of ancient bronzes from the Shang and Zhou dynasties and an exquisite gathering of standing Bodhisattva statues. Resembling a semidivine race of smiling humans, most of the statues are from the Northern Qi, Northern Wei and Tang dynasties. It's a sublime presentation

Left: Waitress serving soup in a Běijīng *hútòng*; **Below:** Calligraphy water painting in the Temple of Heaven Park (p83)

PHOTOGRAPHER: (LEFT)RAY LASKOWITZ/LONELY PLANET IMAGES ©;(BELOW)RICHARD I'ANSON/LONELY PLANET IMAGES ©

and some of the statues have journeyed through the centuries with pigment still attached. In an attached room are four of the Western-styled 12 bronze animals plundered during the sacking of the Old Summer Palace.

NATIONAL STADIUM & NATIONAL AQUATICS CENTER   Stadium

(国家体育场、国家游泳中心; Guójiā Tǐyùchǎng; Guójiā Yóuyǒng Zhōngxīn; Map p64; National Stadium Y50, National Aquatics Center Y30; 🕙9am-6.30pm; Ⓜ Olympic Sport Center or Olympic Green) It's now hard to imagine that this was the scene of rapturous sporting exultation in August 2008, but such is the fate of most Olympics projects. You can enter the inspiring **National Stadium** – colloquially known as the Bird's Nest – in an attempt to recapture the euphoria of '08 and even ascend the medals podium for a further Y200, or simply admire the architecture for free from the outside. In the winter of 2010, it re-emerged as a snow park;

visionaries see its future as a shopping mall and entertainment complex. The nearby **Water Cube** is well worth a gander from the outside, and at the time of writing was set to open as Asia's largest indoor water park.

Xuānwǔ & Fēngtái
宣武区、丰台区

CAPITAL MUSEUM   Museum

(中国首都博物馆; Zhōngguó Shǒudū Bówùguǎn; Map p64; ☎6337 0491; www.capitalmuseum.org.cn; 16 Fuxingmenwai Dajie; admission Y15; 🕙9am-5pm; Ⓜ Muxidi) This rewarding and impressively styled museum contains a mesmerising collection of ancient Buddhist statues and a lavish exhibition of Chinese porcelain. Further displays are dedicated to a chronological history of Běijīng, cultural relics of Peking Opera, a Běijīng Folk Customs exhibition and exhibits of ancient bronzes, jade, calligraphy and paintings.

QIANMEN DAJIE   Historic Street

(前门大街; Map p66; M Qiánmén) Recently reopened after a costly overhaul, this shopping street – now pedestrianised and 'restored' to resemble a late Qing-dynasty street scene – was designed to bring the tourist dollar to a once charmingly tatty area. As late as the 1950s, this road was called Zhengyangmen Dajie (Facing the Sun Gate St), after Front Gate immediately north. Visitors are today treated to the rebuilt **Qiánmén Decorative Arch** (a concrete fake: the original was torn down in the 1950s) and invited to hop on one of the two reproduction trams (Y20) to glide along the street. Qianmen Dajie's former commercial vitality and sense of community is gone and local shops have made way for Zara, H&M *et al*.

DASHILAR   Historic Street

(大栅栏; Dàshílán'er; Map p66; M Qiánmén) Just west of Qianmen Dajie, this recently restored historic shopping street is a fascinating way to reach the antique shop street of Liulichang to the west. A collection of *lǎozi hào* (shops with history) include Ruifuxiang, Tongrentang, the Neiliansheng Shoe Shop and Liubiju. It's also an excellent place to snack and find accommodation.

WHITE CLOUD TEMPLE   Taoist Temple

(白云观; Báiyún Guàn; Baiyun Lu; Map p64 admission Y10; 8.30am-4.30pm May-Sep, to 4pm Oct-Apr; M Muxidi) Founded in AD 739, White Cloud Temple is a lively complex of shrines and courtyards, tended by distinctive Taoist monks with their hair twisted into topknots. Today's temple halls principally date from Ming and Qing times.

To find the temple, walk south on Baiyun Lu and cross the moat. Continue south along Baiyun Lu and turn into a curving street on the left; follow it for 250m to the temple entrance.

Hǎidiàn 海淀区,

SUMMER PALACE   Historic Site

(颐和园; Yíhé Yuán; Map p88; 19 Xinjian Gongmen; ticket Y20, through ticket Y50, audio guide Y40; 8:30am-5pm; M Xīyuán or Běigōngmén) Virtually as mandatory a Běijīng sight as the Great Wall or the Forbidden City, the gargantuan Summer Palace easily merits

South Cháoyáng

◎ **Top Sights**
    Ancient Observatory A3

⌂ Sleeping
  1 China World Hotel.................................D3
  2 Home Inn...D2

✪ Eating
    China World Shopping Mall..........(see 1)
  3 Jenny Lou's..B2
  4 Xiao Wang's Home Restaurant...........C3
  5 Xiao Wang's Home Restaurant...........B2

✪ Entertainment
  6 Cháoyáng Theatre.............................. D1
  7 GT Banana B3

🛍 Shopping
    Chaterhouse Booktrader........... (see 12)
  8 Five Colours Earth D3
  9 Garden Books.......................................A2
 10 Shard Box Store.................................. B1
 11 Silk Street C3
 12 Place C2

an entire day's exploration, although a (high-paced) morning or afternoon may suffice.

The domain had long been a royal garden before being considerably enlarged and embellished by Emperor Qianlong in the 18th century. He marshalled a 100,000-strong army of labourers to deepen and expand **Kūnmíng Lake** (昆明湖; Kūnmíng Hú; Map p88), and reputedly surveyed imperial navy drills from a hilltop perch.

Anglo-French troops vandalised the palace during the Second Opium War (1856–60). Empress Dowager Cixi launched into a refit in 1888 with money earmarked for a modern navy; the marble boat at the northern edge of the lake was her only nautical – albeit quite unsinkable – concession.

Foreign troops, angered by the Boxer Rebellion, had another go at torching the Summer Palace in 1900, prompting further restoration work. By 1949 the palace had once more fallen into disrepair, eliciting a major overhaul.

Glittering Kūnmíng Lake swallows up three-quarters of the park, overlooked by **Longevity Hill** (万寿山; Wànshòu Shān). The principal structure is the **Hall of Benevolence and Longevity** (仁寿殿; Rénshòu Diàn; Map p88), by the east gate, housing a hardwood throne and attached to a courtyard decorated with bronze animals, including the mythical *qílín* (a hybrid animal that only appeared on earth at times of harmony). Unfortunately, the hall is barricaded off so you will have to peer in.

An elegant stretch of woodwork along the northern shore, the **Long Corridor** (长廊; Cháng Láng; Map p88) is trimmed with a plethora of paintings, while the slopes and crest of Longevity Hill behind are adorned with Buddhist temples. Slung out uphill on a north–south axis, the **Buddhist Fragrance Pavilion** (佛香阁; Fóxiāng Gé; Map p88) and the **Cloud Dispelling Hall** (排云殿; Páiyún Diàn; Map p88) are linked by corridors. Crowning the peak is the **Buddhist Temple of the Sea of Wisdom** (智慧海; Zhìhuì Hǎi; Map p88), tiled with effigies of Buddha, many with obliterated heads.

Cixi's **marble boat** (清晏船; Qīngyàn Chuán; Map p88) sits immobile on the north shore, south of some fine Qing **boathouses** (船坞; Chuán Wù; Map p88). When the lake is not frozen, you can traverse Kūnmíng Lake by ferry to **South Lake Island** (南湖岛; Nánhú Dǎo; Map p88), where Cixi went to beseech the **Dragon King Temple** (龙王庙; Lóngwáng Miào; Map p88) for rain in times of drought. A graceful **17-arch bridge** (十七孔桥; Shíqīkǒng Qiáo; Map p88) spans the 150m to the eastern shore of the lake. In warm weather, **pedal boats** (4-/6-person boat per hr Y40/60; ⏰8.30am-4.30pm in summer) are also available from the dock.

Try to do a circuit of the lake along the **West Causeway** (Xīdī) to return along the east shore (or vice versa). It gets you away from the crowds, the views are gorgeous and it's a great cardiovascular workout.

Towards the North Palace Gate, **Sūzhōu Street** (苏州街; Sūzhōu Jiē; Map p88) is an entertaining and light-hearted diversion of riverside walkways, shops

Summer Palace

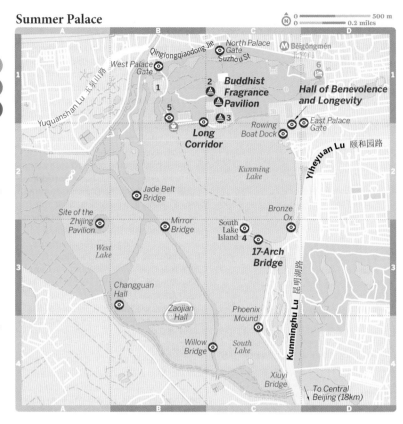

Summer Palace

⊙ Top Sights

17-Arch Bridge.................................C3
Buddhist Fragrance Pavilion..............C1
Hall of Benevolence and Longevity C2
Long Corridor B1

⊙ Sights

1 Boathouses....................................B1
2 Buddhist Temple of the Sea of
  Wisdom......................................C1
3 Cloud Dispelling Hall.......................C1
4 Dragon King Temple.........................C3
5 Marble Boat...................................B1

⊟ Sleeping

6 Aman at Summer Palace....................D1

and eateries designed to mimic the famous Jiāngsū canal town.

The Summer Palace is about 12km northwest of the centre of Běijīng,

accessed via Xīyuàn (Exit C2) or Běigōngmén stations on line 4 of the metro system. In warmer months there's the option of taking a **boat** (☎ 8836 3576; **Houhu Pier; one-way/return incl Summer Palace admission Y70/100)** from behind the Běijīng Exhibition Center near the zoo; the boat voyages via locks along the canal.

OLD SUMMER PALACE　Historic Site
(圆明园; Yuánmíng Yuán; Map p64; admission Y10, palace ruins Y15; ⊙ 7am-7pm; Ⓜ Yuán-míngyuán Park) Forever etched on China's national consciousness for its sacking and destruction by British and French forces during the Second Opium War, the old Summer Palace was originally laid out in the 12th century. Resourceful Jesuits were later employed by Emperor Qianlong to fashion European-style palaces for the gardens, incorporating

elaborate fountains and baroque statuary. During its looting, much went up in flames and considerable booty was sent abroad, but a melancholic tangle of broken columns and marble chunks from the hardier Jesuit-designed stone palace buildings remain.

The subdued marble ruins of the **Palace Buildings Scenic Area** (Xīyánglóu Jǐngqū) can be mulled over in the **Eternal Spring Garden** (Chángchūn Yuán) in the northeast of the park, near the east gate. There were once over 10 buildings here, designed by Giuseppe Castiglione and Michael Benoist.

The **Great Fountain Ruins** (大水法遗址; Dàshuǐfǎ Yízhǐ) themselves are considered the best-preserved relics. Built in 1759, the main building was fronted by a lion's-head fountain. Standing opposite is the **Guānshuǐfǎ** (观水法), five large stone screens embellished with European carvings of military flags, armour, swords and guns.

West of the Great Fountain Ruins are the vestiges of the **Hǎiyàntáng Reservoir** (海宴堂蓄水池台基; Hǎiyàntáng Xùshuǐchí Táijī), where the water for the impressive fountains was stored in a tower and huge water-lifting devices were employed. Also known as the Water Clock, the **Hǎiyàntáng**, where 12 bronze human statues with animal heads jetted water in 12 two-hour sequences, was constructed in 1759. The 12 animal heads from this apparatus was distributed among collections abroad and Běijīng is attempting to retrieve them (four of the animal heads can be seen at the Poly Art Museum). Just west of here is the Fāngwàiguàn, a building turned into a mosque for an imperial concubine; an artful reproduction of a former labyrinth called the **Garden of Yellow Flowers** (迷宫; Mígōng) is also nearby.

The gardens cover a huge area – some 2.5km from east to west – so be prepared for some walking. Besides the ruins, there's the western section, the **Perfection & Brightness Garden** (圆明园; Yuánmíng Yuán) and the southern compound, the **10,000 Spring Garden** (万春园; Wànchūn Yuán).

About a 15-minute walk north from the front gate (follow the signs) near the Magnolia Garden is the **Temple of the Reclining Buddha** (Wòfó Sì; admission Y5; ☺8am-4.30pm). First built in the Tang dynasty, the temple's centrepiece is a huge reclining effigy of Sakyamuni weighing in at 54 tonnes, which 'enslaved 7000 people' in its casting. The reclining form of Buddha represents his moment of death, before entering nirvana. On each side of Buddha are sets of gargantuan shoes, imperial gifts to Sakyamuni.

To get here take the subway to Běijīng Zoo and then hop on fast bus 360; alternatively go to Píngguǒyuán subway station and take bus 318.

 **Courses**

CHINA CULTURE CENTER
Cultural Programs

(☏weekdays 6432 9341, weekends 6432 0141; www.chinaculturecenter.org; Kent Center; 29 Anjialou, Liangmaqiao Lu; ⓜLiangmaqiao) Offers a range of cultural programs, taught in English

Big Underpants

The outlandish 234m-high CCTV Building (Map p86), a continuous loop through horizontal and vertical planes, is a unique addition to the Běijīng skyline. Boldly ambitious and designed by Rem Koolhaas and Ole Scheeren of OMA, the building is an audacious statement of modernity, despite being dubbed 'Big Underpants' by locals. In February 2009, stray fireworks from CCTV's own Lantern Festival display sent the costly TV Cultural Center in the north of the complex up in flames. CCTV famously censored its own reporting of the huge conflagration, even though it was visible for miles around. Big Underpants escaped unsinged.

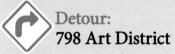

Detour:
798 Art District

Originally flung up by the East Germans, the disused and sprawling electronics factory known as **798 Art District** (798 艺术新区; Map p64; cnr Jiuxianqiao Lu & Jiuxianqiao Beilu; admission free) has for years served as the focus for Běijīng's feisty art community. Stand-out galleries include **Long March Space** (✆6438 7107; www.longmarchspace.com; ⏲11am-7pm Tue-Sun) where paintings, photos, installations and videos get a viewing, and the well-known **Chinese Contemporary Běijīng** (Zhōngguó Dāngdài; ✆8456 2421; www.chinesecontemporary.com; 4 Jiuxianqiao Lu; ⏲11am-7pm); Also check out **Contrasts Gallery** (✆6432 1369; ⏲10am-6pm Tue-Sun), **Běijīng Tokyo Art Projects** (Běijīng Dōngjīng Yìshù Gōngchéng; ✆8457 3245; www.tokyo-gallery.com; 4 Jiuxianqiao Lu) and the excellent **798 Photo Gallery** (Bǎinián Yìnxiàng; ✆6438 1784; www.798photogallery.cn; 4 Jiuxianqiao Lu). Several cafes are at hand when your legs give way.

and aimed squarely at foreign visitors and expats. The club also conducts popular tours around Běijīng and expeditions to other parts of China.

Sleeping

After its Olympic workout, Běijīng has re-emerged with an impressive bevy of accommodation spanning all budgets. The budget bracket – which once scarcely existed for foreign backpackers – is now a fiercely competitive arena of youth hostels and affordable lodgings. Even the staid midrange bracket has been slapped into shape, while the opening of top-flight courtyard and boutique hotels has added more eye-catching choice to the top end.

For hotel bookings, the online agencies **CTrip** (✆400 619 9999; http://english.ctrip.com) and **Elong** (✆400 617 1717; www.elong.net) are useful.

Dōngchéng
CITY WALLS COURTYARD
Courtyard Hotel **$**
(✆6402 7805; www.beijingcitywalls.com; 57 Nianzi Hutong; 碾子胡同57号; 8-/4-bed dm Y100/120, d Y380; ❄ @) Lovely rooms, crumbling *hútòng* setting, a warm courtyard atmosphere and bubbly owner: this excellent hostel is stuffed away within

one of Běijīng's most historic areas. The mazelike web of *hútòng* can be disorientating: from Jingshan Houjie, look for the *hútòng* opening just east of the playground and the Sinopec petrol station. Walk up the *hútòng* and follow it around to the right and then left – the hostel is on the left-hand side. The north gate of the Forbidden City is merely a few minutes' walk away.

PEKING INTERNATIONAL YOUTH HOSTEL
Youth Hostel **$**
(北平国际青年旅社; Běipíng Guójì Qīngnián Lǚshè; Map p70; ✆6526 8855; 5 Beichizi Ertiao; 北池子二条5号; 4-/8-/12-bed dm Y100/100/90, d Y400-500; ❄ @ 🛜) The discreet, central alleyway location is the icing on this particular cake, parcelled away off Nanchizi Dajie, a guidebook's throw from the Forbidden City. The highly relaxing *hútòng* aspect maintains just the right vibe – homey lounge area, small and leafy courtyard, good dorms (doubles are small, though) and an intimate ambience, although it's a tad pricier than many other hostels. Reserve ahead.

RAFFLES BĚIJĪNG HOTEL
Hotel **$$$**
(北京饭店莱佛士; Běijīng Fàndiàn Láifóshì; Map p66; ✆6526 3388; www.beijing.raffles.com; 33 Dongchang'an Jie; 东长安街33号; d incl breakfast Y4100, discount normally 30-40%; 🛜 ❄ 🛜) The seven-storey Raffles oozes

cachet and pedigree, lucratively cashing in on a lineage dating to 1900 (when it was the Grand Hotel de Pekin) and an impeccable location. The elegant lobby yields to a graceful staircase leading to immaculate standard doubles that are spacious and well proportioned, decked out with period-style furniture and large bathrooms.

PARK PLAZA Hotel **$$**
(北京丽亭酒店; Běijīng Lìtíng Jiǔdiàn; Map p66; ☎8522 1999; www.parkplaza.com/beijingcn; 97 Jinbao Jie; 金宝街97号; d Y850; ☒❄@☎) Appealing midrange value with more than a shot of style in the heart of town; the modish Park Plaza has a tip-top location plus a comfortable, modern and well-presented four-star finish. The lobby is mildly jazzy and sedate – but not subdued – arranged with seats in chocolate-brown leather, while rooms are stylish and comfy.

EMPEROR Hotel **$$$**
(皇家驿栈酒店; Huángjiā Yìzhàn Jiǔdiàn; Map p70; ☎6526 5566; www.theemperor.com.cn; 33 Qihelou Jie; 骑河楼街; d Y1600; ☒❄@☎) The location just east of the Forbidden City is certainly regal, although views from the upper-floor rooms merely graze the rooftops of the imperial palace. The funkily designed rooms are named after China's emperors; sink a drink in the excellent rooftop bar. Free internet access and wi-fi.

HǍOYUÁN HOTEL Courtyard Hotel **$$**
(好园宾馆; Hǎoyuán Bīnguǎn; ☎6512 5557; www.haoyuanhotel.com; 53 Shijia Hutong; 史家胡同53号; d standard/deluxe Y760/930, ste Y1080-1380, VIP r Y1590; ❄@☎) The eight standard rooms in the red-lantern-hung front courtyard are delightfully arranged, albeit small. The gorgeous leafy rear courtyard is more enchanting still. For more space, the largest suite's bedroom is set off from a Chinese parlour, complete with calligraphic hangings, vases, rugs and lanterns, while the VIP room is huge. The only discernible drawback is the yawning wasteland eyesore opposite the front gate. The hotel is a short walk from the Dengshikou metro station.

Courtyard 7 Courtyard Hotel **$$$**
(七号院; Qīhàoyuàn; Map p77; ☎6406 0777; www.courtyard7.com; 7 Qiangulouyuan Hutong;

Pedestrian bridge near main train station, Dōngchéng

前鼓楼苑胡同7号; d Y1180, VIP d Y1400, discounts 45%; ai) With tip-top service and three lovely courtyards slung behind a serene old *hútòng* exterior, this is a delightful and fantastically quiet courtyard hotel in a fabulous central location.

Gǔxiàng 20　　　　　　　Hotel **$$**

(古巷20号; Gǔxiàng Èrshí Hào; Map p77; ☎6400 5566; www.guxiang20.com; 20 Nanluogu Xiang; 南锣鼓巷20号; s/d Y888/1280, discounts 35-40%; ❋ @) Nanluogu Xiang courtyard-looking hotel with pleasant but small singles decked out in Qing-style furniture and larger doubles; roof-top tennis court.

Xuānwǔ

QIÁNMÉN HOSTEL　　　　Hostel **$**

(前门客栈; Qiánmén Kèzhàn; Map p66; ☎6313 2370/2369; www.qianmenhostel.com; 33 Meishi Jie; 煤市街33号; 6-8-bed dm Y50, 4-bed dm Y70, tw/d/tr Y200/200/240; @ ❋) This heritage hostel combines a relaxing environment with high-ceilinged original woodwork, charming antique buildings and able staff. Heritage rooms are simple; purpose-built rooms are more modern but with less character. Western breakfasts, bike hire nearby, laundry available.

Xīchéng

RED LANTERN HOUSE

　　　　　　　　Courtyard Hotel **$**

(红灯笼客栈; Hóngdēnglóng Kèzhàn; ☎8328 5771; www.redlanternhouse.com; 5 Zhengjue Hutong; 正觉胡同5号; dm Y55-60, s Y140-180, tw Y160-260, d Y180-260; ❋ @ 🛜) Offers homely *hútòng*-located courtyard-style lodgings a short stroll from Hòuhǎi Lake and run by cheerful staff. Doubles are without shower, but are comfy, clean, cheap and charming. If it's booked out, two sibling branches are nearby. Internet (Y1 for 10 minutes), washing (Y10 per kilo), restaurant-bar in main lobby area (Tsingtao beer Y3 per bottle).

Cháoyáng

OPPOSITE HOUSE HOTEL　Hotel **$$$**

(瑜舍; Yúshè; Map p82; ☎6417 6688; www.theoppositehouse.com; Bldg 1, The Village, 11 Sanlitun Lu; 三里屯路11号院1号楼; d Y1950; 🛏 ❋ @ 🛜 ⛲) Artworks litter the lobby area and rooms are top-drawer chic with American oak bathtubs, open-plan bathrooms, underfloor heating and gorgeous mood lighting; the metal basin swimming pool and fastidiously trendy Mesh bar round out a totally sleek boutique picture. Excellent dining options.

HOTEL G　　　　　　　Hotel **$$**

(北京极栈; Běijīng Jízhàn; Map p82; ☎6552 3600; www.hotel-G.com; A7 Gongti Xilu; 工体西路甲7号; d incl breakfast Y1488; ❋ @ 🛜) Natty boutique hotel featuring a snappy blend of deep purple, charcoal greys, black, floral-print patterns and crushed-velvet textures. Snazzy rooms spoil you with a choice of six different pillows and you won't want to get out of bed, they're that comfy.

Acrobats at Cháoyáng Theatre (p99), Cháoyáng

CHINA WORLD HOTEL   Hotel $$$

(中国大饭店; Zhōngguó Dàfàndiàn; Map p86; ☑6505 2266; www.shangri-la.com; 1 Jianguomenwai Dajie; 建国门外大街1号; d Y2900; ⊜❄🛜➰) The gorgeous five-star China World matches its outstanding level of service to a sumptuous foyer: a masterpiece of Chinese motifs, glittering chandeliers, robust columns and smooth acres of marble. Rooms are modern and amenities extensive, with shopping needs met at the China World Trade Center.

HOME INN   Hotel $

(如家; Rújiā; Map p86; ☑5207 6666; 34 Dongsanhuan Zhonglu; 东三环中路34号; s/d Y259/299, big bed s & d Y299, business r Y339; ❄@) The location, rising up south of the awesome CCTV Building, is as good as we could find. Handy, neat, crisp, modern, fresh and versatile, it's also a bargain. Regularly shaped, simple and unfussy rooms offer no surprises: we're talking Ikea-style work desks, simple flat-screen TVs and ho-hum artwork on the walls. If space is a high priority, go for the luxury business rooms.

Hǎidiàn

MICHAEL'S HOUSE   Courtyard Hotel $$

(迈克之家; Màikè Zhījiā; ☑6222 5620; South yard, 1 Zhiqiang Gardens, Xiaoxitian; 小西天志强北园1号南院; d/ste Y608/1008; @) Elegant, quiet and convivial courtyard-style hotel with grey-brick styling and helpful, traditionally attired staff. Modern but quaintly Chinese, the comfy abode is attractively fringed with greenery, offering very pleasant *hútòng* rooms kitted out with a contemporary finish.

AMAN AT SUMMER PALACE   Hotel $$$

(颐和安缦; Yíhé Ānmàn; Map p88; ☑5987 9999; 15 Gongmenqian Jie; 宫门前街15号; r/courtyard r US$550/650, ste/courtyard ste US$850/$1110; ❄@🛜➰) Just round the corner from the Summer Palace, the elegant Aman resort hotel is an exclusive and palatial escape from Běijīng's fuggy and noisy central districts. Service is discreet and intimate, the courtyard rooms are gorgeous, while choice restaurants, a spa, a library, a cinema, pool and squash courts

---

Běijīng's Best Courtyard Hotels

- **Courtyard 7** (p91)
- **City Walls Courtyard** (p90)
- **Hǎoyuán Hotel** (p91)
- **Peking International Courtyard Hostel** (p90)

round off the refined picture, although prices can be heart-stopping.

Eating

For a proper handle on Chinese food, get the gloves off and sleeves rolled up in Běijīng. Not only is Běijīng cuisine (京菜; *jīngcài*) one of the major Chinese cooking styles, but chefs from all four corners of the land make the culinary pilgrimage here to serve the faddy masses.

Supermarkets

OLÉ SUPERMARKET   Supermarket

Handy branches of this well-stocked supermarket can be found in the basement of **Oriental Plaza** (Map p66; ⊙8.30am-10.30pm), the China World Shopping Mall (Map p86) and the **Ginza Mall** (Map p82; basement, 48 Dongzhimenwai Dajie; ⊙10am-10pm) in Dōngzhímén.

April Gourmet   Deli

(Map p82; 1 Sanlitun Beixiaojie; ⊙8am-9pm) An expat-oriented deli with fine wines and cheeses; three branches in town. Does deliveries.

Jenny Lou's   Deli

(婕妮璐; Jiénílù; Map p86; 6 Sanlitun Beixiaojie; ⊙8am-10pm) Fresh meat, fish, cheeses, wines and a wide array of deli items; six branches in town.

Dōngchéng

For convenient dining and a Pan-Asian selection under one roof, try one of the ubiquitous food courts that can be found in shopping malls throughout the city.

Ghost Street

Hopping at weekends and one of Běijīng's busiest and most colourful restaurant strips at virtually any hour, Ghost St (鬼街；Guǐ Jiē; Map p77) is the nickname of this spirited section of Dongzhimennei Dajie, where scores of restaurants converge to feed legions of locals and out-of-towners. Splendidly lit with red lanterns from dusk to dawn, Ghost St is lined with vocal restaurant staff enticing passers-by into hotpot eateries, spicy seafood restaurants and other heaving outfits. The street is always open so you'll always be able to get fed. Take the subway to Běixīnqiáo, head east along Dongzhimennei Dajie and you will find yourself immediately in Ghost St.

DÀLǏ COURTYARD
Yunnan $$
(大理; Dàlǐ; Map p77; ☎8404 1430; 67 Xiao-jingchang Hutong, Gulou Dongdajie; set menu from Y100; ⏲lunch & dinner) Part of the joy of this restaurant is its lovely courtyard setting; the other essential ingredient is the inventive Yúnnán cuisine from China's southwest. It's necessary to book in advance and, unconventionally, there is no menu. Dishes are devised on impulse by the chef, so communicate any dietary requirements up front.

CRESCENT MOON MUSLIM RESTAURANT
Muslim $$
(新疆弯弯月亮维吾尔穆斯林餐厅; Xīnjiāng Wānwān Yuèliàng Wéiwú'ěr Mùsīlín Cāntīng; 16 Dongsi Liutiao; dishes from Y18; ⏲lunch & dinner; 🗋) The delicious meaty lamb kebabs (羊肉串; yángròu chuàn) at this well-known hútòng-side Uighur restaurant are the talk of the town and there's a far more intimate feel here than at some of Běijīng's other more high-profile Uighur eateries. Try the dàpánjī (大盘鸡). There's a picture menu.

VINEYARD CAFE
European $$
(葡萄园; Pútao Yuán; Map p77; ☎6402 7961; 31 Wudaoying Hutong; set lunch Y55/60; ⏲lunch & dinner, closed Mon; 🗋) Famed for its full-on English breakfasts and excellent pizza, this popular and relaxing hútòng cafe is perfect for lunch after seeing the nearby Lama Temple or as a civilised choice for dinner or drinks.

CAFÉ SAMBAL
Malaysian $$
(Map p77; 43 Doufuchi Hutong; set lunch Y80; ⏲11am-midnight; 🗋) In an uncomplicated but trendy grey-brick, concrete and wood setting with rickety tables, Café Sambal brings Malaysian food to Běijīng with style and panache. The Kumar mutton with vegetables and rice set (Y80) is satisfying, and the menu embraces a wide range of Malaysian treats from Nyonya curry chicken (Y60) to beef rendang (Y60). Good winelist.

WÁNGFǓJǏNG SNACK STREET
Street Food $
(王府井小吃街; Map p66; Wángfǔjǐng Xiǎochījiē; kebabs & dishes from Y5; ⏲9am-10pm) Don't be put off by the starfish (Y20), cicada, seahorse and scorpion kebabs (Y20); this bustling corner of restaurants is a great place to feast elbow-to-elbow with other diners on Xīnjiāng or Muslim Uighur staples such as lamb kebabs (Y5) and flat bread, steaming bowls of málà tàng (麻辣烫; spicy noodle soup), zhájiàngmiàn (炸酱面; noodles in fried bean sauce; Y12), Lánzhōu lāmiàn (兰州拉面; Lánzhōu noodles) and oodles of spicy chuāncài (川菜; Sìchuān food). Round it all off with fried ice cream (Y10). Prices are touristy as it's just west off Wangfujing Dajie.

FOOD REPUBLIC
Food Hall $
(大食代; Dàshídài; Map p66; basement, Oriental Plaza, 1 Dongchang'an Jie; dishes from Y10; ⏲10am-10pm) Perfect for on-the-spot dining, this huge food court has point-and-serve Chinese and other Asian dining options packed under one roof. Purchase a card at the kiosk at the entrance, load up with credits (Y30 to Y500; Y10 deposit) and browse among the canteen-style outlets for whatever grabs your fancy,

from Old Běijīng to Hong Kong, Taiwan and beyond.

DŌNGHUÁMÉN NIGHT MARKET

Street Market **$**

(东华门夜市; Dōnghuámén Yèshì; Map p66; Dong'anmen Dajie; snacks from Y3; ⏱3-10pm, closed Chinese New Year) A sight in itself, the bustling night market near Wangfujing Dajie is a food zoo: lamb kebabs, beef and chicken skewers, corn on the cob, *chòu dòufu* (臭豆腐; smelly tofu), cicadas, grasshoppers, kidneys, quails' eggs, squid, fruit, porridge, fried pancakes, strawberry kebabs, bananas, Inner Mongolian cheese, stuffed aubergines, chicken hearts, pita bread stuffed with meat, shrimps and more. For tourists, expect inflated prices.

QUÁNJÙDÉ ROAST DUCK RESTAURANT

Beijing **$$$**

(全聚德烤鸭店; Quánjùdé Kǎoyādiàn; Map p66; 9 Shuaifuyuan Hutong; set menu incl duck, pancakes, scallions & sauce Y168; ⏱lunch & dinner; 🖳) Less touristy than its revamped Qiánmén sibling, this branch of the celebrated chain has a handy location off Wangfujing Dajie for shopping-laden diners. The roast duck (half duck Y54,

minus pancakes, scallions and sauce) is flavoursome and a key ingredient in a Běijīng sojourn.

Xīchéng

LE LITTLE SAIGON

Vietnamese, French **$$**

(西贡在巴黎; Xīgòng Zài Bālí; Map p77; meals from Y32; 🖳) The French songs and charmingly sedate, easy-going Indo-Chinese vibe are a world away from the fierce traffic noise outside. This yummy corner of French Vietnam hits all the right tastebuds: try scrumptiously scented seafood tamarind soup (Y32), snails in garlic butter (Y48) or Hanoi noodle soup with beef (Y35). Upstairs terrace open in summer.

HÚTÓNG PIZZA

Pizza **$$**

(胡同比萨; Hútóng Bǐsà; Map p77; 9 Yindingqiao Hutong Hou; meals Y80; ⏱11am-11pm; 🖳) The Chinese accuse Marco Polo of stealing pizza from China, and it's come back again. This very relaxing spot near the lakes fires up some enormous pizzas (although they are slow in coming). The *hútòng* house interior is funky and the attic room is handsome, with old painted beams.

Lama Temple arch (p78), Dōngchéng

GREG ELMS/LONELY PLANET IMAGES ©

Cháoyáng

HATSUNE   Japanese $$
(sushi from Y25; ⊙lunch & dinner; ⊜📖)
Chaoyang (2/F Heqiao Bldg C, 8a Guanghua Lu);
Sānlǐtún (Map p82; 3rd fl, The Village; Ⓜ Tuanjiehu) A stylish and relaxed US-style sushi
restaurant much applauded by fickle
and picky expat gastronomes for the
ambience and the standout and novelty-
named hand rolls. Good-value set lunch
deals.

ELEMENT FRESH   Western $$
(新元素; Xīn Yuánsù; Map p82; www.element
fresh.com; 8-3-3 Bldg 8, The Village, 19 Sanlitun
Lu; sandwiches from Y39, pasta from Y58;
⊙11am-11pm Mon-Fri, 8am-11pm Sat & Sun;
📶📖) It was only a matter of time
before the neat, spick-and-span and
perennially popular Shànghǎi outfit
migrated to town, bringing its health-
giving menu of salads, sandwiches,
pastas, smoothies and MSG-free dishes
to an eager tribe of Běijīng expats.
Branches also at a2-112, Qianmen Dajie
and Lido Plaza, 6 Jiangtai Lu.

XIAO WANG'S HOME RESTAURANT
                                            Beijing $$
(小王府; Xio Wngf; Map p86; ☎6594 3602, 6591
3255; 2 Guanghua Dongli; meals Y70; ⊙lunch
& dinner) Treat yourself to home-style
Běijīng cuisine at this excellent restaurant
and go for one of Xiao Wang's specials.
The piāoxiāng páigǔ (deep-fried spareribs

with pepper salt; Y38) are gorgeous: dry,
fleshy, crispy chops with a small pile of
fiery pepper salt. Xiao Wang's fried hot
and spicy Xīnjiāng-style zīran jīchì (chick-
en wings; Y35) is deservedly famous and
the Peking duck is crispy and lean (Y88
per duck, Y5 for sauce, scallions and
pancakes). There's outside seating and a
further attractive branch can be found in
the Rìtán Park (Map p86).

BĚIJĪNG DÀDŎNG ROAST DUCK
RESTAURANT   Beijing $$
(北京大董烤鸭店; Běijīng Dàdǒng Kǎoyādiàn;
Map p82; ☎6582 2892/4003; 3 Tuanjiehu
Beikou; duck Y98; ⊙lunch & dinner; 📖) A long-
term favourite of the Peking duck scene,
the hallmark fowl here is a crispy, lean
bird without the usual high fat content
(trimmed down from 42.38% to 15.22%
for its 'superneat' roast duck, the brochure says), plus plum (or garlic) sauce,
scallions and pancakes. Also carved up is
the skin of the duck with sugar, an imperial predilection.

DŌNGBĚIRÉN   Manchurian $$
(东北人; Map p82; ☎6415 2855; www.dongbeir
en.com.cn; 1a Xinzhong Jie; meals Y50; 📖) This
hearty Manchurian restaurant, overseen
by a smiling gaggle of rouge-cheeked,
pigtailed xiǎojiě (waitresses), cooks up
flavoursome dumplings (jiǎozi) and a fine
range of scrummy northeastern fare.

Běijīng's Best Vegetarian Restaurants

The words wǒ chīsù (我吃素; I am a vegetarian) are only understood in their
literal sense by the professionals, so if you require your vegetarian food to be
100% meat-free, follow your nose to one of the following.

Flee the 'world of dust' (the Buddhist metaphor for the temporal world) to
gracefully presented **Pure Lotus** (净心莲; Jìngxīnlián; Map p82; 12 Nongzhanguan Nanlu;
⊙11am-11pm; mains from Y58; Ⓜ Tuánjiéhú; ⊜📷📖), run by monks, with an attractive
accent on Buddhist cuisine.

Bǎihé Courtyard (百合素食; Bǎihé Sùshí; 23 Caoyuan Hutong; ⊙11am-10pm;
Ⓜ Dōngzhímén or Běixīnqiáo; ⊜📷📖) is one place where you can sample Peking
duck (Y68) without a major calamity for your karma: all dishes are mock-meat
and designed to trick your taste buds.

RAY LASKOWITZ/LONELY PLANET IMAGES ©

Drinking

In the past two decades, Běijīng has morphed from a straitlaced and sober citadel into a modern, drink-dependent capital. Běijīng bars are easing into a more seasoned furrow after years of energetic experimentation, although the bandwagon forever rolls on to occupy any profitable niche in the easily bored expat scene. Approach bars selling preposterously cheap (read possibly fake) alcohol, however, with caution.

Principal bar areas include a now-scattered and thinned-out colony in Sānlǐtún, a hopping slew of bars along Nanluogu Xiang, a long string of samey bars along the northern and southern shores of Hòuhǎi Lake (Hòuhǎi Nan'àn and Hòuhǎi Běi'àn) and nearby Yandai Xiejie; other outfits do their own thing, in their own part of town, including student dives in Wǔdàokǒu.

Cafes

BOOKWORM CAFÉ Cafe
(书虫; Shūchóng; Map p82; www.beijingbook worm.com; Bldg 4, Nansanlitun Lu; ☺8am-1am; 📶) Venue of the annual Běijīng Literary Festival in March, the Bookworm is a great place for breakfast, dining, a solo coffee or a major reading binge.

CAFE ZARA Cafe
(Map p77; www.cafezarah.com; 42 Gulou Dongdajie; coffee Y18, espresso Y15; ☺10am-midnight Wed-Mon; 📶) Peaceful and serene concrete-floor boho enclave on Gulou Dongdajie tranquillised by ambient/chill-out music (occasionally pierced by the squeal of taxi brakes on the road yonder); you *can* sit outside but you may end up swathed in fumes.

Bars

12SQM Bar
(十二平米酒吧; Shí'èr Píngmǐ Jiǔbā; Map p77; cnr Nanluogu Xiang & Fuxiang Hutong; beers from Y15, cocktails from Y35; ☺noon-midnight) The once self-proclaimed smallest bar in Běijīng has expanded to the rear but this much-loved watering hole, run by a welcoming husband-and-wife team, has lost none of its pocket-sized Nanluogu Xiang charm.

PASSBY BAR Bar
(过客; Guòkè; Map p77; 108 Nanluogu Xiang; ☺9am-2am) One of the original bars on

the cafe-bar strip Nanluogu Xiang and still one of the best, with travel-oriented bar staff, a winning courtyard ambience, shelves of books and mags, and a funky ethnic feel.

TREE
Bar

(树酒吧; Shù Jiǔbā; Map p82; ☎ 6415 1954; www.treebeijing.com; 43 Beisanlintun Nan; ⏱ 11am-2am Mon-Sat, 1pm-late Sun) Seriously popular expat dungeon regularly bursting with gregarious drinkers engrossed in conversation, chomping wood-fired pizza and gulping Leffe (Y40), Duvel (Y40) and over 40 Belgian brews, flogged by skilful bar staff.

MAO MAO CHONG BAR
Bar

(毛毛虫吧; Máomáochóng Bā; Map p77; 12 Banchang Hutong; ⏱ 5.30pm-late, closed Tue) Infused with the aroma of freshly baked pizza, this neat and appealing bar in a converted *hútòng* residence oozes style and personality and the location, just off the Nanluogu Xiang drag, enjoys a welcome anonymity. Winning cocktails; homemade vodka.

BED BAR
Bar

(床吧; Chuángbā; Map p77; 17 Zhangwang Hutong; ⏱ 4pm-late Mon-Tue, noon-late Wed-Sun) One of the few bars where you can get horizontal prior to inebriation, this comfortable bar features beds strewn with cushions, an enticing rear courtyard littered with wobbly tables and repro antique chairs, first-rate music and a small dance floor.

FACE
Bar

(妃思; Fēisī; Map p82; 26 Dongcaoyuan, Gongrentiyuchang Nanlu; cocktails from Y65; ⏱ 6pm-late) Sibling of the renowned Shànghǎi French Concession saloon and with the same Southeast Asian accents, Face is elegant if rather pricey (with Tetley's bitter by the pint) but a great bolthole from Běijīng's more sordid taverns. At the time of writing, accommodation was soon to be in the offing.

⭐ Entertainment

Běijīng opera, acrobatics and kung fu are solid fixtures on the tourist circuit, drawing regular crowds. Classical-music concerts and modern theatre reach out to a growing audience of sophisticates, while night owls will find something to hoot about in the live-music and nightclub scene.

Běijīng Opera

Chinese opera has as many regional variations but Běijīng opera (京剧; *Jīngjù*) is by far the most famous, with its colourful blend of singing, dancing, speaking, swordsmanship, mime, acrobatics and dancing. Performances can swallow up an epic six hours, but two hours is more common; at most well-known Běijīng opera venues, around 90 minutes is the norm.

Běijīng opera performer in costume
PHOTOGRAPHER: KEREN SU/LONELY PLANET IMAGES ©

HÚGUĂNG GUILD HALL
Chinese Opera

(湖广会馆; Húguǎng Huìguǎn; 3 Hufang Lu; tickets Y160-680; ⊙performances 7.30pm) With a magnificent red, green and gold interior and balconies surrounding the canopied stage, this theatre dates from 1807. There's also a small **opera museum** (admission Y10; ⊙9-11am & 3-7.30pm) opposite the theatre.

LǍO SHĔ TEAHOUSE
Teahouse

(老舍茶馆; Lǎo Shĕ Cháguǎn; Map p66; 3rd fl, 3 Qianmen Xidajie; evening tickets Y180-380; ⊙performances 7.50pm) This popular teahouse has nightly shows, largely in Chinese. Performances include folk music, tea ceremonies, theatre, puppet shows and matinée Bĕijīng opera. Evening performances of Bĕijīng opera, folk art, music, acrobatics, juggling, kung fu and magic are the most popular; phone or check the website for the latest schedule.

Cháng'ān Grand Theatre
Chinese Opera

(长安大戏院; Cháng'ān Dàxìyuàn; Cháng'ān Bldg, 7 Jianguomennei Dajie; tickets Y80-800; ⊙performances 7.30pm) This theatre offers a genuine experience of Bĕijīng opera, with an erudite audience chattering knowledgeably among themselves during weekend matinée classics and evening performances.

Líyuán Theatre
Theatre

(梨园剧场; Líyuán Jùchǎng; ☎6301 6688, ext 8860; Qiánmén Jiànguó Hotel, 175 Yongan Lu; tickets Y200-500; ⊙performances 7.30pm) Tourist-friendly theatre at the rear of the lobby of the Qiánmén Jiànguó Hotel, with regular performances, matinée kung fu shows and expensive tea-ceremony options.

Acrobatics & Martial Arts

Two thousand years old, Chinese acrobatics is one of the best deals in town. Matinée Shàolín performances are held at the **Líyuán Theatre** (梨园剧场; Líyuán Jùchǎng; ☎6301 6688, ext 8860; Qiánmén Jiànguó Hotel, 175 Yongan Lu).

TIĀNDÌ THEATRE
Acrobatics

(天地剧场; Tiāndì Jùchǎng; Map p82; 10 Dongzhimen Nandajie; tickets Y100-300; ⊙performances 7.15pm) Young performers from the China National Acrobatic Troupe knot themselves into mind-bending and joint-popping shapes. It's a favourite with tour groups, so book ahead. You can also watch the performers training at the **circus school** (☎6502 3984). Look for the white tower resembling something from an airport – that's where you buy your tickets.

Cháoyáng Theatre
Acrobatics

(朝阳剧场; Cháoyáng Jùchǎng; Map p86; 36 Dongsanhuan Beilu; tickets Y180-680; ⊙performances 5.15pm & 7.30pm) Probably the most accessible place for foreign visitors and often bookable through your hotel, this theatre is the venue for visiting acrobatic troupes filling the stage with plate-spinning and hoop-jumping.

Tiānqiáo Acrobatics Theatre
Acrobatics

(天桥杂技剧场; Tiānqiáo Zájì Jùchǎng; ☎6303 7449, English 139 1000 1860; tickets Y100-200; ⊙performances 7.15-8.45pm) West of the Temple of Heaven, this is one of Bĕijīng's most popular venues. The entrance is down the eastern side of the building.

Nightclubs

Bĕijīng's nightclub scene ranges wildly from student dives for the lager crowd to snappy venues and top-end clubs for the preening types, urban poseurs and well-heeled fashionistas.

GT BANANA
Club

(吧那那; Bānànà; Map p86; Scitech Hotel, 22 Jianguomenwai Dajie; tickets Y20-50; ⊙8.30pm-4am Sun-Thu, to 5am Fri & Sat) Banana must be doing something right as it's been around for yonks – perhaps it's the caged dancers and fire-eaters. Spicy Lounge upstairs introduces more variety to the musical mix with regular appearances from international DJs.

Mix
Club

(梅克斯; Méikèsī; Map p82; ⊙8pm-late) Major hip-hop and R&B club west of Sānlǐtún with regular crowd-pulling foreign DJs, inside the Workers' Stadium north gate.

Destination
Club

(目的地; Mùdìdì; Map p82; www.bjdestination.com; 7 Gongrentiyuchang Xilu; admission

weekdays free, weekend incl a drink Y60; ⊗8pm-2pm) Běijīng's sole gay club, Destination's coarse concrete finish wins few awards for its looks, but the crowds at weekends don't seem to mind.

Live Music

A growing handful of international pop and rock acts make it to Běijīng, but there's still a long way to go, although the live-music scene has dynamically evolved in recent years.

East Shore Bar
Bar

(东岸; Dōng'àn; Map p77; ☑8403 2131; 2nd fl, 2 Shishahai Nanyan; Tsingtao beer Y20; ⊗4pm-3am) With views of Qiánhǎi Lake, this excellent bar hits all the right notes with its low-light candlelit mood and live jazz sounds from 9.30pm (Thursday to Sunday).

Yúgōng Yíshān
Live Music

(愚公移山; Map p77; ☑6404 2711; 3 Zhangzi Zhonglu; ⊗7pm-2am) Běijīng's foremost live-music venue ensconced within a haunted Qing-dynasty government building and famed for a host of reliably excellent music acts.

MAO Livehouse
Live Music

(猫; Māo; Map p77; ☑6402 5080; www.maolive. com; 111 Gulou Dongdajie; ⊗4pm-late) This fantastically popular venue for live sounds is one of the busiest in town.

What Bar?
Bar

(什么酒吧; Shénme Bā; Map p70; ☑133 4112 2757; 72 Beichang Jie; admission on live-music nights incl 1 beer Y20; ⊗3pm-late, live music from 9pm Fri & Sat) Microsized and slightly deranged, this broom cupboard of a bar stages regular rotating, grittily named bands to an enthusiastic audience. It's north of the west gate of the Forbidden City.

Classical Music

As China's capital and the nation's cultural hub, Běijīng has several venues where classical music finds an apprecia-tive audience. The annual 30-day **Běijīng Music Festival** (www.bmf.org.cn) is staged between October and November, bring-ing with it international and homegrown classical music performances.

Left: Běijīng boys receiving martial arts training; **Below:** Rabbit sculpture, Poly Art Museum (p84)

PHOTOGRAPHER: (LEFT) KEREN SU/LONELY PLANET IMAGES ©; (BELOW) JINGHUI CAI/LONELY PLANET IMAGES ©

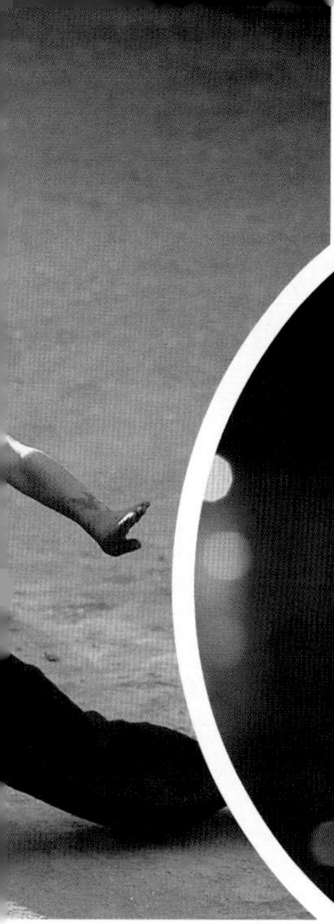

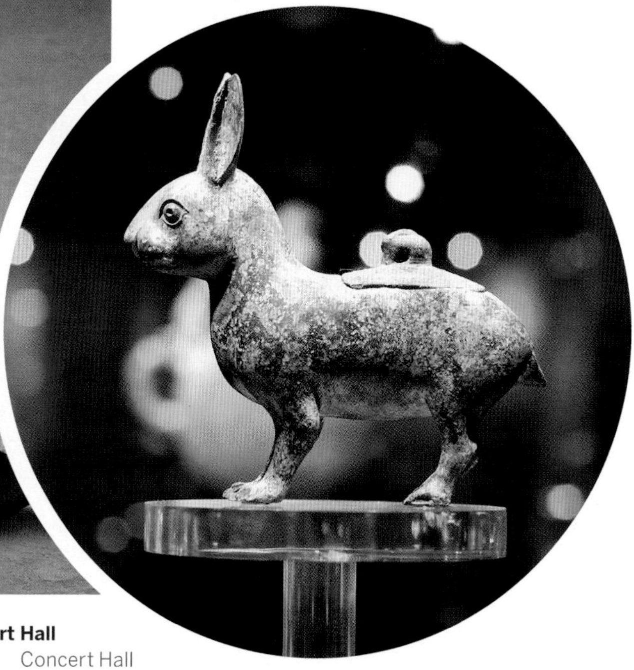

Běijīng Concert Hall Concert Hall

(北京音乐厅; **Běijīng Yīnyuètīng; 1 Beixinhua Jie; tickets Y60-580; ⌚performances 7.30pm)** The 2000-seat Běijīng Concert Hall showcases evening performances of classical Chinese music as well as international repertoires of Western classical music.

Forbidden City Concert Hall Concert Hall

(中山公园音乐堂; **Zhōngshān Gōngyuán Yīnyuè Táng; Map p70; Zhōngshān Park; tickets Y50-500; ⌚performances 7.30pm)** Located on the eastern side of Zhōngshān Park, this is the venue for performances of classical and traditional Chinese music.

Cinemas & Theatre

Only a limited number of Western films are permitted.

Star Cinema City Cinema

(新世纪影城; **Xīnshìjì Yǐngyuàn; Map p66; shop BB65, basement, Oriental Plaza, 1 Dongchang'an Jie; tickets Wed-Mon Y50-70, students Y25)** This six-screen cinema is centrally located and plush (with leather reclining sofa chairs).

China Puppet Theatre Theatre

(中国木偶剧院; **Zhōngguó Mù'ǒu Jùyuàn; 1a Anhua Xili, Beisanhuan Lu; tickets Y30-100; 👪)** This popular theatre has regular events, including shadow play, puppetry, music and dance.

Shopping

Several vibrant Chinese shopping districts offer abundant goods including Wangfujing Dajie (王府井大街), Xīdān (西单) and reconstructed Qianmen Dajie (前门大街; p86) and Dashilar (大栅栏; p86). Delve into fun Yandai Xiejie (烟袋斜街), east of Silver Ingot Bridge, for Tibetan trinkets, glazed tiles, T-shirts, paper cuts, teapots, ceramics and even *qípáo* (cheongsam). Nanluogu Xiang (p80) is also excellent for ceramics and gifts.

More luxurious shopping areas can be found in Sānlǐtún (三里屯); also check out five-star hotel shopping malls. Shopping at open-air markets is an experience not to be missed. Běijīng's most popular markets are Silk Street, the Sānlǐtún Yashou Clothing Market, Pānjiāyuán and the Pearl Market.

Arts & Crafts

LIULICHANG XIJIE   Antiques

Běijīng's premier antique street, not far west of Dashilar, is worth delving along for its quaint, albeit dressed-up, age-old village atmosphere and (largely fake) antiques.

BANNERMAN TANG'S TOYS & CRAFTS
                                        Crafts

(盛唐轩; Shèngtángxuān Chuántǒng Mínjiān Wánjù Kāifā Zhōngxīn; Map p77; 38 Guozijian Jie; ⏰9.30am-7pm) Marvellous collection of handmade toys and delightful collectibles from Chinese Weebles (budao weng; from Y30), puppets, clay figures, tiger pillows

to kites and other gorgeous items; it's just along from the Confucius Temple.

POTTERY WORKSHOP   Ceramics
(Map p77; Nanluogu Xiang)
Another Shànghǎi import on Nanluogu Xiang, this appealing shop sells good-looking ceramics from traditional cool-green celadon teasets to inventive and artistic creations.

SHARD BOX STORE   Boxes
(慎德阁; Shèndé Gé; Map p86; 1 Ritan Beilu; ⏰9am-7pm) Captivating collection of boxes intriguingly pieced together from porcelain fragments from ancient vases shattered during the Cultural Revolution.

Clothing

FIVE COLOURS EARTH   Clothing
(五色土; Wǔsètǔ; Map p86; 1505, 15/F, Bldg 5, Jianwai Soho, 39 Dongsanhuan Zhonglu; ⏰9am-6pm) Unique, distinctive and stylish clothing items – coats, jackets, lovely skirts and sexy tops – featuring embroideries made by the Miao minority from Guìzhōu.

SILK STREET   Clothing
(秀水街; Xiùshuǐ Jiē; Map p86; cnr Jianguomenwai Dajie & Dongdaqiao Lu; ⏰9am-9pm) Seething with shoppers and polyglot (and increasingly tactile) vendors, Silk St was for long synonymous with fake knock-offs, and some pirated labels survive. The market sprawls from floor to floor, shoving piles of rucksacks, shoes, silk, cashmere and tailor-made qípáo into the overloaded mitts of travellers and expats. Haggle fiendishly (credit cards accepted).

SĀNLǏTÚN YASHOU CLOTHING MARKET
                                Clothing
(三里屯雅秀服装市场; Sānlǐtún Yǎxiù Fúzhuāng Shìchǎng; Map p82; 58 Gongrentiyuchang Beilu) After slogging through this hopping, five-floor bedlam of

Chinese dolls at Běijīng market
PHOTOGRAPHER: FELIX RIOUX/LONELY PLANET IMAGES ©

shoes, boots, handbags, suitcases, jackets, silk, carpets, batik, lace, jade, pearls, toys, army surplus and souvenirs, ease the pressure on your bunions with a foot massage (Y50 per hour) or pedicure (Y40) on the 4th floor and restore calories in the 5th-floor food court.

Books

Bookworm Café   Books
(书虫; Map p82; Shūchóng; ☎6586 9507; www.beijingbookworm.com; Bldg 4, Nansanlitun Lu) Growing section of new and almost-new books for sale. Library members can borrow a maximum of two books at a time.

Foreign Languages Bookstore   Books
(外文书店; Wàiwén Shūdiàn; 235 Wangfujing Dajie) Third floor for strong children's, fiction and nonfiction sections plus a smattering of travel guides and seats for tired legs.

Chaterhouse Booktrader   Books
(Map p86; Basement, The Place, 9a Guanghua Lu; ⏱10am-10pm) Excellent kids section and great range of new fiction, even if prices are high.

Department Stores & Malls

ORIENTAL PLAZA   Mall
(东方新天地; Dōngfāng Xīntiāndì; Map p66; www.orientalplaza.com; 1 Dongchang'an Jie; ⏱9.30am-9.30pm) You could spend a day in this staggeringly large shopping megacomplex at the foot of Wangfujing Dajie. Prices may not be cheap, but window-shoppers will be overjoyed.

PLACE   Mall
(世贸天阶; Shìmào Tiānjiē; Map p86; 9 Guanghua Lu) With its vast outdoor video screen, snappy shopping plaza The Place has lured big names Zara, French Connection, Miss Sixty and Mango, as well as Chaterhouse Booktrader; there's a good food court in the basement.

VILLAGE   Mall
(Map p82; 19 Sanlitun Lu; ⏱10am-10pm) Anchoring Sānlǐtún's expensive commercial facelift, this nifty multistorey mall drags in legions of snappy shoppers and diners to its shops, cafes and restaurants; the world's largest branch of Adidas is here.

Markets

PĀNJIĀYUÁN MARKET   Market
(潘家园古玩市场; ⏱dawn-6pm Sat & Sun) Hands-down the best place to shop for gōngyì (crafts) and gǔwán (antiques) in Běijīng is Pānjiāyuán (aka the Dirt Market or the Sunday Market). The market only takes place on weekends and sprawls from calligraphy, Cultural Revolution memorabilia and cigarette-ad posters to Buddha heads, ceramics, Tibetan carpets and beyond. Up to 50,000 visitors scope for treasures here: if you want to join them, early Sunday morning is the best time. Also, ignore the 'don't pay more than half'' rule here – some vendors may start at 10 times the real price, so aim low.

PEARL MARKET   Market
(红桥市场; Hóngqiáo Shìchǎng; Tiantan Donglu; ⏱8.30am-7pm) The cosmos of clutter across from the east gate of Temple of Heaven Park ranges from shoes, leather bags, jackets, jeans, silk by the yard, electronics, Chinese arts, crafts and antiques to a galaxy of pearls (freshwater and seawater, white and black) on the 3rd floor. Prices for the latter vary incredibly with quality and more expensive specimens on the 4th and 5th floors.

ℹ Information

English-language maps of Běijīng can be grabbed for free at most big hotels and branches of the Běijīng Tourist Information Center.

Internet Access

Internet cafes (网吧; wǎngbā) are scarce in the centre of town and tourist areas. Rates are usually Y2 to Y3 (pricier at night). You will need to show your passport and pay a deposit of about Y10; you may be digitally photographed (by the metallic box on the counter). Many cheaper hotels and youth hostels provide internet access, and numerous bars and cafes around Běijīng offer wi-fi.

Dáyǔsù Internet Cafe (达宇速网吧; Dáyǔsù Wǎngbā; 2 Hufang Lu; per hr Y3; ⏱8am-midnight) No English sign, but it's around three shops north of the Bank of China.

Běijīng Museum Pass

To save money and time queuing for tickets, pocket this pass (博物馆通票; Bówùguǎn Tōngpiào; Y80) which allows either complimentary access or discounted admission (typically 50%) to almost 60 museums, temples or tourist sights in and around Běijīng. Not all museums are worth visiting, but you only have to visit a small selection of museums to get your money back. The pass comes in the form of a booklet (Chinese with minimal English), effective from 1 January to 31 December in any one year. Pick it up from participating museums and sights; it can be hard to find (especially as the year progresses), so phone ☎6222 3793 or ☎6221 3256 (www.bowuguan.com.cn, in Chinese) to locate stocks (free delivery within Fifth Ring Rd).

Internet cafe (网吧; wǎngbā; Wusi Dajie; per hr Y3)

Sōngjié Internet Cafe (松杰网吧; Sōngjié Wǎngbā; 140-7 Jiaodaokou Nandajie; per hr Y2; ⏱24hr)

Wǎngjù Internet Cafe (网聚网吧; Wǎngjù Wǎngbā; 449 Dongsi Beidajie; per hr Y2; ⏱24hr)

Medical Services

Běijīng has some of the best medical facilities and services in China. Identified by green crosses, pharmacies selling Chinese (中药; zhōngyào) and Western medicine (西药; xīyào) are widespread.

Bayley & Jackson Medical Center (庇利积臣医疗中心; Bìlì Jíchén Yīliáo Zhōngxīn; ☎8562 9998; www.bjhealthcare.com; 7 Ritan Donglu) Full range of private medical and dental services.

International SOS (北京亚洲国际紧急救援医疗中心; Běijīng Yàzhōu Guójì Jǐnjí Jiùyuán Yīliáo Zhōngxīn; ☎clinic appointments 6462 9112, dental appointments 6462 0333, emergencies 6462 9100; www.internationalsos.com; Suite 105, Wing 1 Kūnshā Bldg, 16 Xinyuanli; ⏱9am-6pm Mon-Fri) Expensive, high-quality clinic with English-speaking staff.

Money

Foreign currency and travellers cheques can be changed at large branches of the Bank of China, CITIC Industrial Bank, the Industrial and Commercial Bank of China, HSBC, the airport and hotel moneychanging counters, and at several department stores (including the Friendship Store), as long as you have your passport. Useful branches of the Bank of China with foreign-exchange counters include a branch next to Oriental Plaza on Wangfujing Dajie and in the China World Trade Center. For international money transfers, branches of Western Union can be found in the Chaoyang branch of China Post (3 Gongrentiyuchang Beilu) and in the International Post Office

ATMs taking international cards are in abundance. The best places to look are in and around the main shopping areas (such as Wangfujing Dajie) and international hotels and their associated shopping arcades; some large department stores also have useful ATMs. There's a Bank of China ATM in the Capital Airport arrivals hall.

Post

The **International Post Office** (国际邮电局; Guójì Yóudiànjú; Jianguomen Beidajie; ⏱8am-7pm) is 200m north of Jiànguómén subway station; poste restante letters (Y3; maximum one month, take passport for collection) can be addressed here. You can also post letters via your hotel reception desk, which may be the most convenient option, or at green post boxes around town.

Public Security Bureau

PSB (公安局; Gōng'ānjú; ☎8402 0101, 8401 5292; 2 Andingmen Dongdajie; ⏱8.30am-4.30pm Mon-Sat) The Foreign Affairs Branch of the PSB handles visa extensions; see p403 for further information. The visa office is on the 2nd floor on the east side of the building.

Tourist Information

Běijīng Tourism Hotline (☎6513 0828; ☻24hr) Has English-speaking operators available to answer questions and hear complaints.

Běijīng Tourist Information Centers (北京旅游咨询服务中心; **Běijīng Lǚyóu Zīxún Fúwù Zhōngxīn;** ☻9am-5pm) Běijīng train station (☎6528 8448; 16 Laoqianju Hutong); Capital Airport (☎6459 8148); Cháoyáng (☎6417 6627/6656; Gongrentiyuchang Beilu); Wangfujing Dajie (Wangfujing Dajie); Xuānwǔ (☎6351 0018; xuanwu@bjta.gov.cn; 3 Hufang Lu) English skills are limited and information is basic, but you can grab a free tourist map of town and handfuls of free literature; some offices also have train-ticket offices.

❶ Getting There & Away

Getting to Běijīng, as the nation's capital, is straightforward. Rail and air connections link the city to virtually every point in China, and fleets of buses head to abundant destinations from Běijīng. Using Běijīng as a starting point to explore the rest of the country makes perfect sense.

Air

Běijīng has direct air connections to most major cities in the world. For more information about international flights to Běijīng, see p405.

Daily flights connect Běijīng to every major city in China. There should be at least one flight a week to smaller cities throughout China.

Purchase tickets for Chinese carriers flying from Běijīng at the **Civil Aviation Administration of China** (中国民航; CAAC; **Zhōngguó Mínháng; Aviation Building;**民航营业大厦; **Mínháng Yíngyè Dàshà;** ☎6656 9118, domestic 6601 3336, international 6601 6667; 15 Xichang'an Jie; ☻7am-midnight) or from one of the numerous other ticket outlets and service counters around Běijīng, and through most midrange and top-end hotels. Discounts are generally available. Also book through www.ctrip.com.cn and www.elong.com.

Make enquiries for all airlines at Běijīng's **Capital Airport** (PEK; ☎from Běijīng only 962 580). Call ☎6454 1100 for information on international and domestic arrivals and departures.

Starfish on sticks for sale, Běijīng

FELIX RIOUX/LONELY PLANET IMAGES ©

Bus

No international buses serve Běijīng, but there are plenty of long-distance domestic routes served by national highways radiating from Běijīng. Běijīng has numerous long-distance bus stations (长途汽车站; *chángtú qìchēzhàn*), positioned roughly on the city perimeter in the direction you want to go. The main three:

BĀWÁNGFÉN LONG-DISTANCE BUS STATION Destinations served by the bus station (八王坟长途客运站; Bāwángfén Chángtú Kèyùnzhàn; 17 Xidawang Lu) in the east of town include **Tiānjīn** (Y31 to Y35) and **Qínhuángdǎo** (Y61 to Y90, 3½ hours, frequent).

SÌHUÌ LONG-DISTANCE BUS STATION Buses from this bus station (四惠长途汽车站; Sìhuì Chángtú Qìchēzhàn) serve locations including **Chéngdé** (Y56 to Y77, four hours, 6am to 4pm).

LIÙLÍQIÁO LONG-DISTANCE BUS STATION Southwest of Běijīng West train station, Liùlíqiáo long-distance bus station (六里桥长途站; Liùlíqiáo Chángtúzhàn) has buses going north, south and west of town including **Chéngdé** (Y73, regular services), **Dàtóng** (Y119, regular services), **Luòyáng** (Y149, six daily), **Xī'ān** (Y259, one at 5.45pm) and **Zhèngzhōu** (Y149, 10 daily).

Train

Travellers arrive and depart by train at Běijīng train station (Běijīng Huǒchēzhàn) near the centre of town, the colossal Běijīng West train station (Běijīng Xīzhàn) in the southwest or at the ultramodern Běijīng South train station (Běijīng Nánzhàn) for trains from Tiānjīn, Shànghǎi and Hángzhōu. Běijīng and Běijīng South train stations are served by their own underground stations, making access simple. International trains to Moscow, Pyongyang (North Korea) and Ulaanbaatar (Mongolia) arrive at and leave from Běijīng train station; trains for Vietnam leave from Běijīng West train station. Bus 122 connects Běijīng train station with Běijīng West train station.

The queues at Běijīng train station can be overwhelming. At the time of writing, there is an English-speaking service window, but it moves around. A foreigners ticketing office (⏲24hr) can be found on the 2nd floor of Běijīng West train station.

If you can't face the queues, ask your hotel to book your ticket or try one of the train-ticket offices (火车票售票处; Huǒchēpiào Shòupiàochù) around town, where you pay a Y5 commission for your ticket. A handy train ticket office (200 Wangfujing Dajie; ⏲9.30am-8.30pm) is at the rear on the right of the 1st floor of the Arts & Crafts Mansion on Wangfujing Dajie. The Běijīng Tourist Information (北京旅游咨询服务中心; Běijīng Lǚyóu Zīxún Zhōngxīn; ☏6417 6627/6656; Gongrentiyuchang Beilu) near Sānlǐtún also has a train ticket office.

Běijīng train station is mainly for T-class trains (*tèkuài*), slow trains and trains bound for the northeast; most fast trains heading south now depart from Běijīng South train station and Běijīng West train station. Slower trains to Shànghǎi (Y327, 13½ hours) also go from here. For high-speed trains to Tiānjīn and Shànghǎi, go to Běijīng South train station.

BĚIJĪNG TRAIN STATION Typical train fares and approximate travel times for hard-sleeper tickets to destinations from Běijīng train station include **Dàtóng** (Y108, 5½ hours), **Hángzhōu** (Y353, 15 hours), **Qīngdǎo** (Y215, nine hours) and **Shànghǎi** (soft-sleeper express Y327, 12 hours).

BĚIJĪNG WEST TRAIN STATION Fast 'Z' class express trains from Běijīng West train station include **Fúzhōu** (Z59, hard seat/hard sleeper Y253/443, 19 hours 40 minutes, at 5.08pm), **Lánzhōu** (Z55, Y377, almost 18 hours, one at 1.35pm) and **Xī'ān** (hard sleeper Y265, 11 hours; Z19 at 9.18pm, Z53 at 9.24pm).

Other typical train fares and approximate travel times for hard-sleeper tickets: **Chéngdū** Y472,

---

Con Artists & Tea Merchants

Beware pesky 'art students' and English students around Wangfujing Dajie, Tiān'ānmén Sq and other tourist areas. They drag Western visitors to exhibitions of overpriced art or extortionate tea ceremonies; the latter may cost Y2000 or more. If approached by overfriendly girls wanting to speak English, refuse to go to a place of their choosing.

MANFRED GOTTSCHALK/LONELY PLANET IMAGES ©

25 hours; **Chóngqìng** Y416, 24 hours; **Kūnmíng** Y578, 38 hours; **Lánzhōu** Y377, 20½ hours; **Lhasa (Tibet)** Y813 (soft sleeper Y1262), 45 hours; **Shíjiāzhuāng** D-class trains Y88, two hours; **Ürümqi** Y652, 40 hours and **Xī'ān** Y274, 13 hours.

BĚIJĪNG SOUTH TRAIN STATION Most D-class trains and the Tiānjīn C-class train depart from slick, Gattica-like Beijing South train station (Běijīng Nánzhàn) to destinations such as **Tiānjīn** (C-series, Y58 to Y69, 30 minutes, every 15 minutes from 6.35am to 10.10pm); **Sūzhōu** (seat/sleeper Y309/620); **Shànghǎi Hóngqiáo** (eight D-class trains – five night trains, Y499, around 10 hours); **Hángzhōu** (D309, Y820, 11½ hours) and **Qīngdǎo** (Y275, 5½ hours, six daily). Fast G-class trains to Shànghǎi should commence shortly.

ⓘ Getting Around

To/From the Airport

Běijīng's Capital Airport is 27km from the centre of town, about 30 minutes to one hour by car depending on traffic.

The 30-minute Airport Express (机场快轨; Jīchǎng Kuàiguǐ; Y25; ⏱6am-10.30pm to airport, 6.30am-11pm from airport) runs every 15 minutes, connecting Capital Airport with Line 2 of the underground system at Dōngzhímén and connecting with Line 10 at Sānyuánqiáo.

Several express bus routes (fare Y16) run every 10 to 20 minutes during operating hours to Běijīng:

Line 3 (⏱7.30am-last flight from Capital Airport, 5.30am-9pm from Běijīng train station) The most popular with travellers, running to the Běijīng International Hotel and Běijīng train station via Cháoyángmén.

Line 2 (⏱7am-last flight from Capital Airport, 5.30am-9pm from Aviation Building) Runs to the Aviation Building in Xīdàn, via Dōngzhímén.

Line 1 (⏱7am-11pm from Capital Airport, 5.30am-11pm from Fāngzhuāng) Runs to Fāngzhuāng, via Dàběiyáo, where you can get onto the metro Line 1 at Guómào. Buses generally make stops at all terminals, but check with the driver. Bus 359 (Y2, one hour, 5.20am to 10pm) also runs to Capital Airport from Dongzhimenwai Xiejie.

Many top-end hotels run shuttle buses from the airport to their hotels.

A taxi (using its meter) should cost about Y85 from the airport to the city centre, including the Y15 airport expressway toll; bank on 30 minutes to one hour to get into town. Join the taxi ranks and ignore approaches from drivers who might try to get a much higher fare from you. When you get into the taxi, make sure the driver uses the meter.

It is also useful to have the name of your hotel written down in Chinese to show the driver.

Bicycle

Ample bicycle lanes are testament to the vehicle's unflagging popularity. The increase in traffic in recent years has made biking along major thoroughfares more dangerous and nerve-racking, however.

Youth hostels often hire out bicycles, which cost around Y20 to Y30 per day; rental at upmarket hotels is far more expensive. A handy network of bike-rental stations (⏱8am-10pm) can be found outside a few underground stations, principally on Line 2 (including Gulou Dajie). Bikes (per four hours Y10, per day Y20, deposit Y400) can be hired and returned to different underground stations. Otherwise there are plenty of other places you can hire bikes. When renting a bike it's safest to use your own lock(s) in order to prevent theft, a common problem in Běijīng.

Car

Visitors to Běijīng are effectively barred from driving around the capital. See p414 for more information.

Public Transport

A rechargeable transport card (公交IC卡; gōngjiāo IC kǎ; deposit Y20) for the underground, buses and taxis is available from subway stations and kiosks. The card typically nets you 60% off the cost of bus trips; merely charge the card at subway stations and swipe as you use.

BUS Buses (公共汽车; gōnggòng qìchē) are a reasonable way to get around: there are ample bus lanes and bus routes, fleet numbers are plentiful and prices are low. It can still be slow going, however, compared to the metro. Routes on bus signs are fiendishly foreigner-unfriendly, although the name of the stop appears in Pinyin and announcements are made in English (but try to work out how many stops you need to go before boarding). Getting a seat can verge on the physical, especially at rush hour.

You generally pay the conductor once aboard the bus, rather than the driver. Using a transport smartcard nets you a big saving of 60% off most bus trips (making most trips just Y0.40); just swipe the touchpad on the bus.

Buses run from 5am to 11pm daily or thereabouts. If you can read Chinese, a useful publication (Y5) listing all the Běijīng bus lines is available from kiosks; alternatively, tourist maps of Běijīng illustrate some of the bus routes. See www.bjbus.com/english/default.htm for a map of Běijīng's bus routes in English.

Buses 1 to 86 cover the city core; the 200 series are yèbān gōnggòng qìchē (night buses), while buses 300 to 501 are suburban lines.

Useful standard bus routes:

1 Runs along Chang'an Jie, Jianguomenwai Dajie and Jianguomennei Dajie, passing Sìhuìzhàn, Bāwángfén, Yonganli, Dōngdān, Xīdān, Mùxīdì, Jūnshì Bówùguǎn, Gōngzhǔfén and Mǎguānyíng along the way.

5 Déshèngmén, Dì'ānmén, Běihǎi Park, Xīhuámén, Zhōngshān Park and Qiánmén.

20 Běijīng South train station, Tiānqiáo, Qiánmén, Wángfǔjǐng, Dōngdān and Běijīng train station.

Ming Tombs statue
PHOTOGRAPHER: GREG ELMS/LONELY PLANET IMAGES ©

44 (outer ring) Xīnjiēkǒu, Xīzhímén train station, Fùchéngmén, Fùxīngmén, Changchunjie, Xuānwǔmén, Qiánmén, Táijīchǎng, Chōngwénmén, Dōngbiànmén, Cháoyángmén, Dōngzhímén, Āndìngmén, Déshèngmèn and Xīnjiēkǒu.

103 Běijīng train station, Dēngshìkǒu, China Art Gallery, Forbidden City (north entrance), Běihǎi Park, Fùchéngmén and Běijīng Zoo.

106 Dōngzhímén Transport Hub Station to Běijīng South train station.

126 Useful for the short hop from Qiánmén to Wangfujing Dajie.

332 Běijīng Zoo, Wèigōngcūn, Rénmín Dàxué, Zhōngguāncūn, Hǎidiàn, Běijīng University and Summer Palace.

823 Dōngzhímén Transport Hub Station to Běijīng West train station.

METRO The metro (地铁; *dìtiě*) is fast and reliable. Currently nine lines are operating (including the Airport Line), with two more under construction, including Line 9 which will link Běijīng West train station with Line 1 and Line 4. The flat fare is Y2 on all lines except the Airport Line (Y25). Trains run every few minutes during peak times, operating from 5am to 11pm daily. Stops are announced in English and Chinese. Metro stations (地铁站; *dìtiě zhàn*) are identified by metro symbols, a blue, encircled English capital 'D'.

Line 1 (一号线; Yīhàoxiàn) Runs east–west from Pínggǔoyuán to Sìhuì East.

Line 2 (二号线; Èrhàoxiàn) The circle line following the Second Ring Rd.

Line 4 (四号线; Sìhàoxiàn) Links Gōngyìxīqiáo and Ānhéqiáo North, connecting with the Summer Palace (Xīyuàn) and the Old Summer Palace (Yuánmíngyuán).

Line 5 (五号线; Wǔhàoxiàn) Runs north–south between Tiāntóngyuàn North and Sōngjiāzhuāng.

Line 8 (八号线; Bāhàoxiàn) Connects Běitǔchéng with South Gate of Forest Park, running through the Olympics Sports Center and Olympic Green.

Line 10 (十号线; Shíhàoxiàn) Follows a long loop from Jìnsōng in the southeast to Bāgōu in the northwest; handy for the Sānlǐtún area.

Line 13 (十三号线; Shísānhàoxiàn) Runs in a northern loop from Xīzhímén to Dōngzhímén.

Batong Line (八通线; Bātōngxiàn) Runs from Sìhuì to Tǔqiáo in the southeastern suburbs.

Airport Line (机场线; Jīchǎngxiàn) Connects Dōngzhímén and Sānyuánqiáo with the terminals at Capital Airport.

Taxi

Běijīng taxis come in different classes, with red stickers on the side rear window declaring the rate per kilometre. Y2 taxis (Y10 for the first 3km, Y2 per kilometre thereafter) include a fleet of spacious Hyundai cars. The most expensive taxis are Y12 for the first 3km and Y2 per kilometre thereafter. Taxis are required to switch on the meter for all journeys (unless you negotiate a fee for a long journey out of town). Between 11pm and 6am there is a 20% surcharge added to the flag-fall metered fare. For extra room and a sense of style, look out for one of the silver London cabs that cruise the streets.

Běijīng taxi drivers speak little, if any, English. If you don't speak Chinese, bring a map or have your destination written down in characters.

Taxis can be hired for distance, by the hour, or by the day (a minimum of Y350 for the day). Taxis can be hailed in the street, summoned by phone or you can wait at one of the designated taxi zones or outside hotels. Call ✆ 6835 1150 to register a complaint. Remember to collect a receipt (ask the driver to *fāpiào*); if you accidentally leave anything in the taxi, the driver's number appears on the receipt so he or she can be located.

AROUND BEIJING

Ming Tombs 十三陵

The **Ming Tombs** (Shísān Líng; ⏱ 8am-5pm), about 50km northwest of Běijīng, are the final resting place of 13 of the 16 Ming emperors. Billed with the Great Wall at Bādálǐng as Běijīng's great double act, the imperial graveyard can unsurprisingly be a rather dormant spectacle, unless you pack a penchant for ceremonial tomb architecture, Confucian symbolism or Ming imperial genealogy.

Three tombs have been opened up to the public: Cháng Líng, Dìng Líng and Zhāo Líng.

Detour:
Chuāndǐxià (Cuàndǐxià)

Nestled in a windswept valley 90km west of Běijīng and overlooked by towering peaks is **Chuāndǐxià** (川底下; admission Y20), a gorgeous cluster of historic courtyard homes and old-world charm. The backdrop is lovely: terraced orchards and fields, with ancient houses and alleyways rising up the hillside.

Chuāndǐxià is also a museum of **Maoist graffiti and slogans**, especially up the incline among the better-preserved houses. The town's friendly residents long ago flung open their doors to overnighting visitors. The lovely-looking **Bǎishùn Kèzhàn** (百顺客栈), behind the spirit wall at No 43 Chunadixiacun at the foot of the village, is a magnificent old courtyard guesthouse.

A bus (Y10, two hours) leaves for Chuāndǐxià from Píngguǒyuán metro station every day at 7.30am and 12.30pm, returning at 10.30am and 3.30pm. If you take the later bus, you may either need to spend the night or find alternative transport. The other option is to take bus 929 (make sure it's the branch line, or *zhīxiàn* 支线, not the regular bus; runs 7am to 5.15pm) from the bus stop 200m to the west of Píngguǒyuán metro station to Zhāitáng (斋堂; Y8, two hours), then hire a taxi van (Y20). The last bus returns from Zhāitáng to Píngguǒyuán at 4.20pm. If you miss the last bus, a taxi will cost around Y80 to Píngguǒyuán. Taxi drivers waiting at Píngguǒyuán metro station will charge around Y140 to Y150 for a round-trip. Some hostels in Běijīng also arrange tours to Chuāndǐxià.

The road leading up to the tombs is the 7km **Spirit Way** (神道; Shéndào; admission winter/summer Y20/30; ⏱7am-8pm). Commencing with a triumphal arch, the path enters the Great Palace Gate, where officials once had to dismount, and passes a giant *bìxì*, which bears the largest stele in China. A magnificent guard of 12 sets of stone animals and officials ensues.

Cháng Líng (长陵; admission winter/summer Y30/45), burial place of the emperor Yongle, is the most impressive, with its series of magnificent halls lying beyond its yellow-tiled gate. Seated upon a three-tiered marble terrace is the most notable structure, the Hall of Eminent Favours, containing a recent statue of Yongle and a breathtaking interior with vast *nanmu* (cedarwood) columns.

Dìng Líng (定陵; admission incl museum winter/summer Y40/60), the burial place of the emperor Wanli, contains a series of subterranean interlocking vaults and the remains of the various gates and halls of the complex. Excavated in the late 1950s,

this tomb is of more interest to some visitors as you are allowed to descend into the underground vault. Accessing the vault down the steps, visitors are confronted by the simply vast marble self-locking doors that sealed the chamber after it was vacated. The tomb is also the site of the absorbing **Ming Tombs Museum** (Shísān Líng Bówùguǎn; admission Y20).

Zhāo Líng (昭陵; admission winter/summer Y20/30), the resting place of the 13th Ming emperor Longqing, follows an orthodox layout and is a tranquil alternative if you find the other tombs too busy.

Tour buses usually combine visits to one of the Ming Tombs with trips to the Great Wall at Bādálǐng; see p114 for information about buses to and from Bādálǐng.

To go independently, take fast bus 345 (345 路快; 345 Lùkuài) from Déshèngménxī, 500m east of Jīshuǐtán subway station, to Chāngpíng (昌平; Y6, one hour, running 5.30am to 10pm). Get off at the Chāngpíng Dōngguān (昌平东关) stop and change to bus 314 (running 6am to 7pm) for the tombs. Alternatively, take the slower standard bus 345 to Chāngpíng Běizhàn (昌平北站) and similarly transfer to bus 314.

Marco Polo Bridge 卢沟桥

Described by the great traveller himself, this 266m-long grey marble **bridge (Lúgōu Qiáo; 88 Lugouqiaochengnei Xijie; admission Y20; ⊙8am-5pm)** is host to 485 carved stone lions. Each animal is different, with the smallest only a few centimetres high, and legend insists they move around during the night.

Dating from 1189, the stone bridge is Běijīng's oldest (but is a composite of different eras; it was widened in 1969), and spans the Yǒngdìng River (永定河) near the small walled town of Wǎnpíng (宛平城), just southwest of Běijīng.

Despite the praises of Marco Polo and Emperor Qianlong, the bridge wouldn't have rated more than a footnote in Chinese history were it not for the famed Marco Polo Bridge Incident, which ignited a full-scale war with Japan. On 7 July 1937, Japanese troops illegally occupied a railway junction outside Wǎnpíng. Japanese and Chinese soldiers started

shooting, and that gave Japan enough of an excuse to attack and occupy Běijīng.

The **Memorial Hall of the War of Resistance Against Japan** is a gory look back at Japan's occupation of China. Also on the site are the Wǎnpíng Castle, Dàiwáng Temple and a hotel.

Take bus 6 from the north gate of Temple of Heaven Park to the last stop at Liùlǐ Bridge (六里桥; Liùlǐ Qiáo) and then either bus 339 or 309 to Lúgōu Xīnqiáo (卢沟新桥); the bridge is just ahead.

THE GREAT WALL

China's greatest engineering triumph and must-see sight, the **Great Wall** (万里长城; Wànlǐ Chángchéng) wriggles haphazardly from its scattered Manchurian remains in Liáoníng province to wind-scoured rubble in the Gobi desert and faint traces in the unforgiving sands of Xīnjiāng.

The most renowned and robust examples undulate majestically over the peaks and hills of Běijīng municipality, but the Great Wall can be realistically visited in many North China provinces. It is mistakenly assumed that the wall is one

Elephant statues at Ming Tombs

continuous entity; in reality, the edifice exists in chunks interspersed with natural defences (such as precipitous mountains) that had no need for further bastions.

History

The 'original' wall was begun over 2000 years ago during the Qin dynasty (221–207 BC), when China was unified under Emperor Qin Shi Huang. Separate walls that had been constructed by independent kingdoms to keep out marauding nomads were linked together. The effort required hundreds of thousands of workers – many of whom were political prisoners – and 10 years of hard labour under General Meng Tian.

Ming engineers made determined efforts to revamp the eroding bastion, facing it with some 60 million cu metres of bricks and stone slabs. The picture-postcard brick-clad modern-day manifestations of the Great Wall date from Ming times.

Despite the wall, the Mongol armies managed to impose foreign rule on China from 1279 to 1368 and the bastion failed to prevent the Manchu armies from establishing two and a half centuries of non-Chinese rule on the Middle Kingdom. The wall did not even register with the 19th-century European 'barbarians' who simply arrived by sea, and by the time the Japanese invaded, the wall had been outflanked by new technologies (such as the aeroplane).

The wall was largely forgotten after that. Mao Zedong encouraged the use of the wall as a source of free building material, a habit that continues unofficially today. Its earthen core has been pillaged and its bountiful supply of shaped stone stripped from the ramparts for use in building roads, dams and other constructions.

Without its cladding, lengthy sections have dissolved to dust and the barricade might have vanished entirely without the tourist industry. Several important sections have been rebuilt, kitted out with souvenir shops, restaurants, toboggan rides and cable cars, populated with squads of unspeakably annoying hawkers and opened to the public.

Consult William Lindesay's website at www.wildwall.com for reams of info on the Great Wall.

Visiting the Wall

The most touristed area of the Great Wall is at Bādálǐng. Also renovated but less overrun are Mùtiányù, Sīmǎtái and Jīnshānlǐng. Unimpressed with the tourist-oriented sections, explorative

Sleeping by the Great Wall

If you want to make your trip to the Great Wall more of an experience or a multiday foray, why not spend the night by the wall. **Commune by the Great Wall** (长城脚下的公社; Chángchéng Jiǎoxià de Gōngshè; ☎ 8118 1888; www.communebythegreatwall.com; r Y1890; ✳ @ 🛜 ➿) is not cheap but the cantilevered geometric architecture, location and superb panoramas are standout. **Red Capital Ranch** (怀柔县雁栖镇下关地村28号; ☎ 8401 8886; www.redcapitalclub.com; 28 Xiaguandi village, Yanxi, Huairou County; Map p53; d 1425; ✳ @ ➿) is Běijīng's escapist option, a Manchurian hunting lodge with 10 individually styled villas, a mountain setting, a 50-acre estate with Great Wall remains and a stress-busting Tibetan Tantric Space Spa (breakfast included). The **Schoolhouse at Mùtiányù** (小园; Xiǎoyuán; ☎ 6162 6506; www.theschoolhouseatmutianyu.com; Mutianyu Village; house from Y1800; 🛜 ✳) has a magnificent range of thoughtfully designed luxury homes – sleeping up to 10 – with gardens, Great Wall views and excellent food.

GREG ELMS/LONELY PLANET IMAGES ©

travellers have long sought out the authentic appeal of unrestored sections of wall (such as at Huánghuā or Jiànkòu).

Some tours make hellish diversions to jade factories, gem-exhibition halls, Chinese medicine centres and whatnot; Buddhist monks may bestow blessings followed by requests for cash. When booking a tour, ensure such scams are not on the itinerary. It can be safest to book through your hotel or youth hostel, but always consider going under your own steam by public transport or hiring a car and a driver. As with most popular destinations in China, avoid weekend trips and definitely shun the big holiday periods (p400).

Take shoes with good grip, water, sunscreen and waterproofs in summer.

Bādálǐng   八达岭

The wall's most-photographed and most-visited manifestation, **Bādálǐng** (Bādálǐng Chángchéng; ☎ 6912 1338, 6912 1423, 6912 1520; admission adult/student Y45/25; ☺ 6am-8pm summer, 7am-6pm winter) is 70km northwest of Běijīng.

The raw scenery yields classic views of the bastion snaking into the distance over undulating hills. The name Bādálǐng sends a shiver down the spines of hard-core wall walkers; however: there are souvenir stalls, T-shirt-flogging hawkers, heavily restored brickwork, guardrails and crowds of sightseers.

The wall here was first built during the Ming dynasty (1368–1644), and heavily restored in both the 1950s and the 1980s. Punctuated with *dílóu* (watchtowers), the 6m-wide masonry is clad in brick, typical of Ming engineering.

Two sections of wall trail off in opposite directions from the main entrance. The restored wall crawls for a distance before nobly disintegrating into ruins; unfortunately you cannot realistically explore these more authentic fragments. Cable cars exist for the weary (Y60 round-trip).

The admission fee also gets you into the **China Great Wall Museum** (☺ 9am-4pm).

Getting There & Away

The easiest and most reliable way to reach Bādálǐng is on bus 919 (Y12, 80 minutes, every 30 minutes 7.30am to 7pm) from the old gate of Déshèngmén, about 500m east of the Jīshuǐtán subway stop. Ask for the 919 branch line (919 支线). A taxi to the wall and back is a minimum of Y400 (eight-hour hire with maximum of four passengers).

Tour Buses

Hotel tours and hostel tours can be convenient (and should avoid rip-off diversions), but avoid high-priced excursions.

Tour buses to Bādálǐng depart from the Běijīng Sightseeing Bus Centre (北京旅游集散中心; Běijīng Lǚyóu Jísàn Zhōngxīn; ☎8353 1111) southwest of Tiān'ānmén Sq.

Line C (return entry to Great Wall Y100; ☉departures 7.30am-11.30am) Runs to Bādálǐng.

Line A (Y160, includes entrance tickets and lunch; ☉departures 6am-10.30am) Runs to Bādálǐng and Dìng Líng at the Ming Tombs.

Mùtiányù 慕田峪

Famed for its Ming-dynasty guard towers and stirring views, the 3km-long section of wall at **Mùtiányù** (Map p53; admission Y45; ☉6.30am-6pm), 90km northeast of Běijīng in Huáiróu County, dates from Ming-dynasty remains, built upon an earlier Northern Qi-dynasty conception. With 26 watchtowers, the wall is impressive and manageable; most hawking is reserved for the lower levels (hawkers go down to around Y15 for cotton 'I climbed the Great Wall' T-shirts). If time is tight, the wall here has a **cable car** (single/return Y35/50; ☉8.30am-4.30pm); a single trip takes four minutes. You can also sweep down on the **toboggan** (滑道; huádào; single/return Y40/55).

Getting There & Away

Public Transport

From Dōngzhímén Transport Hub Station (东直门枢纽站; Dōngzhímén Shūniǔzhàn; Map p82) take fast bus 916 (916路快; Jiǔyīliù Lùkuài; Y12, one hour, regular services) to Huáiróu (怀柔), then change for a minibus to Mùtiányù (Y25 to 30). The normal 916 (Y2, 2½ hours) is much slower. The last fast 916 bus back to Dōngzhímén from Huáiróu is at 5.30pm; the last slow 916 bus is at 7pm. During the summer months, weekend tour bus 6 departs between 7am and 8.30am for Mùtiányù (Y50) from outside the South Cathedral at Xuānwǔmén.

Tours

Youth hostels and hotels run tours to Mùtiányù from around Y200; such tours are very convenient, but some hotels charge sky-high prices.

Sīmǎtái 司马台

In Mìyún County, 110km northeast of Běijīng, the stirring remains at **Sīmǎtái** (Map p53; admission Y40; ☉8am-5pm) make for a more exhilarating Great Wall experience. Built during the reign of Ming-dynasty emperor Hongwu, the 19km section is an invigorating stretch of watchtowers, precarious plunges and scrambling ascents.

Chairlift at the Great Wall, Sīmǎtái

This rugged section of wall can be heart-thumpingly steep and the scenery exhilarating. The eastern section of wall at Sīmătái is the most treacherous, sporting 16 watchtowers and dizzyingly steep ascents that require free hands. The cable car (single/return Y30/Y50) saves valuable time and is an alternative to a sprained ankle.

The breathtaking (four-hour max) walk between Jīnshānlǐng and Sīmătái) is one of the most popular hikes and makes the long journey out here worth it. The walk is possible in either direction, but it's more convenient to return to Běijīng from Sīmătái.

Before heading out to Sīmătái, check if it's open as it was shut for restoration and development at the time of writing.

Getting There & Away

Tours

Most travellers get to Sīmătái on early-morning trips with a youth hostel, which usually involves being dropped off at Jīnshānlǐng and being picked up at Sīmătái; prices are in the region of Y260, including tickets. The entire journey from Běijīng and back can take up to 12 hours. A taxi from Běijīng for the day costs about Y400.

Tour buses (Y160/220/300 for 12 or more/five to 11/four people; price includes entrance ticket) run to Sīmătái at 9am from the **Běijīng Sightseeing Bus Centre** (北京旅游集散中心; **Běijīng Lǚyóu Jísàn Zhōngxīn; Map p64;** ☎ 8353 1111), northwest of Qiánmén alongside Tiān'ānmén Sq, if there are enough people.

Public Transport

To get here by public transport, take fast bus 980 (980 路快; **Jiǔbǎlíng Lùkuài;, Y15, regular services 5.50am to 8pm)** to Miyún (密云) from the **Dōngzhímén Transport Hub Station** (东直门枢纽站; **Dōngzhímén Shūniǔzhàn; Map p82**) and change to a minibus to Sīmătái or a taxi (round-trip Y120). The last fast 980 bus back from Miyún is at 6.30pm; the last slow bus returns at 7pm.

Jīnshānlǐng 金山岭

The Great Wall at Jīnshānlǐng (**Jīnshānlǐng Chángchéng; Map p53;** ☎ 0314 883 0222; admission Y50) marks the starting point of an exhilarating 10km hike to Sīmătái. The journey – through some stunning mountainous terrain – takes around four hours as the trail is steep and parts of the wall have collapsed; it can be traversed without too much difficulty, but some find it tiring. Arriving at Sīmătái you have to buy another ticket and en route you need to cross a rope bridge (Y5). At the time of writing, the Great Wall at Sīmătái was shut so it was not possible to complete the entire hike. Check with your hotel or hostel for the latest. The cable car at the start of Jīnshānlǐng is for the indolent or infirm (one-way/return Y30/50).

You can do the walk in the opposite direction, but getting a ride back to Běijīng from Sīmătái is easier than from Jīnshānlǐng. Of course, getting a ride should be no problem if you've made arrangements with your driver to pick you up (and didn't pay in advance).

ⓘ Getting There & Away

Tours

Most travellers get to Jīnshānlǐng on early morning trips with a youth hostel which usually involves being dropped off at Jīnshānlǐng and being picked up at Sīmătái; prices are in the region of Y260, including tickets. The entire journey from Běijīng and back can take up to 12 hours. A taxi from Běijīng for the day costs about Y400.

Public Transport

Take fast bus 980 (980 路快, Y15, regular services 5.50am to 8pm) to Miyún (密云) from the **Dōngzhímén Transport Hub Station** (东直门枢纽站; Dōngzhímén Shūniǔzhàn; Map p82) and then hire a minivan to drop you off at Jīnshānlǐng and collect you at Sīmătái. This should cost around Y100, but ensure you don't pay the driver in full until he picks you up. If you are heading to Chéngdé (in Héběi province), you will pass Jīnshānlǐng en route. The last fast 980 bus back from Miyún to Dōngzhímén is at 6.30pm; the last slow bus returns at 7pm.

Jiànkòu 箭扣

For gorgeous hikes along an incomparable section of Běijīng's wall, head to the rear of the Jiànkòu **Great Wall** (后箭扣长城; Hòu Jiànkòu Chángchéng; Map p53; admission Y20), accessible from Huáiróu. It's a 40-minute walk uphill from the drop-off at Xīzhàzi Village (Xīzhàzì Cūn; 西栅子村) to a fork in the path among the trees, which leads you to a collapsed section of wall, heading off east and west. Tantalising panoramic views spread out as the brickwork meanders dramatically along a mountain ridge; the setting is truly magnificent.

Tread carefully – sections are badly collapsing and the whole edifice is overgrown with plants and saplings – but its unadulterated state conveys an awe-inspiring and raw beauty.

🛈 Getting There & Away

Public Transport

Take fast bus 916 (ask for the 916路快 or fast bus – the normal 916 is much slower) from Dōngzhímén to Huáiróu (Y12, first/last bus 6.30am/7.50pm, one hour) from Dōngzhímén Transport Hub Station (东直门枢纽站; Dōngzhímén Shūniǔzhàn; Map p82). At Huáiróu you will need to hire a minivan to the rear Jiànkòu wall section; this should cost around Y200 return (one hour each way) as it's a fair distance; alternatively hire a van and driver either in Běijīng or Huáiróu for around Y400 for a day-long Great Wall tour, including Jiànkòu, Huánghuā, Mùtiányù, Xiàngshuǐhú and other sections of wall. The last fast 916 bus back to Dōngzhímén from Huáiróu is at 5.30pm; the last slow 916 bus (Y2, 2½ hours) is at 7pm.

Huánghuā 黄花

The Great Wall at Huánghuā, 60km from Běijīng, affords breathtaking panoramas of partially unrestored brickwork and watchtowers snaking off in two directions. There is also a refreshing absence of amusement park rides, exasperating tourist trappings and the full-on commercial mania of Bādálíng.

Clinging to the hillside on either side of a reservoir, Huánghuā is a classic and

DISCOVER BĚIJĪNG & THE GREAT WALL HUÁNGHUĀ

well-preserved example of Ming defences with high and wide ramparts, intact parapets and sturdy beacon towers. Official on-site signs declare that it's shut and illegal to climb here, but locals pooh-pooh the warnings and encourage travellers to visit and clamber on the wall. Fines are rarely enforced, although a theoretical risk exists.

Shoes with good grip are important for climbing Huánghuā as some sections are either slippery (eg parts of the wall south of the reservoir are simply smooth slopes at a considerable incline) or uneven and crumbling.

From the road, you can go either way along the battlements. Heading east, one route takes you across a small dam, along a path clinging to the side of the wall until the second watchtower, where you climb a metal ladder to the masonry. Alternatively cross a wooden bridge south of the dam (look for the sign to Mr Li's Tavern), pop through an outdoor restaurant and then clamber through someone's back garden to the second watchtower. Whichever route you take, it costs Y2.

In the other direction to the west, climb the steps past the ticket collector (Y2) to the wall, from where an exhilarating walk can be made along the parapet. Things get a bit hairier beyond the third watchtower as there's a steep gradient and the wall is fragile here, but the view of the overgrown bastion winding off into hills is magnificent.

Getting There & Away

Public Transport

To reach Huánghuā, take the fast bus 916 (ask for the 916路快 or fast bus – the normal 916 is much slower, Y12, first/last bus 6.50am/7.50pm, one hour) to Huáiróu (怀柔) from the Dōngzhímén Transport Hub Station (东直门枢纽站; Dōngzhímén Shūniǔzhàn; Map p82) to Huáiróu (怀柔). Get off at Míngzhū

117

KRZYSZTOF DYDYNSKI/LONELY PLANET IMAGES ©

Don't Miss Pǔníng Temple

With its squeaking prayer wheels and devotional intonations of its monks, Chéngdé's only active Buddhist temple was built in 1755 in anticipation of Qianlong's victory over the western Mongol tribes in Xīnjiāng. Supposedly modelled on the earliest Tibetan Buddhist monastery (Samye), the first half of the temple is distinctly Chinese (with Tibetan buildings at the rear).

The mindbogglingly vast gilded statue of **Guanyin** (the Buddhist Goddess of Mercy) towers within the Mahayana Hall; see the boxed text, p382. The effigy is astounding: over 22m high, it's the tallest of its kind in the world and radiates a powerful sense of divinity. Hewn from five different kinds of wood (pine, cypress, fir, elm and linden), Guanyin has 42 arms, with each palm bearing an eye and each hand holding instruments, skulls, lotuses and other Buddhist devices.

If you're fortunate, you may be able to clamber up to the first gallery (Y10) for a closer inspection of Guanyin; torches are provided to cut through the gloom. Sadly, higher galleries are often out of bounds, so an eye-to-eye with the goddess may be impossible. To climb the gallery, try to come in the morning, as it is often impossible to get a ticket in the afternoon, and prepare to be disappointed, as the gallery may simply be shut.

Pǔníng Temple has a number of friendly lamas who manage their domain, so be quiet and respectful at all times. Take bus 6 from in front of the Mountain Villa Hotel.

NEED TO KNOW

普宁寺; Pǔníng Sì; Puningsi Lu; admission Y50, winter Y40; ⏰ 7.30am-6pm, winter 8am-5pm

Guǎngchǎng (明珠广场), cross the road and take a minibus to Huánghuā (Y10, 40 minutes); ask for Huánghuāchéng (黄花城) and don't get off at the smaller Huánghuāzhèn by mistake. Taxi-van drivers charge around Y40 one-way to reach Huánghuā from Huáiróu. The last fast 916 bus back to Dōngzhímén from Huáiróu is at 5.30pm; the last slow 916 (Y2) bus is at 7pm.

Chéngdé 承德

🎵 0314 / POP 457,000

In many respects a typical provincial Chinese town, Chéngdé evolved during the first half of the Qing dynasty from hunting grounds to overblown summer resort and Manchu headquarters of foreign affairs. Beginning with Kangxi, the Qing emperors fled here from the torpid summer heat of the Forbidden City and for closer proximity to the hunting grounds of their northern homelands.

The Bìshǔ Shānzhuāng (Fleeing-the-Heat Mountain Villa) is a grand imperial palace and the walled enclosure behind rings China's largest regal gardens. Beyond the grounds is a remarkable collection of politically chosen temples, built to host dignitaries such as the sixth Panchen Lama.

History

In 1703, when an expedition passed through the Chéngdé valley, Emperor Kangxi was so enamoured with the surroundings that he had a hunting lodge built, which gradually grew into the summer resort. Rèhé – or Jehol (Warm River; named after a hot spring here) – as Chéngdé was then known, grew in importance and the Qing court began to spend more time here – sometimes up to several months a year, with some 10,000 people accompanying the emperor on his seven-day expedition from Běijīng.

The emperors also convened here with the border tribes – undoubtedly more at ease here than in Běijīng – who posed the greatest threats to the Qing frontiers: the Mongols, Tibetans, Uighurs and, eventually, the Europeans. The resort reached its peak under Emperor Qianlong (r 1735–96), who commissioned many of the outlying temples to overawe visiting leaders.

In 1793 British emissary Lord Macartney arrived to open trade with China. The well-known story of Macartney refusing to kowtow before Qianlong probably wasn't the definitive factor in his dismissal (though it certainly made quite an impression on the court) – in any case, China, it was explained, possessed all things and had no need for trade.

The Emperor Xianfeng died here in 1861, permanently warping Chéngdé's feng shui and tipping the Imperial Villa towards long-term decline.

◎ Sights

BÌSHǓ SHĀNZHUĀNG   Historic Site
(避暑山庄; admission Apr-Nov Y120, Dec-Mar Y90; ⊙palace 7am-5pm, park 5.30am-6.30pm)
The imperial summer resort is composed of a main palace complex and vast park-like gardens, all enclosed by a good-looking 10km-long wall. The peak-season entrance price is steep, considering the Forbidden City is half the price.

A huge spirit wall shields the resort entrance from the bad spirits and traffic fumes of Lizhengmen Dajie. Through Lìzhèng Gate (丽正门; Lìzhèng Mén), the **Main Palace** (正宫; Zhèng Gōng) is a series of nine courtyards and five elegant, unpainted halls, with a rusticity complemented by towering pine trees. The wings in each courtyard have various exhibitions (porcelain, clothing, weaponry), and most of the halls are decked out in period furnishings.

Exiting the Main Palace brings you to the **gardens** and forested hunting grounds, with landscapes borrowed from famous southern scenic areas in Hángzhōu, Sūzhōu and Jiāxīng, as well as the Mongolian grasslands. The 20th century took its toll on the park, but you can still get a feel for the original scheme of things.

The double-storey **Misty Rain Tower** (烟雨楼; Yānyǔ Lóu), on the northwestern side of the main lake, served as an imperial study. Further north is the **Wénjīn Pavilion** (文津阁; Wénjīn Gé), built in 1773 to house a copy of the *Siku Quanshu,* a major anthology of classics, history, philosophy and literature commissioned by Qianlong. The anthology took 10 years to compile, and totalled an astounding 36,500 chapters. Four copies were made, only one of which has survived (now in Běijīng).

Padlocks left by worshippers in Pǔníng Temple (p118), Chéngdé

KRZYSZTOF DYDYNSKI/LONELY PLANET IMAGES ©

In the east, elegant **Yǒngyòusì Pagoda** (永佑寺塔; Yǒngyòusì Tǎ) soars above the fragments of its vanished temple.

Almost all of the forested section is closed from November through May because of fire hazard in the dry months, but fear not, you can still turn your legs to jelly wandering around the rest of the park.

GUĀNDÌ TEMPLE   Taoist Temple
(关帝庙; Guāndì Miào; 18 Lizhengmen Dajie; admission Y20; ☽8am-5pm) The restored Taoist Guāndì Temple was first built during the reign of Yongzheng, in 1732. For years the temple housed residents but is again home to a band of Taoist monks, garbed in distinctive jackets and trousers, their long hair twisted into topknots.

EIGHT OUTER TEMPLES 外八庙
Buddhist Temples
(外八庙; wài bā miào) Skirting the northern and eastern walls of the Bìshǔ Shānzhuāng, the eight outer temples were, unusually, designed for diplomatic rather than spiritual reasons. The surviving temples and monasteries were all built between 1713 and 1780; the prominence given to Tibetan Buddhism was as much for the Mongols (fervent Lamaists) as the Tibetan leaders.

Bus 6 taken to the northeastern corner will drop you in the vicinity and bus 118 runs along Huancheng Beilu, though pedalling the 12km (round-trip) by bike is an excellent idea.

PǓTUÓZŌNGCHÉNG TEMPLE
Buddhist Temple
(普陀宗乘之庙; Pǔtuózōngchéng Zhīmiào; Shizigou Lu; admission Y40, winter Y30; ☽8am-6pm, winter 8.30am-5pm) Chéngdé's largest temple is a minifacsimile of Lhasa's Potala Palace and houses the nebulous presence of Avalokiteshvara (Guanyin). A marvellous sight on a clear day, the temple's red walls stand out against its mountain backdrop. Enter to a huge stele pavilion, followed by a large triple archway topped with five small stupas in red, green, yellow, white and black. In between the two gates are two large stone elephants whose knees bend impossibly.

Fronted by a collection of prayer wheels and flags, the Red Palace (also called the Great Red Platform) contains most of the main shrines and halls. Bus 118 (Y1) runs along Huancheng Beilu past the temple.

TEMPLE OF SUMERU, HAPPINESS & LONGEVITY   Buddhist Temple

(须弥福寿之庙; Xūmífúshòu Zhīmiào; Shizigou Lu; admission Y30, winter Y20; ⏰8am-5.30pm, winter 8.30am-5pm) East of the Pǔtuózōngchéng Temple, this huge temple was built in honour of the sixth Panchen Lama, who stayed here in 1781. Incorporating Tibetan and Chinese architectural elements, it's an imitation of a temple in Shigatse, Tibet. Note the eight huge, glinting dragons (each said to weigh over 1000kg) that adorn the roof of the main hall. Bus 118 (Y1) runs along Huancheng Beilu past the temple.

PŪLÈ TEMPLE   Buddhist Temple

(普乐寺; Pǔlè Sì; admission Y30, winter Y20; ⏰8am-6pm, winter 8.30am-5pm) This peaceful temple was built in 1776 for the visits of minority envoys (Kazakhs among them). At the rear of the temple is the unusual Round Pavilion, reminiscent of the Hall of Prayer for Good Harvests at Bēijīng's Temple of Heaven. Inside is an enormous wooden mandala (a geometric representation of the universe).

Pǔyòu Temple   Buddhist Temple

(普佑寺; Pǔyòu Sì; admission Y20; ⏰8am-6pm) East of Pǔníng Temple, this temple is dilapidated and missing its main hall, but it has a plentiful contingent of merry gilded luóhàn in the side wings, although a fire in 1964 incinerated many of their confrères.

Ānyuǎn Temple   Buddhist Temple

(安远庙; Ānyuǎn Miào; admission Y10; ⏰8am-5.30pm) A copy of the Gurza Temple in Xīnjiāng; only the main hall remains, containing deteriorating Buddhist frescos. Take bus 10.

🛏 Sleeping

Chéngdé has an unremarkable and expensive range of tourist accommodation; at the time of writing, foreigners were barred from many cheap hotels. Hotel room prices increase at the weekend and during the holiday periods.

MOUNTAIN VILLA HOTEL   Hotel $$

(山庄宾馆; Shānzhuāng Bīnguǎn; ☎209 1188; www.hemvhotel.com; 11 Lizhengmen Lu; 丽正门路11号; d Y380-680, tr Y400, discounts of 30%; ❄) The Mountain Villa has a plethora of rooms and offers pole position for a trip inside the Bìshǔ Shānzhuāng, making it one of the best choices in town. The cheapest rooms are in the rear block but take a look at rooms first. Take bus 7 from the train station and from there it's a short walk. All major credit cards are accepted.

QĪWÀNGLÓU HOTEL   Hotel $$

(绮望楼宾馆; Qīwànglóu Bīnguǎn; ☎202 2196; 1 Bifengmen Donglu; 碧峰门东路1号; s/d/tr/ste Y480/480/580/1800; ❄) Qīwànglóu boasts a serene green and traditional setting alongside the Summer Villa's walls,

Battle of the Buddhas

Hands down China's largest Buddha gazes out over the confluence of the waters of the Dàdù River and the Mín River at Lèshān (p336) in Sìchuān. The Buddha in the Big Buddha Temple at Zhāngyè may not take it lying down though: he is China's largest 'housed reclining Buddha'. Lounging around in second place is the reclining Buddha in the Mógāo Caves, China's second largest. The vast reclining Buddha at Lèshān is a whopping 170m long and the world's largest alfresco reclining Buddha. Bristling with limbs, the Thousand Arm Guanyin statue in the Pǔníng Temple's Mahayana Hall in Chéngdé also stands up to be counted: she's the largest wooden statue in China (and possibly the world). Not to be outdone, Hong Kong fights for its niche with the Tian Tan Buddha Statue (p274), the world's 'largest outdoor seated bronze Buddha statue'.

Gilded dragons, Temple of Sumeru, Happiness & Longevity (p121), Chéngdé

KRZYSZTOF DYDYNSKI/LONELY PLANET IMAGES ©

accentuated by the hotel's courtyard gardens and wandering peacocks. Aim for the pleasant rooms backing onto courtyards but avoid downstairs rooms, which have bad air.

Eating

XIǍO FÉIYÁNG Hotpot $
(小肥羊; Xīnyìfùlái Hotel; Lizhengmen Dajie; meals Y40; ⏰11am-9pm) Right across the way from Lìzhèng Gate, this downstairs lamb-hotpot restaurant is excellent for post-Imperial Summer Resort ramblings. Best is the two-flavour spicy and mild *yuānyāng* (鸳鸯锅; Y20) base, into which you fling plateloads of lamb (羊肉; Y18), cabbage (白菜; Y4), potatoes (土豆片; Y4), eggs (鸡蛋; Y1) and more. Tick the form and hand to the waitress. It's on the ground floor of the Xīnyìfùlái Hotel (新意富来酒店).

XĪLÁISHÙN FÀNZHUĀNG Muslim $
(西来顺饭庄; ☎202 5554; 6 Zhonggulou Dajie; dishes Y10-40) The gathering place for local Muslims, this unassuming restaurant is a great choice for those undaunted by Chinese-only picture menus. Excellent

choices include beef fried with coriander (烤牛肉; *kǎo niúròu;* Y24) and sesame duck kebabs (芝麻鸭串; *zhīma yāchuàn;* Y25). Look for the mosque-style entrance.

ⓘ Information

Bank of China (中国银行; Zhōngguó Yínháng; 4 Dutongfu Dajie) Also on Xinsheng Lu and Lizhengmen Dajie; 24-hour ATMs.

China Post (中国邮政; Zhōngguó Yóuzhèng; cnr Lizhengmen Dajie & Dutongfu Dajie; ⏰8am-6pm) A smaller branch is on Lizhengmen Dajie, east of the Main Gate of the Imperial Summer Resort.

Public Security Bureau (公安局; PSB; Gōng'ānjú; ☎202 2352; 9 Wulie Lu; ⏰8.30am-5pm Mon-Fri)

Web Cafe (网吧; Wǎngbā; Chaichang Hutong; per hr Y2; ⏰24hr)

Xiàndài Internet Cafe (现代网吧; Xiàndài Wǎngbā; Chezhan Lu; per hr Y2; ⏰24hr) West of the train station.

ⓘ Getting There & Away

Bus
Buses for Chéngdé leave Běijīng hourly from Liùlǐqiáo bus station (Y56 to Y73, four hours);

buses also run from Běijīng's Sìhuì long-distance station (Y50 to Y74, four hours, 6am to 4pm). Minibuses from Chéngdé leave every 20 minutes for Běijīng (Y85, three hours, last bus 6.30pm) from the train-station parking lot, also stopping down the road from the Yúnshān Hotel.

Buses also leave from Chéngdé's east bus station (dōng qìchēzhàn; 212 3566), 8km south of town: destinations include Běijīng (Y73, four hours, every 20 minutes from 6am to 6pm) and Qínhuángdǎo (Y96, five hours, five daily for Shānhǎiguān).

Train

The fastest regular trains from Běijīng train station take over four hours (hard/soft seat Y41/92); slower trains take much longer. The first train from Běijīng departs at 8.07am, arriving in Chéngdé at 12.29am. Alternatively, catch the 00.25am train from Běijīng and reach Chéngdé early next morning. In the other direction, the 1.29pm service from Chéngdé is a useful train, arriving in Běijīng at 5.51pm. The first train to Běijīng is at 5.45am, arriving at 11am. Trains also go to **Shěnyáng** (Y97, 13 hours, 6.53am daily) and **Tiānjīn** (hard seat Y65, nine hours, 9.53pm daily).

Getting Around

Taxis are Y6 at flag fall (then Y1.4 per kilometre); on the meter, a taxi from the train station to the Bìshǔ Shānzhuāng should cost around Y7. There are several minibus lines (Y1), including minibus 5 from the train station to Lizhengmen Dajie, minibus 1 from the train station to the east bus station and minibus 6 to the Eight Outer Temples, grouped at the northeastern end of town. Bus 11 also runs from the train station to the Bìshǔ Shānzhuāng. To reach the east bus station, take bus 118 or a taxi (Y20).

Xī'ān & the North

A monumental trail of antiquity extends across North China. Affluent Chinese may roll their eyes at the mention of impoverished Hénán, yet the province's heritage takes us back to China's earliest days. Neighbouring Shaanxi boasts a similar pedigree, when Emperor Qinshi Huangdi buried Confucian scholars alive, torched their literature and left the Terracotta Warriors to posterity. The Shaanxi capital Xī'ān furthermore marked the beginning and end of the Silk Road, developing into a cosmopolitan Tang capital.

Shaanxi is a traveller's dream. If you only visited Píngyáo and jetted home, you may assume China was bursting with picture-perfect, ancient walled settlements. The mountain fastness of Wǔtái Shān reveals a Buddhist leaning that finds further concentration in the astonishing Buddhist cave sculpture at Yúngāng.

East towards the Yellow Sea, Shāndōng's ancient bedrock is Confucius, the Yellow River and sacred Tài Shān, while the breezy port of Qīngdǎo is a refreshing diversion.

Main street leading to pagoda, Shaanxi

Hired bike on city walls (p147), Xī'ān

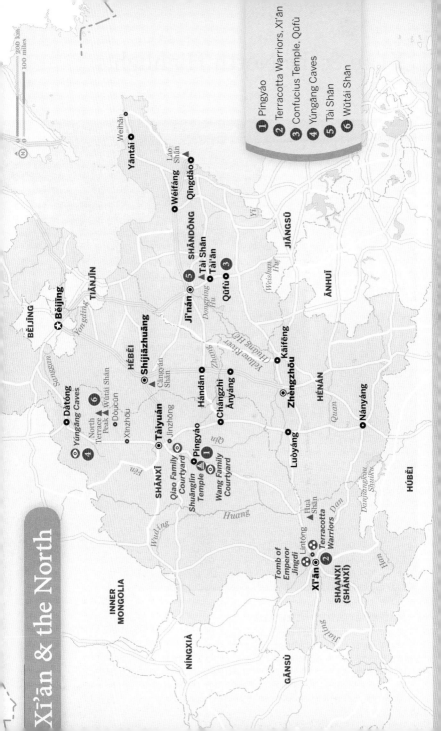

Xī'ān & the North

1. Píngyáo
2. Terracotta Warriors, Xī'ān
3. Confucius Temple, Qūfù
4. Yúngāng Caves
5. Tài Shān
6. Wǔtái Shān

Xī'ān & the North Highlights

1

Potter around Píngyáo

Reaching Píngyáo (p155) is like stepping through a wormhole to some distant age. The town walls are a picture, the courtyard houses simply splendid and the inviting alleyways are brimming with charm. There's every temptation to come to Píngyáo and stay put, in some huge pretence the 20th century never happened.

Need to Know

LOCATION Two hours southeast of Tàiyuán. **BEST PHOTO OP** From the city walls or along Nan Dajie. **MOST PICTURESQUE MOMENT** Evening. **GETTING AROUND** On foot. **For more, see** p155.

Píngyáo Don't Miss List

YANG MAOLIN, PÍNGYÁO LOCAL

1 CITY WALL

I simply love the city wall (p160) around Píngyáo. The fine Ming dynasty ramparts are all around you as soon as you enter town. From the earliest days, residents have clambered onto the fortification, especially at the time of the Spring Festival when locals dress up in their very finest. It is always very satisfying to look out over town and compare the grey bricks and tiles of Píngyáo with the great view beyond.

2 SHUĀNGLÍN TEMPLE

Local people really revere Shuānglín Temple (p158). On the eighth day of the fourth month (on the lunar calendar), worshippers flock down to the temple to light incense and worship Buddha. Some pray to Guanyin for peace for their family, others pray to the Money God for lucrative business; others still entreat Niangniang for a son or daughter.

3 NAN DAJIE

Píngyáo's best-known street – the 440m-long Nan Dajie (p157) – forms the commercial heart of town and has come to symbolise Píngyáo. Most of the buildings down here date to the Ming and Qing dynasties, presenting a genteel and well-preserved portrait of old Píngyáo.

4 CITY TOWER

You've got to climb the 300-year-old City Tower (p155) on Nan Dajie for a fine perspective of the town. With its Qing dynasty tablets and iron bell and original Qing dynasty murals that adorn the eastern and western walls, the views over the old town from here are excellent.

5 PÍNGYÁO BEEF

When you've finished sightseeing, try some of Píngyáo's exquisite and tender beef, which enjoys a nationwide reputation. When the Empress Dowager passed through Píngyáo, she enjoyed the local beef so much it was elevated to the status of an imperial dish. Look out for Zhonghua Laozihao Niurou – a type of locally prepared beef.

Marvel at the Terracotta Warriors

Staring out from the millennia, the silent Terracotta Warriors (p143), on the outskirts of Xī'ān are one of China's most astounding artistic achievements. The warriors stand as an embodiment of the towering creativity of the Qin-dynasty craftsmen that fashioned them. Yet they also represent the overarching megalomania of the emperor whose tomb they protect, a tomb inside which – legends insist – flowed rivers of mercury.

Wonder at the Yúngāng Caves

The ancient Buddhist statuary at Yúngāng (p165) is one of China's three great collections of grotto artwork. Despite the effects of pollution and weathering, the statues retain a magnificent amount of pigment and the eagle-eyed can track down graffiti from the Cultural Revolution and attentions from other eras. The vast seated Buddha in Cave 20 may be the drawcard, but the entire galaxy of effigies is lovely.

Explore Qūfù's Confucius Temple ③

Ancestral home of the Kong family, Qūfù is again elevated in stature as the CCP once again applauds Confucius and his thought. It may be tricky for Westerners to grasp Confucius' often unfathomable dictums, but exploring the sage's temple (p172) is a great cultural primer. It may be steeped in introspection, but the temple stands at the very epicentre of China's Confucian heritage.

Watch the Sunrise from Tài Shān ⑤

China's most climbed mountain (p169) is also its holiest Taoist peak, the easternmost of the five Taoist mountains. In ancient times, the Chinese believed that the sun began its daily journey from Tài Shān. Emperors climbed Tài Shān in search of divine blessing while today's sprightly octogenarians bound up the steps, propelled by faith (or belief in the old adage that you'll live to 100 if you climb the mountain).

Temple Trekking in Wǔtái Shān ⑥

The monastic enclave of Táihuái in Wǔtái Shān (p159) is home to an extraordinary number of temples, and the surrounding peaks are sprinkled with yet more. The five peaks are one of China's four holiest Buddhist mountains and worshippers are drawn from across the land, the scenery and spiritual focus creating an alluring combination.

Xī'ān & the North's Best...

Buddhist Culture

○ **Yúngāng Caves** (p165) A Sutra in stone and one of China's most supreme Buddhist treasures.

○ **Xiăntōng Temple, Wŭtái Shān** (p159) Alluring Buddhist temple decorated with some magnificent architecture.

○ **Lóngmén Caves** (p153) A mesmerising master class in Buddhist statuary.

○ **Shuānglín Temple** (p158) A riveting collection of elegantly painted statues from the Song and Yuan dynasties.

Cuisine

○ **Muslim Quarter, Xī'ān** (p139) Follow your nostrils, snacking on Silk Road staples.

○ **Qīngdăo** (p179) Some of the best seafood and kebabs in north China.

○ **First Noodle under the Sun** (p140) *The* place to come for filling *biáng biáng* noodles.

○ **Máogōng Xiāngcàiguăn** (p140) Add some zest to your northern diet with a blast of spice from Húnán.

Places to Stay

○ **Sofitel, Xī'ān** (p139) At the very apex of luxury in Xī'ān .

○ **Hàn Táng Inn** (p139) Homely hostel with a popular roof terrace and central location in Xī'ān.

○ **Jing's Residence** (p156) Highly sophisticated and stylish courtyard accommodation – traditional meets modern.

○ **Fóyuán Lóu** (p161) Delightfully tucked away behind Shūxiàng Temple in Wŭtái Shān.

Scenery

○ **Huà Shān** (p148) Pine trees, hair-raising ascents and awesome views from Taoism's sacred western mountain.

○ **Wǔtái Shān** (p159) Astonishing Shānxī mountain panorama sprinkled with Buddhist temples.

○ **Tài Shān** (p169) Awesome sunrise panoramas from Taoism's holiest peak.

○ **Qīngdǎo** (p176) On the balmy Shāndōng coastline with superb views of the Yellow Sea.

○ **City Walls, Xī'ān** (p147) Clamber up for excellent view over the city.

Need to Know

ADVANCE PLANNING

○ **One Month Before** Get your accommodation sorted and book your hotel rooms.

○ **One Week Before** Book your onward train or air tickets through and from the region through your hotel or a local travel agent.

RESOURCES

○ **Terracotta Warriors** (www.bmy.com.cn) Website of the Terracotta Warriors.

○ **Wǔtái Shān** (www.wutaishan.cn) Website of the Wǔtái Mountains.

○ **My Red Star** (www.myredstar.com) Qīngdǎo listings and entertainment guide.

○ **That's Qīngdǎo** (www.thatsqingdao.com) Online Qīngdǎo guide with listings and news clips.

GETTING AROUND

○ **Train** Your best bet for getting around between towns and cities at convenience and speed.

○ **Air** Good connections within the region and nationwide.

○ **Long-Distance Bus** Extensive and reasonably efficient network throughout the region.

○ **Taxis** Your primary means of transport within town.

○ **Local Bus** Extensive network within town but not foreigner-friendly.

BE FOREWARNED

○ **Language** English skills are rudimentary in most parts.

○ **Fake Monks** Guard against fake monks asking for alms and donations.

○ **Ticket Price Hikes** Admission ticket prices for top sights regularly go up.

○ **Pollution** Pollution in some big towns can be intense.

○ **Weather** Cold weather or snow may put high-altitude destinations out of reach or uncomfortable to visit.

Sakyamuni Buddha, Yúngāng Caves (p165); **above:** Toffee apples, Muslim Quarter (p139)
(LEFT & ABOVE) MARTIN MOOS/LONELY PLANET IMAGES ©

Xī'ān & the North Itineraries

These tours bring you the highlights of north China, from the Terracotta Warriors to Buddhist caves at Lóngmén and Yúngāng to the ancient town of Píngyáo, and on via Wǔtái Shān to the port town of Qīngdǎo.

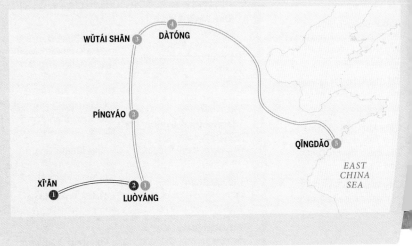

XĪ'ĀN TO LUÒYÁNG
Terracotta Warriors, Warrior Monks

Spend two days exploring the diverse sights of the Shaanxi capital **(1) Xī'ān**, including the outstanding Terracotta Warriors, the Ming city walls, the city's rare collection of Tang-dynasty pagodas, its atmospheric Muslim Quarter, fascinating museums and the excellent range of restaurants. Ensure you sample the scrumptious local Muslim cuisine. If you have more time on your hands and an adventurous streak, consider a journey east to the further-flung Taoist mountain of Huà Shān (where you can spend the night) or an exploration of the scattered imperial tombs and temples around Xī'ān. Then jump aboard an express train to **(2) Luòyáng** to spend the night and visit the old town and the astonishing Lóngmén Caves, one of China's most significant collections of Buddhist statuary, outside town. The White Horse Temple, also outside town, is China's oldest Buddhist temple. A short detour by bus to the legendary birthplace of kung fu – the Shàolín Temple – is also recommended for anyone with either an interest in Buddhism or the magnificence of China's *wǔshù* (martial arts). Visiting the Shàolín Temple is also an opportunity to explore the surrounding Taoist mountain of Sōng Shān, another of China's most sacred Taoist sites.

LUÒYÁNG TO QĪNGDǍO
Old Towns & German Beer

1 WEEK

After seeing the sights of **(1) Luòyáng** – detailed in the first itinerary – head north into Shānxī province to spend a few days in the delightful old walled town of **(2) Píngyáo**. Journey out to some of the sights beyond Píngyáo, but spend most of your time enjoying the age-old textures of the ancient city walls and low-rise architecture. Then make your way north again to the Buddhist mountain fastness of **(3) Wǔtái Shān**, but don't attempt this in winter. In summer, buses run from Wǔtái Shān to **(4) Dàtóng**, which you can also reach from Píngyáo via Tàiyuán, the provincial capital of Shānxī. Visit the astounding

Yúngāng Caves outside town to compare them with the effigies of Lóngmén. To reach **(5) Qīngdǎo** – far away on the coast of the Shāndōng peninsula – take a bus from Dàtóng first to Běijīng and then catch an express D-train to Qīngdǎo. Alternatively, fly from Tàiyuán. Qīngdǎo is a fetching terminus: with its beaches, robust German architecture, historic churches and excellent seafood, the Shāndōng port is a relaxing place to hang your travelling hat. The port city is also the home of Tsingtao beer – so raise a glass to your travels!

Terracotta warriors in battle formation (p143), Bīngmǎyǒng

Discover Xī'ān & the North

At a Glance

○ **Xī'ān** (p136) Pottery warriors, city walls and Taoist peaks.

○ **Píngyáo** (p155) Charming walled town stuffed with historic allure.

○ **Wǔtái Shān** (p159) Monastic retreat replete with Buddhist mystery.

○ **Tài Shān** (p169) China's foremost Taoist summit.

○ **Dàtóng** (p163) Home of the spectacular Yúngāng Caves.

Bicycle commuters passing Bell Tower, Xī'ān

PHOTOGRAPHER: GREG ELMS/LONELY PLANET IMAGES ©

XĪ'ĀN 西安

029 / POP 4.5 MILLION

Xī'ān's fabled past is a double-edged sword. Primed with the knowledge that this legendary city was once the terminus of the Silk Road and a melting pot of cultures and religions – as well as home to emperors, courtesans, poets, monks, merchants and warriors – visitors can feel let down by the roaring, modern-day version. But even though Xī'ān's glory days ended in the early 10th century, many elements of ancient Cháng'ān, the former Xī'ān, are still present.

The city walls remain intact, vendors of all descriptions still crowd the narrow lanes of the warrenlike Muslim Quarter, and there are enough places of interest to keep even the most diligent amateur historian busy. Then there are the Terracotta Warriors (see p143).

Sights

Inside the City Walls

GREAT MOSQUE Mosque

(清真大寺; Qīngzhēn Dàsì; Huajue Xiang; admission Mar-Nov Y25, Dec-Feb Y15, Muslims free; ⏰8am-7.30pm Mar-Nov, to 5.30pm Dec-Feb)
One of the largest mosques in China, the Great Mosque is a fascinating blend of Chinese and Islamic architecture. The present buildings are mostly Ming and Qing, though the mosque is said to have been founded in the 8th century. To get here, follow Xiyang Shi several minutes west and look for a small alley leading south past a gauntlet of souvenir stands.

BELL TOWER & DRUM TOWER
Historic Sites

Now marooned on a traffic island, the **Bell Tower** (钟楼; Zhōng Lóu; admission Y27, combined Drum Tower ticket Y40; ⏱8.30am-9.30pm Mar-Nov, to 6pm Dec-Feb) sits at the heart of Xī'ān and originally held a large bell that was rung at dawn, while its alter ego, the **Drum Tower** (鼓楼; Gǔ Lóu; Beiyuanmen; admission Y27, combined Bell Tower ticket Y40; ⏱8.30am-9.30pm Mar-Nov, to 6pm Dec-Feb), marked nightfall. Both date from the 14th century and were later rebuilt in the 1700s (the Bell Tower initially stood two blocks to the west). Musical performances, included in the ticket price, are held inside each at 9am, 10.30am, 11.30am, 2.30pm, 4pm and 5pm. Enter the Bell Tower through the underpass on the north side.

Outside the City Walls

FREE SHAANXI HISTORY MUSEUM
Museum

(陕西历史博物馆; Shǎnxī Lìshǐ Bówùguǎn; 91 Xiaozhai Donglu; ⏱8.30am-6pm Tue-Sun Apr-Oct, last admission 4.30pm, 9.30am-5pm Tue-Sun Nov-Mar, last admission 4pm) Shaanxi's museum is often touted as one of China's best, but if you come after visiting some of Xī'ān's surrounding sights you may feel you're not seeing much that is new. Nevertheless, the museum makes for a comprehensive and illuminating stroll through ancient Cháng'ān, and most exhibits include labels and explanations in English.

The number of visitors is limited to 4000 a day, so get here early and expect to queue for at least 30 minutes. Make sure to bring your passport to claim your free ticket. Take bus 610 from the Bell Tower or bus 701 from the South Gate.

BIG GOOSE PAGODA
Buddhist Temple

(大雁塔; Dàyàn Tǎ; Yanta Nanlu; admission Y50, incl pagoda climb Y80; ⏱8am-7pm Apr-Oct, to 6pm Nov-Mar) Xī'ān's most famous landmark, this pagoda dominates the surrounding modern buildings. It was completed in AD 652 to house the Buddhist sutras brought back from India by the monk Xuan Zang. Surrounding the pagoda is **Dà Cí'ēn Temple** (大慈恩寺; Dàcí'ēn Sì), one of the largest temples in Tang Cháng'ān.

Bus 610 from the Bell Tower and bus 609 from the South Gate drop you off at the pagoda square; the entrance is on the south side.

FREE XĪ'ĀN MUSEUM
Museum

(西安博物院; Xī'ān Bówùyuàn; 76 Youyi Xilu; ⏱8.30am-7pm, closed Tue) Housed in the pleasant grounds of the Jiànfú Temple is this newish museum featuring relics unearthed in Xī'ān over the years. Don't miss the basement, where a large-scale model of ancient Xī'ān gives a good sense of the place in its former pomp.

Also in the grounds is the **Little Goose Pagoda** (小雁塔; Xiǎoyàn Tǎ; ⏱8.30am-7pm, closed Tue). The top of the pagoda was shaken off by an earthquake in the middle of the 16th century, but the rest of the 43m-high structure is intact. At the time of writing, it was no longer possible to climb the pagoda.

Bus 610 runs here from the Bell Tower; from the South Gate take bus 203.

TEMPLE OF THE EIGHT IMMORTALS
Taoist Temple

(八仙庵; Bāxiān Ān; Yongle Lu; admission Y3; ⏱7.30am-5.30pm Mar-Nov, 8am-5pm Dec-Feb) Xī'ān's largest Taoist temple dates back to the Song dynasty and is still an active place of worship. Supposedly built on the site of an ancient wine shop, it was constructed to protect against subterranean divine thunder. Bus 502 runs close by the temple (eastbound from Xi Xinjie).

Sleeping

If you're arriving by air and have not yet booked accommodation, keep in mind that representatives at the shuttle bus drop-off (outside the Melody Hotel) can often get you discounted rooms at a wide selection of hotels.

All hostels in the city offer a similar range of services, including bike hire, internet, laundry, restaurant and travel services. Ask about free pick-up from the

Xī'ān

1 km
0.5 miles

Train Station 火车站

Long-Distance
Bus Station

To Big Goose Pagoda &
Da Cíen Temple (4km)

To Shaanxi Grand
Opera House (500m)

To CITS; Tang
Dynasty (2km)

City Walls

West Gate

North Gate

South Gate

East Gate

Muslim Quarter

Great Mosque

Lianhu Park

Geming Park

China Eastern Airlines

Kodak

Huancheng Dong Lu 环城东路

Huancheng Bĕilù

Huancheng Xīlù 环城西路

Huancheng Bĕilù

Daqing Lu

Xīguan Zhengjie

Taibai Bĕilù

Qianwei Jie

Lianhu Lu

Xi Qīlù

Xī Balu

Beixin Jie

Houzaimen

Xī Wulu 西五路

Bĕixin Jie

Xiyang Shi

Damaishi Jie

Xī Dajie 西大街

Hongguang Jie

Beiguangji Jie

Dapi Yuan

Beiyuanmen

Bĕi Dàren 北大街

Bĕi Dàjie 北大街

Xī Xīnjie

Dong Xīnjie

Dong Yīlu

Shangde Lu 尚德路

Jiefang Lu 解放路

Dong Balu

Dong Qīlù

Dong Liùlù

Dong Wulu

Dong Sīlù

Dong Sanlu

Dong Erlu

Changle Lu

Yongle Lu

Heping Lu 和平路

Shuncheng Xixiang

Nan Dajie 南大街

Shuyuan Xiang 书院巷

Dongmutou Shi

Juhuayuan Lu

Dong Dajie 东大街

Duanlumen

China Eastern Airlines

Advance Train Ticket
Booking Office

Airport
Shuttle Bus

1
2
3
4
5
6
7
8
9
10
11
12
13
14
15

train station and book ahead at the most popular places.

HÀN TÁNG INN — Hostel $

(汉唐驿; Hàntáng Yì; ☎8728 7772, 8723 1126; www.hostelxian@yahoo.com.cn; 7 Nanchang Xiang; 南长巷7号; dm/s/d Y50/70/160; ☺❄@) Newly ensconced in a more convenient central location, the dorms here are compact but spotless and come with en suite bathrooms. Smaller and more homely than the other hostels in town – the roof terrace provides space to spread out – the staff know what travellers want and do their best to satisfy them. It's tucked down an alley off Bei Dajie; look for the two terracotta warriors standing guard outside.

SOFITEL — Hotel $$$

(索菲特人民大厦; Suǒfēitè Rénmín Dàshà; ☎8792 8888; sofitel@renminsquare.com; 319 Dong Xinjie; 东新街319号; d/ste Y1242/1814; ☺❄@☎) Xī'ān's self-claimed 'six-star' hotel is undoubtedly the most luxurious choice in the city and has a soothing, hushed atmosphere. The bathrooms are top-notch. Reception is in the east wing and room rates change daily, so you can score a deal when business is slow.

BELL TOWER HOTEL — Hotel $$$

(西安钟楼饭店; Xī'ān Zhōnglóu Fàndiàn; ☎8760 0000; www.belltowerhtl.com; 110 Nan Dajie; 南大街110号; d Y850-1080, discounts of 33%; ❄@) Big discounts are on offer during slack periods, making this state-owned four-star more affordable. Some rooms have a bird's-eye view of the Bell Tower and all are spacious and comfortable with cable TV and broadband internet connections.

HÉJIĀ SHĀNGWÙ HOTEL — Hotel $$

(和嘉商务宾馆; ☎8728 2200/8919; www. hj600.cn; 16 Nan Dajie; 南大街16号; s/d/tr Y280/298/368, discounts of 30%; ❄@) The great location means this new place can be noisy, but the rooms are decent-sized with clean bathrooms and they all come with ADSL connections.

Eating

Hit the **Muslim Quarter** for fine eating in Xī'ān. Common dishes here are *májiàng liángpí* (麻酱凉皮; cold noodles in sesame sauce), *fěnzhēngròu* (粉蒸肉; chopped mutton fried in a wok with ground wheat), *ròujiāmó* (肉夹馍; fried pork or beef in pitta bread, sometimes with green peppers and cumin), *càijiāmó* (菜夹馍; the vegetarian version of *ròujiāmó*) and the ubiquitous *ròuchuàn* (肉串; kebabs).

Best of all is the delicious *yángròu pàomó* (羊肉泡馍), a soup dish that involves crumbling a flat loaf of bread into a bowl and adding noodles, mutton and broth.

A good street to wander for a selection of more typically Chinese restaurants is Dongmutou Shi, east of Nan Dajie.

Xī'ān

◉ Top Sights
City Walls	A2
Great Mosque	C3
Muslim Quarter	C2

◎ Sights
1	Bell Tower	D3
2	Drum Tower	C3
3	Forest of Stelae Museum	D4
4	Temple of the Eight Immortals	G3

⊜ Sleeping
5	Bell Tower Hotel	D3
6	Hàn Táng Inn	D3
7	Héjiā Shāngwù Hotel	D4

8	Sofitel	E2

⊗ Eating
9	First Noodle under the Sun	E4
10	Lǎo Sūn Jiā	E3

⊕ Drinking
11	Moonkey Music Bar	D4
12	Old Henry's Bar	C4

⊛ Entertainment
13	1+1	E3
14	Song & Song	D4

⊕ Shopping
15	Northwest Antique Market	F3

JULIET COOMBE/LONELY PLANET IMAGES ©

Don't Miss **Muslim Quarter**

The backstreets leading north from the Drum Tower have been home to the city's Hui community (Chinese Muslims) for centuries. Although Muslims have been here since at least the 7th century, some believe that today's community didn't take root until the Ming dynasty.

The narrow lanes of the Muslim Quarter (回族区) are full of butcher shops, sesame-oil factories, smaller mosques hidden behind enormous wooden doors, men in white skullcaps and women with their heads covered in coloured scarves. Good streets to stroll down are Xiyang Shi, Dapi Yuan and Damaishi Jie, which runs north off Xi Dajie through an interesting Islamic food market.

FIRST NOODLE UNDER THE SUN
Noodles **$**

(天下第一面酒楼; Tiānxià Dìyī Miàn Jiǔlóu; ☑8728 6088; 19 Dongmutou Shi; dishes Y6-58; ☺9am-10.30pm; 🔊) The speciality at this busy place is *biáng biáng miàn*, a giant, 3.8m strip of noodle that comes folded up in a big bowl with two soup side dishes (Y10). English menu.

MÁOGŌNG XIĀNGCÀIGUǍN
Hunan **$$**

(毛公湘菜馆; ☑8782 0555; 99 Youyi Xilu; mains from Y26; ☺11am-10pm; 🔊) A statue of the Chairman overlooks diners at this slick Hunanese place across the road from the Little Goose Pagoda. English menu.

LǍO SŪN JIĀ
Shaanxi **$**

(老孙家; ☑8240 3205; 2nd fl, Dong Dajie; dishes Y12-40; ☺8am-9pm; 🔊) Xī'ān's most famous restaurant (over a century old) is as well known for its perfunctory service as it is for the steaming bowls of *yángròu pàomó* it specialises in. There's no English sign; look for the big red characters on the 2nd-floor window.

GREEN MOLLY RESTAURANT & BAR
Western **$$**

(绿茉莉; Lǜ Mòlì; ☑8188 3339; Keji Lu; 世纪金花商厦后门右200米; mains from Y52; ☺7pm-3am; 🔊) It's a bit of a trek southwest of the city walls (Y20 in a taxi), but if you're craving authentic Western food and beers on tap, then this wood-panelled pub is the place to come. The beers are expensive, but it's buy one, get one free all the time. It's hard to find, so get your taxi driver to call for directions.

 Drinking

Xī'ān's nightlife options range from bars and clubs to cheesy-but-popular tourist shows. The main bar strip is Defu Xiang, close to the South Gate.

Old Henry's Bar (老亨利酒吧; Lǎohēnglì Jiǔbā;48 Defu Xiang; ⏰8pm-3am) is always busy and has outside seating. Opposite the South Gate, **Moonkey Music Bar** (月亮钥匙音乐酒吧; Yuèliàng Yàoshi Yīnyuè Jiǔbā; ⏰5pm-2am) is an appropriately grungy spot to hear local bands while downing a beer.

⭐ Entertainment

TANG DYNASTY Dinner Show
(唐乐宫; Tángyuè Gōng; ☎8782 2222; www.xiantangdynasty.com; 75 Chang'an Beilu; performance with/without dinner Y500/220) The most famous dinner theatre in the city stages an over-the-top spectacle with Vegas-style costumes, traditional dance, music and singing. It's dubbed into English.

SHAANXI GRAND OPERA HOUSE Dinner Show
(陕歌大剧院; Shǎngē Dàjùyuàn; ☎8785 3295; www.xiantangdynasty.com; 165 Wenyi Lu; performance with/without dinner Y198/128) Also known as the Tang Palace Dance Show, this is a cheaper, less flashy alternative to the Tang Dynasty show.

Try **Song & Song** (上上酒吧乐巢会; Shàngshàng Jiǔbā Lècháohuì; 109 Ximutou Shi; ⏰7pm-late), which is more of a big bar with DJs than a genuine club, or the ever-popular **1+1** (壹加壹俱乐部; Yījiāyī Jùlèbù; 285 Dong Dajie; ⏰7pm-late), a neonlit maze of a place that pumps out party hip-hop tunes well into the early hours. Some travellers enjoy the evening **fountain & music show**

(⏰shows 9pm Mar-Nov, 8pm Dec-Feb) on Big Goose Pagoda Sq; it's the largest in Asia.

🔒 Shopping

Stay in Xī'ān for a couple of days and you'll be offered enough sets of miniature terracotta warriors to form your own army. A good place to search out gifts is the Muslim Quarter, where prices are generally cheaper than elsewhere.

Serious shoppers should also visit the **Northwest Antique Market** (西北古玩城; Xīběi Gǔwán Chéng; Dong Xinjie; ⏰10am-5.30pm), by the Zhongshan Gate. This three-storey warren of shops selling jade, seals, antiques and Mao memorabilia sees far fewer foreign faces than the Muslim Quarter.

ℹ️ Information

You should have no trouble finding usable ATMs. When in doubt, try the southeast corner of the Bell Tower intersection.

Bank of China (中国银行; Zhōngguó Yínháng) Juhuayuan Lu (38 Juhuayuan Lu; ⏰8am-8pm); Nan Dajie (29 Nan Dajie; ⏰8am-6pm) Exchanges cash and travellers cheques and has ATMs at both of these branches.

China Post (邮电大楼; Zhōngguó Yóuzhèng; Bei Dajie; ⏰8am-8pm)

Internet cafe (网吧; wǎngbā; 21 Xi Qilu; per hr Y3; ⏰24hr) Around the corner from the long-distance bus station.

Public Security Bureau (PSB; 公安局; Gōng'ānjú; ☎1682 1225; 63 Xi Dajie; ⏰8.30am-noon & 2-6pm Mon-Fri)

ℹ️ Getting There & Away

Air

Xī'ān's Xiányáng Airport is one of China's best connected – you can fly to almost any major Chinese destination from here, as well as several international ones.

China Eastern Airlines (中国东方航空公司; Zhōngguó Dōngfāng Hángkōng; ☎8208 8707; 64 Xi Wulu; ⏰8am-9pm) operates most flights to and from Xī'ān. Daily flights include Běijīng

(Y840), Chéngdū (Y630), Guǎngzhōu (Y890), Shànghǎi (Y1160), Shēnzhèn (Y980) and Ürümqi (Y1640).

Bus

The most central long-distance bus station (长途汽车站; chángtú qìchēzhàn) is opposite Xī'ān's train station. Note that buses to Huà Shān (6am to 8pm) depart from in front of the train station.

Other bus stations around town where you may be dropped off include the east bus station (城东客运站; chéngdōng kèyùnzhàn; Changle Lu) and the west bus station (城西客运站; chéngxī kèyùnzhàn; Zaoyuan Donglu). Both are located outside the Second Ring Rd. Bus 605 travels between the Bell Tower and the east bus station, and bus 103 travels between the train station and the west bus station. A taxi into the city from either bus station costs between Y15 and Y20.

Buses from Xī'ān's long-distance bus station include the following:

Huà Shān one-way/return Y33/55, two hours, three daily (11am, noon & 2.30pm)

Luòyáng Y60.50, four hours, every 40 minutes (7am to 7.30pm)

Píngyáo Y180, seven hours, hourly (8am to 4pm)

Train

Xī'ān's main train station (huǒchē zhàn) is just outside the northern city walls. Buy your onward tickets as soon as you arrive. Most hotels and hostels can get you tickets (Y40 commission); there's also an Advance Train-Ticket Booking Office (代售火车票; Dàishòu Huǒchēpiào; Nan Dajie; ⏰8.30am-noon & 2-5pm) in the ICBC Bank's south entrance. Otherwise, brave the crowds in the main ticket hall.

Xī'ān is well connected to the rest of the country. Deluxe Z-trains run to/from Běijīng West (soft sleeper only Y417, 11½ hours), leaving Xī'ān at 7.23pm and Běijīng at 9.24pm. Several express trains also make the journey (Y265, 12½ hours); departures begin late afternoon.

All prices listed below are for hard sleeper (yìng wò) tickets.

Chéngdū Y201, 16 ½ hours

Chóngqìng Y191, 14 hours

Lánzhōu Y169, 7 ½ to nine hours

Luòyáng Y106, five hours

Left: Army of Terracotta Warriors, Bīngmǎyǒng; **Below:** Caged cicadas for sale, Muslim Quarter (p140)

PHOTOGRAPHER: (LEFT & BELOW) KRZYSZTOF DYDYNSKI/LONELY PLANET IMAGES ©

Píngyáo Y95, nine hours
Shànghǎi Y323, 15 to 22 hours
Ürümqi Y483, 27 to 39 hours

🛈 Getting Around

Xī'ān's Xiányáng Airport is about 40km northwest of Xī'ān. Shuttle buses run every 20 to 30 minutes from 5.40am to 8pm between the airport and the Melody Hotel (Y25, one hour). Taxis into the city charge over Y100 on the meter.

Bus 610 is useful: it starts at the train station and passes the Bell Tower, Little Goose Pagoda, Shaanxi History Museum and Big Goose Pagoda. The city's much-needed and much-delayed first metro line should open in 2011.

Taxi flag fall is Y6. If you can cope with the congested roads, bikes are a good alternative and can be hired at the youth hostels.

AROUND XĪ'ĀN

The plains surrounding Xī'ān are strewn with early imperial tombs, many of which have not yet been excavated. But unless you have a particular fascination for burial sites, you will probably be satisfied after visiting just a couple. Tourist buses run to almost all of the sites from in front of Xī'ān train station, with the notable exception of the Tomb of Emperor Jingdi.

👁 Sights

East of Xī'ān
ARMY OF TERRACOTTA WARRIORS
Museum

(兵马俑; Bīngmǎyǒng; www.bmy.com.cn; admission Mar-Nov Y90, Dec-Feb Y65, students Y45; ⏱8.30am-5.30pm Mar-Nov, to 5pm Dec-Feb) The Terracotta Army isn't just Xī'ān's premier site, but one of the most famous archaeological finds in the world. This subterranean life-sized army of thousands has silently stood guard over the soul of China's first unifier for over two millennia.

143

ALAMY/DORLING KINDERSLEY

Don't Miss **Forest of Stelae Museum**

Housed in Xī'ān's Confucius Temple, this museum holds over 1000 stone stelae (inscribed tablets), including the nine Confucian classics and some exemplary calligraphy. The second gallery holds a Nestorian tablet (AD 781), the earliest recorded account of Christianity in China.

The highlight, though, is the fantastic sculpture gallery (across from the gift shop), which contains animal guardians from the Tang dynasty, pictorial tombstones and Buddhist statuary. To get to the museum, follow Shuyuan Xiang east from the South Gate.

NEED TO KNOW

碑林博物馆; Bēilín Bówùguǎn; 15 Sanxue Jie; admission Mar-Nov Y45, Dec-Feb Y30; 8am-6.15pm Mar-Nov, to 5.15pm Dec-Feb

The discovery of the army of warriors was entirely fortuitous. In 1974, peasants drilling a well uncovered an underground vault that eventually yielded thousands of terracotta soldiers and horses in battle formation. Over the years the site became so famous that many of its unusual attributes are now well known, in particular the fact that no two soldiers' faces are alike.

To really appreciate a trip here, it helps to understand the historical context of the warriors. If you don't want to employ a guide (Y100) or use the audio guide (Y40), the on-site theatre gives a useful primer on how the figures were sculpted. Then visit the site in reverse, which enables you to build up to the most impressive pit for a fitting finale.

Start with the smallest pit, **Pit 3**, containing 72 warriors and horses, which is believed to be the army headquarters due to the number of high-ranking officers unearthed here. In the next pit, **Pit 2**, containing around 1300 warriors and horses (which is still being excavated), you get to examine five of the soldiers up close: a kneeling archer, a standing archer, a cavalryman and his horse, a midranking officer and a general. The level of detail is extraordinary: the expressions, hairstyles, armour and even the tread on the footwear are all unique.

The largest pit, **Pit 1**, is the most imposing. Housed in a building the size of an aircraft hangar, it is believed to contain 6000 warriors (only 2000 are on display) and horses, all facing east and ready for battle. The vanguard of three rows of archers (both crossbow and longbow) is followed by the main force of soldiers, who originally held spears, swords, dagger-axes and other long-shaft weapons. The infantry were accompanied by 35 chariots, though these, made of wood, have long since disintegrated.

Almost as extraordinary as the soldiers is a pair of bronze chariots and horses unearthed just 20m west of the Tomb of Qin Shi Huang. These are now on display, together with some of the original weaponry, in a small **museum** to the right of the main entrance.

The Army of Terracotta Warriors is easily reached by public bus. From the Xī'ān train-station parking lot, take the green Terracotta Warriors minibuses (Y7, one hour) or bus 306 (Y7, one hour), both of which travel via Huáqīng Hot Springs and the Tomb of Qin Shi Huang. The parking lot for all vehicles is a good 15-minute walk from the site. Electric carts do the run for Y5.

HUÁQĪNG HOT SPRINGS

Historic Site

(华清池; Huáqīng Chí; admission Mar-Nov Y70, Dec-Feb Y40; ☺7am-7pm Mar-Nov, 7.30am-6.30pm Dec-Feb) The natural hot springs in this park were once the favoured retreat of emperors and concubines during the Tang dynasty.

An obligatory stop for Chinese tour groups, who pose for photos in front of the elaborately restored pavilions and by the ornamental ponds, it's a pretty place but not really worth the high admission price.

♥ **If You Like…**
Town Walls

If you like the city walls of Píngyáo (p160) and Xī'ān (p147), north China has other towns ringed by ramparts. Their remains usually signify other historic buildings of note.

1 ZHÈNGDÌNG 正定
Walled Zhèngdìng has a fantastic collection of temples, including the outstanding Lóngxīng Temple which houses an astonishing bronze colossus of Guanyin. From Shíjiāzhuāng, minibus 201 (Y2, 45 minutes, first/last bus 6.30am/6.30pm) runs regularly to Zhèngdìng from near the train station; D-trains run from Běijīng West to Shíjiāzhuāng (two hours).

2 KĀIFĒNG 开封
Once the prosperous capital of the Northern Song, the walled town of Kāifēng has an alluring crop of temples and pagodas. West of Zhèngzhōu, Kāifēng is on the railway line between Xī'ān and Shànghǎi, with several D-class trains passing through.

3 JĪMÍNGYÌ 鸡鸣驿
Whipped by dust storms in spring, Jīmíngyì (140km northwest of Běijīng) is China's oldest remaining post station. The town walls still stand although sections have collapsed; ascend the East Gate for fine views. Take a bus to Shāchéng (Y45, 11.50am and 2pm) from Běijīng's Liùlǐqiáo station, then a bus to Jīmíngyì (Y3, 30 minutes, 8.30am to 5pm).

4 ZHŪJIĀYÙ 朱家峪
With its coffee-coloured soil and unspoiled bucolic panoramas, this charming stone village (80km east of Jǐ'nán) provides a fascinating foray into one of Shāndōng's oldest intact hamlets. Take a bus heading to BóShān (博山, Y26, 1½ hours) from Jǐ'nán and get off at the mouth of the village, from where it's a 2km walk.

TOMB OF QIN SHI HUANG

Historic Site

(秦始皇陵; Qín Shǐhuáng Líng; admission Mar-Nov Y40, Dec-Feb Y20; ☺8am-6pm Mar-Nov, to 5pm Dec-Feb) In its time, this tomb must have been one of the grandest mausoleums the world had ever seen.

Historical accounts describe it as containing palaces filled with precious stones, underground rivers of flowing mercury and ingenious defences against intruders. The tomb reputedly took 38 years to complete, and required a workforce of 700,000 people. It is said that the artisans who built it were buried alive within, taking its secrets with them.

Considered too dangerous to excavate, the tomb has little to see but you can climb the steps to the top of the mound for a fine view of the surrounding countryside. The tomb is about 2km west of the Army of Terracotta Warriors. Take bus 306 from Xī'ān train station.

BÀNPŌ NEOLITHIC VILLAGE

Ancient Village

(半坡博物馆; Bànpō Bówùguǎn; admission Mar-Nov Y35, Dec-Feb Y25; ◎8am-6pm) This village is of enormous importance for Chinese archaeological studies, but unless you're desperately interested in the subject it can be an underwhelming visitor experience. Bànpō is the earliest example of the Neolithic Yangshao culture, which is believed to have been matriarchal. It appears to have been occupied from 4500 BC until around 3750 BC.

The village is in the eastern suburbs of Xī'ān. Bus 105 (Y1) from the train station runs past (ask where to get off); it's also often included on tours.

North & West of Xī'ān
TOMB OF EMPEROR JINGDI

Historic Site

(汉阳陵; Hàn Yánglíng; admission Mar-Nov Y90, Dec-Feb Y65; ◎8.30am-7pm Mar-Nov, to 6pm Dec-Feb) Also referred to as the Han Jing Mausoleum, Liu Qi Mausoleum and Yangling Mausoleum, this tomb is easily Xī'ān's most underrated highlight. If you only have time for two sights, then it should be the Army of Terracotta Warriors and this impressive museum and tomb.

A Han-dynasty emperor influenced by Taoism, Jingdi (188–141 BC) based his rule upon the concept of *wúwéi* (nonaction or noninterference) and did much to improve the life of his subjects: he lowered taxes greatly, used diplomacy

to cut back on unnecessary military expeditions and even reduced the punishment meted out to criminals.

The site has been divided into two sections: the museum and the excavation area. The **museum** holds a large display of expressive terracotta figurines (over 50,000 were buried here), including eunuchs, servants, domesticated animals and even female cavalry on horseback. But it's the **tomb** itself, which is still being excavated, that's the real reason to make the trip out here. Inside are 21 narrow pits, some of which have been covered by a glass floor, allowing you to walk over the top of ongoing excavations and get a great view of the relics. In all, there are believed to be 81 burial pits here.

Unfortunately, getting here by public transport is a pain. First, take bus 4 (Y1) from Xī'ān's North Gate. After 30 minutes, it reaches the end of its line at the Zhang Jiabu roundabout. Get off and walk 100m right of the roundabout, where another bus, also numbered 4 (Y2), leaves for the tomb. The catch is that while there are many buses to the roundabout, only three a day do the second leg to the tomb. At the time of writing, they were leaving at 8.30am, 10.50am and 2.30pm, returning to Xī'ān at 12.30pm, 3.30pm and 5.30pm.

Alternatively, you can try to find a Western Tour that visits the site, or hire a taxi (figure on Y200 for a half-day). The tomb is also close to the airport, so you could stop here on your way to or from there.

IMPERIAL TOMBS

Historic Sites

A large number of imperial tombs (皇陵; huáng líng) dot the Guānzhōng plain around Xī'ān. They are sometimes included on tours from Xī'ān, but most aren't so remarkable as to be destinations in themselves. By far the most impressive is the **Qián Tomb** (乾陵; Qián Líng; admission Mar-Nov Y45, Dec-Feb Y25; ◎8am-6pm), where China's only female emperor, Wu Zetian (AD 625–705), is buried together with her husband Emperor Gaozong, whom she succeeded. The long **Spirit Way** (Yù Dào) here is lined with enormous, lichen-encrusted sculptures of animals and

SEAN CAFFREY/LONELY PLANET IMAGES ©

Don't Miss Xī'ān's City Walls

Xī'ān is one of the few cities in China where the old **City Walls** (城墙; Chéngqiáng; admission Y40; ⊙8am-8.30pm Apr-Oct, to 7pm Nov-Mar) are still standing. Built in 1370 during the Ming dynasty, the 12m-high walls are surrounded by a dry moat and form a rectangle with a perimeter of 14km.

Most sections have been restored or rebuilt, and it is now possible to walk the entirety of the walls in a leisurely four hours. You can also cycle from the South Gate (bike hire Y20 for 100 minutes, Y200 deposit). The truly lazy can be whisked around in a golf cart for Y200. To get an idea of Xī'ān's former grandeur, consider this: the Tang city walls originally enclosed 83 sq km, an area seven times larger than today's city centre.

officers of the imperial guard, culminating with 61 (now headless) statues of Chinese ethnic group leaders who attended the emperor's funeral. The mausoleum is 85km northwest of Xī'ān. Tour bus 2 (Y25, 8am) runs close to here from Xī'ān train station and returns in the late afternoon.

 Tours

One-day tours allow you to see all the sights around Xī'ān more quickly and conveniently than if you arranged one yourself. Itineraries differ somewhat, but

there are two basic tours: an Eastern Tour and a Western Tour.

Most hostels run their own tours, but make sure you find out what is included (admission fees, lunch, English-speaking guide) and try to get an exact itinerary, or you could end up being herded through the Terracotta Warriors before you have a chance to get your camera out.

Eastern Tour

The Eastern Tour (Dōngxiàn Yóulǎn) is the most popular as it includes the Army of Terracotta Warriors, the Tomb of Qin Shi Huang, Bànpō Neolithic Village, Huáqīng

Hot Springs and the Big Goose Pagoda. Most travel agencies and hostels charge around Y300 for an all-day excursion, including admission fees, lunch and guide. Sometimes the hostel tours skip Bànpō.

It's perfectly possible to do a shortened version of the eastern tour by using the tourist buses or bus 306, all of which pass by Huáqīng Hot Springs, the Terracotta Warriors and the Tomb of Qin Shi Huang.

Western Tour

The longer Western Tour (Xīxiàn Yóulǎn) includes the Xiányáng City Museum, imperial tombs, Fǎmén Temple and, possibly, the Tomb of Emperor Jingdi. It's far less popular than the Eastern Tour so you may have to wait a couple of days for your hostel or agency to organise enough people. It's also more expensive; expect to pay Y600.

THE NORTH
Huà Shān 华山

One of Taoism's five sacred mountains, the granite domes of Huà Shān used to be home to hermits and sages. These days,

though, the trails that wind their way up to the five peaks are populated by droves of day-trippers drawn by the dreamy scenery. And it is spectacular. There are knifeblade ridges and twisted pine trees clinging to ledges as you ascend, while the summits offer transcendent panoramas of green mountains and countryside stretching away to the horizon.

Sights & Activities

There are three ways up the mountain to the **North Peak** (北峰; Běi Fēng), the first of five summit peaks. Two of these options start from the eastern base of the mountain, at the cable-car terminus. The first option is handy if you don't fancy the climb: an Austrian-built **cable car** (one-way/return Y80/150; ⊙7am-7pm) will lift you to the North Peak in 10 scenic minutes.

The second option is to work your way to the North Peak under the cable-car route. This takes a sweaty two hours, and two sections of 50m or so are quite literally vertical, with nothing but a steel chain to grab onto and tiny chinks cut into the rock for footing.

South Peak, Huà Shān's highest peak

The Man Behind the Army

History is written by the winners. But in China, it was penned by Confucian bureaucrats and for Qin Shi Huang that was a problem, because his disdain for Confucianism was such that he outlawed it, ordered almost all its written texts to be burnt and, according to legend, buried 460 of its top scholars alive. As a result, the First Emperor went down in history as the sort of tyrant who gives tyrants a bad name.

At the same time, though, it's hard to overstate the magnitude of his accomplishments during his 36 years of rule (which began when he was just 19). He created an efficient, centralised government that became the model for later dynasties; he standardised measurements, currency and, most importantly, writing; he built over 6400km of new roads and canals; and he conquered six major kingdoms before turning 40.

The fact that Qin Shi Huang did all this by enslaving hundreds of thousands of people helped ensure that his subsequent reputation would be as dark as the black he made the official colour of his court. But in recent years, there have been efforts by the China Communist Party (CCP), no strangers to autocratic rule themselves, to rehabilitate him, by emphasising both his efforts to unify China and the far-sighted nature of his policies.

The third option is the most popular, but it's still hard work. A 6km path leads to the North Peak from the village of Huà Shān, at the base of the mountain. It usually takes between three and five hours to reach the North Peak via this route. The first 4km up are pretty easy going, but after that it's all steep stairs.

If you want to carry on to the other peaks, count on a minimum of eight hours in total from the base of Huà Shān. To spare your knees, another option is to take the cable car to the North Peak and then climb to the other peaks, ending up back where you started. It takes about four hours to complete the circuit this way and it's still fairly strenuous. Huà Shān has a reputation for being dangerous, especially when the trails are crowded, or if it's wet or icy, so exercise caution.

But the scenery is sublime. Along **Blue Dragon Ridge** (苍龙岭;Cānglóng Lǐng), which connects the North Peak with the **East Peak** (东峰;Dōng Fēng), **South Peak** (南峰; Nán Fēng) and **West Peak** (西峰; Xī Fēng), the way has been cut along a narrow rock ridge with impressive sheer cliffs on either side. The South Peak is the highest at 2160m and the most crowded.

There is accommodation on the mountain, most of it basic and overpriced, but it does allow you to start climbing in the afternoon, watch the sunset and then spend the night, before catching the sunrise from either the East Peak or South Peak. Some locals make the climb at night, using torches (flashlights).

Admission is Y100. To get to the cable car *(suŏdào)*, take a taxi from the village to the ticket office (Y10) and then a shuttle bus (one way/return Y10/20) the rest of the way.

🛏 Sleeping & Eating

You can either spend the night in Huà Shān village or on one of the peaks. Take your own food or eat well before ascending, unless you like to feast on instant noodles and processed meat – proper meals are very pricey on the mountain. Don't forget a torch and warm clothes. Bear in mind that prices for a bed triple during public

Detour:
Fǎmén Temple

(法门寺; Fǎmén Sì; admission Mar-Nov Y120, Dec-Feb Y90; ⏱8am-6pm) This temple dates back to the 2nd century AD and was built to house parts of a sacred fingerbone of the Buddha, presented to China by India's King Asoka. In 1981, after torrential rains had weakened the temple's ancient brick structure, the entire western side of its 12-storey pagoda collapsed. The subsequent restoration of the temple produced a sensational discovery. Below the pagoda in a sealed crypt were over 1000 sacrificial objects and royal offerings – all forgotten for almost two millennia.

Arguably, what's on display here is more impressive than the collection at the Shaanxi History Museum. There are elaborate gold and silver boxes (stacked on top of one another to form pagodas) and tiny crystal and jade coffins that originally held the four sections of the holy finger.

Fǎmén Temple is 115km northwest of Xī'ān. Tour bus 2 (Y25, 8am) from Xī'ān train station runs to the temple and returns to Xī'ān at 5pm. The temple is also generally included on Western Tours.

---

holidays. On the mountain, expect nothing remotely luxurious, especially not private bathrooms.

BĬJIĀYÍ INN   Hotel $$
(比家宜快捷酒店; Bǐjiāyí Kuàijié Jiǔdiàn; ☎0913-465 8000; Yuquan Donglu; 玉泉东路; s & d Y238-281; ❄⌘) A new and welcome choice in a town crying out for a decent midrange hotel. Big, modern rooms and the best option if you want a modicum of comfort without breaking the bank.

HUÁYÁNG HOTEL   Hotel $
(华洋大酒店; Huáyáng Dàjiǔdiàn); ☎0913-436 5288; Yuquan Lu; 玉泉路; s & d Y120) Clean and simple rooms with OK bathrooms make this the pick of the admittedly poor hotels on offer on Yuquan Lu.

DŌNGFĒNG BĪNGUǍN   Hotel $
(东峰宾馆; dm Y100-220, tr/d Y260/320) The top location for watching the sun come up and the best restaurant.

NORTH PEAK HOTEL   Hotel $
(北峰饭店; Běifēng Fàndiàn; dm Y60-180, d Y240-260) The busiest of the peak hotels.

ⓘ Getting There & Away
From Xī'ān to Huà Shān, catch one of the private buses (one-way/return Y33/55, two hours, 6am

to 8pm) that depart from in front of Xī'ān train station. You'll be dropped off on Yuquan Lu, which is also where buses back to Xī'ān leave from 7.30am to 7pm. Coming from the east, try to talk your driver into dropping you at the Huà Shān highway exit if you can't find a direct bus.

Luòyáng 洛阳
☎0379 / POP 1.4 MILLION

Capital of 13 dynasties until the Northern Song dynasty shifted its capital to Kāifēng in the 10th century, Luòyáng was one of China's true dynastic citadels. Today Luòyáng is largely indistinguishable from other fume-laden modern Chinese towns. Nonetheless, the magnificently sculpted Lóngmén Caves by the banks of the Yī River remain one of China's most prized Buddhist treasures and the annual **Peony Festival**, centred on Wángchéng Park in April, is colourful fun. The old town, where the bulk of Luòyáng's history survives, is in the east.

◎ Sights & Activities

WHITE HORSE TEMPLE
(白马寺; Báimǎ Sì; admission Y50; ⏱7am-7pm Apr-Oct, hours vary rest of year) Although its original structures have largely been

replaced and it is likely that older temples have now vanished, this active **monastery** is regarded as being the first surviving Buddhist temple erected on Chinese soil. It originally dating from the 1st century AD.

When two Han-dynasty court emissaries went in search of Buddhist scriptures, they encountered two Indian monks in Afghanistan; the monks returned to Luòyáng on white horses carrying Buddhist sutras and statues. The impressed emperor built the temple to house the monks; it is also their resting place.

Structures of note include the **Big Buddha Hall**, the **Hall of Mahavira** and the **Pilu Hall** at the very rear, while the standout **Qíyún Pagoda** (齐云塔; Qíyún Tǎ), an ancient 12-tiered brick tower, is a pleasant five-minute walk away.

The temple is located 13km east of Luòyáng, around 40 minutes away on bus 56 from the Xīguān (西关) stop.

FREE **LUÒYÁNG MUSEUM** Museum
(洛阳博物馆; Luòyáng Bówùguǎn; 298 Zhongzhou Zhonglu; ☺8.30am-5.30pm Apr-Oct, to 5pm Nov-Mar) One of the few places you can get your finger on the pulse of ancient Luòyáng, this museum has an absorbing collection of Tang-dynasty three-colour *sāncǎi* porcelain and dioramas of the Sui- and Tang-dynasty city: the outer Tang wall was punctured by 18 magnificent gates and embraced the Imperial City with the colossal, five-eaved and circular Tiāntáng (Hall of Heaven) at its heart. Despite plentiful explanations concerning Luòyáng's former grandeur, there is little info on its subsequent loss. Take bus 4 or 11.

OLD TOWN
Historic Area
(老城区; lǎochéngqū) Any Chinese city with a sense of history has its old town. Luòyáng's old town lies east of the rebuilt **Lijīng Gate**

(丽京门; Lìjīng Mén; gate tower admission Y30; ☺8am-10pm), where a maze of narrow and winding streets rewards exploration, and old courtyard houses survive amid modern outcrops.

WÁNGCHÉNG PARK Park
(王城公园; Wángchéng Gōngyuán; Zhongzhou Zhonglu; admission Y3, park & zoo Y15, Peony Festival Y50-55) One of Luòyáng's indispensable green lungs, this attractive park is the site of the annual Peony Festival; held in April, the festival sees the park flooded with colour, floral aficionados, photographers, girls with garlands on their heads and hawkers selling huge bouquets of flowers.

🛏 Sleeping

LUÒYÁNG YOUTH HOSTEL Hostel **$**
(洛阳国际青年旅社; Luòyáng Guójì Qīngnián Lǚshè; ☎6526 0666; 3rd fl, Binjiang Dasha, 72 Jinguyuan Lu; 金谷园路72号滨江大厦3楼; 6-/8-person dm Y60/55, common r Y140, s/d Y238/228, discounts on d 40%; ❄@) Tiled-

Shops in Luòyáng's old town
KRZYSZTOF DYDYŃSKI/LONELY PLANET IMAGES ©

floor doubles are clean and simple; some rooms come with computers. Internet access Y2 per hour.

Peony Hotel Hotel **$$**
(牡丹大酒店; Mǔdān Dàjiǔdiàn; ☎6468 0000; peonyhotel.net; dept@yahoo.com.cn; 15 Zhongzhou Xilu; 中州西路15号; standard d Y550-660, discounts of 30%; ❄) Renovated in 2004, standard 'A' doubles are small, with midget bathrooms, but are prettily laid out and attractively furnished, with free broadband. Nonsmoking room available.

 Eating

Luòyáng's famous 'water banquet' resonates along China's culinary grapevine. The main dishes of this 24-course meal are soups and are served up with the speed of flowing water – hence the name.

TUDALI Korean **$**
(土大力; Tǔdàlì; ☎6312 0513; www.tudali.com, in Chinese; Xinduhui, cnr Jiefang Lu & Tanggong Xilu; meals Y30; ⏰11.30am-2am) With the accent on spiciness, this popular Korean restaurant brings patrons out in a sweat.

The *pàocàitāng* (泡菜汤; kimchi soup; Y15) is refreshingly piquant, as is the *làwèi niúròutāng* (辣味牛肉汤; spicy beef soup; Y22) or you can get your metal chopsticks around a plate of chips (Y10).

ZHĒN BÙ TÓNG FÀNDIÀN Henan **$$**
(真不同饭店; One of a Kind Restaurant; ☎6399 5080; 369 Zhongzhou Donglu; dishes Y15-45, water banquet from Y60) Huge place behind a colourful green, red, blue and gold traditional facade. This is the place to come for a water-banquet experience; if 24 courses seems a little excessive, you can opt to pick individual dishes from the menu.

ⓘ Information

Internet cafes (per hour Y2) are scattered around the train station and sprinkled along nearby Jinguyuan Lu.

Bank of China (中国银行; Zhōngguó Yínháng; ⏰8am-4.30pm) The Zhongzhou Xilu office exchanges travellers cheques and has an ATM that accepts MasterCard and Visa. There's also a branch on the corner of Zhongzhou Lu and Shachang Nanlu that's open until 5.30pm. Another branch just west of the train station has foreign-exchange services.

Buddha statues in the Lóngmén Caves

China Post (中国邮政; Zhōngguó Yóuzhèng; cnr Zhongzhou Zhonglu & Jinguyuan Lu)

Public Security Bureau (PSB;公安局; Gōng'ānjú; ☏6393 8397; cnr Kaixuan Lu & Tiyuchang Lu; ☉8am-noon & 2-5.30pm Mon-Fri) The exit-entry department (Chūrùjìng Dàtīng) is in the south building.

❶ Getting There & Away

Air

You would do better to fly into or out of Zhèngzhōu. Daily flights operate to Běijīng (Y890, one hour), Shànghǎi (Y890, one hour) and other cities.

Bus

Regular departures from the long-distance bus station (长途汽车站; ☏6323 3186; Chángtú Qìchēzhàn; 51 Jinguyuan Lu) across from the train station include the following:

Dēngfēng Y20, two hours, every 30 minutes.

Shàolín Temple Y17, 1½ hours, every 20 minutes (5.20am to 6pm)

Xī'ān Y90, four hours, hourly (8am to 6pm)

Zhèngzhōu Y40, 1½ hours, every 20 minutes

Fast buses to Shàolín (Y20, one to 1½ hours) leave from outside the train station every half-hour until 4.30pm; otherwise, take a bus for Xǔchāng from the long-distance bus station and get off at the temple (Y22, 1½ hours). You can also get to Shàolín on buses to Dēngfēng (Y20, two hours).

Train

Regional destinations include Kāifēng (hard seat Y30, three hours) and Zhèngzhōu (hard seat Y10 to Y20, 1½ hours).

Hard-sleeper destinations include **Běijīng West** seat/sleeper Y106/191, seven to 10 hours, **Shànghǎi** seat/sleeper Y153/254, 13 to 16 hours and **Xī'ān** G-class hard/soft seat Y184/294, two hours; from Lùoyáng Lóngmén Station.

❶ Getting Around

There is no shuttle bus from the CAAC office to the airport, 12km north of the city, but bus 83 (Y1; 30 minutes) runs from the parking lot to the right as you exit the train station; a taxi from the train station will cost about Y30.

If You Like...
Sacred Mountains

If you like the Taoist peak of Huà Shān (p148), north China frequently crumples into spectacular mountain ranges. Many, but by no means all, have been requisitioned by Taoists and Buddhists who have left their slopes littered with temples and myth.

1 WǓDĀNG SHĀN 武当山
Birthplace of the 'soft' martial art of taichi, Wǔdāng Shān is deeply venerated by Taoist monks and nuns who make a continuous pilgrimage to its slopes and temples. Located in northwest Húběi province; the nearest train station is Wǔdāng Shān.

2 HÉNG SHĀN 衡山
Héng Shān is the northernmost peak of Taoism's five holy mountains, the cliff-clinging Hanging Monastery its most celebrated highlight. Southeast of Dàtóng; see the transport information for reaching the Hanging Monastery (p166).

3 SŌNG SHĀN 嵩山
Sōng Shān is best known for the Buddhist Shàolín Temple, although the mountain is itself – paradoxically perhaps – the central peak of China's five Taoist mountains. Located southeast of Luòyáng; all buses from Luòyáng to the Shàolín Temple reach Sōng Shān.

Buses 5 and 41 go to the Old Town from the train station, running via Wángchéng Sq.

Taxis are Y5 at flag fall, making them a more attractive option than taking motor rickshaws, which will cost you around Y4 from the train station to Wángchéng Sq.

Around Luòyáng

Lóngmén Caves
龙门石窟

A sutra in stone, the epic achievement of the **Lóngmén Caves** (Dragon Gate Grottoes; Lóngmén Shíkū; admission Y120, English-speaking guide Y100; ☉6am-8pm summer, 6.30am-7pm winter) was first undertaken by chisellers from the Northern Wei dynasty, after the capital was relocated here from Dàtóng in AD 494. Over the next 200 years or so, more than 100,000 images and statues of Buddha and his disciples emerged from over a kilometre of limestone cliff wall along the Yī River (Yī Hé).

In the early 20th century, many effigies were beheaded by unscrupulous collectors or simply extracted whole, many ending up abroad in such institutions as the Metropolitan Museum of Art in New York, the Atkinson Museum in Kansas City and the Tokyo National Museum. Some effigies are returning and severed heads are gradually being restored to their bodies, but many statues have clearly just had their faces crudely bludgeoned off, vandalism that dates to the Cultural Revolution (the Ten Thousand Buddha Cave was particularly badly damaged during this period) and earlier episodes of anti-Buddhist fervour.

The caves are scattered in a line on the west and east sides of the river. Most of the significant Buddhist carvings are on the west side, but a notable crop can also be admired after traversing the bridge to the east side.

The Lóngmén Caves are 13km south of Luòyáng and can be reached by taxi (Y30) or bus 81 (Y1.50, 40 minutes) from the east side of Luòyáng's train station. The last bus 81 returns to Luòyáng at 8.50pm. Buses 53 and 60 also run to the caves.

THREE BĪNYÁNG CAVES   Caves
Work began on the Three Bīnyáng Caves (宾阳三洞; Bīnyáng Sān Dòng) during the Northern Wei dynasty. Despite the completion of two of the caves during the Sui and Tang dynasties, statues here all display the benevolent expressions that characterised Northern Wei style.

TEN THOUSAND BUDDHA CAVE   Cave
South of Three Bīnyáng Caves, the Tang-dynasty Ten Thousand Buddha Cave (万佛洞; Wànfó Dòng) dates from 680. In addition to its namesake galaxy of tiny bas-relief Buddhas, there is a fine effigy of the Amitabha Buddha. Note the red pigment on the ceiling.

LOTUS FLOWER CAVE   Cave
Cave No 712, also called Lotus Flower Cave (莲花洞; Liánhuā Dòng), was carved between 525 and 527 during the Northern Wei dynasty. The cave contains a large

Hotel courtyard, Píngyáo

PHILIP GAME/LONELY PLANET IMAGES ©

standing Buddha, now faceless and handless. On the cave's ceiling wispy apsaras (celestial nymphs) drift around a central lotus flower, itself a Buddhist metaphor for purity and serenity.

ANCESTOR WORSHIPPING TEMPLE
Cave Temple

The most physically imposing of all the Lóngmén caves, this vast cave temple (奉先寺; Fèngxiān Sì) was carved during the Tang dynasty between 672 and 675; it contains the best examples of sculpture, despite evident weathering.

Nine principal figures dominate the Ancestor Worshipping Temple. The 17m-high seated central Buddha is said to be Losana, whose face is allegedly modelled on Tang empress and Buddhist patron Wu Zetian, who funded its carving. In the corner of the south wall of the temple, next to the semi-obliterated guardian figure, are three statues that have simply been smashed away.

MEDICAL PRESCRIPTION CAVE
Cave

Located south of Ancestor Worshipping Temple is the tiny Medical Prescription Cave (药方洞; Yàofāng Dòng), begun in the Northern Wei and completed in the Northern Qi. The entrance to this cave is carved with 6th-century stone stelae inscribed with remedies for a range of common ailments.

EARLIEST CAVE
Cave

Next door to the Medical Prescription Cave is the larger Earliest Cave (古阳洞; Gǔyáng Dòng), begun in 493. It's a narrow, high-roofed cave featuring a Buddha statue and a profusion of sculptures, particularly of flying apsaras.

Píngyáo 平遥

☎0354 / POP 450,000

China's best-preserved ancient walled town, Píngyáo, is fantastic. This is the China we all think of in flights of fancy: red-lantern-hung lanes set against night-time silhouettes of imposing town walls, elegant courtyard architecture, ancient towers poking into the north China sky and an entire brood of creaking temples and old buildings. Píngyáo is also a living-and-breathing community: locals hang laundry in courtyards, career down alleyways on bicycles, simply sun themselves in doorways or chew the fat with neighbours.

History

Already a thriving merchant town during the Ming dynasty, Píngyáo's ascendancy came during the Qing when merchants created the country's first banks and cheques to facilitate the transfer of vast amounts of silver from one place to another.

◉ Sights & Activities

It's free to walk the streets, but you must pay Y120 to climb the city walls or enter any of the 18 buildings deemed historically significant. Tickets are valid for two days; electronic audio tours are Y40 (Y100 deposit). Opening hours for the sights are from 8am to 7.30pm from 1 May to 30 September, and from 8am to 6.30pm from 1 October to 30 April.

RÌSHĒNGCHĀNG FINANCIAL HOUSE MUSEUM
Museum

(日升昌; Rìshēngchāng; 38 Xi Dajie; 西大街38号) This museum began life as a humble dye shop in the late 18th century before its tremendous success as a business saw it transform into China's first draft bank (1823), eventually expanding to 57 branches nationwide. The museum has nearly 100 rooms, including offices, living quarters and a kitchen, as well as several old cheques.

CONFUCIAN TEMPLE
Hall, Temple

Píngyáo's oldest surviving building is **Dàchéng Hall** (大成殿; Dàchéng Diàn), dating from 1163 and found in the **Confucian Temple** (文庙; Wén Miào), a huge complex where bureaucrats-to-be came to take the imperial exams.

City Tower
Tower

(市楼; Shì Lóu; Nan Dajie; admission Y5; ⊙8am-7pm) The tallest building in the old town. Climb its smooth stone steps for fine views over Píngyáo's magnificent rooftops and inspect its ragged and forlorn shrine to a severe-looking Guandi.

Qīngxū Guàn
Taoist Temple

(清虚观; Dong Dajie) Shānxī dust has penetrated every crevice of this ancient and partly fossilised Taoist temple near the East Gate. With 10 halls and originally dating to the Tang dynasty, it's an impressive complex.

Nine Dragon Screen
Ancient Monument

(九龙壁; Jiǔlóng Bì; Chenghuangmiao Jie) In front of the old Píngyáo Theatre (大戏堂; Dàxìtáng).

🛏 Sleeping

Many of Píngyáo's hotels are delightfully converted from courtyard homes, and finding a bed for the night is not hard. Some hotels and hostels can arrange pick-up from the train or bus station.

JING'S RESIDENCE
Courtyard Hotel $$$

(锦宅; Jǐn Zhái; ☎584 1000; www.jingsresidence.com; 16 Dong Dajie; 东大街16号; luxury r Y1660, discounts of 50%; ❄@🛜) This supremely classy abode features a soothing blend of old Píngyáo and modern flair: it's sleek, modish and fastidiously well finished. The themed courtyards are an absolute picture and the rooms are elegant and stylish, while the upstairs bar is the last word in nattiness.

HARMONY GUESTHOUSE
Courtyard Hotel $

(和义昌客栈; Héyìchāng Kèzhàn; ☎568 4952; www.py-harmony.com; 165 Nan Dajie; 南大街165号; dm Y30-50, s & tw Y80-100, d Y100-180, tr Y150-200; ❄@🛜) Ever popular, Harmony Guesthouse offers rooms off two beautifully preserved courtyards in a lovely 300-year-old Qing building. Most come

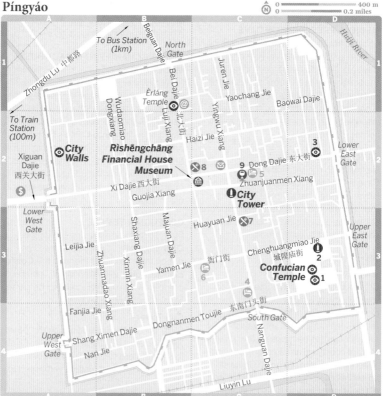

Píngyáo

with traditional stone *kang* beds, wooden bedtop tea tables and delightful wooden inlaid windows. Dorm accommodation can be found in the old guesthouse.

ZHÈNGJIĀ KÈZHÀN
Courtyard Hotel **$**

(郑家客栈; ☎568 4466; 68 Yamen Jie; 衙门街68号; dm/d Y40/168, discounts of 20%; @) All the dorms (no shower) are upstairs under the eaves at this pleasant place with a courtyard atmosphere just east of Listen to the Rain Pavilion. Downstairs doubles are spacious and pleasantly arranged, with shower. Next door there's another lovely courtyard belonging to the same outfit; arranged on two levels, it has pricier double rooms (Y258) elegantly decorated with period furniture, and a gracefully presented main area.

Eating & Drinking

Most hotels can rustle up (Western or Chinese) breakfast, lunch and dinner.

DÉJŪYUÁN
Homestyle Food **$$**

(德居源; 82 Nan Dajie; ☻8.30am-10pm; 📵) This welcoming and popular little Nan Dajie restaurant has a simple and tasty menu of affordable dishes from lamb dumplings (Y15) to stewed aubergine (Y10). It's opposite the Tian Yuan Kui Guesthouse.

Déjūyuán Bīnguǎn
Shaanxi **$$**

(德居源宾馆; Xi Dajie; dishes Y10-35; 📵) Superb Shǎnxī cuisine served in a traditional courtyard. English menu.

Sakura Cafe
Bar **$**

(樱花屋西餐酒吧; Yīnghuāwū Xīcān Jiǔbā; 6 Dong Dajie; beers from Y10; ☻9am-late; 📵) Lively, fun and adorned with red lanterns and flags, this gregarious, warm, entertaining and affordable cafe-bar has good music and is popular with local Chinese.

Shopping

Part of Píngyáo's charms lie in its peeling and weatherbeaten shopfronts, yet to be mercilessly restored. Nan Dajie is stuffed with wood-panelled shops selling ginger sweets (marvel at vendors pulling the golden sugary ginger mass into strips), moon cakes, Píngyáo snacks, knick-knacks and bric-a-brac, Cultural Revolution posters, jade, shoes and slippers, and loads more. Look out for more hats, shoes, slippers, lacquerware and whatnot along Xi Dajie. The shutters start closing around 9pm.

Information

China Post (邮局; yóujú; Xi Dajie; ☻8am-6pm)

Industrial & Commercial Bank of China (工商银行; ICBC; Gōngshāng Yínháng; Xiguan Dajie) Has an ATM that accepts Visa but, like all other Píngyáo banks, does not change money or travellers cheques.

Internet cafe (网吧; wǎngbā; per hr Y2; ☻24hr) Beyond the Lower West Gate.

Public Security Bureau (PSB; 公安局; Gōng'ānjú; ☎563 5010; Shuncheng Lu; ☻8am-noon & 3-6pm Mon-Fri) Twenty minutes' walk south of the train station, on the corner of the junction with Shuguang Lu. Cannot extend visas.

Xīngténg internet cafe (兴腾网吧; Xīngténg Wǎngbā; per hr Y2; ☻24hr) Opposite the Èrláng Temple on Bei Dajie.

Píngyáo

◎ Top Sights

City Tower...C2
City Walls..A2
Confucian Temple.............................D3
Rìshēngchāng Financial
   House Museum................................C2

◎ Sights

1 Dàchéng Hall................................D3
2 Nine Dragon Screen.....................D3
3 Qīngxū Guàn.................................D2

⊜ Sleeping

4 Harmony Guesthouse..................C3
5 Jing's Residence...........................C2
6 Zhèngjiā Kèzhàn...........................C3

⊗ Eating

7 Déjūyuán.......................................C3
8 Déjūyuán Bīnguǎn.......................C2

⊝ Drinking

9 Sakura Café...................................C2

Getting There & Away

Bus

Buses to local destinations such as Jiéxiū (Y9, 40 minutes) usually trawl for passengers at the train station, so it's normally quicker to catch them there.

Píngyáo's **bus station** (汽车新站; qìchēxīnzhàn; ☏ 569 0011) has buses to Tàiyuán (Y25, two hours, frequent, 6.45am to 7.20pm) and Líshí (Y36, three hours, 7am to 12.30pm).

Train

Tickets are tough to get, especially for sleepers, so plan ahead. Your hotel/hostel should be able to help.

Direct trains include **Běijīng** Y117 to Y154, 11 to 12 hours, three daily, **Dàtóng** Y75 to Y80, seven to 8½ hours, four daily, **Tàiyuán** Y8 (hard seat), 1½ to two hours, frequent services (6.14am to 9.53pm) and **Xī'ān** Y83 to Y95, 8½ to 10½ hours, five daily.

Getting Around

Píngyáo can be easily navigated on foot or bicycle (Y10 per day). Bike rental is all over the place; Xi Dajie has several bike-rental spots, including one by the Lower West Gate. Electric carts whiz around town (Y5 to Y10). Some hostels will pay the driver when you first arrive as part of their free pick-up promise.

Around Píngyáo

Shuānglín Temple 双林寺

Within easy reach of Píngyáo, this **Buddhist temple** (Shuānglín Sì; admission Y25; ⏰8am-7pm) was rebuilt in 1571. It houses a number of rare, intricately carved Song and Yuan painted statues. The interiors of the Sakyamuni Hall and flanking buildings are particularly exquisite.

A rickshaw will cost about Y40 return and a taxi about Y50 (but consider cycling out there instead).

Wang Family Courtyard 王家大院

More of a castle than a cosy home, this Qing-dynasty **former residence** (Wángjiā Dàyuàn; admission Y66; ⏰8am-7pm) is grand (123 courtyards) if rather redundant. Of

Left: Guanyin statue, Shuānglín Temple; **Below:** Nan Dajie, leading to City Tower in the old town (p155), Píngyáo

PHOTOGRAPHER: (LEFT & BELOW) MARTIN MOOS/LONELY PLANET IMAGES ©

more interest perhaps are the still-occupied **cave dwellings** (窑洞; *yáodòng*) behind the castle walls. Two direct buses (8.20am and 2.40pm) leave from Píngyáo bus station. Regular buses go to Jièxiū (介休; Y7, 40 minutes), where you can change to bus 11 (Y4, 40 minutes), which terminates at the complex. The Wang residence is behind the Yuan-dynasty **Confucian Temple** (文庙; Wén Miào; admission Y10), housing a beautiful four-storey pagoda. The last bus back to Jièxiū leaves at 6pm.

Wǔtái Shān 五台山

☑ 0350

The gorgeous mountainous, monastic enclave of Wǔtái Shān (Five Terrace Mountains; www.wutaishan.cn) is Buddhism's sacred northern range and the earthly abode of Manjusri (文殊; Wénshū), the Bodhisattva of Wisdom. Chinese students sitting the ferociously competitive *gāokǎo* exams troop here for a nod from the learned Bodhisattva, proffering incense alongside saffron-robed monks and octogenarian pilgrims. A powerful sense of the divine holds sway in Wǔtái Shān, emanating from the port-walled monasteries – the principal sources of spiritual power – and finding further amplification in the astonishing mountain scenery.

The forested slopes overlooking the town eventually give way to alpine meadows where you'll find more temples and great hiking possibilities. Wǔtái Shān is also famed for its mysterious rainbows, which can appear without rain and are said to contain shimmering mirages of Buddhist beings, creatures and temple halls.

There's a steep Y218 entrance fee for the area – including a mandatory Y50 'sightseeing bus' ticket (旅游观光车票; *lǚyóu guānguāng chēpiào*) for transport within the area – valid throughout the duration of your stay. Some of the more

159

Don't Miss Píngyáo's City Walls

A good place to start is the magnificent city walls (城墙; *chéng qiáng*), which date from 1370. At 10m high and more than 6km in circumference, they are punctuated by 72 watchtowers, each containing a paragraph from Sunzi's *The Art of War*. Part of the southern wall, which collapsed in 2004, has been rebuilt, but the rest is original. Píngyáo's **city gates** (城门; *chéngmén*) are fascinating and are some of the best preserved in China; the **Lower West Gate** (also called Fèngyì Mén, or Phoenix Appearing Gate) has a section of the original road, deeply grooved with the troughs left by cartwheels (also visible at the South Gate).

popular temples charge an additional small entrance fee.

Avoid Wǔtái Shān during the holiday periods and high-season weekends; temperatures are often below zero from October to March and roads can be impassable.

Orientation

Enclosed within a lush valley between the five main peaks is an elongated, unashamedly touristy town called **Táihuái** (台怀), which everyone simply calls Wǔtái Shān. It's here that you'll find the largest concentration of temples, as

well as all the area's hotels and tourist facilities.

Climate

Wǔtái Shān is at high altitude and powerful blizzards can sweep in as late as May and as early as September. Winters are freezing and snowbound; the summer months are the most pleasant, but always pack waterproofs and waterproof shoes or boots, as well as warm clothing because temperatures can still fall rapidly at night. If you are climbing up the peaks to see the sunrise, warm coats can be hired.

Sights

Over 50 temples lie scattered in town and across the surrounding countryside, so knowing where to start can be a daunting prospect. Most travellers limit themselves to what is called the **Táihuái Temple Cluster** (Táihuái Sìmiàoqún; 台怀寺庙群), about 20 temples around Táihuái itself, among which Tǎyuàn Temple and Xiǎntōng Temple (see p164) are considered the best.

TǍYUÀN TEMPLE Buddhist Temple
(塔院寺; Tǎyuàn Sì; admission Y7) At the base of **Spirit Vulture Peak** (灵鹫峰; Língjiù Fēng), the distinctive white stupa rising above Tǎyuàn Temple is the most prominent landmark in Wǔtái Shān and virtually all pilgrims come through here to spin the prayer wheels at its base or to prostrate themselves, even in the snow. Hung with small yellow bells chiming in the Wǔtái Shān winds, the marvellous **Great White Stupa** (大白塔; Dàbái Tǎ) dates originally from 1301 and is one of 84,000 *dagobas* built by King Asoka, 19 of which are in China. The **Great Sutra-Keeping Hall** is a magnificent sight; its towering 9th-century revolving Sutra case originally held scriptures in Chinese, Mongolian and Tibetan.

OTHER TEMPLES & VIEWS
You can continue exploring the cluster of temples north beyond Xiǎntōng Temple. **Yuánzhào Temple** (圆照寺; Yuánzhào Sì) contains a smaller stupa than the one at Tǎyuàn Temple. A 10-minute walk south, **Shūxiàng Temple** (殊像寺;Shūxiàng Sì) can be reached up some steep steps beyond its spirit wall by the side of the road; the temple contains Wǔtái Shān's largest statue of Wenshu riding a lion.

For great views of the town, you can trek, take a chairlift (up/down Y35/30, return Y60) or ride a horse (Y30) up to the temple on **Dàiluó Peak** (黛螺顶; Dàiluó Dǐng; admission Y6), on the eastern side of Qīngshuǐ River (清水河; Qīngshuǐ Hé). For even better views of the surrounding hills, walk 2.5km south to the isolated, fortress-like **Nánshān Temple** (南山寺; Nánshān Sì; admission Y4) and its beautiful stone carvings.

Tours

CITS (中国国际旅行社; Zhōngguó Guójì Lǚxíngshè; ☎139 9410 4419; ⏲7am-9pm) has guides for Y300 per day. It can run tours to the five main peaks (as can other tour companies, but most do not have their own transport and just use local taxis, which you may as well arrange yourself). Return trips cost Y60 (south and east) or Y70 (north, west, central) per person, including waiting time at the top. It's on the main strip.

Sleeping & Eating

Cheaper guesthouses can be found in the vicinity of the restaurants and shops in the north of the village.

FÓYUÁN LÓU Hotel **$$**
(佛缘楼; ☎654 2659; Shūxiàng Temple; r standard/deluxe Y260/360, ste Y480, discounts of 40%; ❄) There are lovely and spacious rooms with elegant furnishings at this hotel with a gorgeous monastic aspect behind Shūxiàng Temple. Take the steep flight of steps up to the temple; the hotel is to the rear. Room prices drop when it's quiet.

Loads of small family-run restaurants are tucked away behind hotels and down small alleys off the main strip where you can find standard fare.

Information

Bring cash, as there's nowhere to change money and ATMs only accept Chinese cards.

China Post (邮局; yóujú; h 8am-7pm) By the bus station, half an hour's walk south, just north of a China Mobile shop.

Tiānyuán Internet (天缘网吧; Tiānyuán Wǎngbā; per hr Y3; ⏲24hr) At the back of a courtyard off the road east of the Qīngshuǐ River.

Wǔtái Shān

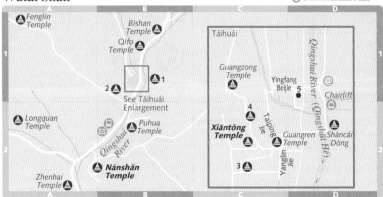

0　　　　2 km
0　　　　1 mile

Wǔtái Shān

◎ Top Sights

    Nánshān Temple B2

    Xiǎntōng Temple C2

◎ Sights

  1 Dàiluó Peak B1

  2 Shūxiàng Temple............................... B1

  3 Tǎyuàn Temple C2

  4 Yuánzhào Temple.............................. C2

Activities, Courses & Tours

  5 CITS D1

Sleeping

    Fóyuán Lóu....................................(see 2)

❶ Getting There & Away

Bus

Buses from **Wǔtái Shān bus station** (汽车站; Qìchē zhàn; ☎654 3101) include the following:

Běijīng Y131, 6½ hours, one to two daily

Dàtóng Y67, four hours, regular (7.30am to 2.30pm; summer only)

Hanging Monastery Y56, three hours, one daily (7.40am)

Shāhé Y20, 1½ hours, hourly (8am to 6pm)

Tàiyuán Y74, four hours, eight daily (5.40am to 3.40pm)

Xīnzhōu Y43, three hours, one daily

Tàiyuán buses all stop in Dòucūn (Y15) and Dōngyě (Y30), the small towns close to Fóguāng Temple and Nánshān Temple, respectively. Dàtóng buses should pass by Húnyuán (浑源), a short taxi ride (Y10) from the monastery. From Dàtóng in winter, first go to Shāhé (Y42, 3½ hours, every 15 minutes, 7am to 4.30pm) then take a minibus taxi (around Y70).

Train

The station known as **Wǔtái Shān** is actually 50km away in the town of Shāhé (砂河). All Dàtóng buses go via here (Y20). Trains include **Běijīng** Y58, six to seven hours, two daily (8.38pm and 1.37am) and **Tàiyuán** Y16, four hours, regular services (8.30am to 3.52pm).

Around Wǔtái Shān

Two of the oldest wooden buildings in China, dating from the Tang dynasty, are at Fóguāng Temple and Nánchán Temple. Few visitors go, so you may have to ask the caretaker to unlock the gates. All Wǔtái Shān–Tàiyuán buses should pass through the small towns where the temples are located, so both can be seen as a day trip.

Fóguāng Temple 佛光寺

The elongated main hall of this Buddhist **temple** (Fóguāng Sì; admission Y15) dates from 857. It contains a central Sakyamuni surrounded by 17 other colourful Tang statues with 296 intriguing Ming arhat statues in the flanks. Fóguāng Temple is set among farmland 6km outside the small town of Dòucūn (豆村). From Wǔtái Shān, take a Tàiyuán-bound bus to

Dòucūn (Y15, one hour) then a minibus taxi (Y20 return, including waiting time) to the temple, or a local bus (Y1) part of the way, leaving you with a pleasant 2km walk.

Nánchán Temple 南禅寺

A further 45km southwest of Fóguāng, near Dōngyě (东冶), this even quieter **temple (Nánchán Sì; admission Y15)** contains a smaller but strikingly beautiful hall built in 782, one of China's oldest temple halls. From Dòucūn take a bus (Y12, one hour) to Dōngyě, then a minibus taxi (Y20 return). The last bus from here to Tàiyuán (Y36, two hours) leaves around 4pm.

Dàtóng 大同

🕿 0352 / POP 1.1 MILLION

Its coal-belt setting and socialist-era refashioning cruelly robbed Dàtóng of much charm. The city has, however, jumped fairly and squarely onto the 'restore-our-greatness' bandwagon, ploughing mountains of cash into a colossal renovation program of its old quarter. Even without its pricey facelift, however, Dàtóng still cuts it as a coal-dusted heavyweight in China's increasingly competitive tourist challenge. Dàtóng is the gateway to one of China's most outstanding Buddhist treasures: the awe-inspiring Yúngāng Caves.

History

Dàtóng first rose to greatness as the capital of the Tuoba, a federation of Turkic-speaking nomads who united northern China (AD 386–534), converted to Buddhism and, like most other invaders, were eventually assimilated into Chinese culture. The Tuoba's outstanding bequest is the Yúngāng Caves, sublime 5th-century Buddhist carvings capturing a quiet, timeless beauty.

◉ Sights

Much of the **old town** (老城区; lǎochéngqū) was pulled down; what replaced it was being levelled at the time of writing to restore it to its former state. It's illogical for sure, but this is China. Buildings being rebuilt from the soles up include the **mosque** (清真寺; Qīngzhēn Sì), a Taoist temple and courtyard architecture.

HUÁYÁN TEMPLE   Buddhist Temple
(华严寺; Huáyán Sì) Shut for refurbishment at the time of writing, Huáyán Temple is divided into two separate complexes, one an active monastery (upper temple), the other a museum (lower temple). Built by the Khitan during the Liao dynasty (AD 907–1125), the temple faces east, not south (it's said the Khitan were sun worshippers).

Dating to 1140, the impressive main hall of the **upper temple** (上华严寺; Shàng Huáyán Sì; Huayansi Jie; admission Y20; ⏲ 8am-6pm summer, to 5.30pm winter) is one of the largest Buddhist halls in China, with Ming statues and Qing murals within. The rear hall of the **lower temple** (下华严寺; Xià Huáyán Sì; Huayansi Jie; admission Y20; ⏲ 8am-6pm summer, to 5.30pm winter) is the oldest building in Dàtóng (1038), containing some remarkable Liao-dynasty wooden sculptures.

NINE DRAGON SCREEN   Ancient Site
(九龙壁; Jiǔlóng Bì; Da Dongjie; admission Y10; ⏲ 8am-6pm year-round) With its nine beautiful multicoloured coiling dragons, this 45.5m-long, 8m-high and 2m-thick Ming-dynasty spirit wall was built in 1392. It's the largest glazed-tile wall in China and is an amazing sight; the palace it once protected burnt down years ago.

🛏 Sleeping & Eating

There are plenty of restaurants around the train station.

TÓNGTIĚ BĪNGUǍN   Hotel $$
(同铁宾馆; 🕿 713 0768; 15 Zhanbei Jie; 站北街 15号; s/d/ste Y280/280/398, discounts of 30%; ❄) There are excellent, spacious and modern rooms with traditional furnishings and elegant touches at this smart, fantastic-value hotel north of the train station. Rooms are clean and well kept, and shower rooms come with heat lamps.

ALAMY/KARL JOHAENTGES

Don't Miss **Xiǎntōng Temple**

Xiǎntōng Temple (显通寺; Xiǎntōng Sì; admission Y10), the largest and most captivating temple in Wǔtái Shān, embraces more than 100 halls and rooms. The **Qiānbō Wénshū Hall** contains a 1000-armed, multifaced Wenshu, whose every palm supports a miniature Buddha. The astonishing brick **Beamless Hall** (无梁殿; Wúliáng Diàn) holds a miniature Yuan-dynasty pagoda, remarkable statues of contemplative monks meditating in the alcoves and a vast seated effigy of Wenshu. Further on, up some steps is the blindingly beautiful **Golden Hall**, enveloped in a constellation of small Buddhas covering all the walls. Five metres high and weighing 50 tonnes, the metal hall was cast in 1606 before being gilded; it houses an effigy of the Wenshu of Wisdom seated atop a lion.

GARDEN HOTEL   Hotel **$$$**
(花园大饭店; Huāyuán Dàfàndiàn; ☎586 5825; www.huayuanhotel.com.cn; 59 Da Nanjie; 大南街59号; d & tw Y880-1180, discounts of 25%; ➌ ❄ @) Impeccable rooms at this intimate hotel feature goose-down quilts, carved pear-wood bed frames, reproduction antique furnishings and lovely bathrooms. It has a lovely atrium, Latin American and Chinese restaurants plus excellent staff, and a Bank of China ATM.

TÓNGHÉ DÀFÀNDIÀN   Chinese **$**
(同和大饭店; Zhanqian Jie; meals Y20-30; ⏱10am-2pm & 5-9pm; 📖) This popular, bright and cheery spot next to the Hongqi

Hotel is perfect for a meal before catching the train. Its big round tables may look intimidating, but solo diners can still take a seat; try the Shānxī fried noodles (Y12), the pancake with meat filling (Y3.5), tasty stirfried mutton slices with Chinese onion, or the egg soup (Y8).

ℹ Information

Bank of China Xiao Nanjie (中国银行; Zhōngguó Yínháng; Xiao Nanjie) ATM; for travellers cheques, you need the Yingbin Xilu branch (⏱8am-noon & 2.30-6pm Mon-Fri).

China Post (中国邮政; Zhōngguó Yóuzhèng; cnr Da Xijie & Xinjian Nanlu; ⏱8am-6.30pm) South of Red Flag Sq; there's another branch near the train station.

Public Security Bureau Entry & Exit Office
(PSB; 公安局出入境接待处; Gōng'ānjú Chūrùjìng Jiēdàichù; Weidu Dadao; ☺9am-noon & 3-5.30pm Mon-Fri)

🛈 Getting There & Away

Air

Located 20km east of the city, Dàtóng's small airport has flights to Běijīng (Y400), Shànghǎi (Y1450), Hǎinán Island (Y2500) and Guǎngzhōu (Y1630). Buy tickets at Aviation Travel Service (航空售票处; Hángkōng Shòupiàochù; Nanguan Xijie; ☺8am-7pm). No public transport goes to the airport. A taxi costs around Y40.

Bus

Buses to Běijīng (Y120, 4½ hours, eight daily) leave from the south bus station (新南站; Xīnnán Zhàn; ☎503 2555; 699 South Xinjian Rd).

For Hanging Monastery (Y35, 1½ hours, regular services 6.30am to 6pm), go to the main bus station (大同汽车站; Dàtóngqìchēzhàn; ☎246 4464; 20 Yantong Xilu).

Train

Services include **Běijīng** Y64 to Y105, six to 7½ hours, frequent services, **Píngyáo** Y75 to Y80, seven to eight hours, five daily and **Xī'ān** Y135, 16½ hours, two daily.

🛈 Getting Around

Dàtóng has an infestation of hand-me-down **taxis** from the rest of China that swarm across town.

Around Dàtóng

Yúngāng Caves
云冈石窟

One of China's most superlative examples of Buddhist cave art, these 5th-century **caves** (Yúngāng Shíkū; ☎0352-302 6230; admission Y100, guide Y80; ☺8.30am-5.20pm, 9am-4.20pm winter) are ineffably sublime. With their 51,000 ancient statues they put virtually everything else in the Shānxī shade.

Carved by the Turkic-speaking Tuoba, the Yúngāng Caves draw their designs from Indian, Persian and even Greek influences that swept along the Silk Road. Work began in AD 460, continuing for 60 years before all 252 caves, the oldest collection of Buddhist carvings in China, had been completed.

At the time of writing only 39 of the 45 caves were open, showcasing some of China's most precious and elegant Buddhist artwork. Despite weathering, many of the statues at Yúngāng still retain their gorgeous pigment, unlike the slightly later statues at Lóngmén.

Some caves contain intricately carved square-shaped pagodas, while others depict the inside of temples, carved and painted to look as though made of wood. Frescos are in abundance and there are graceful depictions of animals, birds and angels, some still brightly painted, and almost every cave contains the 1000-Buddha motif (tiny Buddhas seated in niches).

Eight of the caves contain enormous Buddha statues; the largest can be found in **Cave 5**, an outstanding 17m-high, seated effigy of Sakyamuni with a gilded face. The frescos in this cave are badly scratched, but note the painted vaulted ceiling. Bursting with colour, **Cave 6** is also stunning, resembling a set from an *Indiana Jones* epic with legions of Buddhist angels, Bodhisattvas and other figures. In the middle of the cave a square block pagoda connects with the ceiling, with Buddhas on each side over two levels. Most foreign visitors are oblivious to the graffiti in bright-red oil paint on the right-hand side of the main door frame within the cave, which reads '大同八中' (Dàtóng Bāzhōng; 'Datong No 8 Middle School'), courtesy of pupils probably during the Cultural Revolution. On the priceless fresco to the right is further graffiti in red paint, left by what appears to be a contingent from Píngyáo.

Further damage is much in evidence. Chronic weathering has afflicted **Cave 7** (carved between 470 and 493) and **Cave 8**, both scoured by the Shānxī winds. Atmospheric pollution has also taken its toll.

Caves 16 to 20 are the earliest caves at Yúngāng, carved under the supervision of monk Tanyao. Examine the exceptional quality of the carvings in **Cave 18**; some of the faces are perfectly presented. **Cave 19** contains a vast 16.8m-high effigy of Sakyamuni. The Maitreya Buddha is a popular subject for Yúngāng's sculptors, for example in the vast seated form in **Cave 17** and **Cave 13**; the latter statue has been carved with graffiti by workers from Hohhot (in Inner Mongolia) and other miscreants.

Cave 20 is similar to the Ancestor Worshipping Cave at Lóngmén, originally depicting a trinity of Buddhas (the past, present and future Buddhas). The huge seated Buddha in the middle is the representative icon at Yúngāng, while the Buddha on the left has somehow vanished. Many caves in the western end of Yúngāng have Buddhas with their heads smashed off, as in **Cave 39**. Buddhist figures exposed to the elements, especially near doorways, have been almost totally weathered away.

English-speaking guides are available, although almost every cave comes with English captions. Photography is permitted in some caves but not in others.

🛈 Getting There & Away

At the time of writing, getting to Yúngāng was a nightmare due to roadworks. Things should have eased by the time you read this and bus 3-2 (Y2.50, 50 minutes, from 6am to 6pm) from Dàtóng train station should be running again. At research time you had to take bus 4 (Y1, 30 minutes) to Xīnkāilǐ (新开里), then bus 3-1 (Y1.5) to Jìnhuá Gōng (晋华宫), followed by a taxi (Y10) to the drop-off from where it is a further 1km walk; due to traffic jams, the entire journey was taking 2½ hours or more. A taxi from Dàtóng will cost around Y80.

Hanging Monastery
悬空寺

Built precariously into the side of a cliff, the Buddhist **Hanging Monastery** (Xuánkōng Sì; admission Y130; ⏲7am-7pm summer, 8am-6pm winter) is made all the more stunning by its long support stilts. The halls have been built along the contours of the cliff face, connected by rickety catwalks and corridors.

If passengers on the bus from Dàtóng are scarce you may be transferred into a free taxi for the last 5km from Húnyuán (浑源). The same should, in theory, apply in the opposite direction. To go from the Hanging Monastery to Mùtǎ, you'll need a taxi (Y10) to Húnyuán, from where there are regular buses to Mùtǎ (Y12, 25 minutes, last bus 6pm).

Tài'ān 泰安

☎0538 / POP 933,760

Gateway to Tài Shān's sacred slopes, Tài'ān has a venerable tourist industry that has been in full swing since the time of the Ming dynasty. Though there's not much to see outside of the magnificent Dài Temple, you will need the better part of a day for the mountain, so spending the night either here or at the summit is advised.

◎ Sights

DÀI TEMPLE   Temple
(岱庙; Dài Miào; Daibeng Lu; admission Y20; ⏲8.30am-6pm summer, to 5.30pm winter)
With its eternal-looking trees and commanding location at the hub of Tài'ān, this magnificent temple complex was a traditional pilgrimage stop on the route to the mountain and the site of sacrifices to the god of Tài Shān.

The main hall is the colossal twin yellow-eaved, nine-bay-wide **Hall of Heavenly Blessing** (天贶殿; Tiānkuàng Diàn; slippers required Y1), which dates to AD 1009. The dark interior is decorated with a marvellous, flaking, 62m-long Song-dynasty fresco depicting Emperor Zhenzong as the god of Tài Shān.

To the south of the **south gate** (正阳门; Zhèngyáng Mén) is the splendid Dàimiào Fāng, a *páifāng* (ornamental arch) decorated with four pairs of weathered lions, and dragon and phoenix motifs.

Sleeping

Tài'ān Tourism Information Centre in front of the train station can help you book a room. Basic English is spoken.

YÙZUÒ HOTEL Hotel **$$$**
(御座宾馆; Yùzuò Bīnguǎn; ☎826 9999; www.yuzuo.cn; 3 Daimiao Beijie; 岱庙北街3号; tw/d/ste Y480/680/780; ✱@) Pleasantly positioned next to the Dài Temple and attractively trimmed with lights at night, this traditionally styled three-star hotel is manned by polite staff and ranges among low-rise, two-storey blocks.

ROMAN HOLIDAY Hotel **$$**
(罗马假日商务酒店; Luómǎ Jiàrì Shāngwù Jiǔdiàn; ☎627 9999; 18 Hongmen Lu; 红门路18号; s & tw Y298, d Y398; ✱@) The small, neat rooms come with see-through showers, glass sinks and striped carpets and wallpaper in this bizarrely named modern four-storey hotel. The location and comfort level are quite good and discounts take prices down to Y158 with breakfast.

Eating

The **night market** (夜市; yè shì; ☉5.30pm-late) located in the centre of town along the Nai River has many hotpot stalls. During the day, there's also the **Běixīn Small Eats Street** (北新小吃步行街; Běixīn Xiǎochī Bùxíng Jie) where you can find savoury breads, roast-meat skewers, fried chicken and more.

Ā DŌNG JĪA CHÁNG CÀI Chinese **$**
(阿东家常菜; 25 Hongmen Lu; meals from Y10; 🗐) This handily located, clean restaurant fills you up with shuǐjiǎo (水饺; dumplings), including lamb (Y24 per jīn – half a jīn is enough for one) and vegetable (Y18 per jīn) fillings among other choices.

SHENG TAO YANG COFFEE & TEA International **$$**
(圣淘缘休闲餐厅; Shèngtáoyuán Xiūxián Cāntīng'; 29 Hongmen Lu; dishes Y25-150; 🛜) The ivory baby-grand piano beside the toilet may be overkill but the comfy couches, eager staff and huge 36-page menu are lovely. Yummy pizzas. There's also steak, spaghetti and Chinese dishes with rice. Chinese menu with lots of photos. Free wi-fi.

ℹ Information

Bank of China (中国银行; Zhōngguó Yínháng; Tongtian Jie; ☉8.30am-5pm) The 24-hour ATM accepts foreign cards.

China Post (邮局; Zhōngguó Yóuzhèng; 85 Qingnian Lu; ☉8.30am-5.30pm)

Public Security Bureau (PSB; 公安局; Gōng'ānjú; ☎827 5264; cnr Dongyue Dajie & Qingnian Lu; ☉8.30am-noon & 1-5pm Mon-Fri)

Buddha statue, Yúngāng Caves (p165)
KRZYSZTOF DYDYNSKI/LONELY PLANET IMAGES ©

Visa office is in the eastern side of this huge building.

Tài'ān Tourism Information Centre (泰安市旅游咨询中心; Tài'ānshì Lǚyóu Zīxún Zhōngxī) Hongmen Lu (22 Hongmen Lu; ☎218 7989; ☉8am-8pm); train station (☎688 7358; ☉6am-midnight) Both offices do hotel, train and plane ticket bookings.

World Net Bar Internet (大世界网吧; Dàshìjiè Wǎngbā; 2nd fl, 6 Hongmen Lu; per hr Y1.50; ☉24hr)

❶ Getting There & Away

Bus

Buses leave from the long-distance bus station (长途汽车站; chángtú qìchēzhàn; Panhe Lu), south of the train station:

Běijīng Y134, six hours, two daily (8.30am & 2.30pm)

Jǐ'nán Y22, 1½ hours, every 30 minutes (6.30am to 6pm)

Qīngdǎo Y100, 5½ hours, three daily (6am, 8am & 2.30pm)

Qūfù Y21, one hour, hourly

Shànghǎi Y205, 12 hours, one daily (4.30pm)

From the Tài Shān Bus Station (泰山汽车站; Tàishān Qìchēzhàn; Caiyuan Dajie) there are regular buses to Jǐ'nán (Y20, 1½ hours, every 20 minutes, 6am to 6pm).

Train

Tickets can be hard to get here, so book early. Regular trains (hard seat/sleeper) run to the following:

Běijīng Y158/296, seven to 10 hours, eight daily

Jǐ'nán hard seat Y11, one hour, regular

Qīngdǎo Y70/140, six to seven hours, 11 daily

Shànghǎi Y224/352, eight to 14 hours, 14 daily

Express D trains (hard/soft seat only) run to the following:

Běijīng Y79/176, four hours, four daily

Qīngdǎo Y70/108, 3½ hours, two daily (2.30pm & 7.15pm)

Shànghǎi Y90/140, seven hours, five daily

❶ Getting Around

Taxis start at Y6 (then Y1.50 per kilometre thereafter). Avoid unmetered three-wheelers.

Calligraphy brushes, Xī'ān

Tài Shān 泰山

♪ 0538

Sacred mountains are a dime a dozen in China, but when push comes to shove, the one that matters the most is **Tài Shān (admission Feb-Nov Y125, Dec-Jan Y100)**. Worshipped since at least the 11th century BC, the mountain rises up like a guardian of the Middle Kingdom, bestowing its divine sanction on worthy rulers and protecting the country from catastrophe. Anyone who's anyone in China has climbed it – from Confucius to Du Fu to Mao Zedong – and Qin Shi Huang, the First Emperor, chose the summit as the place from which to first proclaim the unity of the country in 219 BC.

The best time to visit is in autumn when the humidity is low; the clearest weather is from early October onwards. In winter the weather is often fine, but very cold. The tourist season peaks from May to October. The summit can be very cold, windy and wet; army overcoats are available there for hire (Y20 average) and you can buy waterproof coats from vendors.

Tài Shān itself is 1532m above sea level, with a walking distance of 7.5km from base to summit on the central route and an elevation change of about 1400m. Although it's not a major climb (there aren't any trails on the main route), with well over 6000 steps to the top, it can certainly be exhausting and should not be underestimated.

◉ Sights & Activities

There are three routes up the mountain that can be followed on foot: the main **central route** (sometimes referred to as the east route), the **western route** (often used for bus descents) and the lesser-known **Tiānzhú Peak** route up the back of the mountain. The central and western routes converge at the halfway point (Midway Gate to Heaven), from where it's a final 3.5km of steep steps. Figure on about eight to nine hours round-trip (four hours up, one to two hours at the summit, three hours down), which includes time to visit the various sights along the way.

If that sounds like too much walking, or if you have bad knees, take a minibus up to Midway Gate to Heaven and then a cable car up to South Gate to Heaven, near the summit area. You can reverse this by climbing up and taking the cable car and then bus down.

As with all Chinese mountain hikes, viewing the sunrise is considered an integral part of the experience. Stay overnight at one of the summit guest houses and get up early the next morning for the famed sunrise.

Central Route 中路

This has been the main route up the mountain since the 3rd century BC, and over the past 2000 years or so a bewildering number of bridges, trees, rivers, gullies, inscriptions, caves, pavilions and temples have become famous sights in their own right.

Purists can begin their ascents with a south–north perambulation through Dài Temple in Tài'ān, 1.7km south of the trailhead, in imitation of imperial custom. Most climbers, however, begin at the **First Gate of Heaven** (一天门; Yìtiān Mén), at the end of Hongmen Lu (at the foot of Taishan). Nearby is the **Guandi Temple** (关帝庙; Guāndì Miào), containing a large statue of Lord Guan. Beyond is a stone archway overgrown with wisteria upon which is written 'the place where Confucius began his ascent'.

Further along is **Red Gate Palace** (红门宫; Hóng Mén Gōng; admission Y5), with its wine-coloured walls. This is the first of a series of temples dedicated to Bixia. After this is a large gate called **Wànxiān Lóu** (万仙楼), and the **ticket office** (售票处; Shòupiào Chù).

Continuing through the tunnel of cypresses known as Cypress Cave is **Huímǎ Peak** (Huímǎ Lǐng), where Emperor Zhenzong had to dismount and continue by sedan chair because his horse refused to go further. Allow two hours for the climb up to the halfway point, the **Midway Gate to Heaven** (中天门; Zhōng Tiān Mén), where the central and western routes converge.

Beyond is **Five Pine Pavilion** (五松亭; Wǔsōng Tíng), where, in 219 BC, Emperor Qin Shi Huang was overtaken by a violent storm and was sheltered by the pine trees.

Ahead is the arduous **Path of Eighteen Bends** (十八盘) that eventually leads to the summit; climbing it is performed in slow motion by all and sundry as legs turn to lead. You'll pass **Opposing Pines Pavilion** (对松亭; Duìsōng Tíng) and the **Welcoming Pine** (迎客松; Yíngkè Sōng) – every mountain worth its salt in China has one – with a branch extended as if to shake hands.

The final stretch takes you to the **South Gate to Heaven** (南天门; Nán Tián Mén), the third celestial gate, which marks the beginning of the summit area. At the summit, bear right and walk along Tian Jie to **Azure Clouds Temple** (碧霞祠; **Bìxiá Cí; admission Y5**), with its sublime perch in the clouds, where elders offer money and food to the deities of Bixia, Yanguang Nainai and Taishan Songzi Niangniang (the latter helping women bear children).

Climbing higher, you will pass the Taoist **Qīngdì Palace** (青帝宫; Qīngdì Gōng),

before the fog- and cloud-swathed **Jade Emperor Temple** (玉皇顶; Yùhuáng Dǐng) comes into view, perched on the highest point (1532m) of the Tài Shān plateau.

The main sunrise vantage point is the **North Prayer Rock** (拱北石; Gǒngběi Shí); if you're lucky, visibility extends to over 200km, as far as the coast.

Western Route 西路

The most popular way to descend the mountain is by bus (Y30) via the western route. If you want to walk, the footpath intercepts with the road at a number of points, and they are often one and the same. Given the amount of traffic, you might prefer to hop on a bus rather than inhale its exhaust. If you choose to hike up or down, be aware that unless you walk along the road, the trail is not always clearly marked. Buses will not stop for you once they have left the Midway Gate to Heaven.

Either by bus or foot, the western route treats you to considerable variation in scenery, with orchards, pools and flowering plants. The major attraction along this route is **Black Dragon Pool** (黑龙潭; Hēilóng Tán), which is just below **Longevity Bridge** (长寿桥; Chángshòu Qiáo) and is fed by a small waterfall.

An enjoyable conclusion to your descent is a visit to **Pǔzhào Temple** (普照寺; Pǔzhào Sì; Pervading Light Temple; admission Y5; ⏰8am-5.30pm).

Tài Shān

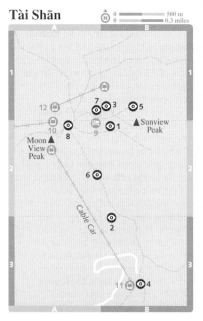

Tài Shān

⊙ Sights

1	Azure Clouds Temple	B1
2	Five Pine Pavilion	B3
3	Jade Emperor Temple	B1
4	Midway Gate to Heaven	B3
5	North Prayer Rock	B1
6	Opposing Pines Pavilion	A2
7	Qingdi Palace	A1
8	South Gate to Heaven	A2
	Welcoming Pine	(see 6)

⊟ Sleeping

9	Shénqí Hotel	A2

Transport

10	Cable Car to Peach Blossom Park	A2
11	Cable Car to Peak	B3
12	Cable Car to Rear Rocky Access	A1

🛏 Sleeping & Eating

There are many hotels at the summit area along Tian Jie, catering to a range of budgets from Y160 and *way* up on weekends. Accommodation prices here don't apply to main holiday periods, when room prices can triple. At other times, always ask for discounts.

There is no food shortage on Tài Shān; the central route is dotted with teahouses, stalls, vendors and restaurants. Your pockets are likely to feel emptier than your stomach, but keep in mind that all supplies are carried up by foot and that the prices rise as you do.

SHÉNQÌ HOTEL   Hotel   **$$$**
(神憩宾馆; Shénqì Bīnguǎn; ☎ 822 3866; fax 821 5399; d/ste Y1480/2080; ❄ @) The fact that all the important guests to the summit stay here means that prices are inevitably high. It's a reasonably smart hotel with a restaurant (serving Taoist banquets) and a bar, and is reached by steep steps. Rooms are clean with a strange boxlike shower hidden in a wooden cubicle.

ℹ Getting There & Away

Bus 3 runs from the Tài'ān train station to the Tài Shān central route trailhead via Hongmen Lu (Y1, 10 minutes) and, in the opposite direction, from Tài'ān's train station to the western-route trailhead (Y1, 10 to 15 minutes) at Tiānwài Village (Tiānwài Cūn).

ℹ Getting Around

At Tiānwài Village (天外村; Tiānwài Cūn), at the foot of the western route, minibuses (Y30 each way) depart every 20 minutes (or when full) to the Midway Gate to Heaven, halfway up Tài Shān. The minibuses operate from 4am to 8pm during high season, and less regularly during low season.

The main cable car (空中索道; kōngzhōng suǒdào; one-way/return Y80/140; ⏰ 7.30am-5.30pm 16 Apr-15 Oct, 8.30am-5pm 16 Oct-15 Apr) is a five-minute walk from Midway Gate to Heaven. Be warned: high-season and weekend queues may force you to wait up to two hours.

Detour:
Tiānzhú Peak Route

The lesser-known route up the back of the mountain through the **Tiānzhú Peak Scenic Area** (天烛峰景区; Tiānzhú Fēng Jǐngqū) provides more adventurous hikers a rare chance to ascend Tài Shān without the crowds. It's mostly ancient pines and peaks back here; visit the mountain's main sights by taking the central route down. Make sure you get an early start; the bus here takes 45 minutes, and the climb itself can take upwards of four hours. To get to the trailhead, take bus Y2 (游2; yóu'èr; Y3) from Caiyuan Dajie opposite the train station in Tài'ān to the terminus, Tiānzhú Fēng Jǐng (天烛峰景).

There is another cable car (桃花源索道; táohuāyuán suǒdào; one-way/return Y80/140; ⏰ 7.30am-5.30pm 16 Apr-15 Oct, 8.30am-5pm 16 Oct-15 Apr) that takes you from north of South Gate to Heaven down to Peach Blossom Park (桃花源; Táohuā Yuán), a scenic area behind Tài Shān that is worth exploring. From here you can take a minibus to Tài'ān (Y25, 40 minutes).

A third, shorter cable car (后石坞索道; hòushíwù suǒdào; one-way Y20; ⏰ 8.30am-4pm Apr-Oct, closed 16 Oct-15 Apr) comes up from the Rear Rocky Recess (后石坞; Hòu Shíwù) on the back of the mountain.

Qūfù 曲阜
☎ 0537 / POP 85,700

Hometown of the great sage, Confucius, and his ancestors, the Kong clan, Qūfù is a testament to just how important Confucian thought was in imperial China. In 2008 the provincial government revealed plans for a controversial US$4.2 billion 'cultural symbolic city' to be built nearby, beginning in 2010. As of writing, construction had yet to begin.

◉ Sights

The main ticket office (售票处; Shòupiào-chù) is at the corner of Queli Jie and Nanma Dao, east of the Confucius Temple's main entrance. This is where you should purchase a combined ticket (Y150) to all three sights and can hire an English-speaking guide (Y100). From 16 November to 14 February, tickets are Y10 cheaper and sights close an hour earlier.

CONFUCIUS TEMPLE   Temple

(孔庙; Kǒng Miào; admission Y90; ⏱8am-5.30pm) China's largest imperial building complex after the Forbidden City, this temple actually started out as a simple memorial hall 2500 years ago, gradually mushrooming into today's compound, which is one-fifth the size of the Qūfù town centre.

The main entrance in the south passes through a series of triple-door gates, leading visitors to two airy, cypress-filled courtyards. About halfway along the north–south axis rises the triple-eaved **Great Pavilion of the Constellation of Scholars** (奎文阁; Kuíwén Gé), an imposing Jin-dynasty wooden structure containing faded prints illustrating Confucius' exploits in *The Analects*. Beyond lie a series of colossal, twin-eaved stele pavilions, followed by **Dàchéng Gate** (大成门; Dàchéng Mén), north of which is the **Xìngtán Pavilion** (杏坛; Xìng Tán), marking the spot from where Confucius allegedly taught his students.

The core of the complex is the huge yellow-eaved **Dàchéng Hall** (大成殿; Dàchéng Diàn), which, in its present form, dates from 1724; it towers 31m on a white marble terrace. Craftspeople carved the 10 dragon-coiled columns so expertly that they had to be covered with red silk when Emperor Qianlong visited, lest he felt that the Forbidden City's Hall of Supreme Harmony paled in comparison.

Inside is a huge statue of Confucius residing on a throne, encapsulated in a red and gold burnished cabinet. The next hall, the **Chamber Hall** (寝殿; Qǐn Diàn), was built for Confucius' wife and is now undergoing extensive renovations. East of Dàchéng Hall, **Chóngshèng Hall** (崇圣祠; Chóngshèng Cí) is also adorned with fabulous carved pillars.

Exit from the east gate, **Dōnghuá Gate** (东华门; Dōnghuá Mén), south of which is the **Bell Tower** (钟楼; Zhōnglóu), spanning the width of Queli Jie. Come early to avoid the hordes of megaphone-blaring tour groups that descend upon the complex.

CONFUCIUS MANSIONS
Museum

(孔府; Kǒng Fǔ; admission Y60; ⏱8am-6pm) Adjacent to the Confucius Temple are the Confucius Mansions, a maze of 450 halls, rooms, buildings and side passages originally dating from the 16th century.

The mansions were the most sumptuous aristocratic lodgings in China, indicative of the Kong family's former power.

Stone statues, Confucius Forest
KRZYSZTOF DYDYNSKI/LONELY PLANET IMAGES ©

Qūfù

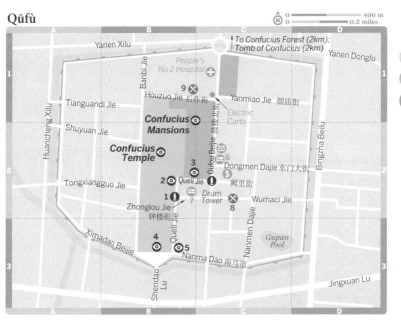

The Confucius Mansions are built on an 'interrupted' north–south axis. Grouped by the south gate are the former administrative offices. The **Ceremonial Gate** (重光门; Chóngguāng Mén) leads to the **Great Hall** (大堂; Dà Táng), two further halls and then the **Nèizhái Gate** (内宅门; Nèizhái Mén), which seals off the residential quarters (used for weddings, banquets and private functions). The **Front Chamber** (前堂楼; Qián Táng Lóu) was where the duke lived and is laid out on two floors – rare for a hall this size.

Located east just before the Nèizhái Gate is the **Tower of Refuge** (避难楼; Bìnàn Lóu) – not open to visitors – where the Kong clan could gather if the peasants turned nasty. It has an iron-lined ceiling on the ground floor, a staircase that could be yanked up into the interior, and provisions for a lengthy retreat.

CONFUCIUS FOREST Cemetery
(孔林; Kǒng Lín; admission Y40; ⏱7.30am-6pm)
Around 2km north of town on Lindao Lu is the peaceful Confucius Forest, the largest artificial park and best-preserved cemetery in China.

Qūfù

◎ **Top Sights**
- Confucius Mansions B1
- Confucius Temple B2

◎ **Sights**
- 1 Bell Tower B2
- 2 Dōnghuá Gate B2
- 3 Entrance to Confucius Mansions B2
- 4 Entrance to Confucius Temple B3
- 5 Main Ticket Office B3

🛏 Sleeping
- 6 Mingya Confucianist Hotel C2
- 7 Quèlǐ Hotel B2

✴ **Eating**
- 8 Night Market C2
- 9 Yù Shū Fáng B1

The pine and cypress forest of over 100,000 trees covers 200 hectares and is bounded by a wall 10km long. Confucius and his descendants have been buried here over the past 2000 years, a tradition that continues today.

Flanking the approach to the **Tomb of Confucius** (孔子墓; Kǒngzǐ Mù) are pairs of stone panthers, griffins and larger-than-life guardians. The tomb itself is a simple grass mound enclosed by a low wall and faced with a Ming-dynasty stele.

Electric carts (电动旅游车; Diàndòng Lǚyóu Chē; return Y15) run to the temple from the corner of Houzuo Jie and Gulou Beijie, near the exit of the Confucius Mansions. Otherwise take a pedicab (Y3 to Y5) or bus 1 (Y2) from along Gulou Beijie. To reach the forest on foot takes about 30 minutes.

🛏 Sleeping

MINGYA CONFUCIANIST HOTEL

Hotel **$$**

(名雅儒家大饭店; Míngyǎ Rújiā Dàfàndiàn; ☑ 505 0888; 8 Gulou Beijie; 鼓楼北街8号; s & d incl breakfast Y388, discounts of 35%; ❋ @) While we're not sure if the great sage would approve of his name on a hotel banner, we assume he would like the fab location (smack-bang in the middle of town) and would be more than pleased with the large comfy rooms and well-mannered staff.

QUÈLǏ HOTEL

Hotel **$$$**

(阙里宾舍; Quèlǐ Bīnshè; ☑ 486 6818; www.quelihotel.com; 15 Zhonglou Jie; 钟楼街15号; s Y398-598, tw Y498-568, ste Y1288; ❋ @) The four-star Quèlǐ might be the highest-rated hotel in town, and with its tile roof and ornate decor it looks very much the part as *the* tourist hotel. In reality, however, it's in dire need of a refurbishment.

🍴 Eating

Head to either the area around **Shendao Lu** (south of the Confucius Temple), or the **night market** (夜市; Yèshì), off Wu-maci Jie, east of Gulou Nanjie.

YÙ SHŪ FÁNG

Chinese Banquet **$$$**

(御书房; ☑ 441 9888; 2nd fl, Houzuo Jie; set meals Y128) With 2nd-floor rooms over-

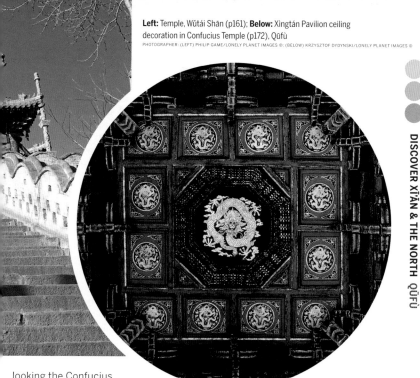

Left: Temple, Wǔtái Shān (p161); **Below:** Xìngtán Pavilion ceiling decoration in Confucius Temple (p172), Qūfù

PHOTOGRAPHER: (LEFT) PHILIP GAME/LONELY PLANET IMAGES ©; (BELOW) KRZYSZTOF DYDYNSKI/LONELY PLANET IMAGES ©

looking the Confucius Mansions, this is a fantastic place to take a breather after having successfully navigated several kilometres of courtyards. Recharge with some divine oolong tea (铁观音; *tiě guānyīn*) – cup (杯) from Y10, pot (壶) from Y30; or splash out on a banquet meal where nine (!) delicious Hong Kong family dishes are served in quick succession. No English is spoken here; enter by the door manned by *qipao*-clad ladies beside the 1st-floor furniture store (the owner is a wood-carver).

ⓘ Information

ATMs accepting international credit cards are along or just off Gulou Beijie. Internet cafes are just off Wumaci Jie (Y3 to Y5 per hour; look out for 网吧).

Bank of China (中国银行; **Zhōngguó Yínháng; 96 Dongmen Dajie;** ☉8.30am-4.30pm) Foreign exchange and ATM.

China Post (邮局; **Zhōngguó Yóuzhèng; 8-1 Gulou Beijie;** ☉7.30am-6.30pm summer, 8am-6pm winter)

Public Security Bureau (PSB; 公安局; **Gōng'ānjú;** ☎443 0049; **1 Wuyuntan Lu;** ☉8.30am-noon & 2-6pm Mon-Fri)

ⓘ Getting There & Away

Bus

Qūfù's **long-distance bus station** (汽车站; **Qìchēzhàn;** ☎441 2554) is 6km southwest of the walled city. **Left luggage** (Y2; ☉6am-6pm) is available here. Buses connect with these destinations:

Běijīng Y160 to Y180, six hours, four daily (8.10am, 11.20am, 3pm & 5.30pm)

Jǐ'nán Y44, three hours, every 30 minutes

Qīngdǎo Y125, five hours, five daily (8.30am, 9.30am, 1.30pm, 2.20pm & 4.40pm)

Tài'ān Y21, one hour, every 30 minutes

Train

When a railway project for Qūfù was first tabled, the Kong family petitioned for a change of routes, claiming that the trains would disturb Confucius' tomb. They won and the nearest tracks were routed to Yǎnzhōu (兖州), 16km west of Qūfù. Eventually another train station (442 1571) was constructed about 6km east of Qūfù, but only slow trains stop there, so it is more convenient to go to Yǎnzhōu train station (346 2965), on the line from Běijīng to Shànghǎi. Minibuses connect Yǎnzhōu bus station (walk straight ahead as you exit the train station, cross the parking lot and turn right; the bus station is 50m on the left) with Qūfù (Y5, 30 minutes, every 15 minutes, 6.30am to 5.30pm). Otherwise, a taxi from Yǎnzhōu train station to Qūfù should cost from Y40 to Y50.

Buy your tickets at the railway booking office (火车售票处; huǒchē shòupiào chù; 335 2276; 8 Jingxuan Lu; 7am-9pm); Y5 commission. Destinations include the following:

Běijīng D train, 2nd/1st class Y75/100, 4½ hours, two daily, other regular trains

Jǐ'nán Y24, two hours, frequent services

Qīngdǎo Y48 to Y144, seven to nine hours, 12 daily

Shànghǎi D train, 2nd/1st class Y77/123, six hours, two daily, other regular trains

Getting Around

Bus 1 travels along Gulou Beijie and Lindao Lu, connecting the bus station with the Confucius Forest. A taxi from the long-distance bus station to the city should cost Y15 and a pedicab Y5.

Pesky pedicabs (Y2 to Y3 to most sights within Qūfù) infest the streets, chasing all and sundry. Decorated tourist horse carts can take you on 30-minute tours (Y20 to the Confucius Forest from Queli Jie).

Qīngdǎo　青岛

 0532 / POP 1.73 MILLION

A breath of (literally) crisp sea air for anyone emerging from China's polluted urban interior, Qīngdǎo is hardly old-school China, but its effortless blend of German architecture and modern city planning puts most Chinese white-tile towns to shame. Its German legacy more or less intact, Qīngdǎo takes pride in its unique appearance: the Chinese call the town 'China's Switzerland'.

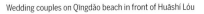

Wedding couples on Qīngdǎo beach in front of Huāshí Lóu

MARTIN MOOS/LONELY PLANET IMAGES ©

Made in Tsingtao

The beer of choice in Chinese restaurants around the world, Tsingtao is one of China's oldest and most familiar brands. Established in 1903 by a joint German-British beer corporation, the red-brick Tsingtau Germania-Brauerei began its life as a microbrewery of sorts, producing two varieties of beer (Pilsener Light and Munich Dark) for the concession town, using natural mineral water from nearby Láo Shān. In 1914 the Japanese occupied Qīngdǎo and confiscated the plant, which, as far as the beer was concerned, wasn't such a bad thing: the rechristened Dai Nippon Brewery increased production and began distributing 'Tsingtao' throughout China. In 1949, after a few years under the Kuomintang, the communists finally got hold of the prized brewery, and over the next three decades (marked by xenophobia and a heavily regulated socialist economy) Tsingtao accounted for an astounding 98% of all of China's exports. Today the company continues to dominate China's beer export market and is partly owned by the beer colossus Anheuser-Busch InBev.

You can buy Tsingtao beer by the bag from streetside vendors, but pouring it requires skill. Of course, a visit to the original Tsingtao brewery should be in order too.

History

German forces wrested the port town from the Chinese in 1898 after the murder of two German missionaries, and Qīngdǎo was ceded to Germany for 99 years. In 1914 the Japanese moved into town after the successful joint Anglo-Japanese naval bombardment of the port. Japan's position in Qīngdǎo was strengthened by the Treaty of Versailles, and they held the city until 1922 when it was ceded back to the Kuomintang. The Japanese returned in 1938, after the start of the Sino-Japanese War, and occupied the town until defeated in 1945. Since then, Qīngdǎo's fortunes have risen. It is one of the largest ports in China and a major manufacturing centre (home to domestic and international brands).

Sights

Most sights are squeezed into the old town, though walkers will prefer hilly Bādàguān to the west, which is generally more picturesque and a better area to wander.

ST MICHAEL'S CATHOLIC CHURCH
Church

(天主教堂; Tiānzhǔ Jiàotáng; ☏ 8286 5960; 15 Zhejiang Lu; admission Y5; ⏱ 8am-5pm Mon-Sat, noon-5pm Sun) Completed in 1934, the twin-spired church, up a steep hill off Zhong-shan Lu, is a grand edifice with a cross on each spire. Put aside time to roam the area round here – a lattice of ancient hilly streets where old folk sit on wooden stools in decrepit doorways, playing cards and shooting the breeze.

PROTESTANT CHURCH
Church

(基督教堂; Jīdū Jiàotáng; 15 Jiangsu Lu; admission Y7; ⏱ 8.30am-5pm, weekend services) On a street notable for its German architecture, this church was designed by Curt Rothkegel and built in 1908. You can climb up to inspect the mechanism of its clock (Bockenem 1909). It is also well worth wandering along nearby Daxue Lu for a marvellous scenic view of old German Qīngdǎo.

Qīngdǎo

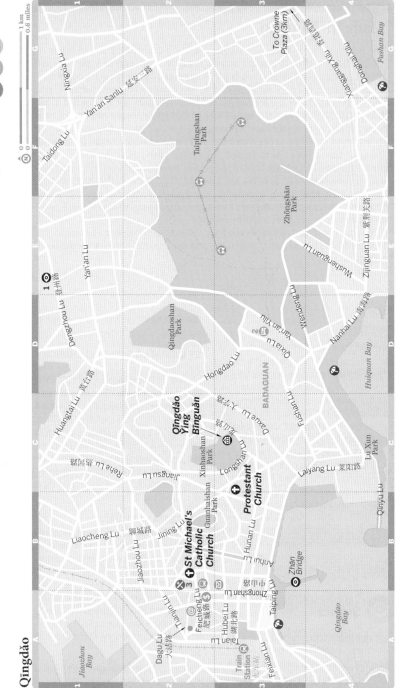

Qīngdǎo

⦿ Top Sights

Protestant Church...............................C3
Qīngdǎo Yíng Bīnguǎn.......................C3
St Michael's Catholic Church B2

⦿ Sights

1 Tsingtao Beer Museum.....................E1

⊟ Sleeping

2 Qīngdǎo International Youth
Hostel D3

⊗ Eating

3 Wángjīe Shāokǎo B2

QĪNGDǍO YÍNG BĪNGUǍN
Concession Building

(青岛迎宾馆; Qīngdǎo Yíng Hotel; admission summer/winter Y15/10; ◷8.30am-5pm) To the east of Xìnhàoshān Park remains one of Qīngdǎo's most interesting pieces of German architecture – the former German governor's residence and a replica of a German palace. It's now a museum.

HUĀSHÍ LÓU
Concession Building

(花石楼; Huāshí Bldg; 18 Huanghai Lu; admission Y6.50; ◷8am-5.30pm) Built in 1930, this castlelike villa was originally the home of a Russian aristocrat, and later the German governor's retreat for fishing and hunting. Clamber up two narrow stairwells to get to the top of the turret.

QĪNGDǍO BEACHES
Beaches

(青岛沙滩; Qīngdǎo Shātān) Qīngdǎo is famed for its six beaches, which are pleasant enough, but don't go expecting the French Riviera.

Qīngdǎo's largest beach is draped along the shore, way off in the east of town. **Shílǎorén Bathing Beach** (石老人; Donghai Donglu) is a 2.5km-long strip of clean sand and seawater-smoothed seashells, occasionally engulfed in banks of mist pouring in from offshore. The area around the beach has undergone heavy development in recent years, and has lost some of its charm. Take bus 304 from Zhàn Bridge (Zhàn Qiáo; Y2.50, 45 minutes) or hop in a taxi (Y20). If you take the bus, stop off at the Hái'er Lú (海尔) stop and head east.

Sleeping

The old town has excellent budget and midrange options. The central business district has no soul – top-end international chains are located there.

QĪNGDǍO INTERNATIONAL YOUTH HOSTEL
Hostel $$

(青岛国际青年旅舍; Qīngdǎo Guójì Qīngnián Lǚshè; ☎8286 5177; www.youthtaylor.com; 7a Qixia Lu; 栖霞路7号甲; dm from Y70, tw & tr Y240/320; ❄@☏) Despite the misleading name, this is more of a cosy midrange hotel than hostel. Set inside a renovated villa, the tidy rooms (and bathrooms) are massive. There's some yesteryear art deco charm, and the location in the plush Bādàguān neighbourhood is ideal for walks through old Qīngdǎo. There's a shared kitchen. Limited dorm rooms. English is limited.

CROWNE PLAZA
Hotel $$$

(青岛颐中皇冠假日酒店; Qīngdǎo Yízhōng Huángguān Jiàrì Jiǔdiàn; ☎8571 8888; www.icho telsgroup.com; 76 Xianggang Zhonglu; 香港中路76号; d/ste Y1200/2324, discounts of up to 40%; ❄@☏☲) At this glittering, 38-floor tower rising above Qīngdǎo's crackling commercial district, you won't be bumping into much old-town charm. Business travellers can content themselves instead with the warm honey-coloured hues of the splendid foyer, the fully equipped rooms, the indoor pool, professional standards of service and a choice of five restaurants – buffets at Café Asia (lunch/dinner Y128/168) are a favourite with expats. Wi-fi in the lobby.

Eating

The waterfront area is brimming with restaurants, from No 6 Bathing Beach almost all the way to No 1 Bathing Beach. Wander at will, or grab a copy of *Red Star* (try the hostels or foreign restaurants) for extensive listings.

BELLAGIO
Taiwanese $$

(鹿港小镇; Lùgǎng Xiǎozhèn; ☎8387 0877; 19 Aomen Sanlu; dishes from Y15; ◷10am-midnight)

Swish Bellagio serves up excellent Tai-wanese cuisine late into the night. It has two equally popular branches in Běijīng, so it must be doing something right! Try the three-cup chicken (三杯鸡; *sān bēijī*). Picture menu.

WÁNGJIĚ SHĀOKĂO   Street Food   **$**
(王姐烧烤; ☎8515 9228; cnr Zhongshan & Dexian Lu; lamb skewers Y2; ◷10am-6pm) Sooner or later, Qīngdǎo's legendary meat skewers will require your undivided attention, and where better to start than to join the throng outside this streetside stall. Squeeze your way to the front and order lamb (羊肉串; *yángròu chuàn*; Y2), pork (猪肉串; *zhūròu chuàn*; Y4) or cuttlefish (鱿鱼串; *yóuyú chuàn*; Y10).

ℹ Information

Book City (书城; Shū Chéng; 67 Xianggang Zhonglu; per hr Y2; ◷9am-midnight) On the 4th floor of Book City at the junction of Xianggang Zhonglu and Yan'erdao Lu; the evening entrance (after Book City closes) is north on Yan'erdao Lu.

Bank of China (中国银行; Zhōngguó Yínháng; 66 & 68 Zhongshan Lu; ◷8.30am-5pm Mon-Fri) On the corner of Feicheng Lu. Foreign-currency exchange. External ATM accepts foreign cards.

China Post (邮局; Zhōngguó Yóuzhèng; 51 Zhongshan Lu; ◷8.30am-6pm) Opposite the large Parkson building.

Public Security Bureau (PSB; 公安局; Gōng'ānjú; ◷9am-noon & 1.30-4.30pm Mon-Fri) East branch (☎8579 2555, ext 2860; 272 Ningxia Lu); Old Town (Zhongshan Lu) For the east branch, bus 301 goes from the train station and stops outside the terracotta-coloured building (stop 14).

ℹ Getting There & Away

Air

There are flights to most large cities in China, including daily services to Běijīng (Y710, 1¼ hours), Shànghǎi (Y740, 1¼ hours) and Hong Kong (Y1810, three hours). International flights include daily flights to Seoul (Y1400) and Tokyo (Y4300) along with four weekly flights to Osaka (Y2700). For flight information call **Liuting International Airport** (☎8471 5139).

Bus

Most out-of-town buses arrive at Qīngdǎo's **long-distance bus station** (长途汽车站; chángtú qìchēzhàn; ☎8371 3833; 2 Wenzhou Lu) in the Sìfāng district north of town. Daily buses include **Běijīng** Y230, nine hours, one daily (8pm), **Qūfù** Y127, five hours, four daily and **Tài'ān** Y116, six hours, four daily.

Train

All prices listed here are for hard seat unless otherwise noted; the express D trains only have 1st- and 2nd-class soft seats. Regular trains run to numerous destinations, including Tài'ān/Tài'shān (Y70, six hours). Express D trains include **Běijīng** Y116, six hours, six daily, **Shànghǎi** Y170, 10 hours, two daily (10.25am & 10.30am), **Tài'ān/Tài'shān** Y70, 3½ hours, one daily (10.30am).

St Michael's Church (p177) and sky-scraper, Qīngdǎo

ⓘ Getting Around

To/From the Airport

Qīngdǎo's Liuting International Airport (☎ 8471 5139) is 30km north of the city. Taxis to/from the airport cost Y50 to Y75. Buses (Y20) leave hourly from the Green Tea Inn (Zhongshan Lu) in the old town from 5.40am to 7.40pm, and half-hourly from the CAAC office in the business district from 6am to 9pm.

Public Transport

Bus 501 runs east from the train station, passing Zhōngshān Park and continuing along the entirety of Xianggang Lu in the central business district. Bus 26 from the train station runs a similar route, although it turns north on Nanjing Lu, just before the start of Xianggang Zhonglu.

Taxi

Flag fall is Y7 for the first 3km and then Y1.20 per kilometre thereafter, plus fuel tax (Y1).

Shànghǎi & the Yangzi Region

Shànghǎi truly feels like it was born yesterday. Don't come here for the Great Wall or creaking old palaces; Shànghǎi doesn't do those. Come instead for crisp modernity, youthful vigour, funky art deco architecture, gorgeous French Concession streetscapes, rocketing modern skyscrapers and charming 19th century *shíkùmén* ('stone gate') buildings. You could also simply come for its restaurants and bars – and never feel short-changed.

Shànghǎi lies at the end of the mighty and turbulent Yangzi River (Cháng Jiāng), which traces its source back to the Tibet-Qīnghǎi plateau in the high-altitude west of China. Within easy reach of Shànghǎi are the ancient Yangzi Region canal towns that dot the lushly watered landscape. Hángzhōu's fabulous West Lake is a speedy train trip away, but many travellers will want to explore Huángshān (the fabled Yellow Mountains), flee the heat to Mògānshān, jump on a boat to the holy Buddhist island of Pǔtuóshān or chart a passage through the magnificent Three Gorges.

Historic town, Shànghǎi

Women practising taichi with fans, Shànghǎi

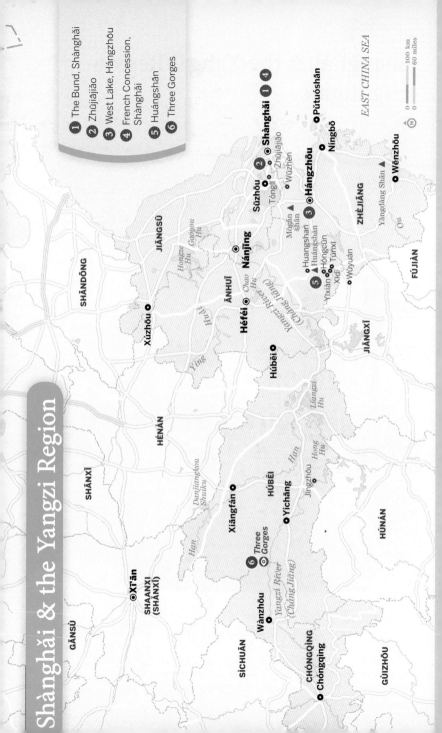

Shànghǎi & the Yangzi Region

1 The Bund, Shànghǎi
2 Zhūjiājiǎo
3 West Lake, Hángzhōu
4 French Concession, Shànghǎi
5 Huángshān
6 Three Gorges

EAST CHINA SEA

0   100 km
0   60 miles

GĀNSÙ

SHAANXI (SHǍNXĪ)

Xī'ān

SHǍNXĪ

HÉNÁN

SHĀNDŌNG

Xúzhōu

JIĀNGSŪ

Hongze Hu

Gaoyou Hu

Huai

Ying

Nánjīng

ÁNHUĪ

Chao Hu

Héféi

Hányǔ

Danjiangkou Shuiku

Han

Xiāngfán

HÚBĚI

Yichāng

6 Three Gorges

Wànzhōu

Yangzi River (Cháng Jiāng)

SÌCHUĀN

CHÓNGQÌNG

Chóngqìng

GUÌZHŌU

HÚNÁN

Jingzhōu

Hong Hu

Han

Liangzi Hu

HÚBĚI

Yangzi River (Cháng Jiāng)

Mògàn Shān

Sūzhōu

Tónglǐ

Wūzhèn

Zhūjiājiǎo

Shànghǎi 1 4

2 Zhūjiājiǎo

Hángzhōu 3

ZHÈJIĀNG

Huángshān
Huángshān
5 Hóngcūn
Yīxiàn Túnxī
Wūyuán

JIĀNGXĪ

Yàndàng Shān

Wēnzhōu

Ōu

FÚJIÀN

Níngbō

Pǔtuóshān

N

Shànghǎi & the Yangzi Region Highlights

1
The Bund

Mainland China's most iconic foreign concession-era architectural backdrop and streetscape is Shànghǎi's supreme standout sight. From neoclassical bombast to art deco elegance, the Bund is a sweeping chronicle built in brick and wreathed in nostalgia for a vanished age.

Need to Know

LOCATION West bank of Huángpǔ River **BEST TIME** Sunset; night **BEST PHOTO OP** The promenade towards Pǔdōng **BEST FOR DRINKS** New Heights **For more, see p212 and Map p195.**

The Bund Don't Miss List

HAN YUQI, 47, ART DIRECTOR, IMAGETUNNEL

1 HISTORIC ALLURE

When I was small, my dad would take me to the Bund. I really wanted to ride the trams with 'plaits' (electric cables) – they are sadly no more. The old vessels that pulled in here and the winged statue of the Goddess of Peace have likewise disappeared. I love the **Customs Building**, the **HSBC Bank building**, the **Peace Hotel** and the overlooked **Meteorological Signal Tower**: it all resembles an old film set!

2 NOSTALGIA

The Bund's historical refrain makes me think of Victor Sassoon. But what does the **Peace Hotel** – back then known as Sassoon House and the tallest building on the Bund, courtesy of Shànghǎi's most successful adventurer – mean today? Several years ago I went to listen to the Peace Hotel Old Jazz Band and it came to me: Shànghǎi is a modern legend.

3 YUANMINGYUAN LU

When admiring the 33 buildings along the bank of the Huángpǔ River, turn into Yuanmingyuan Lu and you'll be even more blown away. You may not know each building's story, you'll be moved by their sheer style and sense of historical drama. I call this street the 'back garden of the Bund'!

4 ROMANCE

Starting at **Waibaidu Bridge**, the 'Bund Sweetheart's Wall' is actually a concrete flood barrier. From the 1970s it became Shànghǎi's most romantic dating spot because of its scenic charms and because Shànghǎi was so densely packed it was one of the few places where people could meet. On China's 'Valentine's Day' (seventh day of the seventh month) this year I passed by Waibaidu Bridge and it was simply a sea of couples among all the lights.

5 NINGBO LU

If you're feeling peckish, I recommend heading to Ningbo Lu – just a few minutes walk from the Bund – for restaurants offering tasty and good-value food. If the weather's good, take a seat outside at twilight and take in its sensations.

Exploring Zhūjiājiǎo

The charming canal-town tempo of Zhūjiājiǎo (p220) within Shànghǎi municipality is an ideal counterpoint to the modernity and urban zeal of metropolitan Shànghǎi. Track down an ancient bridge or two, delve into Zhūjiājiǎo's delightful alleyways and admire some old-town architecture, or spend the night at one of the growing crop of accommodation options to capture the water town at night.

Savouring the French Concession

The brash Pǔdōng skyline may be Shànghǎi's most iconic countenance, but it has little charm. That is kept for the French Concession (p201), Shànghǎi's romantic, civilised, chic, cheeky, fine-looking quarter. Shànghǎi isn't strong on bohemians, but the ones it has all live in the French Concession. From art deco apartment blocks to modish restaurants, funky bars, snappy little boutiques and leafy back lanes, the French Concession is the place to be.

Wandering around West Lake ③

China's archetypal city lake, Hángzhōu's West Lake (p230) is surrounded on all sides by a tranquilising tableau of pagodas, lilting willows, choice temple architecture and some really excellent hotel options. Few urban panoramas in China are so seductively well kept and the lake truly comes into its own at night when couples wander arm-in-arm round the shore or perch themselves on lakeside benches.

⑤ Hiking up Huángshān

When China's most heavenly mountain rises up through a spectral sea of mist and fog it may make other top sights on your itinerary seem quite mundane by comparison. Huángshān (p242) may not be one of China's holy mountains, but that is perhaps beside the point, because the views – in the right weather conditions – are supernaturally sublime. If you only have time for one mountain in China, make it this one.

⑥ Drifting through the Three Gorges

Apocryphally the work of the Great Yu – that mythical tamer of floods – the Three Gorges (p247) are the most dramatic scenic wonders along China's longest river, the Yangzi. A hydrofoil may do the trick if you want the speedy highlights version, otherwise there's a choice of vessels if you want to disengage from road, rail or plane travel for three or four days and fully savour the scenery.

Shànghǎi & the Yangzi Region's Best...

Escapes

○ **Mògānshān** (p235) Make a break for the Zhèjiāng hills.

○ **Huángshān** (p242) Count the steps up to the top of Heavenly Capital Peak.

○ **Pǔtuóshān** (p238) Bounce over the waves to the island home of Guanyin.

○ **Hui Villages** (p244) Trek between the villages of south Ānhuī province.

○ **Wùyuán** (p247) Immerse yourself in the magic of the Jiāngxī countryside.

○ **Three Gorges Cruise** (p247) China's most famous river journey.

Wining & Dining

○ **Fu 1039** (p212) Spot-on Shànghǎi cuisine in a charming old villa setting.

○ **Glamour Bar** (p212) For an elegant perspective on the Bund, and excellent cocktails.

○ **Vue** (p221) Sumptuous views from a North Bund vantage point.

○ **Moganshan Lodge** (p237) Fabulous old Mógānshān villa, great food and a knowledgeable British proprietor.

Beds

○ **Park Hyatt** (p210) Seriously snazzy, and not just the views.

○ **Astor House Hotel** (p206) Grand old perch on the wrong side of Waibaidu Bridge.

○ **Moganshan House 23** (p236) Exquisitely-presented Mògānshān villa accommodation.

○ **West Well** (p220) Lovely old courtyard accommodation in Shànghǎi's top canal town.

○ **Urbn** (p209) Carbon-neutral, nifty and stylish.

Need to Know

Buildings

◦ **Shànghǎi World Financial Center** (p203) Pǔdōng colossus with three observation decks.

◦ **Mògānshān** (p235) Crumbling old European hill-resort architecture.

◦ **French Concession, Shànghǎi** (p201) The city's best villa architecture, art deco and *shíkùmén* buildings.

◦ **Tónglǐ** (p226) Age-old canal town architecture.

◦ **Sūzhōu Museum** (p221) Jiāngnán garden architecture brought bang up to date.

◦ **Hóngcūn & Xīdì** (p244) Magnificent examples of Hui-style village architecture.

ADVANCE PLANNING

◦ **One Month Before** Get your accommodation sorted and your hotel rooms booked.

◦ **One Week Before** Book your onward train or air tickets out of Shànghǎi and through the region via your hotel or a local travel agent.

RESOURCES

◦ **City Weekend** (www.cityweekend.com.cn) Listings website.

◦ **Shanghaiist** (www.shanghaiist.com) Local entertainment and news blog.

◦ **SmartShanghai** (www.smartshanghai.com) For food, fun and frolicking; good entertainment coverage.

◦ **Shanghai Daily** (www.shanghaidaily.com) (Censored) coverage of local news.

◦ **CTrip** (www.english.ctrip.com) Discounted hotels and ticketing; recommended.

GETTING AROUND

◦ **Metro** From Pǔdōng International Airport into Shànghǎi; extensive, efficient and fast system reaching all major sights.

◦ **Bus** Into Shànghǎi from Pǔdōng International Airport; extensive urban network, nonuser-friendly for foreign travellers.

◦ **Long-distance Bus** For reaching regional destinations.

◦ **Maglev** Links Pǔdōng International Airport with the Shànghǎi metro system.

◦ **Train** Efficient rail system out of Shànghǎi to the region and beyond.

◦ **Air** For regional and more long-distance flights.

◦ **Boat** For journeys to Pǔtuóshān and along the Three Gorges.

BE FOREWARNED

◦ **Scams** Guard against English-speaking girls on East Nanjing Rd and elsewhere press-ganging you to extortionate tea ceremonies.

◦ **Taxi Sharks** At Pǔdōng International Airport.

◦ **Language** English rarely used outside of tourist hotels and restaurants.

◦ **Museums** Some shut on Monday.

Left: Boats on Wu Gorge (p249), Three Gorges; **Above:** View over Huángshān

Shànghǎi & the Yangzi Region Itineraries

Five days is enough for Hángzhōu and the standout canal towns of Jiāngsū; in a week the mountain panoramas of Zhèjiāng and Ānhuī, including Huángshān and the sacred island of Pǔtuóshān, are within reach.

5 DAYS

SHÀNGHǍI TO HÁNGZHŌU
Water Towns & West Lake

After you have seen the sights in swinging **(1) Shànghǎi**, jump on a bus to the nearby picturesque canal town of **(2) Zhūjiājiǎo** for a day trip. Wander through the village's charming streets, popping into temples and churches, crossing humpbacked bridges that vault the waters and snacking as you go. Spend the night in Zhūjiājiǎo and continue by bus to the charming water town of **(3) Tónglǐ** in Jiāngsū province, or spend the night in Tónglǐ. Explore the old town, pop into Tónglǐ's Chinese Sex Culture Museum, take a boat tour along the canal, admire the Tuìsī Garden and the Ming-dynasty Gēnglè Táng. From Tónglǐ, it's a short bus journey

to **(4) Sūzhōu** for a day's exploration of the top sights, including the eye-catching Sūzhōu Museum, the Garden of the Master of the Nets, the Humble Administrator's Garden, the town's canal views and temple vistas. **(5) Hángzhōu** is another short hop away by bus and constitutes a delightful terminus, with several days of unhurried sightseeing opportunities around the good-looking West Lake and beyond, and the option to return to Shànghǎi by either bus or train.

SHÀNGHǍI TO HUÁNGSHĀN
Mounting Mountains

1 WEEK

From **(1) Shànghǎi**, take the fast boat to **(2) Pǔtuóshān** (Pǔtuó Mountain) to spend a night on China's easternmost Buddhist mountain and insular home of the bodhisattva Guanyin, the Goddess of Mercy. Explore the island's many shrines to the goddess and climb up Foding Mountain from the Fǎyǔ Temple near the centre of the island. Returning to Shànghǎi, head down by bus or train to **(3) Hángzhōu** for several days' sightseeing around stunning West Lake. If the weather is hot, set off from Hángzhōu to spend a night on delightfully cool **(4) Mògānshān**, a mountainous retreat decorated with old European villa architecture and shaded walks. Returning to Hángzhōu, jump on a bus to **(5) Túnxī** en route to the stunning mountain panoramas of **(6) Huángshān**, China's fabled mountain of mists and photogenic pine trees. Aim to spend a night on the mountain so you can catch the famous sunrise from the peak and descend the next morning. After clambering down Huángshān, return to terra firma to explore the surrounding **(6) Hui villages** around Túnxī, including Hóngcūn and Xidì, where you can also spend the night before returning to Shànghǎi from Túnxī.

Bar in French Concession, Shànghǎi
PHOTOGRAPHER: GREG ELMS/LONELY PLANET IMAGES ©

Discover Shànghǎi & the Yangzi Region

At a Glance

- **Shànghǎi** (p194) Paris of the East, New York of China.

- **Sūzhōu** (p221) Ancient Jiāngsū canal town and silk capital.

- **Hángzhōu** (p229) Home of the superlative West Lake.

- **Huángshān** (p242) China's most idyllic mountain panoramas.

- **Yangzi River Cruise** (p247) The magnificent Three Gorges.

Yùyuán bazaar (p201), Old Town, Shànghǎi
PHOTOGRAPHER: GREG ELMS/LONELY PLANET IMAGES ©

SHÀNGHǍI

♪021 / POP 15 MILLION

Shànghǎi is a city of action, not ideas. You won't spot many Buddhist monks contemplating the dharma, or wild-haired poets handing out flyers, but skyscrapers will form before your eyes. Shànghǎi folk chat about fashion and food, but what they really talk about is money. One of the country's most massive, rich and vibrant cities, Shànghǎi is heading places the rest of China can only dream about. But Shànghǎi is also about its past, most recognisably in its standout foreign concession architecture and European-style streets.

As the gateway to the Yangzi River (Cháng Jiāng), Shànghǎi (the name means 'by the sea') has long been an ideal trading port. However, although it supported as many as 50,000 residents by the late 17th century, it wasn't until after the British opened their concession here in 1842 that modern Shànghǎi – in some ways the most influential city in 20th-century China – really came into being.

The British presence in Shànghǎi was soon followed by the French and Americans, and by 1853 Shànghǎi had overtaken all other Chinese ports. Built on the trade of opium, silk and tea, the city also lured the world's great houses of finance, which erected grand palaces of plenty. Shànghǎi also became a byword for exploitation and vice; its countless opium dens, gambling joints and brothels managed by gangs were at the heart of Shànghǎi life. Guarding it all were the US, French and Italian marines, British Tommies and Japanese bluejackets.

After Chiang Kaishek's coup against the communists in 1927, the Kuomintang cooperated with the foreign police and the Shànghǎi gangs, and with Chinese and foreign factory owners, to suppress labour unrest. Exploited in workhouse conditions, crippled by hunger and poverty, sold into slavery, excluded from the high life and the parks created by the foreigners, the poor of Shànghǎi had a voracious appetite for radical opinion. The Chinese Communist Party (CCP) was formed here in 1921 and, after numerous setbacks, 'liberated' the city in 1949. Later Shànghǎi was the power base of the infamous Gang of Four during the Cultural Revolution.

Shànghǎi's burgeoning economy, its leadership and its intrinsic self-confidence have put it miles ahead of other cities in China.

 Sights

Shànghǎi municipality covers a huge area, but the city proper is more modest. Broadly, central Shànghǎi is divided into two areas: Pǔxī (west of the Huángpǔ River) and Pǔdōng (east of the Huángpǔ River). The historical attractions belong to Pǔxī, where Shànghǎi's personality is also found: the Bund (officially called East Zhongshan No 1 Rd) and the former foreign concessions, the principal shopping districts, and Shànghǎi's trendiest clusters of bars, restaurants and nightclubs. Pǔdōng is a more recent invention and is the location of the financial district and the famous Shànghǎi skyline. Remember that Shànghǎi is developing at a breakneck pace and there is consequently an even higher rate of change here than in most other major world cities.

The last entrance to many Shànghǎi museums is one hour before closing.

The Bund　　外滩

The area around the Bund is the tourist centre of Shànghǎi and is the city's most famous mile.

EAST NANJING ROAD　　Architecture
Once known as Nanking Rd, East Nanjing Rd (南京东路; Map p198) was where the

Shànghǎi In...

ONE DAY

Rise with the sun for early-morning riverside scenes on the **Bund** as the vast city stirs from its slumber. Then stroll down East Nanjing Rd to **People's Square** and either the **Shànghǎi Museum** or the **Urban Planning Exhibition Hall**. After a dumpling lunch on Huanghe Rd food street, hop on the metro at People's Square to shuttle east to Pǔdōng. Explore the fun and interactive **Shànghǎi History Museum** or contemplate the Bund from the breezy Riverside Promenade, then take a high-speed lift to the world's highest observation deck, in the **World Financial Center**, to put Shànghǎi in perspective. Stomach rumbling? Time for dinner in the French Concession, followed by a nightcap on the Bund if you want to go full circle.

TWO DAYS

Pre-empt the crowds with an early start at the Old Town's **Yùyuán Gardens** before poking around for souvenirs on Old St and wandering the alleyways. Make your next stop **Xīntiāndì** for lunch and a visit to the **Shíkùmén Open House Museum**. Taxi it to **Tiánzǐfáng** for the afternoon, before another French Concession dinner. Caught a second wind? Catch the acrobats, hit the clubs or unwind with a traditional Chinese massage.

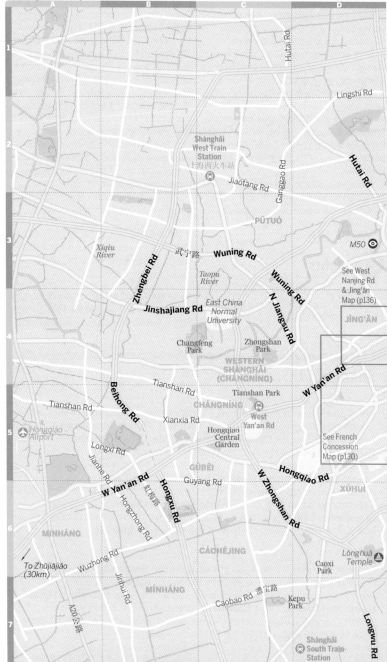

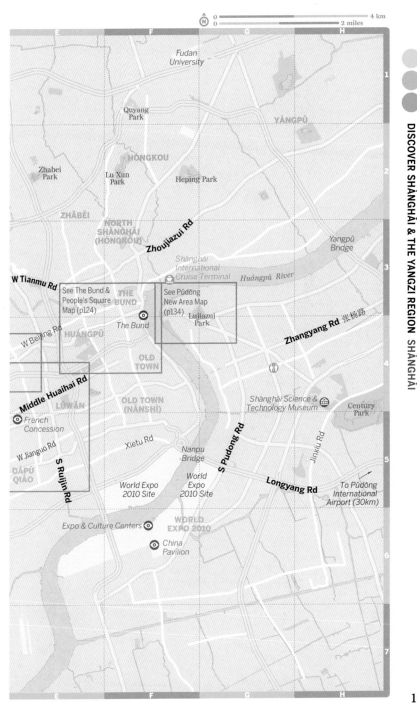

0 — 4 km
0 — 2 miles

Fudan University

Quyang Park

YÁNGPǓ

HÓNGKŌU

Zhabei Park

Lu Xun Park

Heping Park

ZHÁBĚI

NORTH SHÀNGHǍI (HÓNGKŌU)

Zhoujiazui Rd

Yangpǔ Bridge

W Tianmu Rd

Shànghǎi International Cruise Terminal

Huángpǔ River

See The Bund & People's Square Map (p124)

THE BUND

See Pǔdōng New Area Map (p134)

The Bund

Lùjiāzuǐ Park

W Beijing Rd

HUÁNGPǓ

Zhangyang Rd 张杨路

OLD TOWN

OLD TOWN (NÁNSHÌ)

LÚWĀN

Shànghǎi Science & Technology Museum

Century Park

French Concession

S Pudong Rd

Jinxiu Rd

W Jianguo Rd

Xietu Rd

Nanpu Bridge

Longyang Rd

To Pǔdōng International Airport (30km)

DǍPǓ QIÁO

S Ruijin Rd

World Expo 2010 Site

World Expo 2010 Site

Expo & Culture Centers

WORLD EXPO 2010

China Pavilion

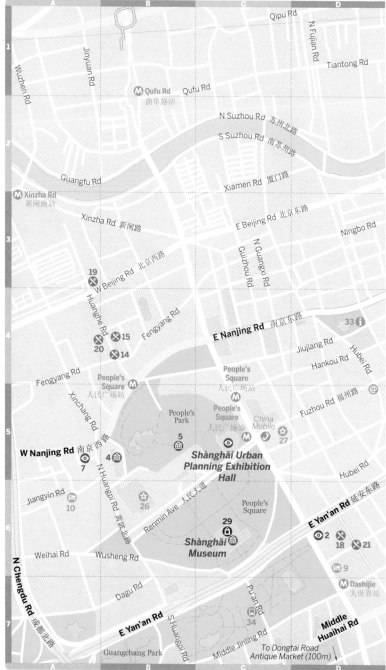

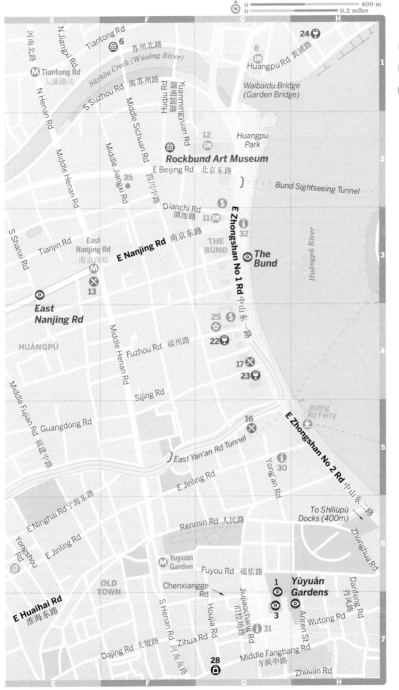

N 0 _____ 400 m
  0 _____ 0.2 miles

河南北路 N Henan Rd

N Jiangxi Rd

Tiantong Rd

苏州北路
N Suzhou Rd

6

苏州河 Sūzhōu Creek (Wúsōng River)

S Suzhou Rd 南苏州路

M Tiantong Rd
天潼路站

Middle Sichuan Rd

Yuanmingyuan Rd 圆明园路

Hubin Rd 湖滨路

24

8

Huangpu Rd 黄浦路

Waibaidu Bridge
(Garden Bridge)

N Henan Rd

Middle Jiangxi Rd

35

12

Huangpu
Park

Rockbund Art Museum

E Beijing Rd 北京东路

四川中路

S Shanxi Rd

Tianjin Rd

East
Nanjing Rd
南京路站

M

East
Nanjing Rd

13

Dianchi Rd
滇池路

11

E Zhongshan No 1 Rd 中山东一路

THE
BUND

The
Bund

32

Bund Sightseeing Tunnel

Huángpǔ River

HUÁNGPǓ

Middle Henan Rd

Fuzhou Rd 福州路

25

22

Middle Fujian Rd

Guangdong Rd

Sijing Rd

17

23

Jinling
Rd Ferry

E Zhongshan No 2 Rd 中山东二路

16

East Yan'an Rd Tunnel

E Jinling Rd

30

Yong'an Rd

To Shíliùpù
Docks (400m)

Zhonghua Rd

Yongshou
Rd

E Ninghai Rd 宁海东路

E Jinling Rd

Renmin Rd 人民路

M Yuyuan
Garden

Fuyou Rd 福佑路

1

Yùyuán
Gardens

Danfeng Rd 丹凤路

OLD
TOWN

Chenxiangge
Rd

S Henan Rd

Houjia Rd

Jiujiaochang Rd 旧校场路

3

31

Anren St

Wutong Rd

E Huaihai Rd
淮海东路

Dajing Rd 大境路

Zihua Rd

28

Middle Fangbang Rd
方浜中路

Zhoujin Rd

199

The Bund & People's Square

◎ Top Sights
East Nanjing Rd.................................E3
Rockbund Art Museum.....................F2
Shànghǎi Museum.............................C6
Shànghǎi Urban Planning
　Exhibition Hall..............................C5
The Bund..G3
Yùyuán Gardens & Bazaar..................H7

◎ Sights
1 Entrance to Yùyuán Gardens &
　Bazaar G6
2 Great World D6
3 Húxīntíng Teahouse G7
4 Shànghǎi Art Museum B5
5 Shànghǎi Museum of
　Contemporary Art.......................B5
6 Shànghǎi Post Museum................F1
7 Tomorrow Square A5

◎ Sleeping
8 Astor House Hotel G1
9 Marvel Hotel D6
10 Mingtown Etour Youth Hostel..............A6
11 Peace Hotel G3
12 Peninsula G2

◎ Eating
13 Hóngyī Plaza..................................E3
14 Huanghe Rd Food Street B4
15 Jiājiā Soup Dumplings.................B4
16 Lost Heaven...................................G5
17 M on the Bund G4

18 Wǔ Fāng Zhāi D6
19 Xiǎo Nán Guó A3
20 Yang's Fry Dumplings...................A4
21 Yunnan Rd Food Street D6

◎ Drinking
22 Captain's Bar G4
　Glamour Bar..........................(see 17)
23 New Heights G4
24 Vue H1

◎ Entertainment
25 House of Blues & Jazz...................G4
26 Shànghǎi Grand Theatre...............B6
27 Yifū Theatre....................................C5

◎ Shopping
28 Old Street G7
29 Shànghǎi Museum Shop C6
　Sūzhōu Cobblers.....................(see 22)

Information
30 Huángpǔ Tourist Centre................G5
31 Tourist Information & Service
　Centre..G7
32 Tourist Information & Service
　Centre..G3
33 Tourist Information & Service
　Centre..D4

Transport
34 Pu'an Rd Bus Station C7
35 Train Ticket Office.........................F2

first department stores in China were opened in the 1920s, and where the modern era – with its new products and the promise of a radically different lifestyle – was ushered in. Guard against English-speaking Chinese women (or students) shanghaiing you towards extortionate 'tea ceremonies'.

ROCKBUND ART MUSEUM
Art Museum

(上海外滩美术馆; **Shànghǎi Wàitān Měishùguǎn; Map p198;** www.rockbundartmuseum.org; 20 Huqiu Rd; 虎丘路20号; adult Y15; ⏰10am-6pm Tue-Sun; Ⓜ East Nanjing Rd) Housed in the former Royal Asiatic Society building (1932) and the adjacent former National Industrial Bank, this private museum behind the Bund focuses on contempo-

rary art, with rotating temporary exhibits throughout the year.

People's Square 人民广场

Once the site of the Shànghǎi Racecourse, People's Sq is the modern city's nerve centre. Overshadowed by the dramatic form of **Tomorrow Square** (明天广场; Míngtiān Guǎngchǎng), the open space is peppered with museums, performing-arts venues and leafy People's Park.

SHÀNGHǍI ART MUSEUM
Art Museum

(上海美术馆; **Shànghǎi Měishùguǎn; Map p198;** www.sh-artmuseum.org.cn; 325 West Nanjing Rd; 南京西路325号; adult Y20; ⏰9am-5pm, last entry 4pm; Ⓜ People's Sq) The exhibits of modern Chinese art (often 20th century) are hit-and-miss, but the building (the former Shànghǎi Racecourse Club) and its period details are simply gorgeous. English captions are sporadic.

GREAT WORLD Entertainment
(大世界; Dà Shìjiè; Map p198; Middle Xizang Rd; 西藏中路; Ⓜ Dashijie) Shànghǎi's most famous house of ill repute in the 1930s, Great World was rehabilitated by the Communists and then closed for renovations for the past decade. It should be open by the time you read this.

Old Town 南市

Known to locals as Nán Shì (Southern City), the Old Town is the most traditionally Chinese part of Shànghǎi. Its circular layout still reflects the footprint of its 16th-century walls, erected to keep marauding Japanese pirates at bay.

YÙYUÁN GARDENS & BAZAAR
Gardens, Bazaar
(豫园、豫园商城; Yùyuán & Yùyuán Shāngchéng; Map p198) With its shaded alcoves, glittering pools churning with carp, pavilions, pines sprouting wistfully from rockeries, and roving packs of Japanese tourists, the **gardens** (豫园; Yùyuán; admission Y30; ⏱ 8.30am-5.30pm, last entry 5pm; Ⓜ Yuyuan Garden) is one of

Shànghǎi's premier sights – but overpoweringly crowded at weekends.

The Pan family, rich Ming-dynasty officials, founded the gardens, which took 18 years (1559–77) to be nurtured into existence before bombardment during the Opium War in 1842. Restored, they are a fine example of Ming garden design.

Next to the garden entrance is the **Húxīntíng Teahouse** (湖心亭; Húxīntíng; Map p198; ⏱ 8.30am-9.30pm), once part of the gardens and now one of the most famous teahouses in China.

The adjacent **bazaar** may be tacky, but it's good for a browse if you can handle the push and pull of the crowds and vendors. Just outside the bazaar is **Old Street** (老街; Lǎo Jiē; Map p198), known more prosaically as Middle Fangbang Rd, a busy street lined with curio shops and teahouses.

French Concession 法租界

Once home to the bulk of Shànghǎi's adventurers, revolutionaries, gangsters, prostitutes and writers, the French Concession is the most graceful part of the city.

TIÁNZĬFÁNG Art Galleries, Shops
(田子坊; Map p201; Lane 210, Taikang Rd; 泰康路210弄; Ⓜ Dapuqiao) Xīntiāndì and Tiánzǐfáng are based on a similar

The Bund

Symbolic of colonial Shànghǎi, the Bund (Wàitān; Map p199) was the city's Wall St, a place of feverish trading and fortunes made and lost. Originally a towpath for dragging barges of rice, the Bund (an Anglo-Indian term for the embankment of a muddy waterfront) was once situated only a few feet from the Huángpǔ River before the road was widened and a flood barrier was built (the river now lies above the level of Nanjing Rd due to subsidence). In 2009 most traffic was diverted underground with the aim of making the area more pedestrian-friendly.

Today the Bund has emerged as a designer retail and restaurant zone, and the city's most exclusive boutiques, restaurants and hotels see the Bund as the only place to be. The optimum activity here is to simply stroll, contrasting the bones of the past with the futuristic geometry of Pǔdōng's skyline. Evening visits are rewarded by electric views of Pǔdōng and the illuminated grandeur of the Bund.

idea – an entertainment complex housed within a warren of traditional *lòngtáng* (alleyways) – but when it comes to genuine charm and vibrancy, Tiánzǐfáng is the one that delivers. Also known as Taikang Lu (泰康路) or Taikang Rd, this community of design studios, wi-fi cafes and boutiques is the perfect antidote to Shànghǎi's oversized malls and intimidating sky-scrapers.

XĪNTIĀNDÌ
Shops

(新天地; Map p201; www.xintiandi.com; cnr Taicang & Madang Rds; 太仓路与马当路路口; M South Huangpi Rd, Xintiandi) An upmarket retail and dining complex consisting of largely rebuilt *shíkùmén* houses (low-rise tenement buildings built in the early 1900s), this was the first development in the city to prove that historic architecture does, in fact, have economic value.

The small **Shíkùmén Open House Museum** (屋里厢石库门民居陈列馆; Wūlǐxiāng Shíkùmén Mínjū Chénlièguǎn; Map p201; admission Y20; ⏰10.30am-10.30pm Sun-Thu, 11am-11pm Fri & Sat) depicts traditional life in a 10-room Shànghǎi *shíkùmén*.

FREE SITE OF THE 1ST NATIONAL CONGRESS OF THE CCP
Communist Museum

(中共一大会址纪念馆; Zhōnggòng Yīdà Huìzhǐ; Map p201; 76 Xingye Rd; 兴业路76号; ⏰9am-5pm; M South Huangpi Rd, Xintiandi) The CCP was founded in July 1921 in this French Concession *shíkùmén* building in one fell swoop, converting an unassuming block into one of Chinese communism's holiest shrines.

West Nanjing Road & Jìng'ān
南京西路、静安

Lined with sharp top-end shopping malls, clusters of foreign offices and a dense crop of embassies and consulates, West Nanjing Rd is where Shànghǎi's streets are paved with gold, or at least Prada and Gucci.

JADE BUDDHA TEMPLE
Buddhist Temple

(玉佛寺; Yùfó Sì; Map p210; 170 Anyuan Rd; 安远路170号; adult Y20; ⏰8am-4.30pm; M Changshou Rd) One of Shànghǎi's few active Buddhist monasteries, this temple was built between 1911 and 1918. The centrepiece is the 1.9m-high pale-green **Jade Buddha** (Yùfó), seated upstairs in his own hall. Visitors are not able to approach the statue, but can admire it from a distance. An additional charge of Y10 is levied to see the statue (no photographs).

FREE M50
Art Galleries

(创意产业集聚区; M50 M Wǔshí Chuàngyì Chǎnyè Jíjùqū; Map p194; 50 Mogan-shan Rd; 莫干山路50号; ⏰10am-6pm Tue-Sun; taxi or M Shanghai Railway Station) Běijīng may dominate the art scene in China, but Shànghǎi has its own

Japanese cafe, French Concession
PHOTOGRAPHER: GREG ELMS/LONELY PLANET IMAGES ©

Shànghǎi Museum

The must-see **Shànghǎi Museum** (上海博物馆; Shànghǎi Bówùguǎn; Map p204; www.shanghaimuseum.net; 201 Renmin Ave – entrance East Yan'an Rd; 人民大道201号; admission free; ☻9am-5pm; M People's Sq) guides you through the craft of millennia while simultaneously escorting you through the pages of Chinese history. Expect to spend half, if not most of, a day here.

Designed to resemble the shape of an ancient Chinese *dǐng* vessel, the building is home to one of the most impressive collections in China. Take your pick from the archaic green patinas of the **Ancient Chinese Bronzes Gallery** through to the silent solemnity of the **Ancient Chinese Sculpture Gallery**; from the exquisite beauty of the ceramics in the **Zande Lou Gallery** to the measured and timeless flourishes captured in the **Chinese Calligraphy Gallery**. Chinese painting, seals, jade, Ming and Qing furniture, coins and ethnic costumes are also on offer in this museum, intelligently displayed in well-lit galleries.

Photography is allowed in some galleries. The audio guide (available in eight languages) is well worth the Y40 (deposit Y400 or passport). The excellent **museum shop** sells postcards, a rich array of books and faithful replicas of the museum's ceramics and other pieces.

thriving gallery subculture, centred on this complex of industrial buildings down dusty Moganshan Rd in the north of town.

Pǔdōng New Area 浦东新区

SHÀNGHǍI WORLD FINANCIAL CENTER
Skyscraper

(SWFC; 上海环球金融中心; Shànghǎi Huánqiú Jīnróng Zhōngxīn; Map p208; www.swfc-observatory.com; 100 Century Ave; 世纪大道100号; observation deck 94th/97th/100th fl, adult Y100/110/150; ☻8am-midnight; M Lujiazui) Opening its doors in late August 2008, the SWFC boasts the world's highest observation deck (there are three decks in total, on the 94th, 97th and 100th floors) and is the world's 2nd-highest hotel above ground level (at time of press). Even the dazzling Jīnmào Tower is now in the shade. Take the ear-popping lift up to the top or visit the restaurant-bar **100 Century Avenue** (Map p208; 91st fl, access via the Park Hyatt; coffee/weekday lunch Y55/180; ☻11am-10.30pm; 🛜) to truly put your head in the clouds.

JĪNMÀO TOWER
Skyscraper

(金茂大厦; Jīnmào Dàshà; Map p208; 88 Century Ave; 世纪大道88号; adult Y88; ☻8.30am-9.30pm; M Lujiazui) The crystalline Jīnmào Tower has an observation deck on the 88th floor, but consider sinking a drink in the **Cloud 9 Bar** on the 87th floor and time your visit for dusk for both day and night views.

SHÀNGHǍI HISTORY MUSEUM
History Museum

(上海城市历史发展陈列馆; Shànghǎi Chéngshì Lìshǐ Fāzhǎn Chénlièguǎn; Map p208; Oriental Pearl Tower basement; adult Y35, audio tour Y30; ☻8am-9.30pm; M Lujiazui) This modern museum, in the basement of the Oriental Pearl Tower, has fun multimedia presentations and imaginative displays that recreate the history of Shànghǎi, with an emphasis on the pre-1949 era. Ticket prices go up each year almost as fast as the surrounding high rises.

ORIENTAL PEARL TOWER
Skyscraper

(东方明珠电视塔; Dōngfāng Míngzhū Diànshì Tǎ; Map p208; 1 Century Ave; 世纪大道1号; tickets Y100-150; ☻8am-10pm; M Lujiazui) Best viewed when it's illuminated at night, this poured-concrete shocker of a tripod

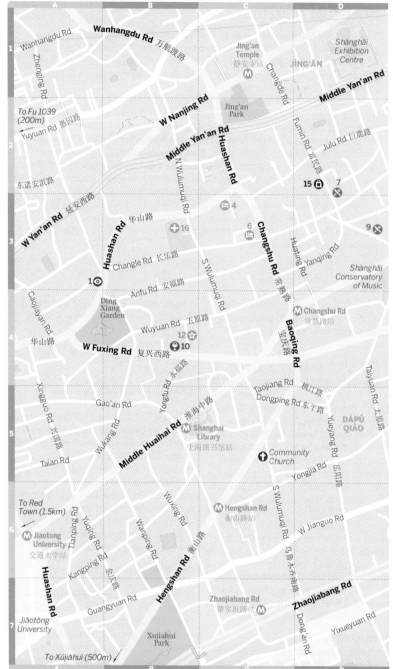

DISCOVER SHÀNGHǍI & THE YÁNGZǏ REGION SHÀNGHǍI

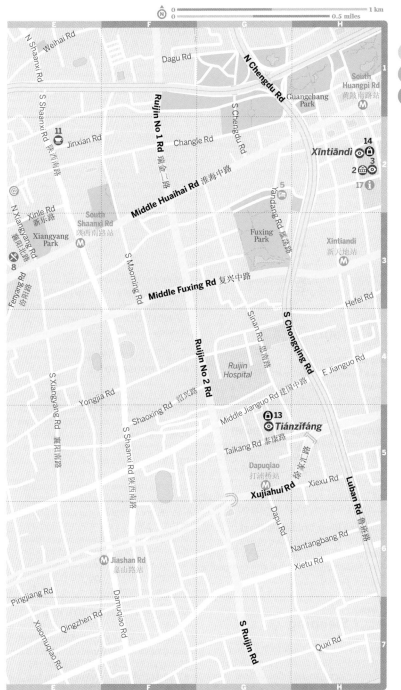

N Weihai Rd

N Shaanxi Rd

Dagu Rd

N Chengdu Rd

Guangchang Park

South Huangpi Rd 黄陂南路站

S Shaanxi Rd 陕西南路

Ruijin No 1 Rd 瑞金一路

Jinxian Rd

11

Changle Rd

S Chengdu Rd

Xīntiāndì

14

3

2

17

Middle Huaihai Rd 淮海中路

Xinle Rd 新乐路

N Xiangyang Rd 襄阳北路

Xiangyang Park

South Shaanxi Rd 陕西南路站

Yandang Rd 雁荡路

5

Fuxing Park

Xintiandi 新天地站

8

Fenyang Rd 汾阳路

S Maoming Rd

Middle Fuxing Rd 复兴中路

Hefei Rd

Sinan Rd 思南路

S Chongqing Rd

S Xiangyang Rd

Ruijin No 2 Rd 瑞金二路

Ruijin Hospital

E Jianguo Rd

Yongjia Rd

Shaoxing Rd 绍兴路

S Shaanxi Rd 陕西南路

Middle Jianguo Rd 建国中路

13

Tiánzǐfáng

Taikang Rd 泰康路

Xujiahui Rd

Dapuqiao 打浦桥站

Xiexu Rd

Luban Rd 鲁班路

Dapu Rd

Nantangbang Rd

Jiashan Rd 嘉善路站

Xietu Rd

Pingjiang Rd

Damuqiao Rd

S Ruijin Rd

Xiaomuqiao Rd

Qingzhen Rd

Quxi Rd

0   1 km
0   0.5 miles

French Concession

◎ Top Sights
Tiánzǐfáng G5
Xīntiāndì H2

◎ Sights
1 Propaganda Poster Art Centre............ A3
2 Shíkùmén Open House Museum.......... H2
3 Site of the 1st National Congress
   of the CCP...................................... H2

◎ Sleeping
4 Old House Inn.................................. C3
5 Púdǐ Boutique Hotel G2
6 Quintet... C3

◎ Eating
7 Bǎoluó Jiǔlóu.................................. D2
8 El Willy E3
9 Sìchuān Citizen D3

◎ Drinking
10 Boxing Cat Brewery B4
11 Citizen Cafe E2

◎ Entertainment
12 Shelter.. B4

◎ Shopping
13 Tiánzǐfáng G5
14 Xīntiāndì...H2
15 Yú...D2

◎ Information
16 Huàshān Hospital............................. B3
17 Shànghǎi Information Centre for
   International Visitors H2

TV tower has become symbolic of the Shànghǎi renaissance.

Tours

Big Bus Tours   Bus
(www.bigbustours.com; tickets US$44)
Shànghǎi's first hop-on, hop-off bus service (22 stops). Tickets are valid for 24 hours and include a boat tour.

Huángpǔ River Cruise (The Bund)   Boat
(黄浦江游船船; Huángpǔjiāng yóulǎnchuán; 501 East Zhongshan No 2 Rd; 中山东二路501号; tickets Y100; ◷10.30am-10.15pm) The classic Shànghǎi tour. Fifty-minute cruises run from the Shíliùpù Docks (aka 'The 16 Pu'; 十六铺; off Map p198; Shíliùpù) south of the Bund.

Huángpǔ River Cruise (Pǔdōng)   Boat
(黄浦江游船; Huángpǔjiāng yóulǎnchuán; Pearl Dock; 明珠码头; tickets Y50-70; ◷10am-8pm; M Lujiazui) Forty-minute cruises departing hourly in Pǔdōng.

Sleeping

In general, hotels fall into five main categories: slick new skyscraper hotels, historic hotels in old villas or apartment blocks, boutique hotels, Chinese chain hotels and hostels. For hotel bookings, the online agencies **CTrip** (✆400 619 9999; http://english.ctrip.com) and **Elong** (✆400 617 1717; www.elong.net) are good choices.

The Bund & People's Square

ASTOR HOUSE HOTEL
   Historic Hotel $$
(浦江饭店; Pǔjiāng Fàndiàn; Map p198; ✆6324 6388; www.astorhousehotel.com; 15 Huangpu Rd; 黄浦路15号; d Y1280, discounts 40%; ✳@; taxi) Etched with history, this venerable old-timer is a dream come true for travellers needing a perch near the Bund, a yesteryear nobility and a pedigree that reaches back to the earliest days of concession-era Shànghǎi. Rooms are colossal (you could fit a bed in the capacious bathrooms) and no other hotel has its selling points: doormen in kilts, original polished wooden floorboards and the overall impression of British public school meets Victorian asylum. No metro.

MINGTOWN ETOUR YOUTH HOSTEL
   Hostel $
(上海新易途国际青年旅舍; Shànghǎi Xīnyìtú Guójì Qīngnián Lǔshè; Map p198; ✆6327 7766; 55 Jiangyin Rd; 江阴路55号; 6-bed dm Y65, d Y220-340; ✳@✶; M People's Sq) The

Etour has a choice location just behind People's Sq, and pleasant rooms (many with reproduction antique furniture). But it's the tranquil courtyard with fish pond and split-level bar-restaurant that really sells this one.

PEACE HOTEL   Historic Hotel **$$$**
(和平饭店; Hépíng Fàndiàn; Map p198; ☏6321 6888; www.fairmont.com; 20 East Nanjing Rd; 南京东路20号; d Y2500-3100, discounts 20%; ➡✳@🛜✈; **M**East Nanjing Rd) After three-plus years of renovations, the city's definitive art deco building, the Peace Hotel, finally reopened in 2010 under the direction of the Fairmont group. The main challenge in modernising the building was balancing out the architectural integrity of such a historic place with the pressing need to upgrade a building that was not originally designed to be a hotel.

MARVEL HOTEL   Hotel **$$**
(商悦青年会大酒店; Shāngyuè Qīngniánhuì Dàjiǔdiàn; Map p198; ☏3305 9999; www.marvelhotels.com.cn; 123 South Xizang Rd; 西藏南路123号; d Y1080-1580; ✳@🛜; **M**Dashijie) Occupying the former YMCA

building (1931) just south of People's Sq, the Marvel is one of the city's standout midrange hotels. The successful mix of history, central location and modern comfort (broadband access via the TV, soundproofed windows, comfy down pillows) makes it one of Shànghǎi's best-value hotels.

PENINSULA   Luxury Hotel **$$$**
(上海半岛酒店; Shànghǎi Bàndǎo Jiǔdiàn; Map p198; ☏2327 2888; www.peninsula.com; 32 East Zhongshan No 1 Rd; 中山东一路32号; d Y3200-5400, discounts 40%; ➡✳@🛜✈; **M**East Nanjing Rd) This new luxury hotel on the Bund combines art deco motifs with Shànghǎi modernity, but it's the little touches that distinguish it from the numerous other five-star places in the neighbourhood: a TV in the tub, valet box and fabulous views across the river or out onto the gardens of the former British consulate.

French Concession

OLD HOUSE INN   Boutique Hotel **$$**
(老时光酒店; Lǎoshíguāng Jiǔdiàn; Map p201; ☏6248 6118; www.oldhouse.cn; 16 Lane 351, Huashan Rd; 华山路351弄16号; s Y580,

Bar in the French Concession

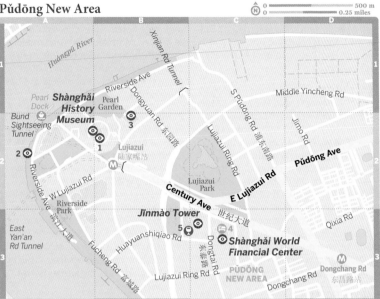

Pǔdōng New Area

◎ Top Sights

Jīnmào Tower..C3
Shànghǎi History Museum..................A2
Shànghǎi World Financial Center......C3

◎ Sights

1 Oriental Pearl Tower...........................B2
2 Riverside Promenade...........................A2
3 Shànghǎi Ocean Aquarium B2

🛏 Sleeping

4 Park Hyatt...C3

🍸 Drinking

5 Cloud 9 ....B3

d Y880-1250, all include breakfast; ❄ @ 🛜;
Ⓜ Changshu Rd) This 1930s red-brick
building has been lovingly restored to
create an exclusive, yet affordable place
to stay. All 12 rooms are decorated
with care and attention and come with
wooden floors, traditional Chinese
furniture, stylish artwork, and a few
antiques.

QUINTET   B&B $$

(Map p201; ☎ 6249 9088; www.quintet-shanghai.
com; 808 Changle Rd; 长乐路808号; d Y800-
1200; ❄ ❄ 🛜; Ⓜ Changshu Rd) This chic
B&B has six beautiful double rooms in a
1930s town house not short on charac-
ter. Some of the rooms are on the small
side, but each is decorated with style,
incorporating modern luxuries such as
big-screen satellite TV, wi-fi and laptop-
sized safes with more classic touches
like wood-stripped floorboards and deep
porcelain bathtubs. There's no sign – just
buzz on the gate marked 808 and wait to
be let in.

PǓDǏ BOUTIQUE HOTEL
    Boutique Hotel $$$

(璞邸精品酒店; Pǔdǐ Jīngpǐn Jiǔdiàn; Map p201;
☎ 5158 5888; www.boutiquehotel.cc; 99 Yandang Rd; 雁荡路99号; d from Y1577, discounts
20%; ❄ @ 🛜; Ⓜ Xintiandi) This exquisite
52-room boutique hotel gets excellent
reviews for its trendy, ultramodern rooms,
professional staff and elite but accessible
atmosphere. The interior is super-
stylish and alluringly dark hued; rooms
are beautifully attired and spacious.

West Nanjing Road & Jìng'ān

LE TOUR TRAVELER'S REST YOUTH HOSTEL Hostel $
(乐途静安国际青年旅舍; Lètú Jìng'ān Guójì Qīngnián Lǚshè; Map p210; ☏ 6267 1912; www.letourshanghai.com; 36, Alley 319, Jiaozhou Rd; 胶州路319弄36号; dm Y60, d Y220-300; ❄@⏰; ⓂJìng'ān Temple) Housed in a former towel factory, this fabulous youth hostel leaves most others out to dry. Sitting quietly in a *lílòng* (alleyway), this great place has bundles of space, and the old-Shànghǎi textures continue once inside, with red-brick interior walls and reproduced stone gateways above doorways. It's bright, spacious and airy with attractive, gaily painted rooms and very amiable staff.

URBN Boutique Hotel $$$
(Map p210; ☏ 5153 4600; www.urbnhotels.com; 183 Jiaozhou Rd; 胶州路183号; d & tw Y2000-2500, discounts 30%; ➖❄⏰; ⓂChangping Rd) China's first carbon-neutral

Shànghǎi Museums

If you liked the outstanding Shànghǎi Museum (p203) or if Shànghǎi's awesome plum rains are preparing to inundate town, the city has a riveting selection of museums and exhibition spaces with collections ranging from Maoist propaganda to the imperial postal service and beyond.

1 PROPAGANDA POSTER ART CENTRE 宣传画黏画艺术中心
(Xuānchuánhuà Niánhuà Yìshù Zhōngxīn; Map p201; ☏ 6211 1845; www.shanghaipropagandaart.com; Room B-OC, President Mansion, 868 Huashan Rd; admission Y20; ⏰10am-5pm; ⓂShanghai Library, Jiangsu Rd) Size up a collection of 3000 original propaganda posters from the 1950s, '60s and '70s. The centre divides into a showroom and a shop.

2 SHÀNGHǍI URBAN PLANNING EXHIBITION HALL 上海城市规划展示馆
(Chéngshì Guīhuà Zhǎnshìguǎn; Map p198; www.supec.org; 100 Renmin Ave – entrance Xizang Rd; 人民大道100号; admission Y30; ⏰9am-5pm Mon-Thu, to 6pm Fri-Sun; ⓂPeople's Sq) Featuring Shànghǎi's idealised future (circa 2020), with an incredible model layout of the megalopolis-to-come plus a self-applauding Virtual World 3-D wraparound tour.

3 SHÀNGHǍI MUSEUM OF CONTEMPORARY ART (MOCA SHÀNGHǍI) 上海当代艺术馆
(Shànghǎi Dāngdài Yìshùguǎn; Map p198; www.mocashanghai.org; People's Park; 人民公园; admission Y20; ⏰10am-9.30pm; ⓂPeople's Sq) Temporary exhibits here range from the work of local artist Zhou Tiehai and urban dystopia instalments to Japanese ecodesign and multimedia instalments.

4 SHÀNGHǍI POST MUSEUM 上海邮政博物馆
(Shànghǎi Yóuzhèng Bówùguǎn; Map p198; 250 North Suzhou Rd; 北苏州路250号; admission free; ⏰9am-5pm Wed, Thu, Sat & Sun; ⓂTiantong Rd) Located in a magnificent 1924 post office, with panoramic views from the rooftop garden.

5 SHÀNGHǍI SCIENCE & TECHNOLOGY MUSEUM 上海科技馆
(Shànghǎi Kējìguǎn; Map p194; www.sstm.org.cn; 2000 Century Ave; 世纪大道2000号; adult Y60; ⏰9am-5.15pm Tue-Sun; ⓂScience & Technology Museum) Some exhibits are past their prime here, but it's still a fun outing for kids, with four theatres (two IMAX, one 4-D and one outer space) showing themed films.

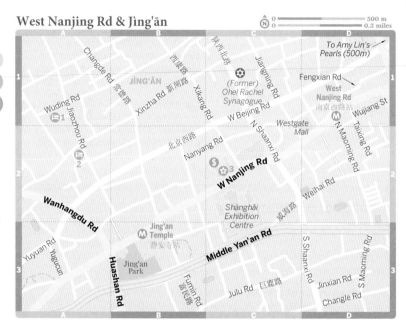

West Nanjing Rd & Jìng'ān

Sleeping
1 Le Tour Traveler's Rest Youth
   Hostel A1
2 Urbn A2

Entertainment
3 Shànghǎi Centre C2

Shopping
   Chaterhouse Booktrader .... (see 3)

hotel not only uses recyclable materials and low-energy products where possible, it also calculates its complete carbon footprint – including staff commutes and delivery journeys – then offsets it by donating money to environmentally friendly projects. The 26 open-plan rooms are beautifully designed with low furniture and sunken living areas exuding space.

Pǔdōng New Area

PARK HYATT Luxury Hotel $$$
(柏悦酒店; Bóyuè Jiǔdiàn; Map p208; 6888 1234; www.parkhyattshanghai.com; 100 Century Ave; 世纪大道100号; d from Y3600, discounts 20%; 🐾 @ 🛜 🛫; Ⓜ Lujiazui) Spanning the 79th to 93rd floors of the towering Shànghǎi World Financial Center, this jaw-dropper is the world's highest hotel above ground level and could easily lay claim to being the coolest hotel in China, never mind Shànghǎi. High-walled corridors with brown-fabric and grey-stone textures lead to luxurious rooms with quirky features such as a mist-free bathroom mirror containing a small TV screen, a rainforest shower in the bathroom ceiling, a plug socket in the safe for your laptop and a toilet seat that opens automatically as you approach it.

🍴 Eating

In true Shànghǎi style, today's restaurant scene is a reflection of the city's craving for foreign trends and tastes, whether it comes in the form of Hunanese chilli peppers or French foie gras. Shànghǎi cuisine itself is generally sweeter than other Chinese cuisines, and is heavy on fish and seafood.

The Bund & People's Square

A lot's cooking near the Bund: from elegant gourmet palaces to delicious local restaurants hidden in malls, all are staking out a spot along the sumptuous skyline.

LOST HEAVEN   Yunnanese   **$$$**
(花马天堂; Huāmǎ Tiāntáng; Map p198; www.lostheaven.com.cn; ☎ 6330 0967; 17 East Yan'an Rd; 延安东路17号; dishes Y30-90; 🖲; Ⓜ East Nanjing Rd) Lost Heaven might not have the views that keep its rivals in business, but why go to the same old Western restaurants when you can get sophisticated Bai, Dai and Miao folk cuisine from China's mighty southwest? Specialities are flowers (banana and pomegranate), wild mushrooms, chillies, Burmese curries, Bai chicken and superb pu-erh teas, all served up in gorgeous Yúnnán-meets-Shànghǎi surrounds.

HÓNGYĪ PLAZA   Chinese   **$$**
(宏伊国际广场; Hóngyī Guójì Guǎngchǎng; Map p198; 299 East Nanjing Rd; 南京东路299号; meals from Y30; 🖲; Ⓜ East Nanjing Rd) Not all malls are created equal: the Hóngyī effortlessly slices and dices the competition with its star-studded restaurant line-up, and the whole shebang is a mere stone's throw from the waterfront. Top picks here are **South Memory** (6th floor), which specialises in spicy Hunanese drypots (a kind of personal miniwok); **Dolar Hotpot** (5th floor), whose delicious sauce bar makes it popular even outside of winter; **Charme** (4th floor), a Taiwanese restaurant with try-it-to-believe-it shaved-ice desserts; **Wagas** (ground floor), Shànghǎi's own wi-fi cafe chain; and **Ajisen** (basement), king of Japanese ramen.

M ON THE BUND   Continental   **$$$**
(米氏西餐厅; Mǐshì Xīcāntīng; Map p198; ☎ 6350 9988; www.m-onthebund.com; 7th fl, 20 Guangdong Rd; 广东路20号7楼; mains from Y198, 2-course lunches Y186; 🖲; Ⓜ East Nanjing Rd) With table linen flapping in the breeze alongside exclusive rooftop views to Pǔdōng, the grand dame of the Bund still elicits applause from Shànghǎi's gastronomes.

French Concession

BǍOLUÓ JIǓLÓU   Shanghainese   **$$**
(保罗酒楼; Map p201; ☎ 6279 2827; 271 Fumin Rd; 富民路271号; dishes Y18-68; ⏱ 11am-3am; 🖲; Ⓜ Changshu Rd, Jing'an Temple) Gather up a boisterous bunch of friends for a fun-filled meal at this typically chaotic and cavernous Shànghǎi institution, which

Food Streets

Shànghǎi's food streets are great spots for gourmands to search for something new. It's not really street food like elsewhere in Asia, but rather a collection of tiny restaurants, each specialising in a different Chinese cuisine.

With a prime central location near People's Park, **Huanghe Road** (黄河路美食街; Huánghé Lù Měishí Jiē; Map p198; Ⓜ People's Sq) covers all the bases from cheap lunches to late-night post-theatre snacks. You'll find excellent Shanghainese further north at **Xiǎo Nán Guó** (小南国; No 214), but it's best for dumplings – get 'em fried at **Yang's Fry Dumplings** (小杨生煎馆; No 97) or served up in bamboo steamers across the road at **Jiājiā Soup Dumplings** (佳家汤包; No 90).

South Yunnan Road (云南路美食街; Yúnnán Lù Měishí Jiē; Ⓜ Dashijie) has some interesting speciality restaurants and is just the spot for an authentic meal after museum-hopping at People's Sq. Look out for Shaanxi cuisine at No 15 and five-fragrance dim sum at **Wǔ Fāng Zhāi** (五芳斋; Map p198; No 28). You can also find cold salted chicken (咸鸡; *xiánjī*) – it's better than it sounds – and Uighur kebabs here.

Accommodation Price Indicators

The price ranges for this chapter are as follows:

$	less than Y400 a night
$$	Y400 to Y1300
$$$	more than Y1300

has lines out the door late into the night. Try the excellent lion's-head meatballs, lotus-leaf roasted duck or the *bǎoluó kǎomàn* (保罗烤鳗; baked eel).

SÌCHUĀN CITIZEN Sichuanese **$**
(龙门陈茶屋; Map p201; Lóngmén Chénchá Wū; ☎ 5404 1235; 30 Donghu Rd; 东湖路30号; dishes Y18-58; 🖥 📶; Ⓜ South Shaanxi Rd) Citizen has opted for the 'rustic chic' look, the wood panelling and whirring ceiling fans conjuring up visions of an old-style Chéngdū teahouse that's been made over for an *Elle* photoshoot. But the food is the real stuff, prepared by a busy Sìchuān kitchen crew to ensure no Shanghainese sweetness creeps into the peppercorn onslaught.

EL WILLY Spanish **$$$**
(Map p201; ☎ 5404 5757; www.elwilly.com.cn; 20 Donghu Rd; 东湖路20号; tapas Y65-165, rice for 2 Y188-218; 📶; Ⓜ South Shaanxi Rd) The unstoppable energy of colourful-sock-wearing Barcelona chef Willy fuels this restored 1920s villa, which ups its charms with creative tapas and succulent rice dishes. The set lunch (Y78) is a steal.

West Nanjing Road & Jìng'ān

FU 1039 Shanghainese **$$$**
(福一零三九; Fú Yào Líng Sān Jiǔ; off Map p201; ☎ 6288 1179; 1039 Yuyuan Rd; 愚园路1039号; dishes Y40-288; 🕙 11am-2.30pm & 5-11pm; 📶; Ⓜ Jiangsu Rd) Set in a three-storey 1913 villa, Fu is upmarket Shanghainese all the way, with an unusual old-fashioned charm in a city hell-bent on modern design. Not easy to find, it rewards the

persistent with succulent standards such as the smoked fish starter and stewed pork in soy sauce. The entrance, down an alley and on the left, is unmarked.

🍷 Drinking

Shànghǎi is awash with watering holes, their fortunes cresting and falling with the vagaries of the latest vogue. Bars regularly sink without a trace, while others suddenly pop up like corks from nowhere. Bars usually open late afternoon (but many open earlier), calling it a night at around 2am.

🎯 The Bund

GLAMOUR BAR Cocktail Bar
(魅力酒吧; Mèilì Jiǔbā; Map p198; www.m-the glamourbar.com; 6th fl, 20 Guangdong Rd; 广东路20号6楼; 🕙 5pm-late; Ⓜ East Nanjing Rd) Michelle Garnaut's stylish bar is set in a splendidly restored space just beneath M on the Bund. In addition to mixing great drinks, it hosts film screenings, an annual literary festival, music performances and China-related book launches.

CAPTAIN'S BAR Bar
(船长青年酒吧; Chuánzhǎng Qīngnián Jiǔbā; Map p198; 6th fl, 37 Fuzhou Rd; 福州路37号6楼; 🕙 11am-2am; 📶; Ⓜ East Nanjing Rd) There's the odd drunken sailor and the crummy lift needs a rethink, but this is a fine Bundside terrace-equipped bar atop the Captain Hostel. Come for phosphorescent nocturnal Pǔdōng views, with pizza and without wall-to-wall preening sophisticates.

NEW HEIGHTS Bar
(新视角; Xīn Shìjiǎo; Map p198; 7th fl, Three on the Bund, 3 East Zhongshan No 1 Rd; 中山东一路3号7楼; 🕙 11am-1.30am; 🖥; Ⓜ East Nanjing Rd) The terrace of this casual Three on the Bund bar pretty much has *the* definitive angle on Lùjiāzuǐ's neon nightfall overture. Try the cocktails, but skip the food.

French Concession

CITIZEN CAFE   Cafe
(天台餐厅; Tiāntái Cāntīng; Map p201; 222 Jinxian Rd; 进贤路222号; ⏱11am-12.30am; 🛜; Ⓜ South Shaanxi Rd) Citizen's burgundy-and-cream colours, antique ceiling fans and well-worn parquet offer calming respite from the Shànghǎi crush. Cappuccinos, cocktails and club sandwiches.

BOXING CAT BREWERY   Bar
(拳击猫啤酒屋; Quánjīmāo Píjiǔwū; Map p201; www.boxingcatbrewery.com; 82 West Fuxing Rd; 复兴西路82号; ⏱5pm-2am Mon-Fri, 11am-2am Sat & Sun; 🛜; Ⓜ Shanghai Library/Changshu Rd) Deservedly popular three-floor micro-brewery with Southern-style grub.

 # Entertainment

There's something for most moods in Shànghǎi: opera, rock, hip-hop, techno, salsa and early-morning waltzes in People's Sq. Venues open and close all the time. Check out Shànghǎi's entertainment websites and magazines for guidance.

Traditional Performances

Chinese acrobatic troupes are among the best in the world, and Shànghǎi is a good place for performances.

SHÀNGHǍI CENTRE   Acrobatics
(上海商城剧院; Shànghǎi Shāngchéng Jùyuàn; Map p210; 📞6279 8948; www.pujiangqing.com; 1376 West Nanjing Rd; 南京西路1376号; tickets Y100-280; Ⓜ Jing'an Temple) The Shànghǎi Acrobatic Troupe (Shànghǎi Zájì Tuán) has short but entertaining performances here most nights at 7.30pm.

YÌFŪ THEATRE   Chinese Opera
(逸夫舞台; Yìfū Wǔtái; Map p198; 📞6322 5294; www.tianchan.com; 701 Fuzhou Rd; tickets Y30-280; Ⓜ People's Sq) A block east of People's Sq, this is the main opera theatre in town, staging a variety of regional operatic styles, including Běijīng opera, Kunqu opera and Yue opera, with a Běijīng opera highlights show several times a week. A shop in the foyer sells CDs.

Live Music

In addition to the places listed here, other bars, cafes and restaurants, such as the

Acrobats performing at the Shànghǎi Centre

GREG ELMS/LONELY PLANET IMAGES ©

Shànghǎi for Children

Shànghǎi isn't exactly at the top of most kids' holiday wish-list, but the new Disney theme park in Pǔdōng (estimated completion 2014) will no doubt improve its future standing. Also in or near Pǔdōng (Map p208):

○ Shànghǎi History Museum

○ Shànghǎi Ocean Aquarium

○ Science & Technology Museum

○ A ride on the Maglev train

In central Shànghǎi see an acrobatics show, but if sightseeing mutiny strikes, you can also check out the **Happy Valley** (欢乐谷; Huānlè Gǔ; http://sh.happyvalley. com.cn, in Chinese; adult/child 1.2-1.4m Y200/100; Linyin Ave, Sheshan, Songjiang County; 松江区佘山林荫大道; ⊙9am-6pm; Ⓜ Sheshan, line 9) amusement park, an hour from Shànghǎi by metro.

Glamour Bar and Bǎndù Cabin (traditional Chinese music), stage musical performances. The Peace Hotel jazz band had just been resuscitated as this book went to press.

YÙYĪNTÁNG   Rock
(育音堂; www.yuyintang.org; 1731 West Yan'an Rd, 延安西路1731号; cover Y40; ⊙Thu-Sun 8pm-midnight; Ⓜ West Yan'an Rd) Small enough to feel intimate, but big enough for a sometimes pulsating atmosphere, Yùyīntáng has long been the place in the city to see live music. Rock is the staple diet, but anything goes, from hard punk to gypsy jazz.

HOUSE OF BLUES & JAZZ   Jazz
(布鲁斯与爵士之屋; Bùlǔsī Yǔ Juéshì Zhī Wū; Map p198; ☎6323 2779; 60 Fuzhou Rd; 福州路 60号; ⊙4.30pm-2am; Ⓜ East Nanjing Rd) Jazz-and blues-lovers should make a beeline to this classy restaurant and bar where the in-house band (which changes every three months) whips up live music from 10pm to 1am.

Nightclubs

There's a high turnover, so check listings websites and magazines for the latest on the club scene.

SHELTER   Club
(Map p201; 5 Yongfu Rd; 永福路5号; ⊙9pm-4am Wed-Sun; Ⓜ Shanghai Library) The darling of the underground crowd, Shelter is a reconverted bomb shelter where you can count on great music and cheap drinks. A good line-up of DJs and hip-hop artists passes through; cover for big shows is around Y30.

MUSE   Club
(www.museshanghai.cn; New Factories, 68 Yuyao Rd; 余姚路68号同乐坊; ⊙8.30pm-4.30am; Ⓜ Changping Rd) One of the city's hottest clubs (house, hip-hop) over the past few years, Muse has three locations. The main club is in north Jìng'ān, the other two (both smaller) are in the French Concession; check the website for details.

Classical Music, Opera & Theatre

ORIENTAL ART CENTER
                                    Classical, Opera
(东方艺术中心; Dōngfāng Yìshù Zhōngxīn; ☎6854 7796; www.shoac.com.cn; 425 Dingxiang Rd, Pǔdōng; 浦东丁香路425号; tickets Y30-680; Ⓜ Science & Technology Museum) Home of the Shànghǎi Symphonic Orchestra, the Oriental Art Center was designed to resemble five petals of a butterfly orchid.

There are three main halls that host classical, jazz, dance and Chinese and Western opera performances.

SHÀNGHǍI GRAND THEATRE
Classical, Opera, Dance

(上海大剧院; Shànghǎi Dàjùyuàn; Map p198; ☏6386 8686; www.shgtheatre.com; 300 Renmin Ave; 人民大道300号; tickets Y50-2280; Ⓜ People's Sq) This state-of-the-art venue is in People's Sq and features both national and international opera, dance, music and theatre performances.

Shopping

The Bund & Old Town
The Bund is all about luxury shopping.

SŪZHŌU COBBLERS
Shoes

(上海起想艺术品; Shànghǎi Qǐxiǎng Yìshùpǐn; Map p198; www.suzhou-cobblers.com; Room 101, 17 Fuzhou Rd; ⏱10am-6pm; Ⓜ East Nanjing Rd) For hand-embroidered silk slippers and shoes, pop into this minute shop just off the Bund.

DONGTAI ROAD ANTIQUE MARKET
Souvenirs

(东台路古商品市场; Dōngtáilù Gǔshāngpǐn Shìchǎng; off Map p198; Dongtai Rd; 东台路; ⏱8.30am-6pm) A short shuffle west of the Old Town towards Xīntiāndì, the Dongtai Rd Antique Market is a hefty sprawl of curios, knick-knacks and Mao-era nostalgia, though only a fraction of the items qualify as antique. Haggle hard.

French Concession

The French Concession is where it's at for shoppers; there are boutiques on almost every corner.

TIÁNZǏFÁNG
Fashion, Souvenirs

(田子坊; Map p201; Taikang Rd; 泰康路; Ⓜ Dapuqiao) Burrow into the *lǐlòng* here for a rewarding haul of creative boutiques, selling everything from hip jewellery and yak-wool scarves to retro communist dinnerware.

XĪNTIĀNDÌ
Fashion

(新天地; Cnr Taicang & Madang Rds; 太仓路与马当路路口; ⏱11am-11pm; Ⓜ South Huangpi Rd, Xīntiāndì) Browse the north block for upmarket boutiques, from the fluorescent chic of **Shanghai Tang** (Bldg 15) and clever design at **Simply Life** (Unit 101, 159 Madang Rd) to the eco-fabrics of **Shanghai Trio** (No 4, enter via Taicang Rd), iridescent glass sculptures at **Líulìgōngfáng** (Bldg 11) and embroidered accessories at **Annabel Lee** (Bldg 3).

YÚ
Ceramics

(萸; Map p201; 164 Fumin Rd; 富民路164号; ⏱11am-9pm; Ⓜ Changshu Rd) Man Zhang and her husband create the personable porcelain at this tiny shop, the latest link in the Shànghǎi-Jǐngdézhèn connection, which is an excellent place to browse for

Calligraphy shop, Shànghǎi.

handmade and hand-painted teaware, bowls and vases.

Jìng'ān

AMY LIN'S PEARLS   Pearls
(艾敏林氏珍珠; Àimǐn Línshì Zhēnzhū; Room 30, 3rd fl, 580 West Nanjing Rd; 南京西路580号3楼30号; ⏰10am-8pm; Ⓜ West Nanjing Rd) Shànghǎi's most reliable retailer of pearls of all colours and sizes, which come for a fraction of the price that you'd pay back home.

CHATERHOUSE BOOKTRADER   Books
(Map p210; Shanghai Centre, Unit 104, 1376 West Nanjing Rd; 南京西路1376号104室; ⏰9am-9pm; Ⓜ Jing'an Temple) A great hit with literature-starved expats for its selection of books and mags.

ℹ Information

Internet Access

Internet cafes have become much more scarce in touristy areas – it's generally more convenient to get online at your hotel or at a wi-fi hotspot if you have a laptop.

Míngwàng Internet Cafe (名旺网吧; Míngwàng Wǎngbā; 515 Fuzhou Rd; 福州路515号; per hr Y3.5; ⏰24hr) On the corner of Hubei Rd.

Media

Grab a free copy of the monthly *That's Shanghai* from an expat-centric restaurant or bar, followed swiftly by issues of *City Weekend* and *Time Out* for an instant plug into what's on in town, from art exhibitions and club nights to restaurant openings.

Medical Services

Huàshān Hospital (华山医院; Huàshān Yīyuàn; Map p201; ☎5288 9998; www.sh-hwmc.com.cn; 12 Middle Wulumuqi Rd; 乌鲁木齐中路12号; Ⓜ Changshu Rd) Hospital treatment and outpatient consultations are available at the 8th-floor foreigners clinic (open 8am to 10pm daily), with 24-hour emergency treatment on the 15th floor in Building 6.

Parkway Health (以极佳医疗保健服务; Yǐjíjiā Yīliáo Bǎojiàn Fúwù; 24hr hotline ☎6445 5999;

Left: Amusement park chair ride, Shànghǎi; **Below:** Artificial flowers floating on a pond at Jade Buddha Temple (p202)

PHOTOGRAPHER: (LEFT) ZHANG YI/LONELY PLANET IMAGES ©; (BELOW) RICHARD I'ANSON/LONELY PLANET IMAGES ©

www.parkwayhealth.cn) Seven locations around Shànghǎi, including at the Shànghǎi Centre (上海商城; Shànghǎi Shāngchéng; Suite 203, Shànghǎi Centre, 1376 West Nanjing Rd; 南京西路1376号203室; MWest Nanjing Rd) Private medical care by expat doctors, dentists and specialists.

Money

ATMs are everywhere; most accept major cards.

Bank of China (中国银行; Zhōngguó Yínháng; Map p198; The Bund; ⊙9am-noon & 1.30-4.30pm Mon-Fri, 9am-noon Sat)

Citibank (花旗银行; Huāqí Yínháng; Map p198; The Bund) Useful ATM open 24 hours.

Hong Kong & Shanghai Bank (汇丰银行; HSBC; Huìfēng Yínháng) Shànghǎi Centre (Map p210; West Nanjing Rd); The Bund (Map p198; 15 East Zhongshan No 1 Rd) Has ATMs in the above locations; also an ATM at Pǔdōng Airport arrivals hall.

Post

Post offices and postboxes are green.

International Post Office (国际邮局; Guójì Yóujú; Map p198; 276 North Suzhou Rd; 苏州北路276号; ⊙7am-10pm; MTiantong Rd) Just north of Sūzhōu Creek in Hóngkǒu.

Public Security Bureau

(PSB;公安局; Gōng'ānjú; ☎2895 1900 ext 2; 1500 Minsheng Rd; 民生路1500号; ⊙9am-4.30pm Mon-Sat; MScience & Technology Museum) Handles visas and registrations; 30-day visa extensions cost around Y160. In Pǔdōng.

Tourist Information

Your hotel should be able to provide you with maps and most of the tourist information you require.

Shànghǎi Information Centre for International Visitors (Map p201; ☎6384 9366; No 2, Alley 123, Xingye Rd) Xīntiāndì information centre.

Eating Price Indicators

The price ranges for this chapter are as follows:

$	less than Y60
$$	Y60 to Y160
$$$	more than Y160

Shànghăi Call Centre (☎ 962 288; ⏱ 24hr) This toll-free English-language hotline is possibly the most useful telephone number in Shànghăi – they can even give your cab driver directions if you've got a mobile phone.

Tourist Information & Service Centres (旅游咨询服务中心; Lǚyóu Zīxún Fúwù Zhōngxīn; The Bund (**Map p204; beneath the Bund promenade, opposite the intersection with East Nanjing Rd);** East Nanjing Rd (**Century Sq, 518 Jiujiang Rd);** Old Town (**149 Jiujiaochang Rd)**

Travel Agencies

CTrip (☎ 400 619 9999; http://english.ctrip. com) Online agency good for hotel and flight bookings.

Elong (☎ 400 617 1717; www.elong.net) Online agency good for hotel and flight bookings.

Websites

City Weekend (www.cityweekend.com.cn) Listings website.

Shanghaiist (www.shanghaiist.com) Local entertainment and news blog.

SmartShanghai (www.smartshanghai.com) For food, fun and frolicking. Good entertainment coverage.

Urbanatomy (www.urbanatomy.com) Listings website from *That's Shanghai*.

ⓘ Getting There & Away

Air

Shànghăi has international flight connections to most major cities, many operated by China Eastern, which has its base here.

All international flights (and a few domestic flights) operate out of **Pŭdōng International Airport** (PVG; 浦东国际机场; Pŭdōng Guójì Jīchăng; flight information ☎ 96990; www.shairport.com; Ⓜ Pudong International Airport), with most (but not all) domestic flights operating out of **Hóngqiáo Airport** (SHA; 虹桥机场; Hóngqiáo Jīchăng; flight information ☎ 96990; www.shairport. com; Ⓜ Hongqiao Airport) on Shànghăi's western outskirts. If you are making an onward domestic connection from Pŭdōng it is essential that you find out whether the domestic flight leaves from Pŭdōng or Hóngqiáo, as the latter will require *at least* an hour to cross the city.

Daily (usually several times) domestic flights connect Shànghăi to major cities in China, including **Bĕijīng** Y1220, 1½ hours, **Chéngdū** Y1700, two hours 20 minutes, **Guìlín** Y1390, two hours, **Qīngdăo** Y810, one hour and **Xī'ān** Y1350, two hours.

You can buy air tickets almost anywhere, including at major hotels, travel agencies and online sites such as ctrip.com and elong.net.

Bus

Shànghăi has a number of long-distance bus stations, though given the traffic gridlock it's best to take the train when possible. The massive **Shànghăi Long-Distance Bus Station** (上海长途汽车总站; Shànghăi Chángtú Qìchē Kèyùn Zŏngzhàn; 1666 Zhongxing Rd; Ⓜ Shanghai Railway Station), north of Shànghăi train station, has buses to destinations as far away as Gānsù province and Inner Mongolia.

Handier is the **Hengfeng Road Bus Station** (恒丰路客运站; Héngfēnglù Kèyùnzhàn; Map p210; Ⓜ Hanzhong Rd), which serves cities including Bĕijīng (Y311, 5pm), Hángzhōu (eight daily), Nánjīng (frequent) and Sūzhōu (frequent).

The vast **Shànghăi South Long-Distance Bus Station** (上海长途客运南站; Shànghăi Chángtú Kèyùn Nánzhàn; 666 Shilong Rd; Ⓜ Shanghai South Railway Station) serves cities in south China, including Hángzhōu (frequent), Nánjīng (four daily), Níngbō (frequent), Sūzhōu (frequent), Túnxī/Huángshān (Y135, six hours, eight daily) and Wùyuán (Y175, five hours, two daily).

Buses also depart for Hángzhōu and Sūzhōu from the long-distance bus stations at Hóngqiáo Airport and Pŭdōng International Airport.

Train

Many parts of the country can be reached by direct train from Shànghǎi. The city has three useful stations: the main Shànghǎi railway station (Shànghǎi zhàn; M Shanghai Railway Station), the Shànghǎi South railway station (Shànghǎi Nánzhàn; M Shanghai South Railway Station) and the Hóngqiáo railway station (上海 虹桥站; Shànghǎi Hóngqiáo zhàn; M Hongqiao Railway Station) near Hóngqiáo Airport. Most trains depart from the main station, though some southern destinations, like Hángzhōu, leave from Shànghǎi South. The Hóngqiáo station is for new express trains (many Nánjīng and Sūzhōu trains leave from here) and will ultimately serve as the terminus for the Shànghǎi–Běijīng express, which is estimated to begin in 2012.

At the main station there are two ticket halls (售票厅; shòupiàotīng), one in the main building (same-day tickets) and another on the east side of the square (advance tickets). One counter will claim to have English-speakers. Bilingual automated machines (自助售票处; zìzhù shòupiàochù; ☉24hr) just east of the same-day ticket hall sell tickets to many major destinations.

Alternatively, tickets can also be purchased from one of the numerous train-ticket offices (火车票预售处; huǒchēpiào yùshòuchù); Bund (384 Middle Jiangxi Rd; 江西中路384号; ☉8am-8pm); Jìng'ān (77 Wanhangdu Rd; 万航渡路77号; ☉8am-5pm); Pǔdōng (1396 Lujiazui Ring Rd; 陆家嘴环路1396号; ☉8am-7pm) around town.

Prices and times listed here are always for the fastest train. Slower, less expensive trains have not been listed. Some trains leaving from Shànghǎi Railway Station are Běijīng (D-train) Y327/Y655 (seat/sleeper), 10 hours, seven daily, Huángshān Y169, 12 hours, two daily, Sūzhōu Y41, 30 minutes, frequent services and Xī'ān Y323, 14 hours, 10 daily.

A note on the Běijīng-bound trains: schedules will probably change once the new express starts service from Hóngqiáo (estimated 2012), which will cut the trip down to four hours and stop off at several cities, including Nánjīng. If the D-trains (the ones listed here) are still in service be aware that you'll want to get a bed (soft sleeper only) instead of a seat if you're on an overnight train. There are/were three slower sleeper trains that require 10 days advance booking.

Trains leaving from Shànghǎi South Railway Station include Hángzhōu (Y58, 1½ hours, frequent).

❶ Getting Around

The best way to get around Shànghǎi is the metro, which now gets to most places in the city, followed by cabs, which are reasonably cheap and easy to flag down. In general, buses (Y2) should be avoided as they're hard to figure out, even for Mandarin speakers.

To/From the Airport

Pǔdōng International Airport handles most international flights and some domestic flights. There are four ways to get from the airport to the city: taxi, Maglev train, metro and bus.

A taxi ride into central Shànghǎi will cost around Y160 and take about an hour; to Hóngqiáo Airport costs around Y200. Most taxi drivers in Shànghǎi are honest, though make sure they use the meter;

Roast chickens, Shànghǎi

PHOTOGRAPHER: GREG ELMS/LONELY PLANET IMAGES ©

French Concession restaurant, Shànghǎi

RICHARD I'ANSON/LONELY PLANET IMAGES ©

avoid monstrous overcharging by using the regular taxi rank outside the arrivals hall. Regular buses also run to Sūzhōu (Y84) and Hángzhōu (Y100).

The bullet-fast **Maglev train (www.smtdc. com)** runs from Pǔdōng Airport to Pǔdōng in just eight minutes, from where you can transfer to the metro (Longyang Rd station) or take a taxi (Y40 to People's Sq). Economy single/return tickets cost Y50/80; but show your same-day air ticket and it's Y40 one-way. Children under 1.2m travel free (kids taller than this are half price). The train departs every 20 minutes from roughly 6.45am to 9.40pm.

Metro Line 2 runs from Pǔdōng Airport to Hóngqiáo Airport, passing through central Shànghǎi. It is certainly convenient, though not for those in a hurry. From Pǔdōng Airport, it takes about 75 minutes to People's Sq (Y6) and one hour 45 minutes to Hóngqiáo Airport (Y8).

There are also **airport buses**, taking between 60 and 90 minutes to run to destinations in Pǔxī.

Hóngqiáo Airport is 18km from the Bund, a 30- to 60-minute trip. Most flights now arrive at Terminal 2, which is connected to downtown via metro Lines 2 and 10 (30 minutes to People's Sq). If you arrive at Terminal 1, you can also catch the airport shuttle bus (Y4, 7.50am to 11pm) to the Airport City Terminal on West Nanjing Rd. Airport bus 1 (Y30, 6am to 9.30pm) runs to Pǔdōng International Airport. Taxis cost Y70 to Y100 to central Shànghǎi.

Public Transport

METRO The Shànghǎi metro system (indicated by a red M) currently runs to 11 lines after huge expansion; three additional lines (12, 13, 21) are expected to open in 2012. Lines 1, 2 and 10 are the principal lines that travellers will use. Tickets cost between Y3 and Y10 depending on the distance and are only sold from bilingual automated machines (except in rare cases); keep your ticket until you exit. A one-day metro pass is also sold from information desks for Y18.

TAXIS Shànghǎi's taxis are reasonably cheap, hassle-free and easy to flag down outside rush hour, although finding a cab during rainstorms is impossible. Flag fall is Y12 (for the first 3km) and Y16 at night (11pm to 5am).

AROUND SHÀNGHĂI

Thirty kilometres west of Shànghǎi, **Zhūjiājiǎo** (朱家角 optional ticket incl entry to 4/8 sights Y30/60) is both easy to reach and truly delightful – as long as your visit does not coincide with the arrival of phalanxes of tour buses.

Chinese guidebooks vaguely identify human activity in these parts 5000 years ago and a settlement was here during the Three Kingdoms period 1700 years ago. It was during the Ming dynasty, however, that a commercial centre built on Zhūjiājiǎo's network of waterways was truly developed. What survives today is a charming tableau of Ming- and Qing-dynasty alleys, bridges and old-town (古镇; *gǔzhèn*) architecture.

In the past few years, Zhūjiājiǎo has developed into something of a bohemian getaway from busy Shànghǎi, and there's now an admirable selection of tiny hotels, cafes and arty shops scattered around town. Top picks for overnighting are the quaint **1, 2, 3** (☏5923 2101; www.byways.asia; 3 Lane 123, Xijing St; 西井街123弄3号; dm/d Y60/150) and the **Uma Hostel** (☏189 1808 2961; umahostel@gmail.com; 103 Xijing St; 西井街103号; dm/d Y50/200), both near the **Kèzhí Gardens** (课植园; Kèzhí Yuán). A bit fancier is **West Well** (☏5924 2675; xijinghui@gmail.com; 54 Xijing St; 西井街56号; dY350), set in a huge old courtyard house.

To get to Zhūjiājiǎo, it's easiest to go to the **Pu'an Rd Bus Station** (普安路汽车站; Pǔ'ān Lù Qìchē Zhàn; Ⓜ Dashijie) just south of People's Sq, where you can take the Hùzhū Gāosù Kuàixiàn bus (沪朱高速快线, Y12, one hour, every 30 minutes from 6am to 10pm) direct to the village. Alternatively, you can take the Shànghǎi Sightseeing Bus day tour (Y85, departs 9am and 10am); it returns for Shànghǎi at 3.45pm and 4.45pm. The ticket includes admission to the town. Zhūjiājiǎo can also be reached from the bus station in Tónglǐ (Y15, 90 minutes, nine buses daily).

YANGZI REGION

Sūzhōu 苏州

☏0512 / POP 1.6 MILLION

Sūzhōu's fame was immortalised in the proverb 'In heaven there is paradise, on earth Sūzhōu and Hángzhōu' – a line still very much plugged in the tourist campaigns. But while you won't fall for its hackneyed 'Venice-of-the-East' chat-up line, Sūzhōu – once described by Marco Polo as one of the most beautiful cities in China – still contains enough pockets of charm to warrant two to three days' exploration.

You could easily spend an enjoyable several days here.

 **Sights & Activities**

High-season prices listed are for March to early May and September to October. Gardens and museums stop selling tickets 30 minutes before closing.

GARDEN OF THE MASTER OF THE NETS
网师园   Classical Garden
(Wǎngshī Yuán; low/high season Y20/30; ⏰7.30am-5pm) Off Shiquan Jie (enter),

Shang High

With so many towers scattered around town, a high-altitude view of the metropolis is inevitable, so why not choose a spot where you can relax with a drink?

○ **Cloud 9** (九重天酒廊; Jiǔchóngtiān Jiǔláng; Map p208; 87th fl, Jīnmào Tower, 88 Century Ave; 世纪大道88号金茂大厦87; ⏰5pm-1am Mon-Fri, 11am-2am Sat & Sun; Ⓜ Lujiazui) Atop the Grand Hyatt, this is no longer the highest bar in the city, but it's still the coolest in the stratosphere.

○ **Vue** (非常时髦; Fēicháng Shímáo; Map p198; 32nd & 33rd fls, Hyatt on the Bund, 199 Huangpu Rd; 外滩茂悦大酒店黄浦路199号32-33楼; ⏰6pm-1am; Ⓜ Tiantong Rd) Fabulous views down the Bund and an outdoor jacuzzi to accompany bottles of bubbly and Vue martinis (vodka and mango purée).

this pocket-sized garden, the smallest in Sūzhōu, is considered one of the best preserved in the city. It was laid out in the 12th century, went to seed and was later restored in the 18th century as part of the home of a retired official turned fisherman (thus the name).

Music performances are held for tourists in the evening (see p225).

HUMBLE ADMINISTRATOR'S GARDEN
Classical Garden

(拙政园; Zhuōzhèng Yuán; 178 Dongbei Jie; low/high season Y50/70, audio guide free; ☺7.30am-5.30pm) First built in 1509, this 5.2-hectare garden is clustered with water features, a museum, a teahouse and at least 10 pavilions such as 'the listening to the sound of rain' and 'the faraway looking' pavilions – hardly humble, we know. It is the largest of all the gardens and considered by many to be the most impressive.

WEST GARDEN TEMPLE
Classical Garden

(西园寺; Xīyuán Sì; Xiyuan Lu; admission Y25; ☺8am-5pm) This attractive temple was once part of the Garden to Linger In, but was given to a Buddhist temple in the early 17th century. The West Garden Temple, with its mustard-yellow walls and gracefully curved eaves, was burnt to the ground during the Taiping Rebellion and rebuilt in the late 19th century.

NORTH TEMPLE PAGODA
Pagoda

(北寺塔; Běisì Tǎ; 1918 Renmin Lu; admission Y25; ☺7.45am-5.30pm) The tallest pagoda south of the Yangzi, at nine storeys North Temple Pagoda dominates the northern end of Renmin Lu. Climb it for sweeping views of hazy modern-day Sūzhōu.

SŪZHŌU SILK MUSEUM
Museum

(丝绸博物馆; Sūzhōu Sīchóu Bówùguǎn; 2001 Renmin Lu; admission Y15; ☺9am-5pm) Sūzhōu was the place for silk production and weaving, and the Sūzhōu Silk Museum houses a number of fascinating exhibitions that detail the history of Sūzhōu's 4000-year-old silk industry.

PÁN GATE
Ancient Wall

(盘门; Pán Mén; 1 Dong Dajie; admission Pán Gate only/with Ruìguāng Pagoda Y25/31; ☺7.30am-6pm) Straddling the outer moat in the city's southwest corner, this stretch of the city wall has Sūzhōu's only remaining original

Garden of the Master of the Nets (p221), Sūzhōu

Transport Card

If you are going to be doing a lot of travelling in Shànghǎi, it's worth investing in a transport card (交通卡; *jiāotōng kǎ*) as it can save you queuing. Sold at metro stations and some convenience stores, cards can be topped up with credits and used on the metro, most buses and in taxis. Credits are electronically deducted from the card as you swipe it over the sensor at metro turnstiles and near the door on buses; when paying your taxi fare, hand the card to the driver, who will swipe it for you.

coiled gate, Pán Gate, which dates from 1355. This overgrown gate, actually really a wall, straddles the canal and it's the only remaining land-and-water gate in China.

To get there, take tourist bus Y5 from the train station or Changxu Lu.

OLD STREETS (PÍNGJIĀNG LÙ & SHÀNGTÁNG JIĒ)   Old Streets

While most of the canals in the city have been sealed and paved into roads, there are two outstanding areas which give visitors a clue to Suzhou's 'Venice of the East' moniker. On the eastern side of the city, **Píngjiāng Lù** (平江路) is undoubtedly the prettier and more popular of the two. This pedestrian road (watch out for electric bikes though!) is set alongside a canal.

At the foot of Tiger Hill is the start of a grittier version of Píngjiāng Lù. **Shàngtáng Jiē** (上塘街) eschews espresso and beer for tacky souvenir shops, but keep on walking and the dross is soon replaced by grimy Ming- and Qing-dynasty houses and locals pottering about. You can get a ticket (Y45) to several tourist spots including old residences, but you can do without.

Tours

Evening boat tours wind their way around the outer canal leaving nightly from 7pm to 8.30pm (Y35, 80 minutes, half-hourly). Buy tickets at the port near Rénmín Bridge, which shares the same quarters with the Grand Canal boat ticket office.

Sleeping

SŪZHŌU MINGTOWN YOUTH HOSTEL
Hostel **$**

(苏州浮生四季青年旅舍; Sūzhōu Míngtáng Qīngnián Lǚshè; ☎6581 6869; 28 Pingjiang Lu; 平江路28号; 6-bed dm Y50, r Y140-180; ❄@) Sūzhōu's most pleasant youth hostel by a long shot, this lovely place is located canalside in a traditional part of town rich in old-world flavour (if you overlook the trendy cafes). The only thing that bugs us is hot water: it's only on in the mornings and after 7pm.

PÍNGJIĀNG LODGE
Boutique Hotel **$$$**

(苏州平江客站; Sūzhōu Píngjiāng Kèzha'n; ☎6523 2888; www.pingjianglodge.com; 33 Niujia Xiang; 钮家巷33号; r Y988-2588; ❄@) Fab little hotel spread across two 400-year-old residences. There are well-kept gardens, quiet courtyards and rooms splashed out in traditional furniture. Rooms at the pointy end are suites with split-level living spaces and beautiful bathrooms. Standard rooms are lovely too. Discounts of up to 50% are common.

Eating

Restaurants abound along Guanqian Jie, especially down the road from the Temple of Mystery. Shiquan Jie, between Daichengqiao Lu and Xiangwang Lu, is lined with bars, restaurants and bakeries.

A **B** **C** **D**

0 — 1 km
0 — 0.5 miles

Train Station

14

15

Guangji Lu

Pingqi Lu

Qimen Lu

To Shàngtáng Jie (1.5km)

Humble Administrator's Garden

Sūzhōu Museum

Dongbei Jie

17

5

2

Baita Dōnglù

Dong Zhongshi

Baita Xilu

Renmin Lu 人民路

13

Lindun Lu

Qiaosikong Xiang

Daru Xiang

8

Cang Jie

Watcheng River

Ping'an Fang

16

6

7

Pingjiāng Lù

Guanqian Jie

Jingde Lu

Taijian Long

Furen Fang

Ganjiang Lu

Jia Yu Fang

11

Dashitou Xiang

Twin Pagodas

Wuquaanlu 五峰路

Fenghuang Jie

Shizi Jie

Daoqian Jie

Renmin Lu 人民路

Shiquan Jie 十全街

9

Dong Dajie 东大街

Wuquequao Lu

Daichengbao Lu

Xiangwang Lu

10

Changxu Lu

1

Zhuhui Lu

Xinshi Lu

Sūzhōu to Hángzhōu Boat Wharf

12

4

3

Wumen Bridge

Renmin Bridge

To South Long-Distance Bus Station (0.5km); Train Ticket Office (0.5km)

A **B** **C** **D**

Sūzhōu

◎ Top Sights
Humble Administrator's Garden C2
Píngjiāng Lù C4
Sūzhōu Museum C2

◎ Sights
1 Garden of the Master of the Nets C5
2 North Temple Pagoda B2
3 Pán Gate A7
4 Ruìguāng Pagoda A7
5 Sūzhōu Silk Museum B2

◎ Sleeping
6 Píngjiāng Lodge C4
7 Sūzhōu Mingtown Youth Hostel C4

◎ Eating
8 Pingvon C3
9 Xīshèngyuán C5

◎ Drinking
10 Bookworm D5

Entertainment
Garden of the Master of the Nets ... (see 1)

Transport
11 China Eastern Airlines B4
12 Grand Canal Boat Ticket Office C6
13 Liánhé Ticket Centre B3
14 Local Buses A1
15 North Long-Distance Bus Station B1
16 Train Ticket Office (Guanqian Jie) B4
17 Yángyáng Bike Rental Shop B2

PINGVON Teahouse **$**

(☎ 139 1352 1204; 94 Pingjiang Lu; dishes from Y4) A cute little teahouse perched beside one of Sūzhōu's most popular canalside streets. Pingvon serves up excellent dumplings and delicate little morsels served in baskets and on small plates. Try the green-tea Buddha biscuit and pan-fried dumplings. English menu available.

XĪSHÈNGYUÁN Dumplings **$**

(熙盛源; 43 Fenghuang Jie; dumplings from Y6) Crowds pay and gather near the entrance to wait for the steaming fresh *xiǎolóng bāo* (小龙跑; soup dumplings, Y6) to come out of the kitchen. If you don't want to jostle, grab a seat and order several other great dishes including assorted *húntūn* (馄饨; dumplings; Y6 to Y10).

🍷 Drinking & Entertainment

Bustling Shiquan Jie surges late into the night, but prices are dear. There are also stacks of trendy cafe-bars scattered along Pingjiang Lu.

BOOKWORM Cafe, Bar

(☎ 6526 4720; 77 Gunxiu Fang; ⏰ 9am-1am) Beijing's Bookworm has wormed its way down to Sūzhōu. The service could be quicker but the food is crowd-pleasers (lots of Western options) and the beer is cold. There are occasional events and books you can buy.

GARDEN OF THE MASTER OF THE NETS Music

(Wǎngshī Yuán; tickets Y100) From March to November, music performances are held nightly from 7.30pm to 9.30pm for tourist groups at this garden.

ℹ️ Information

Bank of China (Zhōngguó Yínháng; 1450 Renmin Lu) Changes travellers cheques and foreign cash. There are ATMs that take international cards at most larger branches of the Bank of China.

Hóng Qīngtíng Internet Cafe (Hóng Qīngtíng Wǎngbā; 916 Shiquan Jie; per hr Y2.5; ⏰ 24hr)

China Post (Zhōngguó yóuzhèng'; cnr Renmin Lu & Jingde Lu)

Public Security Bureau (PSB; Gōng'ānjú; ☎ 6522 5661, ext 20593; 1109 Renmin Lu) Can help with emergencies and visa problems. The visa office is about 200m down a lane called Dashitou Xiang.

Sūzhōu Tourism Information Center (Sūzhōu Lǚyóu Zīxún Zhōngxīn; ☎ 6530 5887;

Sūzhōu Museum

This IM Pei–designed **Sūzhōu Museum** is a soothing contrast of water, bamboo and straight lines in a stunning geometric interpretation of a Sūzhōu garden. Inside – a fascinating array of jade, ceramics, wooden carvings, textiles and other displays, all with good English captions.

THINGS YOU NEED TO KNOW

苏州博物馆; Sūzhōu Bówùguǎn; 204 Dongbei Jie; admission free, audio guide Y30; ☺9am-5pm

www.classicsuzhou.com; 345 Shiquan Jie) Several branches in town including bus stations.

ℹ Getting There & Away

Boat

You can get tickets for the Sūzhōu to Hángzhōu boat (Y80 to Y210, 11 hours, 5.30pm daily) at the Liánhé Ticket Centre (Liánhé Shòupiàochù; ☎65206681; 1606 Renmin Lu; ☺8am-5pm). Boats leave from the **wharf** at 306 Renmin Lu.

Bus

Buses leave frequently for Hóngqiáo Airport in Shànghǎi. Tickets are Y50. Tickets for all buses can also be bought at the Liánhé Ticket Centre (Liánhé Shòupiàochù; 1606 Renmin Lu; ☺bus tickets 8.30-11.30am & 1-5pm).

The principal station is the North long-distance bus station (qìchē běizhàn; ☎6577 6577) at the northern end of Renmin Lu, next to the train station, where buses run to many places including Hángzhōu (Y69, two hours, regular).

The South long-distance bus station (qìchē nánzhàn; cnr Yingchun Lu & Nanhuan Donglu) has buses to Hángzhōu (Y70, two hours, every 20 minutes) and Shànghǎi (Y33, 1½ hours, every 30 minutes)

Train

Sūzhōu is on the Nánjīng–Shànghǎi express D line. Book train tickets on the 2nd floor of the Liánhé Ticket Centre (Liánhé Shòupiàochù; 1606 Renmin Lu; ☺train tickets 7.30-11am & noon-5pm). Trains go to Běijīng (hard/soft sleeper

Y158/256, 10 hours, 1.10pm) and Shànghǎi (Y31, 30 mins, 20 daily).

ℹ Getting Around

Bicycle

The Yángyáng Bike Rental Shop (Yángyáng Chēháng; 2061 Renmin Lu; h 7am-6pm), a short walk north of the Silk Museum, offers bike rentals (Y20 per day plus Y200 deposit).

Public Transport

Bus Y5 goes around the western and eastern sides of the city. **Bus Y2** travels from Tiger Hill, Pán Gate and along Shiquan Jie. **Buses Y1** and **Y4** run the length of Renmin Lu.

At the time of writing, Sūzhōu was constructing its first metro line. The first line is expected to be completed by the end of 2010.

Taxi

Fares start at Y10 and drivers generally use their meters. Pedicabs hover around the tourist areas and can be persistent (Y5 for short rides is standard).

Around Sūzhōu

Tónglǐ 同里

☎0512

The lovely canal town of Tónglǐ, only 18km southeast of Sūzhōu, has been around since at least the 9th century and is *the* sight to visit outside Sūzhōu. Rich in historic canalside atmosphere and weather-beaten charm, many of Tónglǐ's buildings have kept their traditional facades, with stark whitewashed walls (faded white if you venture off the tourist trails), black-tiled roofs, cobblestone pathways and willow-shaded canal views adding to a picturesque allure.

You can reach Tónglǐ from either Sūzhōu or Shànghǎi, but aim for a weekday visit.

Sights

The **Old Town** (老城区; Lǎochéngqū; ☏6333 1140; admission Y80; ⊙7.30am-5.30pm) of Tónglǐ is best explored the traditional way: aimlessly meandering the canals and alleys until you get lost. The whitewashed houses and laundry hanging out to dry are all so charming that it doesn't really matter where you go, as long as you can elude the crowds.

There are three old residences that you'll pass at some point (unless you're really lost), the best of which is **Gēnglè Táng** (耕乐堂), a sprawling Ming-dynasty estate with 52 halls spread out over five courtyards in the west of town.

In the north of town is the **Pearl Pagoda** (珍珠塔; Zhēnzhū Tǎ), which dates from the Qing dynasty, but has recently been restored.

In the east of the Old Town you'll find **Tuìsì Garden** (退思园; Tuìsì Yuán), a gorgeous 19th-century garden that delightfully translates as the 'Withdraw and Reflect Garden', so named because it was a Qing government official's retirement home.

Last but not least and definitely not for infant Tónglǐ-goers, you can't miss the **Chinese Sex Culture Museum** (中华性文化博物馆; Zhōnghuá Xìngwénhuà Bówùguǎn; admission Y20). If you thought Confucius was a prude, think again.

Slow-moving **six-person boats** (30/60 minutes, Y40/70) ply the waters of Tónglǐ's canal system. The boat trip on Tónglǐ Lake is free, though of no particular interest.

Sleeping & Eating

Guesthouses (客栈; kèzhàn) are plentiful, with basic rooms starting at about Y80. Restaurants are everywhere, but resist being steered towards the priciest dishes.

ZHÈNGFÚ CǍOTÁNG
Boutique Hotel **$$$**
(正福草堂; ☏6333 6358; www.zfct.net; 138 Mingqing Jie; 明清街138号; d Y380-1380; ❉@)
The best accommodation in town. There are 14 luxe rooms, all tastefully furnished in Qing-style furniture and antiques. Rooms wouldn't be out of place in a *Wallpaper* spread, with hues of gold, brown and ultramodern toilets. The larger, more expensive rooms have private spaces for musing.

TONGLI INTERNATIONAL YOUTH HOSTEL
Hostel **$**
(同里国际青年旅舍; ☏6333 9311; 210 Xintian Jie; 新填街210号; dm Y40, r Y100-160; ❉@☎)
The main location is hard to find (walk across the main bridge onto 中川北路, look on your right for a sign that says

Traditional wooden boats, Tónglǐ
PHOTOGRAPHER: BRUCE BI/LONELY PLANET IMAGES ©

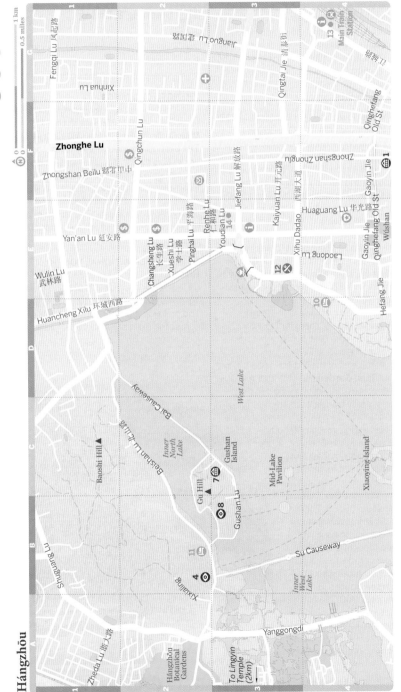

Hángzhōu

1 km
0.5 miles

Fengqi Lu 凤起路

Xinhua Lu

Jianguo Lu 建国路

Qingtai Jie 清泰街

Qingchun Lu

Zhonghe Lu

Zhongshan Beilu 中山北路

Jiefang Lu 解放路

Kaiyuan Lu 开元路

Zhongshan Zhonglu

Qinghefang Old St

Huaguang Lu 华光路

Yan'an Lu 延安路

Changsheng Lu 长生路

Xueshi Lu 学士路

Pinghai Lu 平海路

Renhe Lu 仁和路

Youdian Lu

Xihu Dadao 西湖大道

Gaoyin Jie · Gaoyin Lu

Gaoyin Jie

Qinghefang Old St

Wushan

Wulin Lu 武林路

Laodong Lu

Hefang Jie

Huancheng Xilu 环城西路

West Lake

Baoshi Hill ▲

Bai Causeway

Inner North Lake

Gushan Island

Gu Hill ▲

Mid-Lake Pavilion

Xiaoying Island

Gushan Lu

Shuguang Lu 曙光路

Su Causeway

Inner West Lake

Xixiling

Yanggongdi

Hángzhōu Botanical Gardens

To Linyin Temple (2km)

Zheda Lu 浙大入路

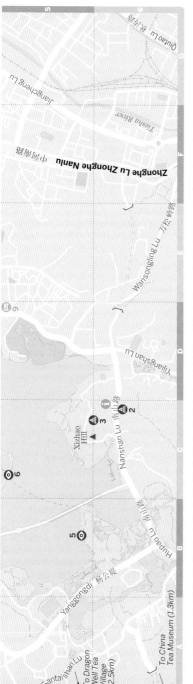

根和民居 and walk inside the tiny alley), but it's a stunner. Rooms are decked out in the owner's antique Ming furniture and the wooden pillars and stone courtyard ooze atmosphere.

ⓘ Getting There & Away

From Sūzhōu, take a bus (Y8, 50 minutes, every 30 minutes) from the South long-distance bus station to Tónglǐ. Grab an electric cart (Y2) from beside the Tónglǐ bus station to the Old Town, or you can walk it in about 15 minutes. Pedicabs might offer you rides into town to dodge the entry fee, but you really need the ticket to see the sights in the town so avoid them.

Buses return to Sūzhōu every 30 minutes (last bus 7.25pm). The last bus to drop you at the South long-distance bus station departs at 4.30pm. Buses thereafter drop you off behind Súzhóu's train station.

From Shànghǎi, sightseeing buses depart daily from the Shànghǎi Stadium at 8.30am and depart from Tónglǐ at 4.30pm; the journey takes up to 1¾ hours depending on traffic. Tickets are Y130 and include admission to Tónglǐ and its sights, bar the Chinese Sex Culture Museum. 10 daily buses (Y32) leave Tónglǐ bus station for Shànghǎi.

Hángzhōu 杭州

♪ 0571 / POP 6.16 MILLION

One of China's most revered tourist drawcards, Hángzhōu's dreamy West Lake panoramas and fabulously green and hilly environs can easily lull you into long sojourns. Religiously cleaned by armies of street sweepers and litter collectors, its scenic vistas draw you into a classical Chinese watercolour of willow-lined banks, ancient pagodas, mist-covered hills and the occasional *shíkùmén* building and old *lǐlòng*. West Lake is a delight to explore, either on foot or by bike. You'll need about three days to fully savour the picturesque Jiāngnán ('south of the Yangzi River') ambience, but the inclination is to take root – like one of the lakeside's lilting willows – and stay put.

◎ Sights
1 Húqìngyú Táng Chinese Medicine
   Museum F4
2 Jìngcí Temple C6
3 Léifēng Pagoda C6
4 Mausoleum of General Yue Fei B2
5 Red Carp Pond B5
6 Three Pools Mirroring the Moon..........C5
7 Zhèjiāng Provincial Museum................C3
8 Zhōngshān Park...................................B3

◎ Sleeping
9 Crystal Orange Hotel...........................D5

10 Mingtown Youth Hostel.......................D4
11 Shangri-La Hotel B2

◎ Eating
12 Lǎomǎjiā Miànguǎn..............................E3

Drinking
  Mingtown Youth Hostel...............(see 10)

Transport
13 Bus Ticket Office................................G4
14 Train Ticket Office..............................E3

History

Hángzhōu's history dates from the start of the Qin dynasty (221 BC). Marco Polo passed through in the 13th century, calling Hángzhōu Kinsai and noting in astonishment that Hángzhōu had a circumference of 100 miles while its waters were vaulted by 12,000 bridges.

Hángzhōu flourished after being linked with the Grand Canal in AD 610 but fully prospered after the Song dynasty was overthrown by the invading Jurchen, who captured the Song capital Kāifēng, along with the emperor and the leaders of the imperial court, in 1126. The remnants of the Song court fled south, finally settling in Hángzhōu and establishing it as the capital of the Southern Song dynasty.

With 10 city gates by Ming times, Hángzhōu took a hammering from Taiping rebels, who besieged the city in 1861 and captured it; two years later the imperial armies reclaimed it. Few monuments survived the devastation; much of what can be seen in Hángzhōu today is of fairly recent construction.

◎ Sights & Activities

Hángzhōu grants free admission to all museums and gardens. Other sights offer half-price tickets for children between 1m and 1.3m, free for shorties under 1m.

WEST LAKE   Lake

The very definition of classical beauty in China, West Lake (西湖; Xīhú) continues to mesmerise and methodical prettification has worked a cunning magic. Pagoda-topped hills rise over willow-lined waters as boats drift slowly through a vignette of leisurely charm.

Originally a lagoon adjoining the Qiántáng River, the lake didn't come into existence until the 8th century, when the governor of Hángzhōu had the marshy expanse dredged. As time passed the lake's splendour was gradually cultivated: gardens were planted, pagodas built, and causeways and islands constructed from dredged silt.

Celebrated poet Su Dongpo himself had a hand in the lake's development, constructing the **Su Causeway** (苏堤; Sūdī) during his tenure as local governor in the 11th century.

Connected to the northern shores by the Bai Causeway is **Gūshān Island** (孤山岛; Gūshān Dǎo), the largest island in the lake and the location of the **Zhèjiāng Provincial Museum** (浙江省博物馆; Zhèjiāng Shěng Bówùguǎn; 25 Gushan Lu; admission free, audio guide Y10; ◷8.30am-4.30pm Tue-Sun), **Zhōngshān Park** (中山公园; Zhōngshān Gōngyuán) and the Lóuwàilóu Restaurant.

The smaller island in the lake is **Xiǎoyíng Island** (小瀛洲; Xiǎoyíng Zhōu), where you can look over at **Three Pools Mirroring the Moon** (三潭印月; Sāntán Yìnyuè), three small towers in the water on the south side of the island;

each has five holes that release shafts of candlelight on the night of the mid-autumn festival. From Lesser Yíngzhōu Island, you can gaze over to **Red Carp Pond** (花港观鱼; Huāgǎng Guānyú), home to a few thousand red carp.

Cruise boats (游船; yóuchuán; incl entry to Three Pools adult/child Y45/22.5; ⏱7am-4.45pm) shuttle frequently from four points (Hubin Park, Red Carp Pond, Zhōngshān Park and the Mausoleum of General Yue Fei) to the Mid-Lake Pavilion (Húxīn Tíng) and Xiǎoyíng Island (Xiǎoyíng Zhōu). **Buggies** (⏱8am-6.30pm) speed around West Lake; just raise your hand to flag one down. A complete circuit is Y40, otherwise Y10 takes you to the next stop. Tourist buses Y1 and Y2 also run around West Lake.

LÉIFĒNG PAGODA   Pagoda
(雷峰塔; Léifēng Tǎ Jǐngqū; admission Y40; ⏱7.30am-9pm Mar-Nov, 8am-5.30pm Dec-Feb) Topped with a golden spire, the eye-catching Léifēng Pagoda can be climbed for fine views of the lake. The original pagoda, built in AD 977, collapsed in 1924. During renovations in 2001, Buddhist scriptures written on silk were discovered in the foundation, along with other treasures.

JÌNGCÍ TEMPLE   Buddhist Temple
(净慈寺; Jìngcí Sì; admission Y10; ⏱6am-5.30pm) The serene Chan (Zen) Jìngcí Temple was originally built in AD 954 and is now fully restored. The main hall – the **Great Treasure Hall** – contains a simply vast seated effigy of Sakyamuni. Hunt down the awesome **1000-arm Guanyin** (千手观音) in the Guanyin Pavilion with her huge fan of arms.

LÍNGYǏN TEMPLE   Buddhist Temple
(灵隐寺; Língyǐn Sì; Lingyin Lu; grounds Y35, grounds & temple Y65; ⏱7am-5pm) Hángzhōu's most famous Buddhist temple, Língyǐn Temple was built in AD 326. The main **temple buildings** are restorations of Qing-dynasty structures. Behind the Hall of the Four Heavenly Guardians stands the Great Hall and a magnificent 20m-high statue of Siddhartha Gautama (Sakyamuni), sculpted from 24 blocks of camphor wood in 1956 and based on a Tang-dynasty original. During the time of the Five Dynasties (907–60) about 3000 monks lived in the temple.

Boats parked at West Lake, Hángzhōu

WIBOWO RUSLI/LONELY PLANET IMAGES ©

The walk up to the temple skirts the flanks of **Fēilái Peak** (Fēilái Fēng; Peak Flying from Afar), magically transported here from India according to legend. The **Buddhist carvings** lining the riverbanks and hillsides, all 470 of them, date from the 10th to 14th centuries. To get a close-up view of the best carvings, including the famed 'laughing' Maitreya Buddha, follow the paths along the far (east) side of the stream.

Bus K7 and tourist bus Y2 (both from the train station), and tourist bus Y1 from the roads circling West Lake, go to the temple.

QĪNGHÉFĀNG OLD STREET

Shopping Street

At the south end of Zhongshan Zhonglu is this fun and fascinating bustling pedestrian street (清河坊历史文化街; Qīnghéfāng Lìshǐ Wénhuà Jiē), with makeshift puppet theatres, teahouses and curio stalls. It's also the home of several traditional medicine shops, including the **Húqìngyú Táng Chinese Medicine Museum** (中药

博物馆; Zhōngyào Bówùguǎn; 95 Dajing Gang; admission Y10; 8.30am-5pm), which is an actual dispensary and clinic.

 **Sleeping**

Book well ahead in the summer months, at weekends and during the busy holiday periods.

MINGTOWN YOUTH HOSTEL

Hostel **$**

(明堂杭州国际青年旅社; Míngtáng Hángzhōu Guójì Qīngnián Lǚshè; 8791 8948; 101-11 Nanshan Lu; 南山路101-11号; dm Y50, s Y180, d Y130-240; ✿ @) With its handy lakeside location, this friendly hostel is often booked out so reserve well ahead. It offers ticket booking, internet access, and rental of bikes and camping gear.

CRYSTAL ORANGE HOTEL   Hotel **$$$**

(桔子水晶酒店; Júzi Shuǐjīng Jiǔdiàn; 2887 8988; www.orangehotel.com; 122 Qingbo Jie; 清波街122号; tw Y788, ste Y1388, discounts of

Left: Sunset over West Lake, Hángzhōu (p230); **Below:** Laughing Buddha of Língyǐn Temple, Hángzhōu (p231)

PHOTOGRAPHER: (LEFT) JULIET COOMBE/LONELY PLANET IMAGES ©; (BELOW) KEREN SU/LONELY PLANET IMAGES ©

50%; ❄ @ 🛜) Uncluttered
and modern business hotel
with a crisp and natty interior,
Warhol prints in the lobby, glass lift and
only four floors, but sadly no views of
West Lake from the neat rooms.

SHANGRI-LA HOTEL Hotel **$$$**
(杭州香格里拉饭店; Hángzhōu Xiānggélǐlā
Fàndiàn; ☎ 8797 7951; fax 8707 3545; www.
shangri-la.com; 78 Beishan Lu; 北山路78号; d
Y1650, with lake view Y2500, discounts of 30%;
❄ @ 🛜 ≋) Surrounded by forest on the
north shore of the lake, this hotel enjoys a
winning, picturesque location. The hotel
has been around for a long time, so view
rooms first, as quality varies. Health club.

 Eating

Hángzhōu cuisine emphasises fresh,
sweet flavours and makes good use
of freshwater fish, especially eel and
carp. Hángzhōu's most popular res-
taurant street is Gaoyin Jie, parallel to

Qīnghéfāng Old St. Hángzhōu's leafy
answer to Shànghǎi's Xīntiāndì, **Xīhú
Tiāndì** (西湖天地; 147 Nanshan Lu) has an
attractive panoply of smart cafes and
restaurants.

GRANDMA'S KITCHEN Hangzhou **$**
(外婆家; Wàipójiā; 8 fl, Bldg B, Hangzhou Tower,
Huancheng Beilu; mains Y6-55; ⏲10.30am-2pm
& 4-9pm; 🗉)
Highly popular with locals, this chain
restaurant cooks up classic Hángzhōu
favourites; try the *hóngshāo dōngpō ròu*
(红烧东坡肉; braised pork). There are
several other branches in town.

LǍOMǍJIĀ MIÀNGUǍN Noodles **$**
(老马家面馆; 232 Nanshan Lu; meals Y15;
⏲7am-10.30pm)
Simple, popular and unfussy Muslim
restaurant stuffed into an old *shíkùmén*
building with a handful of tables and
spot-on *niúròu lāmiàn* (牛肉拉面,

233

beef noodles, Y7) and superscrummy *ròujiāmó* (肉夹馍, meat in a bun, Y5).

LÓUWÀILÓU RESTAURANT
Hangzhou $$$

(楼外楼; Lóuwàilóu; 30 Gushan Lu; mains Y30-200; ⏱10.30am-3.30pm & 4.30-8.45pm; 📖)
Founded in 1838, this is Hángzhōu's most famous restaurant. The local speciality is *xīhú cùyú* (西湖醋鱼, sweet and sour carp) and *dōngpō ròu* (东坡肉; braised pork) but there's a good choice of other well-priced standard dishes.

🍷 Drinking

For drinking, Shuguang Lu north of West Lake is the place; a brash clutch of lesser bars also operates opposite the China Academy of Art on Nanshan Lu (南山路).

MINGTOWN YOUTH HOSTEL
Bar

(明堂杭州国际青年旅社; 101-11 Nanshan Lu; ⏱7pm-1am) The hostel's lovely bar area is one of the most chilled-out spots in town, with comfy sofas, sensuous music, great atmosphere and a roof garden. Great range of brews, including Franziskaner Weissbier (Y32), or you can just sit back with a Tsingtao (Y18).

ℹ️ Information

Twenty-four-hour internet cafes are in abundance around the train station (typically Y4 or Y5 per hour); look for the neon signs '网吧'.

Bank of China (中国银行; Zhōngguó Yínháng; **177 Laodong Lu**) Offers currency exchange plus 24-hour ATM.

China Post (中国邮政; Zhōngguó Yóuzhèng; **Renhe Lu**) Close to West Lake.

Hángzhōu Tourist Information Center (杭州旅游咨询服务中心; Hángzhōu Lǚyóu Zīxún Fúwù Zhōngxīn; **Hángzhōu train station**) Provides basic travel info, free maps and tours. Other branches include one at Léifēng Pagoda and at **228 Yan'an Lu**.

Public Security Bureau Exit & Entry Administration Service Center (PSB; 公安局; Gōng'ānjú Bànzhèng Zhōngxīn; 📞8728 0600; **35 Huaguang Lu**; ⏱8.30am-noon & 2-5pm Mon-Fri) Can extend visas.

ℹ️ Getting There & Away

Air

Hángzhōu has flights to all major Chinese cities (bar Shànghǎi) and international connections to Hong Kong, Macau, Tokyo, Singapore and other destinations. Several daily flights connect to Běijīng (Y1050) and Guǎngzhōu (Y960).

One place to book air tickets is at the **Civil Aviation Administration of China** (CAAC; 中国民航; Zhōngguó Mínháng; 📞8666 8666; **390 Tiyuchang Lu**; ⏱7.30am-8pm). Most hotels will also book flights, generally with a Y20 to Y30 service charge.

Sculpture exhibition at a Shànghǎi gallery
PHOTOGRAPHER: ALAMY/ZHENG XIANZHANG

Bus

All four bus stations are outside the city centre; tickets can be conveniently bought for all stations from the bus ticket office (长途汽车售票处; Chángtú Qìchē Shòupiàochù; ☉6.30am-5pm) near the exit from Hángzhōu's main train station.

The east bus station (汽车东站; Qìchē Dōngzhàn;71 Genshan Xilu) is the most comprehensive, with buses to Shànghǎi (Y54, 2½ hours) and Wēnzhōu (Y140, 4½ hours).

The north bus station (汽车北站; Qìchē Běizhàn; 766 Moganshan Lu) has buses to Běijīng (Y410, 15 hours, one daily at 3.15pm) and Wūkāng (Y15, 45 minutes).

From Shànghǎi, buses leave frequently for Hángzhōu's **east bus station** (Y65, 2½ hours) from Shànghǎi's Hengfeng Rd bus station, the Shànghǎi south bus station and the main long-distance bus station. Buses (Y85, two hours) to Hángzhōu also run every 30 minutes between 10am and 9pm from the Hóngqiáo airport long-distance bus station. Regular buses (Y100, three hours) also run to Hángzhōu from Shànghǎi's Pǔdōng International Airport long-distance bus station.

Buses for Huáng Shān (Y59 to Y88, six hours) leave from the west bus station (汽车西站; Qìchē Xīzhàn; 357 Tianmushan Lu).

Train

Regular D-class express trains (Y54, 75 to 90 minutes) run daily to Hángzhōu from Shànghǎi South train station (Shànghǎi Nánzhàn); book weekend tickets in advance. Numerous other slow trains run between the two cities.

A handy evening express D-class train runs to Běijīng (soft seat/soft sleeper Y354/821, 11 hours, 8.15pm); book in advance. Z class and T class trains to Běijīng cost Y539 and take 13 hours.

Other trains from Hángzhōu include Xiàmén (D class, Y309, 6½ hours) and Xī'ān (Y341, 19 to 23 hours).

ⓘ Getting Around

To/From the Airport

Hángzhōu's airport is 30km from the city centre; taxi drivers ask around Y100 to Y130 for the trip. Shuttle buses (Y20, one hour) run every 15 minutes between 5.30am and 9pm from the CAAC office.

Bicycle

You'll be tripping over bike-hire outfits around West Lake (Y5 to Y10 per hour); the city's public bicycle scheme is cheaper. Youth hostels also rent out bikes.

Public Transport

BUS Hángzhōu has a clean, efficient bus system and getting around is easy. 'Y' buses are tourist buses; 'K' is simply an abbreviation of '*kōngtiáo*' (air-con). Tickets are Y2 to Y5. Following are popular bus routes:

Bus K7 Usefully connects the main train station to the western side of West Lake and Língyǐn Temple.

Tourist bus Y1 Circles West Lake in a return loop to Língyǐn Temple.

Tourist bus Y2 Goes from the main train station, along Beishan Lu and up to Língyǐn Temple.

Tourist bus Y3 Travels around West Lake to the China Silk Museum, China Tea Museum, Dragon Well Tea Village and the Southern Song-dynasty Guan Kiln.

METRO The No 1 Line of Hángzhōu's new metro system is due to open by 2012 and will run through the Main Train Station.

TAXI Metered Hyundai taxis are ubiquitous and start at Y10; figure on around Y20 to Y25 from the main train station (queues can be horrendous though) to Hubin Lu.

Around Hángzhōu

Mògānshān 莫干山

☏0572

A blessed release from the suffocating summer torpor roasting north Zhèjiāng, this delightful **hilltop resort** (admission Y80) was developed as a resort by 19th-century Europeans from Shànghǎi and Hángzhōu during the concession era, in the style of Lúshān and Jīgōngshān in Hénán. Refreshingly cool in summer and sometimes smothered in spectral fog, Mògānshān is famed for its scenic, forested views, towering bamboo and stone villa architecture; the mountain remains a weekend bolthole for expat *tàitai*'s (wives) fleeing the simmering lowland heat.

The best way to enjoy Mògānshān is just to wander the winding forest paths and stone steps, taking in some of the architecture en route. There's Shànghǎi gangster **Du Yuesheng's old villa** (杜月笙别墅; Dù Yuèshēng Biéshù) – now serving as a hotel – Chiang Kaishek's lodge, a couple of churches (375 Moganshan and 419 Moganshan) and many other villas linked (sometimes tenuously) with the rich and famous, including the **house** (毛主席下榻处; Máo Zhǔxí Xiàtàchù; 126 Moganshan) where Chairman Mao rested his chubby limbs.

Containing **Ta Mountain** (塔山; Tǎshān) in the northwest, the **Da Keng Scenic Area** (大坑景区; Dàkēng Jǐngqū) is great for rambling. You can pick up a Chinese map (Y4) at your hotel for some sense of orientation, otherwise there are billboard maps dotted about.

The **main village** (Mògānshān Zhèn) is centred around **Yinshan Jie** (荫山街), where you will find **China Post** (40 Moganshan; ◷8.30-11am & 1-4pm), a branch of the PSB (opposite the post office) and several hotels. For information on hikes or for suggestions for activities on Mògānshān, contact well-informed Mark

Kitto, at Moganshan Lodge, but he may appreciate it if you bought a coffee.

🛏 Sleeping

Mògānshān is full of hotels of varying quality, most housed in crumbling villas; room prices peak at weekends (Friday to Sunday). Don't expect to find any backpacker spots, but haggle your socks off to drive prices down; if you come off-season (eg early spring) you can expect good rates, but be warned that many hotels either shut up shop or close for renovation over the winter.

MOGANSHAN HOUSE 23   Hotel   **$$$**
(莫干山杭疗23号; Mògānshān Hángliáo 23 Hào; ☎803 3822; 23 Moganshan; 莫干山23号; weekday/weekend d Y900/1200, Y1250/1500; ❄️🛜) This exquisitely restored villa hits the Mògānshān nail squarely on the head, bursting with period charm, from art deco-style sinks, black-and-white tiled bathroom floors, wooden floorboards, and the original staircase to a lovely English kitchen. It's also kid-friendly with a family room, baby chairs and swings in the garden. There's only six rooms, so book well in advance, especially for weekend stays.

Picturesque water town, Wūzhèn

NAKED RETREATS

Farmhouses $$

(☏ 021 5465 9577; www.nakedretreats.cn; 329 Moganshan; 莫干山329号; per person rates weekday lodges/bungalows Y350/520, weekend Y450/750; ❄) Naked Retreats offers a selection of ecolodges, farmhouses and bungalows enveloped in bamboo forest sleeping anything from a couple to a crowd, plus lovely views. Range of activities also organised, from biking to fishing, trekking, stargazing, yoga and massage.

Eating

Yinshan Jie has a number of restaurants and hotels with restaurants.

MOGANSHAN LODGE

International $$

(马克的咖啡厅; Mǎkè de Kāfēitīng; ☏ 803 3011; www.moganshanlodge.com; Songliang Shanzhuang, just off Yinshan Jie; ⏰ 9am-11pm; 🛜) English Mògānshān resident Mark Kitto can cook up a treat, brew up a fine coffee and give you the low-down on Mògānshān's charms at this elegantly presented villa up some steps from Yinshan Jie.

Getting There & Away

From Hángzhōu, buses leave from the north bus station to Wǔkāng (武康; Y15, 40 minutes, every 30 minutes) from 6.20am to 7pm; in the other direction, buses run every 30 minutes from 6.30am to 7pm; note that Wǔkāng is also known as Déqīng (德清).

From Wǔkāng minivans run to the top of Mògānshān for around Y50; a taxi will cost around Y70 to Y80. Buses from Shànghǎi run to Wǔkāng (Y53, four hours) and leave from a small bus station near Baoshan Rd metro, at 80 Gongxing Rd. Buses depart from Shànghǎi at 6.30am, 11.50am and 12.50pm; buses depart from Wǔkāng for Shànghǎi at 6.30am, 7.40am, 1pm and 3.30pm. Buses also run between Shànghǎi north bus station and Wǔkāng (Y60).

Wūzhèn 乌镇

☏ 0573

Wūzhèn is a water town whose network of waterways and access to the Grand Canal once made it a prosperous place for its trade and production of silk.

Sights

Wūzhèn is tiny and it's possible to see everything in a couple of hours. Most people come here on a day trip from Hángzhōu or Shànghǎi. The main street of the old town, Dongda Jie, is a narrow path paved with stone slabs and flanked by wooden buildings. You pay an exorbitant entrance fee at the **main gate** (入口; rùkǒu; Daqiao Lu; through ticket Y150; ⏰ 8am-5pm), which covers entry to all of the exhibits. Some of these are workshops, such as the **Gongsheng Grains Workshop** (三白酒坊; Sānbái Jiǔfáng), an actual distillery churning out a pungent rice wine ripe for the sampling. Next door, the **Blue Prints Workshop** (蓝印花布作坊; Lán Yìnhuābù Zuòfang) shows the dyeing and printing process for the traditional blue cloth of the Jiāngnán region.

At the western end of the old town, around the corner on Changfeng Jie, is an interesting exhibit many visitors miss. The **Huìyuán Pawn House** (汇源当铺; Huìyuán Dàngpù) was once a famous pawnshop that eventually expanded to branches in Shànghǎi.

One of the best reasons to visit Wūzhèn is for the regular live performances of local **Flower Drum opera** (Huāgǔ xì) held throughout the day in the village square, and shadow-puppet shows (píyǐngxì) in the small theatre beside the square. The puppet shows in particular are great fun and well worth watching. You can hire a boat at the main gate (Y80 per person) for a ride down the canal.

Getting There & Away

From Hángzhōu, buses run from the east bus station to Wūzhèn (Y26, 1½ hours) leaving every hour or so from 6.25am to 6.25pm.

From Shànghǎi, the easiest (but most expensive) way is to take a tour bus (Y165 return, ticket includes the entrance fee to Wūzhèn and a Chinese-speaking guide, 9am and 9.30am, two hours) from Shànghǎi Stadium. A cheaper option is to take a bus from Shànghǎi's south bus station (Y46).

Minibuses (Y10) connect Wūzhèn with the canal town of Nánxún.

Pǔtuóshān 普陀山

0580

The lush and well-tended Buddhist island of Pǔtuóshān – the Zhōushān Archipelago's most famed isle – is the enchanting abode of Guanyin, the eternally compassionate Goddess of Mercy. With its clean beaches and fresh air, it's a perfect retreat, but try to visit midweek, as the island is bombarded by tourists come weekends. Spring can be fogged out with sporadic boat services, so phone ahead.

◉ Sights

The central part of town is around Pǔjì Temple about 1km north of the ferry terminal. This is where many hotels are located. You can reach the central square by taking the roads leading east or west from the ferry terminal; either way takes about 20 minutes. Alternatively, minibuses from the ferry terminal run to Pǔjì Temple and to other points of the island.

The first thing you see as you approach the island by boat is a 33m-high glittering statue of Guanyin, the **Nánhǎi Guānyīn** (南海观音; **admission Y6**), overlooking the waves at the southernmost tip of the island.

An entrance fee (summer/winter Y160/140) is payable when you arrive; entry to some other sights is extra.

PǓJÌ TEMPLE   Temple
(普济禅寺; **Pǔji Sì; admission Y5**; ⏱5.30am-6pm)
Fronted by large ponds and overlooked by towering camphor trees and Luóhàn Pines, this temple stands by the main square and dates to at least the 17th century. Chubby Milefo – the future Buddha – sits in a red, gold and green burnished cabinet in the Hall of Heavenly Kings. Buses leave from the west side of the temple to various points around the island.

FǍYǓ TEMPLE   Temple
(法雨禅寺; **Fǎyǔ Chánsì; admission Y5**; ⏱5.30am-6pm) Colossal camphor trees and a huge gingko tree tower over this temple, where a vast glittering statue of Guanyin is seated in the main hall, flanked by rows of histrionic *luóhàn* (arhat) effigies. In the hall behind stands a 1000-arm Guanyin. Get to the temple by bus from the ferry terminal (Y6).

Pǔjì Temple pavilion, Pǔtuóshān

ALAMY/MARK DUNN

Water Towns

If you liked either Zhūjiājiǎo (p220), Tónglǐ (p226) or Wūzhèn (p237), the provinces of Jiāngsū and Zhèjiāng are dotted with picturesque canal towns, characterised by ancient bridges, worn and ancient lanes, Qing-dynasty architecture and charming waterway vistas.

1 **LÙZHÍ** 甪直
(Jiāngsū Province; bus 518 from Sūzhōu's train station, Y4, one hour, first/last bus 6am/8pm)
A short bus journey from Sūzhōu, ancient Lùzhí's humpbacked bridges are delightful. Take a half-hour boat ride (Y40) to sample the canal views.

2 **MÙDÚ** 木渎
(Jiāngsū Province; tourist bus Y4 from Sūzhōu's train station, Y3) While Mùdú is neither the largest nor the most appealing of Jiāngsū's canal towns, it's location on the edges of Sūzhōu makes for convenient half-day tours.

3 **NÁNXÚN** 南浔
(Zhèjiāng Province; buses, Y10, link Nánxún and Wūzhèn) Nestling in Zhèjiāng near the border with Jiāngsū, this 1400-year-old town has an intriguing mix of Chinese and European architecture, introduced by affluent silk merchants.

FODING MOUNTAIN Mountain
(佛顶山; Fódǐng Shān; admission Y5) A fantastic, shaded half-hour climb can be made from Fǎyǔ Temple to Fódǐng Mountain – Buddha's Summit Peak – the highest point on the island. This is also where you will find the less elaborate **Huiji Temple** (慧济禅寺; Huìjì Chánsì; admission Y5; ⊙5.30am-6.30pm). In summer the climb is much cooler in the late afternoon; watch devout pilgrims and Buddhist nuns stop every three steps to either bow or kneel in supplication. The less motivated take the **cable car** (one way/return Y30/50; ⊙6.40am-5pm).

BEACHES Beach
Pǔtuóshān's two large beaches, **One Hundred Step Beach** (百步沙; Bǎibùshā; ⊙6am-6pm) and **One Thousand Step Beach** (千步沙; Qiānbùshā) on the east of the island are attractive and largely unspoilt, although periodically you may have to pay for access (admission Y15); swimming (May through August) is not permitted after 6pm.

🛏 Sleeping

Room prices are generally discounted from Sunday to Thursday; the prices given here refer to Friday and Saturday and holiday periods. Several hotels have shuttle buses to and from the pier.

PǓTUÓSHĀN HOTEL Hotel $$$
(普陀山大酒店; Pǔtuóshān Dàjiǔdiàn; ☎609 2828; www.putuoshanhotel.com; 93 Meicen Lu; 梅岑路93号; d Y1188-1288, ste Y1988; ❄ @)
Backing onto a green hill, Pǔtuóshān's best hotel is pleasant and uncluttered, with decent amenities and service to match. Midweek rooms are discounted to Y650.

HǍITŌNG HOTEL Hotel $$$
(海通宾馆; Hǎitōng Bīnguǎn; ☎609 2569; d Y680-780, t with seaview Y980, midweek/weekend discounts of 60%/30%; ❄) Across the road as you exit the ferry terminal, this agreeable place has helpful staff and a tempting traditional feel.

✖ Eating

Pǔtuóshān isn't famed for its food; what you get is generally brought in from the mainland and is expensive. Some of the best places to eat are in the temples, where vegetarian meals are usually served at lunch and sometimes at breakfast and dinner for Y2 to Y10.

ℹ Information

Bank of China (中国银行; Zhōngguó Yínháng; Meicen Lu; ⊙8-11am & 2-5pm) Has Forex currency exchange. ATMs (24-hour) taking international cards are close by down the side of the block.

China Post (邮局; yóujú; 124 Meicen Lu) Southwest of Pǔjì Temple.

Clinic (诊所; Zhěnsuǒ; ☎609 3102; Meicen Lu) Situated behind the Bank of China.

Industrial & Commercial Bank of China (工行; Gōngháng; Meicen Lu; ⊙8-11am & 2-5pm)

Tourist Service Center (旅游咨询中心; Lǚyóu Zīxún Zhōngxīn; ☎609 4921) Near Pǔjì Temple.

ℹ Getting There & Away

The nearest airport is on the neighbouring island of Zhūjiājiān (朱家尖).

Regular boats link Pǔtuóshān and Zhūjiājiān, while a nightly boat leaves Pǔtuóshān at 4.40pm for the 12-hour voyage to Shànghǎi's Wúsōng Wharf. Tickets cost Y109 to Y499, offering numerous grades of comfort; it's easy to upgrade once you're on board. From Shànghǎi, the boat leaves Wúsōng Wharf at 8pm, with an extra two services on Friday at 7.20pm and 8.40pm. To reach Wúsōng Wharf, take **metro Line** 3 to Songbin Lu from where it's a 15-minute walk. Cross the eight-lane highway and follow the signs to the wharf. Bank on a 90-minute journey from People's Square.

A **fast boat** (Y258) departs Pǔtuóshān for the port of Xiǎo Yáng Shān (小洋山) south of Shànghǎi at 1pm, where passengers are then bused to Nanpu Bridge; the whole trip takes four hours. The twice-daily bus/ferry from Shànghǎi to Pǔtuóshān departs from Xiǎo Yáng Shān; shuttle buses leave depart Nanpu Bridge in Shànghǎi at 7.20am and 8am to connect with them. From Pǔtuóshān, the ferry departs at 1pm.

Tickets for both ferry and bus/ferry services are available at the Shanghai Port Wusong Passenger Transport Centre (Shànghǎi Gǎng Wúsōng Kèyùn Zhōngxīn Shòupiàochù; ☎5657 5500) or Huángpǔ Tourist Centre (黄浦旅游集散中心; Huángpǔ Lǚyou'u Jísàn Zhōngxīn; ☎6336 9051; 21 East Jinling Rd; 金陵东路21号; ⊙9am-6pm)

ℹ Getting Around

Walking around Pǔtuóshān is the most relaxing option if you have time. If not, minibuses zip from the passenger ferry terminal to various points around the island, including Pǔjì Temple (Y5), One Thousand Step Beach (Y6), Fǎyǔ Temple (Y6), Fànyīn Cave (Y8) and the cable-car station (Y10). There are more bus stations at Pǔjì Temple, Fǎyǔ Temple and other spots around the island serving the same and other destinations.

Túnxī 屯溪

☎0559 / POP 75,000

Ringed by low-lying hills, the old trading town of Túnxī (also called Huángshān Shì) is the main springboard for trips to Huángshān and the surrounding Huīzhōu villages.

🛏 Sleeping

OLD STREET HOSTEL Hostel **$**
(老街国际青年旅舍; Lǎojiē Guójì Qīngnián Lǚshè; ☎254 0386; www.hiourhostel.com; 266 Lao Jie; 老街266号; dm/d/tw/tr/f Y40/129/149/188/200; ✳@🛜) With its convenient location and decent rooms – the four-person dorms come with proper mattresses and private bathrooms, while the private rooms sport wood-lattice decor and flat-screen TVs – this place clearly has an appeal that extends beyond the backpacking crowd.

✖ Eating & Drinking

There are cheap street eats and a variety of local restaurants in the area just east of the eastern end of Old St. The streets abutting Old St are constantly being renovated and are home to a bunch of restaurants and cute coffees shops and bars.

MĚISHÍ RÉNJIĀ
Hui Cuisine **$**

(美食人家; Lao Jie; dishes Y6-38; ☺lunch & dinner) At the offical entrance to Lao Jie, this bustling restaurant – spread over two floors and hung with traditional Chinese *mǎdēng* lanterns – seethes with satisfied customers. Peruse the counter for a range of dishes – *húntun* (wontons; dumpling soup), *jiǎozi* (stuffed dumplings), *bāozi* (steamed buns stuffed with meat or vegetables), noodles, claypot and more – on display, have them cooked fresh to order and sink a delicious glass of sweet *zǐmǐlù* (紫米露), made from purple glutinous rice.

ℹ Information

Bank of China (中国银行; Zhōngguó Yínháng; cnr Xin'an Beilu & Huangshan Xilu; ☺8am-5.30pm) Changes travellers cheques and major currencies; 24-hour ATM takes international cards.

China Post (中国邮局; Zhōngguó Yóuqū; 183 Lao Jie)

Public Security Bureau (PSB; 公安局; Gōng'ānjú; ☎232 3093; 1st fl, 108 Changgan Zhonglu; ☺8am-noon & 2.30-5pm)

ℹ Getting There & Away

Air

There are flights from **Huángshān City Airport** (黄山市飞机场; **Huángshānshì Fēijīchǎng**) to Běijīng (Y1090, two hours, one daily), Guǎngzhōu (Y960, 1½ hours, one daily) and Shànghǎi (Y580, one hour, one daily), and thrice-daily flights to Hong Kong (Y2188, 1¾ hours).

Bus

The **long-distance bus station** (客运总站; kèyùn zǒngzhàn; Qiyun Dadao) is roughly 2km west of the train station on the outskirts of town. Destinations include Hángzhōu (Y85, three hours, hourly from 6.50am to 5.50pm), Shànghǎi (Y132, five hours, five daily – last bus 3.50pm), Sūzhōu (Y100, six hours, 6am daily) and Wùyuán (Y34, two hours, 8.20am and 12.30pm daily).

Within Ānhuī, buses go to Shèxiàn (Y6, 45 minutes, frequent services) and Yīxiàn (Y12.50, one hour, frequent services 6am to 5pm).

Buses to Huángshān go to the main base at Tāngkǒu (Y13, one hour, frequent, 6am to 5pm) and on to the north entrance, Tàipíng (Y20, two hours). There are also minibuses to Tāngkǒu (Y15) from in front of the train station.

Inside the bus station (to the right as you enter) is the separate **Huángshān Tourist Distribution Center** (黄山市旅游集散中心; Lǚyóu Jísàn Zhōngxīn; ☎255 8358; ☺7.30am-6pm) with special tourist buses to popular destinations. Return buses operate hourly from 8am to 4pm with a two-hour break from 11am to 1pm. They include Hóngcūn (Y14, 1½ hours) and Xīdì (Y12, one hour).

Climbing Huángshān

Bus 9 (Y1) runs between the bus station and train station; otherwise, a taxi should cost Y7 to Y10.

Train

Train connections are abysmal. Trains from Běijīng (Y195 to Y330, 20 hours, 9.21am), Shànghǎi (Y94 to Y175, 13 hours, 7.10pm and 10.11pm) and Nánjīng (Y64 to Y108, six to 7½ hours, 15 daily) stop at Túnxī (generally called Huángshān). For better connections to southern destinations, first go to Yīngtán (Y51 to Y196, five to seven hours, nine daily) in Jiāngxī and change trains there.

🛈 Getting Around

Taxis are Y5 at flag fall, with the 5km taxi ride to the airport costing about Y30. Competition among pedicab drivers is fierce, so they are the cheapest way of getting around, costing approximately Y4 for a trip to Old St from the train station area. Short rides start at Y2.

Huángshān 黄山

📞 0559 / ELEV 1873M

When its archetypal granite peaks and twisted pines are wreathed in spectral folds of mist, Huángshān's idyllic views easily nudge it into the select company of China's top 10, nay, top five, sights. Yesterday's artists seeking an escape from the hustle

Tour group photographing scenery, Huángshān

and bustle of the temporal world may have been replaced by crowds of tourists, who bring the hustle and bustle with them, but Huángshān still rewards visitors with moments of tranquillity, and the unearthly views can be simply breathtaking.

Climate

Spring (April to June) generally tends to be misty, which means you may be treated to some stunning scenery, but you're just as likely to encounter a thick fog that obscures everything except for a line of yellow ponchos extending up the trail. Summer (July to August) is the rainy season, though storms can blow through fairly quickly. Autumn (September to October) is generally considered to be the best travel period. Even at the height of summer, average temperatures rarely rise above 20°C at the summit, so come prepared.

 Sights & Activities

Buses from Túnxī (Huángshān Shì) drop you off in Tāngkǒu, the sprawling town

DIANA MAYFIELD/LONELY PLANET IMAGES ©

Huángshān

⊚ Sights

1 Bànshān Temple A3
2 Front Gate B4
3 Mercy Light Temple A3
   Mt Huángshān Visitors Centre .... (see 3)
4 Refreshing Terrace A1
5 West Sea Canyon (Ring Road 1) A1
6 West Sea Canyon (Ring Road 2) A1

⊖ Sleeping

7 Běihǎi Hotel A1
8 Páiyúnlóu Hotel A1

Transport

9 Long-Distance Bus Station B4
10 Mercy Light Temple Station A3
11 Yungu Station B2

at the foot of Huángshān. A base for climbers, this is the place to stock up on supplies (maps, raincoats, food, money), store your excess luggage and arrange onward transport.

Spend some time in the perfectly preserved Hui villages of Xīdì and Hóngcūn around the mountain's base.

Ascending & Descending the Mountain

Regardless of how you ascend **Huángshān** (admission 1 Mar–30 Nov Y230, 1 Dec–29 Feb Y130, seniors year-round Y60, child 1.1-1.3m in height year-round Y60), you will be stung by the dizzying entrance fee. You can pay at the eastern steps near the **Yúngǔ Station** (云谷站; Yúngǔ Zhàn) or at the **Mercy Light Temple Station** (慈光阁站; Cíguāng Gé Zhàn), where the western steps begin. Shuttle buses (Y13) run to both places from Tāngkǒu.

Three basic routes will get you up to the summit: the short, hard way (eastern steps); the longer, harder way (western steps); and the very short, easy way (cable car). The eastern steps lead up from the Yúngǔ Station; the western steps lead up from the parking lot near Mercy Light Temple. It's possible to do a 10-hour circuit going up the eastern steps and then down the western steps in one day, but you'll have to be slightly insane, in good shape and you'll definitely miss out

Huángshān

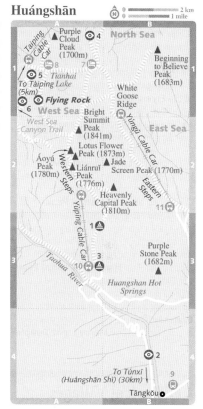

on some of the more spectacular, hard-to-get-to areas.

Make sure to bring enough water, food, warm clothing and rain gear before climbing; taking sunscreen is also recommended. Bottled water and food prices increase the higher you go.

EASTERN STEPS

A medium-fast climb of the 7.5km eastern steps from **Yúngǔ Station** (890m) to **White Goose Ridge** (白鹅峰; Bái'é Fēng; 1770m) can be done in 2½ hours. The route is pleasant, but lacks the awesome geological scenery of the western steps. Much of the climb is comfortably shaded and although it can be tiring, it's a doddle compared with the western steps. Slow-moving porters use the eastern steps for ferrying up their loads, so considerable traffic plies the route.

WESTERN STEPS

The 15km western steps route has some stellar scenery, but it's twice as long and strenuous as the eastern steps, and much easier to enjoy if you're clambering down rather than gasping your way up.

The western steps descent begins at the **Flying Rock** (飞来石; Fēilái Shí), a boulder perched on an outcrop half an hour from Běihǎi Hotel, and goes over **Bright Summit Peak** (光明顶; Guāngmíng Dǐng; 1841m).

Further on, **Lotus Flower Peak** (莲花峰; Liánhuā Fēng; 1873m) marks the highest point, but is occasionally sealed off, preventing ascents. **Liánruǐ Peak** (莲蕊峰; Liánruǐ Fēng; 1776m) is decorated with rocks whimsically named after animals, but save some energy for the much-coveted and staggering climb – 1321 steps in all – up **Heavenly Capital Peak** (天都峰; Tiāndū Fēng; 1810m) and the stunning views that unfold below.

Further below, the steps lead to **Bànshān Temple** (半山寺; Bànshān Sì) and below that the **Mercy Light Temple** (慈光阁; Cíguāng Gé), where you can pick up a minibus back to Tāngkǒu (Y13) or continue walking to the hot springs area.

YÚNGǓ CABLE CAR

Shuttle buses (Y13) ferry visitors from Tāngkǒu to the **Cable Car** (云谷索道; Yúngǔ Suǒdào; one-way 1 Mar-20 Nov Y80, 1 Dec-29 Feb Y65; ⏱7am-4.30pm). Shuttle buses (Y13) also run from Tāngkǒu to Mercy Light Temple, which is linked by the **Yùpíng Cable Car** (玉屏索道; Yùpíng Suǒdào; one-way 1 Mar-20 Nov Y80, 1 Dec-29 Feb Y65; ⏱7am-4.30pm) to the area just below the Yùpínglóu Hotel.

On the Summit

The summit is essentially one huge network of connecting trails and walks that meander up, down and across several different peaks. **Refreshing Terrace** (清凉台; Qīngliáng Tái) is five minutes' walk from Běihǎi Hotel and attracts sunrise crowds (most hotels supply thick padded jackets for the occasion). Lucky visitors are rewarded with the luminous spectacle of *yúnhǎi* (literally 'sea of

Historical Villages

Dating to AD 1047, the village of **Xīdì** (西递; admission Y80) has for centuries been a stronghold of the Hu (胡) clan, descended from the eldest son of the last Tang emperor who fled here in the twilight years of the Tang dynasty. Typical of the Huīzhōu style, Xīdì's 124 surviving buildings reflect the wealth and prestige of the prosperous merchants who settled here. This Unesco World Heritage village is a picturesque tableau of slender lanes, cream-coloured walls topped with horse-head gables, roofs capped with dark tiles, and doorways ornately decorated with carved lintels. When you're done with the village, pop out on paths leading out to nearby hills where there are suitable spots for your picture-postcard panoramas of the village.

Dating to the southern Song dynasty, the delightful village and Unesco World Heritage site of **Hóngcūn** (宏村; admission Y80), 11km northeast of Yīxiàn, has at its heart the crescent-shaped Moon Pond and is encapsulated by South Lake, West Stream and Léigng Mountain. The village is a charming and unhurried portrait of bridges, lakeside views, narrow alleys and traditional halls. If the bridge at the entrance to the village looks familiar, it's because it featured in a scene from Ang Lee's *Crouching Tiger, Hidden Dragon*. The busy square by Hóngjì Bridge on the West Stream is shaded by two ancient trees (the 'horns' of the ox), a red poplar and a gingko. Admission includes a guide.

Lookout over West Sea scenic area, Huángshān

DIANA MAYFIELD/LONELY PLANET IMAGES ©

clouds'): idyllic pools of mist that settle over the mountain, filling its chasms and valleys with fog and turning its peaks into islands that poke from the clouds.

The staggering and other-worldly views from the summit reach out over huge valleys of granite and enormous formations of rock, topped by gravity-defying slivers of stone and the gnarled forms of ubiquitous Huángshān pine trees (*Pinus taiwanensis*).

West Sea Canyon 西海大峡谷

A strenuous and awe-inspiring 8.5km hike, this route descends into a **gorge** (Xīhǎi Dàxiágǔ) and has some impressively exposed stretches (it's not for those afraid of heights), taking a minimum four hours to complete. Avoid the area in bad weather.

 **Sleeping**

Tāngkǒu 汤口
Mediocre midrange hotels line Tāngkǒu's main strip, Feicui Lu.

HUÁYÌ BĪNGUǍN   Hotel **$$**
(华艺宾馆; ☎ 556 6888; South Gate; 南大门; tw Y480-680; ❄) A large white edifice on the west side of the river on the Huángshān access road, this four-star hotel offers the priciest and nicest (the word being relative in this context) accommodation in Tāngkǒu. Prices in the three-star building are lower.

The Summit 山顶
Ideally, Huángshān visits include nights on the summit. Note that room prices will rise on Saturday and Sunday and are astronomical during major holiday periods.

BĚIHǍI HOTEL   Hotel **$$$**
(北海宾馆; Běihǎi Bīnguǎn; ☎ 558 2555; www.hsbeihaihotel.com; dm Y200, s & d Y1680, discounts of 30%; @) The four-star Běihǎi comes with professional service, money exchange, a mobile-phone charging point, cafe and 30% discounts during the week. Larger doubles with private bathroom have older fittings than the smaller, better-fitted-out doubles (same price). Although the best-equipped hotel, it's also the busiest and least charming.

245

PÁIYÚNLÓU HOTEL Hotel $$

(排云楼宾馆; Páiyúnlóu Bīnguǎn; ☎558 1558; dm/d/tr Y280/1280/1480; @) With an excellent location near Tiānhǎi Lake (Tiānhǎi Hú) and the entrance to the West Sea Canyon, plus four-star comfort, this place is recommended for those who prefer a slightly more tranquil setting. Ironically, none of the regular rooms has any views, but the newer dorms are unobstructed and come with attached showers.

ℹ Information

Tāngkǒu

If you have extra luggage, leave your bags (Y2 to Y5) at one of the travellers' restaurants, which are also good sources of information.

Bank of China (中国银行; Zhōngguó Yínháng; ☺8am-5pm) Southern end of Yanxi Jie.

Public Security Bureau (PSB; 公安局; gōng'ānjú; ☎556 2311) Western end of the bridge.

On the Mountain

Most hotels on the mountain have internet access areas for guests and nonguests, with hourly rates of Y15 to Y20.

Bank of China (中国银行; Zhōngguó Yínháng; ☺8-11am & 2.30-5pm) Opposite Běihǎi Hotel. Money can be changed here. There is an ATM that accepts international cards.

Police station (派出所; pàichūsuǒ; ☎558 1388) Beside the bank.

ℹ Getting There & Away

Buses from Túnxī (aka Huángshān Shì) take around one hour to reach Tāngkǒu from either the long-distance bus station (Y13, one hour, frequent departures, 6am to 5pm) or the train station (Y15, departures when full, 6.30am to 5pm, may leave as late as 8pm in summer). Buses back to Túnxī from Tāngkǒu are plentiful, and can be flagged down on the road to Túnxī (Y13). The last bus back leaves at 5.30pm.

Tāngkǒu's long-distance bus station (东岭换乘分中心; Dōnglǐng Huànchéng Fēnzhōngxīn) is east of the town centre. Your hotel should be able to help with bookings and even pick-up or transfers. Buses run to **Hángzhōu** Y90 to Y95, 3½ hours, seven daily, **Héféi** Y77, four hours, four daily, **Shànghǎi** Y120, 6½ hours, 6.30am daily and **Yīxiàn** Y15, one hour, four daily.

ℹ Getting Around

Official tourist shuttle buses run between the bus station and the hot springs area (Y7), Yúngǔ Station (云谷站; Yúngǔ Zhàn; eastern steps, Y13) and Mercy Light Temple Station (慈光阁站; Cíguānggé Zhàn; western steps, Y13). Officially they depart every 20 minutes from 6am to 5.30pm, though they usually don't budge until enough people are on board. Taking a taxi to the eastern or western steps will cost Y50; to the hot springs area Y30m.

Cable car from hotel, Huángshān

Wùyuán 婺源

♪0793 / POP 81,200

The countryside around Wùyuán is home to some of southeastern China's most immaculate views. Parcelled away in this hilly pocket is a scattered cluster of picturesque Huīzhōu villages, where old China remains preserved in enticing panoramas of ancient bridges, glittering rivers and stone-flagged alleyways.

Despite lending its name to the entire area, Wùyuán itself – also called Zǐyángzhèn (紫阳镇) – is a far-from-graceful town and best avoided.

There are two main ticketing options to see the countryside: either a **five-day pass** (Y180), which grants you admission to 12 sights, or the **single tickets** at each village (Y60 each). The pass covers a number of villages (only the most interesting are listed here), including Sīxī/Yáncūn, Little Lǐkēng (Xiǎo Lǐkēng) and Xiǎoqǐ, plus various other sights such as the Rainbow Bridge (Qīnghuá). Big Lǐkēng (Dà Lǐkēng) has a separate admission fee.

Hire an English-speaking guide (Y200 per day) and driver at the **CITS office** (中国国际旅行社; Zhōngguó Guójì Lǚxíngshè; ♪0798 862 9999) in nearby Jǐngdézhèn.

The Wùyuán **main bus station** (婺源汽车站; Wùyuán qìchēzhàn) is located west of town; a motorbike or taxi here should cost you Y5. Note that buses that arrive at night (such as the Shànghǎi one) will drop you off at the north end of town, not at the station. There are also buses to/from **Hángzhōu** (Y123, 3½ hours, two daily) and **Túnxī** (Y40, 2½ hours, two daily).

CRUISING THE YANGZI

Few river panoramas have inspired as much awe as the Three Gorges (三峡; Sānxiá). Well-travelled Tang dynasty poets have gone weak-kneed before them. Voluble emperors and hard-boiled communist party VIPs have been rendered speechless. Flotillas of sightseers have megapixelled their way from Chóngqìng to Yíchāng.

Yet the gorges these days get mixed press. Some travellers have their socks well and truly blown away; others arrive in Yíchāng scratching their heads and wondering what all the fuss was about. The reservoir that has built up behind the Three Gorges Dam – a body of water almost the length of England – is also taking its toll.

Apart from bringing some binoculars with you, here are four handy tips to maximise your enjoyment of the Three Gorges:

○ Try to ensure the Three Gorges aren't just one of three things on your China tour

○ Disregard the roar of a marketing machine selling the Three Gorges like there was no tomorrow

○ Treat the journey as an occasion to unwind from the effort of getting around China

○ Take along a good read

If you don't have the time for the *Three Gorges* Director's Cut, hop on the hydrofoil and jet down for the shorter and edited (but perhaps equally enjoyable) highlights version.

The Effects of the Dam

The dwarfing chasms of rock, sculpted over aeons by the irresistible volume of water, are the Yangzi River's most fabled reach. In brief, the gorges have been undoubtedly affected by the rising waters. The peaks are not as towering as they once were, nor are the flooded chasms through which boats travel as narrow and pinched. The effect is more evident to seasoned boat hands or repeat visitors who are more inclined to repeat the 'you should have seen them in the old days' mantra, accompanied by a knowing look.

The Route

Apocryphally the handiwork of the Great Yu, a legendary architect of the river, the gorges – Qútáng, Wū and Xīlíng – commence just east of Fèngjié in Chóngqìng and level out west of Yíchāng in Húběi province, a distance of around 200km.

Chóngqìng to Wànzhōu
重庆 – 万州

Passing the drowned town of Fúlíng (涪陵), the first port of call is at **Fēngdū** (丰都), 170km from Chóngqìng. Long nicknamed the **City of Ghosts** (鬼城; Guǐchéng), the town is just that: inundated in 2009, its residents were moved across the river. This is the stepping-off point for crowds to clamber up – or take the cable car (Y20) up – **Míng Shān** (名山; admission Y60), with its theme-park crop of ghost-focused temples.

Drifting through the county of Zhōngzhōu, the boat takes around three hours to arrive at **Shíbǎozhài** (石宝寨; Stone Treasure Stockade; admission Y80; ⊙8am-4pm) on the northern bank of the river. A 12-storey, 56m-high wooden pagoda built on a huge, river-encircled rock bluff, the structure originally dates to the reign of Qing-dynasty emperor Kangxi (1662–1722).

Most morning boats moor for the night at partially inundated **Wànzhōu**

(万州; also called Wànxiàn). Travellers aiming to get from A to B as fast as possible while taking in the gorges can skip the Chóngqìng to Wànzhōu section by hopping on a three-hour bus and then taking either the hydrofoil or a passenger ship from the Wànzhōu jetty.

Wànzhōu to Yíchāng
万州–宜昌

Boats departing from Wànzhōu soon pass the relocated **Zhāng Fēi Temple** (张飞庙; Zhāngfēi Miào; admission Y20), where short disembarkations may be made. The ancient town of **Fèngjié** (奉节), capital of the state of Kui during the the 'Spring and Autumn' (722–481 BC) and 'Warring States' (475–221 BC) periods, overlooks **Qútáng Gorge** (瞿塘峡; Qútáng Xiá), the first of the three gorges. The town – where most ships and hydrofoils berth – is also the entrance point to half-submerged **White King Town** (白帝城; Báidìchéng; admission Y50), where the King of Shu, Liu Bei, entrusted his son and kingdom to Zhu

Geliang, as chronicled in *The Romance of the Three Kingdoms*.

Qútáng Gorge – also known as Kui Gorge (夔峡; Kuí Xiá) – rises dramatically into view, towering into huge vertiginous slabs of rock, its cliffs jutting out in jagged and triangular chunks. The shortest and narrowest of the three gorges, 8km-long Qútáng Gorge is over almost as abruptly as it starts, but is considered by many to be the most awe-inspiring.

After Qútáng Gorge the terrain folds into a 20km stretch of low-lying land before boats pull in at the riverside town of **Wūshān** (巫山), situated high above the river. Many boats stop at Wūshān for five to six hours so passengers can transfer to smaller tour boats for trips along the **Little Three Gorges** (小三峡; Xiǎo Sānxiá; tickets Y150-200) on the Daning River (大宁河; Dàníng Hé).

Back on the Yangzi River, boats pull away from Wūshān to enter the **Wū Gorge** (巫峡; Wū Xiá), under a bright red bridge. The 'Gorge of Witches' is stunning, cloaked in green and carpeted in shrubs, its cliffs frequently disappearing into ethereal layers of mist. About 40km in length, its towering cliffs are topped by sharp, jagged peaks on the northern bank.

At 80km, **Xīlíng Gorge** (西陵峡; Xīlíng Xiá) is the longest and perhaps least impressive gorge; sections of the gorge in the west have been submerged. Then the monumental **Three Gorges Dam** (三峡大坝; Sānxiá Dàbà; admission Y105) looms up and boats stop so passengers can shuttle across to the dam's observation deck for a bird's-eye view of this mammoth project.

Boats & Tickets

In Chóngqìng, most hotels, hostels and travel agents can sell you a trip, some on the luxury cruise ships aimed primarily at Western tourists. You can also buy

249

tickets for the ordinary ferries at the **ferry port ticket hall** (重庆港售票大厅; Chóngqìnggǎng Shòupiào Dàtīng; ⏰6am-10pm), accessed from under the bridge on Chaoqian Lu (朝千路) in Chóngqìng. An option is **Chongqing Port International Travel Service** (重庆港国际旅行社; Chóngqing Gǎng Guójì Lǚxíngshè; ☎023-6618 3683; www. cqpits.com.cn; 18 Xinyi Jie), where staff speak English. In Yíchāng, **China International Travel Service** (CITS; 中国国际旅行社; Zhōngguó Guójì Lǚxíngshè; ☎625 3088; Yunji Lu; ⏰8.30am-5.30pm) can arrange tickets. Alternatively buy tickets for passenger ships and the hydrofoil from the **Yíchāng Ferry Terminal** (宜昌港客运站; Yíchāng Gǎng Kèyùnzhàn; Yanjing Dadao).

Luxury Cruises

The most luxurious passage is on international standard cruise ships, where maximum comfort and visibility accompany a leisurely agenda. Trips include shore visits to all the major sights (Three Gorges Dam, Little Three Gorges et al), allowing time to tour the attractions, (often secondary to the scenery). Cabins have air-con, TV (perhaps satellite), fridge/minibar and perhaps more. These vessels are ideal for travellers with time, money and negligible Chinese skills. The average duration for such a cruise is three nights and three to four days.

Tourist Boats

Typically departing from Chóngqìng at around 9pm, Chinese tourist cruise ships usually take around 2½ days to reach Yíchāng. Some Chinese cruise ships stop at all the sights; others stop at just a few (or none at all). They are less professional than the luxury tour cruises and are more aimed at domestic travellers (Chinese food, little spoken English).

Prices for cruise ships that do not stop at the tourist sights:

1st class Y1042, two-bed cabin with shower

2nd class upper/lower bunk Y483/530, four-bed cabins

3rd class upper/lower bunk Y317/347, six-bed cabins

Vessels that stop at six tourist sights:

1st class Y1525, two-bed cabin with shower

2nd class upper/lower bunk Y992/1060, four-bed cabins

3rd class from Y620, six-bed cabins

Passenger Ships

A further alternative is to board a straightforward passenger ship from Chóngqìng to Yíchāng. They are cheap, but can be disappointing: you will sail through the first two gorges in the dead of night and only catch the last gorge. Stops are frequent but hasty and they pass tourist sights by. Journeys take 36 hours (38 hours from Yíchāng to Chóngqìng). Shared toilets and showers can be grotty. Meals on board are average, so take along your

Chóngqìng cruise

Chóngqìng & Yíchāng

CHÓNGQÌNG 重庆

Most visitors tend to agree there's a unique feel to Chóngqìng (重庆), an allure not found in other major Chinese cities. Once a striking feature of the Chóngqìng skyline, stilt houses (吊脚楼; *diàojiǎo lóu*) were, in many ways, the predecessor to the modern skyscraper: sprawling vertically to save space. However, modernisation has turned stilt housing into a symbol of poverty and as a result they have all but disappeared in the city centre.

Chóngqìng has excellent air, bus and rail connections to many destinations within China.

YÍCHĀNG 宜昌

A scruffy city of four million souls, Yíchāng is on the map as a hopping-on or hopping-off point for ferries to the spectacular Three Gorges.

The huge **Three Gorges Dam** (三峡大坝; Sānxiá Dàbà; admission Y105) hulks away upstream. The world's largest due to length (2.3km), it isn't the most spectacular. Take a bus from the long-distance station to Máopíng (茅坪; Y15), but get off at Bālù Chēzhàn (八路车战). Alternatively, take bus 4 from the ferry terminal to Yèmíngzhū (夜明珠; Y1) then change to bus 8 (Y10), which terminates at Bālù Chēzhàn. Tours (Y150 inclusive of admission) leave from **Hubei Xiazhou International Travel Service** (☎644 0001; 78 Yiling Lu).

Hotel options include **Yíchāng Hotel** (宜昌饭店; Yíchāng Fàndiàn; ☎644 1616; 113 Dongshan Dadao; 东山大道113号; s/d Y288/268; ❄ @) and **25 Hours Hotel** (25 Hours 块捷 酒店; 25 Hours Kuàijié Jiǔdiàn; ☎691 0000; 1 Guoyuan Lu; 果园路1号; s/d Y288/298; ❄ 📶).

Zili Lu has loads of cheap restaurants offering filling bowls of *zhōu* (粥; porridge; Y4) and various noodle dishes.

Daily flights from Three Gorges Airport (三峡机场; Sānxiá Jīchǎng) go to Běijīng, Shànghǎi and Xī'ān. Trains and buses connect Yíchāng with Wǔhàn.

Bus 4 (Y1) goes from one block north of the train station to the **Yíchāng Ferry Terminal** (宜昌港客运站; Yíchāng Gǎng Kèyùnzhàn; Yanjing Dadao), where boat tickets are sold.

own food and drinks. Functional accommodation costs:

1st class (一等; yīděng) Twin cabin; Y800

2nd class (二等; èrděng) Y490 to Y510

3rd class (三等; sānděng) Y400 to Y424

4th class (四等; sìděng) eight-bed dorm Y302 to Y332

Hydrofoil

Hydrofoils depart hourly from Wànzhōu (Y410, including a bus from Chóngqìng to Wànzhōu, or Y300 for the hydrofoil ticket only) downriver, running to the hydrofoil terminal west of Yíchāng. The journey takes 10 hours: three hours for the bus trip from Chóngqìng to Wànzhōu, six hours for the hydrofoil journey from Wànzhōu to Yíchāng and an hour by bus from the Yíchāng hydrofoil terminal into town. Note that Wànzhōu is also called Wànxiàn (万县).

Hydrofoils are passenger vessels and are not geared towards tourists, so there's no outside seating. Visibility is OK (albeit through perspex windows), but if you stand by the door you can get a good view. For those who find a day of gorge-viewing sufficient, hydrofoils are ideal, but tourist sights are skipped.

Hong Kong & the South

Hong Kong is more than just a snappy-looking international gateway to China: in many ways it is China – and always has been – in its language, cooking, people and folk traditions. The mellifluous singsong sounds of Cantonese are everywhere on the harbour breeze, as is the aroma of dim sum. But British rule lent Hong Kong a uniqueness and this is nowhere more evident than in its vigorous cosmopolitanism. Across the water, Macau is equally special: call it China with a pinch of Portuguese. Over the border, southern China ranges across a tantalising spectrum of landscapes, from the picture-perfect karst peaks of Yángshuò and Déhāng to the Hakka-round-house-dotted hills of southwest Fújiàn, the ancient and noble river town of Fènghuáng and the genteel island retreat of Gǔlàng Yǔ, offshore from Xiàmén and facing Táiwān.

Central, Hong Kong (p267) at night
PHOTOGRAPHER: RICHARD I'ANSON/LONELY PLANET IMAGES ©

Tian Tan Buddha statue (p274), Lantau island

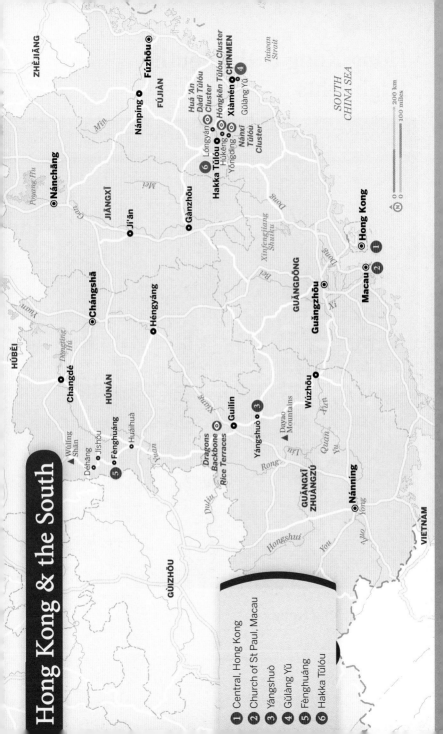

Hong Kong & the South

1 Central, Hong Kong
2 Church of St Paul, Macau
3 Yángshuò
4 Gǔlàng Yǔ
5 Fènghuáng
6 Hakka Tǔlóu

Hong Kong & the South Highlights

① Central, Hong Kong

Every traveller takes in Hong Kong's glittering business hub, Central, which is also home to the Peak Tram, historic buildings, skyrocketing towers and fine wining and dining. The best introduction is on the wide-angled approach aboard the Star Ferry, while the night-time vista from Tsim Sha Tsui is simply awesome.

Need to Know
LOCATION Hong Kong Island GETTING AROUND Tram, on foot, taxi, metro or escalator BEST PHOTO OP From Tsim Sha Tsui or Victoria Peak For more, see p267 and Map p278

Central, Hong Kong Don't Miss List

JONATHAN SILVER, 39, LAWYER

1 STAR FERRY

When I take guests around Hong Kong, we first hop aboard the Star Ferry (p282) for a short trip across the harbour from Tsim Sha Tsui to Central. Central's lights are spectacular at night. If you've time to spare, stop for a quick beer at the little-known rooftop bar at Pier 7 before hitting the bars and clubs of Lan Kwai Fong.

2 PEAK TRAM

Rub shoulders with tourists and wealthy residents alike on the Peak Tram (p268). The train leans 27 degrees at times during its ascent up Victoria Peak, so ensure you claim a seat before take-off. Stop at Peak Tower for a coffee (or ice cream!) or a stroll around the shops, and admire perhaps Hong Kong's best views (clouds permitting).

3 TRAM TO SHEUNG WAN

Journey back in time on a Hong Kong tram (p267) from Central to Sheung Wan or Happy Valley. Squeeze up to the front of the top deck for the best vantage point, but prepare early for disembarking – after 14 years, I am still amazed by the number of people who cram into one small tram.

4 SEVVA

Look for the lift serving only the 25th floor in the office lobby of Princes Building. Once you've mastered the lift button system, whiz up. Sevva (p284) is something of a secret oasis: the tree-lined outdoor area has stunning 360-degree views over Central and the Mandarin Hotel. Its honeycomb cream cake is hard to beat – order it to go, too.

5 CENTRAL-MIDLEVELS ESCALATOR

Worth a trip all on its own, the **escalator** (Cochrane St, cnr Shelley & Peel Sts; admission free; ⏰down 6-10am, up 10.30am-midnight; Ⓜ Central, exit C) takes you past antique shops, the traditional grocery stores of Hollywood Road, the hole-in-the-wall restaurants and bars of Staunton St – and the occasional bondage shop. Along the way or at the top, step off and straight into a shop from a bygone age, a bar or any number of restaurants serving food from almost every continent on earth.

Ruins of the Church of St Paul

South China's most sublime architectural ruin, the facade of the Church of St Paul (p295), is an almost mandatory pilgrimage for the godless and faithful alike. Macau isn't short of churches, but this staggering edifice – gorgeously illuminated at night – has its own unique magic and story to tell. Macau's casinos and big-spending gamblers are bywords for the ex-Portuguese territory, but this is its most poignant and enduring icon.

Amble Around Gǔlàng Yǔ

Xiàmén saves its best treasures offshore. It's only a matter of miles to the Taiwan-controlled island of Jīnmén, and the overseas connection doesn't finish there. A short boat trip from Xiàmén, Gǔlàng Yǔ's (p322) colonial-era architecture and European layout is a perfect restorative for anyone inured to the numbing socialist planning of Chinese towns. The island is small and compact and exploration straightforward, but get your room booked early; it's a popular bolthole.

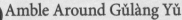

ALAMY/BETTY JOHNSON

Explore Yángshuò

3

For some travellers the town of Yángshuò (p311) is a turn-off: Western food, colloquial-English-speaking support staff and backpackers aplenty. But this is more than made up for by the surrounding, unbelievably lovely karst peaks: possibly *the* last word in iconic China landscapes. And vices aside, the town is loads of fun, and for anyone who has travelled at length around China, cap-doffing to its sheer energy and commercial vitality comes naturally.

5

Discover Fènghuáng

With its classic riverine setting, brooding gate towers, ancient temples and riverside rooms precariously supported on stilts, this lovely Húnán walled town (p316) is a superlative slice of old China. Get lost down Fènghuáng's old lanes, size up the covered Hóng Bridge and pick up all manner of souvenirs from streetside ethnic-minority hawkers; but try to book a room in advance (it's popular with Chinese tourists).

6

LEE FOSTER/LONELY PLANET IMAGES ©

Explore the Hakka Tǔlóu

Get exploring in the rural wilds of southwest Fújiàn province (p324), where a strong sense of community survives among the Hakka Chinese. Unique to this region of China, the breathtaking *tǔlóu* – effectively vast castles made of wood and tamped earth – are among the most astonishing sights in the Middle Kingdom. Some have been damaged by war and conflagration, but many – some arranged in imposing clusters – still house residents.

Hong Kong & the South's Best…

Lodgings

○ **Upper House** (p275) Elegant and composed boutique hotel on Hong Kong Island.

○ **Hyatt Regency Tsim Sha Tsui** (p277) Choice views from a definitive Tsim Sha Tsui hotel.

○ **Pousada de Mong Há** (p298) For a hilltop perspective of the Macau Peninsula.

○ **Yángshuò Village Inn** (p311) Lovely accommodation in a drop-dead-gorgeous location.

○ **Mogo Cafe Hotel** (p323) Lovely, stylish rooms on leisurely Gǔlàng Yǔ.

Wining and Dining

○ **Luk Yu Teahouse** (p281) *The* place to yum cha in Central, Hong Kong.

○ **Ye Shanghai** (p283) Fabulous Shànghǎi flavours, with superb dim sum as a concession to local tastes.

○ **Alfonso III** (p299) Outstanding Macanese cuisine on the south China coast.

○ **Luna** (p312) Scrumptious Italian cuisine, with a side of priceless views.

○ **L'Atelier de Joel Robuchon** (p282) Stylish dining, excellent tapas.

Architecture

○ **Hong Kong Island** (p275) From colonial elegance to stratospheric towers.

○ **Macau** (p292) A rich seam of ecclesiastical architecture and Portuguese-era grandeur.

○ **Fènghuáng** (p316) Charming vistas of traditional riverside Chinese architecture and bridges.

○ **Yǒngdìng** (p324) Awesome Hakka-built earth roundhouses rising up from the Fújiàn countryside.

○ **Gǔlàng Yǔ** (p322) Graceful south China island enclave of European villas and church architecture.

Scenic Exploration

◦ **Dragon's Backbone Rice Terraces** (p308) Hike from Dàzhài to Píng'ān through glittering rice terraces.

◦ **Yángshuò** (p311) Hire a bike and delve into southwest China's most idyllic landscape.

◦ **Yǒngdìng** (p324) Hike around the Fújiàn countryside in search of Hakka *tǔlóu*.

◦ **Lamma** (p284) Trek across the island from Yong Shue Wan to Sok Kwu Wan.

◦ **Taipa and Coloane** (p294) Explore Macau's breezy islands.

Need to Know

ADVANCE PLANNING
◦ **One Month Before** Get your hotel room booked; get your visa sorted.

◦ **Two Weeks Before** Book tickets for entertainment events.

◦ **One Week Before** Book a table at Hong Kong or Macau restaurants.

RESOURCES
◦ **Hong Kong Tourism Board** (www. discoverhongkong.com) Very efficient and useful website.

◦ **HK Magazine** (http://hk-magazine.com) Hong Kong listings and entertainment; free magazine available from restaurants, bars and hotels.

◦ **Time Out** (www. timeout.com. hk) Informative entertainments website; look out for the hard copy from news-stands.

◦ **bc Magazine** (www. bcmagazine.net) Hong Kong entertainment magazine; free hard copy.

GETTING AROUND
◦ **Airport Express** The fastest way into town from Hong Kong International Airport.

◦ **MTR** Hong Kong's metro system is very fast and highly efficient.

◦ **Boats** Ply the waters of Hong Kong and Macau.

◦ **Train** Trains criss-cross the entire southern region.

◦ **Air** Planes service the region, China and to international destinations from Hong Kong.

◦ **Local Bus** The Hong Kong and Macau bus system is efficient; urban buses elsewhere are not foreigner-friendly.

◦ **Long-distance Buses** Serve numerous destinations across the region.

BE FOREWARNED
◦ **Summer Heat** Hot and very humid in Hong Kong and Macau, with lots of rain.

◦ **Museums** Some museums in Hong Kong close for a weekday, sometimes Tuesday (often Monday in Macau).

◦ **Language** English-language skills are poor outside of Hong Kong and Yángshuò.

◦ **Touts** Highly annoying in drawcard destinations such as Yángshuò.

.eft: Rice-field workers resting, Yángshuò (p311);
Above: Largo do Senado, Macau (p292)

Hong Kong & the South Itineraries

From Hong Kong, these tours take you via Macau to the spectacular karst scenery of Yángshuò to the rice terraces of northern Guǎngxī and on to sedate Xiàmén and the Hakka earth buildings of Fújiàn province.

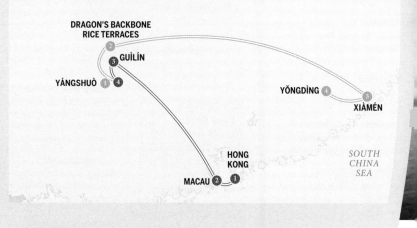

HONG KONG TO YÁNGSHUÒ
Cosmopolitan Cityscape, Karst Capital

Start your journey in **(1) Hong Kong**, which is simply overflowing with sights. Explore Hong Kong Island's Central district, ride the Peak Tram up to Victoria Peak, visit the Man Mo Temple along Hollywood Rd, jump aboard one of the island's antique trams and pop across Victoria Harbour to Tsim Sha Tsui aboard the Star Ferry. Dining on dim sum will be a culinary highlight of your Hong Kong experience, so make the most of the restaurants in this book. Speed across the water to **(2) Macau** to explore the ex-Portuguese territory, including the Ruins of the Church of St Paul, the Monte Fort and Macau Museum and the Mandarin's House,

and enjoy some mouth-watering Macanese food. Don't overlook the islands of Taipa and Coloane. Fly from Macau to **(3) Guìlín** in Guǎngxī province. Do some sightseeing in town before jumping aboard a boat down the Lí River to **(4) Yángshuò**. You'll drift past an astonishing panorama of verdant karst peaks. Spend a few days in Yángshuò, to hike and cycle through the surrounding karst countryside – the opportunities for exploration are almost endless – or turn your hand to some taichi lessons.

YÁNGSHUÒ TO YǑNGDÌNG
Rural Idylls, Hakka Houses

1 WEEK

From **(1) Yángshuò** return to Guìlín to make a diversion north to the **(2) Dragon's Backbone Rice Terraces** to hike from the village of Dàzhài to Píng'ān past some jaw-dropping vistas of sparkling terraced rice fields. Spend a night in one of the charming guesthouses in Dàzhài, Tiántóuzhài or Píng'ān before returning to Guìlín to take a flight to **(3) Xiàmén** in Fújiàn province. Base yourself on the charming, carless island of Gǔlàng Yǔ; you'll need to have some accommodation prebooked and hop on a ferry with your suitcases to check in. Gǔlàng Yǔ is worth careful exploration and is tailor-made for slow and lazy apprecia-

tion. You may find there is little reason to leave the island – except perhaps for a visit to the Nánpǔtuó Temple – until it's time for an excursion to the Hakka *tǔlóu* of **(4) Yǒngdìng**, Nánjǐng and Huá'ān. These colossal – usually round but sometimes oval or rectangular – earth buildings are essentially fortified villages for the Hakka families who dwell within them. Do spend the night in one – it's easy to find a room and it's a unique experience.

Man squatting by Li River, Yángshuò (p311)
PHOTOGRAPHER: MERTEN SNIJDERS/LONELY PLANET IMAGES ©

Discover Hong Kong & the South

At a Glance

○ **Hong Kong Island** (p267) Home of glittering Central district and Victoria Peak.

○ **Kowloon** (p269) High-density shopping and tourist warren.

○ **Macau** (p291) Gorgeous slice of yester-century Portugal with island escapes.

○ **Xiàmén** (p320) Gateway to Gǔlàngyǔ and Hakka territory.

○ **Yángshuò** (p311) Backpacker Mecca and karst wonderland.

HONG KONG

☑852 / POP 7 MILLION

Like a shot of adrenaline, Hong Kong quickens the pulse. Skyscrapers march up jungle-clad slopes by day and blaze neon by night across a harbour crisscrossed by freighters and motor junks. Above streets teeming with traffic, five-star hotels stand next to ageing tenement blocks.

This is also a city that lives to eat, offering diners the very best of China and beyond. Hong Kong, above all, rewards those who grab experience by the scruff of the neck, who'll try that jellyfish, explore half-deserted villages or stroll beaches far from neon and steel.

History

Until European traders started importing opium into the country, Hong Kong really was an obscure backwater in the Chinese empire.

China's attempts to stamp out the opium trade gave the British the pretext they needed for military action. Gunboats were sent in. In 1841, the Union flag was hoisted on Hong Kong Island and the Treaty of Nanking, which brought an end to the so-called First Opium War, ceded the island to the British crown 'in perpetuity'. At the end of the Second Opium War in 1860, Britain took possession of Kowloon Peninsula, and in July 1898 a 99-year lease was granted for the New Territories.

In 1984 Britain agreed to return what would become the Special Administrative Region (SAR) of Hong Kong to China in 1997, on the condition it would retain its free-market economy as well as its social and legal systems for 50 years.

Taxi on Nathan Rd, Kowloon (p269)

PHOTOGRAPHER: GREG ELMS/LONELY PLANET IMAGES ©

Hong Kong City Overview

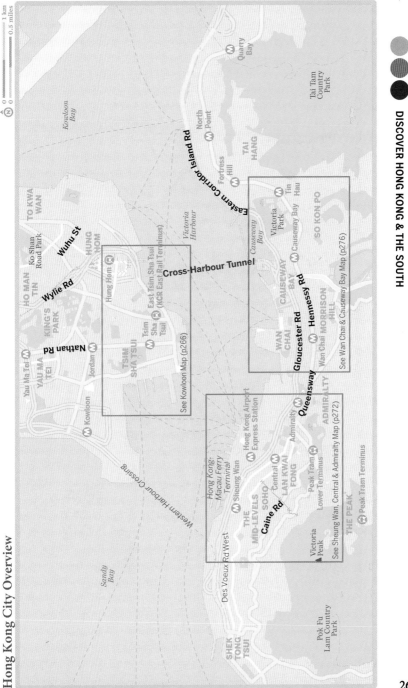

0 — 1 km
0 — 0.5 miles

Quarry Bay

Tai Tam Country Park

Kowloon Bay

North Point

Fortress Hill

TAI HANG

Eastern Corridor Island Rd

Victoria Park

Tin Hau

Causeway Bay

SO KON PO

Victoria Harbour

Causeway Bay

See Wan Chai & Causeway Bay Map (p276)

TO KWA WAN

Ko Shan Road Park

Wuhu St

HUNG HOM

HO MAN TIN

Wylie Rd

KING'S PARK

Hung Hom

East Tsim Sha Tsui (KCR East Rail Terminus)

Cross-Harbour Tunnel

CAUSEWAY BAY

WAN CHAI

MORRISON HILL

Hennessy Rd

Yau Ma Tei

YAU MA TEI

Nathan Rd

Jordan

TSIM SHA TSUI

Tsim Sha Tsui

See Kowloon Map (p266)

Gloucester Rd

Wan Chai

Kowloon

Queensway

ADMIRALTY

Western Harbour Crossing

Hong Kong-Macau Ferry Terminal

Hong Kong Airport Express Station

Sheung Wan

SOHO

Admiralty

Central

LAN KWAI FONG

Peak Tram Lower Terminus

THE MID-LEVELS

Caine Rd

Des Voeux Rd West

Victoria Peak

See Sheung Wan, Central & Admiralty Map (p272)

THE PEAK

Peak Tram Terminus

Sandy Bay

Pok Fu Lam Country Park

SHEK TONG TSUI

265

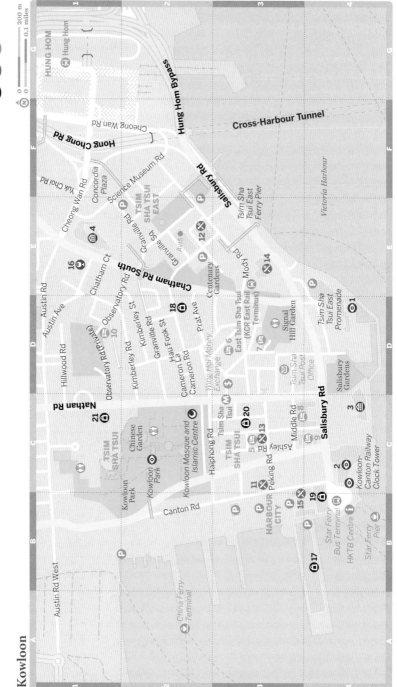

Kowloon

Kowloon

⊙ Sights
1 Avenue of the Stars D4
2 Hong Kong Cultural Centre C4
3 Hong Kong Museum of Art C4
4 Hong Kong Museum of History E1

🛏 Sleeping
5 Hop Inn C3
6 Hyatt Regency Tsim Sha Tsui D3
7 Minden D3
8 Peninsula Hong Kong C3
9 Salisbury C4
10 Stanford Hillview Hotel D1

⊗ Eating
11 Hutong C3
12 Sabatini E2

13 T'ang Court C3
14 Woodlands E3
15 Ye Shanghai B3

⊙ Drinking
Felix .... (see 8)
16 Phonograph E1

🔒 Shopping
17 Harbour City B4
18 Initial D2
K11 .... (see 6)
19 Star Computer City B4
20 Swindon Books C3
21 Yue Hwa Chinese Products
Emporium C1

Climate

Hong Kong rarely gets especially cold, but it would be worth packing something at least a little bit warm between November and March. Between May and mid-September temperatures in the mid-30s combined with stifling humidity can turn you into a walking sweat machine. This time is also the wettest, accounting for about 80% of annual rainfall – partly due to typhoons.

The best time to visit Hong Kong is between mid-September and February. At any time of the year pollution can be diabolical.

⊙ Sights

The **Hong Kong Museum Pass** (www. discoverhongkong.com/eng/attractions/ museum-major.html; 7 days HK$30), which allows multiple entries to all museums mentioned in this book, is available from the participating museums. Museums are free on Wednesdays.

Hong Kong Island – Central

Central is where high finance meets haute couture, and megadeals are closed in towering skyscrapers. To the west is history-rich Sheung Wan, while quiet Admiralty lies to the east.

MAN MO TEMPLE   Temple
(文武廟; Map p272; 124-126 Hollywood Rd, Sheung Wan; ⊙8am-6pm; bus 26) Taoist Man Mo Temple was built in 1847 by Chinese merchants and dedicated to the gods of literature ('man') and of war ('mo'). Besides a place of worship, it was a court of arbitration for local disputes.

HONG KONG ZOOLOGICAL & BOTANICAL GARDENS   Park
(Map p272; ☎ 2530 0154; Albany Rd, Central; ⊙terrace gardens 6am-10pm, zoo & aviaries to 7pm; buses 3B, 12) Built over a century ago in the style of an English park, the gardens feature a pleasant collection of arbored paths, fountains, aviaries and a zoo.

STATUE SQUARE & AROUND
                    Historic monuments
(Map p272; Edinburgh Pl, Central; Ⓜ Central, exit K) This leisurely square used to house effigies of British royalty. Now it pays tribute to a single sovereign – the founder of HSBC, the banking giant which owns the square. To the east is the **Legislative Council Building** (立法會大樓; Map p272; 8 Jackson Rd), a neoclassical edifice. To the north is the **Cenotaph** (和平紀念碑; Map p272; Chater Rd), a memorial to Hong Kong residents killed during the two world wars.

GREG ELMS/LONELY PLANET IMAGES ©

Don't Miss Peak Tram

The gravity-defying **Peak Tram** (Map p272; www.thepeak.com.hk; one-way/return HK$25/36; ☉7am-midnight; M Central, exit J2) is one of Hong Kong's most memorable attractions, though the ride itself takes only five minutes. Rising steeply above skyscrapers, the funicular runs every 15 minutes from the lower terminus up the side of 552m Victoria Peak (Map p278). On clear days and at night, the views from the top are spectacular.

OLD WAN CHAI   Old Neighbourhoods
The area around Queen's Rd E (Wan Chai metro station, exit A3) is filled with pockets of local culture that are best explored on foot. The historic **Blue House** (Map p276; 72-74A Stone Nullah La) is a prewar building with cast-iron Spanish balconies reminiscent of those found in New Orleans. Conservationists love it; tenants loathe it (old Bluesy's loos don't flush!).
Wan Chai market (Map p276; ☉7.30am-7pm) vendors flaunt their wares on Cross St and Stone Nullah Lane.

TIN HAU TEMPLE   Temple
(天后廟; Map p276; 10 Tin Hau Temple Rd, Causeway Bay; ☉7am-5pm; M Tin Hau, exit B) This listed 300-year-old temple is dedicated to the most famous deity in coastal South

China – Tin Hau, goddess of the sea and guardian angel for fishermen. There are almost 60 temples dedicated to her in Hong Kong alone.

VICTORIA PARK   Park
(Map p276; Causeway Rd, Causeway Bay; M Tin Hau, exit B) Hong Kong's largest patch of public greenery is best visited on weekday mornings, when it becomes a slow-motion forest of taichi practitioners. You can join the (non)action if you like.

Hong Kong Island – The South

The rugged coastline of the south coast of Hong Kong Island makes for decent beaches and protection from typhoons for boat people. From Central, below Exchange Square, buses 6, 6A and 260 leave for Stanley and Repulse Bay, and buses 70 and 70P for Aberdeen. From Repulse Bay, buses 73 and 973 take you to Aberdeen. Bus 9 from Shau Kei Wan MTR station (exit A3) goes to Shek O.

STANLEY Market, Beach
(Map p278) This crowd-pleaser is best visited on weekdays. Its maze of covered alleyways is called **Stanley Market** (Stanley Village Rd; ☉10am-6pm), which has (pricey) bargain clothing, including a variety of children's wear (haggling a must!).

ABERDEEN Typhoon Shelter
(Map p278) Aberdeen's main attraction is the typhoon shelter it shares with sleepy **Ap Lei Chau**, where the sampans of Hong Kong's boat-dwelling fisherfolk used to moor. On weekday evenings, you may spot dragonboat teams practising here. The best way to see the area is by sampan. A half-hour tour of the typhoon shelter costs about HK$55 per person.

REPULSE BAY Beach
(Map p278) At the southeastern end of Hong Kong's most popular beach stands the eccentric Kwun Yam shrine (觀音廟) and a garish gallery of deities – from goldfish and a monkey god to the more familiar Tin Hau.

OCEAN PARK Amusement Park
(香港海洋公園; www.oceanpark.com.hk; Ocean Park Rd; admission HK$250; ☉10am-6pm) Ocean Park, the worthy nemesis of Hong

Kong Disneyland, is a massive marine-themed amusement park complete with white-knuckle rides, giant pandas, an **atoll reef**, and an amazing **aquarium**. Bus 629 from Admiralty MTR Station (Map p272) or Central Pier No 7 (Map p272) takes you there.

SHEK O Beach
(Map p278) Shek O is the kind of place where villagers drying algae on clotheslines live alongside Vespa-riding 'bourgeois bohemians'. Ragged cliffs and a laid-back vibe complete the picture.

Kowloon

Tsim Sha Tsui, known for its dining and shopping options, is Hong Kong's most (charmingly) eclectic district, with a population comprising Chinese, Indians, Filipinos, Nepalese, Africans and Europeans, and the glamorous often only a stone's throw from the pedestrian.

TSIM SHA TSUI EAST PROMENADE & STAR FERRY Harbour
(尖沙嘴東部海濱花園和天星小輪; Map p266; Salisbury Rd; M Tsim Sha Tsui, exit E) The resplendent views of Victoria Harbour make this walkway one of the best strolls in Hong Kong. Begin your journey at the old **Kowloon-Canton Railway clock tower**, a landmark of the Age of Steam, near the **Star Ferry concourse**.

Hong Kong In...

ONE DAY
Catch a tram up to **Victoria Peak** for a good view of the city, stopping in **Central** for lunch on the way down. Then head to **Man Mo Temple** for a taste of history before taking the Star Ferry to Kowloon. Enjoy the views along **Tsim Sha Tsui East Promenade** as you make your way to the **Museum of History** for some context to all you've seen. After dinner in Tsim Sha Tsui, take the MTR to **Lan Kwai Fong** for drinks and dancing.

TWO DAYS
In addition to the above, you could head to **Aberdeen** for a boatride or hike across **Lamma Island**, followed by a seafood lunch in Sok Kwu Wan. After dark, make your way to the **Temple Street Night Market**.

To your left is the windowless **Hong Kong Cultural Centre** (香港文化中心), passing which you'll arrive at the **Avenue of the Stars** (星光大道), Hong Kong's tribute to its film industry. Though uninspiring, it's the vantage point for watching the **Symphony of Lights** (⊙shows 8-8.20pm), a laser-light show à la *Star Wars* projected from the top of skyscrapers.

HONG KONG MUSEUM OF HISTORY
Museum

(香港歷史博物館; Map p266; 100 Chatham Rd South; admission HK$10; ⊙10am-6pm Mon & Wed-Sat, to 7pm Sun; Ⓜ Tsim Sha Tsui, exit B2) If you only have time for one museum, do make it this one. It takes you on a fascinating journey through Hong Kong's past, from prehistoric times to 1997.

HONG KONG MUSEUM OF ART
Museum

(香港藝術博物館; Map p266; 10 Salisbury Rd; admission HK$10; ⊙10am-6pm Fri-Wed, to 8pm Sat; Ⓜ Tsim Sha Tsui, exit J) The museum's six floors of Chinese antiquities, paintings, calligraphy and contemporary Hong Kong art are a must if you're remotely interested in art. The thematic exhibitions featuring modern works by local and overseas artists are also inspiring. Free English-language tours at 11am.

TEMPLE STREET NIGHT MARKET
Street Market

(廟街夜市; ⊙6pm-midnight; Ⓜ Yau Ma Tei, exit C) Extending from Man Ming Lane (north) to Nanking St (south), this famous bazaar hawks everything under the moon from pirated designer bags to sex toys. Remember to bargain.

TIN HAU TEMPLE
Temple

(天后廟; cnr Temple & Public Square Sts; ⊙8am-5pm; Ⓜ Yau Ma Tei, exit C) This large, incense-filled sanctuary built in the 19th century is one of Hong Kong's most famous Tin Hau temples.

JADE MARKET

Jade Market, Old Streets

(Cnr Kansu & Battery Sts, Yau Ma Tei; ⏰10am-5pm; Ⓜ Yau Ma Tei (exit C)) Some 450 stalls sell all varieties and grades of jade, but unless you know your nephrite from your jadeite, it's wise not to buy expensive pieces here.

YUEN PO ST BIRD GARDEN   Garden

(園圃街雀鳥花園; Flower Market Rd, Mong Kok; ⏰7am-8pm; Ⓜ Prince Edward, exit B1) To the east of the Prince Edward MTR station is this delightful place where birds are preened, bought, sold and fed bugs with chopsticks by their fussy owners (usually men).

New Territories (New Kowloon)

The southernmost 31 sq km of the New Territories is officially called New Kowloon. Full of high-rise apartments, it's less frantic than its neighbours to the south.

New Kowloon is serviced by the Tsuen Wan and Kwun Tong MTR lines.

CHI LIN NUNNERY   Temple

(志蓮淨苑; Map p278; www.chilin.org; 5 Chin Lin Dr, Diamond Hill; ⏰9am-4.30pm; Ⓜ Diamond Hill, exit C2) This beautiful replica of a Tang-dynasty monastery comes complete with temples, lotus ponds, Buddhist relics and timber structures assembled without the use of a single iron nail. It's the world's largest cluster of handcrafted timber buildings.

SIK SIK YUEN WONG TAI SIN TEMPLE

Temple

(嗇色園黃大仙祠; www.siksikyuen.org.hk; Lung Cheung Rd, Wong Tai Sin; admission by donation HK$2; ⏰7am-5.30pm; Ⓜ Wong Tai Sin, exit B3) This Taoist temple is dedicated to Wong Tai Sin, who was said to have transformed boulders into sheep. In fact, the whole area, an MTR station and a residential property near the temple are

271

Sheung Wan, Central & Admiralty

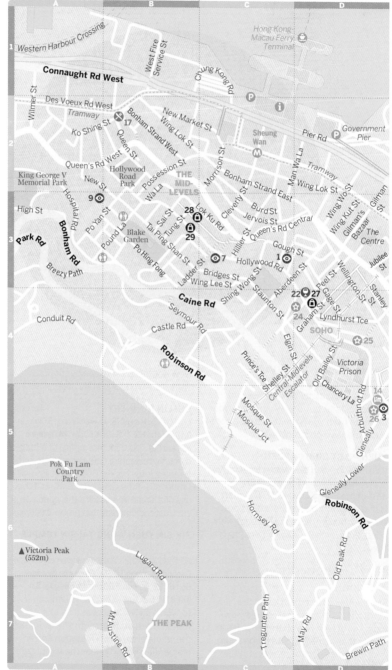

DISCOVER HONG KONG & THE SOUTH   HONG KONG

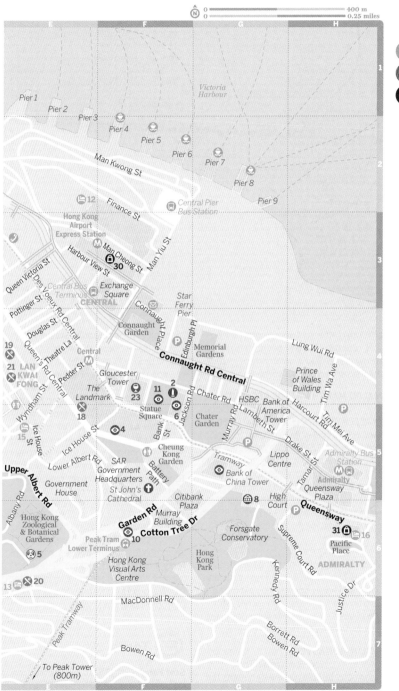

0   400 m
0   0.25 miles

Victoria Harbour

Pier 1
Pier 2
Pier 3
Pier 4
Pier 5
Pier 6
Pier 7
Pier 8
Pier 9

Man Kwong St

Central Pier Bus Station

Finance St

12

Hong Kong Airport Express Station

Harbour View St

Man Cheong St

30

Man Yiu St

Queen Victoria St

Des Voeux Rd Central

Pottinger St

Central Bus Terminus

Exchange Square

CENTRAL

Connaught Place

Star Ferry Pier

Douglas St

Connaught Garden

Edinburgh Pl

Memorial Gardens

Lung Wui Rd

19

21 LAN KWAI FONG

Queen's Rd Central

Queen's Theatre La

Central

Pedder St

Connaught Rd Central

Chater Rd

Prince of Wales Building

Tim Wa Ave

Gloucester Tower

23

11

2

Jackson Rd

HSBC

Lambeth St

Bank of America Tower

Harcourt Rd

The Landmark

Wyndham St

18

Statue Square

6

Chater Garden

Murray Rd

Drake St

P

Ice House St

15

4

Bank St

Cheung Kong Garden

Tramway

Lippo Centre

Admiralty Bus Station

Tamar St

Lower Albert Rd

SAR Government Headquarters

Battery Path

Bank of China Tower

Admiralty

M

Upper Albert Rd

St John's Cathedral

Citibank Plaza

High Court

8

Queensway Plaza

Albany Rd

Government House

Garden Rd

Murray Building

Cotton Tree Dr

Queensway

Hong Kong Zoological & Botanical Gardens

10

Forsgate Conservatory

Supreme Court Rd

31

16

5

Peak Tram Lower Terminus

Hong Kong Visual Arts Centre

Hong Kong Park

Pacific Place

ADMIRALTY

13

20

MacDonnell Rd

Kennedy Rd

Justice Dr

Peak Tramway

Bowen Rd

Borrett Rd

Bowen Rd

To Peak Tower (800m)

Sheung Wan, Central & Admiralty

◎ Sights
1	Amelia Johnson Contemporary	C3
2	Cenotaph	F4
3	Grotto Fine Art	D5
4	Hanart TZ Gallery	F5
5	Hong Kong Zoological & Botanical Gardens	E6
6	Legislative Council Building	F5
7	Man Mo Temple	C3
8	Museum of Tea Ware	G5
9	Para/Site Art Space	A3
10	Peak Tram Lower Terminus	F6
11	Statue Square	F4

⊜ Sleeping
12	Four Seasons Hotel	E2
13	Garden View YWCA	E6
14	Hotel LKF	D5
15	Ice House	E5
16	Upper House	H6

⊗ Eating
17	ABC	B2
18	L'Atelier de Joel Robuchon	E5
19	Luk Yu Teahouse	E4
20	Pure Veggie House	E6
	San Xi Lou	(see 20)
21	Yung Kee	E4

⊙ Drinking
22	Club 71	D4
23	Sevva	F4

◉ Entertainment
24	Peel Fresco	D4
25	Propaganda	D4
26	Tazmania Ballroom	D5

⊙ Shopping
27	Arch Angel Antiques	D4
28	Cat Street	B3
	Dymocks	(see 30)
29	Hollywood Rd	B3
30	IFC Mall	F3
31	Pacific Place	H6

all named after this poor immortal who was supposed to have been a hermit. Just below the temple is an arcade of fortune-tellers, some of whom speak English.

MAI PO MARSH NATURE RESERVE
Nature Reserve

(米埔自然保護區; Map p278; ☎ 2471 3480, www.wwf.org.hk; San Tin, Yuen Long; ⊙9am-5pm Mon-Fri) The 2700-hectare protected wetland is home to an amazing range of flora and fauna, including up to 300 species of birds. Three-hour guided tours (HK$70), most in Cantonese, leave the visitor centre four times between 9am and 2.30pm on weekends.

Lantau

Twice the size of Hong Kong Island, Lantau has only about 50,000 residents and you could easily spend a day exploring its trails and enjoying its beaches. **Mui Wo** (Map p278) or Silver Mine Bay is the arrival point for ferries from Central.

PO LIN MONASTERY
Monastery

(寶蓮禪寺; ⊙9am-6pm; Lantau) This enormous temple complex contains the 26m-tall **Tian Tan Buddha statue** (天壇大佛; ⊙10am-5.30pm), the world's largest seated bronze Buddha statue. From Mui Wo, board bus 2 to **Ngong Ping** (Map p278), a plateau 500m above sea level, where a cable-car system called **Ngong Ping 360** (昂平360纜車; www.np360.com.hk; Lantau; one-way/return HK$58/88; ⊙10am-6pm Mon-Fri, 9am-6.30pm Sat & Sun) whizzes you past breathtaking views to the monastery. Ngong Ping 360 has another terminal in **Tung Chung** (東涌), a two-minute walk from Tung Chung MTR station.

TAI O
Fishing Village

(大澳; Map p278; Lantau) One of Hong Kong's oldest fishing villages, picturesque Tai O is famous for its **stilt houses**, **rope-tow ferry** and temple dedicated to Kwan Yu (God of War). It's reachable by bus 1 from Mui Wo, bus 11 from Tung Chung, or bus 21 from Ngong Ping.

 Tours

Star Ferry (☎ 2118 6201; www.starferry.com.hk) runs a 60-minute **Harbour Tour** (per day/night HK$55/110; ⏱11.05am-9.05pm), beginning at Tsim Sha Tsui and stopping at Central, Wan Chai and Hung Hom.

Tours run by the **HKTB** (☎2508 1234; www.discoverhongkong.com; ⏱9am-6pm):

Island Tour Includes Man Mo Temple, the Peak, Aberdeen, Repulse Bay and Stanley Market; HK$350/490 per half-/full day.

Land Between Tour Covers temples, villages and the China boundary; HK$350/450 per half-/full day.

 # Sleeping

Hong Kong offers the full gamut of accommodation, from cell-like spaces to palatial suites in some of the world's finest hotels. Compared with those in other cities in China, rooms are relatively expensive, though they can still be cheaper than their US or European counterparts. The rates listed here are the rack rates.

Hong Kong Island

Most of Hong Kong Island's top-end hotels are in Central and Admiralty, while Wan Chai and Sheung Wan cater to the midrange market.

UPPER HOUSE
Boutique Hotel **$$$**

(奕居; Map p272; ☎2918 1838; www.upperhouse.com; Pacific Place, 88 Queensway, Admiralty; r from HK$2800, ste from HK$4500; @ 🛜; M Admiralty, exit F) Every corner of this boutique hotel spells serenity – the understated and classy lobby, the sleek 'paperless' rooms, the elegant sculptures, and the manicured lawn where guests can join free yoga classes.

ICE HOUSE
Studio Apartment **$$**

(Map p272; ☎2836 7333; www.icehouse.com.hk; 38 Ice House St, Central; r HK$900-1050, low-season discounts of 20%; @; M Central, exit G) The location, in the heart of Central and staggering distance from Lan Kwai Fong, and the 64 spacious, open-plan 'suites' make the Ice House excellent value. Each room has a kitchenette, a work desk and internet access.

HOTEL LKF
Hotel **$$$**

(蘭桂芳酒店; Map p272; ☎3518 9688; www.hotel-lkf.com.hk; 33 Wyndham St, Central; r from HK$3500, low-season discounts of up to 50%; @; M Central, exit D2) Right in the thick of the Lan Kwai Fong action (but far enough above it not to be disturbed by it), the stylish LKF offers spacious rooms in muted earth tones containing all the trimmings: fluffy dressing gowns, espresso machines, and free bedtime milk and cookies. Internet access is for the top three floors only.

Seafood, New Territories
PHOTOGRAPHER: MICHAEL COYNE/LONELY PLANET IMAGES ©

Wan Chai & Causeway Bay

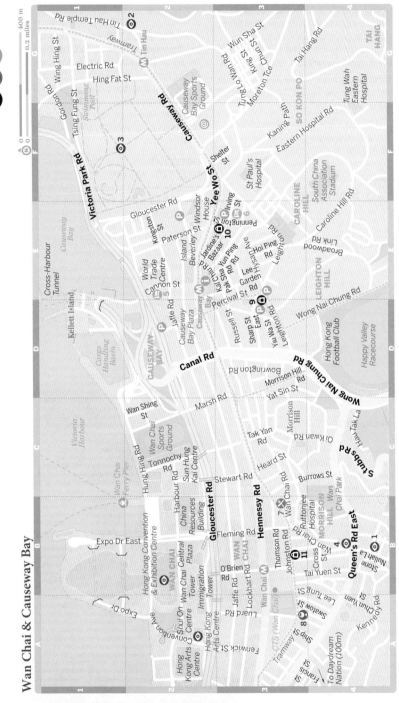

Wan Chai & Causeway Bay

◎ Sights
1 Blue House...B4
2 Tin Hau Temple....................................G2
3 Victoria Park..F1
4 Wan Chai Market B4

◎ Sleeping
5 Alisan Guest House E2
6 Jia..E3

✦ Eating
7 Hang Zhou Restaurant........................B3

◎ Drinking
8 Pawn...A3

◎ Shopping
9 G.O.D. D3
10 Jardine's Bazaar E3
11 Johnston Rd B3

Y-LOFT YOUTH SQUARE HOSTEL
Hostel $$
(☎3721 8989; 238 Chai Wan Rd; tw/d/tr HK$600/750/990, ste HK$1200-1800, low-season discounts of 25%; @ ☎; Ⓜ Chai Wan, exit A) If you don't mind living a little further away in Chai Wan (not Wan Chai!), you'll be rewarded with large, clean and cheerful rooms. Stanley is only 15 minutes away by bus from the 16X bus stop opposite the MTR station. To reach the hostel from exit A, go straight through the mall to the footbridge and take the first exit on your right. Reception's on the 12th floor.

FOUR SEASONS HOTEL
Luxury Hotel $$$
(四季酒店; Map p272; ☎3196 8888; www.fourseasons.com/hongkong; IFC 3, 8 Finance St, Central; r from HK$4300, ste from HK$8800; @ ☎ ☒; Ⓜ Tung Chung Line, Hong Kong station, exit F) Everything about the Four Seasons is class, from the fine rooms and restaurants to the panoramic harbour views from its location in the International Financial Centre. There's also a great spa. But it's the sophisticated service that is most memorable.

JIA
Boutique Hotel $$$
(Map p276; ☎3196 9000; www.jiahongkong. com; 1-5 Irving St, Causeway Bay; r HK$2500, ste from HK$3500, low-season discounts of up to 40%; @ ☎; Ⓜ Causeway Bay, exit F) Inspired by French designer Philippe Starck, this boutique hotel is chic as hell, from the stunning staff uniforms and postmodern furnishings to the guests: models in sunglasses loitering in the lobby. Standard rooms are poky, but the service is smooth.

Garden View YWCA
Hotel $$
(女青園景軒; Map p272; ☎2877 3737; http://hotel.ywca.org.hk; 1 MacDonnell Rd, Central; r HK$1550-1750, ste from HK$2350, all include breakfast, low-season discounts of up to 50%; @ ☎ ☒; green minibus 1A) Straddling the border of Central and Mid-Levels, the YWCA-run Garden View has fine views and is one of the better midrange places in Central.

Alisan Guest House
Guest House $
(阿里山賓館; Map p276; ☎2838 0762; http://home.hkstar.com/~alisangh; Flat A, 5th fl, Hoito Ct, 23 Cannon St, Causeway Bay; s/d/tr HK$350/450/550; ☎; Ⓜ Causeway Bay, exit D1) Spread through several apartments, the rooms in this small family-run place are clean, the welcome warm and the advice good.

Kowloon

Kowloon has an incredible array of accommodation: from the Peninsula, the 'grand dame' of hotels, to its infamous neighbour, Chungking Mansions, plus plenty in between.

HYATT REGENCY TSIM SHA TSUI
Luxury Hotel $$$
(香港尖沙咀凱悅酒店; Map p266; ☎2311 1234; http://hongkong.tsimshatsui.hyatt.com; 18 Hanoi

---

Accommodation Price Indicators

The price ranges for the Hong Kong section are as follows:

$	less than HK$$900
$$	HK$900-1500
$$$	more than HK$1500

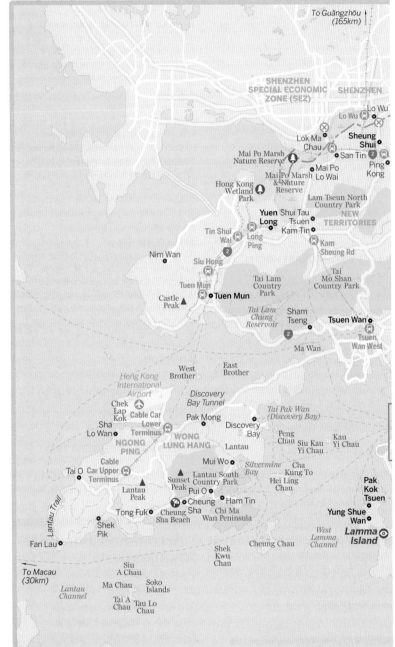

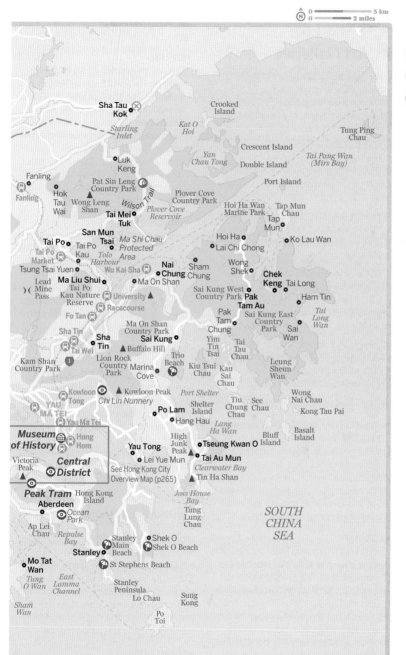

N 0 —————— 5 km
   0 —————— 2 miles

Sha Tau Kok

Crooked Island

Starling Inlet

Kat O Hoi

Tung Ping Chau

Fanling

Luk Keng

Yan Chau Tong

Crescent Island

Double Island

Tai Pang Wan (Mirs Bay)

Hok Tau Wai

Pat Sin Leng Country Park

Wong Leng Shan

Wilson Trail

Plover Cove Country Park

Port Island

Tai Mei Tuk

Plover Cove Reservoir

Hoi Ha Wan Marine Park

Tap Mun Chau

San Mun Tsai

Ma Shi Chau Protected Area

Hoi Ha

Tap Mun

Tai Po

Tai Po Kau

Lai Chi Chong

Ko Lau Wan

Tai Po Market

Tsung Tsai Yuen

Tolo Harbour

Wu Kai Sha

Nai Chung

Sham Chung

Wong Shek

Chek Keng

Tai Long

Lead Mine Pass

Ma Liu Shui

Tai Po Kau Nature Reserve

University

Ma On Shan

Sai Kung West Country Park

Pak Tam Au

Ham Tin

Fo Tan

Racecourse

Pak Tam Chung

Sai Kung East Country Park

Sai Wan

Tai Long Wan

Sha Tin

Tai Wei

Sha Tin

Ma On Shan Country Park

Buffalo Hill

Sai Kung

Yim Tin Tsai

Tai Tau Chau

Leung Sheun Wan

Kam Shan Country Park

Lion Rock Country Park

Marina Cove

Trio Beach

Kiu Tsui Chau

Kau Sai Chau

Kowloon Tong

Kowloon Peak

Chi Lin Nunnery

Port Shelter

Tiu Chung Chau

See Chau

Wong Nai Chau

Kong Tau Pai

YAU MA TEI

Yau Ma Tei

Po Lam

Hang Hau

Shelter Island

Lang Ha Wan

Bluff Island

Basalt Island

Museum of History

Hung Hom

Yau Tong

High Junk Peak

Tseung Kwan O

Victoria Peak

Central District

Lei Yue Mun

Tai Au Mun

Clearwater Bay

See Hong Kong City Overview Map (p265)

Tin Ha Shan

Peak Tram

Hong Kong Island

Joss House Bay

SOUTH CHINA SEA

Aberdeen

Ocean Park

Tung Lung Chau

Ap Lei Chau

Repulse Bay

Stanley Main Beach

Shek O

Shek O Beach

Stanley

Mo Tat Wan

St Stephens Beach

Tung O Wan

East Lamma Channel

Stanley Peninsula

Lo Chau

Sung Kong

Sham Wan

Po Toi

If You Like…
Art Galleries

Besides the commercial galleries listed here, you should also check out the nonprofit **Para/Site Artspace** (藝術空間; Map p272; www.para-site.org.hk; 4 Po Yan St, Sheung Wan; ⊙noon-7pm Wed-Sun).

Amelia Johnson Contemporary (Map p272; www.ameliajohnsoncontemporary.com; 6-10 Sin Hing St, Central; ⊙11am-7pm Tue-Fri, to 6pm Sat) Showcases the works of artists from Hong Kong and overseas.

Grotto Fine Art (Map p272;www.grottofineart.com; 2nd fl, 31C-31D Wyndham St, Central; ⊙11am-7pm Mon-Sat) The only gallery that represents exclusively Hong Kong artists.

Hanart TZ Gallery (Map p272; www.hanart.com; room 202, 2nd fl, Henley Bldg, 5 Queen's Rd, Central; ⊙10am-6.30pm Mon-Fri, to 6pm Sat) Hanart was instrumental in introducing contemporary Chinese art to the world.

Osage Gallery (www.osagegallery.com; 5th fl, Kian Dai Industrial Bldg, 73-75 Hung To Rd; ⊙10am-7pm Tue-Sun & public holidays) Specialising in Hong Kong, Chinese and Asian art.

Rd, Tsim Sha Tsui; r HK$1500-2900; ste from HK$3300; @ 🛜 🏊; Ⓜ Tsim Sha Tsui, exit D2) This Tsim Sha Tsui classic, reopened at this convenient address, features plush, medium-sized rooms, many with great views, and impeccable service. The photos of Tsim Sha Tsui captured by a local photographer are a refreshing touch.

SALISBURY   Hostel, Hotel   **$$**
(香港基督教青年會; Map p266; 📞2268 7888; www.ymcahk.org.hk; 41 Salisbury Rd, Tsim Sha Tsui; dm/s HK$240/750, d HK$800-1050, ste from HK$1500; @ 🛜 🏊; Ⓜ Tsim Sha Tsui, exit E) Operated by the YMCA. The rooms here are simple, but the facilities and the five-star views are not. The location makes it great value. Budgeters who book ahead might get a bed in the four-bed dorms. However, no-one can stay more than seven consecutive nights, and walk-in

guests for the dorms aren't accepted if they've been in Hong Kong more than 10 days.

HOP INN   Hostel   **$**
(樸樸旅舍; Map p266; 📞2881 7331; www.hopinn.hk; Flat A, 2nd fl, Hanyee Bldg, 19-21 Hankow Rd, Tsim Sha Tsui; s HK$350-450, d HK$480-610, tr HK$580-760; @; Ⓜ Tsim Sha Tsui, exit A1) This guest house has a youthful vibe and nine spotless little rooms, each featuring illustrations by a Hong Kong artist. Our favourite is the first room by Gukzik Lau. Some rooms have no windows, but they're quieter than the ones that do.

MINDEN   Boutique Hotel   **$$**
(Map p266; 📞2739 7777; www.theminden.com; 7 Minden Ave, Tsim Sha Tsui; r HK$900-1500, ste HK$2500; Ⓜ Tsim Sha Tsui (exit G); @) The boutique-ish Minden is centrally located, the rooms are comfortable and the lobby is packed with an eclectic mix of Asian and Western curios and furnishings.

STANFORD HILLVIEW HOTEL
     Hotel   **$$**
(仕德福山景酒店; Map p266; 📞2722 7822; www.stanfordhillview.com; 13-17 Observatory Rd, Tsim Sha Tsui; s & d HK$1480-1680, ste from HK$2680, low-season discounts of up to 45%; 🛜; Ⓜ Tsim Sha Tsui, exit B1) At the eastern end of Knutsford Tce, the Stanford is a quality hotel in just about our favourite location in Tsim Sha Tsui, with little traffic noise but seconds from loads of bars and restaurants.

PENINSULA HONG KONG
     Luxury Hotel   **$$$**
(香港半島酒店; Map p266; 📞2920 2888; www.peninsula.com; Salisbury Rd, Tsim Sha Tsui; r HK$4200-5800, ste from HK$6800; @ 🛜 🏊; Ⓜ Tsim Sha Tsui, exit E) Hong Kong's colonial classic is pure elegance, with service and up-to-the-minute facilities to match. If you can afford it, the Pen is somewhere everyone should stay at least once.

BOOTH LODGE   Hostel   **$**
(卜維廉賓館; 📞2771 9266; http://boothlodge.salvation.org.hk; 11 Wing Sing Lane, Yau Ma Tei;

s & tw incl breakfast HK$620-1500; M Yau Ma Tei, exit C) This wedge-shaped, Salvation Army–run place is spartan and clean but fair value in the lower midrange. Standard rooms are about HK$500 low season. Reception is on the 7th floor.

Eating

One of the world's greatest food cities, Hong Kong offers culinary excitement whether you're spending HK$20 on a bowl of noodles or megabucks on haute cuisine.

The best of China is well represented, be it Cantonese, Shanghainese, Northern or Sichuanese cuisine. What's more, the international fare on offer – French, Italian, Spanish, Japanese, Thai, Indian, Indonesian or fusion – is the finest and most diverse in all of China. There are also great vegetarian options.

If you can't decide what you fancy, following your nose along certain streets in the main districts can be rewarding.

While you're in Hong Kong do try dim sum, uniquely Cantonese dishes normally steamed and served for breakfast, brunch or lunch.

Chef carving Peking Duck

Hong Kong Island

The island's best range of cuisines is in Central and Wan Chai.

LUK YU TEAHOUSE   Cantonese   **$$**
(陸羽茶室; Map p272; ☎ 2523 5464; 24-26 Stanley St, Central; mains HK$100-350; ⏰7am-10pm; M Central, exit D2) Hong Kong's most famous teahouse is known for its divine dim sum (available 7am to 5pm) and delectable Cantonese dishes. The elegant Eastern art deco furnishings are also much raved about. All this more than compensates for the sometimes cavalier service by the wrinkly waiters (though that too is a classic). Luk Yu comes recommended by the Michelin inspectors.

HANG ZHOU RESTAURANT
   Hangzhou   **$$**
(杭州酒家; Map p276; ☎ 2591 1898; 1st fl, Chinachem Johnston Plaza, 178-188 Johnston Rd, Wan Chai; lunch HK$70-200, dinner HK$200-1800; ⏰11.30am-2.30pm & 5.30-10.30pm; M Wan Chai, exit A5) A food critics' favourite, this establishment with one Michelin star excels at Hangzhou cooking, the delicate sister of Shanghainese cuisine. Dishes such as shrimp stirfried with tea leaves

Star Ferry

On a smoggy day, they're the only stars you'll see from Victoria Harbour. The iconic **Star Ferry** (天星小輪), founded in 1888, is a fleet of 12 passenger ferries (each named after a star) that plies Victoria Harbour between Hong Kong and Kowloon.

For a modest fare, you can cross the harbour on one of four routes. It's a little hard to imagine, therefore, that in 1966, thousands gathered here to protest against a five-cent fare increase. The protest eventually erupted into the 1966 Riot, the first in a series of important social protests leading to colonial reform.

The Star Ferry has borne witness to major events in Hong Kong history. In 1910, the Kowloon–Canton Railway was built near its Kowloon concourse, linking Hong Kong with the mainland. On Christmas Day 1941, the colonial governor, Sir Mark Aitchison Young, took the ferry to Tsim Sha Tsui, where he surrendered to the Japanese at the Peninsula Hotel.

In 2006, amid vehement opposition, the government tore down the old pier at Edinburgh Pl on Hong Kong Island. Taking over its functions is an ugly Edwardian replica at Piers 4 to 7 further west. The pier in Kowloon remains untouched.

show how the best culinary creations should engage all your senses.

PURE VEGGIE HOUSE
Vegetarian Chinese **$$**

(心齋; Map p272; 3rd fl, Coda Plaza, 51 Garden Rd, Admiralty; meals HK$150-250; ⏰11am-10pm; 🖋; Ⓜ Admiralty, then bus 12A) Hong Kong's best vegetarian restaurant shows how, in the hands of a master, a Chinese vegetarian menu doesn't have to read like the rundown of a meat-lookalike contest. All dishes and dim sum, some unique to this place, are delicious and msg-free. The service is immaculate.

TUNG PO SEAFOOD RESTAURANT
Cantonese **$**

(📞2880 9399; 2nd fl, Municipal Services Bldg, 99 Java Rd, North Point; meals HK$80-180; ⏰5.30pm-12.30am, reservations 2.30-5.30pm; Ⓜ North Point, exit A1) This institution has revolutionised *dai pai dong* (hawker-style) cooking in Hong Kong. There's no end to the novelty in its menu, which has featured items such as steamed glutinous rice with duck jus. Even beer is served in big rice bowls, to be downed bandit style. Book ahead or go before seven.

L'ATELIER DE JOEL ROBUCHON
French **$$$**

(Map p272; 📞2166 9000; www.joel-robuchon.com; Shop 401, Landmark, Queen's Rd Central, Central; lunch HK$400-1500, dinner HK$560-1800; ⏰7.30-10am, noon-2.30pm & 6.30-10.30pm, no breakfast Sun; Ⓜ Central, exit F) We think this latest 'workshop' of the celebrity chef is everything it's cracked up to be. What's more, sampling its Michelin-starred wonders doesn't have to cost the earth. Go for breakfast or share a few tapas with a friend.

SAN XI LOU
Sichuanese **$$**

(三希樓; Map p272; 7th fl Coda Plaza, 51 Garden Rd, Admiralty; meals HK$100-350; ⏰11am-10.30pm; Ⓜ Admiralty, then bus 12A) The fresh ingredients and the complexity of the spices should tell you this is Hong Kong's finest Sichuanese kitchen. If still in doubt, ask the Sichuanese expats at the neighbouring tables.

YUNG KEE
Cantonese **$$**

(鏞記酒家; Map p272; www.yungkee.com.hk; 32-40 Wellington St, Central; meals HK$300-600; ⏰11am-11.30pm; Ⓜ Central, exit D2) Operating since 1942, Yung Kee is famous for its roast goose and dim sum (served 2pm to 5.30pm Monday to Saturday, 11am to 5.30pm Sunday).

ABC
Western **$**

(Map p272; ☎ 9278 8227; CF7, Queen St Cooked Food Market, 38 Des Voeux Rd West, Sheung Wan; meals HK$80-200; ⏱ noon-2.30pm & 6.30-10pm Mon-Sat, evenings only Sun) Mediterranean fare served hawker-style in a Chinese food market. Booking advised for dinner.

Kowloon

There's plenty of choice in both cuisine and budget, especially in Tsim Sha Tsui. More local places can be found further north.

T'ANG COURT
Cantonese **$$$**

(唐閣; Map p266; ☎ 2375 1133; http://hongkong. langhamhotels.com; Langham Hotel, 8 Peking Rd, Tsim Sha Tsui; lunch HK$200-2000, dinner HK$360-2000; ⏱ 11am-2.30pm & 6-10.30pm Mon-Fri, noon-2.30pm & 6-10.30pm Sat & Sun; ⚲; Ⓜ East Tsim Sha Tsui, exit L4) As befitting a restaurant named after China's greatest dynasty, T'ang Court has honed its speciality, Cantonese cooking, into an art, whether it's baked oysters on the half-shell or an honest plate of greens. T'ang Court has two Michelin stars.

YE SHANGHAI
Shanghainese **$$$**

(夜上海; Map p266; ☎ 2376 3322; www.elite -concepts.com; 6th fl, Marco Polo Hotel, Harbour City, Canton Rd, Tsim Sha Tsui; meals HK$300-600; ⏱ 11.30am-3pm & 6-11pm; Ⓜ East Tsim Sha Tsui, exit L4) The name means 'Shànghǎi nights'. Dark woods and subtle lighting inspired by 1920s Shànghǎi fill the air with romance. The modern Shanghainese creations, which are lighter and easier on the eye than traditional Shanghainese fare, are also exquisite. The only exception to this Jiangnan harmony is the Cantonese dim sum being served at lunch, though that too is wonderful. Ye Shanghai has one Michelin star.

SABATINI
Italian **$$$**

(Map p266; ☎ 2733 2000; www.rghk.com.hk; 3rd fl, Royal Garden Hotel, 69 Mody Rd, Tsim Sha Tsui; lunch HK$200-800, dinner HK$600-900; ⏱ noon-2.30pm & 6-11pm; ⚲; Ⓜ East Tsim Sha Tsui, exit P2) One of two branches of Sabatini Ristorante Italiano in Rome, this place serves up excellent Italian favourites in a jovial, faux-rustic setting. Want romance with your risotto? An avuncular Filipino trio will serenade you at your table till you're weak at the knees. Booking advised.

WOODLANDS
Vegetarian, Indian **$**

(活蘭印度素食; Map p266; Upper Ground fl, 16 & 17 Wing On Plaza, 62 Mody Rd, Tsim Sha Tsui; meals HK$55-100; ⏱ noon-3.30pm & 6.30-10.30pm; ⚲; Ⓜ East Tsim Sha Tsui, exit P1) Woodlands comes highly recommended for its excellent Indian fare (mostly South Indian) and modest charm. Dithering gluttons should choose the thali meal, a round metal tray with samplings of different curries, soup, rice and dessert.

HUTONG
Chinese **$$$**

(胡同; Map p266; ☎ 3428 8342; 28th fl, 1 Peking Rd, Tsim Sha Tsui; lunch HK$250-400, dinner HK$400-1000; ⏱ noon-2.30pm & 6pm-midnight; Ⓜ Tsim Sha Tsui, exit C1) Muted lighting and interiors just this side of kitsch lend Michelin-starred Hutong a dramatic air. Like the decor, the tasty contemporary dishes are a tad contrived, but never mind, the real gem is out the window – the Kowloon waterfront in all its splendour.

TIM HO WAN
Dim Sum **$**

(☎ 2332 2896; Shop 8, 2-20 Kwong Wa St, Mong Kok; meals $30-50; ⏱ 10am-9.15pm) A former Four Seasons dim sum chef recreates magic in the world's cheapest Michelin-starred eatery for those who'd wait for a table.

Detour: Lamma & Cheung Chau

Laid-back **Lamma** (Map p278) has decent beaches, excellent walks and a plethora of restaurants in **Yung Shue Wan** and **Sok Kwu Wan**.

Dumbbell-shaped **Cheung Chau** (Map p278), with a harbour filled with fishing boats, a windsurfing centre, several temples and some bars and restaurants, makes a fun day out.

Drinking

Lan Kwai Fong (LKF) in Central is synonymous with nightlife in Hong Kong, attracting everyone from expat and Chinese suits to travellers.

Hong Kong Island

CLUB 71 Bar
(七一吧; Map p272; basement, 67 Hollywood Rd, Central; ☉3pm-2am Mon-Sat, 6pm-1am Sun; bus 26) Named after a protest march that took place on 1 July 2003, this is one of the best drinking spots for nonposeurs. It's also a great place to meet Hong Kong's musicians, artists and writers (plus wannabes of all of the above).

SEVVA Designer Bar
(Map p272; www.sevva.hk; 25th fl, Prince's Bldg, 10 Chater Rd, Central; ☉noon-midnight Mon-Thu, to 2am Fri & Sat; M Central, exit H) If there was a million-dollar view in Hong Kong, it'd be the one from the balcony of this stylish number – iconic skyscrapers up so close you see their arteries of steel, with the harbour and Kowloon in the distance.

PAWN Gastropub
(Map p276; 62 Johnston Rd, Wai Chai; ☉11am-late; M Wan Chai, exit B2) Occupying a period building that used to house a century-old pawn shop, the Pawn serves a huge range of beers and wines from stylishly beaten-up sofas and cool terrace tables overlooking tram tracks.

Kowloon

PHONOGRAPH Bar
(Map p266; shop A&B, ground fl, 2 Austin Ave, Tsim Sha Tsui; ☉6pm-4am; M Tsim Sha Tsui, exit B2) With dark, velvety interiors opening onto a quiet corner of Tsim Sha Tsui, Phonograph is a breath of fresh air on Kowloon's bar scene. Musicians and artist types come for the mellow vibe and eclectic music selection.

Felix Bar, Restaurant
(Map p266; 28th fl, Peninsula Hong Kong, Salisbury Rd, Tsim Sha Tsui; ☉6pm-2am; M East Tsim Sha Tsui, exit L2) Designed by Philippe Starck, swanky Felix is where to head for amazing views and expensive drinks.

Entertainment

Hong Kongers work hard and play harder. To find out what's on, pick up a copy of **HK Magazine** (http://hk-magazine.com), an entertainment listings magazine. It's free, appears on Friday and can be found in restaurants, bars and hotels. For more comprehensive listings buy the fortnightly **Time Out** (www.timeout.com.hk) from newsstands. Also worth checking out is the freebie **bc magazine** (www.bcmagazine.net).

The main ticket providers, **Urbtix** (✆2734 9009; www.urbtix.hk/; ☉10am-8pm), **Cityline** (✆2317 6666; www.cityline.com.hk), and **Hong Kong Ticketing** (✆3128 8288; www.hkticketing.com; ☉10am-8pm), have among them tickets to every major event in Hong Kong.

Cantonese Opera

Hong Kong is one of the best places to watch Cantonese opera. **Sunbeam Theatre** (www.ua-sunbeam.com; 423 King's Rd, North Point) is dedicated to the art form. Performances are also being staged at **Ko Shan Theatre** (📞 2330 5661; www.lcsd. gov.hk/CE/CulturalService/KST/; 77 Ko Shan Rd, Hung Hom). The best way to book if you don't speak Cantonese is through the Urbtix or CityLine systems.

Live Music & Clubbing

PEEL FRESCO   Music Bar
(Map p272; www.peelfresco.com; 49 Peel St, Central; ⏰5pm-late Mon-Sat; Midlevels escalator) This charming place has great live jazz six nights a week, with local and overseas acts performing next to huge Renaissance-style paintings. The action starts around 9.30pm, but go at 9pm to secure a seat.

TAZMANIA BALLROOM   Club
(Map p272; www.tazmaniaballroom.com; 1st fl, LKF Tower, 33 Wyndham St, Central; ⏰5am-late; Ⓜ Central, exit D2) This sexy, futuristic lair hasn't forgotten how to be playful. At any one time, you'll see people dressed to the hilt smoking on the balcony, or in sweatpants playing pool at gold-plated tables.

Gay & Lesbian Venues

For more venues and the latest events, try **Utopia Asia** (www.utopia-asia.com/hkbars.htm) or **Gay HK** (www.gayhk.com).

Propaganda   Club
(Map p272; lower ground fl, 1 Hollywood Rd, Central; weekend cover HK$100; ⏰9pm-late Tue-Sat; Midlevels escalator) Hong Kong's premier gay dance club. The weekend cover

charge gets you into Works below on Friday. Enter from Ezra's Lane.

🛍 Shopping

It's not the bargain destination it was, but Hong Kong is crammed with retail space, making it a delight for shoppers.

If you prefer everything under one roof, some of the sleeker options:

IFC Mall (國際金融商場; Map p272; www.ifc.com.hk; 1 Harbour View St, Central; Ⓜ Tung Chung Line, Hong Kong station)

Pacific Place (太古廣場; Map p272; 88 Queensway, Admiralty; Ⓜ Admiralty)

In Kowloon, head for these:

Harbour City (海港城; Map p266; Canton Rd, Tsim Sha Tsui) An enormous complex.

K11 (Map p266; 18 Hanoi Rd, Tsim Sha Tsui; Ⓜ East Tsim Sha Tsui, exit D2) Interesting shops and art spaces.

For antiques and curios, Central's **Hollywood Road** (Map p272) should be your first stop, while

Shopping Centre, Tsim Sha Tsui
PHOTOGRAPHER: RICHARD I'ANSON/LONELY PLANET IMAGES ©

cheaper **Cat St** (Map p272), also in Central, specialises in younger (ie retro) items like old postcards and Mao paraphernalia.

You can buy clothes you'll enjoy wearing for less than you'd pay at home in Hong Kong's malls. For cheap attire, try **Jardine's Bazaar** (渣甸街; Map p276) in Causeway Bay, and **Johnston Rd** (Map p276) in Wan Chai. In Kowloon, besides **Temple Street night market** (p270) you can try **Ladies Market** (女人街; Tung Choi St, Fa Yuen St & Sai Yeung Choi St, Mong Kok; ⊙noon-10.30pm; Ⓜ Mong Kok, exit B2) in Mong Kok.

Hong Kong is one of the best places in Asia to buy English-language books and the city's computer malls have some of the lowest prices on earth. Similarly, there are some fantastic camera stores, though most are *not* on Nathan Rd in Tsim Sha Tsui.

Hong Kong Island

Central and Causeway Bay are the main shopping districts on Hong Kong Island.

G.O.D.   Lifestyle
(住好啲; Map p276; www.god.com.hk; Leighton Centre, Sharp St East, Causeway Bay; ⊙noon-10pm; Ⓜ Causeway Bay) This spunky shop is where to go for really cool Hong Kong–style accessories and souvenirs. It has five stores in town, including this one.

Arch Angel Antiques   Antiques
(Map p272; 53-55 Hollywood Rd, Central; ⊙9.30am-6.30pm; bus 26) This well-respected shop has knowledgable staff and a wide selection of antiques and curios, including many at affordable prices. Everything is authenticated.

Dymocks   Books
(Map p272; ☏ 2117 0360; Shop 2007-2011, 2nd fl, IFC Mall, 1 Harbour View St, Central; ⊙9.30am-9pm; Ⓜ Tung Chung Line Hong Kong station)

Daydream Nation   Fashion
(www.daydream-nation.com; ☏ 3741 0758; 21 Wing Fung St, Star St, Wan Chai; noon-8.30pm; Ⓜ Admiralty, exit F) Daydream Nation is a 'Vogue Talent 2010' brand created by a fashion designer and her musician brother. The highly wearable clothes come with a touch of theatricality.

HONG KONG SHOPPING

Kowloon

Shopping in Kowloon is a mix of the down-at-heel and the glamorous; you can find just about anything – especially in Tsim Sha Tsui – and you don't even have to look very hard.

Yue Hwa Chinese Products Emporium

Chinese Products

(裕華國貨; Map p266; 301-309 Nathan Rd, Yau Ma Tei; ⏱10am-10pm; Ⓜ Yau Ma Tei. exit D) This enormous place has seven floors of ceramics, furniture, souvenirs, clothing and traditional medicines.

Initial
Fashion

(Map p266; www.initialfashion.com; Shop 2, 48 Cameron Rd, Tsim Sha Tsui; 11.30am-10.30pm; Ⓜ Tsim Sha Tsui) Initial's 10-plus branches carry stylish, multifunctional urbanwear.

Swindon Books
Books

(Map p266; ✆ 2366 8001; www.swindonbooks. com; 13-15 Lock Rd, Tsim Sha Tsui; ⏱10am-8pm Mon-Sat, 12.30-6.30pm Sun; Ⓜ Tsim Sha Tsui) Carries stationery as well as books.

Star Computer City
Computers

(星光電腦城; Map p266; 2nd fl, Star House, 3 Salisbury Rd, Tsim Sha Tsui; ⏱10am-8pm; Ⓜ Tsim Sha Tsui) Conveniently near the Star Ferry Pier and hence relatively expensive, and only two dozen computer shops!

ⓘ Information

Hong Kong is awash with free maps – the airport is full of them. The *Hong Kong Map,* distributed by the HKTB, is enough for most travellers.

Emergency

Fire, police & ambulance (✆999)

Internet Access

Internet cafes may be hard to come by, but wi-fi is widely available. Wi-fi is free at the following:

○ Parks, public libraries, sports centres, museums, cooked-food markets, community halls, and government premises listed at www. gov.hk/en/theme/wifi/location.

○ Over 30 MTR stations (see www.mtr.com.hk/eng/facilities/wifi.html).

○ Hong Kong International Airport.

○ McDonald's (www.mcdonalds.com.hk), Pacific Coffee (www.pacificcoffee.com) and Starbucks (www.starbucks.com.hk) outlets with purchase.

Medical Services

Medical care is of a high standard in Hong Kong (general enquiries, call 2300 6555), though private hospital care is costly. Hospitals with 24-hour emergency services:

Matilda International (明德國際醫院; 41 Mt Kellett Rd, Peak) Pricey private hospital atop Victoria Peak.

Queen Elizabeth (伊利沙伯醫院; 30 Gascoigne Rd, Yau Ma Tei) Public hospital in Kowloon.

Money

The Hong Kong dollar is pegged to the US dollar at a rate of US$1 to HK$7.80.

ATMs Available throughout Hong Kong, including at the airport.

Banks Best exchange rates, but some levy commissions of HK$50 or more for each transaction.

Licensed moneychangers Abundant in tourist districts and ground floor of Chungking Mansions. Wing Hoi Money Exchange (ground fl, Shop No 9b, Mirador Arcade, 58 Nathan Rd, Tsim Sha Tsui; 8.30am-8.30pm Mon-Sat, to 7pm Sun) in Mirador Mansion can change most major currencies and travellers cheques; rates at the airport are poor.

Post

Hong Kong Post (www.hongkongpost.com) has offices including the following:

General post office (中央郵政局; Map p272; 2 Connaught Pl, Central; 8am-6pm Mon-Sat, 9am-5pm Sun)

Tsim Sha Tsui post office (尖沙咀郵政局; Map p266; ground & 1st fl, Hermes House, 10 Middle Rd, Tsim Sha Tsui; 9am-6pm Mon-Sat, to 2pm Sun)

Telephone

Facts to know before making calls in Hong Kong:

○ All phone numbers have eight digits (except 800 toll-free numbers) and no area codes.

○ Local calls are free on private phones and cost HK$1 for five minutes on pay phones.

○ A phonecard, available at convenience stores, will let you make international direct-dial calls.

○ A SIM card (from HK$50) with prepaid call time will connect you to the local mobile-phone network.

Some handy phone numbers:

International directory assistance (10015)

Local directory assistance (1081)

Reverse charge/collect calls (10010)

Weather & time (18501)

Tourist Information

The enterprising and efficient HKTB (香港旅遊發展局; visitor hotline 2508 1234 9am-6pm; www.discoverhongkong.com) runs an immensely useful visitor hotline and excellent website. It also maintains Visitor Information & Service Centres:

Hong Kong International Airport (Buffer Halls A & B, Arrivals Level, Terminal 1; 7am-11pm)

Hong Kong Island (The Peak Piazza; 9am-9pm)

Kowloon (Map p266; Star Ferry Concourse, Tsim Sha Tsui; 8am-8pm)

Lo Wu (2nd fl, Arrival Hall, Lo Wu Terminal Bldg; 8am-4pm) At the border to mainland China.

Travel Agencies

Phoenix Services Agency (峯寧旅運社; 2722 7378; info@phoenixtrvl.com; room 1404-5, 14th fl, Austin Tower, 22-26a Austin Ave, Tsim Sha Tsui; 9am-6pm Mon-Fri, to 4pm Sat)

ⓘ Getting There & Away

Air

Some 90 airlines operate between Hong Kong International Airport (HKG; Map p278; 2181 8888; www.hkairport.com) and about 150 destinations worldwide. Competition keeps fares relatively low, and Hong Kong is a great place to find discounted tickets.

There are few bargain airfares between Hong Kong and China, however, as the government regulates the prices. Seats can be difficult to book due to the enormous volume of business travellers and Chinese tourists, so book well in advance.

However, if you're prepared to travel a couple of hours to Guǎngzhōu or Shēnzhèn, in nearby Guǎngdōng province, then you can find much cheaper flights. Shēnzhèn airport, in particular, has flights to just about everywhere in China. For an idea of price, check out www.elong.net.

See p405 for international airlines flying to/from Hong Kong.

Boat

For sea transport to/from Macau, see p303.

Bus

You can reach virtually any major destination in Guǎngdōng province by bus (HK$100 to HK$220).

CTS Express Coach (☎2764 9803; http://ctsbus.hkcts.com) Has the most extensive cross-border bus services to destinations in Guǎngdōng province.

Trans-Island Limousine Service (☎3193 9333; www.trans-island.com.hk) Has buses to a dozen destinations in Guǎngdōng province.

Train

You can get the latest train schedules and ticket prices from the MTR's excellent website, www.mtr.com.hk. Other handy train-related facts:

Immigration formalities at Hung Hom Completed before boarding, including checking your visa for China; arrive at station 45 minutes before departure.

Tickets Can be booked in advance at CTS (p288), East Rail stations in Hung Hom, Mong Kok, Kowloon Tong and Sha Tin, and MTR Travel at Admiralty Station; tickets booked with credit card by phone (☎2947 7888) must be collected at least one hour before departure.

Trains to Guǎngzhōu, Shànghǎi, Běijīng and Zhàoqìng Daily from Hung Hom station; HK$235 to HK$934.

Trains to Shēnzhèn Board East Rail train at Hung Hom station or any East Rail station along the way, and ride it to Lo Wu; from Shēnzhèn you can take a local train or bus to Guǎngzhōu and beyond.

ⓘ Getting Around

Hong Kong's public-transport system is the envy of cities the world over. It's fast, easy to navigate, relatively inexpensive and ridiculously easy with the Octopus card payment system.

To/From the Airport

Airport Express (www.mtr.com.hk; 24-/21-/13-min ride from Central/Kowloon/Tsing Yi HK$100/90/60) Fastest and costliest public route to the airport; most airlines allow Airport Express passengers to check in at the Central or Kowloon stations up to a day ahead of departure; trains depart from HONG KONG AIRPORT EXPRESS STATION (Map p272) in Central every 12 minutes.

Bus (www.nwstbus.com.hk; fares HK$21-45) Services connect the airport with Lantau, the New Territories, Kowloon and Hong Kong Island.

Lighting incense, Man Mo Temple (p267)
PHOTOGRAPHER: RICHARD I'ANSON/LONELY PLANET IMAGES ©

Ferry For info on service to Shēnzhèn airport, see the boxed text, p291.

Taxi To Central about HK$300 plus luggage charge of HK$5 per item.

Bicycle

In quiet areas of the Outlying Islands or New Territories, a bike can be a lovely way of getting around as long as you don't mind a few hills.

Car & Motorcycle

Hong Kong's maze of one-way streets and dizzying expressways isn't for the faint-hearted. But if you're hell-bent on ruining your holiday, **Avis** (Map p266; ☎2890 6988; shop 46, ground fl, Peninsula Centre, 67 Mody Rd, Tsim Sha Tsui; ⏰8am-7pm Mon, 9am-7pm Tue-Fri, 9am-4pm Sat & Sun) will rent you a Honda Civic for HK$790/3500 a day/week with unlimited kilometres.

Public Transport

No more rummaging in your purse for small change: **Octopus card** (www.octopuscards.com; HK$150, plus refundable deposit HK$50) Reusable 'smart card' that can be used on most forms of public transport and in a number of stores. To put money on your card, go to an add-value machine/ticket office at MTR stations, or 7-Eleven stores.

MTR Tourist 1-Day Pass (HK$55) This pass, allowing unlimited travel on the MTR for 24 hours, is good for short stays.

CROSS-HARBOUR FERRY The **Star Ferry** (p282; www.starferry.com.hk; from HK$2) operates on four routes:

Central-Hung Hom

Central-Tsim Sha Tsui

Wan Chai-Hung Hom

Wan Chai-Tsim Sha Tsui

OUTLYING ISLANDS FERRIES Most ferries depart from the Outlying Islands Piers close to the IFC building in Central. The main companies serving the islands:

New World First Ferry (NWFF; www.nwff.com. hk) Services to Lantau and Cheung Chau, and an interisland service connecting Peng Chau, Mui Wo (Lantau) and Cheung Chau.

Hong Kong & Kowloon Ferry Co (www.hkkf. com.hk) Serves Lamma and Peng Chau.

BUS Hong Kong's extensive **bus system** (fares HK$2.5-40; ⏰5.30 or 6am-midnight or 12.30am), including a handful of night buses, will get you almost anywhere. Note that exact change or an

Health food store in Sheung Wan

HKIA to China the Fast Way

If you're heading straight from Hong Kong International Airport (HKIA) to airports in Macau, Shēnzhèn and Guǎngzhōu try the following:

Chu Kong Passenger Transportation Co (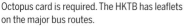2858 3876; www.cksp.com.hk/eng/home.html) buses go from HKIA to Shēnzhèn airport (HK$295, 50 minutes, six times daily from 10am to 7.50pm); they also run to Macau, Shékǒu, Dōngguǎn, Zhūhǎi and Zhōngshān.

CTS Express Coach (2261 2147), **Eternal East Cross Border Coach** (2261 0176) and **Go Go Bus** (2261 0886; www.gogobus.com), all with counters at HKIA, have buses going to points in southern China.

Octopus card is required. The HKTB has leaflets on the major bus routes.

There are myriad bus stops and stations; major ones:

Central Bus Terminus (Map p272; Exchange Sq) Gets you to the southern side of the island. Buses 6, 6A and 260 leave for Stanley and Repulse Bay, and buses 70 and 70P for Aberdeen.

Admiralty (Map p272) Above Admiralty MTR station. Gets you to the southern side of the island.

Star Ferry Pier (Map p266) Has buses to Hung Hom station and points in eastern and western Kowloon.

PUBLIC LIGHT BUS 'Public light buses', better known as 'minibuses', have no more than 16 seats and come in two varieties:

With red roof/stripe Fares HK$2 to HK$20; supplement bus services. Get on or off almost anywhere – just yell 'ni do, m gói' (here, please); pay with Octopus card/coins as you exit.

With green roof/stripe Operate on over 350 set routes and make designated stops.

TRAIN The Mass Transit Railway (MTR;www.mtr.com.hk; fares HK$4-26) runs 10 lines composing arguably the best railway service on earth – fast, convenient and always on time. You can buy individual tickets or use an Octopus card (slightly cheaper). Once you go past the turnstile, you must complete the journey within 150 minutes.

The MTR also runs overland services on two main lines and two smaller lines, offering excellent transport to the New Territories:

East Rail From Hung Hom station in Kowloon to Lo Wu (HK$33) and Lok Ma Chau, gateway to Shēnzhèn; a spur runs from Tai Wai to Wu Kai Sha.

West Rail From Hung Hom station to Tuen Mun via Yuen Long.

Light Rail Fares HK$3.70 to HK$5.80. Operates on routes in western New Territories between Tuen Mun and Yuen Long, and feeds the West Rail.

TRAM Hong Kong's century-old trams, operated by Hong Kong Tramways Ltd (www.hktramways.com; fares HK$2), comprise the only all double-decker wooden-sided tram fleet in the world. They operate on six overlapping routes, on 16km of track running east–west along the northern side of Hong Kong Island.

Taxi

Hong Kong is served by taxis of three colours:

Red Serving Hong Kong Island and Kowloon; HK$18 flag fall for the first 2km, then HK$1 for every additional 200m.

Green Serving the New Territories; HK$14.5 flag fall, then HK$1.30 for every subsequent 200m.

Blue Serving Lantau; HK$13 flag fall, then HK$1.30 for every 200m.

MACAU
POPULATION: 549,500 / 853

Such has been its explosive growth since 2002 that it is commonplace to refer to Macau as the Vegas of the East. It might be more appropriate to put that the other way round, since Macau has eclipsed its

American rival in gambling income. And there are other things that Macau does better. Beyond the gaming halls, it offers cobblestoned streets punctuated with Chinese temples and baroque churches, pockets of greenery, a historic centre of Unesco World Heritage status, and balmy beaches.

Macau's history has also created a one-of-a-kind cuisine that celebrates the marriage of European, Latin American, African and Asian flavours. Prices in this chapter are quoted in patacas (MOP$) unless otherwise stated.

History

Portuguese galleons first visited southern China to trade in the early 16th century, and in 1557, as a reward for clearing out pirates endemic to the area, they were allowed to establish a tiny enclave in Macau. As trade with China grew, so did Macau, which became the principal centre for Portuguese trade with China, Japan and Southeast Asia. However, after the Opium Wars between the Chinese and the British, and the subsequent establishment of Hong Kong, Macau went into a long decline.

In 1999, under the Sino-Portuguese Joint Declaration, Macau was returned to China and designated a Special Administrative Region (SAR). Like Hong Kong, the pact ensures Macau a 'high degree of autonomy' in all matters (except defence and foreign affairs) for 50 years. Since the handover, casinos have mushroomed.

👁 Sights

For a small place (just 29 sq km), Macau is packed with important cultural and historical sights. The **Macau Museums Pass** (MOP$25) allows entry to a half-dozen museums over a five-day period.

Central Macau Peninsula

Running from Avenida da Praia Grande to the Inner Harbour, Avenida de Almeida Ribeiro – called San Ma Lo (新馬路 New Thoroughfare) in Cantonese – is the peninsula's main thoroughfare and home to the charming **Largo do Senado** (Map p296), a black-and-white-tiled square close to several major sights.

MONTE FORT & MACAU MUSEUM
Fort, Museum

(大炮台; **Fortaleza do Monte; Map p296; admission free;** ☉7am-7pm Mon-Sun) Built by the Jesuits between 1617 and 1626, Monte Fort is accessible by escalator just east of the Church of St Paul. Barracks and storehouses were designed to allow the fort to survive a long siege, but the cannons were fired only once: during an aborted invasion by the Dutch in 1622. Housed in the fort is the remarkable **Macau Museum** (澳門博物館; Museu de Macau; Map p296; ☎2835 7911; www.macau museum.gov.mo; admission MOP$15; ☉10am-5.30pm Tue-Sun), which has exhibits on the history and traditions of Macau.

CHURCH OF ST DOMINIC
Church

(聖母堂; **Igreja de São Domingos; Map p296; Largo de São Domingos;** ☉10am-6pm) This lovely 17th-century baroque church occupies the site of a convent built by the Spanish Dominicans in 1587. It contains the **Treasury of Sacred Art** (聖物寶庫; Tresouro de Arte Sacra; Map p296; admission free; ☉10am-6pm), an Aladdin's cave of ecclesiastical art, including dismembered relics and a skull, exhibited over three floors.

ST JOSEPH'S SEMINARY CHURCH
Church

(聖若瑟修院及聖堂; **Capela do Seminario São Jose; Map p296; Rua do Seminario;** ☉10am-5pm) One of Macau's most beautiful buildings and the best example of tropicalised baroque, the church was consecrated in 1758 as part of the Jesuit seminary.

LEAL SENADO
Senate

(民政總署大樓; **Map p296; ☎2857 2233; 163 Av de Almeida Ribeiro**) The 'Loyal Senate' is home to Macau's main municipal administrative body. If you walk through, there's a peaceful courtyard and the stately **Senate Library** (☉1pm-7pm) out the back. Inside, the **IACM Gallery** (☉9am-9pm Tue-Sun) holds well-curated exhibitions.

MANDARIN'S HOUSE
Historic Residence

(鄭家大屋; Caso do Mandarim; Map p296; www.
wh.mo/mandarinhouse; 10 Travessa de Antonio
da Silva; admission free; ⏰10am-5.30pm Fri-Tue)
Built in 1869, this sprawling complex with
over 60 rooms was the ancestral home
of Zheng Guanying, an author-merchant
whose readers included emperors, Dr Sun
Yatsen and Chairman Mao.

Sir Robert Ho Tung Library
Library

(何東圖書館; Map p296; ☎2837 7117; 3 Largo
de St Agostinho; ⏰10am-7pm Mon-Sat, 11am-7am
Sun; @) This stunner comprises a 19th-century
villa and a glass-and-steel extension rising
above a back garden, with Piranesi-like bridges
shooting out between the two.

Southern Macau Peninsula

The southern Macau Peninsula features
a number of old colonial houses and
baroque churches.

COLONIAL MACAU
Historic Neighbourhoods

From Avenida de Almeida Ribeiro, follow
Calçada do Tronco Velho to the **Church of
St Augustine** (聖奧斯定教堂; Igreja de Santo
Agostinho; Map p296; Largo de Santo Agostinho;
⏰10am-6pm), built in 1814, and facing it,
China's first Western theatre, the **Dom
Pedro V Theatre** (崗頂劇院; Teatro Dom
Pedro; Map p296; Calçada do Teatro), a 19th-
century pastel-green building not open to
the public. Next you will see the **Church
of St Lawrence** (聖老楞佐教堂; Igreja de São
Lourenço; Map p296; Rua da Imprensa Nacional;
⏰10am-6pm Tue-Sun, 1-2pm Mon) with its
magnificent painted ceiling. Walk down
Travessa do Padre Narciso to the pink
Government House (特區政府總部; Sede
do Goberno; Map p296; cnr Av da Praia Grande
& Travessa do Padré Narciso), originally built
for a Portuguese noble in 1849 and, for
now, headquarters of the Macau SAR
(Special Administrative Region) government. The oldest section of Macau is a
short distance southwest of here, via the
waterfront promenade **Avenida da República** (Map p296). Along here are several
colonial villas and civic buildings not open
to the public. These include the **residence
of the Portuguese consul-general**

(葡國駐澳門領事官邸; Consulado-Geral de
Portugal em Macau; Map p296; Rua do Boa Vista),
which was once the Hotel Bela Vista, one
of the most storied hotels in Asia.

MACAU MUSEUM OF ART
Museum

(澳門藝術博物館; Museu de Arte de Macau;
Map p296; www.artmuseum.gov.mo; Macau
Cultural Centre, Av Xian Xing Hai; admission
MOP$5, ⏰10am-6.30pm Tue-Sun) This vast,
excellent museum houses rotating
exhibits as well as permanent collections
of works by established Chinese and
Western artists such as George Chinnery
(1774–1852), who spent most of his adult
life in Macau painting. Also inside the
Cultural Centre is **Creative Macau** (Map
p296; ☎2875 3282; www.creativemacau.org.mo;
⏰2-7pm Mon-Sat), an art space featuring
some fine exhibitions.

A-MA TEMPLE
Temple

(媽閣廟; Templo de A-Ma; Map p296; Rue de São
Tiago da Barra; ⏰10am-6pm) The A-Ma Temple is dedicated to A-Ma (better known
as Tin Hau, the goddess of the sea), from
which the name Macau is derived.

Northern Macau Peninsula

The northern peninsula sees fewer tourists and thus is good to just wander around in, get lost and find yourself some *hung yan bang* (almond biscuits).

GUIA FORT — Fort

(東望洋山堡壘; Fortaleza de Guia; Map p296; ⏰9am-5.30pm) As the highest point on the Macau Peninsula, this fort affords panoramic views of the city and, on a clear day, across to the islands and China. At the top you'll find a **lighthouse**, built in 1865 and the oldest on the China coast, and the lovely **Chapel of Our Lady of Guia** (聖母雪地殿聖堂; Capela de Nossa Señora da Guia; Map p296; ⏰10am-5pm Tue-Sun), built in 1622 and retaining almost 100% of its original features, including one of the most valuable mural paintings in East Asia. You can walk up or take the **Guia Cable Car** (東望洋山纜車; Teleférico da Guia; Map p296; one-way/return MOP$3/5; ⏰8am-6pm Tue-Sun) that runs from the entrance to **Flora Garden** (二龍喉公園; Jardim da Flora; Map p296; Travessa do Túnel; ⏰7.30am-8.30pm), Macau's largest public park.

LOU LIM IOC GARDEN — Garden

(盧廉若公園; Jardim Lou Lim Ioc; Map p296; 10 Estrada de Adolfo de Loureiro; ⏰6am-9pm) A cool and shady Sūzhōu-style garden with pavilions, lotus ponds, bamboo groves, grottoes and a bridge with nine turns (to escape from evil spirits, who can only move in straight lines).

KUN IAM TEMPLE — Temple

(觀音堂; Templo de Kun Iam; Map p296; Av do Coronel Mesquita; ⏰10am-6pm) Dating back four centuries, Kun Iam Temple is Macau's oldest and most interesting temple. The likeness of Kun Iam, the Goddess of Mercy, is in the main hall; to the left of the altar and behind glass is a statue of a bearded arhat rumoured to represent Marco Polo. The first treaty of trade and friendship between the USA and China was signed in the temple's terraced gardens in 1844.

The Islands

Connected to the Macau mainland by three bridges and joined together by an ever-growing area of reclaimed land called Cotai, Coloane and, to a lesser extent, Taipa are oases of calm and greenery. By contrast, the Cotai Strip is development central, with megacasinos sprouting up.

TAIPA — Island

Taipa Village, in the north-central part of the island, is a window to the island's past. Here you'll find the stately **Taipa House Museum** (龍環葡韻; Casa Museum da Taipa; Map p301; Av da Praia; admission MOP$5; ⏰10am-5.30pm Tue-Sun), housed in five waterfront villas that give a sense of how the Macanese middle class lived in the early 20th century. Also in the village is the **Church of Our Lady of Carmel** (嘉模聖母堂; Igreja de Nossa Senhora de Carmo; Map p301; Rue da Restauração) and temples including **Pak Tai Temple** (北帝廟; Templo Pak Tai; Map p301; Rua do Regedor).

Bikes can be rented in Taipa Village at **Aluguer de Bicicletas** (Map p301; 📞2882 7975; 36 Largo Governador Tamagini Barbosa); there's no English sign but it's next to the Don Quixote restaurant. You are not allowed to cross the Macau–Taipa bridges on a bicycle.

COLOANE — Island

A haven for pirates until the start of the 20th century, Coloane (路環; Lo Wan in Cantonese), considerably larger than Taipa, is the only part of Macau that doesn't seem to be changing at a head-spinning rate, which is a relief.

All buses stop at the roundabout in **Coloane Village** on the western shore, which overlooks mainland China across

---

Accommodation Price Indicators

The price ranges for the Macau section are as follows:

$	less than MOP$700
$$	MOP$700-2000
$$$	more than MOP$2000

GREG ELMS/LONELY PLANET IMAGES ©

Don't Miss Ruins of the Church of St Paul

A gateway to nowhere in the middle of the city is all that remains of the **Church of St Paul** (大三巴牌坊; Ruinas de Igreja de São Paulo; Map p296; Rua de São Paulo), considered by some to be the greatest monument to Christianity in Asia. The church was designed by an Italian Jesuit and built in 1602 by Japanese Christian exiles and Chinese craftsmen. In 1835 a fire destroyed everything except the facade. Like much of Macau's colonial architecture, its European appearance belies the fascinating mix of influences (in this case, Chinese, Japanese, Indochinese) that contributed to its aesthetics (look at the gargoyles).

the water. The main attraction in the village is the **Chapel of St Francis Xavier** (聖方濟各教堂; Capela de São Francisco Xavier; Map p302; Av de Cinco de Outubro; ◔10am-8pm), built in 1928 and which contains a relic of the saint's armbone. The village has some interesting temples, including the **Tam Kong Temple** (譚公廟; Templo Tam Kong; Map p302; Largo Tam Kong Miu; ◔8.30am-6pm), where you'll find a dragon-boat made of whalebone.

About 1.5km southeast of Coloane Village is **Cheoc Van Beach** (Bamboo Bay; Map p302); while larger and more popular **Hác Sá Beach** lies to the northeast.

 Tours

Quality Tours, coach trips organised by the MGTO (Macau Government Tourist Office) and tendered to such agents as **Gray Line** (錦倫旅行社; Map p296; ☎2833 6611; Room 1015, ground fl, Macau Ferry Terminal; adult/child 3-11 MOP$118/108), take about five hours.

 **Sleeping**

Rates shoot up on Friday or Saturday, while during the week you can find some incredible deals. These discounts can be found at travel agencies, hotel websites

Macau Peninsula

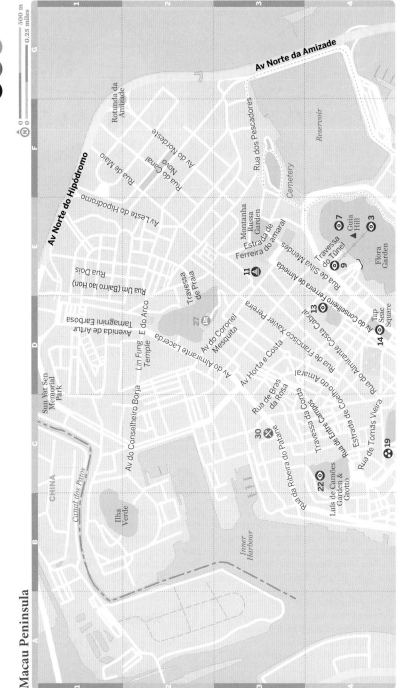

CHINA

Canal dos Patos

Ilha Verde

Inner Harbour

Sun Yat Sen Memorial Park

Av do Conselheiro Borja

Lin Fung Temple

E do Arco

Avenida de Artur Tamagnini Barbosa

Rua Dois

Rua Um (Bairro Iao Hon)

Rua da Ribeira do Patane

Av do Almirante Lacerda

Av do Coronel Mesquita

Travessa de Praia

27

Av Horta e Costa

Rua de Bras da Rosa

Travessa da Corda

Rua de Entre Campos

30

Luís de Camões Garden & Grotto

22

Rua de Coelho do Amaral

Estrada de Coelho do Amaral

Rua de Tomás Vieira

19

Rua de Francisco Xavier Pereira

Rua de Almirante Costa Cabral

13

Av do Conselheiro Ferreira de Almeida

Rua da Silva Mendes

Estrada de Ferreira do amaral

Montanha Russa Garden

11

9

Tap Seac Square

14

Travessa de Túnel

Guia Hill

7

3

Flora Garden

Rua dos Pescadores

Cemetery

Reservoir

Av Norte da Amizade

Rotunda da Amizade

Rua de Maio

Rua do Canal Novo

Av do Nordeste

Av Leste do Hipódromo

Av Norte do Hipódromo

500 m
0.25 miles

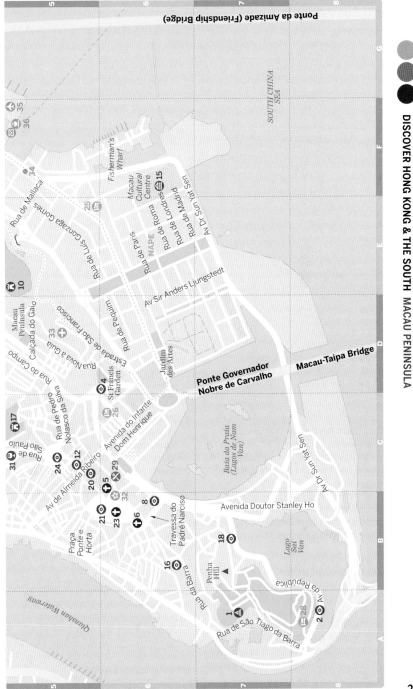

Ponte da Amizade (Friendship Bridge)

SOUTH CHINA SEA

Fisherman's Wharf

Macau Cultural Centre 15

NAPE

Rua de Paris
Rua de Roma
Rua de Londres
Rua de Madrid
Av Dr Sun Yat Sen

25

Rua de Malaca

34

35
36

10

Av Sir Anders Ljungstedt

Rua de Luís Gonzaga Gomes

Macau Peninsula

Calçada do Gaio

33

Rua Nova à Guia

Estrada de São Francisco

Rua de Pequim

Jardim des Artes

Ponte Governador Nobre de Carvalho

Macau-Taipa Bridge

Rua do Campo

St Francis Garden

4

26

Avenida do Infante Dom Henrique

Rua de Pedro Nolasco da Silva

17

31

Rua de São Paulo

24

12

20

5

29

32

Av de Almeida Ribeiro

Baía da Praia (Lagos de Nam Van)

Av Dr Sun Yat Sen

21

23

6

8

Travessa do Padré Narciso

Avenida Doutor Stanley Ho

Praça Ponte e Horta

16

Rua da Barra

18

Lago Sai Van

Penha Hill

Av da República

Quinshan Waterway

1

Rua de São Tiago da Barra

2

28

Macau Peninsula

◎ Sights

1 A-Ma Temple A7
2 Avenida da Republica..............................A8
3 Cable Car Terminus.....................................E4
  Chapel of Our Lady of Guia..........(see 10)
4 Chinese Reading Room.........................D6
5 Church of St Augustine.........................C6
  Church of St Dominic....................(see 24)
6 Church of St Lawrence B6
  Creative Macau ....(see 15)
7 Flora Garden...E4
8 Government House...................................B6
9 Guia Cable Car..E4
10 Guia Fort & Lighthouse........................E5
11 Kun Iam Temple..E3
12 Largo do Senado.......................................C5
  Leal Senado ....(see 20)
13 Lou Lim Ioc Garden.................................D4
14 Macao Central Library D4
  Macau Museum.................................(see 17)
15 Macau Museum of Art............................F6
16 Mandarin's House......................................B6
17 Monte Fort...C5
18 Residence of the Portuguese
  Consul General...B7
19 Ruins of the Church of St Paul............C4
20 Senate Library..C5
21 Sir Robert Ho Tung Library B6
22 Sr Wong Ieng Kuan Library...................C4
23 St Joseph's Seminary Church.............B6
24 Treasury of Sacred Art C5

◎ Sleeping

25 Mandarin Oriental E5
26 New Nam Pan Hotel.................................C6
27 Pousada de Mong Há..............................D2
28 Pousada de Saõ Tiago A8

◎ Eating

29 Alfonso III..C6
  Corner's Wine Bar & Tapas Café..(see 19)
30 Lung Wah Tea House...............................C3

◎ Drinking

31 Macau Soul..C5

◎ Entertainment

32 Dom Pedro V Theatre............................B6

Information

33 Centro Hospitalar Conde Saõ
  Januário...D5
34 Macau Immigration
  Department...F5
  MGTO (Ferry Terminal)................(see 36)
  MGTO (Guia Lighthouse) .... (see 10)

Transport

35 Heliport F5
36 Macau Ferry Terminal F5

and specialist sites such as www.macau. com. **Shun Tak Centre** (200 Connaught Rd, Sheung Wan) in Hong Kong, from where the Macau ferries depart, is also good, as are the booths in the arrivals hall of the Macau Ferry Terminal.

All rooms listed here have air-con and bathroom unless otherwise stated. Most midrange and top-end hotels have shuttle buses from the ferry terminal.

Macau Peninsula

MANDARIN ORIENTAL
Luxury Hotel **$$$**
(文華東方酒店; Map p296; ☏ 8805 8888; www. mandarinoriental.com/macau; Av Dr Sun Yat Sen; r MOP$3500-4900, ste from MOP$6100; ⊖ @ 🛜 🏊) A great high-end option, the new Mandarin has elegance, superlative service, comfortable rooms and excellent facilities.

POUSADA DE MONG HÁ
Inn **$$**
(望廈賓館; Map p296; ☏ 2851 5222; www. ift.edu.mo/pousada; Colina de Mong Há; s/d/ ste all incl breakfast MOP$680/960/1360, discounts midweek & low season of up to 30%; @ 🛜) This attractive Portuguese-style inn atop Mong Há Hill is an old barracks and is now run by tourism students. The rooms are simple, homely and squeaky clean.

Pousada de São Tiago
Luxury Hotel **$$$**
(聖地牙哥酒店; Map p296; ☏ 2837 8111; www. saotiago.com.mo; Fortaleza de São Tiago da Barra, Av da República; ste MOP$5800-9800, discounts low season of 35-50%; @ 🏊) The 'St James Inn', built into the ruins of a 17th-century fort, has 12 balconied suites with splendid views of the harbour. It's romantic, old-fashioned and expensive.

New Nam Pan Hotel — Guesthouse $
(新南濱賓館; Map p296; 📞 2848 2842, www. cnmacauhotel.com; 2nd fl, 8 Av de Do João IV; s/d/tr/q MOP$280/380/480/580, plus weekends MOP$100-200; 🛜) Central location, a rustic vibe and eight spotless rooms make New Nam Pan a good budget option.

The Islands

POUSADA DE COLOANE — Hotel $$
(竹灣酒店; Map p302; 📞 2882 2143; www. hotelpcoloane.com.mo; Estrada de Cheoc Van, Coloane; r from MOP$750, discounts low season of 20-40%; 🏊) This 30-room hotel with its Portuguese-style rooms (all with balconies and sea views) is excellent value. And the location above Cheoc Van Beach is about as chilled as you'll find. It's served by buses 25 and 26A.

GRAND HYATT MACAU — Luxury Hotel $$$
(澳門君悅酒店; off Map p296; 📞 8868 1234; http://macau.grand.hyatt.com; City of Dreams, Estrada do Istmo, Cotai; r MOP$1488-2688, ste MOP$1588-2788; 🛏@🛜🏊) The most tasteful of the casino-hotels on the Cotai Strip, the Grand Hyatt is part of the City of Dreams casino-shopping-performance complex. The massive rooms come with glass-and-marble showering areas and a full battery of technology.

 Eating

Browse a typically Macanese menu and you'll find an enticing stew of influences from Chinese and Asian cuisines, as well as from those of former Portuguese colonies in Africa, India and Latin America.

ALFONSO III — Macanese $
(亞豐素三世餐廳; Map p296; 📞 2858 6272; 11a Rua Central; meals MOP$70-200; ⏰noon-3pm & 6-10.30pm Mon-Sat) With a diverse menu featuring liver and tripe dishes in addition to popular classics, all fabulously executed, it's clear this unpretentious eatery doesn't just cater for the weekend crowds. It's always packed with Macanese families, so book ahead.

ANTONIO — Portuguese $$$
(安東尼奧; Map p301; 📞 2899 9998; www. antoniomacau.com; 3 Rua dos Negociantes, Taipa; starters MOP$100-255, mains MOP$150-300; ⏰noon-3pm & 6.30-10.30pm Mon-Fri, noon-10.30pm Sat & Sun) Dark mahogany set off by blue-and-white azulejo tiles prepare you for an authentic Portuguese meal at this Michelin-recommended restaurant known for whipping up a mean goat's cheese with honey (MOP$145) and a lavish seafood stew (MOP$480 for two people).

LUNG WAH TEA HOUSE — Cantonese $
(龍華茶樓; Map p296; 📞 2857 4456; 3 Av do Almirante Lacerda; dim sum from MOP$14, tea MOP$10; ⏰7am-2pm; 🚌) There's grace in the retro furniture and the casual air of this Cantonese teahouse (c 1963) with a Michelin Bib Gourmand. Take a booth by windows overlooking the Almirante Lacerda (Red Market), where the teahouse buys its produce every day.

Restaurante Fernando — Macanese $
(法蘭度餐廳; off Map p302; www.fernando-restaurant.com; 9 Praia de Hác Sá, Coloane; mains MOP$55-160, rice dishes MOP$60-75; ⏰noon-9.30pm) A Macau institution famed for seafood and the perfect place for a protracted, boozy lunch by the sea.

 **Drinking & Entertainment**

LORD STOW'S CAFE — Cafe
(澳門澳門安德魯餅店; Map p302; www. lordstow.com; Largo do Matadouro, Coloane Village; ⏰10am-6pm) This cosy cafe serves

Eating Price Indicators

The price ranges for the Macau section (per meal) are as follows:

$	less than MOP$200
$$	MOP$200-400
$$$	more than MOP$400

MACAU EATING

If You Like…
Macau Libraries

If you liked the Sir Robert Ho Tung Library (p293) then why not further explore Macau's libraries. Each one shows by the way they relate to their surroundings how tiny proportions can also be beautiful.

1 CHINESE READING ROOM
(八角亭; Map p296; Rua de Santa Clara; ☺9am-noon, 7pm-midnight) This former drinks booth known as 'Octagonal Pavilion' (c. 1926) in Chinese has red windows and a slip of a staircase linking up two floors.

2 SENATE LIBRARY
(民政總處大樓圖書館; Map p296; ☎2857 2233; 163 Avenida de Almeida Ribeiro; ☺1-7pm Mon-Sat) On the first floor of the 18th-century Leal Senado (Loyal Senate) building is this library containing wonderful carved wooden furnishings, panelled walls and an extensive book collection

3 SR WONG IENG KUAN LIBRARY
(白鴿巢公園黃營均圖書館; Map p296; ☎2895 3075; Praca de Luis de Camoes; ☺8am-8pm, closed Mon; @) An oasis of calm between a boulder (which juts into its interior) and a banyan tree (which frames its entrance) in the Luis de Camoes Garden.

4 COLOANE LIBRARY
(路環圖書館; Map p302; ☎2888 2254; ☺Mon-Sat 1-7pm; @) A mini Grecian temple c. 1917 with a pediment containing the words, in Chinese and Portuguese: Library.

5 MACAO CENTRAL LIBRARY
(澳門中央圖書館; Map p296; ☎2856 7576, 2855 8049; 89 A-B, Avenida Conselheiro Ferreira de Almeida; ☺10am-8pm; @) A modern library inside a restored heritage building.

baked goodies from the famous bakery around the corner, including the popular pastéis de nata (egg-custard tarts with a flaky crust), and cheesecake in unusual flavours.

Corner's Wine Bar & Tapas Cafe
Bar, Cafe

(大三巴角落餐廳; Map p296; 3 Travessa de São Paulo; ☺cafe noon-5pm daily, bar 5pm-midnight Sun-Thu, to 1am Fri & Sat) This artsy rooftop bar has plush pink couches and stunning views of the St Paul ruins.

BLUE FROG
Bar

(藍蛙; Map p301; ☎2882 8281; www.blue frog.com.cn; Venetian Macao-Resort-Hotel, Estrada da Baía de N Senhora da Esperança, Taipa; ☺11am-late) This bar inside the Venetian is a smoking stage for indie gigs. Here, almost every weekend, you'll see psych-rockers or synth-punkers who look completely out of place in a casino, smack in the middle of one, having the time of their lives.

MACAU SOUL
Bar

(澳感廊; Map p296; ☎2836 5182; www.macausoul.com; 31a Rua de São Paulo; ☺9.30am-8.30pm Mon-Thu, 9.30am-midnight Fri-Sun) Huddled in the shadows of the Ruins of St Paul, Macau Soul is elegantly decked out in woods and stained-glass windows, with a basement where blues bands perform. Opening hours vary, so phone ahead.

ℹ Information

The Macau Government Tourist Office (MGTO) distributes the excellent (and free) *Macau Tourist Map,* with tourist sights and streets labelled in Portuguese and Chinese. Small inset maps highlight the Taipa and Coloane areas and show bus routes.

Emergency

Emergency tourist hotline (English-speaking staff; ☎112)

Fire services (☎2857 2222)

Official emergency services (☎999)

Police (☎2857 3333)

Internet Access

Macau's few internet cafes come and go quickly. The good news is that wi-fi coverage is expanding. Most libraries, museums and some parks and squares have free wi-fi.

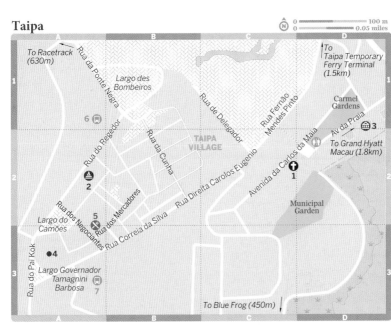

Taipa

Taipa

◉ Sights
1 Church of Our Lady of Carmel C2
2 Pak Tai Temple.......................................A2
3 Taipa House Museum D1

Activities, Courses & Tours
4 Aluguer de Bicicletas A3

⊗ Eating
5 Antonio...A2

🚌 Transport
6 Bus Stop.. A1
7 Main Bus Stop A3

Internet Resources

GoMacau (www.gomacau.com) Latest information on hotels, flights, sights, entertainment and activities.

Macau Government Tourist Office (www. macautourism.gov.mo) The best source of information for visiting Macau.

Medical Services

The first two hospitals listed here have 24-hour emergency services:

Centro Hospitalar Conde São Januário (山頂醫院; Map p296; ☏ 2831 3731; Estrada do Visconde de São Januário) Southwest of Guia Fort.

Money

ATMs are everywhere, especially just outside the Hotel Lisboa, where you'll find half a dozen.

You can change cash and travellers cheques at the banks lining Avenida da Praia Grande and Avenida de Almeida Ribeiro.

Post

China Post (郵政局) main post office **(Av de Almeida Ribeiro; ⊙9am-6pm Mon-Fri, to 1pm Sat);** ferry terminal branch **(⊙10am-7pm Mon-Sat)** Red vending machines dispense stamps throughout Macau. Poste restante service is available at counters 1 and 2 of the main post office.

Telephone

Some handy phone-related facts:

Local calls Free from private phones and most hotel telephones; calls from public payphones cost MOP$1 for five minutes.

Coloane

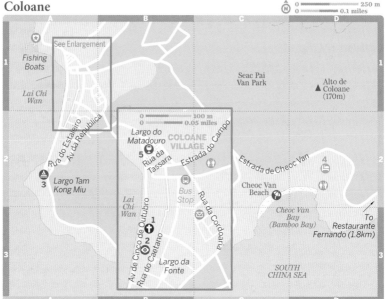

Coloane

⊙ Sights

1 Chapel of St Francis Xavier	B3
2 Coloane Library	B3
3 Tam Kong Temple	A2

⊜ Sleeping

| 4 Pousada de Coloane | D2 |

⊖ Drinking

| 5 Lord Stow's Cafe | B2 |

Prepaid IDD/local cards (from **MOP\$50**) Can be used in most mobile phones; purchase from CTM stores or the ferry terminal.

Some useful numbers:

International directory assistance (☎101)

Local directory assistance (☎181)

Weather (☎1311)

Tourist Information

Pick up themed leaflets on Macau's sights and bilingual maps at outlets of the Macau Government Tourist Office (MGTO; 澳門旅遊局; ☎2831 5566; www.macautourism.gov.mo).

Largo do Senado (旅遊諮詢處; ☎8397 1120; ⊙9am-6pm)

Guia Lighthouse (旅遊局東望洋燈塔分局; ☎2856 9808; ⊙9am-1pm & 2.15-5.30pm)

Macau Ferry Terminal (旅遊局外港碼頭分局; Map p296; ☎2872 6416; ⊙9am-10pm)

Hong Kong (澳門政府旅遊局; Map p272; ☎2857 2287; Room 336-337, Shun Tak Centre, 200 Connaught Rd, Sheung Wan; ⊙9am-10pm)

❶ Getting There & Away

Air

For details of airlines, check the website of Macau International Airport (www.macau-airport.gov. mo); the airport itself is on Taipa. Air Macau (澳門航空; NX; Map p296; www.airmacau. com.mo; ground fl, 398 Alameda Doutor Carlos d'Assumpção) has at least one flight a day to mainland cities, including Běijīng, Hángzhōu, Nánjīng, and Shànghǎi, as well as to Taipei and Kaohsiung in Taiwan, and to Bangkok and Seoul.

Sky Shuttle (www.skyshuttlehk.com; Mon-Thu HK\$2600, Fri-Sun HK\$2800) runs a 15-minute helicopter shuttle between Macau and Hong Kong up to 54 times a day from 9am to 11pm.

Boat

TO HONG KONG Services to/from Hong Kong operate virtually 24 hours a day:

TurboJet (www.turbojet.com.hk; economy/superclass Mon-Fri HK$142/244, Sat & Sun HK$154/260, night crossing HK$176/275) Most frequent; 55-minute trip; departs from Hong Kong–Macau Ferry Terminal (200 Connaught Rd, Sheung Wan) and from Macau Ferry Terminal. See the website for services to Hong Kong International Airport.

CotaiJet (www.cotaijet.com.mo; economy/superclass Mon-Fri MOP$142/244, Sat & Sun MOP$154/260, night crossing MOP$176/275) Every half-hour from 7am to 1am; runs between Taipa Ferry Terminal and Hong Kong–Macau Ferry Terminal. A feeder shuttle-bus service drops off at destinations on the Cotai Strip. Check the website for services to Hong Kong International Airport.

New World First Ferry (www.nwff.com.hk; economy/deluxe Mon-Fri HK$140/245, Sat & Sun HK$155/260, night crossing MOP$175/275) Every half-hour from 7am to 10.30pm. The 60–75-minute trip runs between Macau Ferry Terminal and Hong Kong's China Ferry Terminal.

🛈 Getting Around

To/From the Airport

Airport bus AP1 (MOP$4.20) Airport to Macau Ferry Terminal and Border Gate; stops at major hotels en route. Runs every 15 minutes from 7am to midnight. Extra charge of MOP$3 for each large piece of luggage.

Airport buses MT1 and MT2 (MOP$4.20) Airport to Praça de Ferreira do Amaral near Casino Lisboa; from 7am to 10am, then 4pm to 8pm.

Buses 21 and 26 Airport to Coloane.

Bus 21 Airport to A-Ma Temple.

Taxi (about MOP$40) Airport to town centre.

Car

Avis Rent A Car (www.avis.com.mo; room 1022, ground fl, Macau Ferry Terminal) hires out cheap Smart City Coupes/Toyota Corollas (MOP$600 to MOP$850).

Public Transport

Macau has about 50 public bus and minibus routes, running from 6am to midnight. Fares cost MOP$3.20 on the peninsula, MOP$4.20 to Taipa, MOP$5 to Coloane Village, MOP$6.40 to Hác Sá Beach. Destinations are displayed in Portuguese and Chinese.

Macau Transmac Bus Co (www.transmac.com.mo) and **Macau TCM Bus Co** (www.tcm.com.mo) have information on routes and fares. The *Macau Tourist Map*, available at MGTO outlets, also has a list of both bus companies' routes and a pamphlet listing all bus routes.

Useful services on the peninsula include buses 3 and 3A, between the ferry terminal and city centre; buses 3 and 5, which go to the Border Gate; and bus 12, which runs from the ferry terminal, past Hotel Lisboa to Lou Lim Ioc

Bright Lights, Sin City

Macau's seafront is a space occupied by gargantuan monuments. Of course, casinos are no stranger to a city known as 'the Vegas of the East', but while previously there was only one landmark house of cards, now the sky's the limit. There are at present some 30 casinos in Macau.

Over 80% of gamblers and 95% of high rollers come from mainland China. The latter play in members-only rooms where the total amount wagered on any given day can exceed a country's GDP, and where money allows you to do wonderful things such as smash a chandelier with an ashtray and not pay for it. These VIP rooms are also assumed to be convenient sites for money laundering.

All casinos operate 24 hours a day.

Garden and Kun Iam Temple. Buses 21, 21A, 25 and 26A go to Taipa and Coloane.

Taxi

Not many taxi drivers speak English, so it can help to have your destination written in Chinese. Flag fall is MOP$13 (first 1.6km); then it's MOP$1.50 for each additional 230m. There's a MOP$5/2 surcharge to Coloane from Macau peninsula/Taipa, and a MOP$5 surcharge for journeys from the airport. Large bags cost an extra MOP$3. Call ☎2851 9519 or ☎2893 9939 for yellow radio taxis.

THE SOUTH
Guǎngzhōu (广州)

Huge Guǎngzhōu (population 12 million), known to many in the West as Canton, is south China's busiest transport and trade hub. Otherwise, it holds little interest to the traveller. Good maps of Guǎngzhōu can be found at newsstands. Bookshops also have a variety of maps for sale.

If you find yourself with time on your hands here check out the ultramodern

New Guangdong Museum (广东省博物馆新馆; Guǎngdōngshěng Bówùguǎn Xīnguǎn; ☎020-3804 6886; 2 Zhujiang Donglu; ⏰9am-5pm Tue-Sun; ⓂZhujiang New Town) and the **Mausoleum of the Nanyue King** (南越王墓; Nányuèwáng Mù; ☎020-8666 4920; 867 Jiefang Beilu; admission Y12, audio guide Y10; ⏰9am-5.30pm).

Guǎngzhōu's choices in the budget and lower-midrange accommodation ranges are dreary but there are plenty of excellent top-end and upper-midrange hotels; check out **White Swan Hotel** (白天鹅宾馆; Báitiān'é Bīnguǎn; ☎8188 6968; www.whiteswanhotel.com; 1 Shamian Nanjie; 沙面南街1号; s & d Y1300-1500, ste from Y3100; ❄@) or **Guǎngdōng Victory Hotel** (胜利宾馆; Shènglì Bīnguǎn; ☎8121 6688; www.vhotel.com; 53 & 54 Shamian Beijie; 沙面北街53 & 54号; r from Y320; ❄@) on Shāmiàn Island, the quietest and most attractive area in the city.

The city has a gastronomic culture and legendary cuisine. Dim sum, or yum cha as it's called in these parts, is the heart of Cantonese cuisine.

Left: Largo do Senado (p292), Macau; **Below:** Festival in Largo do Senado

PHOTOGRAPHER: (LEFT) MANFRED GOTTSCHALK/LONELY PLANET IMAGES ©; (BELOW) OLIVER STREWE/LONELY PLANET IMAGES ©

Báiyún International Airport (Báiyún Guójì Jīchǎng; www.baiyunairport.com; M Airport South, bus Jīchǎng Nán) services numerous international and domestic destinations; it can be reached on an airport shuttle bus or via metro.

Guǎngzhōu has several long-distance bus stations and three long-distance train stations:

Guǎngzhōu main train station (Guǎngzhōu zhàn; Huanshi Xilu; M Guǎngzhōu Huǒchēzhàn)

Guǎngzhōu south station (Guǎngzhōu nánzhàn; Shibi, Pānyú; M Guǎngzhōu South)

Guǎngzhōu east station (Guǎngzhōu dōngzhàn; M Guǎngzhōu Dōngzhàn)

The extensive metro is the speediest and cleanest way to get around the city; free maps are available at all stations.

Guìlín 桂林

☎ 0773 / POP 740,000

Whether you're going north to the highlands, or south to Yángshuò and beyond, Guìlín is where you're likely to spend a night or two. The city is a good introduction to Guǎngxī's dreamlike scenery.

 Sights

SOLITARY BEAUTY PEAK Park
(独秀峰; Dúxiù Fēng; 1 Wangcheng; 王城1号; admission Y70; ⊙ 7.30am-6pm) A peaceful, leafy retreat from the city centre, the entrance fee for this famous pinnacle includes admission to **Wáng Chéng** (王城), a 14th-century Ming prince's mansion, now home to Guǎngxī Normal University (lucky students!).

OTHER HILLS Hills
Just west of Solitary Beauty Peak is **Wave-Subduing Hill** (伏波山; Fúbō Shān; admission Y25; ⊙ 7am-6pm), which offers more great views as well as the chance to see Song- and Tang-dynasty Buddhist carvings etched into the walls of **Returned**

305

Pearl Cave (还珠洞; Huánzhū Dòng). Just south of the city centre is **Elephant Trunk Hill** (象鼻山; Xiàngbí Shān; admission Y40; ⏰7am-6.30pm), perhaps best viewed from one of the bamboo rafts (about Y5) that float down the Lí River.

Tours

The popular Lí River trip from Guìlín to Yángshuò lasts about 4½ hours and includes a wonderfully scenic boat trip to Yángshuò, lunch, and a bus ride back to Guìlín. Expect to pay Y350 to Y450 for a boat with an English-speaking guide or Y245 for the Chinese version. China International Travel Service (CITS; 中国国际旅行社; Zhōngguó Guójì Lǚxíngshè), p307, can arrange it, as can most hotel and tourist information service centres in Guìlín.

Sleeping

RIVERSIDE HOSTEL Inn $$
(九龙商务旅游酒店; Jiǔlóng Shāngwù Lǚyóu Jiǔdiàn; ☎258 0215; www.guilin-hostel.com; 6 Zhumu Xiang, Nanmen Qiao; 南门桥竹木巷6号; s/d Y100-220; ❄@) This cosy inn by the Táohuā River (桃花江) is highly recommended by travellers (especially couples). Staff are attentive and rooms are comfy. The tatami rooms fill up fast. Its three-room branch, **Lakeside Inn** (背包驿站; Bēibāo Yìzhàn; ☎280 6806; 1-1-2 Shanhu Beilu; 杉湖北路杉湖综合楼1-1-2号) by Shān Lake is equally good. Advance bookings by phone or via the website are essential.

JÌNGGUĀN MÍNGLÓU HOTEL
 Hotel $$$
(静观茗楼度假酒店; Jìngguān Mínglóu Dùjià Jiǔdiàn; ☎228 3265; 9 Ronghu Nanlu; 榕湖南路9号; standard/deluxe d Y380/480, deluxe ste Y1380; ❄) If luxury chain hotels are not your cup of tea, book this one. This adorable hotel with stunning views of Róng Lake and Guìlín's surrounding karst scenery is simply exquisite. Reproduction antique Chinese furniture adorns the lobby and extends into the fabulous rooms.

The friendly staff don't speak English and there's nowhere to eat here, but small restaurants and cafes line the lakeside, so you won't have far to walk.

Eating

Local specialities include Guìlín rice noodles (桂林米粉; Guìlín mǐfěn), beer duck (啤酒鸭; píjiǔ yā) and Guìlín snails (桂林田螺; Guìlín tiánluó), while the ubiquitous chǎoguō fàn (炒锅饭; claypot rice dishes; from Y6) make a great snack.

ZHÈNGYÁNG TĀNGCHÉNG Soup $$
(正阳汤城; 8 Zhengyang Lu; dishes Y25-78; ⏰11.30am-3am; 🖱) Easily one of the most popular soup restaurants in the city serving local specialities. The alfresco dining area is a prime people-watching spot. We especially recommend the grilled Lí River fish and soup with sea bass and chrysanthemum.

AMANI Pizza $$
(阿玛尼; Āmǎní; ☎210 6351; Binjiang Lu; pizzas from Y38; ⏰10am-1am) Customers flock here for the tasty pizza, possibly the best in town. The laid-back setting makes this an easy place to while away the hours. It has a more hectic **branch** (☎280 9351; 159 Zhengyang Lu; ⏰10am-2am) on the pedestrianised street.

Drinking

Guìlín's streets are dotted with trendy little cafes, while Zhengyang Lu has a short stretch of bars with outdoor seating.

LE FEITZ Bar
(翡翠酒吧; Fěicuì Jiǔbā; ☎137 3773 4082; 1-8 Chaoyang Lu, University Residence; 朝阳路大学生公寓1-8号; ⏰10am-midnight) Frequented by local college students and expats alike, Le Feitz is arguably the most popular Irish pub in Guilin. It has live music almost every evening. It's near the north gate of Guangxi Normal University (朝阳路师大北门; Cháoyáng Lù Shìdàběimén).

Paulaner Bar

(柏龙酒吧; Bólóng Jiǔbā; 2 Zhengyang Lu; ⏰4pm-1.30am) Prices surged after its recent facelift but it still serves the best German beer in town. The big-screen TV is still there for sports fans.

ℹ Information

Medical Services

People's Hospital (人民医院; Rénmín Yīyuàn; Wenming Lu)

Money

The Bank of China (中国银行; Zhōngguó Yínháng) branches on Zhongshan Nanlu (near the main bus station) and Jiefang Donglu change money and travellers cheques, give credit-card advances and have 24-hour ATMs.

Post

China Post (中国邮政; Zhōngguó Yóuzhèng; Zhongshan Beilu; ⏰8am-7pm) A large branch of China Post: it's 500m north of the roundabout of Jiefang Donglu. There's another handy branch by the train station.

Public Security Bureau

PSB (公安局; Gōng'ānjú; ☎582 3492; 16 Shijiayan Lu; ⏰8.30am-noon & 3-6pm Mon-Fri) Can extend visas.

Tourist Information

Guìlín Tourist Information Service Centre (桂林旅游咨询服务中心; Guìlín Lǚyóu Zīxún Fúwù Zhōngxīn; ☎280 0318; South Gate, Ronghu Beilu; ⏰8am-10pm) These helpful centres dot the city. There's a good one by the South Gate on Róng Lake.

Travel Agencies

China International Travel Service (CITS; 中国国际旅行社; Zhōngguó Guójì Lǚxíngshè; www.guilintrav.com; Binjiang Lu) Helpful staff. There are other branches everywhere.

ℹ Getting There & Away

Air

Air tickets can be bought from the Civil Aviation Administration of China (CAAC; 中国民航; Zhōngguó Mínháng; ☎384 7252; cnr Shanghai Lu & Anxin Beilu; ⏰7.30am-8.30pm). Direct flights to/from Guìlín include Běijīng (Y1440),

Guǎngzhōu harbour

CHRIS MELLOR/LONELY PLANET IMAGES ©

Chéngdū (Y980), Chóngqìng (Y840), Guǎngzhōu (Y990), Hong Kong (Xiānggǎng; Y1410), Kūnmíng (Y840), Shànghǎi (Y1300) and Xī'ān (Y1090).

International destinations include Seoul, Korea and Osaka, Japan.

Bus

Guìlín's **main bus station** (客运总站; Guìlín kèyùn zǒngzhàn; ☎ 382 2666; Zhongshan Nanlu) is north of the train station. There are regular buses to **Lóngshèng** Y30, two hours, every 40 minutes and **Yángshuò** Y15 to Y18, 1½ hours, every 15 minutes.

Train

Few trains start in Guìlín, so it's often tough to find tickets, especially for hard sleepers. Buy them at least a couple of days in advance if possible. Most trains leave from Guìlín Station (桂林站; Guìlín Zhàn), but some may leave from Guìlín North Train Station (桂林北站; Guìlín Běizhàn), 9km north of the city centre.

Direct services include **Běijīng** Y416, 23 hours, four daily (1.56am, 1.28pm, 3.36pm and 7.02pm), **Chóngqìng** Y272, 19 hours, one daily (8.42am), **Guǎngzhōu** Y207, 12 hours, two daily (6.28pm and 9.23pm), **Kūnmíng** Y281, 18½ hours, three daily (3.34pm, 4.30pm and 4.56pm), **Shànghǎi** Y341, 22 hours, four daily (12.12pm, 2.05pm,

5.02pm and 5.33pm) and **Xī'ān** Y385, 27 hours, one daily (5.54pm).

ⓘ Getting Around

Guìlín's Liǎngjiāng International Airport (两江国际机场; Liǎngjiāng Guójì Jīchǎng) is 30km west of the city. Half-hourly shuttle buses (Y20) run from the CAAC office between 6.30am and 9pm. From the airport, shuttle buses meet every arrival. A taxi costs about Y80 (40 minutes).

Dragon's Backbone Rice Terraces 龙脊梯田
☎0773

This part of Guǎngxī boasts stunning views of terraced paddy fields, and the clear standout is **Dragon's Backbone Rice Terraces** (Lóngjǐ Tītián; adult Y50). The rice fields rise up to 1000m high and are an amazing feat of farm engineering on hills dotted with minority villages. The best time to visit is after the summer rains, which leave the fields glistening with reflections. The fields turn golden just before harvesting (October), and become snow white in winter (December). Avoid visiting in early spring (March), when the mountains are shrouded in mist.

Hotel overlooking the Dragon's Backbone Rice Terraces near Lóngshèng

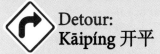

Detour:
Kāipíng 开平

The town centre of Kāipíng (Hoi Ping in Cantonese; population 680,000), 140km southwest of Guǎngzhōu, is sleepy and scruffy, but don't let that disappoint you. The World Heritage–listed *diāolóu* (碉楼), a photogenic cluster of flamboyant fortified residences and watchtowers scattered across the 20km periphery of Kāipíng, are one of the most arresting man-made attractions in Guǎngdōng. These towers, displaying an eclectic mix of European architectural styles from Roman to rococo, were built in the early 20th century by villagers who were 'sold' as coolies to California and Southeast Asia. Out of the nearly 3000 original *diāolóu*, only 1833 remain. Each was built with sturdy walls, iron gates and ports for defence and observation.

The must-see attraction in Kāipíng is the village of Zìlì, 11km west of Kāipíng, which boasts the largest collection of *diāolóu*. Fifteen towers rise beautifully amid the paddy field, but only three towers, built in the 1920s, are open to the public.

Buses to Kāipíng will drop you off at one of two bus stations: the bigger Yìcí bus station or the more convenient Chángshā bus station. Both stations run frequent buses to Guǎngzhōu (Y55 to Y60, two hours), Shēnzhèn (Y90, 2½ hours) and Zhūhǎi (Y52 to Y71, 2½ hours) between 6.20am and 7.30pm. The former also has buses to Hong Kong (HK$150, four hours, 9.15am, 2pm and 4.10pm). Local buses 7 and 13 link the two stations, or it's Y8 by taxi. In Guǎngzhōu, the Guǎngfó Bus Station also has buses to Kāipíng (Y58, every 30 minutes, from 7am to 8.30pm).

Dàzhài (大寨) is a laid-back Yao village that has an idyllic rural allure with a bubbling stream (look out for the snakes in the water). The number of guesthouses has mushroomed in recent years, but it remains relatively unspoilt by tourism. Continue uphill to the more remote village of **Tiántóuzhài** (田头寨) atop the mountain. It's a sublime place to marvel at the panoramic views of the terraces, not to mention the sunrise or a starry night sky. **Píng'ān** (平安), a beautiful 600-year-old Zhuang village, is the biggest settlement and most popular among tourists. It has the best facilities, but expect to share your experience with the masses.

Most locals here are Zhuang or Yao, but you'll also find Dong and Miao people in the area.

There's nowhere in this area to change money, not even in Lóngshèng, so come prepared.

Activities

The four- to five-hour trek between the villages of Dàzhài and Píng'ān, passing through the villages of Tiántóuzhài and Zhōngliù (中六) is highly recommended. The route is clearly signposted, but if you want a local to guide you, there will be plenty of offers. Expect to pay Y30 to Y40.

Sleeping & Eating

You can stay in traditional wooden homes of minority villagers (offer locals around Y20 for a simple bed), but three in particular – Dàzhài, Tiántóuzhài and Píng'ān – are set up for tourists. Nearly all guesthouses offer food. Most have English menus. Look out for *zhútǒng fàn*, a rice meal barbecued inside bamboo sticks.

MINORITY CAFE & INN Guesthouse $

(龙脊咖啡店; Lóngjǐ Kāfēidiàn; Dàzhài; ☎758 5605; r Y30-45) Perched above the village on the trail leading up to Tiántóuzhài, this small, friendly guesthouse has a cute terrace and an English menu (dishes Y10 to Y25). It's about a 20-minute walk (1km) uphill from the main gate. Shared bathroom only.

WÀNJǏNGLÓU Inn $

(万景楼; Tiántóuzhài; ☎758 5665; www.wanjinglou.com, in Chinese; tw Y70-90) This excellent guesthouse is located above Tiántóuzhài. Rooms with sweeping views don't have bathrooms (but rooms without views do). The staff don't speak English but are helpful enough. To get there, take the path up to the right (the left is to Píng'ān) after you leave the village of Tiántóuzhài. From there it's another 15-minute walk (about 800m) and the guesthouse is above Dazhai Hostel. It can arrange direct shuttle buses to/from Guìlín.

Jīntián Guesthouse Guesthouse $

(金田酒店; Jīntián Jiǔdiàn; Tiántóuzhài; ☎758 5683; www.ljjtjd.com; r Y80-100, weekday discount of 10-30%) All rooms are adequate and comfortable, and the owner, Hanna, speaks excellent English. It's on the left as you walk up the hill from Dàzhài.

LÓNGYǏNG HOTEL Hotel $$

(龙颖饭店; Lóngyǐng Fàndiàn; Píng'ān; ☎758 3059; tw without/with air-con incl breakfast Y220/280; ✳@) Located near the top of the village, this is the best-quality option in Píng'ān. Decent rooms with air-con often go for Y120. The manager speaks English and there are terrific views from the terrace. A new branch next to Dazu Hotel, with cheaper rooms (Y70 to Y100), is now open.

🛈 Getting There & Away

Hotels in Tiántóuzhài, including Wànjǐnglóu and Quánjǐng Lóu (全景楼; ☎758 5688), arrange direct **shuttle service** between Guìlín and Dàzhài for their guests. They also take other passengers if seats are available. The bus (Y40, three hours) usually leaves Guìlín train station at 8.30am. Reservations are a must. Buses return to Guìlín at 11.30am.

All hotels in Píng'ān provide a similar service. The bus (Y30) leaves Guìlín train station at 1pm and returns at 10am. Again, reservations (☎138 7735 0504) are necessary.

If you opt for **public transport**, take a bus to Lóngshèng (龙胜) and get off at Hépíng (和平). From that road junction, minibuses trundle back and forth between Lóngshèng and the rice terraces, stopping to pick up passengers to Dàzhài (Y8, 45 minutes, every 20 minutes, 7am to 6pm) and Píng'ān (Y7, 30 minutes, every 30 minutes between 7.40am and 5pm). Buses to Guìlín (Y27, 1½ hours, 6.30am to 7pm) also stop over there.

Limestone pinnacles, Li River (p314)
PHOTOGRAPHER: MARTIN MOOS/LONELY PLANET IMAGES ©

Yángshuò 阳朔

📞0773 / POP 310,000

One of the most popular destinations for foreigners in southern China, Yángshuò's dramatic karst landscape is at times other-worldly. Take a leisurely bamboo-raft ride and/or cycle through the dreamy valleys and you'll see. Once you've had your fill of natural beauty, there's also a host of well-run courses and activities to keep you occupied far beyond your original intended length of stay. Travelling with kids is easy here. It's one of the more family-friendly Chinese destinations, with English-speaking locals, well-set-up hostels and food for the finicky.

Touts are an almost constant nuisance here; fend them off firmly but politely.

🏃 Activities & Courses

Yángshuò Taichi Health Centre   Taichi
(阳朔太极拳健康中心; Yángshuò Tàijíquán Jiànkāng Zhōngxīn; 📞890 0125; www.chinasouth-taichi.com; Baoquan Lu; classes per hr/week/month Y80/1500/4000; ⏰office 8-11.30am & 2.30-5.30pm) Runs classes for both the Yang and Chen styles of taichi. Cheap accommodation is available for students.

ROCK CLIMBING   Climbing
Yángshuò is fast becoming one of the hottest climbing destinations in Asia. **China Climb** (中国攀岩; Zhōngguó Pānyán; 📞881 1033; www.chinaclimb.com; 45 Xianqian Jie; ⏰9am-9pm), located inside Lizard Lounge bar, is the biggest climbing club in China and the most professional outfit in town. It offers local advice for experienced climbers and fully guided, bolted climbs for beginners. Also ask here for information on renting kayaks (from Y150 per day).

CYCLING   Cycling
There's no shortage of places to rent bikes (from Y15 per day), but for the best equipment and strong advice on possible trips, try **Bike Asia** (📞882 6521; www.bikeasia.com; 42 Guihua Lu; 桂花路42号; ⏰9am-6pm), above Bar 98.

🛏 Sleeping

Yángshuò is teeming with hotels run by English-speaking staff, especially at the budget end of the market, and all provide internet access. While the Xi Jie neighbourhood has abundant options, some of the best lodgings are located on the outskirts of Yángshuò.

🌿 YÁNGSHUÒ VILLAGE INN
Boutique Hotel $$$
(听月楼; Tīngyuè Loú; 📞139 7836 9849; www.yangshuoguesthouse.com; Moon Hill Village; Yuèliàng Shān Lìcūn; 月亮山历村; d Y380-390, ste Y500; ❄) Located below Moon Hill (9km south of Yángshuò centre), the inn is proud of its ecofriendly practices and high-quality services. Indeed, it exceeded all our expectations. Rooms with local handmade bamboo furniture are beyond fabulous, especially those in the tastefully renovated mudbrick farmhouse. Refillable water bottles are provided for guests to use. Staff are attentive and speak excellent English. From Yángshuò bus station, take a minibus to Gāotián (高田) and tell the driver to drop you at Lì Cūn (历村; Y5, every 15 minutes). A taxi from Xi Jie costs around Y30.

Its equally excellent sister hotel **Yangshuo Mountain Retreat** (阳朔胜地; Yángshuò Shèngdì; 📞877 7091; www.yangshuomountainretreat.com; Gāotián Zhèn Fēnglóu Cūnwěi Wánggōng Shānjiǎo; 高田镇凤楼村委王公山脚; r from Y500; ❄ @) is located by the Yùlóng River (遇龙河; Yùlóng Hé).

TRIPPERS CARPE DIEM   Hostel $$
(山景假日酒店; Shānjǐng Jiàrì Jiǔdiàn; 📞882 2533; www.guesthouseyangshuo.com; 35 Shibanqiaocun; 石板桥村35号; dm/s Y35/120, d Y160-300; ❄ @) This brand-new hostel is run by a Belgian-Chinese family. It has stunning views of the rice fields and karst peaks, excellent staff, spotless rooms and an MSG-free cafe. It's 1.5km north of Xi Jie.

YANGSHUO OUTSIDE INN   Hostel $
(荷兰饭店; Hélán Fàndiàn; 📞881 7109; www.yangshuo-outside.com; Cháolóng Village, Jìmǎ; 骥马朝龙村; dm/s Y50/100, d Y120-200; ❄ @) This farmhouse-turned-hostel surrounded by rural vistas is located 4km

southwest of Yángshuò. The complex is filled with rustic charm and a communal feel, which gives you a glimpse of rural life in China without compromising the standard of hygiene and comfort. An annexe with modern-furnished family suites (Y300 to Y500) was recently added. It's close to the Yùlóng River; a taxi here will cost Y25 or it's 20 minutes by bike.

HÓNGFÚ PALACE HOTEL Hotel **$$**

(鸿福饭店; Hóngfú Fàndiàn; 📞137 3739 7888; www.yangshuohongfuhotel.com; 79 Xi Jie; 西街79号; d Y380-480, tw/ste Y660/880; ❄) Cracking location, set back from Xi Jie in the historic Jiangxi Guildhall and sharing its premises with Le Vôtre (see later this page). Roomy doubles, regularly discounted to Y220, overlook a Qing-style courtyard. Identical rooms without the courtyard view go for as little as Y170.

🍴 Eating & Drinking

LUNA Italian **$$$**

(📞139 7836 9849; Moon Hill Village; Yuèliàng Shān Lìcūn; 月亮山历村; dishes from Y38; ⏰7.30am-midnight) The spectacular view of Moon Hill definitely makes Luna worth a visit, but what really seems to keep customers coming are its organic salad and exquisitely cooked pasta. The menu features a wide selection of Italian fare, and the winelist is impressive. It's

located on the rooftop of Yangshuo Village Inn.

LE VÔTRE French **$$$**

(乐德法式餐厅; Lèdé Fǎshì Cāntīng; 79 Xi Jie; dishes from Y38; ⏰8am-midnight) The first French restaurant in town, and still the best. This one shares its historic premises with the Hóngfú Palace Hotel. The interior, flanked by a dazzling array of Christian and Buddhist statues and hung with portraits of Chairman Mao, oozes an eccentric charm. The huge outdoor seating area draws big crowds, as does the fine menu and home-brewed beer.

RIVER BAR Bar **$$**

(漓湾酒吧; Líwān Jiǔbā; Binjiang Lu; drinks from Y25, dishes from Y28; ⏰5pm-late) It's all in the name – stunningly situated by Lí River, this outdoor bar has a hideaway vibe and provides sublime river views while you sip a bewildering array of cocktails. The varied menu includes steaks, pasta, kebabs and a big list of teas and coffees.

Yángshuò

Activities, Courses & Tours
| 1 Bike Asia | C1 |
| 2 China Climb | C1 |

🛏 **Sleeping**
| 3 Hóngfú Palace Hotel | C2 |

Eating
| Le Vôtre | (see 3) |

Yángshuò

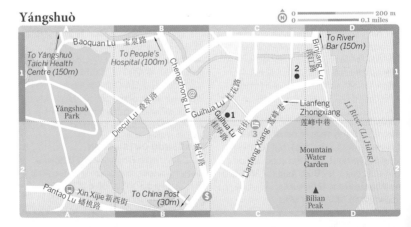

DIANA MAYFIELD/LONELY PLANET IMAGES ©

Don't Miss **Moon Hill 月亮山**

For mind-blowing views of the surrounding countryside, head to the surreal limestone pinnacle **Moon Hill**, famed for its moon-shaped hole. To get here by bike, take the main road south of Yángshuò towards the river and turn right onto the road about 200m before the bridge. Moon Hill is another 8km down the road on your right.

THINGS YOU NEED TO KNOW
Yuèliàng Shān; admission Y15

⭐ Entertainment

IMPRESSIONS LIÚ SĀNJIĚ
Outdoor Performance **$$**
(印象刘三姐; **Yìnxiàng Liú Sānjiě**; ☎881 7783; tickets Y198-680; ⊙shows 8-9pm) The top show in town is directed by moviemaker Zhang Yimou, the man who also directed the opening ceremony at the Beijing Olympics. Six hundred performers, including local fishermen, take to the Lí River each night. Twelve surrounding karst peaks are illuminated as part of the show, which gets rave reviews from many travellers. Hotels often arrange slight discounts.

❶ Information

Travel agencies are all over town, while backpacker-oriented cafes and bars, as well as most hotels, can often dispense good advice. Shop around for the best deals.

Bank of China (中国银行; **Zhōngguó Yínháng**; Xi Jie; ⊙9am-5pm) Foreign exchange and 24-hour ATM for international cards.

Café Too & Hostel (自游人旅店; **Zìyóurén Lüdiàn**; ☎882 8342; 7 Chengzhong Lu; ⊙8am-midnight) Friendly, bite-sized cafe with fresh coffee, free internet and an impressive range of foreign-language books that you can buy, sell or swap.

China Post (中国邮政; **Zhōngguó yóuzhèng'**; Pantao Lu; ⊙8am-5pm) English-speaking staff.

People's Hospital (人民医院; Rénmín Yīyuàn; 26 Chengzhong Lu) English-speaking doctors available.

Public Security Bureau (PSB; 公安局; Gōng'ānjú; Chengbei Lu; ⏱8am-noon & 3-6pm summer, 2.30-5.30pm winter) Doesn't issue visa extensions.

ⓘ Getting There & Away

AIR The closest airport is in Guìlín; see p307.
BUS Direct bus links include **Guìlín** Y15 to Y18, one hour, every 10 minutes (6.45am to 8.30pm), **Xīngpíng** Y7, one hour, every 15 minutes (6.30am to 6pm) and **Yángdī** Y10, 30 minutes, every 20 minutes (6.30am to 6pm).
TRAIN Yángshuò has no train station, but train tickets for services from Guìlín can be bought from hotels and travel agencies around town. Expect to pay Y50 commission.

ⓘ Getting Around

The best way to get around is by bicycle; you can rent one at almost all hostels, and from streetside outlets for Y15 per day.

Around Yángshuò

The highlight of a trip to Guǎngxī is to get out into the countryside of Yángshuò. There are weeks of exploring possibilities here, by bike, boat, foot or any combination thereof.

Unfortunately, the local authority has plans to privatise the whole area. It's very likely that you'll be forced to pay admission fees just for entering the territory by the time you read this book.

Lí River   漓江

There are also a number of picturesque, ancient villages to visit, and the river here far outstrips anything you'll see around Guìlín. Classic rural scenes of wallowing water buffalo and farmers tending to crops are dominated by a backdrop of prominent limestone peaks. There are also a number of picturesque, ancient villages to visit.

Xīngpíng (兴坪), the location of the photo on the back of Y20 banknotes, is more than 1000 years old and houses a number of historic residences, some laid-back cafes and a handful of guesthouses. Most travellers base themselves here to explore the surrounding countryside. The HI-affiliated **This Old Place** (老地方; Lǎo Dìfang; ☏870 2887; www.topxingping.com; 5 Rongtan Lu; dm Y30-40, s Y60, d Y80-180) is an excellent place to stay. The stunning 16km **hiking trail** between Xīngpíng and Yángdī (扬堤) takes around four to five hours to complete, crossing the river

---

Great Guǎngxī Bike Ride

YÁNGSHUÒ TO DRAGON BRIDGE & BACK (20KM ROUND-TRIP, FOUR HOURS)

Soak up the rural charm as you follow the beautiful Yùlóng River (遇龙河) past rice paddies, fish farms and water buffalo to the 600-year-old Dragon Bridge (p315). From Yángshuò, cycle along Pantao Lu and take the first main road on the left after the Farmers Trading Market. Continue straight, past the hospital on your right, and through the village of Jìmǎ (骥马) before following the road round to the right to reach the start of a bumpy track. Follow this all the way to Dragon Bridge (遇龙桥; Yùlóng Qiáo). Note: the last few hundred metres are on a main road. Cross the bridge and follow another track south for 20 minutes (around 8km) until it becomes a small, paved road, which eventually stops at the river's edge. Take a bamboo raft across the river (Y5), then turn left off a small paved road down a tiny pathway, which leads you back to the Jìmǎ village road.

Crowds on Xi Jie, Yángshuò (p311) at night

SARA-JANE CLELAND/LONELY PLANET IMAGES ©

three times. The admission fee is Y16, which includes two ferry crossings.

Also popular, and much closer to Yángshuò, is the historic village of **Fúlì** (福利), with its stone houses and cobbled lanes. Fúlì is famous in these parts for its handmade fans. It takes about an hour to get here by bike. There are also regular buses from Yángshuò to a drop-off point within walking distance of Fúlì (Y3, 15 minutes).

Yùlóng River   遇龙河

The scenery along this smaller, quieter river, about 4km southwest of Yángshuò, is simply breathtaking. There are a number of great swimming spots and countless exploring possibilities. Just rent a bike and get out there.

One option is to aim for **Dragon Bridge** (遇龙桥; Yùlóng Qiáo), about 10km upstream. This 600-year-old stone arched bridge is among Guǎngxī's largest and comes with higgledy-piggledy steps and sides that lean inwards with age. To get here by bike, see the boxed text, p314. Alternatively, take a bus to Jīnbǎo (金宝) and ask to get off at the bridge (Y5, 35 minutes), just after Báishā (白沙).

Déhāng   德夯

In a seductive riverine setting overlooked by towering, other-worldly karst peaks, the Miao hamlet of **Déhāng** (admission Y60), to the northwest of Jíshǒu in western Húnán province, offers a tantalising spectrum of treks into picturesque countryside. Rising into columns, splinters and huge foreheads of stone, the local karst geology climbs over verdant valleys layered with terraced fields and flushed by waterfalls and clear streams.

◉ Sights & Activities

Surplus to its charming village views, Déhāng is itself located within a huge 164-sq-km geological park, where some delightful treks thread into the hills.

The beautiful **Nine Dragon Stream Scenic Area** (九龙溪景区; Jiǔlóngxī Jǐngqū) winds along a stream out of the village, past Miao peasants labouring in the terraced fields, over bridges, alongside fields croaking with toads or seething with tadpoles (depending on the season), and into an astonishing landscape of peaks blotched with green

315

and valleys carpeted with lush fields. Continue to the end of the trail for the fantastic **Liúshā Waterfall** (流沙瀑布; Liúshā Pùbù; admission free) – China's highest waterfall at 216m – which descends in fronds of spray onto rocks above a green pool at its foot. Climb the steps behind the waterfall for stirring views through the curtain of water (a small umbrella is handy at this point) – the sight is particularly impressive after rainfall. The return walk to the Liúshā Waterfall takes about two hours.

Cross the bridge over the river to visit the 2.6km-long scenic **Yùquánxī Scenic Area** (玉泉溪景区; Yùquánxī Jǐngqū), where you follow a path along a valley by the Yùquán Stream, past haystacks (consisting of stout wooden poles sunk into the ground onto which are tossed clumps of hay) and gorgeous belts of layered terraced fields.

🛏 Sleeping & Eating

Several simple inns (客栈; kèzhàn) can be found in the village, near the square, stuffed down alleyways or picturesquely suspended over the river. You'll need a torch (flashlight) to avoid tumbling into the water at night. Travellers aiming for more midrange comfort can stay overnight in nearby (and unattractive) Jíshǒu.

JIĒLÓNGQIÁO INN   Inn $
(接龙桥客店; Jiēlóngqiáo Kèdiàn; ☏135 1743 0915; s/d Y40/50) This small, all-wood inn is next door to the Jiēlóng Inn – the owners play mah jong together much of the time – and the well-kept, heavily varnished rooms, with fan and TV, are the best in the village. The drawback is the communal shower and toilet, located two flights down in the dank basement.

Jiēlóng Inn   Inn $
(接龙客栈; Jiēlóng Kèzhàn; ☏135 7432 0948; s/d Y40/60; ❄) Right next to the Jiēlóng Bridge, this popular spot has a handful of air-con rooms with shared shower and toilet and a restaurant-seating area with views along the river.

ℹ Getting There & Away

The best way to reach Déhāng is to travel via Jíshǒu, a railway town to the south of the village. Regular buses to Déhāng (Y6, 50 minutes) leave from outside Jíshǒu's train station, arriving at and departing (every 20 minutes) from the square/parking lot in Déhāng.

Fènghuáng 凤凰
☏0743

Under round-the-clock siege from domestic tourists – the Taiping Rebellion of the modern age – this riveting riverside town of ancient city walls, disintegrating gate towers, rickety houses on stilts and hoary temples can easily fill a couple of days.

◉ Sights & Activities

Strolling willy-nilly is the best way to see Fènghuáng. Many of the back alleys in the old town maintain an intriguing charm, a treasure trove of old family pharmacists, traditional shops, temples, ancestral halls and crumbling dwellings.

Strips of riverweed hang out to dry and cured meats (including flattened pig faces!) swing from shopfronts. Elsewhere, platters of garlic, peanuts and fish are left out to dry.

Most sights can only be visited if you buy the Y148 **through ticket** (通票; tōngpiào), which includes entrance to the Yang Family Ancestral Hall, the Former Home of Shen Congwen, the Former Home of Xiong Xiling (熊希龄故居), Gǔchéng Museum, Wànshòu Temple, a boat ride along the Tuó River, the East Gate Tower and a few other sights. You don't have to buy the through ticket, and much of Fènghuáng can be seen for free, but you will need it if you simply have to see the included sights. Through tickets are sold at several places in town, including the North Gate Tower and the Tourism Administrative Bureau of Fènghuáng. Boat trips ferry passengers along the Tuó River for Y30 from the North Gate Tower (atmospheric night trips included). Sights are generally all open from 8am to 5.30pm.

Fènghuáng

Fènghuáng

⦿ Top Sights

City Wall B2
East Gate Tower C2
Hóng Bridge D2

⦿ Sights

1 Former Home of Shen Congwen B3
2 Gǔchéng Museum B2
3 Jiāngxīn Buddhist Temple D2
4 Laoying Shao B1
5 North Gate Tower B2
6 Stepping Stones B1
7 Wànmíng Pagoda D3

8 Wànshòu Temple D2
9 Wooden Footbridge B1

🛏 Sleeping

10 Koolaa's Home C2
11 Phoenix Jiāngtiān Holiday Village C2

🍽 Eating

12 Night Market D2
13 Soul Too C2

🍷 Drinking

14 Elope Bar C2

Wander along Fènghuáng's restored salmon-pink **city wall** (城墙; *chéngqiáng*) with its defensive aspect along the southern bank of the Tuó River. Halfway along its length, the **North Gate Tower** (北门城楼; Běimén Chénglóu) is in a tragic state of neglect, downtrodden and scratched with names, but it remains a magnificent structure.

To the east is the **East Gate Tower** (东门城楼; Dōngmén Chénglóu), a Qing-dynasty twin-eaved tower dating from 1715. Spanning the river is the magnificent covered **Hóng Bridge** (虹桥; Hóng Qiáo; **upstairs galleries on through ticket**), from the east of which runs Huilong Ge, a narrow alley of shops, hotels, restaurants and the small **Jiāngxīn Buddhist Temple** (江心禅寺; Jiāngxīn Chánsì).

One of several former residences in town, the **Former Home of Shen Congwen** (沈从文故居; Shěn Cóngwén Gùjū) is where the famous modern novelist was born and bred. (The author's tomb can

317

also be found in the east of town.) The **Gǔchéng Museum** (古城博物馆; Gǔchéng Bówùguǎn; Dengying Jie; ☺7.30am-6pm) is dedicated to the history of the old town.

Crossing the river over the **stepping stones** (跳岩; tiàoyán), best navigated when sober, or by the **wooden footbridge** (木头桥; Mùtou Qiáo), brings you to ever-developing **Laoying Shao**, a street of bars, cafes and shops overlooking the river. Further along, is **Wànshòu Temple** (万寿宫; Wànshòu Gōng), close to the distinctive **Wànmíng Pagoda** (万名塔; Wànmíng Tǎ) right on the riverbank.

🛏 Sleeping

Inns (客栈; kèzhàn) can be found everywhere in Fènghuáng and provide a cheap and atmospheric means of sampling the village's pleasant nocturnal mien. Beibian Jie, which is sandwiched between the city wall and the river on the north side of town, is a good place to look for decent digs with a river view. Note that

many inns are quite rudimentary, often coming with squat toilets, and proximity to the water means some can be damp, but comfortable enough. During the peak holiday crush, rooms will be more expensive and in very short supply, so book ahead.

KOOLAA'S HOME   Inn $

(考拉小屋; Kǎolā Xiǎowū; ☏151 7433 9597; 18-2 Beibian Jie; 北边街18-2号; d Y120; ❄@🛜📶) There are only four sweet and snug rooms at Koolaa's, but their popularity has inspired the inn imitators proliferating along the same street, so book ahead. It's simple and unfussy, but has a definite charm. The top-floor double rooms have balconies, but all have river views, showers, TVs and air-con, and are clean and dry. The downstairs cafe has an English menu and wi-fi. To reach Koolaa's, walk through the North Gate Tower and turn right, walking down the alley between the city wall and the river. It's around 200m along on your left – look for the English sign.

Left: Bamboo rafts on Yulong River (p315); **Below:** Girls in Tujia traditional dress playing drums, Fènghuáng

PHOENIX JIĀNGTIĀN HOLIDAY VILLAGE

Hotel **$$$**

(凤凰江天旅游度假村; Fènghuáng Jiāngtiān Lǚyóu Dùjiàcūn; ☎326 1998; www.fhjt-hotel. com; Jiangtian Sq; 虹桥路江天广场; s & d Y588, tr Y688, discounts of 40%; ❄ @) Tucked behind Laoying Shao in a square that can also be accessed from Hongqiao Lu, the Phoenix offers spacious rooms with decent bathrooms, all with ADSL, although there are no river views. To get here, turn right at the arch on Laoying Shao.

 Eating

NIGHT MARKET

Street Market **$**

(虹桥夜市; Hóngqiáo Yèshì; Hongqiao Donglu; ☾5pm-1am) Hands down the best place to eat in Fènghuáng is this fantastic, lively night market. From the late afternoon, just north of the Hóng Bridge, food stalls set up shop ready to barbecue all manner of meat, fish and vegies.

SOUL TOO

Western **$$**

(亦素咖啡; Yìsù Kāfēi; ☎326 0396; 18 Laoying Shao; ☾8am-midnight) An upmarket cafe serving a wide variety of proper coffee (from Y25), as well as good pizza (from Y45), pasta and tempting chocolate cake, Soul Too makes for a pleasant pit stop away from the tour-group madness. It's not cheap, but then there aren't many places in Fènghuáng with an extensive list of foreign wines and Cuban cigars.

 Drinking

Laoying Shao is full of extremely loud bars with river views, live music and throngs of vacationing Chinese letting their hair down. Some bars don't welcome foreigners. Other bars can be found along Huilong Ge on the other side of the river.

ELOPE BAR   Bar

(25 Laoying Shao; ⏰1pm-2am) More mellow than most of the bars on this strip, and with a raised balcony that enables you to sip a drink while contemplating the river. Beers start at Y20, cocktails at Y35.

ℹ Information

Note that no banks can exchange foreign currency in Fènghuáng. The nearest bank that can exchange money is in Jíshŏu.

Industrial & Commercial Bank of China (ICBC: 工商银行; Gōngháng; Nanhua Lu) Has a 24-hour ATM.

China Post (中国邮政; Zhōngguó Yóuzhèng)

Tourism Administrative Bureau of Fènghuáng (凤凰旅游中心; Fènghuáng Lǚyóu Zhōngxīn; ☎322 9364; 46 Daomen Kou) Alongside Culture Sq.

Xīndōngli Internet Cafe (新动力网吧; Xīndōngli Wǎngbā; 2nd fl, Jianshe Lu; per hr Y2; ⏰24hr) Just west of the road at the southern foot of Hóng Bridge.

ℹ Getting There & Around

To get here you'll first have to get to Jíshŏu (which has a train station). Regular buses (Y15, 70 minutes) go to and from Jíshŏu stop outside the old town. A motorcycle taxi will ferry you in for Y5. Other destinations include **Chángshā** Y120, five hours, eight daily, **Huáihuà** Y33, two hours, every 20 minutes (depart from a car park off Hongqiao Donglu), and **Zhāngjiājiè** Y60, four hours, four daily.

There's no train station in Fènghuáng, but you can book tickets for elsewhere at the **Train Ticket Booking Office** (火车售票处; Huŏchē Shòupiàochù; ☎322 2410; Hongqiao Zhonglu; ⏰8am-10pm). It's just south of Hóng Bridge opposite the Xīndōngli internet cafe.

Xiàmén 厦门

☎0592 / POP 637,000

Xiàmén, also known to the West as Amoy, ranks as the most attractive city in Fújiàn province. Many of its old colonial buildings have been carefully restored, and its clean, well-kept streets and lively waterfront district give it a captivating old-world charm rarely seen in Chinese cities.

History

Xiàmén was founded around the mid-14th century in the early years of the Ming dynasty, when the city walls were built and the town was established as a major seaport and commercial centre. The Portuguese arrived in the 16th century, followed by the British in the 17th century, and later by the French and the Dutch, all attempting, rather unsuccessfully, to establish Xiàmén as a trade port. The port was closed to foreigners in the 1750s and it was not until the Opium Wars that the tide turned. In August 1841 a British naval force of 38 ships carrying artillery and soldiers sailed into Xiàmén harbour, forcing the port to open. Xiàmén then became one of the first treaty ports.

Japanese and Western powers followed soon after, establishing consulates and making Gŭlàng Yŭ a foreign enclave. Xiàmén was in Japanese hands from 1938 to 1945.

◎ Sights

The most absorbing part of Xiàmén is near the western (waterfront) district, directly opposite the small island of Gŭlàng Yŭ (see p322).

NÁNPŬTUÓ TEMPLE   Temple

(南普陀寺; Nánpŭtuó Sì; Siming Nanlu; admission Y3; ⏰8am-6pm) On the southern side of Xiàmén, this Buddhist temple was originally built over a millennium ago but has been repeatedly destroyed and rebuilt. Its latest incarnation dates to the early 20th century, and today it's an active and busy temple.

Take bus 1 from the train station or bus 21, 45, 48 or 503 from Zhongshan Lu to reach the temple.

 Sleeping & Eating

Gŭlàng Yŭ beats Xiàmén hands down as a more memorable and relaxing place to stay. Beng a port city, Xiàmén is known

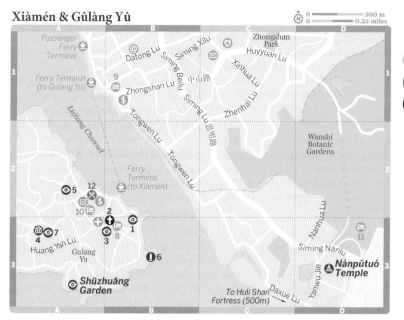

Xiàmén & Gŭlàng Yŭ

◉ Top Sights
Nánpŭtuó Temple.................................D3
Shūzhuāng Garden............................A3

◉ Sights
1 Bo'ai Hospital.................................B3
British Consulate.......................(see 1)
2 Ecclesia Catholica........................B3
3 Former Japanese Consulate...............B3
Former Spanish Consulate............(see 3)
4 Koxinga Memorial Hall...................A3
5 Organ Museum...............................A2

6 Statue of Koxinga..........................B3
Sunlight Rock............................(see 7)
7 Sunlight Rock Park........................A3

🛏 Sleeping
8 46Howtel......................................B3
9 Lùjiāng Harbourview Hotel...............B1
10 Mogo Cafe Hotel...........................A2
11 Shángkètáng...............................D3

🍽 Eating
12 Babycat Café...............................A2

for its fresh fish and seafood, especially oysters and shrimp. You'll find good places to eat around Zhongshan Lu near the harbour.

SHÁNGKÈTÁNG   Hotel **$$**
(上客堂; Shángkètáng; ☏252 1988; 515 Siming Nanlu; 思明南路515号; s Y280, tw 260-380, discounts of 20%; ❄ @) It could be us, but we swear the soap at this Buddhist-run hotel smells like incense. An excellent midrange choice perched on a small hill right beside the Nánpŭtuó Temple. Note: access to the hotel is via Nanhua Lu after 8pm.

LÙJIĀNG HARBOURVIEW HOTEL
                    Hotel **$$$**
(鹭江宾馆; Lùjiāng Bīnguǎn; ☏202 2922; www.lujiang-hotel.com; 54 Lujiang Dao; 鹭江道54号; s Y600-800, sea-view d Y920-1070, discounts of 30%; ❄ @) This 1940s-era four-star hotel has great panoramas from its more spacious sea-view rooms, some with balcony. Rooms are large and complete with spiffy orange-coloured walls and chairs. Staff are helpful and the rooftop restaurant is excellent.

LUCKY FULL CITY SEAFOOD

Dim Sum $$

(潮福城; Cháofú Chéng; 28 Hubin Bei Lu; dim sum from Y10; ⏰10am-10pm; 📖) You'll have to be really lucky (or wait at least 30 minutes) for a table at this popular restaurant. English and picture menu available.

ℹ️ Information

Bank of China (中国银行; Zhōngguó Yínháng; 6 Zhongshan Lu) The 24-hour ATM accepts international cards.

China International Travel Service (CITS; 中国国际旅行社; Zhōngguó Guójì Lǚxíngshè; 335 Hexiang Xilu) This branch near Yundang Lake is recommended.

China Post (中国邮政; Zhōngguó Yóuzhèng; cnr Xinhua Lu & Zhongshan Lu) Telephone services available.

Public Security Bureau (PSB; 公安局外事科; Gōng'ānjú; 📞226 2203; 45-47 Xinhua Lu) Opposite the main post and telephone office. The visa section (chūrùjìng guǎnlǐchù; open 8.10am to 11.45am and 2.40pm to 5.15pm Monday to Saturday) is in the northeastern part of the building on Gongyuan Nanlu.

Yúyuè Internet Cafe (娱悦网吧; Yúyuè Wǎngbā; 113 Datong Lu; per hr Y4; ⏰24hr)

ℹ️ Getting There & Away

Air

Air China, China Southern, Xiàmén Airlines and several other domestic airlines operate flights to/ from Xiamen to all major domestic airports in China. There are international flights to/from Bangkok, Hong Kong, Jakarta, Kuala Lumpur, Los Angeles, Manila, Osaka, Penang, Singapore and Tokyo.

Boat

There is a ferry service to Jīnmén, Taiwan (Y180, one hour, hourly), though you need a multiple-entry visa if you want to return to Xiàmén. You will get a Taiwanese visa upon arrival.

Bus

Destinations from the long-distance bus station (长途汽车站; chángtú qìchēzhàn; 58 Hubin Nanlu) include **Guǎngzhōu** Y208, nine hours, two daily, **Guìlín** Y253, 8.50am daily,

Lóngyán Y46, three hours, regular services, and **Yǒngdìng** Y65, four hours, four daily.

ℹ️ Train

From Xiàmén's **train station** (Xiahe Lu), in the city's northeast, there are services to **Běijīng West** Y253 to Y705, 34 hours, **Hángzhōu** (D train) Y198, six hours and **Shànghǎi** (D train), Y237, 7½ hours.

ℹ️ Getting Around

Xiàmén airport is 15km from the waterfront district, about 8km from the eastern district. From the waterfront, taxis cost around Y35.

Gǔlàng Yǔ 鼓浪屿

☑️0592

Gǔlàng Yǔ is a sedate retreat of meandering lanes and shaded warrens of backstreets, set in an architectural twilight of over 1000 (!) colonial villas, crumbling buildings and ancient banyan trees, and it's well worth spending a few days soaking up its charms.

The foreign community was well established on Gǔlàng Yǔ by the 1880s, with a daily English newspaper, churches, hospitals, post and telegraph offices, libraries, hotels and consulates. In 1903 the island was officially designated an International Foreign Settlement, and a municipal council with a police force of Sikhs was established to govern it. Today, memories of the settlement linger in the many charming colonial buildings and the sound of classical piano wafting from speakers (the island is nicknamed 'piano island' by the Chinese).

Sights

Old colonial residences and **consulates** are tucked away in the maze of streets leading from the pier, particularly along Longtou Lu and the back lanes of Huayan Lu. You can buy a through ticket to the island's main sights for Y80, but you can skip these without detracting too much from the overall experience.

Southeast of the pier you will see the two buildings of the former **British Consulate**

(原英国领事馆; 14–16 Lujiao Lu) above you, while further along at 1 Lujiao Lu (鹿礁路) is the cream-coloured former Japanese **Bo'ai Hospital**, built in 1936. Residents have now barred access to the public via a warning near the entrance slathered in black paint. Up the hill on a different part of Lujiao Lu at No 26 stands the red-brick **former Japanese Consulate**, just before you reach the magnificent snow-white **Ecclesia Catholica** (天主堂; Roman Catholic Church; Tiānzhǔtáng; 34 Lujiao Lu), dating from 1917. The white building next to the church is the **former Spanish Consulate**.

The highly distinctive **Bāguà Lóu** (八卦楼) at No 43 Guxin Lu (鼓新路) is now the **Organ Museum** (风琴博物馆; Fēngqín Bòwùguǎn; admission Y20, incl in through ticket for island; ☉8.40am-5.30pm), with a fantastic collection including a Norman & Beard organ from 1909.

Hàoyuè Garden (皓月园; Hàoyuè Yuán; admission Y15, incl in through ticket; ☉6am-7pm) is a rocky outcrop containing an imposing **statue of Koxinga** in full military dress. **Sunlight Rock** (Rìguāng Yán) is the island's highest point at 93m. On a clear day you can see the island of Jīnmén. At the foot of Sunlight Rock is a large colonial building known as the **Koxinga Memorial Hall** (郑成功纪念馆; Zhèngchénggōng Jìniànguǎn; ☉8-11am & 2-5pm).

The waterfront **Shūzhuāng Garden** (菽庄花园; Shūzhuāng Huāyuán; admission Y30, incl in through ticket) on the southern end of the island is a lovely place to linger for a few hours.

🛏 Sleeping & Eating

Gǔlàng Yǔ groans under the weight of its accommodation choices. However, its popularity means that you should book in advance, especially over the weekend. Cars aren't allowed.

Gǔlàng Yǔ is a great place for fish and seafood, especially at the restaurants in the centre of town. You'll find a collection of small eateries in the streets around the ferry terminal, and off Longtou Lu there are many small restaurants and stalls.

46HOWTEL　　　　　　　　Hotel　$$$
(☎206 5550; www.46howtel.com; 46 Fujian Lu; 福建路46号; r Y360-780; ❄ @) While the rest of the hotels on the island are happy with quirky and the antique styles (oh, how plebeian), this 'howtel' opts for cutting-edge modern. Expect rooms straight out of a *Wallpaper* spread: sharp lines, glossy surfaces and plush carpets. Service is top notch too.

MOGO CAFE HOTEL　　　　Hotel　$$
(蘑菇旅馆; Mógū Lǚguǎn; ☎208 5980; www.mogo-hotel.com; 3-9 Longtou Lu; 龙头路3-9号; r Y280-580; ❄ @) Book ahead if you want rooms at this fab joint, perched just 100m from the ferry terminal. Each of the 19 rooms has designer flair: textured wallpaper, mood lighting, rain showers. You've got to lug your luggage up three flights of stairs, though, so pack light.

BABYCAT CAFÉ　　　　　　Cafe　$$
(☎206 4119; 8 Longtou Lu; ☉10.30am-11pm; 📶) Trendy cafe (that actually reminds us of Luke Skywalker's home on Tattoine) with a large range of coffees, Amoy handmade pie, Tsingtao beer (Y15), and smoothies (from Y18). Further, non-Tattoine-style branch at 143 Longtou Lu. Free wi-fi.

❶ Information

Bank of China (中国银行; Zhōngguó Yínháng; 2 Longtou Lu; ☉9am-7pm) Forex and 24-hour ATM.

Hospital (Yīyuàn; 60 Fujian Lu) Has its own miniature ambulance for the small roads.

China Post (中国邮政; Zhōngguó Yóuzhèng; 102 Longtou Lu)

Xiàmén Gǔlàng Yǔ Visitor Center (Xiàmén Gǔlàng Yǔ Yóukè Zhōngxīn; Longtou Lu) Left luggage Y2 to Y5.

❶ Getting There & Around

Ferries for the five-minute trip to Gǔlàng Yǔ leave from the ferry terminal just west of Xiàmén's Lùjiāng Harbourview Hotel. Outbound, it's a free ride on the bottom deck and Y1 for the upper deck. Xiàmén-bound it's Y8 (free between 10pm and midnight). Boats run between 5.30am and midnight. Waterborne circuits of the island can be done by boat (Y15), with hourly departures from the passenger ferry terminal off Lujiang Lu between 7.45am and 8.45pm. Round-island buggies take 30 minutes for a circuit (Y10 to Y40).

Hakka Tǔlóu 客家土楼

The stunning rural area of rolling farmland and hills in southwestern Fújiàn is the heartland of the Hakka (客家; *kèjiā*) people and their remarkable *tǔlóu* (土楼; roundhouses). These vast, packed-earth edifices resembling fortresses are scattered throughout the surrounding countryside. Today over 30,000 survive, many still inhabited and open to visitors.

There are thousands of *tǔlóu,* some a few centuries old, but the big-ticket ones are all lumped into various clusters. There are three major counties: the **Yǒngdìng**, **Nánjǐng** and **Huá'ān.** Except for the Huá'ān cluster, the rest can be visited in a day or three. The first two are in the general vicinity of each other and you can base yourself in the small village of Liùlián (六联) – also called the Tǔlóu Mínsú Wénhuàcūn (土楼民俗文化村) – which you can reach by bus from Xiàmén, Lóngyán or Yǒngdìng.

Huá'ān is over 100km northeast away and is best visited as a separate trip if you're not hiring a vehicle.

A short walk from Liùlián, **Zhènchéng Lóu** (振成楼) is a grandiose structure built in 1912, with two concentric circles

and 222 rooms. In the centre of the *tǔlóu* is a large ancestral hall, complete with Western-style pillars, for special ceremonies and greeting guests.

Near Zhènchéng Lóu, the much older, square **Kuíjù Lóu** (奎聚楼) dates back to 1834. Also worth visiting is the late-19th-century and (comparatively) pea-sized **Rúshēng Lóu** (如升楼) with only one ring and 16 rooms. Along the river is the five-storey-square **Fúyù Lóu** (福裕楼), which boasts some wonderfully carved wooden beams and pillars.

Spending the night in a *tǔlóu* will reward you with unforgettable memories of a vanishing dimension of life in China.

The owners of the **Fúyù Lóu** (福裕楼常棣客栈; ☏ 553 5900, 1386 0221 798; tulou@126. com; d incl breakfast Y60) have converted some rooms at the rear into basic but comfy doubles complete with fan and small TV. The owners are friendly, speak some English and serve tasty Hakka food (dishes from Y20). They can also organise a pick-up from Xiàmén and transport for touring the area.

With the infrastructure still in flux, the easiest way to see the *tǔlóu* is to book a tour or hire a vehicle from Xìamén. Alternatively, take a bus from Xiàmén. From Xiàmén long-distance bus station, take a bus headed to Yǒngdìng (永定县, Y65, four hours, four per day from 5.30am to 12.30pm). It will pass Liùlián. In the other direction, there is a bus at 7.20am and 12.20pm from Yǒngdìng.

Best of the Rest

Yúnnán (p326)
Lìjiāng and Dàlǐ are two of China's most attractive ancient towns; they are embedded in a fantastic landscape that includes the dramatic Tiger Leaping Gorge.

Sìchuān (p334)
Home of China's spiciest cuisine and a mountainous frontier with Tibet – Sìchuān is also the habitat of the reclusive Giant Panda.

The Silk Road (p338)
China's ancient Silk Road – running through Gānsù – passes by the astonishing Mògāo Caves and the dramatic Great Wall fort of Jiāyùguān.

Above: Buddhist monks outside a temple; **Left**: The three pagodas (p326), Dàlǐ, Yúnnán

PHOTOGRAPHER: (ABOVE)AUSTIN BUSH/LONELY PLANET IMAGES ©; (LEFT) DIANA MAYFIELD/LONELY PLANET IMAGES ©

Yúnnán

HIGHLIGHTS

① Dàlǐ (p326) Funky Bai town surrounded by stunning scenery.

② Lìjiāng (p328) Extraordinary Naxi town with riveting ethnic textures.

③ Yùlóng Xuěshān (p330) One of China's most stunning mountains.

④ Tiger Leaping Gorge (p330) Yúnnán's – and possibly China's – greatest trek.

Man praying at temple, Zhōngdiàn
PHOTOGRAPHER: DIANA MAYFIELD/LONELY PLANET IMAGES ©

Dàlǐ 大理

☏ 0872 / POP 40,000

Dàlǐ, the original funky banana-pancake backpacker hang-out in Yúnnán, was once *the* place to chill, with its stunning location sandwiched between mountains and Ěrhǎi Hú (Ěrhǎi Lake). Loafing here for a couple of weeks was an essential Yúnnán experience.

Today, though, Dàlǐ routinely gets bashed for being – you guessed it – too 'touristy'. Then again, this sniffy attitude has resulted in fewer Westerners heading here, so you won't be as taken for granted as in years past. Forget the whingers, for there are fascinating possibilities for exploring, especially by bicycle and in the mountains above the lake, and getting to know the region's Bai culture.

Sights

Absolutely *the* symbol of the town/region, the **three pagodas** (三塔寺; Sān Tǎ Sì; admission incl Chongsheng Temple full/student Y121/62; ⏱7am-7pm) 2km north of the north gate are among the oldest standing structures in southwestern China. The tallest of the three, **Qianxun Pagoda**, has 16 tiers that reach a height of 70m.

The **Dàlǐ Museum** (Dàlǐ Shì Bówùguǎn; Fuxing Lu; admission free; ⏱8.30am-5.30pm) houses a small collection of archaeological pieces relating to Bai history, including some fine figurines.

Merrymaking – along with buying, selling and general horse-trading – takes place during the **Third Moon Fair** (Sānyuè Jié), which begins on the 15th day of the third lunar month (usually April) and ends on the 21st day.

The **Torch Festival** (Huǒbǎ Jié) is held on the 24th day of the sixth lunar month (normally July) – see p44 for more details.

Sleeping & Eating

JIM'S TIBETAN HOTEL   Hotel **$$**
(Jímǔ Zàngshì Jiǔdiàn; ☏ 267 7824; www.china-travel.nl; 13 Yuxiu Lu; 玉秀路13号; d Y280; @)

The rooms here are the most distinctive in Dàlǐ, packed with antique Chinese-style furniture, and manage to be both stylish and cosy. There's a garden, a rooftop terrace, a restaurant and bar below and wi-fi throughout.

CĀNG ĚR CHŪN   Yúnnán   **$**
(苍洱春; ☎ 690 0907; 84 Renmin Lu; dishes from Y6; ⏱ 9am-10.30pm) A great place for classic Bai dishes such as Grandma's potato (*lǎo nǎi yángyù*) and Yunnan staples such as *táozá rǔbǐng*. There's a limited English menu, but you can also point at anything that takes your fancy.

TOWER CAFÉ   Western   **$$**
(钟楼咖啡; Zhōnglóu Kāfēi; ☎ 267 1883; 44 Yangren Jie; mains from Y26; ⏱ 11am-11pm) Comfortable, professionally run three-storey place with a roof terrace, that serves up solid Western comfort food and a selection of tasty Thai dishes. There's a good range of foreign beer and wine too.

ⓘ Information

Bank of China (Zhōngguó Yínháng; Fuxing Lu) Changes cash and travellers cheques and has an ATM that accepts all major credit cards.

China Post (yóujú; cnr Fuxing Lu & Huguo Lu; ⏱ 8am-8pm)

ⓘ Getting There & Away

Coming from Lìjiāng, Xiàguān-bound buses stop at the eastern end of Dàlǐ to let passengers off before continuing on to the north bus station.

From Kūnmíng's west bus station, there are numerous buses to Dàlǐ (Y100, four to five hours, every 20 minutes from 7.30am to 7.30pm). Heading north, it's easiest to pick up a bus on the roads

Lìjiāng

Lìjiāng

◉ **Top Sights**
Old Market Square C3
White Horse Dragon Pool B4

⊜ **Sleeping**
1 Dōngbā Hotel D3

⊗ **Eating**
2 Mama Fu's..C3

⊕ **Entertainment**
3 Naxi Orchestra....................................C3

outside the west or east gates; buy your ticket in advance from your guesthouse or a travel agent.

ⓘ Getting Around

From Dàlǐ, a taxi to Xiàguān airport takes 45 minutes and costs around Y100; to Xiàguān's train station it costs Y50.

Buses (Y2, 30 minutes, marked 大理) run between the old town and Xiàguān from as early as 6.30am; get on along Yu'er Lu or where it meets the road one block west of Boai Lu (coming in it will drop you off along Boai Lu). Bus 8 runs between Dàlǐ and central Xiàguān (Y2, 30 minutes) on the way to the train station every 15 minutes from 6.30am.

Lìjiāng 丽江

♩ NEW TOWN 08891, OLD TOWN 0888 / POP OLD TOWN 40,000

A UN World Heritage Site since 1999, Lìjiāng is a city of two halves: the old town and the very different and modern new town. The old town is where you'll be spending your time and it's a jumble of lanes that twist and turn. If you get lost, head upstream and you'll make your way back to the main square.

Sights

Note that the old town technically has a Y80 entrance fee. Nobody usually pays this, but you may be asked for it if you try to buy a ticket for other sights around town.

OLD TOWN Historic Site

The old town (古城) is dissected by a web of arterylike canals that once brought the city's drinking water from Yuquan Spring, in what is now Black Dragon Pool Park. Several wells and pools are still in use around town (but hard to find). Where there are three pools, these were designated into pools for drinking, washing clothes and washing vegetables. A famous example of these is the **White Horse Dragon Pool** (Báimǎlóng Tán; ⏱7am-10pm) in the deep south of the old town, where you can still see the odd local washing their veggies after buying them in the market.

The focus of the old town is the busy **Old Market Square** (Sìfāng Jiē), once the haunt of Naxi traders. They've long since made way for tacky souvenir stalls and food stands. However, the views up the hill and the surrounding lanes are still extraordinary.

BLACK DRAGON POOL PARK
Scenic Area

(黑龙潭公园 Hēilóngtán Gōngyuán; Xin Dajie; admission with Y80 town entrance ticket free; ⏱7am-8.30pm) On the northern edge of town is the Black Dragon Pool Park; its view of Yùlóng Xuěshān (Jade Dragon Snow Mountain) is the most obligatory photo shoot in southwestern China. The **Dongba Research Institute** (Dōngbā Wénhuà Yánjiùshì; ⏱8am-5pm Mon-Fri) is part of a renovated complex on the hillside here. You can see Naxi cultural artefacts and scrolls featuring a unique pictograph script.

The **Museum of Naxi Dongba Culture** (Nàxī Dōngbā Wénhuà Bówùguǎn; admission free; ⏱9am-5pm) is at the park's northern entrance and is a decent introduction to traditional Naxi lifestyle and religion, complete with good English captions.

Sleeping & Eating

Throw a stick and you'll hit a charming Naxi guesthouse in the old town. There are well over 700 places to stay in the old city, with more appearing all the time. In peak seasons (especially holidays), prices double (or more).

DONGBA HOTEL Hotel $

(东巴客栈; Dōngbā Kèzhàn; ☎512 1975; www. dongbahotel.com; 109 Wenzhi Alley; 文治巷 109号; s & d Y120-280; @) A family-style atmosphere (free laundry and tea and coffee), great staff, and cute rooms (some on two levels) with huge, comfy beds and nice bathrooms make this very well-maintained inn a lovely place to stay. It gets a lot of repeat guests, which says it all.

MAMA FU'S Yúnnán $

(Māmāfù Cāntīng; ☎512 2285; Mishi Xiang; dishes from Y18; ⏱9am-10.30pm) An original Lìjiāng culinary cornerstone from way back. Alfresco dining here beside a tranquil stream provides one of the best people-watching opportunities in the Old Town. The Chinese dishes are very solid, especially the Naxi ones (try the *chǎo hǎicài*).

Entertainment

NAXI ORCHESTRA Music

(Nàxī Gǔyuè Huì; Naxi Music Academy; ☎512 7971; tickets Y120-160; ⏱performances 8pm) One of the few things you can do in the evening in Lìjiāng is attend performances of this orchestra inside a beautiful building in the old town. Not only are all two dozen or so members Naxi, but they play a type of Taoist temple music (known as *dòngjīng*) that has been lost elsewhere in China.

Information

Bank of China (Zhōngguó Yínháng; Dong Dajie) This branch is in the old town and has an ATM machine. There are other banks around town with ATM's too.

China Post (yóujú; Minzhu Lu; ⏰8am-8pm) Offers EMS (Express Mail Service). Another post office is in the old town just north of the Old Market Sq.

Public Security Bureau (PSB; Gōng'ānjú; Fuhui Lu; ⏰8.30-11.30am & 2.30-5.30pm Mon-Fri) Is reputedly very speedy with visa extensions.

ⓘ Getting There & Away

AIR Lìjiāng's airport is 25km east of town. Most hotels in the old town also offer an air-ticket booking service.

BUS The main long-distance bus station is south of the old town; to get there take bus 8 or 11 (Y1; the latter is faster) from along Minzhu Lu.

An **express bus station** (Gāo Kuài Kèyùnzhàn; Shangrila Dadao) for Kūnmíng is in the north of town. Buses to Xiàguān run from both the long-distance station and the express bus station; the long-distance station has more services, however.

TRAIN There is one train daily to Dàlǐ at 9.58am (Y15, two hours) and one sleeper to Kūnmíng (Y92, nine hours) at 10.12pm.

ⓘ Getting Around

Buses to the airport (Y15) leave from outside the CAAC office 90 minutes before flight departures. The long-distance bus station also has buses to the airport (Y7).

Taxis start at Y7 in the new town and are not allowed into the old town. Bike hire is available at most hostels and **N's Kitchen** (Y30 per day).

Yùlóng Xuěshān 玉龙雪山

Also known as Mt Satseto, **Yùlóng Xuěshān** (Jade Dragon Snow Mountain; adult Y190, protection fee Y80) soars to some 5500m. Its peak was first climbed in 1963 by a research team from Běijīng and now, at some 35km from Lìjiāng, it is regularly mobbed by hordes of Chinese tour groups and travellers.

This area is extremely expensive (add in transport, entrance fees and chairlifts, and you'll be lucky to pay less than Y450).

Tiger Leaping Gorge 虎跳峡

📞0887

One of the world's deepest gorges, Tiger Leaping Gorge (Hǔtiào Xiá; admission Y50)

measures 16km long and is a giddy 3900m from the waters of Jīnshā River (Jīnshā Jiāng) to the snowcapped mountains of Hābā Shān (Hābā Mountain) to the west and Yùlóng Xuěshān to the east and, despite the odd danger, it's gorgeous almost every single step of the way.

The gorge trek is not to be taken lightly. Even for those in good physical shape, it's a workout. The path constricts and crumbles; it certainly can wreck the knees. When it's raining (especially July and August), landslides and swollen waterfalls can block the paths, in particular on the low road. (The best time to come is May and the start of June, when the hills are afire with plant and flower life.)

A few people – including a handful of foreign travellers – have died in the gorge. Over the last decade, there have also been cases of travellers being assaulted on the trail. As always, it's safer in all ways not to do the trek alone.

Plan on three to four days away from Líjiāng for the hike but it can be done in two. Check with cafes and lodgings in Lìjiāng or Qiáotóu for trail and weather updates. Most have fairly detailed gorge maps; just remember they're not to scale and occasionally out of date.

Make sure you bring plenty of water on this hike – 2L to 3L is ideal – as well as plenty of sunscreen and lip balm. There are plenty of guesthouses along the way so you can break up the journey.

 Hiking

There are two trails: the higher (the older route) and the lower, which follows the new road and is best avoided, unless you enjoy being enveloped in clouds of dust from passing tour buses and 4WDs. While the scenery is stunning wherever you are in the gorge, it's absolutely sublime from the high trail. Make sure you don't get too distracted by all that beauty, though, and so miss the arrows that help you avoid getting lost on the trail.

It's six hours to Běndìwān or a strenuous eight hours to Walnut Garden.

Man tending field in front of the three pagodas

AMERENS HEDWICH/LONELY PLANET IMAGES ©

It's much more fun, and a lot less exhausting, to do the trek over two days. By stopping overnight at one of the many guesthouses along the way, you'll have the time to appreciate the magnificent vistas on offer at almost every turn of the trail.

Ponies can be hired (their owners will find you) to take you to the gorge's highest point for between Y100 and Y150; it's not uncommon to see three generations of a family together, with the oldies on horseback and the young ones panting on foot behind them.

The following route starts at **Jane's Guesthouse** (p333). Walk away from Qiáotóu, past the school, for five minutes or so, then head up the paved road branching to the left; there's an arrow to guide you. After about 2.5km on the road, you'll reach the **Sunrise Guesthouse**. It's here that the gorge trail proper starts and the serious climbing begins. Note that locals may try and hit you up for an additional 'fee' at this point, which they will claim is reward for them keeping the trail litter-free.

From here on, you start to ascend past mountain goats who scatter out of the way as you approach, as well as the odd, old geezer smoking a reflective pipe by the side of the trail. In places, the path clings to the sides of the cliffs.

The toughest section of the trek comes after Nuòyú village, when the trail winds through the 28 agonising bends, or turns, that lead to the highest point of the gorge. Count on five hours at normal pace to get through here and to reach Yǎchà village. It's a relatively straightforward walk on to Běndìwān. About 1½ hours on from there, you begin the descent to the road on slippery, poor paths. Watch your step here; if you twist an ankle, it's a long hop down.

After the path meets the road at **Tina's Guesthouse**, there's a good detour that leads down 40 minutes to the middle rapids and Tiger Leaping Stone, where a tiger is once said to have leapt across the Yangzi, thus giving the gorge its name.

From Tina's to Walnut Garden, it is a further 40-minute walk along the road. A new alternative trail to Walnut Garden keeps high where the path descends to Tina's, crosses a stream and a 'bamboo forest' before descending into Walnut Garden.

The next day's walk is shorter at four to six hours. There are two ferries and so

331

two route options to get to Dàjù. After 45 minutes you'll see a red marker leading down to the new (winter) ferry (*xīn dùkǒu*; one-way Y20); the descent includes one hairy section with a sheer drop.

Many trekkers call it a day when they reach the bottom and flag down anything heading back to Qiáotóu. The road to Dàjù and the village itself is pretty uninteresting. If you do decide to go on, it's a hard climb to the car park, where you may have to register with the PSB (Gōng'ānjú).

The second, lesser-used option continues along the road from Walnut Garden until it reaches the permanent ferry crossing (Y20). From here paths lead to Dàjù, where there are two buses a day back to Lìjiāng (Y40, 3 hours, 7.30am, 1.30pm)

If you're doing the walk the other way round and heading for Qiáotóu, walk north through Dàjù, aiming for the white pagoda at the foot of the mountains.

🛏️ Sleeping & Eating

The following list of accommodation options along the way (listed in the order that you'll come to them) is not exhaustive. In the unlikely event that everywhere is full, basic rooms will be available with a local. We've never heard of anyone who had to sleep rough in the gorge.

All the guesthouses double as restaurants and shops, where you can pick up water and snacks.

NAXI FAMILY GUESTHOUSE
Guesthouse **$**

(Nàxī Kèzhàn; ☎880 6928; dm Y20, s & d Y120; @) Taking your time to spend a night here instead of double-timing it to Walnut Garden isn't a bad idea. It's an incredibly friendly, well-run place (organic veggies and wines, and the only internet access in the gorge), set around a pleasant courtyard.

TEA HORSE GUESTHOUSE
Guesthouse **$**

(Chámǎ Kèzhàn; ☎139 8871 7292; dm Y20, s & d Y120) Just after Yāchà village, this bigger place has a great 'Naxi mama' running

things and even has a small spa and massage parlour where aching limbs can be eased.

HALFWAY GUESTHOUSE
Guesthouse **$**

(Zhōngtú Kèzhàn, Běndìwān; ☎139 8870 0522; dm Y20, s & d Y120-150) Once a simple home to a guy collecting medicinal herbs and his family, this is now a busy-busy operation. The vistas here are awe-inspiring and perhaps the best of any lodging in the gorge; the view from the communal toilets is worth the price of a bed alone.

FIVE FINGERS MOUNTAIN GUESTHOUSE
Guesthouse **$**

(Wǔzhǐ Kèzhàn; ☎139 8877 6286; dm Y25, s Y50) An endearingly rustic place, where chickens run around and you're part of the family during your stay. The 200m climb up from the road to get here is a killer after five hours of walking, though.

TINA'S GUESTHOUSE
Guesthouse **$**

(Zhōngxiá Lǚdiàn; ☎820 2258; tina999@live.cn; dm Y25, s & d Y60-280). It's a bit concrete-blocky and lacks the charm of other places on the mountain, but it has lots of beds and the location is perfect for those too knackered to make it to Walnut Garden.

SEAN'S SPRING GUESTHOUSE
Guesthouse **$**

(Shānquán Kèzhàn; ☎820 2223; www.tigerleapinggorge.com; dm Y25, s & d Y60-200) is one of the original guesthouses on the trail, and still the spot for lively evenings and socialising. It's run by the eponymous Sean, a true character. Recently refurbished, the best rooms have great views of Yùlóng Xuěshān.

CHATEAU DE WOODY
Guesthouse **$**

(Shānbáiliǎn Lǚguǎn; ☎139 8871 2705; s & d Y60) Another old-school gorge guesthouse, the rooms here all have views and bathrooms and are a very good deal. Across the road, the less attractive modern extension has rooms for the same price.

JANE'S GUESTHOUSE

Guesthouse **$**

(Xiágǔ Xíng Kèzhàn; Qiáotóu; ☏880 6570; dm/s & d Y20/50-80; @) This two-storey place with tidy, clean rooms is where many people start their trek. The breakfasts here make for good walking fuel and there are left-luggage facilities (Y5 a bag).

. . . .

❶ Getting There & Away

From the Lìjiāng long-distance bus station, buses run to Zhōngdiàn (Shangri-La) every 40 minutes (7.30am to 5pm) and pass through Qiáotóu (Y21).

Returning to Lìjiāng from Qiáotóu, buses start running through from Zhōngdiàn around 10am. The last one rolls through around 7.40pm (Y20). The last bus to Zhōngdiàn passes through at around 7pm.

At the time of writing, there were no buses to Báishuǐtái from Lìjiāng. There is one bus a day from Zhōngdiàn to Báishuǐtái (Y25, three hours, 9.10am).

Eventually, paved roads will connect Qiáotóu, Walnut Garden and the settlement across the river from Dàjù, then north to connect Báishuǐtái and Zhōngdiàn.

Tiger Leaping Gorge to Báishuǐtái

An adventurous add-on to the gorge trek is to continue north all the way to Hābā village and the limestone terraces of Báishuǐtái. This turns it into a four-day trek from Qiáotóu and from here you

can travel on to Zhōngdiàn. From Walnut Garden to Hābā, via Jiāngbiān, is seven to eight hours. From here to the Yi village of Sānbà is about the same, following trails. You could just follow the road and hitch with the occasional truck or tractor, but it's longer and less scenic. Some hardy mountain bikers have followed the trail. This is really only fun from north to south, elevations being what they are. The best way would be to hire a guide in Walnut Garden for around Y100 per day, depending on the number of people. For Y150 per day you should be able to get a horse and guide.

In Hābā most people stay at the **Hābā Snow Mountain Inn** (哈巴雪山客栈; Hābā Xuěshān Kèzhàn; ☏0887 886 6596; beds Y30; @). In Sānbà, beds can also be found for around Y25. From Sānbà there is an 8am bus to Zhōngdiàn (Y40, five hours), or you could get off at the turn-off to Bìtǎ Hǎi (Emerald Pagoda Lake) and hike there.

If you plan to try the route alone, assume you'll need all provisions and equipment for extremes of weather. Ask for local advice before setting out.

Sìchuān

HIGHLIGHTS

1 **Éméi Shān (p334)** Awe-inspiring mountain scenery and Buddhist place of veneration.

2 **Grand Buddha (p336)** Buddhist China's most colossal statue.

3 **Jiǔzhàigōu Nature Reserve (p337)** Idyllic landscape of lakes, forests, waterfalls and mountains.

Five-month-old giant panda

Giant Panda Breeding Research Base
大熊猫繁殖研究中心

One of Chéngdū's most popular tourist attractions, this **reserve (Dàxióngmāo Fánzhí Yánjiū Zhōngxīn; www.panda.org.cn; admission Y58; ⊙8am-6pm)**, 18km north of the city centre, is the easiest way to catch a glimpse of Sìchuān's most famous resident outside of a zoo. The enclosures here are large and kept in good condition.

Home to nearly 50 giant and red pandas, the base focuses on getting these sexually reluctant creatures to breed; March to May is the 'falling in love period', wink wink. If you visit in autumn or winter, you may see tiny newborns in the nursery.

There's a corny but informative 15-minute film about panda mating habits and an old-fashioned museum has detailed exhibits on panda evolution, habits, habitats and conservation efforts, all with English captions.

Try to visit the base in the morning, when the pandas are most active. Feeding takes place around 9.30am, although you'll see them eating in the late afternoon too. During the middle of the day they spend most of their time sleeping, particularly during the height of midsummer when they sometimes disappear into their living quarters (air-conditioned, apparently).

Tourist bus 902 (Y2, one hour, 8am to 4pm) runs here from outside **Traffic Inn (Jiāotōng Qīngnián Lǚshè; ✆8545 0470; www.redcliffinn.cn; 6 Linjiang Zhonglu)**, and goes past **Sim's Cosy Garden Youth Hostel (Lǎoshěn Qīngnián Lǚshè; ✆8196 7573; www.gogosc.com; 211 Yihuan Lu Bei Siduan)** en route. Last bus back is 6pm. All decent youth hostels run trips here too, which cost more but get you to the base earlier.

Éméi Shān 峨眉山
✆0833 / ELEV 3099M

A cool, misty retreat from the Sìchuān basin's sweltering heat, stunning **Éméi Shān (entrance Y150/80 adult/student)** is one of China's four most famous Buddhist mountains (the others are Pǔtuóshān,

Wǔtái Shān and Jiǔhuá Shān). Here you'll find fabulous forested mountain scenery, ramshackle wooden temples and macaques demanding tribute for safe passage. There's also the wonderful opportunity to spend the night in one of the many monasteries that dot the mountain range.

The magnificent Buddhist **Jīndǐng Temple** (金顶寺; Jīndǐng Sì; Golden Summit Temple) is at the Golden Summit (Jīn Dǐng; 3077m), commonly referred to as the mountain's highest peak. Covered with glazed tiles and surrounded by white marble balustrades, the renovated temple, which now occupies 1695 sq metres, is quite striking. In front of the temple, the unmissable 48m-tall golden statue **Multi-dimensional Samantabhadra** (十方普贤; Shífāng Pǔxián) honours mountain protector Pǔxián and was added in 2006.

 **Sleeping**

On the Mountain
Almost all the temples on the mountain (with the notable exception of Jīndǐng Temple at the summit) offer cheap lodgings in dormitory-style accommodation with shared bathrooms but usually no showers.

There are also two hotels on the mountain; **Jīndǐng Dàjiǔdiàn** (金顶大酒店; ☑509 8088/77; from foot 9½ hours, from summit 30 minutes; tw/tr Y780/580, discounted to Y620/460) and **Cableway Company Hotel** (索道公司招待所; Suǒdào Gōngsī Zhāodàisuǒ; ☑155 2030 0955; from foot 8½ hours, from summit 90 minutes; tr/tw Y150/260), although standards are low considering the prices.

XIĀNFĒNG TEMPLE Monastery $
(仙峰寺; Xiānfēng Sì; dm/tw with shared bathroom Y30-260, tw Y280; approx walking time from foot of mountain 6 hours; from summit 4 hours) This pretty remote temple, with a lovely forested location backed by rugged cliffs, is set around a large shaded front courtyard and has a wonderfully peaceful atmosphere.

In Bàoguó Village
TEDDY BEAR HOTEL Youth Hostel $$
(玩具熊酒店; Wánjùxióng Jiǔdiàn; ☑559 0135, 138 9068 1961; www.teddybear.com.cn; 43 Baoguo Lu; dm Y35, d/tw from Y260, tr Y180; ✳@🛜) This 'backpacker central' place has cute, well-maintained rooms and English-speaking staff. Guests are also given an excellent hand-drawn map of the mountain trails for free. Call for a free pick-up from Éméi bus or train station.

ℹ Information
Agricultural Bank of China (农业银行; Nóngyè Yínháng; ☺9am-5pm) Has foreign-exchange desk and foreign-friendly ATM.
Internet cafe (网吧; wǎngba; per hour Y2; ☺24hr) Walk five minutes north from mountain entrance then climb steps on right to level of road bridge. At top, turn right and walk 200m.

ℹ Getting Around
Bàoguó (报国) village is your gateway to the mountain. Buses from the village bus station travel to three bus depots on the mountain: Wǔxiǎngǎng (五显冈, Y20, 15 minutes), about a 20-minute walk below Qīngyīn Pavilion; Wànnián (万年, Y20, 45 minutes), below Wànnián Temple; and Léidòngpíng (雷洞坪; Y40, 90 minutes), a few minutes' walk from Jīngdǐng Cable Car.

Buses run roughly half-hourly from 6am to 5pm from 26 April to 31 October and from 7am to 4pm from 1 November to 25 April.

The last buses back down the mountain leave at 6pm (5pm in winter) from each of the three mountain bus depots.

ℹ Getting There & Away
The town of Éméi (峨眉山市; Éméi Shān Shì) lies 6.5km east of the mountain Éméi Shān and is the transport hub for the mountain. All buses to Éméi Shān terminate here – at the new Emei Shan Passenger Traffic Centre (峨眉山客运中心; Éméi Shān Kèyùn Zhōngxīn), directly opposite Éméi train station (峨眉火车站; Éméi Huǒchēzhàn). From here, it's a Y20 cab to Bàoguó Village, the gateway to the mountain. Alternatively, take bus 1 (Y1) from outside Éméi bus station to Pēnshuǐ Chí (喷水池) bus stop, then take bus 5 (Y1.5) from across the square to Bàoguó (报国).

Buses from **Bàoguó Bus Station** include **Chéngdū** Y45, 2½ hours, 8am to 6pm, **Lèshān** Y11, one hour, 8am-5.30pm and **Chóngqìng** Y115, six hours, 8.30am.

Destinations from **Éméi Train Station** include **Chéngdū** Y24 (seat), 2½ hours, 7 daily, 5.53am to 11.28pm and **Xī'ān** Y232 (sleeper), 19 hours, 10.28am daily.

Lèshān 乐山

🎵0833 / POP 156,000

With fingernails bigger than the average human, the world's tallest Buddha draws plenty of tourists to this relaxed riverside town. It's an easy day trip from Chéngdū or a convenient stopover en route to or from Éméi Shān.

◉ Sights

Lèshān's pride and joy is the serene, 1200-year-old **Grand Buddha** (Dàfó; admission Y90, students Y50; ⏰7.30am-6.30pm Apr-early Oct, 8am-5.30pm early Oct-Mar) carved into a cliff face overlooking the confluence of the Dàdù River (Dàdù Hé) and the Mín River (Mín Hé). And at 71m tall, he's definitely big. His ears stretch for 7m, his shoulders span 28m, and each of his big toes is 8.5m long.

To fully appreciate the Buddha's magnitude, get an up-close look at his head, then descend the steep, winding stairway for the Lilliputian view. Avoid visiting on weekends or holidays, when traffic on the staircase can come to a complete standstill.

Bus 13 (Y1) travels from Xiàobà Bus Station and loops through the town centre (you can catch it on Dong Dajie) before crossing the river to reach the Grand Buddha Scenic Area and Wūyóu Temple.

⊖ Tours

Tour boats pass by for panoramic views of the Grand Buddha (hovering in front for about 10 minutes), which reveal two guardians in the cliffside, not visible from land. Large **tour boats** (Y50, 30 minutes) and smaller **speedboats** (Y50, 15 to 20

minutes) both leave regularly from the ferry dock (旅游船码头; lǚ\"yóuchuán mǎtóu). They run from 7.30am to 6.30pm (1 April to 7 October) or from 8am to 5.30pm (8 October to 31 March).

Sleeping & Eating

JIĀZHŌU HOTEL   Hotel $$
(Jiāzhōu Bīnguǎn; 🎵213 9888; 85 Baita Jie; 白塔街85号; r incl breakfast from Y360; ❄ @)
Rooms aren't quite as grand as the lobby suggests, but this is more upscale than most and makes for a very comfortable stay. Third-floor rooms and above have internet connection for laptop users and many rooms, even some of the cheapies, have river views.

For dumplings, noodles and other quick bites, try Dong Dajie and the surrounding streets between the post office and the river.

YANG'S RESTAURANT   Sichuan $
(Yángjiā Cāntīng; 2f 186 Baita Jie; 白塔街186号 2层; dishes Y15-25; ⏰6-9pm) Octogenarian and travel guru Mr Yang and his wife run this small restaurant in the living room of their home. They serve simple but tasty local food and he may regale you with tales of his life while you eat.

❶ Information

Bank of China (Zhōngguó Yínháng; 16 Renmin Nanlu) Changes money and travellers cheques, offers cash advances on credit cards and has foreign-friendly ATM.

China Post (yóujú; 62 Yutang Jie)

Public Security Bureau (PSB; Gōng'ānjú; 🎵518 2555; 243 Jiading Beilu; 嘉定北路243号; ⏰9am-noon & 1-5pm Mon-Fri) Visa extensions in two days. North of town, on corner of Bailu Lu (白禄路); take bus 1 (Y1) or a taxi (Y5 to Y6) from the centre.

❶ Getting There & Around

Lèshān has three bus stations, all north of the centre. Buses from Chéngdū's Xīnnánmén station arrive at Xiàobà bus station (Xiàobà Chēzhàn), but Central bus station (乐山客运中心车站; Lèshān

Kèyùn Zhōngxīn Chēzhàn) is bigger and has more frequent services to more destinations. You may also be dropped at Liányùn bus station (联运车站; Liányùn chēzhàn).

Pedicab rides cost Y2 to Y5. Taxis start at a flat rate of Y3 for the first 3km.

Jiǔzhàigōu Nature Reserve
九寨沟风景名胜区

☎ 0837 / POP 62,000 / ELEV 2000M

This stunning Unesco World Heritage site (Jiǔzhàigōu Fēngjǐng Míngshèngqū; www.jiuzhai.com; Nine Village Valley National Park; www.jiuzhai.com; entrance adult/student May-mid-Nov Y220/170, mid-Nov-Apr Y80/70; plus shuttle bus Y90; ⏱ 7am-6pm) is one of Sìchuān's star attractions. An incredible 1.5 million people visit the park every year to gawp at its famous bluer-than-blue lakes, it's rushing waterfalls and its deep-green trees backed by snowy mountains.

The best time to visit is September through to November, when you're most likely to have clear skies and (particularly in October) blazing autumn colours to contrast with the turquoise lakes.

Sleeping

There's an almost endless supply of hotels around Péngfēng Village (彭丰村; Péngfēng Cūn) and Bianbian Jie (although Bianbian Jie tends to close down in winter) so don't worry if the options below are full. Staying inside the park is not allowed any more, although villagers may still offer you a bed.

ZHUO MA'S   Homestay **$**
(卓玛; Zhuómǎ; ☎ 135 6878 3012; www.zhuomajiuzhaigou.hostel.com; beds Y180) A genuine Tibetan homestay, this beautifully decorated wood cabin in a tiny village about 10km up the valley from the main park has three simple rooms and a wonderfully accommodating family. The lovely Zhuo Ma speaks some English and is on hand to welcome foreign guests. There's a common bathroom with shower and prices include three meals a day. It costs around Y50 to get here in a taxi from Péngfēng Village.

Eating & Drinking

Péngfēng Village and Bianbian Jie are stuffed full of cheap restaurants.

STAR CAFE   Cafe **$**
(Tàibái Lóu; ☎ 773 9839; 23 Bianbian Jie; 边边街23号; coffee Y10-30, food & snacks Y5-36; ⏱ noon-late; 🛜) The coolest hang-out in town, Star Cafe has a good selection of fresh coffee, beers and spirits and some OK food. There's also patio seating by the river.

ℹ Information

An **ATM** at the park entrance accepts foreign cards as does the China Construction Bank and Agricultural Bank of China where you can also change cash.

ℹ Getting There & Away

AIR More than a dozen daily flights link Chéngdū with Jiǔzhàigōu Airport (officially called Jiǔhuáng Airport). Other direct flights include Běijīng, Shànghǎi, Hángzhōu, Chóngqìng, Kúnmíng, Xī'ān.

Buses to Jiǔzhàigōu (Y45, 1½ hours) meet arriving flights. A taxi from the airport is about Y200.

There's also an airport bus that stops first at Huánglóng National Park, waiting long enough for passengers to tour the park, and then continues on to Jiǔzhàigōu (Y100).

BUS The new tunnel-tastic route from Jiǔzhàigōu to Chéngdū, via Sōngpān, should be open by the time you read this and was reportedly set to cut journey times down to four or five hours! Check www.jiuzhai.com for the latest. At the time of research, buses leaving from Jiǔzhàigōu Bus Station include **Chéngdū** Y140, 10 hours (at 7.30am and 8am).

ℹ Getting Around

Hop-on, hop-off buses (Y90) travel within the park itself, and are pretty much essential because of the size of the park.

Outside the park, there's no public bus service. To get around you have to walk, cycle or take a taxi. Taxi fares begin at Y5.

The Silk Road

HIGHLIGHTS

1 **Labrang Monastery (p339)** Vast Tibetan monastery and sacred place of pilgrimage.

2 **Jiāyùguān Fort (p341)** Sublime Great Wall fort framed by snow-capped mountains.

3 **Mògāo Caves (p341)** China's most astonishing collection of Buddhist cave art.

4 **Kashgar (p342)** The Silk Road's most distinctive Uighur town.

Labrang Monastery, Xiàhé
PHOTOGRAPHER: MARTIN MOOS/LONELY PLANET IMAGES ©

Lánzhōu 兰州

0931 / POP 3.2 MILLION

This sprawling city along the southern banks of the Yellow River (Huáng Hé) is a major transport hub for the area.

If you need to spend some time here, visit the free **Gānsù Provincial Museum** (甘肃省博物馆; Gānsù Shěng Bówùguǎn; Xijin Xilu; audio guide for Silk Road exhibition Y10; 9am-5pm Tue-Sun), which has an intriguing collection of Silk Road artefacts.

The most practical area to base yourself is in the east, home of the train station; most budget hostels near the station won't accept foreigners. Try the **Zǐjīnghuā Jiǔdiàn** (紫荆花酒店; Bauhinia Hotel; 863 8918; 36 Tianshui Nanlu; 天水南路36号; d & tw Y388-400, tr Y380; ✳) or the **JJ Sun Hotel** (锦江阳光酒店; Jǐnjiāng Yángguāng Jiǔdiàn; 880 5511; www.jjsunhotel.com; 589 Donggang Xilu; 东岗西路589号; s/tw Y900/800; ✳ @).

The **Hézhèng Lù night market** (和政路夜市场入口; Hézhèng Lù Yèshìchǎng) is a terrific place for savouring the flavours of the northwest.

Among other cities, Lánzhōu has flights to Běijīng, Dūnhuáng, Shànghǎi and Xī'ān.

Lánzhōu has several bus stations, all with departures for Xīníng. The **main long-distance bus station** (长途车站; chángtú chēzhàn; Pingliang Lu) and the **south bus station** (汽车南站; qìchē nánzhàn; Langongping Lu) are the most useful. Buses to Xiàhé (Y45.50, six hours, three daily) depart from the south bus station in the far west of the city. Hidden off the main street, the **Tiānshuǐ bus station** (天水汽车站; Tiānshuǐ Qìchēzhàn; Tianshui Lu) has buses for eastern Gānsù.

The city is a major stop for trains heading to western China.

Xiàhé 夏河

0941 / POP 70,000

The alluring monastic town of Xiàhé attracts an astonishing band of visitors, from backpack-laden students, insatiable wanderers, shaven-headed Buddhist nuns, Tibetan nomads in their most colourful finest, camera-toting tour groups and dusty, itinerant beggars. Most visitors are rural Tibetans, whose purpose is to pray, prostrate themselves and seek spiritual fulfilment at holy Labrang monastery (Lābǔléng Sì). The area was long part of the Tibetan region of Amdo.

 Sights

LABRANG MONASTERY
Tibetan Monastery

(拉卜楞寺; Lābǔléng Sì; admission Y40) Even the most illustrious of China's incense-wreathed temples pale in comparison with the vast magnitude of this astounding complex.

Labrang monastery was founded in 1709 by Ngagong Tsunde (E'angzongzhe in Chinese), the first-generation Jamyang (a line of reincarnated rinpoches or living Buddhas ranking third in importance after the Dalai and Panchen Lamas), from nearby Gānjiā. At its peak the monastery housed nearly 4000 monks, but their ranks greatly declined during the Cultural Revolution. Numbers are recovering, and are currently restricted to 1200 monks, drawn from Qīnghǎi, Gānsù, Sìchuān and Inner Mongolia.

With its endless squeaking prayer wheels, hawks circling overhead and the deep throb of Tibetan trumpets resonating from the surrounding hills, Labrang is a monastery in the entire sense of the word. In addition to the chapels, residences, golden-roofed temple halls and living quarters for the monks, Labrang is also home to six *tratsang* (monastic colleges or institutes), exploring esoteric Buddhism, theology, medicine, astrology and law. Many of the chapel halls are illuminated in a yellow glow by yak-butter lamps, their strong-smelling fuel scooped out from voluminous tubs.

The only way to visit the interior of these buildings is with a tour, which generally includes the Institute of Medicine, the Manjushri Temple, the Serkung (Golden Temple) and the main Prayer Hall (Grand Sutra Hall), plus a museum of relics and yak-butter sculptures. English tours (Y40) of the monastery leave the ticket office

(售票处; Shòupiàochù) around 10.15am and 3.15pm.

The rest of the monastery can be explored by walking the *kora* (pilgrim circuit) and although many of the temple halls are padlocked shut, there are a couple of separate smaller chapels you can visit. Over three floors, the **Barkhang** (admission Y10; ☺9am-noon & 2-5pm) is the monastery's traditional printing press (with rows upon rows of over 20,000 wood blocks for printing).

Its interior illuminated by a combination of yak-butter lamps and electric light bulbs by the thousand, the 31m-tall **Gòngtáng Chörten** (贡唐宝塔; Gòngtáng Bǎotǎ; admission Y10) is a spectacular stupa with lovely interior murals and fantastic views from the roof.

The **Dewatsang Chapel** (德哇仓文殊佛殿; Déwācāng Wénshū Fódiàn; admission Y10), built in 1814, ranges over four floors and houses a vast 12m-statue of Manjushri (Wenshu) and thousands of Buddhas in cabinets around the walls. The **Hall of Hayagriva** (马头明王殿; Mǎtóu Míngwáng Diàn; Hall of Horsehead Buddha), destroyed during the Cultural Revolution, was reopened in 2007. Containing vivid and bright murals, the hall also encapsulates a startlingly fierce 12m-high effigy of Hayagriva with six arms and three faces.

The best morning views of the monastery come from the **Thangka Display Terrace**, a popular picnic spot, or the forested hills south of the main town.

The welcoming **nunnery** (*ani gompa* in Tibetan, 尼姑庵, *nígū'ān* in Chinese) is on the hill above the Tibetan part of town.

Next door is the small Nyingmapa (Red Hat) school monastery of **Ngakpa Gompa** (红教寺; Hóngjiào Sì; admission Y5) whose lay monks wear striking red and white robes and long, braided hair.

 **Festivals & Events**

The **Monlam (Great Prayer) Festival** starts three days after the Tibetan New Year, which is usually in February or early March. On the morning of the 13th day of

Xiàhé

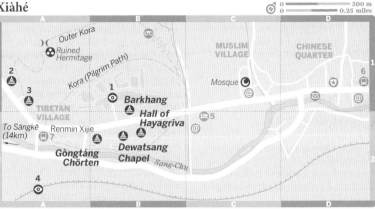

Xiàhé

◉ Top Sights
Barkhang..B1
Dewatsang Chapel............................B2
Gòngtáng Chörten..............................B2
Hall of Hayagriva.................................B2

◉ Sights
1 Monastery Ticket Office.....................B1
2 Ngakpa Gompa A1
3 Nunnery A1
4 Thangka Display Terrace....................A2

⊖ Sleeping
5 Overseas Tibetan
  Hotel...C2

Eating
Everest Café....................................(see 5)

Transport
6 Bus Station.......................................D1
7 Buses to Dájiǔtān A2

the festival, more than 100 monks carry a huge *thangka* (sacred painting on cloth) of the Buddha and unfurl it on the hill facing the monastery. This is accompanied by spectacular processions and prayer assemblies.

🛏 Sleeping

OVERSEAS TIBETAN HOTEL   Hotel   **$**
(华侨饭店; Huáqiáo Fàndiàn; ☏ 712 2642; www.overseastibetanhotel.com; 77 Renmin Xijie; 人民西街77号; dm Y20, d Y160-200; @)
Well-run and bustling place, owned by the energetic and bouncy Jesuit-educated Lohsang, a likeable Tibetan with faultless English who runs the *kora* most mornings. Dorms are simple, pricier doubles are well laid out and attractive, coming with bath. Also here is the Everest Cafe; as well

as internet (Y5 per hour), bike hire and a travel agency.

❶ Information

China Post (邮局; yóujú; ⊙ 8am-6pm)

Industrial & Commercial Bank of China (工商银行; Gōngshāng Yínháng; ICBC) Has an ATM and changes US dollars. No one in Xiàhé changes travellers cheques.

Public Security Bureau (公安局; PSB; Gōng'ānjú; ☏ 333 8010; ⊙ 9am-noon & 3-6pm Mon-Fri) Does not handle visa extensions; you'll need to go to Hézuò, Línxià or Sōngpān.

❶ Getting There & Away

Xiàhé is serviced by regular bus service. Most travellers head on to either Lánzhōu or Sìchuān. If you can't get a direct ticket to/from Lánzhōu, take a bus to Línxià and change there.

Jiāyùguān Fort 嘉峪关城楼

One of the classic images of western China, the **Jiāyùguān Fort** (Jiāyùguān Chénglóu; May-Oct/Nov-Apr Y100/80; 🕐8.30am-7.30pm) guards the pass between the snowcapped Qílián Shān peaks and Hēi Shān (Black Mountains) of the Mǎzōng Shān range.

Built in 1372, the fort was christened the 'Impregnable Defile Under Heaven'. Although the Chinese often controlled territory far beyond the Jiāyùguān area, this was the last major stronghold of imperial China – the end of the 'civilised world', beyond which lay only desert demons and the barbarian armies of Central Asia.

Admission also includes an excellent **Jiāyùguān Museum of the Great Wall** (🕐8.30am-7.30pm), with photos, artefacts, maps and Silk Road exhibits.

As it's only 5km west of the town of Jiāyùguān, it's possible to cycle here. A taxi trip to the fort costs about Y10.

Mògāo Caves 莫高窟

The Mògāo Caves (Mògāo Kū) are, simply put, one of the greatest repositories of Buddhist art in the world. At its peak, the site housed 18 monasteries, over 1400 monks and nuns, and countless artists, translators and calligraphers. The traditional date ascribed to the founding of the first cave is AD 366.

The caves fell into disuse after the collapse of the Yuan dynasty and were largely forgotten until the early 20th century when they were 'rediscovered' by a string of foreign explorers.

Entrance to the **caves** (📞886 9060; admission low/high season Y80/160; 🕐8.30am-6pm May-Oct, 9am-5.30pm Nov-Apr, tickets sold till one hour before closing) is strictly controlled – it's impossible to visit them on your own. The general admission ticket grants you a two-hour tour of 10 caves, including the infamous Library Cave (No 17) and a related exhibit containing rare fragments of manuscripts in classical Uighur and Manichean. Excellent English-speaking guides (Y20) are always available, and you can generally arrange tours in many other languages as well.

Of the 492 caves, 20 'open' caves are rotated fairly regularly, so recommendations are useless, but tours always include the two **big Buddhas**, 34.5m and 26m tall respectively. It's also possible to visit 12 of the more unusual caves for an additional fee; prices range from Y100 (No 217, early Tang) to Y500 (No 465, tantric art).

Note that if the weather is bad, the caves will be closed.

After the tour it's well worth visiting the **Dūnhuáng Research Centre**, where eight more caves, each representative of a different period, have been flawlessly reproduced, along with selected murals.

Dūnhuáng itself has some impressive, large sand dunes.

❶ Getting There & Away

The Mògāo Caves are 25km from Dūnhuáng. A green bus (one-way Y8) leaves at 8.30am from the intersection across from the Dunhuang Hotel; it returns at noon, which isn't really enough time at the caves. A return taxi costs from Y100 to Y150 for a day.

Singing Sands Mountain & Crescent Moon Lake 鸣沙山、月牙泉

Six kilometres south of Dūnhuáng at **Singing Sands Mountain** (Míngshā Shān; admission low/high season Y80/120; 🕐6am-10pm), the desert meets the oasis in most spectacular fashion. The climb to the top of the dunes – the highest peak swells to 1715m – is sweaty work, but the view across the undulating desert sands and green poplar trees below is awesome. Hire a pair of bright-orange shoe protectors (防沙靴; fángshāxuē; Y10) or just shake your shoes out later. At the base of the dunes lies a miraculous pond, known as **Crescent Moon Lake** (Yuèyáquán).

You can ride a bike to the dunes in around 20 minutes. Minibus 3 (Y1) shuttles between Dūnhuáng and the dunes from from 7.30am to 10pm, departing from opposite the Yǒuhǎo Bīnguan. A taxi costs Y10 one-way. Most people head out here at about 6pm when the weather starts to cool down.

Kashgar 喀什

📞 0998 / POP 340,000

The westernmost metropolis of China's New Frontier, Kashgar (Kāshí) has been the epicentre of cultural conflict and cooperation for over two millennia.

Modernity has swept in like a sandstorm. The highways and railroads that connect it to the rest of China have brought waves of Han migrant workers. Taxis and motorbikes are everywhere, and much of the Old City is being bulldozed in the name of 'progress'.

Yet the spirit of Kashgar lives on. The great-grandsons of craftsmen and artisans still hammer and chisel away in side alleys; everything sellable is hawked and haggled over; and not a few donkey carts still trundle their way through the crowds.

So soak it in for a few days, eat a few kebabs, chat with a local medicine man in a back alley.

 Sights

SUNDAY MARKET & LIVESTOCK MARKET
Bazaar

A Uighur primer: 'Boish-boish!' means 'Coming through!' You'd best hip yourself to this phrase, or risk being ploughed over by a push cart at the **Sunday Market** (星期天市场; Yengi Bazaar; Xīngqītiān Shìchǎng; Aizirete Lu; ⊙daily), which, despite its name, is open every day. A section on the northern side of the market contains everything of interest to foreign visitors, including the spice market, musical instruments, fur caps and kitschy souvenirs and carpets.

Southeast of the city is the **Livestock Market** (动物市场; Mal Bazaar; Dòngwù Shìchǎng), with an equal livestock-to-people ratio. It's only open on Sunday from 8am to 6pm and is busiest around lunchtime. It's jam-packed with tourists in the morning so visit in the late afternoon.

A taxi to the Sunday Market is Y5, and to the Livestock Market Y12. Otherwise, bus 8 runs to the Livestock Market from Id Kah Mosque.

OLD TOWN
Old Town

Sprawling on both sides of Jiefang Lu are roads full of Uighur shops and narrow alleys lined with adobe houses right out of an early-20th-century picturebook. Houses range in age from 50 to 500 years old and the lanes twist haphazardly through neighbourhoods where Kashgaris have lived and worked for centuries. It's a great place for strolling, peeking through gates, chatting to the locals and admiring the craftsmen as they create their wares.

Avoid the residential area to the east, which has been turned into a tourist trap and requires a ticket to enter.

At the eastern end of Seman Lu stands a 10m-high section of the old town walls, which are at least 500 years old.

ID KAH MOSQUE
Mosque

(艾提尕尔清真寺; Ài Tígǎ'ěr Qīngzhēn Sì; admission Y20) The yellow-tiled Id Kah Mosque, which dates from 1442, is the heart of the city – and not just geographically. Enormous, its courtyard and gardens can hold 20,000 people during the annual Qurban Baiyram celebrations. Non-Muslims may enter, but Fridays are usually no-go. Dress modestly, including a headscarf for women. Take off your shoes if entering carpeted areas and be discreet when taking photos.

Sleeping & Eating

INTERNATIONAL HOTEL
Hotel $$$

(Zhōngxīyà Guójì Dàjiǔdiàn; 📞 280 2222; fax 280 2266; 8 Renmin Donglu; 人民东路8号; tw incl breakfast Y598, discounts 20%; ❄ @) Next to Main Sq, this four-star hotel is the most upmarket option in Kashgar. Rooms from the upper floors have sweeping views of Kashgar.

ALTUN ORDA
Restaurant $$

(Jīnào'ěrdà Tèsècài; 📞 258 1555; 320 Renmin Xilu; dishes from Y25) A sumptuously designed restaurant, famous for its roasted mutton (Y55). Other tasty dishes include *ghoush nan* (meat pie) and *mirizlig manta* (pastry with raisins and walnuts).

ℹ️ Information

Money

The **Bank of China** (Zhōngguó Yínháng main branch; ⏰9.30am-1.30pm & 4-7.30pm; Main Sq) can change travellers cheques and cash and it has a 24-hour ATM. You can also sell yuan back into US dollars at the main branch's foreign-exchange desk if you have exchange receipts; this is a good idea if you are headed to Tashkurgan, where the bank hours are erratic.

Post

China Post (yóujú; 40 Renmin Xilu; ⏰9.30am-8pm) The 2nd floor handles all foreign letters and packages.

Public Security Bureau

PSB (Gōng'ānjú; 111 Youmulakexia Lu; ⏰9.30am-1.30pm & 4-8pm) Extend your visa here.

Dangers & Annoyances

Travellers have lost money or passports to pickpockets at the Sunday Market and even on local buses, so keep yours tucked away.

Some foreign women walking the streets alone have been sexually harassed. The Muslim Uighur women dress in long skirts and heavy stockings, and here one sees more veils of brown gauze hiding female faces. It is wise for women travellers to dress as would be appropriate in any Muslim country, covering arms and legs.

ℹ️ Getting There & Away

It's imperative when you buy tickets in Kashgar to verify 'which time' the ticket is for. It should be Běijīng time, but this isn't always the case.

AIR There are seven daily flights to Ürümqi (Y1230), which are sometimes cancelled due to poor turnout or sandstorms. A handy **Air Ticket Agent** (Jīpìao Dàishòuchù; 📞296 6666; 8 Renmin Donglu) is located at the International Hotel.

BUS Domestic buses use the **long-distance bus station** (kāshí zhàn; Tian Nanlu). Sleeper buses to Ürümqi (24 hours, Y229 to Y248) depart from the international bus station.

TRAIN Daily trains to Ürümqi depart at 8.18am and 1.16pm and take 32 and 24 hours, respectively. Lower-berth sleeper tickets on the faster train are Y345. You can buy tickets from the **train booking office** (huǒchē shòupiàochù; Tian Nanlu; commission Y5; ⏰9.30am-1pm & 3-7pm) at the main bus station.

ℹ️ Getting Around

TO/FROM THE AIRPORT The airport is 13km northeast of the town centre. One shuttle bus (Y10) meets all incoming flights. Just tell the driver your destination in town. A taxi should cost the same. From Main Sq, bus 2 goes directly to the airport.

BICYCLE A bicycle is the cheapest and most versatile way to get around Kashgar. Mountain bikes can be hired at the Chini Bagh Hotel for Y25/50 per half-/full day. The Giant Bike Shop (捷安特自行车行; Jíeāntè Zìxíngchē Háng; 📞640 1616; 37 Jiangkang Lu) also rents bikes for Y30 per day. It's located opposite the Three Fortune Hotel (三运宾馆).

BUS Useful bus routes are buses 2 (Jiefang Lu to the international bus station and the airport), 9 (international bus station to the Chini Bagh Hotel and Sèmǎn Bīnguǎn), 8 (Id Kah Mosque to the Livestock Market), 20 (Post Office to Abakh Hoja Tomb) and 28 (Id Kah Mosque to the train station). The fare is Y1.

TAXIS Taxis are metered and the flag fall is Y5.

China
In Focus

CHINA TODAY 346
China's economy is growing at a breathtaking pace but for many, little has changed and most Chinese are poor.

HISTORY 348
China has, for much of its history, been in conflict either internally or with outsiders.

FAMILY TRAVEL 358
Travelling with young children is challenging but rewards those with a sense of adventure.

THE PEOPLE OF CHINA 360
The Chinese are an exceptionally proud people: proud of their civilisation and history, their written language and achievements.

CHINESE CUISINE 366
Food plays a central and prominent role in both Chinese society and the national psyche.

ARTS & ARCHITECTURE 374
China is custodian of one of the world's richest cultural and artistic legacies.

RELIGION & BELIEFS 380
Religious belief in China is generally marked by great tolerance: although each faith is distinct, some crossover exists between Buddhism, Taoism and Confucianism.

CHINA'S LANDSCAPES 384
China is home to the world's highest mountain range, one of its hottest deserts, and a colossal web of waterways.

Miao girls in traditional costume celebrating Flower Dance Festival
PHOTOGRAPHER: KEREN SU/LONELY PLANET IMAGES ©

China Today

> **A certain fragility exists in China's increasing sense of confidence and growing self-assurance.**

Temple portico, Lángmùsì

belief systems
(% of population)

70 Atheist
22 Buddhist
4 Christian
1-2 Taoist
1-2 Islam

if China were 100 people

92 would be Han Chinese

8 would be ethnic minorities, eg Zhuang, Manchu, Uighur ect

population per sq km

= 820 people

Shanghai   Kunming   Hong Kong

China Superpower?

For decades, the world has been awe-struck by China's potential. Gazing into the statistics of growth, it's all too easy to fall in with those who perceive China as an emergent superpower. Books such as *When China Rules the World* by Martin Jacques triumphantly declare the establishment of a new world order.

China's apparent ability to shrug off the financial crisis through a massive stimulus package revealed a robust resilience to ride out the worst. Despite a slowing in the rate of economic growth, the Chinese economy continues to expand at a rate of around 10% and the growing middle-classes are upbeat. China has it sewn up, say the pundits.

From a Western perspective, there is understandable agreement. China can be both ultramodern (space missions, the Pǔdōng skyline, Maglev trains) and very powerful (a vast standing army, a gigantic economy), despite only three decades of growth. Naysayers discern a coming crash,

KRZYSZTOF DYDYNSKI/LONELY PLANET IMAGES ©

What the world saw was a vast and poorly-equipped mobilisation of one of China's greatest resources – its people – to tackle the spill. It worked, but it wasn't modern.

Harmony

The Chinese leadership under Hu Jintao has taken pains to stress 'harmony' throughout society, as part of China's formula of a 'peaceful rise'. Some analysts suggest that ostensible harmony is easier to achieve in authoritarian states like China, because the press is muffled, free speech disallowed and dissent quashed. The 11-year sentencing of Liu Xiaobo for his democratic agenda in Charter 08 is only harmonious in the sense he has been silenced, perhaps explaining why Běijīng reacted with such venom to his Nobel Peace Prize in 2010.

The laws of social entropy apply in China as elsewhere, however, and tensions inevitably ripple across the surface of society, or suddenly explode with eye-blinking ferocity. A series of bizarre kindergarten massacres in 2010 shocked the nation. Many Chinese called for greater understanding of those afflicted by mental-health problems, a malady that carries great stigma in Chinese society.

Ethnic relations remain prickly. The underlying tensions that ignited deadly riots in Tibet in 2008 and Xīnjiāng in 2009 are perhaps yet to be fully addressed.

A certain fragility exists in China's increasing sense of confidence and growing self-assurance. Some of this transmutes into a worrying nationalism, which is particularly appealing to young Chinese who perhaps lack other ideologies they can believe in.

initiated perhaps by the pricking of a property-market bubble, but just as many pundits insist the only way is up.

China's more balanced perspective is that it is a developing nation. It is wise to remember that China's per capita GDP puts it roughly on a level with Namibia's. China possesses colossal latent power by virtue of its size and huge population, but these dimensions have also created unequal growth. Inequality in China is among the most extreme in the world.

China dazzles in its big cities, but often lacks even the most basic equipment and systems. The Dàlián oil spill in July 2010 came in the same week that China overtook the US as the world's largest energy consumer – making the nation a superpower at least in oil dependency terms. But the ensuing clean-up operation saw a ragtag navy of fishing boats tackling the spill, as workers used their bare hands, straw mats, pots and stockings full of human hair to battle the oil.

History

Lion guarding bridges at Gate of Heavenly Peace, Tiān'ānmén Sq

MANFRED GOTTSCHALK/LONELY PLANET IMAG

The epic sweep of China's history paints a perhaps deceiving impression of long epochs of peace occasionally convulsed by break-up, internecine division or external attack. Yet China has, for much of its history, been in conflict either internally or with outsiders. Although China's size and shape has also continuously changed – from tiny beginnings by the Yellow River to the subcontinent of today – an uninterrupted thread of history runs through China from its earliest roots to the full flowering of the Chinese civilisation.

From Oracle Bones to Confucius

The earliest 'Chinese' dynasty, the Shang, was long considered apocryphal; however, archaeological evidence (unearthed cattlebones and turtle shells covered in mysterious scratches, recognised as an early form of Chinese writing) proved that a society known as the Shang developed in central China from around 1766 BC.

c 4000 BC

Archaeological evidence for the first settlements along the Yellow River (Huáng Hé).

Sometime between 1050 and 1045 BC, a neighbouring group known as the Zhou conquered Shang territory. The Zhou was one of many states competing for power in the next few hundred years, but developments during this period created some of the key sources of Chinese culture that would last till the present day. A constant theme of the first millennium BC was conflict, particularly the periods known as the 'Spring and Autumn' (722–481 BC) and 'Warring States' (475–221 BC).

From this disorder emerged the thinking of Confucius (551–479 BC), whose system of thought and ethics underpinned Chinese culture for 2500 years. Confucius' desire for an ordered and ethical world seems a far cry from the warfare of the time he lived in.

Early Empires

The Warring States period ended decisively in 221 BC when the Qin kingdom conquered other states in the central Chinese region and Qin Shi Huang declared himself emperor. Later histories portrayed Qin Shi Huang as particularly cruel and tyrannical, but Qin Shi Huang also oversaw vast public-works projects, including walls built by some 300,000 men, connecting defences into what would become the Great Wall. He unified the currency, measurements and written language, providing the basis for a cohesive state.

The dynasty was overturned by a peasant, Liu Bang, who rose up and founded the Han dynasty, a dynasty so important that the name Han still refers to ethnic Chinese. Critical to the centralisation of power, Emperor Wu (140–87 BC) institutionalised Confucian norms in government. Promoting merit as well as order, he was the first leader to experiment with examinations for entry into the bureaucracy, but his dynasty was plagued by endemic economic problems and the inability to exercise control over a growing empire, which led to the collapse of the Han.

Disunity Restored

Between the early 3rd and late 6th centuries AD, north China witnessed a succession of rival kingdoms vying for power while a potent division formed between north and south. Riven by warfare, the north was controlled by non-Chinese rule, most successfully by the Northern Wei dynasty (386–534). A succession of rival regimes followed until nobleman Yang Jian (d 604) reunified China under the fleeting Sui dynasty (581–618). His son Sui Yangdi contributed greatly to the unification of south and north through construction of the Grand Canal, which was later extended and remained the empire's most important communication route between south and north until the late 19th century. After instigating three unsuccessful incursions onto Korean soil, resulting

551 BC
The birth of Confucius. His thoughts were collected in *The Analects* – deeply influential ideas of an ethical, ordered society.

214 BC
Emperor Qin indentures thousands of labourers to link existing city walls into one Great Wall.

c 100 BC
Buddhism first arrives in China from India.

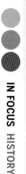

The Best Confucius Temples

1 Confucius Temple, Qūfù p172

2 Confucius Temple, Běijīng p79

3 Confucius Temple, Píngyáo p155

in disastrous military setbacks, Sui Yangdi faced revolt on the streets and was assassinated in 618 by one of his high officials.

The Tang

The Chinese nostalgically regard the Tang (618–907) as their cultural zenith. The output of the Tang poets is still regarded as China's finest, as is Tang sculpture, while its legal code became a standard for the whole East Asian region.

The Tang was founded by the Sui general Li Yuan, his achievements consolidated by his son Taizong (626–49). Cháng'ān (modern Xī'ān) became the world's most dazzling capital, with its own cosmopolitan foreign quarter, a population of a million, a market where merchants from as far away as Persia mingled with locals and an astonishing city wall that eventually enveloped 83 sq km.

Taizong was succeeded by Chinese history's sole reigning woman emperor, Wu Zetian (625–705). Under her leadership the empire reached its greatest extent, spreading well north of the Great Wall and far west into inner Asia. Her strong promotion of Buddhism, however, alienated her from the Confucian officials and in 705 she was forced to abdicate in favour of Xuanzong.

Xuanzong appointed minorities from the frontiers as generals, in the belief that they were so far removed from the political system and society that ideas of rebellion or coups would not enter their minds. Nevertheless, it was An Lushan, a general of Sogdian-Turkic parentage, who took advantage of his command in north China to make a bid for imperial power. The fighting lasted from 755 to 763, and although An Lushan was defeated, the Tang's control over China was destroyed forever.

In its last century, the Tang withdrew from its former openness, turning more strongly to Confucianism, while Buddhism was outlawed by Emperor Wuzong from 842 to 845. The Tang decline was marked by imperial frailty, growing insurgencies, upheaval and chaos.

Open Markets

Further disunity – the fragmentary-sounding Five Dynasties or Ten Kingdoms period – followed the fall of the Tang until the Northern Song dynasty (960–1127) was established. The Song dynasty existed in a state of constant conflict with its northern neighbours, being eventually driven from Kāifēng to its southern capital in Hángzhōu for the period of the Southern Song (1127–1279).

874 AD
The Huang Chao rebellion breaks out, which will help reduce the Tang empire to chaos and lead to the fall of the capital in 907.

1215
Genghis Khan conquers Běijīng as part of his creation of a massive Eurasian empire under Mongol rule. Hall of Preserving Harmony, Forbidden City (right)

MANFRED GOTTSCHALK/LONELY PLANET IMAGES ©

The period was culturally rich and economically prosperous. The full institution of a system of examinations for entry into the Chinese bureaucracy was brought to fruition during the Song. Young Chinese men sat tests on the Confucian classics, obtaining office if successful.

China's economy prospered during the Song, as cash crops and handicraft products became far more central to the economy.

Mongols to Ming

Genghis Khan (1167–1227) began his rise to power, turning his sights on China; he took Běijīng in 1215, destroying and rebuilding it; his successors seized Hángzhōu, the Southern Song capital, in 1276. The court fled and, in 1279, Southern Song resistance finally expired. Kublai Khan, grandson of Genghis, now reigned over all of China as emperor of the Yuan dynasty. Under Kublai, the entire population was divided into categories of Han, Mongol and foreigner, with the top administrative posts reserved for Mongols, even though the examination system was revived in 1315. An innovation was the use of paper money, although overprinting created a problem with inflation.

The Mongols ultimately proved less able at governance than warfare, their empire succumbing to rebellion within a century and eventual vanquishment. Ruling as Ming emperor Hongwu, Zhu Yuanzhang established his capital in Nánjīng, but by the early 15th century the court had begun to move back to Běijīng where a hugely ambitious reconstruction project was inaugurated by Emperor Yongle (r 1403–24), building the Forbidden City and devising the layout of the city we see today.

In 1405 Yongle launched the first of seven great maritime expeditions. Led by the eunuch general Zheng He (1371–1433), the fleet consisted of more than 60 large vessels and 255 smaller ones, carrying nearly 28,000 men. The fourth and fifth expeditions departed in 1413 and 1417, and travelled as far as the present Middle East. The emperors after Yongle however, had little interest in continuing the voyages, and China dropped anchor on its global maritime explorations.

The Great Wall was re-engineered and clad in brick while ships also arrived from Europe, presaging an overseas threat that would develop from entirely different directions. Traders were quickly followed by missionaries, and the Jesuits, led by the formidable Matteo Ricci, made their way inland and established a presence at court.

The Ming was eventually undermined by internal power struggles. Natural disasters, including drought and famine, combined with a menace from the north. The Manchu, a nomadic warlike people, saw the turmoil within China and invaded.

The Qing: the Path to Dynastic Dissolution

After conquering just a small part of China and assuming control in the disarray, the Manchu named their new dynasty the Qing (1644–1911). Like the Mongols before them, the conquering Manchu found themselves in charge of a civilisation whose government they had defeated, but whose cultural power far exceeded their own. They

1406
Ming Emperor Yongle begins construction of the 800 buildings of the Forbidden City.

1644
Běijīng falls to peasant rebel Li Zicheng. Last Ming emperor Chongzhen hangs himself in Jīngshān Park; Qing dynasty is established.

1842
The Treaty of Nánjīng ends the first Opium War. China is forced to hand over Hong Kong island and open five ports to foreign trade.

The Best Ruins

1 Ruins of the Church of St Paul, p295

2 Jiànkòu Great Wall, p116

3 Old Summer Palace, p88

4 Ming City Wall Ruins Park, p75

enforced strict rules of social separation between the Han and Manchu, and tried to maintain – not always very successfully – a culture that reminded the Manchu of their nomadic warrior past. The Qing flourished most greatly under three emperors who ruled for a total of 135 years: Kangxi, Yongzheng and Qianlong.

Much of the map of China that we know today derives from the Qing period. Territorial expansion and expeditions to regions of Central Asia spread Chinese power and culture further than ever.

War & Reform

For the Manchu, the single most devastating incident was not the Opium Wars, but the far more destructive anti-Qing Taiping War of 1856–64, an insurgency motivated partly by a foreign credo (Christianity). The Qing eventually reconquered the Taiping capital at Nánjīng, but upwards of 20 million Chinese died in the uprising.

The events that finally brought the dynasty down, however, came in quick succession. Foreign imperialist incursions continued and Western powers nibbled away at China's coastline. Hong Kong was a British colony and Macau was administered by the Portuguese. Attempts at self-strengthening – involving attempts to produce armaments and Western-style military technology – were dealt a brutal blow by the Sino-Japanese War of 1894–95. Not only was Chinese influence in Korea lost, but Taiwan was ceded to Japan.

One of the boldest proposals for reform, which drew heavily on the Japanese model, was the program put forward in 1898 by reformers including the political thinker Kang Youwei (1858–1927). However, in September 1898 the reforms were abruptly halted, as the Dowager Empress Cixi, fearful of a coup, placed the emperor under house arrest and executed several of the leading advocates of change. In a major misjudgement, the dynasty declared in June that it supported the Boxers in their rebellion. Eventually, a multinational foreign army forced its way into China and defeated the uprising that had besieged the foreign Legation Quarter in Běijīng. The imperial powers then demanded huge financial compensation from the Qing.

The Cantonese revolutionary Sun Yatsen (1866–1925) remains one of the few modern historical figures respected in both China and Taiwan. Sun and his Revolutionary League made multiple attempts to undermine Qing rule in the late 19th century, raising sponsorship and support from a wide-ranging combination of the Chinese diaspora, the newly emergent middle class, and traditional secret societies.

1904–05

The Russo-Japanese War is fought entirely on Chinese territory. Japan's victory is the first by an Asian power over a European one.

1911

Revolution spreads across China as local governments withdraw support for the dynasty, and instead support a republic.

1925

The shooting of striking factory workers in Shànghǎi by foreign-controlled police (the 'May Thirtieth Incident') fires nationalism.

The end of the Qing dynasty arrived swiftly. A local uprising in the city of Wǔhàn in October 1911 was discovered early, leading the rebels to take over command in the city and declare independence from the Qing dynasty. Within a space of days, then weeks, most of China's provinces did likewise. Provincial assemblies across China declared themselves in favour of a republic, with Sun Yatsen (who was not even in China at the time) as their candidate for president.

The Republic: Instability & Ideas

The Republic of China lasted less than 40 years on the mainland with the country under threat from what many described as 'imperialism from without and warlordism from within'. There was breathing room for new ideas and culture, yet the period was marked by repeated disasters.

Sun Yatsen returned to China and only briefly served as president, before having to make way for militarist leader Yuan Shikai. In 1912 China held its first general election, and it was Sun's newly established Kuomintang (Nationalist; Guómíndǎng, literally 'Party of the National People') party that emerged as the largest grouping. Parliamentary democracy did not last long, as the Kuomintang itself was outlawed by

The Great Wall, Jīnshānlǐng (p115)

PHOTOGRAPHER: DIANA MAYFIELD/LONELY PLANET IMAGES ©

1937

On 7 July the Japanese and Chinese clash at Wanping, sparking conflict between China and Japan which only ends in 1945.

1946

Communists and the Kuomintang fail to form a coalition government, plunging China back into civil war.

1949

Mao Zedong stands on top of the Gate of Heavenly Peace in Běijīng on 1 October, and announces the creation of the PRC.

Yuan, and Sun fled to exile in Japan. However, after Yuan's death in 1916, the country split into rival regions ruled by militarist warlord-leaders. Also, in reality, the foreign powers still had control over much of China's domestic and international situation. The city of Shànghǎi became the focal point for the contradictions of Chinese modernity. The racism that accompanied imperialism was visible every day, as Europeans kept themselves separate from the Chinese. Amid the glamour of modernity, its inequalities and squalor also inspired the first congress of the Chinese Communist Party (CCP).

Double-dealing by the Western Allies and Chinese politicians who had made secret deals with Japan led to some 3000 students gathering in central Běijīng in 1919 and marching to the house of a Chinese government minister closely associated with Japan. Once there, they broke in and destroyed the house. This event, over in a few hours, became a legend.

The student demonstration came to symbolise a much wider shift in Chinese society and politics. The May Fourth Movement, as it became known, was associated closely with the New Culture. In literature, a May Fourth generation of authors wrote works attacking the Confucianism that they felt had brought China to its current crisis, and explored new issues of sexuality and self-development while the CCP was founded in the intellectual turmoil of the movement.

The Northern Expedition & the Long March

After years of vainly seeking international support for his cause, Sun Yatsen found allies in the newly formed Soviet Russia. The Soviets ordered the fledgling CCP to ally itself with the Kuomintang. Their alliance was attractive to Sun: the Soviets would provide political training, military assistance and finance. From their base in Guǎngzhōu, the Kuomintang and CCP trained together from 1923, in preparation for their mission to reunite China.

Sun died of cancer in 1925. Under Soviet advice, the Kuomintang and CCP prepared for their 'Northern Expedition', the big 1926 push north that was supposed to finally unite China. The most powerful military figure turned out to be an officer from Zhèjiāng named Chiang Kaishek (1887–1975). Chiang moved steadily forward and finally captured Shànghǎi in March 1927. Using local thugs and soldiers, Chiang organised a lightning strike by rounding up CCP activists and union leaders in Shànghǎi and killing thousands of them.

Chiang Kaishek's Kuomintang government officially came to power in 1928 through a combination of military force and popular support. Marked by corruption, it ruthlessly suppressed political dissent. Yet Chiang's government also kick-started a major industrialisation effort, greatly augmented China's transport infrastructure, and successfully renegotiated what many Chinese called 'unequal treaties' with Western powers.

A major centre of CCP activity was the base area in impoverished Jiāngxī province. However, by 1934, Chiang's previously ineffective 'Extermination Campaigns' were making the CCP's position in Jiāngxī untenable. The CCP commenced their Long

1962

Mass starvation from the Great Leap Forward; Liu Shaoqi and Deng Xiaoping reintroduce market reforms leading to condemnation.

1966

The Cultural Revolution breaks out. The movement is marked by a fetish for violence as a catalyst for transforming society.

1972

US President Richard Nixon visits China, marking a major rapprochement and the start of full diplomatic relations.

March, travelling over 6400km. Four thousand of the original 80,000 communists who set out eventually arrived, exhausted, in Shaanxi (Shǎnxī) province in the northwest.

Events came to a head in December 1936, when the militarist leader of Manchuria (General Zhang Xueliang) and the CCP kidnapped Chiang. As a condition of his release, Chiang agreed to an openly declared United Front: the Kuomintang and communists would put aside their differences and join forces against Japan.

War & the Kuomintang

The Japanese invasion of China, which began in 1937, was merciless, with the notorious Nanjing Massacre just one of a series of war crimes committed by the Japanese Army. The government had to operate in exile from the far southwestern hinterland of China as China's eastern seaboard was lost to Japanese occupation.

In China itself, it is now acknowledged that both the Kuomintang and the communists had important roles to play in defeating Japan. Chiang, not Mao, was the internationally acknowledged leader of China during this period, and despite his government's multitude flaws, he maintained resistance to the end. The communists had an important role as guerrilla fighters, but did far less fighting in battle than the Kuomintang.

The real winners from WWII, however, were the communists. By the end of the war with Japan, the communist areas had expanded massively, with some 900,000 troops in the Red Army, and party membership at a new high of 1.2 million.

The Kuomintang and communists plunged into civil war in 1946 and after three long years the CCP won. On 1 October 1949 in Běijīng, Mao declared the establishment of the People's Republic of China.

Mao's China

Mao's China desired, above all, to exercise ideological control over its population.

The US refused to recognise the new state at all. The 1950s marked the high point of Soviet influence on Chinese politics and culture. However, the decade also saw rising tension between the Chinese and the Soviets, fuelled in part by Khrushchev's condemnation of Stalin (which Mao took, in part, as a criticism of his own cult of personality).

Mao's experiences had convinced him that only violent change could shake up the relationship between landlords and their tenants, or capitalists and their employees, in a China that was still highly traditional. The first year of the regime saw some 40% of the land redistributed to poor peasants. At the same time, some one million or so people condemned as 'landlords' were persecuted and killed.

As relations with the Soviets broke down in the mid-1950s, the CCP leaders' thoughts turned to economic self-sufficiency. Mao, supported by Politburo colleagues, proposed the policy known as the Great Leap Forward (Dàyuèjìn), a highly ambitious plan to harness the power of socialist economics to boost production of steel, coal and electricity.

1976
Mao Zedong dies, aged 83. The Gang of Four are arrested by his successor and put on trial.

1989
Student demonstrations in Tiān'ānmén Sq end tragically.
Statue, Tiān'ānmén Sq (left)

GLENN BEANLAND/LONELY PLANET IMAGES ©

The Best Foreign Concessions & Colonies

1 Shànghǎi, French Concession, p201

2 Gǔlàng Yǔ, near Xiàmén, p322

3 Qīngdǎo, p176

4 Hong Kong, p252

5 Macau, p291

However, the Great Leap Forward was a monumental failure. Its lack of economic realism caused a massive famine and at least 20 million deaths.

Cultural Revolution

Mao had decided that a massive campaign of ideological renewal, in which he would attack his own party, must be launched.

Still the dominant figure in the CCP, Mao used his prestige to undermine his own colleagues. Top leaders suddenly disappeared from sight, only to be replaced by unknowns, such as Mao's wife Jiang Qing and her associates, later dubbed the 'Gang of Four'. Meanwhile, an all-pervasive cult of Mao's personality took over. One million youths at a time, known as Red Guards, would flock to hear Mao in Tiān'ānmén Sq. Immense violence permeated throughout society: teachers, intellectuals and landlords were killed in their thousands.

Worried by the increasing violence, the army forced the Red Guards off the streets in 1969. And the early 1970s saw a remarkable rapprochement between the US and China. Secretive diplomatic manoeuvres led, eventually, to the official visit of US President Richard Nixon to China in 1972, which began the reopening of China to the West. Slowly, the Cultural Revolution began to cool down, but its brutal legacy survives today.

Reform

Mao died in 1976, to be succeeded by the little-known Hua Guofeng (1921–2008). Within two years, Hua had been outmanoeuvred by the greatest survivor of 20th-century Chinese politics, Deng Xiaoping. Deng enlisted a policy slogan originally invented by Mao's pragmatic prime minister, Zhou Enlai – the 'Four Modernisations'. The party's task would be to set China on the right path in four areas: agriculture, industry, science and technology, and national defence.

The first, highly symbolic move of the 'reform era' (as the post-1978 period is known) was the breaking down of the collective farms. Farmers were able to sell a proportion of their crops on the free market, and urban and rural areas were also encouraged to establish small local enterprises. As part of this encouragement of entrepreneurship, Deng designated four areas on China's coast as Special Economic Zones (SEZs).

1997
Hong Kong is returned to the PRC.

2001
China joins the World Trade Organization, giving it a seat at the top table that decides global norms on economics and finance.

2008
Běijīng hosts the 2008 Summer Olympic Games and Paralympics, burnishing China's image overseas.

The new freedoms that the urban middle classes enjoyed created the appetite for more. After the death in April 1989 of relative liberal Hu Yaobang, Tiān'ānmén Sq was the scene of an unprecedented demonstration. At its height, nearly a million Chinese workers and students, in a rare cross-class alliance, filled the space in front of the Gate of Heavenly Peace. On the nights of 3 and 4 June, the military were enlisted to quell the demonstration, which ended tragically.

For some three years, China's politics were almost frozen, but in 1992 Deng undertook what Chinese political insiders called his 'southern tour', or *nánxún*. By visiting Shēnzhèn, Deng indicated that the economic policies of reform were not going to be abandoned.

21st-Century China

Since 2002, President Hu Jintao and prime minister Wen Jiabao have made more efforts to deal with the inequality and poverty in the countryside, but this remains a major concern, along with reform of the CCP itself.

China has placed scientific development at the centre of its quest for growth, sending students abroad in their tens of thousands to study science and technology and develop a core of scientific knowledge within China itself.

As a permanent member of the UN Security Council and in its quest for economic and diplomatic influence in Africa and South America, China has a powerful international role. It is, however, hesitant to assume a more influential position in international affairs. China's preference for remaining neutral but friendly and businesslike may also be tested: crises such as the ever-volatile North Korean situation and Iran's nuclear ambitions mean that China is having to make hard choices.

2009
July riots in Ürümqi leave hundreds dead as inter-ethnic violence flares between Uighurs and Han Chinese.

2010
Yushu earthquake on 14 April kills or injures thousands of people; the largest ever World Expo is held in Shànghǎi in spring.

2011
The 100th anniversary of the Xinhai Revolution and the founding of the Republic of China is celebrated on 10 October.

Family Travel

China is full of potential as a travel destination for families, but this potential remains largely undeveloped. As parents, you will need to be adventurous and should treat any journey to China with your children as an educational experience. If you expect to find the kind of kid-friendly service that you find in the West, you will arrive unprepared.

The Basics

Foreign children will be more comfortable in the large cities of Hong Kong, Macau, Běijīng and Shànghǎi, where there is a service industry (hotels, restaurants and sights) attuned to the needs of parents, but in smaller towns and rural areas, little provision is made.

Travelling long distances with children in China has its own challenges. Hiring a car is now possible, but it remains an unrealistic way of seeing China, partly because the car-hire network remains in its infancy. Trains are fun, but are often crowded; on long-distance trains, food options are limited. Long-distance buses are also crowded and seatbelts often not provided.

Food is another challenge. While larger towns will have Western restaurants, outside of fast food, smaller towns may only have a Chinese menu (fine for adults, not necessarily for kids).

Sightseeing also needs to be varied. Teenagers may not share your enthusiasm for China's ancient sights, but they may fall for the great scenic outdoors. Again, the larger cities are much better provided with museums aimed at children.

Safety

The Chinese love children and pay them a lot of attention; expect your children to receive even more attention for the colour of their hair or eyes.

China is generally very safe for non-Chinese children. Trafficking in Chinese children in China does occur and is a source of anxiety for Chinese mothers, but non-Chinese-looking children are generally left alone. Your biggest concerns may be what your children eat and keeping an eye on them when they cross the road.

Practicalities

For train travel, children shorter than 1.4m can get a hard sleeper for 75% of the full price or a half-price hard seat. Children shorter than 1.1m ride free, but you have to hold them the entire journey.

Many sights and museums have children's admission prices, which usually apply to children under 1.3m in height. Infants under the age of two fly for 10% of the full airfare, while children between the ages of two and 11 pay half the full price for domestic flights and 75% of the adult price for international flights.

Strollers are hard to come by, and you may wish to take your own. If so, prepare for the inconvenience of uneven pavements. Escalators at metro stations are often up only.

Always ensure that your child carries a form of ID and a hotel card in case they get lost.

Baby food and milk powder are widely available in supermarkets, as are basics like nappies, baby wipes, bottles, medicine, dummies and other paraphernalia. Few restaurants have highchairs or kids menus, and finding baby-changing rooms is next to impossible. Hotels with cots are also rare.

Ask a doctor specialising in travel medicine for information on recommended immunisations for your child.

The Best
For Children

1 Star Ferry (p282)

2 Shànghǎi History Museum (p203)

3 Acrobatics Show (p213)

4 Yángshuò (p311)

5 Qīngdǎo's beaches (p179)

6 Peak Tram (p268)

The People of China

Despite being the world's most populous nation – stamping ground of roughly one-fifth of humanity – China is often regarded as being homogenous. This is probably because Han Chinese – the majority ethnic type in this energetic and bustling nation – make up over nine-tenths of the population. But as with China's mystifying linguistic babel, you only have to get your travelling shoes on to encounter a vibrant patchwork of different ethnicities.

Ethnic Make-up

Han Chinese – the predominant clan in China and the nation's 56th recognised ethnic group – make up the lion's share of China's people, 92% of the total figure. Because Han civilisation is the dominant culture of the land, when we think of China – from its writing system to its visual arts, calligraphy, literature and politics – we associate it with Han culture.

The Han Chinese are distributed throughout China but predominantly concentrate along the Yellow River, Yangzi River and Pearl River basins. A glance however, at the map of China reveals that these core heartland regions of Han China are fragments of contemporary China's vast expanse. The colossal regions of Tibet, Qīnghǎi, Xīnjiāng, Inner Mongolia and the three provinces of the northeast (Manchuria) are all historically non-Han regions, areas of which remain essentially non-Han today.

Many of these regions are peopled by some of the remaining 8% of the population: China's 55 other ethnic minorities, known collectively as *shǎoshù mínzú* (少数民族; minority nationals). The largest minority groups in China include the Zhuang (壮族), Manchu (满族), Miao (苗族), Uighur (维吾尔族), Yi (彝族), Tujia (土家族), Tibetan (藏族), Hui (回族), Mongolian (蒙古族), Buyi (布依族), Dong (侗族), Yao (瑶族), Korean (朝鲜族), Bai (白族), Hani (哈尼族), Li (黎族), Kazak (哈萨克族) and Dai (傣族). Population sizes differ dramatically, from the sizeable Zhuang in Guǎngxī to minute numbers of Menba (门巴族) in Tibet. Ethnic labelling can be reasonably fluid: the Hakka (客家) were once regarded as a separate minority, but are today considered Han Chinese.

China's minorities tend to cluster along border regions, in the northwest, the west, the southwest, the north and northeast of China, but are also distributed throughout the land. Some minority peoples are found in one area alone (such as the Hani in Yúnnán); others, such as the Muslim Hui, are found across China.

Wedged into the southwest corner of China between Tibet, Myanmar (Burma), Vietnam and Laos, fecund Yúnnán province alone is home to over 20 ethnic groups, making it one of the most ethnically diverse and culturally rich provinces in the country.

China Demographics

- **Population** 1.33 billion
- **Birth Rate** 12.17 births per 1000 people
- **Percentage of people over 65 years of age** 8.6%
- **Urbanisation rate** 2.7%
- **Sex Ratio (under age of 15)** 1.17 (boys to girls)
- **Life expectancy** 74.5 years

The Chinese Character

As a race of people, the Han Chinese are quite reserved. Shaped by Confucian principles, the Chinese of today's China are thoughtful and discreet, but also highly pragmatic and practically minded. Conservative and somewhat introverted, they favour dark clothing over bright or loud colours.

The Chinese (apart from the Shanghainese, some Chinese may insist) are particularly generous. Don't be surprised if a Chinese person you have just met on a train invites you for a meal in the dining carriage. They will insist on paying, in which case do not attempt to thwart their efforts. The Chinese also simply adore children and are particularly warm to them: don't be too surprised if you see a Chinese man pinch the buttocks of a small boy (it's not rare to see children naked from the waist down)! It's all part of an innocent playfulness that is highly endearing.

A sense of subtlety can be also said to pervade the Chinese character but the Chinese are also an exceptionally proud people. They are proud of their civilisation and history, their written language and of their inventions and achievements. This pride rarely comes across as arrogance or self-assurance, however, and may be tinged with a lack of confidence. The Chinese may, for example, be very proud of the railway to Tibet or of China's newfound world status, but there is little self-satisfaction in the nation's opaque political culture or manifest corruption.

The modern Chinese character has been shaped by recent political realities and while Chinese people have always been reserved and circumspect, in today's China they may appear even more careful and prudent. While Chinese people are often very honest and frank about certain things (asking your age and how much you

earn or expressing a dislike for Japan), they can be painfully tight-lipped on other subjects, such as the relevance of free speech in a China context. This can be as much due to shame (and therefore an unwillingness to discuss it with foreigners) as due to caution and circumspection. Chinese are often very uncomfortable discussing these things if other Chinese are listening. All of this makes the Chinese sometimes appear very complicated indeed, despite their reputation for being straightforward.

Women in China

Chairman Mao once said that women hold up half the sky. Women in today's China officially share complete equality with men; however, as with other nations that profess sexual equality, the reality is often far different. Chinese women do not enjoy strong political representation; the Chinese Communist Party (CCP) is a largely patriarchal organisation. Iconic political leaders from the early days of the CCP were all men and the influential echelons of the party remain a largely male domain.

High-profile, successful Chinese businesswomen are very much in the public eye. But the relative lack of career opportunities for females in other fields also indicates a continuing bias against women in employment. Women in today's China enjoy more freedom than ever before and a revolution in their status has taken place since 1949, but sexual discrimination in the workplace survives.

In traditional China, an ideal woman's behaviour was governed by the 'three obediences and four virtues' of Confucian (p381) thought. The three obediences were submission to the father before marriage, husband after marriage and sons in the case of widows. The four virtues were propriety in behaviour, demeanour, speech and employment.

Women practising taichi with fans on the Bund, Shànghǎi
PHOTOGRAPHER: JOHN BANAGAN/LONELY PLANET IMAGES ©

The CCP after 1949 tried to outlaw old customs and put women on equal footing with men. They abolished arranged marriages and encouraged women to get an education and join the workforce. Pictures from this time show sturdy, ruddy-cheeked women with short cropped hair and overalls, a far cry from the corpulent palace ladies of the Tang or the pale, willowy beauties featured in later traditional paintings. In their quest for equality, the CCP successfully desexualised women in the 1950s and 1960s, manufacturing a further form of imprisonment that contemporary Chinese women regard with disdain.

Women's improved social status today has meant that more women are putting off marriage until their late 20s, instead choosing to focus on education and career opportunities. This has been enhanced by the rapid rise in house prices, further encouraging women to leave marriage (and having children) till a later age. Equipped with a good education and a high salary, they have high expectations of their future husbands (some of whom may be wary of courting girls with doctorates, in case they are outshone). Premarital sex and cohabitation before marriage are increasingly common in larger cities and lack the stigma they had several years ago.

Again, there is a strong rural-urban divide and all is not well down on the farm. Urban women are far more optimistic and freer, while women from rural areas, where traditional beliefs are at their strongest, fight an uphill battle against discrimination. Rural China is heavily weighted against girls; a marked preference for baby boys over baby girls exists. This has resulted in an imbalance between China's population of men to women, a consequence of female foeticide, selective abortions and even infanticide. China's women are more likely to commit suicide than men (bucking the global trend), while rural Chinese women are up to five times as likely to kill themselves. When one considers the fact that most of the Chinese population lives in rural areas, the problem comes into frightening perspective.

China's One-Child Policy

The one-child policy (actually a misnomer) was railroaded into effect in 1979 in a bid to keep China's population to one billion by the year 2000; the latest government estimate claims the population will peak at 1.5 billion in 2033. The policy was originally harshly implemented but rural revolt led to a softer stance; nonetheless, it has generated much bad feeling between local officials and the rural population. All non-Han minorities are exempt from the one-child policy.

Rural families are now allowed to have two children if the first child is a girl, but some have upwards of three or four kids. Additional children often result in fines and families having to shoulder the cost of education themselves, without government assistance. Official stated policy opposes forced abortion or sterilisation, but allegations of coercion continue as local officials strive to meet population targets. The government is taking steps to punish officials who force women to undergo inhumane sterilisation procedures. Families who do abide by the one-child policy will often go to great lengths to make sure their child is male. In parts of China, this is creating a serious imbalance of the sexes – in 2007, 111 boys were born for every 100 girls. That could mean that by 2020, over 30 million Chinese men may be unable to find a wife.

The law can also be vicious, with handcuffed prostitutes shamefully paraded in public. Very few women smoke in public and do so in private, revealing a taboo in this area.

Chinese suspicions of most '-isms' and avoidance of collective action not proscribed by the authorities perhaps contribute to the scarcity of a feminist movement in China.

Lifestyle

Economic liberalisation measures mean that the people of China today enjoy a far more diverse array of lifestyles than at any other time in their history. Young, ambitious Chinese are presented with a totally modern and sophisticated set of urban living choices. Unlike the West, very few young Chinese are idealists driven by anti-establishment goals, so the generation may appear brash and materialistic. This mindset is not their fault, but a reflection of government policy to create – through propaganda and education – a generation that is largely in agreement with its mandate. It is a crucial element in the 'harmonious' society that Hu Jintao is attempting to mould. As such, this lifestyle may look Western in appearance, but in fact is very different.

Beyond ethnic differences, the big divide is between the city and the countryside. The culture of the big city – with its bars, white-collar jobs, desirable schools, dynamism and opportunities – stands in marked contrast to rural China, where little may have changed in the past three decades. Many of China's cities – take Tiānjīn for example – are clearly international in aspiration, but the countryside remains deeply poor, especially in the southwest. China calls itself a 'developing country', which it is, but tremendous imbalances divide fully developed areas from regions that have seen little or no development. This high-paced urban development over the past three decades means there remains a great difference from countries such as the UK where urban-rural house price differences are not stark. In China, for example, there is not the drift of retirees to the countryside and rural areas in China remain a place to escape from, rather than to.

Who's in the Middle?

China's middle class (*zhōng chǎn*) is a controversial subject: for starters, no one agrees on how it should be defined. China's State Information Centre takes a numbers approach, identifying the middle class as those whose annual income is between US$7300 and US$73,000 (Y50,000 to Y500,000). International banks and market research groups tend to raise the bar slightly higher, identifying the minimum cut-off at US$10,000 (Y68,382) and looking at factors such as whether or not households own a car, apartment, eat out regularly and so on.

Other economists, however, are less enthusiastic. Dragonomics, which publishes the *China Economic Quarterly*, believes that 'middle class' is a misleading term; many Chinese described as such are in fact considerably poorer than their counterparts in developed countries. Their study argues that the country consists of 'consuming China' – 110 million people living in the Běijīng, Shànghǎi and Guǎngzhōu metropolitan areas – and 'surviving China' – everyone else. But however you define it, everyone does agree that the middle class – or the consumers – are on the rise. According to the state, over half of China's urban population will have an annual income of over $7300 by 2025.

Further polarisations include the generation gap. A vivid absence of sympathy exists between youngsters and their parents, and in particular their grandparents', generation. This misunderstanding can, in a Western context, be explained by youthful rebellion and nonconformity. Chinese youths however, are generally more conformist than their Western counterparts; what is more evident is the juxtaposition of two completely opposing political cultures and generations, one that was communist and the other which is staunchly materialist and more egocentric.

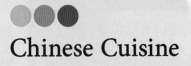

Chinese Cuisine

Eggs at a stall in Jardine's Bazaar (p286), Hong Kong

WILL ROBB/LONELY PLANET IMAGES ©

China is simply obsessed with food. Cuisine plays a central role in both Chinese society and the national psyche. Work, play, romance, business and the family all revolve around food. Meals are occasions to clinch deals, strike up new friendships and rekindle old ones. All you need to fully explore this tasty domain is a pair of chopsticks, an explorative palate and a passion for the unusual and unexpected.

Real Chinese Food

Your very first impressions of China may have been via your taste buds. Chinatowns the world over teem with the aromas of Chinese cuisine, ferried overseas by China's versatile and hard-working cooks. Chinese food is a wholesome point of contact – and a very tasty one at that – between an immigrant Chinese population and local people. Chinatowns across the globe swarm with diners on Sundays looking to yum cha and heartily feast on dim sum.

But what you see – and taste – at home is usually just a wafer-thin slice of a very hefty and wholesome pie. Chinese cuisine in the West is culled from the cookbook of an emigrant community that largely emerged from China's southern seaboard. So although though you may be hard pressed to avoid dim sum and *cha siu* in your local Chinatown, discovering more 'obscure' specialities from Yúnnán, the northeast or Xīnjiāng can be a tough (fortune) cookie.

Remember that China is not that much smaller than Europe. Although Europe is a patchwork of different nation states, languages, cultural traditions and climates, China is also a smorgasbord of dialects, languages, ethnic minorities and often extreme geographic and climatic differences. Eating your way around China is one of the best ways to journey the land, so pack a sense of culinary adventure along with your travelling boots!

Regional Cooking

China's immense geographical, topographical and climatic disparities combined with millennia of local cooking traditions have forged China's various schools of cuisine. While many regions proudly lay claim to their own distinctive style of cooking and considerable shades exist in between, China is traditionally carved up into four principal schools: northern, eastern, western and southern.

The development of China's varied regional cuisines has been influenced by the climate, abundance of certain crops and animals, the type of terrain, proximity to the sea and last, but not least, the influence of neighbouring nations and the importation of ingredients and aromas. Naturally fish and seafood is prevalent in coastal regions of China, while in Inner Mongolia and Xīnjiāng there is a dependence on meat such as beef and lamb.

Of their various cooking schools, the Chinese traditionally say '南甜北咸东辣西酸' or 'Sweet in the south, salty in the north, hot in the east and sour in the west'. It's a massive generalisation, but as with most generalisations, there's more than a grain of truth.

Northern School

In the dry north Chinese wheat belt there's an accent on millet, sorghum, maize, barley and wheat rather than rice (which requires an abundance of water). Northern cooking is rich and wholesome: filling breads – such as *mántou* (馒头) or *bǐng* (饼; flat breads) – are steamed, baked or fried while noodles may form the basis of any northern meal, although the ubiquitous availability of rice means it can always be found. Northern cuisine is frequently quite salty and appetising dumplings (饺子; *jiǎozi*) are widely eaten.

Imperial cooking is also a chief characteristic of the northern school. Peking duck is Běijīng's signature dish, served with typical northern ingredients – pancakes, spring onions and fermented bean paste. You can find it all over China, but it's only true to form in the capital, roasted in ovens fired up with fruit-tree wood.

The influence of Manchurian cooking and the cold climate of the three northeastern provinces – Liǎoníng, Jílín and Hēilóngjiāng – have left a legacy of rich and hearty stews, dense breads and dumplings. The cooking of the nomadic Mongolians has also left a pronounced mark on northern meat cooking, especially in the Mongolian hotpot and the Mongolian barbecue.

Hallmark northern dishes include the following:

Běijīng kǎoyā	北京烤鸭	Peking duck
jiāo zhá yángròu	焦炸羊肉	deep-fried mutton
qīng xiāng shāo jī	清香烧鸡	chicken wrapped in lotus leaf
shuàn yángròu	涮羊肉	lamb hotpot
mántou	馒头	steamed buns

367

jiǎozi	饺子	dumplings
ròu bāozi	肉包子	steamed meat buns
sān měi dòufu	三美豆腐	sliced bean curd with Chinese cabbage

Southern School

The southern Chinese – particularly the Cantonese – spearheaded successive waves of immigration overseas, leaving an aromatic constellation of Chinatowns around the world as outposts of the Chinese culinary empire. Southern cooking may lack the richness and saltiness of northern cooking, but more subtle aromas are tempted to the surface instead. The Cantonese astutely believe that good cooking does not require much flavouring, for it is the *xiān* (natural freshness) of the ingredients that mark a truly high-grade dish. Hence the near obsessive attention paid to the freshness of ingredients in southern cuisine.

Nonsouthern Chinese accuse southern cooking of lacking flavour. The hallmark dish is dim sum (点心; Mandarin: *diǎnxīn*), the signature dining experience of every Chinatown the world over and a standard Sunday institution. Yum cha (literally 'drink tea') – another name for dim sum dining – in Guǎngzhōu and Hong Kong can actually be enjoyed any day of the week. Dishes – often in steamers – are wheeled around on trolleys so you can see what you want to order.

Rice is the primary staple of southern cooking. Sparkling paddy fields glitter across south China; the humid climate, plentiful rainfall and well-irrigated land means that rice has been farmed in the south since the Chinese first populated the region during the Han dynasty (206 BC–AD 220).

Southern dishes include the following:

bái zhuó xiā	白灼虾	blanched prawns with shredded scallions
mì zhī chāshāo	密汁叉烧	roast pork with honey
háoyóu niúròu	蚝油牛肉	beef with oyster sauce
kǎo rǔzhū	烤乳猪	crispy suckling pig
shé ròu	蛇肉	snake
tángcù páigǔ	糖醋排骨	sweet and sour spare ribs

Western School

The cuisine of landlocked western China, a region heavily populated by ethnic minorities, enters an entirely different spectrum of flavours and sensations. The trademark ingredient of the western school is the fiercely hot red chilli, a potent firecracker of a herb. Aniseed, coriander, garlic and peppercorns are also thrown in for that extra pungency.

The standout cuisine of the western school is fiery Sìchuān (川菜; *chuāncài*), renowned for its eye-watering peppery aromas. One of the herbs that differentiates Sìchuān cooking from other spicy cuisines is the use of 'flower pepper' (huājiāo), a numbing peppercornlike herb that floods the mouth with an anaesthetising fragrance. Meat, particularly in Húnán, is marinated, pickled or otherwise processed before cooking, which is generally by stir- or explode-frying.

Sìchuān restaurants are everywhere in China, swarming around train stations, squeezed away down food streets or squished into street markets with wobbly stools and rickety tables parked out the front. Húnán food (湘菜; *xiāngcài*) is similarly extremely spicy, without the numbing sensations of Sìchuān cooking.

Dishes from the western school include the following:

gōngbào jīdīng	宫爆鸡丁	spicy chicken with peanuts
shuǐ zhǔ niúròu	水煮牛肉	spicy fried and boiled beef
suāncàiyú	酸菜鱼	sour cabbage fish soup
shuǐzhǔyú	水煮鱼	fried and boiled fish, garlic sprouts and celery
dāndanmiàn	担担面	spicy noodles
huíguō ròu	回锅肉	boiled and stirfried pork with salty and hot sauce
Chóngqìng huǒguō	重庆火锅	Chóngqìng hotpot
yú xiāng ròusī	鱼香肉丝	fish-flavour pork strips
bàngbàng jī	棒棒鸡	shredded chicken in a hot pepper and sesame sauce
málà dòufu	麻辣豆腐	spicy tofu

Eastern School

The eastern school of Chinese cuisine derives from a fecund and fertile region of China, cut by waterways and canals, dotted with lakes, fringed by a long coastline and nourished by a subtropical climate. Jiāngsū province itself – one of the core regions of the eastern school – is famed as the Land of Fish and Rice, a tribute to its abundance of food and produce. The region was also historically prosperous and in today's export-oriented economy, today's eastern provinces are among China's wealthiest. This combination of riches and bountiful food created a culture of epicurism and gastronomic appreciation.

Generally more oily and sweeter than other Chinese schools, the eastern school revels in fish and seafood, in reflection of its geographical proximity to major rivers and the sea. Fish is usually *qīngzhēng* (清蒸; steamed) but can be stirfried, panfried or grilled. Hairy crabs (*dàzháxiè*) are a Shànghǎi speciality between October and December. Eaten with soy, ginger and vinegar and downed with warm Shàoxīng wine, the best crabs come from Yangcheng Lake.

Hitting the Hot Spot

The Sìchuān hotpot sets foreheads streaming and tummies aquiver all over China from sultry Hǎinán Island to the frigid borderlands of Hēilóngjiāng. It is a fierce and smouldering concoction, bursting with fire and boiling with volcanic flavour.

The Mongolian hotpot is a very different and more subtle creature indeed. Mutton or lamb is the principal meat in a Mongolian hotpot, with scalded strips of meat rescued from the boiling soup and doused in thick sauces, especially sesame sauce (芝麻酱; *zhīmajiàng*). Vegetables – cabbage, mushrooms and potatoes – are also cast into the boiling froth and eaten when soft. The hotpot dates to when Mongolian soldiers would use their helmets as a pot, cooking them up over a fire with broth, meat, vegetables and condiments.

As with Cantonese food, freshness is a key ingredient in the cuisine and sauces and seasonings are only employed to augment essential flavours. Stirfrying and steaming are also used, the latter with Shànghǎi's famous *xiǎolóngbāo*, steamer buns filled with nuggets of pork or crab swimming in a scalding meat broth.

Famous dishes from the eastern school include the following:

jiāng cōng chǎo xiè	姜葱炒蟹	stirfried crab with ginger and scallions
xiǎolóngbāo	小笼包	steamer buns
mìzhī xūnyú	蜜汁熏鱼	honey-smoked carp
níng shì shànyú	宁式鳝鱼	stirfried eel with onion
qiézhī yúkuài	茄汁鱼块	fish fillet in tomato sauce
qīng zhēng guìyú	清蒸鳜鱼	steamed Mandarin fish
sōngzǐ guìyú	松子鳜鱼	Mandarin fish with pine nuts
yóubào xiārén	油爆虾仁	fried shrimp
zhá hēi lǐyú	炸黑鲤鱼	fried black carp
zhá yúwán	炸鱼丸	fish balls

Dining: the Ins & Outs

Chinese Restaurants

Restaurants in China serve scrumptious food, but finding eateries with any sense of warmth or charm can be a real task, outside the big cities. With their huge round tables and thousand-candle-power electric lights, large banqueting-style restaurants are impersonal with little sense of intimacy or romance. At the lower end of the scale

Making dumplings at a restaurant in Shànghǎi's Old Town

are the cheap Chinese restaurants, where diners leave chicken bones on the tabletop, loudly slurp their noodles, chain-smoke and shout into mobiles. At each extreme, the food is the focal point of the meal and that is what diners are there for. Many restaurants charge for the prepacked moist tissues which may be handed to you; you are not charged if you refuse them.

Dining Times

The Chinese eat early. Lunch usually commences from around 11.30am, either self-cooked or a takeaway at home, or in a street side restaurant. Rushed urban diners may just grab a sandwich, a fast-food burger or a lunchbox. Dinner usually kicks off from around 6pm. Reflecting these dining times, some restaurants open at around 11am to close for an afternoon break at about 2.30pm before opening again at around 5pm and closing in the late evening.

Menus

In Běijīng, Shànghǎi and other large cities, you may be proudly presented with an English menu (英文菜谱; Yīngwén Càipǔ). In lesser towns and out in the sticks, don't expect anything other than a Chinese-language menu and a hovering waitress with zero English. The best is undoubtedly the ever-handy photo menu, even though what appears on your table may be a very distant relative of what appears on the menu. If

Ordering Essentials

rice	*báifàn*	白饭
noodles	*miàntiáo*	面条
salt	*yán*	盐
pepper	*hújiāo*	胡椒
sugar	*táng*	糖
soy sauce	*jiàngyóu*	酱油
chilli	*làjiāo*	辣椒
egg	*jīdàn*	鸡蛋
beef	*niúròu*	牛肉
pork	*zhūròu*	猪肉
chicken	*jīròu*	鸡肉
lamb	*yángròu*	羊肉
vegetables	*shūcài*	蔬菜
potato	*tǔdòu*	土豆
broccoli	*xīlánhuā*	西兰花
carrots	*húluóbo*	胡萝卜
sweet corn	*yùmǐ*	玉米
green peppers	*qīngjiāo*	青椒
soup	*tāng*	汤
chopsticks	*kuàizi*	筷子
knife	*dāozi*	刀子
fork	*chāzi*	叉子
spoon	*sháozi*	勺子
hot	*rède*	热的
ice cold	*bīngde*	冰的

you like the look of what other diners are eating, just point over with your chopsticks (我要那个; *wǒ yào nèi gè*; 'I want that' is a very handy phrase). Alternatively, pop into the kitchen and point out the meats and vegetables you would like to eat.

Table Manners

Chinese mealtimes are generally relaxed affairs with no strict rules of etiquette. Meals can commence in Confucian vein before spiralling into total Taoist mayhem, fuelled by incessant toasts with *báijiǔ* (a white spirit) or beer and furious smoking by the men.

Meals typically unfold with one person ordering on behalf of a group. When a group dines, a selection of dishes is ordered for everyone to share rather than individual diners ordering a dish just for themselves. As they arrive, dishes are placed communally in the centre of the table or on a lazy Susan, which may be revolved by the host so that the principal guest gets first choice of whatever dish arrives. Soup may arrive midway through the meal or at the end. Rice often arrives at the end of the meal; if you would like it earlier, just ask.

It is good form to fill your neighbours' teacups or beer glasses when they are empty. Show your appreciation to the pourer by gently tapping your middle finger on the table. To serve yourself tea or any other drink without serving others first is bad form. When your teapot needs a refill, signal this to the waiter by taking the lid off the pot.

It's best to wait till someone has announced a toast before drinking your beer; if you want to get a quick shot in, propose a toast to the host. The Chinese do in fact toast each other much more than in the West, often each time they drink.

Smokers can light up during the meal, unless you are in the nonsmoking area of a restaurant. Depending on the restaurant, smokers may smoke through the entire meal. If you are a smoker, ensure you hand around your cigarettes to others as that is standard procedure.

Hong Kong dim sum

Last but not least, never insist to the last on paying for the bill if someone is tenaciously determined on paying – usually the person who invited you to dinner. By all means offer but then raise your hands in mock surrender when resistance is met; to pay for a meal when another person is determined to pay is to make them lose face.

Chinese toothpick etiquette is similar to that found in other Asian nations: one hand excavates with the toothpick, while the other hand shields the mouth.

Street Food

Snacking your way around China is a fine way to sample the different flavours of the land while on the move. Most towns have a street market or a night market (夜市; yèshì) for good-value snacks and meals so you can either take away or park yourself on a wobbly stool and grab a beer. Vocal vendors will be forcing their tasty creations on you but you can also see what people are buying, so all you have to do is join the queue and point.

Vegetarianism

If you'd rather chew on a legume than a leg of lamb, it can be hard going trying to find truly vegetarian dishes. China's history of famine and poverty means the consumption of meat has always been a sign of status and symbolic of health and wealth. Eating meat is also considered to enhance male virility, so vegetarian men raise eyebrows. As a Westerner, trying to explain your secular and ethical reasons for not eating meat may inspire bemusement.

When trying to pursue a vegetarian diet in China, you will find that vegetables are often fried in animal-based oils, while vegetable soups may be made with chicken or beef stock, so simply choosing vegetable items on the menu is ineffective. In Běijīng and Shànghǎi you will, however, find a generous crop of vegetarian restaurants to choose from.

Out of the large cities, you may be hard pressed to find a vegetarian restaurant. Your best bet may to head to a sizeable active Buddhist temple or monastery, where you could well find a Buddhist vegetarian restaurant that is open to the public. Buddhist vegetarian food typically consists of 'mock meat' dishes created from tofu, wheat gluten, potato and other vegetables. Some of the dishes are almost works of art, with vegetarian ingredients sculpted to look like spare ribs or fried chicken.

If you want to say 'I am a vegetarian' in Chinese, say '我吃素' (wǒ chī sù).

Arts & Architecture

Chinese ceramics at Pānjiāyuán market (p103), Běijīng

MANFRED GOTTSCHALK/LONELY PLANET IMAGES

China is custodian of one of the world's richest cultural and artistic legacies. Until the 20th century, China's arts were deeply conservative and resistant to change; in the last hundred years revolutions in technique and content have fashioned a dramatic transformation. Despite this evolution, China's arts – whatever the period – remain united by a common aesthetic that taps into the very soul and essence of the nation.

Painting

Traditional Painting

Traditional Chinese paintings – especially landscapes – have long been treasured in the West for their beauty.

As described in Xie He's 6th-century-AD treatise, the *Six Principles of Painting*, the chief aim of Chinese painting is to capture the innate essence or spirit (*qì*) of a subject and endow it with vitality. The brush line, varying in thickness and tone, was the second principle (referred to as the 'bone method') and is the defining technique of Chinese painting. Traditionally, it was imagined that brushwork quality could reveal the artist's moral character. As a general rule, painters were less concerned with achieving outward resemblance (that was the third principle) than with conveying intrinsic qualities.

Early painters dwelled on the human figure and moral teachings, while also conjuring up scenes from everyday life. By the time of the Tang dynasty, a new genre, known as landscape painting, had begun to flower. Reaching full bloom during the Song and Yuan dynasties, landscape painting meditated on the environment around man.

On a technical level, the success of landscapes depended on the artists' skill in capturing light and atmosphere. Blank, open spaces devoid of colour create light-filled voids, contrasting with the darkness of mountain folds, filling the painting with qì and vaporous vitality. Specific emotions are not aroused, but instead nebulous sensations permeate.

Modern Art

After 1949, classical Chinese techniques had been abandoned and foreign artistic techniques imported wholesale. Washes on silk were replaced with oil on canvas and China's traditional obsession while the mysterious and ineffable made way for attention to detail and realism.

By 1970, Chinese artists had aspired to master the skills of socialist-realism, a vibrant communist-endorsed style that drew from European neoclassical art, the lifelike canvases of Jacques Louis David and the output of Soviet Union painers. Saturated with political symbolism and propaganda, the blunt artistic style was produced on an industrial scale. Traditional Taoist and Buddhist philosophy was overturned; man was now a master of nature, which would bend to his will.

It was only with the death of Mao Zedong in September 1976 that the shadow of the Cultural Revolution – when Chinese aesthetics was conditioned by the threat of violence – began its retreat and a voracious appetite for Western art began to introduce fresh concepts and ideas.

Much Chinese art since 1990 dwelled obsessively on contemporary socio-economic realities with consumer culture, materialism, urbanisation and social change a repetitive focus. More universal themes have become apparent however, as the art scene has matured. Meanwhile, many artists who left China in the 1990s have returned, setting up private studios and galleries.

Ceramics

The Yuan dynasty saw the first development of China's iconic 'blue-and-white' (qīnghuā) porcelain. Cobalt-blue paint, from Persia, was applied as an underglaze directly to white porcelain with a brush, the vessel was covered with another transparent glaze, and fired. This technique was perfected during the Ming dynasty and such ceramics became hugely popular all over the world, eventually acquiring the name 'Chinaware', whether produced in China or not.

Chinese Aesthetics

In reflection of the Chinese character, Chinese aesthetics have traditionally been marked by restraint and understatement, a preference for oblique references over direct explanation, vagueness in place of specificity and an avoidance of the obvious and a fondness for the subtle. Traditional Chinese aesthetics instead sought to cultivate a more reserved artistic impulse and these principles compellingly find their way into virtually every Chinese art form, from painting to sculpture, ceramics, calligraphy, film, poetry and literature.

During the Qing dynasty, porcelain techniques were further refined and developed, showing superb craftsmanship and ingenuity. British and European consumers dominated the export market, displaying an insatiable appetite for Chinese vases and bowls decorated with flowers and landscapes. The Qing is also known for its stunning monochromatic ware, especially the ox-blood vases and highly meticulous imperial yellow bowls, enamel decorated porcelain and elaborate and highly decorative wares.

Literature

Classical novels evolved from the popular folk tales and dramas that entertained the lower classes. During the Ming dynasty they were penned in a semi-vernacular (or 'vulgar') language, and are often irreverently funny and full of action-packed fights.

The most well-known novel outside China is *Journey to the West* (Xīyóu Jì) – more commonly known as *Monkey*. Written in the 16th century, it follows the misadventures of a cowardly Buddhist monk (Tripitaka; a stand-in for the real-life pilgrim Xuan Zang) and his companions – a rebellious monkey, lecherous pig-man and exiled monster-immortal – on a pilgrimage to India.

The Water Margin/Outlaws of the Marsh/All Men Are Brothers (Shuǐhǔ Zhuàn) is, on the surface, an excellent tale of honourable bandits and corrupt officials along the lines of Robin Hood. On a deeper level, though, it is a reminder to Confucian officials of their right to rebel when faced with a morally suspect government (at least one emperor officially banned it).

A revolutionary moment in literature arrived when modernist author Lu Xun wrote his short story *Diary of a Madman* in 1918, the first short story to be penned in colloquial Chinese. Other notable contemporaries of Lu Xun include Ba Jin (*Family*; 1931), Mao Dun (*Midnight*; 1933), Lao She (*Rickshaw Boy/Camel Xiangzi*; 1936) and the modernist playwright Cao Yu (*Thunderstorm*). Lu Xun and Ba Jin also translated a great deal of foreign literature into Chinese.

As with the other arts, the communist tenure from 1949 resulted in a suffocation of the literary impulse. Today's writers have, however, returned to pushing the literary envelope, despite the strong hand of the state censor. Although few contemporary voices have been translated into English, there's enough material to keep any serious reader busy. The provocative Mo Yan (*Life and Death Are Wearing Me Out*; 2008), Yu Hua (*To Live*; 1992) and Su Tong (*Rice*; 1995) have each written momentous historical novels set in the 20th century; all are excellent, though not for the faint of heart.

'Hooligan author' Wang Shuo (*Please Don't Call Me Human*; 2000) remains China's bestselling author with his political satires and convincing depictions of urban slackers. Chun Sue (*Beijing Doll*; 2004) and Mian Mian (*Candy*; 2003) examine the dark urban underbellies of Běijīng and Shànghǎi respectively. Alai (*Red Poppies*; 2002), an ethnic Tibetan, made waves by writing in Chinese about early-20th-century Tibetan Sìchuān – whatever your politics, it's both insightful and a page-turner. Émigré Ma Jian (*Red Dust*; 2004) writes more politically critical work; his debut was a Kerouacian tale of wandering China as a spiritual pollutant in the 1980s. China's most renowned dissident writer, Gao Xingjian, won the Nobel Prize for Literature in 2000 for his novel *Soul Mountain*, an account of his travels along the Yangzi after being misdiagnosed with lung cancer. All of his work has been banned in the PRC since 1989.

Film

The moving image in the Middle Kingdom dates to 1896, when Spaniard Galen Bocca unveiled a film projector and blew the socks off wide-eyed crowds in a Shànghǎi teahouse. Shànghǎi's cosmopolitan verve and exotic looks would make it the capital of China's film industry, but China's very first movie – *Conquering Jun Mountain* (an excerpt from a piece of Beijing Opera) – was actually filmed in Běijīng in 1905.

Shànghǎi opened its first cinema in 1908. In those days, cinema owners would cannily run the film for a few minutes, stop it and collect money from the audience before allowing the film to continue. The golden age of Shànghǎi film-making came in the 1930s when the city had over 140 film companies. Japanese control of China eventually brought the industry to a standstill and sent many film-makers packing.

China's film industry was stymied after the communist revolution, which sent film-makers scurrying to Hong Kong and Taiwan where they played key roles in building up the local film industries that flourished there. Cinematic production in China was co-opted to glorify communism and generate patriotic propaganda. The days of the Cultural Revolution (1966–76) were particularly dark: between 1966 and 1972, just eight movies were made on the mainland.

It wasn't until two years after the death of Mao Zedong that the Běijīng Film Academy, China's premier film school, reopened in September 1978. Its first intake of students included Zhang Yimou, Chen Kaige and Tian Zhuangzhuang – masterminds of the celebrated 'Fifth Generation'. A bleak but beautifully shot tale of a CCP cadre who travels to a remote village in Shaanxi province to collect folk songs, Chen Kaige's *Yellow Earth* aroused little interest in China but proved a sensation when released in the West in 1985.

It was followed by Zhang's *Red Sorghum*, which introduced Gong Li and Jiang Wen to the world. Gong became the poster girl of Chinese cinema in the 1990s and the first international movie star to emerge from the mainland. Jiang, the Marlon Brando of Chinese film, has proved both a durable leading man and an innovative, controversial director of award-winning films such as *In the Heat of the Sun* and *Devils on the Doorstep*.

Rich, seminal works such as *Farewell My Concubine* (1993; Chen Kaige) and *Raise the Red Lantern* (1991; Zhang Yimou) were garlanded with praise, receiving standing ovations and being rewarded with major film awards.

In 1993, Tian Zhuangzhuang made the brilliant *The Blue Kite*. A heart-breaking account of the life of one Běijīng family during the Cultural Revolution, it so enraged the censors that Tian was banned from making films for years.

Each generation charts its own course and the ensuing Sixth Generation – graduating from the Beijing Film Academy post-Tiān'ānmén Square protests – was no different. Sixth Generation film directors eschewed the luxurious beauty of their forebears, and sought to capture the angst and grit of modern urban Chinese life.

Independent film-making found an influential precedent with Zhang Yuan's 1990 debut *Mama*. Zhang is also acclaimed for his candid and gritty documentary-style *Beijing Bastards* (1993). *The Days*, directed by Wang Xiaoshui, follows a couple drifting apart in the wake of the Tiān'ānmén Square protests. Wang also directed the excellent *Beijing Bicycle* (2001), inspired by De Sica's *Bicycle Thieves*.

Jia Zhangke has emerged as the most acclaimed of China's new film-makers. His meditative and compassionate look at the social impact of the construction of the Three Gorges Dam on local people, *Still Life* (2006), scooped the Golden Lion at the 2006 Venice Film Festival.

Architecture

Traditional Architecture

Four principal styles governed traditional Chinese architecture: imperial, religious, residential and recreational. The imperial style was naturally the most grandiose, over-seeing the design of buildings employed by successive dynastic rulers; the religious

style was employed for the construction of temples, monasteries and pagodas, while the residential and recreational style took care of the design of houses and private gardens.

Whatever the style, Chinese buildings traditionally followed a similar basic ground plan, consisting of a symmetrical layout oriented around a central axis (ideally running north–south, to conform with basic feng shui dictates and to maximise sunshine) with an enclosed courtyard (*yuàn*) flanked by buildings on all sides.

In many aspects, imperial palaces are glorified courtyard homes (south-facing, a sequence of courtyards, side halls and perhaps a garden at the rear) completed on a different scale. Apart from the size, the main dissimilarity would be guard towers on the walls and possibly a moat, imperial-yellow roof tiles, ornate dragon carvings (signifying the emperor), the repetitive use of the number nine and the presence of temples.

Chinese temples are very different from Christian churches, with a sequence of halls and buildings interspersed with breezy open-air courtyards. The roofless courtyards allows the weather to permeate within the temple and also permits the *qì* (气; energy) to circulate, dispersing stale air and allowing incense to be burned.

Modern Architecture

China is one of today's most exciting nations for breaking the architectural mould, ripping up the rule book, risk taking, and a healthy but chancy dose of leaping-before-looking. You only have to look at the Pǔdōng skyline to witness a melange of competing modern designs, some dramatic, inspiring and novel, others cheesy and rash.

If modern architecture in China is regarded as anything post-1949, then China has ridden a roller coaster of styles and fashions. Stand between the Great Hall of the People (1959) in Běijīng and the National Centre for the Performing Arts (2008) and weigh up how far China has travelled in the past 50 years. Interestingly, neither building possesses evident Chinese motifs; both are united by foreign styling, soviet

Historic town, Shànghǎi
PHOTOGRAPHER: RICHARD I'ANSON/LONELY PLANET IMAGES ©

design for the former and French imagination for the latter. The same applies to the complex form of Běijīng's CCTV Building, where a continuous loop through horizontal and vertical planes required some audacious engineering.

Many of the top names in international architecture – IM Pei, Rem Koolhaas, Norman Foster, Kengo Kuma, Jean-Marie Charpentier, Herzog & de Meuron – have designed at least one building in China in the past decade.

The Best Modern Architecture

1 CCTV Building (p89)

2 Shànghǎi World Financial Center (p203)

3 Jīnmào Tower (p203)

4 National Stadium (aka the 'Bird's Nest', p85)

5 Tomorrow Square (p200)

Religion & Beliefs

Writing Buddhist scriptures in Xīshuāngbǎnnà

BRADLEY MAYHEW/LONELY PLANET IMAGES

Ideas have always possessed a particular volatility in China. The Taiping Rebellion (1850–64) fused Christianity with revolutionary principles of social organisation, leaving 20 million dead in its bloody 20-year spasm. Communism itself is – or was – an ideology that briefly assumed colossal authority over the minds of China's citizens. Today's Chinese may be more down-to-earth and pragmatic, but they are increasingly returning to religion after decades of state-orchestrated atheism.

Buddhism

Although not an indigenous faith, Buddhism (Fo' Jiào) is the religion most deeply associated with China, Tibet and Chinatowns abroad. Many Chinese may not be regular templegoers but they possess an interest in Buddhism; they may merely be 'cultural Buddhists', with a fondness for Buddhist civilisation.

Buddhism in China

Like other faiths such as Christianity, Nestorianism, Islam and Judaism, Buddhism originally reached China via the Silk Road. The earliest recorded Buddhist temple in China proper dates back to the 1st century AD at Luòyáng but it was not until the 4th century when a period of warlordism coupled with nomadic invasions plunged the country into disarray, that Buddhism gained mass appeal. Buddhism's sudden growth during this period is often attributed to its sophisticated ideas concerning the afterlife (such as karma and reincarnation), a dimension unaddressed by either Confucianism or Taoism. At a time when existence was especially precarious, spiritual transcendence was understandably popular.

As Buddhism converged with Taoist philosophy (through terminology used in translation) and popular religion (through practice), it went on to develop into something distinct from the original Indian tradition. The most famous example is the esoteric Chan school (Zen in Japanese), which originated sometime in the 5th or 6th century, and focused on attaining enlightenment through meditation.

Buddhist Schools

Regardless of its various forms, most Buddhism in China belongs to the Mahayana school, which holds that since all existence is one, the fate of the individual is linked to the fate of others. Thus, Bodhisattvas, those who have already achieved enlightenment but have chosen to remain on earth, continue to work for the liberation of all other sentient beings.

Ethnic Tibetans and Mongols within the People's Republic of China (PRC) practise a unique form of Mahayana Buddhism known as Tibetan or Tantric Buddhism (Lǎma Jiào). Tibetan Buddhism, sometimes called Vajrayana or 'thunderbolt vehicle', has been practised since the early 7th century AD and is influenced by Tibet's pre-Buddhist Bon religion, which relied on priests or shamans to placate spirits, gods and demons. Priests called lamas are believed to be reincarnations of highly evolved beings; the Dalai Lama is the supreme patriarch of Tibetan Buddhism.

The Best Buddhist Temples

1 Lama Temple (p78)

2 Labrang Monastery (p339)

3 Pǔníng Temple (p120)

4 Xiǎntōng Temple (p164)

5 Língyǐn Temple (p231)

6 Pǔtuózōngchéng Temple (p120)

Taoism

A home-grown philosophy/religion, Taoism is also perhaps the hardest of all China's faiths to grasp. Controversial, paradoxical, and – like the Tao itself – impossible to pin down, it is a natural counterpoint to rigid Confucianist order and responsibility.

Taoism predates Buddhism in China and much of its religious culture connects to a distant animism and shamanism, despite the purity of its philosophical school. In its earliest and simplest form, Taoism draws from *The Classic of the Way and its Power* (Dàodé Jìng), penned by the sagacious Laotzu (Laozi; c 580–500 BC).

The Classic of the Way and its Power is a work of astonishing insight and sublime beauty. Devoid of a godlike being or deity, Laotzu's 's writings instead endeavour to address the unknowable and ineffable principle of the universe which he calls Dao (道; dào), or 'the Way'. This way is the way or method by which the universe operates, so it can be understood to be a universal or cosmic principle.

Confucianism

The very core of Chinese society for the past two millennia, Confucianism (Rújiā Sīxiǎng) is a humanist philosophy that strives for social harmony and the common good. In China, its influence can be seen in everything from the emphasis on education and respect for elders to the patriarchal role of the government.

Confucianism is based upon the teachings of Confucius (Kǒngzǐ), a 6th-century-BC philosopher who lived during a period of constant warfare and social upheaval. While Confucianism changed considerably throughout the centuries, some of the principal ideas remained the same – namely an emphasis on five basic hierarchical relationships: father-son, ruler-subject, husband-wife, elder-younger and friend-friend. Confucius believed that if each individual carried out his or her proper role in society (ie a son served his father respectfully while a father provided for his son, a subject served his ruler respectfully while a ruler provided for his subject, and so on) social order would be achieved. Confucius' disciples later gathered his ideas in the form of short aphorisms and conversations, forming the work known as *The Analects* (Lúnyǔ).

In the 20th century, intellectuals decried Confucian thought as an obstacle to modernisation and Mao further levelled the sage in his denunciation of 'the Four Olds'. Confucius' call for social harmony has, however, resurfaced in government propaganda.

Christianity

Christianity first arrived in China with the Nestorians, a sect from ancient Persia which spilt with the Byzantine Church in AD 431, who arrived in China via the Silk Road in the 7th century. A celebrated tablet in Xī'ān (p144) records their arrival. Much later, in the 16th century, the Jesuits arrived and were popular figures at the imperial court, although they made few converts.

Some estimates point to as many as 100 million Christians in China. However, the exact population is hard to calculate as many groups – outside of the four official Christian organisations – lead a strict underground existence (in what are called 'house churches') out of fear of a political clampdown.

Islam

Islam (Yīsīlán Jiào) in China dates to the 7th century, when it was first brought to China by Arab and Persian traders along the Silk Road. Later, during the Mongol Yuan dynasty, maritime trade increased, bringing new waves of merchants to China's coastal regions, particularly the port cities of Guǎngzhōu and Quánzhōu. The descendants of these groups – now scattered across the country – gradually

Guanyin 观音

The boundlessly compassionate countenance of Guanyin, the Buddhist Goddess of Mercy, can be encountered in temples across China. The goddess (more strictly a Bodhisattva or a Buddha-to-be) goes under a variety of aliases: Guanshiyin (literally 'Observing the Cries of the World') is her formal name, but she is also called Guanzizai, Guanyin Dashi and Guanyin Pusa, or, in Sanskrit, Avalokiteshvara. Known as Kannon in Japan and Guanyam in Cantonese, Guanyin shoulders the grief of the world and dispenses mercy and compassion.

integrated into Han culture, and are today distinguished primarily by their religion. In Chinese, they are referred to as the Hui.

Other Muslim groups include the Uighurs, Kazaks, Kyrgyz, Tajiks and Uzbeks, who live principally in the border areas of the northwest. It is estimated that 1.5% to 3% of Chinese today are Muslim.

China's Landscapes

Singing Sands Mountain (p341)

MARTIN MOOS/LONELY PLANET IMAGES

The world's third-largest country – roughly the same size as the United States of America – China covers a colossal 9.5 million sq km, only surpassed in area by Russia and Canada. Straddling natural environments as diverse as subarctic tundra in the north and tropical rainforests in the south, the land embraces the world's highest mountain range and one of its hottest deserts in the west to the steamy, typhoon-lashed coastline of the South China Sea.

The Land

Mountains & Deserts

China's terrain is in large parts mountainous and hilly, commencing in dramatically precipitous fashion in the vast and sparsely populated Tibetan west and levelling out gradually towards the fertile, well-watered, populous and wealthy provinces of eastern China.

Averaging 4500m above sea level, the Tibet and Qīnghǎi region's highest peaks thrust up in the Himalayan mountain range along its southern rim, where mountains average about 6000m above sea level, with 40 peaks rising dizzyingly to 7000m or more.

This vast high-altitude region (Tibet alone constitutes one eighth of China's landmass) is home to an astonishing 37,000 glaciers, the third-largest mass of ice on the planet after the Arctic and Antarctic. This colossal body of frozen water ensures that the Tibet-Qīnghǎi region is the source of many of China's largest rivers.

This mountainous disposition finds repeated refrain throughout China, albeit on a less dramatic scale, as the land continually wrinkles into spectacular mountain ranges. China's hills and mountains may form a dramatic and sublime backdrop, but they generate huge agricultural complications. Many farmers cultivate small plots of land assiduously eked out in patchworks of land squashed between hillsides, in the demanding effort to feed 20% of the world's population, with just 10% of its arable land.

China also contains head-spinningly vast – and growing – desert regions that occupy almost a fifth of the country's landmass, largely in its mighty northwest. These are inhospitably sandy and rocky expanses where summers are torturously hot and winters bone-numbingly cold. North towards Kazakhstan and Kyrgyzstan from the plateaus of Tibet and Qīnghǎi lies Xīnjiāng's Tarim Basin, the largest inland basin in the world. This is the location of the mercilessly thirsty Taklamakan Desert – China's largest desert and the world's second-largest mass of sand after the Sahara Desert.

East of Xīnjiāng extend the epic grasslands and steppes of Inner Mongolia in a huge and elongated belt of land that stretches to the region once called Manchuria.

The Best Mountains

1 Huángshān (p243)

2 Wǔtái Shán (p229)

3 Huà Shān (p148)

4 Pǔtuóshān (p238)

5 Éméi Shān (p334)

6 Tài Shān (p169)

IN FOCUS CHINA'S LANDSCAPES

Rivers & Plains

The other major region comprises roughly 45% of the country and contains 95% of the population. This densely populated part of China descends like a staircase from west to east, from the inhospitable high plateaus of Tibet and Qīnghǎi to the fertile but largely featureless plains and basins of the great rivers that drain the high ranges. These plains are the most important agricultural areas of the country and the most heavily populated.

The Yellow River, about 5460km long and the second-longest river in China, is often touted as the birthplace of Chinese civilisation. China's longest river, the Yangzi, is one of the longest rivers in the world. Its watershed of almost 2 million sq km – 20% of China's landmass – supports 400 million people. Dropping from its source high on the Tibetan plateau, it runs for 6300km to the sea, of which the last few hundred kilometres is across virtually flat alluvial plains.

Wildlife

China's vast size, diverse topography and climatic disparities support an astonishing range of habitats for a wide-ranging diversity of animal life. Scattered from steamy tropical rainforests in the deep southwest to subarctic wilderness in the far north, from the precipitous mountains of Tibet to the low-lying deserts of the northwest and the huge Yangzi River, China's wild animals comprise nearly 400 species of mammal (including some of the world's rarest and most charismatic species), more than 1300 bird species, 424 reptile species and over 300 species of amphibian.

Plants

China is home to more than 32,000 species of seed plants and 2500 species of forest trees, plus an extraordinary plant diversity that includes some famous 'living fossils'. Major habitats include coniferous forests; deciduous broadleaf forests; tropical and subtropical rainforests; and less well-endowed habitats such as wetlands, deserts and alpine meadows. Many reserves remain where intact vegetation ecosystems can be seen firsthand, but few parts of the country have escaped human impact and vast areas are under cultivation with monocultures such as rice.

Apart from rice, the plant probably most often associated with China and Chinese culture is bamboo, of which China boasts some 300 species. Bamboos grow in many parts of China, but bamboo forests were once so extensive that they enabled the evolution of the giant panda, which eats virtually nothing else, and a suite of small mammals, birds and insects that live in bamboo thickets. Some bamboo species have long been cultivated by people for building materials, tools and food.

Deforestation has levelled huge tracts of China's once vast and beautiful primeval forests. At the end of the 19th century, 70% of China's northeast was still forest. Unsustainable clear-cutting in the 20th century – especially during the Great Leap Forward – was not banned there until the mid-1980s, by which time only 5% of old growth woodland remained. Logging controls were more strictly enforced after the great floods of 1998, when deforestation was identified as contributing to the floodwaters. Since then a vigorous replanting campaign was launched to once again cover huge tracts of China with trees, but these cannot restore the rich biodiversity that once existed.

Endangered Species

Almost every large mammal you can think of in China has crept onto the endangered-species list, as well as many of the so-called 'lower' animals and plants. The snow leopard, Indochinese tiger, chiru antelope, crested ibis, Asiatic elephant, red-crowned crane and black-crowned crane are all endangered. Snakes are sought after for food and medicine, and consequently 43 of China's 200 snake species are endangered.

Deforestation, pollution, hunting and trapping for fur, body parts and sport are all culprits. The Convention on International Trade in Threatened and Endangered Species (CITES) records legal trade in live reptiles and parrots, and astonishingly high numbers of reptile and wildcat skins. The number of such products collected or sold unofficially is anyone's guess.

Despite the threats, a number of rare animal species cling to survival in the wild in small and remote areas, including the Chinese alligator in Ānhuī, the giant salamander

The Yangzi Dolphin

The Yangzi dolpin (*baiji*), one of just a few freshwater dolphin species in the world and by far the rarest, migrated to the Yangzi River from the Pacific Ocean over 20 million years ago. From being quite commonplace, around 6000 dolphins still lived in the Yangzi River during the 1950s but numbers fell drastically during the three decades of explosive economic growth from the 1970s, and the last confirmed sighting was in 2002. The creature is a victim – one of many – of human activity in the region, succumbing to drowning in fishing nets and lethal injuries from ships' propellers.

in the fast-running waters of the Yangzi and Yellow Rivers, the Yangzi River dolphin in the lower and middle reaches of the river, and the pink dolphin of the Hong Kong islands of Sha Chau and Lung Kwu Chau. The giant panda is confined to the fauna-rich valleys and ranges of Sìchuān, but your best chances for sighting one is in Chéngdū's Giant Panda Breeding Research Base.

A Greener China?

In 2010, China overtook the USA as the world's largest energy consumer; in the same year the nation replaced Japan as the world's second-largest economy. China is also the world's largest generator of carbon dioxide (although not per capita). Twenty of the world's 30 most polluted cities are in China. Due to its size and sheer thirst for energy and resources, China has the potential to profoundly affect the environment of the entire planet.

The World Bank calculates the annual cost of pollution alone in China at almost 6% of the national GDP; when all forms of environmental damage are incorporated, the figure leaps as high as 12%, meaning China's environmental costs may outweigh economic growth.

China is paradoxically painfully aware of its accelerated desertification, growing water shortages, shrinking glaciers and progressively polluted environment, but remains unclear whether or how to fully champion the development of greener and cleaner energy sources.

Evidence of ambitious and bold thinking is easy to find: in 2010 China announced it would pour billions into developing electric and hybrid vehicles; more than 2000 environmental groups have sprung up since the mid-1990s; Běijīng is committing itself to overtaking Europe in investment in renewable energy by 2020; the construction of vast wind farms (in blustery Gānsù, for example) continues apace; and China leads the world in production of solar cells.

Giant panda at Ocean Park (p269), Hong Kong

PHOTOGRAPHER: HUW JONES/LONELY PLANET IMAGES ©

Its authoritarian system of governance allows China to railroad through daring initiatives. However, the authorities tend to rely heavily on technological 'solutions' and huge engineering programs to combat environmental problems.

One of China's main quandaries is coal. Coal is cheap, easy to extract and remains China's number-one energy source, generating almost 70% of power requirements. Huge untapped reserves in the northwest await exploitation, vast coalfields in Inner Mongolia are now being mined and the economics of coalmining in China make it a cheap fuel source.

Survival
Guide

DIRECTORY	**390**	Legal Matters	398	**TRANSPORT**	**404**
Accommodation	390	Money	399	GETTING THERE & AWAY	404
Activities	394	Passports	400	GETTING AROUND	411
Business Hours	394	Public Holidays	400		
Customs Regulations	394	Safe Travel	401	**LANGUAGE**	**419**
Discount Cards	395	Telephone	402		
Gay & Lesbian Travellers	395	Time	402		
Health	395	Visas	402		
Insurance	398	Volunteering	404		
Internet Access	398				

The Great Wall, Mùtiányù (p114)
PHOTOGRAPHER: MERTEN SNIJDERS/LONELY PLANET IMAGES ©

Directory

Accommodation

Accommodation in China has undergone a revolution in recent years. Whether you are looking for rustic home-steads, homestays, youth hostels, student dormitories, guesthouses, courtyard lodgings, boutique hotels or five-star towers, the choice is growing by the day. There are few places where you can legally go camping and as most of China's flatland is put to agricultural use, you will largely be limited to remote, hilly regions.

ROOMS & PRICES

Most rooms in China are twins, with two single beds. **Single rooms** (单间; *dānjiān*) are rarer. **Double rooms** (双人房、标准间; *shuāng rén fáng* or *biāozhǔn jiān*) will often be twins, but hotels may also have large-bed rooms (大床房; *dàchuáng fáng*), which are rooms with a large single bed. **Suites** (套房; *tàofáng*) are available at most midrange and top-end hotels. **Dorms** (多人房; *duōrénfáng*) are usually, but not always, available at youth hostels (and at a few hotels). All rooms in this book

come with private bathroom/ shower room, unless other-wise stated.

Accommodation in this book is divided by price category, identified by the symbols $ (budget), $$ (midrange) or $$$ (high end); accommodation prices vary across China, so for some selected locations we have given specific budget breakdowns for that location. Generally speaking, hostels, guesthouses and one- to two-star hotels fall into the budget category; midrange hotels are typically three to four stars, while top-end hotels are four to five stars.

You usually have to check out by noon. If you check out between noon and 6pm you will be charged 50% of the room price; after 6pm you have to pay for another full night.

BOOKING ONLINE

Booking online can secure good prices on rooms, and should be the first place you look. You can get a substantial discount (up to 50% off the walk-in rate) by booking through an online agency, although some simply offer rates you can get from the hotels or youth hostels yourself. Airports at major cities often have hotel-booking counters that offer discounted rates.

Useful accommodation websites:

Asia Hotels (www.asia-hotels.com)

China Hotels (www.china-hotelguide.com)

Redflag (www.redflag.info)

SinoHotel (www.sinohotel.com)

Tripadvisor (www.tripadvisor.com) Excellent source of accommodation reviews.

Once in China, book discounted rooms on the following sites:

Ctrip (☎ 800 820 6666; www.english.ctrip.com)

Elong (☎ 800 810 1010; www.elong.com)

CHECKING IN

At check-in you will need your passport; a registration form will ask what type of visa you have. For most travellers, the visa will be L; for a full list of visa categories, see p402. A deposit (押金; *yājīn*) is required at most hotels; this will be paid either with cash or by providing your credit-card details. If your deposit is paid in cash, you will be given a receipt.

GUESTHOUSES

The cheapest of the cheap are China's ubiquitous **guest-houses** (招待所; *zhāodàisuǒ*). Often found clustering near train or bus stations but also dotted around cities and towns, not all guesthouses accept foreigners. Many are on the 2nd floor above street level, accessed by a crummy flight of steps (look out for the signs). Reception is usually a simple counter, staffed by the owner in everyday clothes, mop in hand and fag in mouth. Rooms (doubles, twins, triples, quads) are primitive and grey, with tiled floors and possibly a shower room or shabby bathroom; showers may be communal. There

Book Your Stay Online

For more accommodation reviews by Lonely Planet authors, check out hotels.lonelyplanet.com/China. You'll find independent reviews, as well as recommendations on the best places to stay. Best of all, you can book online.

may be air-con and/or a dated TV. Guesthouses do not tend to have restaurants and are more commonly used by men than women.

Other terms you may encounter for guesthouses:

o 旅店 (lǚdiàn)

o 旅馆 (lǚguǎn)

o 有房 means 'rooms available'

o 今日有房 means 'rooms available today'

o 住宿 (zhùsù) means 'accommodation'

HOMESTEADS

In more rural destinations, small towns and villages, you should be able to find a **homestead** (农家; nóngjiā). The owner of the house will have a handful of rooms that cost in the region of Y50 (bargaining is possible); you will not need to register. The owner will be more than happy to cook up meals for you. Showers and toilets are generally communal.

HOSTELS

If you're looking for efficiently-run budget accommodation, turn to China's youth hostel sector. **Hostelling International** (☏ 400 886 0808; www.yhachina.com) hostels are generally well-run, with a growing network of member hostels. **Utels hostels** are

generally inferior and not as widespread; some may also not take foreigners. You may discover other private youth hostels scattered around China that are unaffiliated; standards at these may be variable.

Youth hostels are typically staffed by youthful English-speakers who are also well-informed on local sightseeing. The foreigner-friendly vibe in youth hostels stands in marked contrast to Chinese hotels that are often unaware of Western requirements. They are also superb for meeting like-minded travellers. Double rooms in youth hostels are often better than midrange equivalents, often just as comfortable, better located and levels of service may be superior. Many offer wi-fi, while most have at least one internet terminal (free perhaps, free for 30 minutes or roughly Y5 to Y10 per hour). Laundry, book-lending, kitchen facilities, bike rental, lockers, noticeboard, bar and cafe should all be available.

Dorms usually cost between Y40 and Y55 (discount of around Y5 for members). They typically come with bunk beds but may have standard beds. Most dorms won't have an en suite shower, though some do; they should have air-con. Many

hostels also have doubles, singles, twins and maybe even family rooms; prices vary but are often around Y150 to Y250 for a double, again with discounts for members. Hostels can arrange ticketing or help you book a room in another affiliated youth hostel. Book ahead (online if possible) as rooms are frequently booked out, especially at weekends or the busy holiday periods.

HOTELS

Hotels are called bīnguǎn (宾馆), jiǔdiàn (酒店), dàjiǔdiàn (大酒店), fàndiàn (饭店) or dàfàndiàn (大饭店) in Chinese.

Hotels vary wildly in quality within the same budget bracket. The star rating system employed in China can be misleading: hotels are frequently awarded four or five stars when they are patently a star lower in ranking. A Chinese-run 'five star' hotel may have achieved its ranking by installing an unimpressive swimming pool or by supplying gifts and lavish dinners to inspectors. Deficiencies may not be immediately apparent, so explore and make an inspection of the overall quality of the hotel. Viewing the room up front pays dividends. English skills are often poor, even in some five-star hotels; sometimes they are nonexistent.

Largely confined to Běijīng, courtyard hotels have rapidly mushroomed. Arranged around traditional sìhéyuàn (courtyards), rooms are usually on ground level. Courtyard hotels are charming and romantic,

Hotel Discounts & Tips

Always ignore the rack rate and ask for the discounted price or bargain for a room, as discounts apply in generally all but youth hostels (except for hostel members) and the cheapest accommodation; you can do this in person at reception, or book online. Apart from during the busy holiday periods (the first week of May and October, and Chinese New Year), rooms should be priced well below the rack rate and rarely booked out. Discounts of 10% to 50% off the tariff rate (30% is typical) are the norm, available by simply asking at reception, by phoning in advance to reserve a room or by booking online at Ctrip. We have listed both the rack rate and the discount you should expect to receive at each hotel, where they apply.

Some tips:

o Ask your hotel concierge for a local map

o The standard of English is often better at youth hostels than at midrange, or high-end, hotels

o Your hotel can help with ticketing, for a commission

o See the Language section (p419) for a handy primer of Chinese phrases

o Almost every hotel has a left-luggage room, which should be free if you are a guest

o Always bargain for a room

liúxuéshēng lóu) or more expensive rooms at their experts building (专家楼; *zhuānjiā lóu*), where visiting teachers often stay.

ROOM CATEGORIES

TWO STARS

Apart from at youth hostels, budget accommodation can be found in hotels rated two stars or unranked. Expect basic facilities, possibly grimy bathrooms or shower rooms, threadbare carpets, very basic or nonexistent English-language skills at reception and a simple restaurant or none at all. All two-star hotel rooms should come with air-con and TV, but may not have telephones or internet access, so ask beforehand. Rooms may have water coolers or a thermos flask (in old establishments). If it's an old-fashioned place, you may find a *fúwùyua'n* (female assistant) on each floor. Breakfast, if available, may consist of boiled eggs, rice porridge, pickled vegetables and so forth.

THREE TO FOUR STARS

Three- to four-star hotels offer comfort and a greater measure of flair than two-star hotels; they are also often bland and uninspiring. When making a choice, opt for Sino-foreign joint-venture hotels over Chinese-owned hotels wherever possible. Opt for newer establishments, as three- to four-star hotels rapidly get set in their ways. Staff should speak some English, but language skills can be highly mechanical, even

but are often expensive and rooms are small, in keeping with the dimensions of courtyard residences. Facilities will be limited so don't expect a swimming pool, gym or subterranean garage.

Practically all hotels will change money for guests, and most midrange and top-end hotels accept credit cards. All hotel rooms are subject to a 10% or 15% service charge. Most hotels in the midrange bracket will have broadband internet access and may have wi-fi.

The Chinese method of designating floors is the same as that used in the USA, but different from, say, that used in Australia. What would be the ground floor in Australia is the 1st floor in China, the 1st is the 2nd, and so on.

OTHER ACCOMMODATION

Some **temples** and **monasteries** (especially on China's sacred mountains) provide accommodation. They are cheap, but ascetic, and may not have running water or electricity.

Some **universities** provide cheap and basic accommodation either in their foreign-student dorm buildings (留学生楼;

at reception. There should be a Western restaurant and a bar (if it's a three-star hotel, expect it to be cheesy).

Rooms in three- to four-star hotels all have a bathroom or shower room, air-con and telephone; they should also come with a kettle (and coffee sachets), water cooler, safe and minibar. Rooms may also have satellite TV, cable TV or an in-house movie channel, and broadband internet connection. No-smoking rooms should be available; the hotel may have a health centre or gym. You may receive a free newspaper slipped under your door, at best perhaps the anodyne *China Daily*. A Western breakfast may be available, certainly at four-star establishments.

In large cities such as Běijīng and Shànghǎi, a growing number of courtyard and boutique hotels fall within this category, offering a more personal level of service, a more intimate environment in which to stay and perhaps a more unique sense of personality and style.

FIVE STARS

China has very few independent hotels of real distinction, so it's generally advisable to select chain hotels that offer a proven standard of international excellence. Shangri-La, Marriott, Hilton, St Regis, Ritz-Carlton, Marco Polo and Hyatt all have a presence in China and can generally be relied upon for high standards of service and comfort.

Some Chinese-owned hotels display five stars when they are, at best, four stars, so be warned (however the tariff should be cheaper).

Five-star hotels should have top-quality recreational, shopping and sport facilities (including swimming pool, health centre or gym and tennis courts), a wide selection of Chinese and international dining options, and a decent bar.

Five-star hotel rooms will have a kettle (and coffee sachets), safe, minibar, satellite or cable TV, broadband internet connection, wi-fi, mp3-player dock perhaps, both shower and bath, free newspaper (typically the *International Herald Tribune*) and nightly turndown service. No-smoking rooms will be available, as will Western breakfasts. Superior comfort should also be available on executive floors, which typically provide business facilities, free drinks upon arrival and in the afternoon, and complimentary breakfast. Service should be top-notch and English *should* be spoken well, although prepare for uncomprehending staff and blank looks.

Hotel Hassles

About a decade ago, an upbeat official announcement insisted foreigners would be able to stay at any hotel of their choosing. Today, however, foreign travellers still find themselves routinely barred from cheap hotels, even if they speak Chinese. The official line is that this is for the security and safety of 'foreign guests', and the Public Security Bureau (PSB) decides which hotels or guesthouses are safe. Many 'foreign guests' however argue that they should be allowed to decide whether a place is safe or not and choose accordingly. In fact many guesthouses that refuse foreigners are quite safe, but foreigners are directed to more expensive midrange hotels. The list of hotels that accept foreigners varies: during our last visit to Chéngdé, for example, budget hotels that were once fine for foreigners were off-limits.

In China's poorly regulated hotel industry, reverse-racism is also inflicted on Chinese travellers. Some hotels and hostels aimed at Westerners do not accept Chinese guests, recommending instead they find somewhere else to spend the night. These hotels seek to separate Westerners and Chinese, to create a Westerner-only atmosphere that fundamentally conflicts with the purpose of visiting China in the first place. Chinese-looking guests need to be warned that they may be told to find a room elsewhere.

If you are really keen to stay in one particular hostel, it may be a good idea to phone the hostel beforehand and book your room in English.

Most top-end hotels list their room rates in US dollars, but you will have to pay in local currency.

Activities

Grab copies of expat magazines in Běijīng, Hong Kong, Guǎngzhōu and Shànghǎi for information on activities such as running, cycling, football, cricket, swimming, ice skating, skateboarding and waterskiing.

Express Business Hotels

Clean and natty express business chains have expanded across China, offering lower-midrange comfort, good hygiene and convenience. They are often centrally located, generally purpose-built, with smallish Ikea-kitted rooms and no wardrobes in their standard doubles. Some of these chains offer membership schemes that bring rates down.

Home Inn (☏ 800 820 3333; www.homeinns.com)

Jinjiang Inn (www.jinjianginns.com)

Motel 168 (www.motel168.com)

HIKING

Hiking is an excellent way to see some of China's most dramatic landscapes; the sacred mountains are great places to consider. Outfits in China, such as **Wildchina** (www.wildchina.com), offer a host of dramatic treks in remote parts of the country.

MARTIAL ARTS

Martial-arts classes are easy to find in Běijīng, Hong Kong, Shànghǎi and Yángshuò, and other places.

ROCK CLIMBING

Rock climbing is popular in Yángshuò (p311) in Guǎngxī, where increasing numbers of foreigners are seeking out the region's bolted climbs.

Business Hours

China officially has a five-day working week. Banks, offices and government departments are open Monday to Friday, roughly from around 9am until 5pm or 6pm; some may close for two hours in the middle of the day. Many banks also open on Saturdays and may also open on Sundays. Post offices are generally open seven days a week.

Saturday and Sunday are public holidays. Most museums stay open on weekends and may make up for this by closing for one day during the week; they also tend to stop selling tickets half an hour before they close.

Travel agencies and foreign-exchange counters in tourist hotels are usually open seven days a week.

Department stores, shopping malls and shops are generally open from 10am to 10pm, seven days a week.

Parks tend to open soon after sunrise and close at twilight, so hours are much longer during the summer months.

Internet cafes are typically open 24 hours, but some open at 8am and close at midnight.

Restaurants are generally open from around 10.30am to midnight, but some shut at around 2pm and reopen at 5pm or 6pm; others open early for breakfast. The Chinese eat much earlier than Westerners, lunching at around midday and dining at about 6pm. Many bars open in the late afternoon and shut around midnight or later.

Customs Regulations

Chinese customs generally pay tourists little attention. There are clearly marked 'green channels' and 'red channels' at the airport. Some travellers have had their Lonely Planet guides confiscated at the (usually Vietnam) border.

Duty free, you're allowed to import 400 cigarettes or the equivalent in tobacco products; 1.5L of alcohol; 50g of gold or silver; and a camera, video camera, laptop and similar items for personal use only. Importation of fresh fruit and cold cuts is prohibited.

You can legally only bring in or take out Y6000 in Chinese currency, although there are no restrictions on foreign currency (but declare any cash exceeding US$5000 or its equivalent in another currency).

You are not allowed to import or export illegal drugs, or animals and plants (including seeds). Pirated DVDs and CDs are illegal exports from China as well as illegal imports into most other countries – if found they will be confiscated. You can take Chinese medicine up to a value of Y300 when you depart China.

Objects considered to be antiques require a certificate and a red seal to clear customs when leaving China. Anything made before 1949 is considered an antique, and if it was made before 1795 it cannot legally be taken out of the country. To get the proper certificate and red seal, your antiques must be inspected by the **Relics Bureau** (Wénwù Jú; ☏ 010-6401 9714, no English spoken) in Běijīng.

Practicalities

o **Electricity** There are four types of plugs – three-pronged angled pins, three-pronged round pins, two flat pins or two narrow round pins. Electricity is 220 volts, 50 cycles AC.

o **Newspapers** The standard English-language newspaper is the *China Daily* (www.chinadaily.com.cn). China's largest circulation Chinese-language daily is the *People's Daily* (*Rénmín Rìbào*). It has an English-language edition on www.english.peopledaily.com.cn. Imported English-language newspapers can be bought from five-star hotel bookshops.

o **TV & Radio** Listen to the BBC World Service (www.bbc.co.uk/worldservice/tuning) or Voice of America (www.voa.gov); however, the websites can be jammed. Chinese Central TV (CCTV) has an English-language channel – CCTV9. Your hotel may have ESPN, Star Sports, CNN or BBC News 24.

o **Weights & Measures** China officially subscribes to the international metric system, but you will encounter the ancient Chinese weights and measures system that features the *liǎng* (tael, 37.5g) and the *jīn* (catty, 0.6kg). There are 10 *liǎng* to the *jīn*.

Discount Cards

Seniors over the age of 65 are frequently eligible for a discount, so make sure you take your passport when visiting sights as proof of age.

An **International Student Identity Card** (ISIC; €12) can net students half-price discounts at many sights. Firstly examine the ticket price board at sights to see whether students are eligible for a discount and then, forcefully if necessary, insist on a discount.

Gay & Lesbian Travellers

Despite China's florid homosexual traditions, the puritanical overseers of the Chinese Communist Party (CCP) have worked hard to suppress them. There is greater tolerance in the big cities than in the more conservative countryside. However, even in urban areas, gay and lesbian visitors should not be too open publicly about their sexual orientation. You will often see Chinese same-sex friends holding hands or putting their arms around each other, but this usually has no sexual connotation.

Utopia (www.utopia-asia.com/tipschin.htm) has tips on travelling in China and a complete listing of gay bars nationwide. Useful publications include the *Spartacus International Gay Guide* (Bruno Gmunder Verlag).

Health

China is a reasonably healthy country to travel in, but some health issues should be noted. Pre-existing medical conditions and accidental injury (especially traffic accidents) account for most life-threatening problems, but becoming ill is not unusual. Outside the major cities, medical care is often inadequate, and food- and waterborne diseases are common. Malaria is still present in some parts of the country, and altitude sickness can be a problem.

Climate

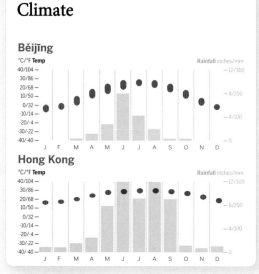

Běijīng

Hong Kong

The following advice is a general guide only and does not replace the advice of a doctor trained in travel medicine.

o Pack medications in their original, clearly labelled containers.

o If you take any regular medication, bring double your needs in case of loss or theft.

o Take a signed and dated letter from your physician describing your medical conditions and medications (using generic names).

o If you have a heart condition, bring a copy of your ECG taken just prior to travelling.

o Get your teeth checked before you travel.

In China you can buy some medications over the counter, but not all, without a doctor's prescription. In general it is not advisable to buy medications locally without a doctor's

advice. Fake medications and poorly stored or out-of-date drugs are also common, so try and take your own.

AVAILABILITY OF HEALTH CARE

Good clinics catering to travellers can be found in major cities. They are more expensive than local facilities but you may feel more comfortable dealing with a Western-trained doctor who speaks your language.

Self-treatment may be appropriate if your problem is minor (eg traveller's diarrhoea), you are carrying the relevant medication and you cannot attend a clinic. If you think you may have a serious disease, especially malaria, do not waste time, get to the nearest quality facility. To find the nearest reliable medical facility, contact your insurance company or your embassy.

INFECTIOUS DISEASES

DENGUE

This mosquito-borne disease occurs in some parts of southern China. There is no vaccine so avoid mosquito bites.

HEPATITIS A

A problem throughout China, this food- and waterborne virus infects the liver, causing jaundice (yellow skin and eyes), nausea and lethargy. There is no specific treatment for hepatitis A; you just need to allow time for the liver to heal. All travellers to China should be vaccinated.

HEPATITIS B

The only sexually transmitted disease that can be prevented by vaccination, hepatitis B is spread by contact with infected body fluids. The long-term consequences can include liver cancer and cirrhosis. All travellers to China should be vaccinated.

JAPANESE B ENCEPHALITIS

A rare disease in travellers; however, vaccination is recommended if you're in rural areas for over a month during summer months, or more than three months in the country. No treatment available; one-third of infected people die, another third suffer permanent brain damage.

MALARIA

Before you travel, ensure you seek medical advice to see if you need antimalaria medication and receive the right medication and dosage for you.

Malaria has been nearly eradicated in China; it is not generally a risk for visitors to the cities and most tourist areas. It is found mainly in rural areas in the southwestern region bordering Myanmar (Burma), Laos and Vietnam - principally Hǎinán, Yúnnán and Guǎngxī. More limited risk exists in remote rural areas of Fújiàn, Guǎngdōng, Guǎngxī, Guìzhōu and Sìchuān. Generally medication is only advised if you are visiting rural Hǎinán, Yúnnán or Guǎngxī.

Malaria is caused by a parasite transmitted by the bite of an infected mosquito. The most important symptom of malaria is fever, but general symptoms such as headache, diarrhoea, cough or chills may also occur. Diagnosis can only be made by taking a blood sample.

To prevent malaria: avoid mosquitos and take antimalaria medications. Most people who catch malaria are taking inadequate or no antimalaria medication.

Always take these insect-avoidance measures in order to help prevent all insectborne diseases (not just malaria):
- Use an insect repellent containing DEET on exposed skin.

- Choose accommodation with screens and fans (if it's not air-conditioned).

- Sleep under a mosquito net impregnated with permethrin.

- Impregnate clothing with permethrin in high-risk areas.

- Wear long sleeves and trousers in light colours.

- Use mosquito coils.

- Spray your room with insect repellent before going out for your evening meal.

RABIES

An increasingly common problem in China, this fatal disease is spread by the bite or lick of an infected animal, most commonly a dog. Seek medical advice immediately after any animal bite and commence postexposure treatment.

SCHISTOSOMIASIS (BILHARZIA)

This disease is found in the central Yangzi River (Cháng Jiāng) basin, carried in water by minute worms that infect certain varieties of freshwater snail found in rivers, streams, lakes and, particularly, behind dams. The infection often causes no symptoms until the disease is well established (several months to years after exposure); any resulting damage to internal organs is irreversible.

TYPHOID

Serious bacterial infection spread via food and water. Symptoms include headaches, a high and slowly progressive fever, perhaps accompanied by a dry cough and stomach pain.

Recommended Vaccinations

The World Health Organization (WHO) recommends the following vaccinations for travellers to China:
- Adult diphtheria and tetanus (ADT)

- Hepatitis A

- Hepatitis B

- Measles, mumps and rubella (MMR)

- Typhoid

- Varicella

The following immunisations are recommended for travellers spending more than one month in the country or those at special risk:
- Influenza

- Japanese B encephalitis

- Pneumonia

- Rabies

- Tuberculosis

Pregnant women and children should receive advice from a doctor who specialises in travel medicine.

Health Advisories

It's usually a good idea to consult your government's travel-health website before departure, if one is available:

○ Australia (www.dfat.gov.au/travel)

○ Canada (www.travelhealth.gc.ca)

○ New Zealand (www.mfat.govt.nz/travel)

○ UK (www.dh.gov.uk) Search for travel in the site index.

○ USA (www.cdc.gov/travel)

Insurance

A travel-insurance policy to cover theft, loss, trip cancellation and medical problems is a good idea. Travel agents can sort this out for you, although it is often cheaper to find good deals with an insurer online or with a broker. Worldwide travel insurance is available at www.lonelyplanet.com/travel_services. You can buy, extend and claim online anytime – even if you're already on the road.

Some policies specifically exclude 'dangerous activities' such as scuba diving, skiing and even trekking. A locally acquired motorcycle licence is not valid under some policies. Check that the policy covers ambulances or an emergency flight home.

Paying for your airline ticket with a credit card often provides limited travel-accident insurance – ask your credit-card company what it's prepared to cover.

You may prefer a policy that pays doctors or hospitals directly rather than reimbursing you for expenditures after the fact. If you have to claim later, ensure you keep all documentation.

Internet Access

The number of internet-cafe licences is strictly controlled, users need to show ID before going online and in some internet cafes (网吧; *wǎngbā*), eg in Běijīng, you will be digitally photographed (by a camera in an innocuous metal box on the registration counter). Rules are rigorously enforced in big cities such as Běijīng, but are more relaxed in small towns. At the time of writing, however, internet cafes in some regions of China were insisting users provide a valid Chinese ID (impossible for foreign travellers to produce).

Internet cafes are listed under the Information section for destinations throughout the book. In large cities and towns, the area around the train station is generally a good place to find internet cafes.

Rates at internet cafes should be around Y2 to Y5 per hour for a standard, no-frills outlet. Deposits of Y10 are sometimes required.

Internet-cafe opening hours vary, but can be 8am to midnight or, more commonly, 24 hours.

Youth hostels and other backpacker hotels should have internet access in common areas; if access is not gratis, rates will be around Y5 per hour. Many midrange and top-end hotels provide free broadband internet access as standard; many also have wi-fi areas. Throughout this book the internet icon (@) is used in hotel reviews to indicate the presence of an internet cafe or a terminal where you can get online; wi-fi areas are indicated with a wi-fi icon (📶).

Legal Matters

Anyone under the age of 18 is considered a minor; the minimum age at which you can drive is also 18. The age of consent for marriage is 22 for men and 20 for women. There is no minimum age restricting the consumption of alcohol or use of cigarettes.

China's laws against the use of illegal drugs are harsh, and foreign nationals have been executed for drug offences; in 2009 a British citizen was executed for smuggling drugs (despite protestations that he was mentally impaired). The Chinese criminal justice system does not ensure a fair trial and defendants are not presumed innocent until proven guilty. Note that China conducts more judicial executions than the rest of the world together – up to 10,000 per year (27 per day) according to some estimates. If arrested, most foreign citizens have the right to contact their embassy.

Money

Consult the Need to Know chapter (p48) for a table of exchange rates.

The Chinese currency is the renminbi (RMB), or 'people's money'. The basic unit of RMB is the yuán (元; Y), which is divided into 10 jiǎo (角), which is again divided into 10 fēn (分). Colloquially, the yuán is referred to as kuài and jiǎo as máo (毛). The fēn has so little value these days that it is rarely used.

The Bank of China issues RMB bills in denominations of Y1, Y2, Y5, Y10, Y20, Y50 and Y100. Coins come in denominations of Y1, 5 jiǎo, 1 jiǎo and 5 fēn. Paper versions of the coins remain in circulation.

Hong Kong's currency is the Hong Kong dollar (HK$), which is divided into 100 cents. Bills are issued in denominations of HK$10, HK$20, HK$50, HK$100, HK$500 and HK$1000. Copper coins are worth 50c, 20c and 10c, while the $5, $2 and $1 coins are silver and the $10 coin is nickel and bronze. The Hong Kong dollar is pegged to the US dollar at a rate of US$1 to HK$7.80, though it is allowed to fluctuate a little.

Macau's currency is the pataca (MOP$), which is divided into 100 avos. Bills are issued in denominations of MOP$10, MOP$20, MOP$50, MOP$100, MOP$500 and MOP$1000. There are copper coins worth 10, 20 and 50 avos and silver-coloured MOP$1, MOP$2, MOP$5 and MOP$10 coins. The pataca is pegged to the

Hong Kong dollar at a rate of MOP$103.20 to HK$100. In effect, the two currencies are interchangeable and Hong Kong dollars, including coins, are accepted in Macau. The Chinese renminbi is also accepted in many places in Macau at one-to-one. You can't spend patacas anywhere else, however, so use them before you leave Macau. Prices quoted in this book are in yuán unless otherwise stated.

ATMS

Bank of China and the Industrial & Commercial Bank of China (ICBC) 24-hour ATMs are plentiful, and you can use Visa, MasterCard, Cirrus, Maestro Plus and American Express to withdraw cash. All ATMs accepting international cards have dual language ability. The network is largely found in sizeable towns and cities. If you plan on staying in China for a long period, it is advisable to open an account at a bank with a nationwide network of ATMs, such as the Bank of China. In larger cities, you will be able to find HSBC and Citibank ATMs.

The exchange rate on ATM withdrawals is similar to that for credit cards, but there is a maximum daily withdrawal amount.

ATMs are listed in the Information sections of destinations throughout this book.

CREDIT CARDS

Credit is not big in China. Although it is increasingly fashionable for young Chinese to use credit cards, numbers remain low compared to the West. Banks such as Bank of

China, ICBC, China Construction Bank and Zhaoshang Bank all issue credit cards and are trying to encourage the Chinese to spend. In large tourist towns such as Běijīng, credit cards are relatively straightforward to use, but don't expect to be able to use them everywhere, and always carry enough cash; the exception is in Hong Kong, where international credit cards are accepted almost everywhere (although some shops may try to add a surcharge to offset the commission charged by credit companies, which can range from 2.5% to 7%).

Where they are accepted, credit cards often deliver a slightly better exchange rate than in banks. Money can also be withdrawn at certain ATMs in large cities on credit cards such as Visa, MasterCard and Amex. Credit cards generally can't be used to buy train tickets, but Civil Aviation Administration of China (CAAC; 中国民航; Zhōngguó Mínháng) offices readily accept international Visa cards for buying air tickets.

MONEYCHANGERS

It's best to wait till you reach China to exchange money as the exchange rate will be better. Foreign currency and travellers cheques can be changed at border crossings, international airports, branches of the Bank of China, tourist hotels and some large department stores; hours of operation for foreign-exchange counters are 8am to 7pm (later at hotels). Top-end hotels will generally change money for hotel guests only. The official rate is given almost everywhere and the exchange charge is standardised, so there is little need to shop around for the best deal.

Australian, Canadian, US, UK, Hong Kong and Japanese currencies and the euro can be changed in China. In some backwaters, it may be hard to change lesser-known currencies; US dollars are still the easiest to change.

Keep at least a few of your exchange receipts. You will need them if you want to exchange any remaining RMB you have at the end of your trip.

TIPPING

Almost no one in China (including Hong Kong and Macau) asks for tips. Tipping used to be refused in restaurants, but nowadays many midrange and top-end eateries include their own (often huge) service charge; cheap restaurants do not expect a tip. Taxi drivers throughout China do not ask for or expect tips.

TRAVELLERS CHEQUES

These are worth taking if you are principally travelling in large cities and tourist areas. Travellers cheques cannot be used everywhere, however; as with credit cards, always ensure you carry enough ready cash. You should have no problem cashing travellers cheques at tourist hotels, but they are of little use in budget hotels and restaurants. Bear in mind that most hotels will only cash the cheques of guests. If cashing them at banks, aim for the larger banks such as the Bank of China or the Industrial & Commercial Bank of China.

Some banks won't change travellers cheques at the weekend.

Cheques from most of the world's leading banks and issuing agencies are now accepted in China; stick to the major companies such as Thomas Cook, Amex and Visa, however. In big cities travellers cheques are accepted in almost any currency, but in smaller destinations it's best to stick to big currencies such as US dollars or UK pounds. Keep your exchange receipts so you can change your money back to its original currency when you leave.

Passports

You must have a passport with you at all times; it is the most basic travel document and all hotels (and some internet cafes) will insist on seeing it. The Chinese government requires that your passport be valid for at least six months after the expiry date of your visa. You'll need at least one entire blank page in your passport for the visa.

Take an ID card with your photo in case you lose your passport. Even better, make photocopies of your passport because your embassy may need these before issuing a new one. You should also report the loss to the local Public Security Bureau (PSB). Be careful who you pass your passport to, as you may never see it again.

Long-stay visitors should register their passport with their embassy.

Public Holidays

The People's Republic of China has 11 national holidays, as follows. Hong Kong and Macau have different holidays.

New Year's Day 1 January

Chinese New Year 23 January 2012, 10 February 2013

International Women's Day 8 March

Tomb Sweeping Festival 5 April

International Labour Day 1 May

Youth Day 4 May

International Children's Day 1 June

Birthday of the Chinese Communist Party 1 July

Anniversary of the Founding of the People's Liberation Army 1 August

Moon Festival end of September

National Day 1 October

Many of the above are nominal holidays that do not result in leave. The 1 May holiday is a three-day holiday, while National Day marks a week-long holiday from 1 October; the Chinese New Year is also a week-long holiday for many. It's not a great idea to arrive in China or go travelling during these holidays as things tend to grind to a halt. Hotel prices all over China rapidly shoot up during the May and October holiday periods.

●●●●

Safe Travel

CRIME

Travellers are more often the victims of petty economic crime, such as theft, than serious crime. Although an American was stabbed to death in broad daylight in Běijīng in 2008, such crimes are rare. Foreigners are natural targets for pickpockets and thieves – keep your wits about you and make it difficult for thieves to get at your belongings. Incidences of crime increase around the Chinese New Year.

High-risk areas in China are train and bus stations, city and long-distance buses (especially sleeper buses), hard-seat train carriages and public toilets. Don't leave anything of value in your bicycle basket.

Hotels are generally safe and some have attendants on every floor. Dormitories obviously require more care. Don't be overly trusting of your fellow travellers; some of them are considerably less than honest. All hotels have safes and storage areas for valuables – use them.

Carry as much cash as you need and keep the rest in travellers cheques. Obviously you will need to equip yourself with more cash if you're travelling to remote areas, as you may not be able to cash your travellers cheques; take a money belt for your cash, passport and credit cards.

Foreigners have been attacked or killed for their valuables, especially in more rural locations, so be vigilant at all times. Travelling solo carries obvious risks; it's advisable to travel with someone else or in a small group. Female travellers in particular should avoid travelling solo. Even in Běijīng, single women taking taxis have been taken to remote areas and robbed by taxi drivers, so don't assume anywhere is safe.

LOSS REPORTS

If something of yours is stolen, report it immediately to the nearest Foreign Affairs Branch of the PSB. Staff will ask you to fill in a loss report before investigating the case.

If you have travel insurance it is essential to obtain a loss report so you can claim compensation. Be prepared to spend many hours, perhaps even several days, organising it. Make a copy of your passport in case of loss or theft.

SCAMS

Con artists are not just increasingly widespread in China – methods are becoming ever more audacious. Well-dressed girls flock along Shànghǎi's East Nanjing Rd and Běijīng's Wangfujing Dajie, dragging single men to expensive cafes or Chinese teahouses, leaving them to foot monstrous bills.

Also watch out for itinerant Buddhist monks preying on foreigners for alms. Another common tactic is for the monk to give you a Buddhist talisman, and then ask for a donation.

Taxi scams at Běijīng's Capital Airport are legendary; always join the queue at the taxi rank and insist that the taxi driver uses his or her meter. Try to avoid pedicabs and motorised three-wheelers wherever possible; we receive a litany of complaints against pedicab drivers who originally agree on a price and then insist on an alternative figure (sometimes 10 times the sum) once arriving at the destination.

Be alert at all times if changing money on the black market. If buying a black-market train ticket, ensure the date, time, destination and ticket type (eg soft sleeper) are correct before handing over your cash.

TRANSPORT

Traffic accidents are the major cause of death in China for people aged between 15 and 45, and the World Health Organization (WHO) estimates there are 600 traffic deaths per day. At long-distance bus stations across China you may be subjected to posters graphically portraying victims of road crashes; then when you get on the bus you find there are no seatbelts (most of the time) or the seatbelts are virtually unusable through neglect, inextricably stuffed beneath the seat.

Your greatest danger in China will almost certainly be crossing the road, so develop 360-degree vision and a sixth sense. Note that cars can frequently turn on red lights in China, so the green 'walk now' man does not mean it is safe to cross.

Telephone

If making a domestic call, look out for very cheap public phones at newspaper stands (报刊亭; bàokāntíng) and hole-in-the-wall shops (小卖部; xiǎomàibù); you make your call and then pay the owner. Domestic and international long-distance phone calls can also be made from main telecommunications offices and 'phone bars' (话吧; huàbā). Cardless international calls are expensive and it's far cheaper to use an IP card.

Area codes for all cities, towns and destinations appear in the relevant chapters.

MOBILE PHONES

China Mobile outlets can sell you a SIM card, which will cost from Y60 to Y100 depending on the phone number and will include Y50 of credit. When this runs out, you can top up the number by buying a credit-charging card (chōngzhí kǎ) from China Mobile outlets and some newspaper stands.

PHONECARDS

If you wish to make international calls, it is much cheaper to use an IP card. International calls on IP cards (IP卡; IP kǎ) are Y1.80 per minute to the USA or Canada, Y1.50 per minute to Hong Kong, Macau and Taiwan, and Y3.20 to all other countries; domestic long-distance calls are Y0.30 per minute. You dial a local number, then punch in your account number, followed by a pin number and finally the number you wish to call. English-language service is

usually available. IP cards can be found at newspaper kiosks, hole-in-the-wall shops, internet cafes and from any China Telecom office, although in some cities they can be hard to find. Some IP cards can only be used locally, while others can be used nationwide, so it is important to buy the right card (and check the expiry date).

Time

The Chinese live by both the Gregorian and the lunar calendar. Time throughout China is set to Běijīng time, which is eight hours ahead of GMT/UTC. There is no daylight saving time in China.

When it's noon in Běijīng the time is 2pm in Sydney, 4am in London, 11pm in New York (previous day) and 8pm in Los Angeles (previous day).

Visas

APPLYING FOR VISAS

FOR CHINA

Apart from citizens of Japan, Singapore and Brunei, all visitors to China require a visa, which covers the whole of China, although there remain restricted areas that require an additional permit from the PSB. Permits are also required for travel to Tibet, a region that the authorities can suddenly bar foreigners from entering.

Your passport must be valid for at least six months after the expiry date of your visa and you'll need at least

one entire blank page in your passport for the visa.

At the time of writing, prices for a standard 30-day visa were as follows:

- o £30 for UK citizens

- o US$140 for US citizens

- o US$30 for citizens of other nations

Double-entry visas:
- o £45 for UK citizens

- o US$140 for US citizens

- o US$45 for all other nationals

Six-month multiple-entry visas:
- o £90 for UK citizens

- o US$140 for US citizens

- o US$60 for all other nationals

A standard 30-day single-entry visa can be issued from most Chinese embassies abroad in three to five working days. Express visas cost twice the usual fee. In some countries (eg the UK and the US), the visa service has been outsourced from the Chinese embassy to a Chinese Visa Application Service Centre, which levies an extra administration fee. In the case of the UK, a single-entry visa costs £30, but the standard administration charge levied by the centre is a further £35.25, making visa applications expensive.

A standard 30-day visa is activated on the date you enter China, and must be used within three months of the date of issue. Sixty-day and 90-day travel visas are harder to get. To stay longer, you can extend your visa in China (see later).

Visa applications require a completed application form (available at the embassy or downloaded from its website) and at least one photo (normally 51mm x 51mm). You normally pay for your visa when you collect it. A visa mailed to you will take up to three weeks. In the US and Canada, mailed visa applications have to go via a visa agent, at extra cost. In the US, many people use the **China Visa Service Center** (☏ in the USA 800 799 6560; www.mychinavisa.com), which offers prompt service. The procedure takes around 10 to 14 days.

Hong Kong is a good place to pick up a China visa. China Travel Service (CTS) will be able to obtain one for you, or you can apply directly to the **Visa Office of the People's Republic of China** (Map p276; ☏ 3413 2300; 7th fl, Lower Block, China Resources Centre, 26 Harbour Rd, Wan Chai; ☉9am-noon & 2-5pm Mon-Fri). Visas processed here in one/two/three days cost HK$400/300/150. Double-entry visas are HK$220, while six-month/one-year multiple-entry visas are HK$400/600 (plus HK$150/250 for express/urgent service). Be aware that American and UK passport holders must pay considerably more for their visas. You must supply two photos.

Five-day visas (Y160 for most nationalities, Y469 for British, US citizens excluded) are available at the Luóhú border crossing between Hong Kong and Shēnzhèn, valid for Shēnzhèn only.

Three-day visas are also available at the Macau–Zhūhǎi border (Y160 for most nationalities, Y469 for British, US citizens excluded). US citizens have to buy a visa in advance in Macau or Hong Kong.

Be aware that political events can suddenly make visas more difficult to procure or renew.

When asked about your itinerary on the application form, list standard tourist destinations; if you are considering going to Tibet or western Xīnjiāng, just leave it off the form. The list you give is not binding. Those working in media or journalism may want to profess a different occupation, otherwise a visa may be refused or a shorter length of stay than that requested may be given. There are eight categories of visas (for most travellers, an L visa will be issued).

FOR HONG KONG

At the time of writing, most visitors to Hong Kong, including citizens of the EU, Australia, New Zealand, the USA and Canada, could enter and stay for 90 days without a visa. British passport holders get 180 days, while South Africans are allowed to stay 30 days visa-free. If you require a visa, apply at a Chinese embassy or consulate before arriving. If you visit Hong Kong from China, you will need to either have a multiple-entry visa to re-enter China or a new visa.

FOR MACAU

Most travellers, including citizens of the EU, Australia, New Zealand, the USA, Canada and South Africa, can enter Macau without a visa for between 30 and 90 days. Most other nationalities can get a 30-day visa on arrival, which will cost MOP$100/50/200 per adult/child under 12/family. If you're visiting Macau from China and plan to re-enter China, you will need to be on a multiple-entry visa.

VISA EXTENSIONS

FOR CHINA

The Foreign Affairs Branch of the local PSB deals with visa extensions.

First-time extensions of 30 days are usually easy to obtain on single-entry tourist visas; further extensions are harder to get, and may only give you another week.

Types of Visas

TYPE	DESCRIPTION	CHINESE NAME
C	flight attendant	*chéngwù* 乘务
D	resident	*dìngjū* 定居
F	business or student	*fǎngwèn* 访问
G	transit	*guòjìng* 过境
J	journalist	*jìzhě* 记者
L	travel	*lǚxíng* 旅行
X	long-term student	*liúxué* 留学
Z	working	*gōngzuò* 工作

Travellers report generous extensions in provincial towns, but don't bank on this. Popping across to Hong Kong to apply for a new tourist visa is another option.

Extensions to single-entry visas vary in price, depending on your nationality. At the time of writing, US travellers paid Y185, Canadians Y165, UK citizens Y160 and Australians Y100. Expect to wait up to five days for your visa extension to be processed.

The penalty for overstaying your visa in China is up to Y500 per day. Some travellers have reported having trouble with officials who read the 'valid until' date on their visa incorrectly. For a one-month travel (L) visa, the 'valid until' date is the date by which you must enter the country (within three months of the date the visa was issued), not the date upon which your visa expires.

FOR HONG KONG

For tourist-visa extensions, inquire at the **Hong Kong Immigration Department** (Map p276; ☏ 2852 3047; www.immd.gov.hk; 2nd fl, Immigration Tower, 7 Gloucester Rd, Wan Chai; ⏱8.45am-4.30pm Mon-Fri, 9-11.30am Sat). Extensions (HK$160) are not readily granted unless there are extenuating circumstances such as illness.

FOR MACAU

If your visa expires, you can obtain a single one-month extension from the **Macau Immigration Department** (Map p296; ☏ 2872 5488;

Ground fl, Travessa da Amizade; ⏱9am-5pm Mon-Fri).

RESIDENCE PERMITS

The 'green card' is a residence permit, issued to English teachers, foreign expats and long-term students who live in China. Green cards are issued for a period of six months to one year and must be renewed annually. Besides needing all the right paperwork, you must also pass a health exam, for which there is a charge. Families are automatically included once the permit is issued, but there is a fee for each family member. If you lose your card, you'll pay a hefty fee to have it replaced.

Volunteering

Large numbers of Westerners work in China with international development charities such as **VSO** (www.vso.org.uk), which can provide you with useful experience and the chance to learn Chinese.

Joy in Action (JIA; www.jia-workcamp.org) Establishing work camps in places in need in south China.

Global Vision International (GVI; www.gvi.co.uk) Teaching in China.

Global Volunteer Network (www.globalvolunteernetwork.org) Connecting people with communities in need.

World Teach (www.worldteach.org) Volunteer teachers.

Transport

GETTING THERE & AWAY

Flights, tours and rail tickets can be booked online at www.lonelyplanet.com/bookings.

ENTERING CHINA

No particular difficulties exist for travellers entering China. The main requirements are a passport that's valid for travel for six months after the expiry date of your visa, and a visa (see p402). As a general rule, visas cannot be obtained at the border (apart from five-day visas for Shēnzhèn at the Hong Kong–Shēnzhèn border and three days visas at the Zhūhǎi–Macau border). In general, visas are not required for Hong Kong or Macau; if you enter Hong Kong or Macau from China and wish to re-enter China, you will need either a multiple-entry visa or a new visa. A permit is required for travel to Tibet. Chinese immigration officers are scrupulous and highly bureaucratic, but not overly officious. Travellers arriving in China will be given a health declaration form and an arrivals form to complete.

AIR

AIRPORTS

Hong Kong, Běijīng and Shànghǎi are China's principal international air gateways.

Báiyún International Airport (CAN; Xīnbáiyún Jīchǎng; ☏ 020-36066999) In Guǎngzhōu; receiving an increasing number of international flights.

Capital Airport (PEK; Shǒudū Jīchǎng; ☏ 010-6454 1100; http://en.bcia.com.cn) Běijīng's international airport; three terminals.

Hong Kong International Airport (HKG; ☏ 852-2181 8888; www.hkairport.com) Located at Chek Lap Kok on Lantau island in the west of the territory.

Hóngqiáo Airport (SHA; Hóngqiáo Jīchǎng; ☏ 021-6268 8899/3659) In Shànghǎi's west; domestic flights.

Pǔdōng International Airport (PVG; Pǔdōng Guójì Jīchǎng; ☏ 021-96990; http://www.shanghaiairport.com) In Shànghǎi's east; international flights.

AIRLINES FLYING TO/FROM CHINA

The following list comprises a selection of airlines flying into Běijīng, Hong Kong, Shànghǎi, Kūnmíng and Macau.

Aeroflot Russian Airlines (SU; www.aeroflot.ru) Běijīng (☏ 010-6500 2412); Hong Kong (☏ 852-2537 2611); Shànghǎi (☏ 021-6279 8033)

Air Canada (AC; www.aircanada.ca) Běijīng (☏ 010-6468 2001); Hong Kong (☏ 852-2867 8111); Shànghǎi (☏ 021-6279 2999)

Air China (CA; www.airchina.com.cn) Běijīng (☏ 4008 100 999); Hong Kong (☏ 852-3970 9000); Shànghǎi (☏ 021-5239 7227)

Air France (AF; www.airfrance.com) Běijīng (☏ 010-6588 1388); Hong Kong (☏ 852-2501 9433); Shànghǎi (☏ 4008 808 808)

Air Macau (NX; www.airmacau.com.mo) Běijīng (☏ 010-6515 8988); Macau (☏ 853-396 5555); Shànghǎi (☏ 021-6248 1110)

Air New Zealand (NZ; ☏ in Hong Kong 852-2862 8988; www.airnewzealand.com)

AirAsia (FD; ☏ in Macau 853-2886 1388; www.airasia.com)

Alitalia (AZ; www.alitalia.com) Běijīng (☏ 010-6501 4861); Shànghǎi (☏ 021-6103 1133)

All Nippon Airways (NH; www.ana.co.jp) Běijīng (☏ 800 820 1122); Hong Kong (☏ 852-2810 7100); Shànghǎi (☏ 021-5696 2525)

American Airlines (AA; www.aa.com) Běijīng (☏ 010-5879 7600); Shànghǎi (☏ 021-6375 8686)

Asiana Airlines (OZ; www.us.flyasiana.com) Běijīng (☏ 010-6468 4000); Hong Kong (☏ 852-2523

Climate Change & Travel

Every form of transport that relies on carbon-based fuel generates CO_2, the main cause of human-induced climate change. Modern travel is dependent on aeroplanes, which might use less fuel per kilometre per person than most cars but travel much greater distances. The altitude at which aircraft emit gases (including CO_2) and particles also contributes to their climate-change impact. Many websites offer 'carbon calculators' that allow people to estimate the carbon emissions generated by their journey and, for those who wish to do so, to offset the impact of the greenhouse gases emitted with contributions to portfolios of climate-friendly initiatives throughout the world. Lonely Planet offsets the carbon footprint of all staff and author travel.

8585); Shànghǎi (☏ 4006 508 000)

Austrian Airlines (OS; www.aua.com) Běijīng (☏ 010-6462 2161); Shànghǎi (☏ 021-6340 3411)

British Airways (BA; www.british-airways.com) Běijīng (☏ 010-6512 4070); Hong Kong (☏ 852-3071 5083); Shànghǎi (☏ 1080 0440 0031)

Cathay Pacific (CX; www.cathaypacific.com) Běijīng (☏ 010-8486 8532); Hong Kong (☏ 852-2747 1888)

China Airlines (CI; ☏ in Hong Kong 852-2868 2299; www.china-airlines.com)

China Eastern Airlines
(MU; www.ce-air.com)
Běijīng (☎ 010-6602 4070);
Hong Kong (☎ 852-2861 1898);
Shànghǎi (☎ 021-95108)

China Southern Airlines
(CZ; www.cs-air.com)
Běijīng (☎ 010-950 333); Hong
Kong (☎ 852-2929 5033);
Shànghǎi (☎ 021-950 333)

Dragonair (KA; www.
dragonair.com)
Běijīng (☎ 010-6518 2533);
Hong Kong (☎ 852-3193 3888);
Kūnmíng (☎ 0871-356 1208/9);
Shànghǎi (☎ 021-6375 6375)

Emirates Airline (EK; ☎ in
Hong Kong 852-2801 8777; www.
emirates.com)

EVA Airways (BR; www.evaair.
com)
Hong Kong (☎ 852-2380 3362);
Macau (☎ 853-2872 6866)

Garuda Indonesia (GA;
www.garuda-indonesia.com)
Běijīng (☎ 010-6505 2901);
Hong Kong (☎ 852-2840 0000)

Hong Kong Airlines (HX;
☎ Hong Kong 852-2155 1888;
www.hkairlines.com)

Japan Airlines (JL; www.
jal.com)
Běijīng (☎ 010-6513 0822);
Hong Kong (☎ 852-2523 0081);
Shànghǎi (☎ 021-6288 3000)
Also flies to Qīngdǎo, Dàlián
and Xiàmén.

Kenya Airways (KQ; ☎ in
Hong Kong 852-3678 2000;
www.kenya-airways.com)

KLM (KL; www.klm.nl)
Běijīng (☎ 010-6505 3505);
Hong Kong (☎ 852-2808 2168);
Shànghǎi (☎ 4008 808 222)

Korean Air (KE; www.
koreanair.com)
Běijīng (☎ 010-8453 8137);
Hong Kong (☎ 852-2366 2001);
Shànghǎi (☎ 021-6275 2000)
Also flies to Qīngdǎo and
Shěnyáng.

Koryo Air (JS; ☎ in Běijīng
010-6501 1557)

Lao Airlines (QV; ☎ in
Kūnmíng 0871-312 5748; www.
laoairlines.com)

Lufthansa Airlines (LH;
www.lufthansa.com)
Běijīng (☎ 010-6468 8838);
Shànghǎi (☎ 021-5352 4999)

Malaysia Airlines (MH; www.
malaysia-airlines.com.my)
Běijīng (☎ 010-6505 2681);
Hong Kong (☎ 852-2916 0088);
Kūnmíng (☎ 0871-316 5888);
Shànghǎi (☎ 021-6279 8607)

MIAT Mongolian Airlines
(OM; ☎ in Běijīng 010-6507
9297; www.miat.com)

Northwest Airlines (NW;
www.nwa.com)
Běijīng (☎ 010-6505 1353);
Hong Kong (☎ 852-2810 4288);
Shànghǎi (☎ 4008 140 081)

**Pakistan International
Airlines** (PK; www.piac.com.
pk) Běijīng (☎ 010-6505 1681);
Hong Kong (☎ 852-2366 4770)

Philippine Airlines (PR;
☎ in Hong Kong 852-2301
9300; www.philippineairlines.
com)

Qantas Airways (QF; www.
qantas.com.au)
Běijīng (☎ 010-6567 9006);
Hong Kong (☎ 852-2822 9000);
Shànghǎi (☎ 021-6145 0188)

Qatar Airways (QR; ☎ in
Hong Kong 852-2868 9833;
www.qatarairways.com)

Scandinavian Airlines (SK;
www.sas.dk)
Běijīng (☎ 010-8527 6100);
Shànghǎi (☎ 021-5228 5001)

Shanghai Airlines (www.
shanghai-air.com)
Hong Kong (☎ 852-3586 2238);
Shànghǎi (☎ 021-6255 0550,
800 620 8888)

Singapore Airlines (SQ;
www.singaporeair.com)
Běijīng (☎ 010-6505 2233);
Hong Kong (☎ 852-2520 2233);
Shànghǎi (☎ 021-6288 7999)

**Swiss International
Airlines** (LX; ☎ in Hong Kong
852-3002 1330; www.swiss.
com)

Thai Airways International
(TG; www.thaiairways.com)
Běijīng (☎ 010-6460 8899);
Hong Kong (☎ 852-2179 7777);
Kūnmíng (☎ 0871-351 1515);
Shànghǎi (☎ 021-8515 0088)

Tiger Airways (TR; ☎ in
Hong Kong 852-2116 8730; www.
tigerairways.com)

Trans Asia Airways
(GE; ☎ in Macau 853-2870
3438/1777; www.tna.com.tw)

United Airlines (UA; www.
ual.com)
Běijīng (☎ 010-6463 1111);
Hong Kong (☎ 852-2810 4888);
Shànghǎi (☎ 021-3311 4567)

Uzbekistan Airways (HY;
www.uzairways.com)
Běijīng (☎ 010-6500 6442);
Shànghǎi (☎ 021-6307 1896)

Vietnam Airlines (VN; ☎ in Hong Kong 852-2810 4896; www.vietnamair.com.vn)

Virgin Atlantic (VS; www.virgin-atlantic.com)
Hong Kong (☎ 852-2532 6060); Shànghǎi (☎ 021-5353 4600)

Viva Macau (ZG; www.flyvivamacau.com)

TICKETS

The cheapest tickets to Hong Kong and China can often be found either online or in discount agencies in Chinatowns around the world. Budget and student-travel agents offer cheap tickets, but the real bargains are with agents that deal with the Chinese, who regularly return home. Airfares to China peak between June and September.

The cheapest flights to China are with airlines requiring a stopover at the home airport, such as Air France to Běijīng via Paris, or Malaysia Airlines to Běijīng via Kuala Lumpur.

The best direct ticket deals are available from China's international carriers, such as China Eastern.

The cheapest available airline ticket is called an APEX (advance purchase excursion) ticket, although this type of ticket includes expensive penalties for cancellation and changing dates of travel. For browsing and buying tickets on the internet, try **Fly China** (www.flychina.com).

To bid for last-minute tickets online, try **Skyauction** (www.skyauction.com). **Priceline** (www.priceline.com) aims to match the ticket price to your budget.

Discounted air-courier tickets are a possibility, but they carry restrictions. As a courier, you transport documents or freight internationally and see it through customs, so you usually have to sacrifice your baggage allowance. Generally trips are on fixed round-trip tickets and offer an inflexible period in the destination country. For more information, check out organisations such as **Courier Association** (www.aircourier.org) and **International Association of Air Travel Couriers** (IAATC; www.courier.org).

AUSTRALIA & NEW ZEALAND

Hong Kong is a popular gateway. However, fares from Australia to Hong Kong are generally not that much cheaper than fares to Běijīng or Shànghǎi.

Flight Centre (☎ 133 133; www.flightcentre.com.au) Offices throughout Australia.

Flight Centre (☎ 0800 24 35 44; www.flightcentre.co.nz)

STA Travel (☎ 0800 474 400; www.statravel.co.nz)

STA Travel (☎ 1300 733 035; www.statravel.com.au) Offices in all major cities and many university campuses.

CANADA

Browse agency ads in the *Globe & Mail*, the *Toronto Star*, the *Montreal Gazette* and the *Vancouver Sun*. From Canada, fares to Hong Kong are often higher than those to Běijīng.

Air Canada has daily flights to Běijīng and Shànghǎi from Vancouver. Air Canada, Air China and China Eastern Airlines sometimes run supercheap fares.

Expedia (www.expedia.ca) Online bookings.

M's Travel (☎ 604 232 0288; www.mstravel.ca/english) Discount tickets to China; its main customers are overseas Chinese.

Travel CUTS (☎ 1866 246 9762; www.travelcuts.com) Canada's national student travel agency; offices in all major cities.

Travelocity (☎ 877 282 2925; www.travelocity.ca)

CONTINENTAL EUROPE

Generally there is not much variation in airfare prices from the main European cities. The major airlines and travel agents usually have a number of deals on offer, so shop around. **STA Travel** (www.statravel.com) and **Nouvelles Frontières** (www.nouvelles-frontieres.fr) have branches throughout Europe.

Recommended agencies include the following.

CTS Viaggi (☎ in Italy 02 584 751; www.cts.it)

ISSTA (☎ in the Netherlands 020 618 8031; www.isstadirect.nl)

Voyages Wasteels (☎ in France 01 42 61 69 87; www.wasteels.fr)

JAPAN

Daily flights operate between Tokyo and Běijīng, as well as regular flights between Osaka and Běijīng. Daily flights link Shànghǎi to Tokyo and Osaka, and there are flights from Japan to other major cities in China, including Dàlián and Qīngdǎo.

STA Travel (☏ in Tokyo 03-5391 2922; www.statravel.co.jp) Reliable.

SINGAPORE

Chinatown Point Shopping Centre on New Bridge Rd has a good selection of travel agents.

STA Travel (☏ 6737 7188; www.statravel.com.sg) Three offices in Singapore.

SOUTH KOREA

Xanadu Travel (☏ 02-795 7771; fax 02-797 7667; www.xanadu.co.kr) Good discount travel agency in Seoul.

THAILAND

STA Travel (☏ 02-236 0262; www.statravel.co.th; Room 1406, 14th fl, Wall Street Tower, 33/70 Surawong Rd) Good and reliable place to start.

UK & IRELAND

Discount air travel is big business in London. Advertisements for many travel agencies appear in the travel pages of the weekend broadsheet newspapers, and in *Time Out*, the *Evening Standard* and *TNT*. The cheapest flights include KLM to China via Amsterdam, Air France via Paris or Singapore Airlines via Singapore.

Travel agents in London's Chinatown dealing with flights to China include the following:

Jade Travel (☏ 0870 898 8928; www.jadetravel.co.uk; 5 Newport Pl)

Omega Travel (☏ 0844 493 8888; www.omegatravel.ltd.uk; 53 Charing Cross Rd)

Reliance Tours Ltd (☏ 0800 018 0503; www.reliance-tours.co.uk; 12-13 Little Newport St)

Sagitta Travel Agency (☏ 0870 077 8888; www.sagitta-tvl.com; 9 Little Newport St)

USA

Discount travel agents in the USA are known as consolidators. San Francisco is the ticket-consolidator capital of America, although some good deals can also be found in Los Angeles, New York and other big cities. Consolidators can be found through the *Yellow Pages* or the travel sections of major daily newspapers.

Air Brokers International (☏ 1 800 883 3273; www.airbrokers.com)

STA Travel (☏ 800 781 4040; www.sta-travel.com) Offices in most major US cities.

VIETNAM

Air China and Vietnam Airlines fly between Ho Chi Minh City and Běijīng; China Southern Airlines flights are via Guǎngzhōu. Shanghai Airlines has five flights weekly to Ho Chi Minh City from Shànghǎi.

From Běijīng to Hanoi there are two flights weekly with either China Southern Airlines or Vietnam Airlines.

BORDER CROSSINGS

China shares borders with Afghanistan, Bhutan, India, Kazakhstan, Kyrgyzstan, Laos, Mongolia, Myanmar, Nepal, North Korea, Pakistan, Russia, Tajikistan and Vietnam; the borders with Afghanistan, Bhutan and India are closed. There are also official border crossings between China and its special administrative regions, Hong Kong and Macau; see p289 and p302, respectively, for overland transport details.

Lonely Planet *China* guides may be confiscated by officials, primarily at the Vietnam–China border.

KAZAKHSTAN

Border crossings from Ürümqi to Kazakhstan are via border posts at Korgas, Tǎchéng and Jímùnǎi. Ensure you have a valid Kazakhstan visa (obtainable, at the time of writing, in Ürümqi, or from Běijīng) or China visa.

Apart from Ālāshànkǒu, which links China and Kazakhstan via train, all border crossings are by bus; you can generally get a bike over, however. Two trains weekly also run between Ürümqi and Almaty.

Remember that borders open and close frequently due to changes in government policy; additionally, many are only open when the weather permits. It's always best to check with the Public Security Bureau (PSB; Gōng'ānjú) in Ürümqi for the official line.

KYRGYZSTAN

There are two routes between China and Kyrgyzstan: one between Kashgar and Osh, via the Irkeshtam Pass; and one between Kashgar and Bishkek, via the dramatic 3752m Torugart Pass.

LAOS

From the Měnglà district in China's southern Yúnnán province, you can enter Laos via Boten in Luang Nam Tha province. A daily bus runs between Vientiane and Kūnmíng; a daily bus also runs from Jǐnghóng to Luang Nam Tha in Laos.

You can now get an on-the-spot visa for Laos at the border, the price of which depends on your nationality (although you cannot get a China visa here).

MONGOLIA

From Běijīng, the Trans-Mongolian Railway trains (see the boxed text, p410) and the K23 trains travel to Ulaanbaatar. Two trains weekly run between Hohhot and Ulaanbaatar, and there are also buses between Hohhot and the border town of Erenhot.

MYANMAR (BURMA)

The famous Burma Road runs from Kūnmíng in Yúnnán province to the Burmese city of Lashio. The road is open to travellers carrying permits for the region north of Lashio, although you can legally cross the border in only one direction – from the Chinese side (Jiěgào) into Myanmar. Myanmar visas can only be arranged in Kūnmíng or Běijīng.

International Train Routes

The number of international train routes to China is limited, but visionary plans are being hatched to lash China and Europe tighter together. Within 15 years, express trains may be racing from Běijīng to London on high-speed tracks as part of a vast Chinese £65-billion project aiming to complete three transnational high-speed routes: to Singapore from Kūnmíng, to Berlin from Běijīng and the rest of Europe and Eastern Europe via Moscow.

In addition to the **Trans-Siberian** and **Trans-Mongolia rail services**, the following trains run international routes:

○ Hung Hom station in **Kowloon** (Jiǔlóng; Hong Kong; www.throughtrain.kcrc.com; p289) to **Guǎngzhōu**, **Shànghǎi** and **Běijīng**

○ **Pyongyang** (North Korea) to **Běijīng**

○ **Almaty** (Kazakhstan) to **Ürümqi**

○ **Běijīng** to **Ulaanbaatar**

○ **Běijīng** to **Hanoi**

NEPAL

The 865km road connecting Lhasa with Kathmandu is known as the Friendship Hwy. It's a spectacular trip across the Tibetan plateau, the highest point being Gyatso-la Pass (5100m).

Visas for Nepal can be obtained in Lhasa, or even at the border at Kodari.

When travelling from Nepal to Tibet, foreigners still have to arrange transport through tour agencies in Kathmandu. Access to Tibet can, however, be restricted for months at a time without warning.

NORTH KOREA

Visas for North Korea are difficult to arrange, and at the time of writing it was impossible for US and South Korean citizens. Those interested in travelling to North Korea from

Běijīng should contact Nicholas Bonner or Simon Cockerell at **Koryo Tours** (☎ 010-6416 7544; www.koryogroup.com; 27 Beisanlitun Nan, Běijīng).

There are five weekly flights and four international express trains (K27 and K28) between Běijīng and Pyongyang.

PAKISTAN

The exciting trip on the Karakoram Hwy, said to be the world's highest public international highway, is an excellent way to get to or from Chinese Central Asia. There are buses from Kashgar for the two-day trip to the Pakistani town of Sost via Tashkurgan when the pass is open.

RUSSIA

A once-weekly train runs from Hā'ěrbīn to Vladivostok via

Suífēnhé; the train runs twice-weekly in the other direction.

The Trans-Mongolian and Trans-Manchurian branches of the Trans-Siberian Railway run from Běijīng to Moscow.

There's a border crossing 9km from Mǎnzhōulǐ; there is also a border crossing at Hēihé.

TAJIKISTAN

At the time of writing, the Kulma Pass, linking Kashgar with Murghob was not open to foreign travellers.

VIETNAM

Visas are unobtainable at the border crossings; Vietnam visas can be acquired in Běijīng, Kūnmíng and Nánníng. Chinese visas can be obtained in Hanoi.

China's busiest border with Vietnam is at the obscure Vietnamese town of Dong Dang, 164km northeast of Hanoi. The closest Chinese town to the border is Píngxiáng in Guǎngxī province, about 10km north of the actual border gate. There are also seven Hanoi-bound buses from Nánníng, running via the Friendship Pass.

The Hékǒu–Lao Cai border crossing is 468km from Kūnmíng and 294km from Hanoi. At the time of writing, the only way to reach Vietnam via Hékǒu was by bus from Kūnmíng.

A third, but little-known, border crossing is at Mong Cai in the northeast corner of the country, just opposite the Chinese city of Dōngxīng and around 200km south of Nánníng.

There are also two weekly trains from Běijīng to Hanoi.

RIVER

Fast ferries leave Jǐnghóng in Yúnnán three times a week for the seven-hour trip to Chiang Saen in Thailand.

 SEA

JAPAN

There are weekly ferries between Osaka and Shànghǎi. From Tiānjīn (Tánggū), a weekly ferry runs to Kōbe in Japan. There are also twice-weekly boats from Qīngdǎo to Shimonoseki. Check in two hours before departure for international sailings.

SOUTH KOREA

International ferries connect the South Korean port of Incheon with Wēihǎi, Qīngdǎo, Yāntái, Tiānjīn (Tánggū, Dàlián and Dāndōng. There are also boats between Qīngdǎo and Gunsan.

In Seoul, tickets for any boats to China can be bought from the **International Union Travel Agency** (☏ 822-777 6722; Room 707, 7th fl, Daehan Ilbo Bldg, 340 Taepyonglo 2-ga, Chung-gu). In China, tickets can be bought cheaply at the pier, or from China International Travel Service (CITS; Zhōngguó Guójì Lǚxíngshè) for a very steep premium.

To reach the International Passenger Terminal from Seoul, take the Seoul–Incheon commuter train (subway line 1 from the city centre) and get off at the Dongincheon station. The train journey takes 50 minutes. From Dongincheon station it's either a 45-minute walk or five-minute taxi ride to the ferry terminal.

🚆 TRAIN

TRANS-SIBERIAN RAILWAY

Rolling out of Europe and into Asia, through eight time zones and over 9289km of taiga, steppe and desert, the Trans-Siberian Railway and its connecting routes constitute one of the most famous and most romantic of the world's great train journeys.

There are, in fact, three railways. The 'true' **Trans-Siberian** line runs from Moscow to Vladivostok. But the routes traditionally referred to as the Trans-Siberian Railway are the two branches that veer off the main line in eastern Siberia for Běijīng.

Since the first option excludes China, most readers of this book will be choosing between the **Trans-Manchurian** and the **Trans-Mongolian**. The Trans-Mongolian (Běijīng to Moscow, 7865km) is faster, but requires an additional visa and another border crossing, but you get to see the Mongolian countryside. The Trans-Manchurian is longer (Běijīng to Moscow, 9025km).

See Lonely Planet's *Trans-Siberian Railway* for further details. Another useful source of information is **Seat 61** (www.seat61.com/Trans-Siberian.htm).

ROUTES

TRANS-MONGOLIAN RAILWAY

Trains offer deluxe two-berth compartments (with shared shower), 1st-class four-berth compartments and 2nd-class four-berth compartments. Fares for 2nd-class/deluxe compartments cost from around Y3737/Y5501 to Moscow, Y1128/1619 to Ulaanbaatar and Y2661/3909 to Novosibirsk. Ticket prices are cheaper if you travel in a group.

o From **Běijīng**: train K3 leaves Běijīng on its five-day journey to Moscow at 7.45am every Wednesday, passing through Dàtóng, Ulaanbaatar and Novosibirsk, arriving in Moscow the following Monday at 2.28pm.

o From **Moscow**: train K4 leaves at 10.03pm on Tuesdays arriving in Běijīng on the following Monday at 2.04pm. Departure and arrival times may fluctuate slightly.

Trans-Manchurian Railway Trains have 1st-class two-berth compartments and 2nd-class four-berth compartments; prices are similar to those on the Trans-Mongolian Railway.

o From **Běijīng**: train K19 departs Běijīng at 10.56pm on Saturday (arriving in Moscow the following Friday at 5.57pm) before arriving at the border post Mǎnzhōulǐ, 2347km from Běijīng. Zabaykal'sk is the Russian border post; from here, the train continues to Tarskaya, where it connects with the Trans-Siberian line.

o From **Moscow**: train K20 leaves Moscow at 11.58pm every Friday, arriving in Běijīng the following Friday at 5.31am. Departure and arrival times may fluctuate slightly.

VISAS

Travellers will need Russian and Mongolian visas for the Trans-Mongolian Railway, as well as a Chinese visa. These can often be arranged along with your ticket by travel agents such as China International Travel Service.

Mongolian visas take three to five days to process, coming as two-day **transit visas** (US$15) or 30-day **tourist visas** (US$30). A transit visa is easy to get (present a through ticket and a visa for your onward destination). The situation regarding visas changes regularly, so check with a Mongolian embassy or consulate. All Mongolian embassies shut for the week of National Day (Naadam), which officially falls around 11 to 13 July.

Russian transit visas (one-week/three-day/one-day process US$50/80/120) are valid for 10 days if you take the train, but will only give you three or four days in Moscow at the end of your journey. You need one photo, your passport and the exact amount in US dollars. You will also need a valid entry visa for a third country plus a through ticket from Russia to the third country. You can also obtain a 30-day Russian tourist visa, but the process is complicated.

BUYING TICKETS

In Běijīng, tickets can be conveniently purchased from **China International Travel Service** (CITS, Zhōngguó Guójì Lǚxíngshè; ☎ 010-6512 0507; www.cits.com.cn; Beijing International Hotel, 9 Jianguomen Neidajie). **Monkey Business Shrine** (www.monkeyshrine.com; Youyi Youth Hostel, 43 Beisanlitun Lu) in Běijīng also arranges trips, and has an informative website with a downloadable brochure. There's another **branch** (☎ 852-2723 1376; Liberty Mansion, Kowloon) in Hong Kong.

Abroad, tickets and sometimes visas can be arranged through one of the following agencies.

Intourist Travel (www.intourist.com) With branches in the UK, USA, Canada, Finland and Poland.

Russia Experience (☎ 020-8566 8846; www.trans-siberian.co.uk; Research House, Fraser Rd, Perivale, Middlesex, England)

White Nights (☎/fax 1800 490 5008; www.wnights.com; 610 Sierra Dr, Sacramento, CA, USA)

●●●

GETTING AROUND

✈ AIR

Despite being a land of vast distances, it's quite straightforward to navigate your way terrestrially around China by rail and bus if you have time; if you are in more of a rush, get airborne.

China's air network is extensive and growing. China's civil aviation fleet is expected to triple in size over the next two decades; airports are constantly being built and upgraded all over the land. Air safety and quality have improved considerably, resulting in a shortage of suitable pilots.

Shuttle buses often run from **Civil Aviation**

Administration of China (CAAC; Zhōngguó Mínháng) offices in towns and cities throughout China to the airport; see the Getting Around sections of relevant chapters. For domestic flights, arrive at the airport one hour before departure.

Remember to keep your baggage receipt label on your ticket as you will need to show it when you collect your luggage. Planes vary in style and comfort. You may get a hot meal, or just a small piece of cake and an airline souvenir. On-board announcements are delivered in Chinese and English.

AIRLINES IN CHINA

The CAAC is the civil aviation authority for numerous airlines, including the following:

Air China (☎ in Běijīng 4008 100 999; www.airchina.com.cn)

China Eastern Airlines (☎ in Shànghǎi 95530; www.ce-air.com)

China Southern Airlines (☎ in Guǎngzhōu 95539; www.cs-air.com) Serves a nationwide web of air routes, including Běijīng, Shànghǎi, Xī'ān and Tiānjīn.

Hainan Airlines (☎ in Hǎinán 950718; www.hnair.com)

Shandong Airlines (☎ in Jǐnán 96777; www.shandongair.com.cn)

Shanghai Airlines (☎ in Shànghǎi 1010 5858; www.shanghai-air.com)

Sichuan Airlines (☎ in Chéngdū 4008 300 999; www.scal.com.cn)

Spring Airlines (☎ in Shànghǎi 800 820 6222; www.china-sss.com) Has connections between Shànghǎi and tourist destinations such as Qīngdǎo, Guìlín and Xiàmén. No food or drink served on board. Some of the above airlines also have subsidiary airlines. Not all Chinese airline websites have English-language capability. Some airline information is listed within the relevant chapters.

The CAAC publishes a combined international and domestic timetable in both English and Chinese in April and November each year. This timetable can be bought at some airports and CAAC offices in China. Individual airlines also publish timetables, which you can buy from ticket offices throughout China.

TICKETS

Except during major festivals and holidays, tickets are easy to purchase. Tickets can be purchased from branches of the CAAC nationwide, airline offices, travel agents or the travel desk of your hotel; travel agents will usually offer a better discount than airline offices. Discounts are common, except when flying into large cities such as Shànghǎi and Běijīng on the weekend, when the full fare can be the norm; prices quoted in this book are the full fare. To book online and obtain good discounts, visit www.Ctrip.com, www.elong.com or www.9588.com. Fares are calculated according to one-way travel, with return tickets simply costing twice the single fare.

You can use credit cards at most CAAC offices and travel agents. Departure tax is included in the ticket price.

⚲ BICYCLE

Except in seriously bike-free hilly cities such as Chóngqìng, bicycles (自行车; zìxíngchē) are an excellent method for getting around China's cities and tourist sights. They can also be invaluable for exploring the countryside surrounding towns such as Yángshuò.

HIRE

Bicycle-hire outlets that cater to travellers can be found in many but not all traveller centres; some addresses are listed in destination chapters. Most youth hostels rent out bicycles, as do many hotels, although the latter are more expensive.

Bikes can be hired by the day or by the hour and it's also possible to hire for more than one day. Rental rates vary depending on where you find yourself, but rates start at around Y10 to Y15 per day in cities such as Běijīng.

Most hire outlets will ask you for a deposit of anything up to Y500 (get a receipt); you'll also need to leave some sort of ID.

TOURING

Cycling through China allows you to go when you want, to see what you want and at your own pace. It can also be an extremely cheap, as well as a highly authentic, way to see the land.

You will have virtually unlimited freedom of movement but, considering the size of China, you will need to combine your cycling days with trips by train, bus, boat, taxi or even planes, especially if you want to avoid particularly steep regions, or areas where the roads are poor or the climate is cold.

Bikechina (www. bikechina.com) is a good source of information for cyclists coming to China. The Yángshuò-based company offers tours around southwest China, ranging from one-day bike tours of Chéngdū to five-day round trips from Chéngdū to Dānbā and eight-day trips around Yúnnán.

A basic packing list for cyclists includes a good bicycle-repair kit, water, sunscreen and other protection from the sun, waterproofs, fluorescent strips and camping equipment. Ensure you have adequate clothing, as many routes will be taking you to considerable altitude. Road maps in Chinese are essential for asking locals for directions.

🚢 BOAT

Boat services within China are limited. They're most common in coastal areas, where you are likely to use a boat to reach offshore islands such as Pǔtuóshān or Hǎinán, or the islands off Hong Kong. The Yāntái–Dàlián ferry will probably survive because it saves hundreds of kilometres of overland travel.

The best-known river trip is the three-day boat ride along the Yangzi (Cháng Jiāng) from Chóngqìng to Yíchāng (p251). The Lí River (Lí Jiāng) boat trip from Guìlín to Yángshuò (p306) is a popular tourist ride.

Hong Kong employs a veritable navy of vessels that connect with the territory's myriad islands, and a number of popular boats run between the territory and other parts of China, including Macau, Zhūhǎi, Shékǒu (for Shēnzhèn) and Zhōngshān. See p289 for details.

Boat tickets can be purchased from passenger ferry terminals or through travel agents.

🔜 BUS

Long-distance bus (长途公 共汽车; *chángtú gōnggòng qìchē*) services are extensive and reach places you cannot get to by train; with the increasing number of intercity highways, journeys are getting quicker. Tickets are cheaper and easier to get than train tickets.

However, tickets are getting more expensive, breakdowns can be a hassle, and some rural roads and provincial routes (especially in the southwest, Tibet and the northwest) remain in bad condition. Precipitous drops, pot holes, dangerous road surfaces and reckless drivers mean accidents remain common. Long-distance journeys can also be cramped and noisy, with Hong Kong films and cacophonous karaoke looped over overhead TVs. Drivers continuously lean on the horn. In such conditions, taking an MP3 player is crucial for one's sanity. Astonishingly, **seat belts** are a rarity in many provinces; if you find one knotted in a cat's cradle beneath your seat, it may look like it's been used to clean a wheel axle.

Routes between large cities sport larger, cleaner and more comfortable fleets of private buses, some equipped with toilets; shorter and more far-flung routes still rely on rattling minibuses into which as many fares as possible are crammed. On countless routes, buses wait till they fill up before leaving or exasperatingly trawl the streets looking for fares.

Sleeper buses (卧铺客车; *wòpù kèchē*) ply popular long-haul routes, costing around double the price of a normal bus service. Bunks can be short, however, and buses claustrophobic.

Take plenty of warm clothes on buses to high-altitude destinations in winter. A breakdown in frozen conditions can prove lethal for those unprepared. Take a lot of extra water on routes across areas such as the Taklamakan Desert.

Bus journey times given throughout this book should be used as a rough guide only. You can estimate times for bus journeys on non-highway routes by calculating the distance against a speed of 25km per hour.

All cities and most towns have one or more **long-distance bus station** (长途 汽车站; *chángtú qìchēzhàn*), generally located in relation to the direction the bus heads in. Tickets are easy to purchase; often just turn up at the bus station and buy your ticket there and then, rather than booking in advance. Booking in advance, however, can secure you a better seat, as many buses have numbered seats.

In many cities, the train station forecourt doubles as a bus station.

🚗 CAR & MOTORCYCLE

Cars in China drive on the right-hand side of the road. Even skilled drivers will be unprepared for China's roads: in the cities, cars lunge from all angles and chaos abounds.

DRIVING LICENCE

To drive in Hong Kong and Macau, you will need an International Driving Permit. Foreigners can drive motorcycles if they are residents in China and have an official Chinese motorcycle licence.

HIRE

Both Běijīng's Capital Airport or Shànghǎi's Pudong International Airport have a **Vehicle Administration Office** (车管所; chēguǎnsuǒ; ☎ 6453 0010, Mon-Sun 9am-6pm) where you can have a temporary three-month driving licence issued. This will involve checking your driving licence and a simple medical exam (including an eyesight test). You will need this licence before you can hire a car from **Hertz** (☎ 800-988-1336), which has branches at Capital Airport and Pǔdōng International Airport. Hire cars from Hertz start from Y450 per day (up to 150km per day; Y20000 deposit). **Avis** (☎ 400 882 1119) also has a growing network around China, with car rental starting from Y200 per day (Y5000 deposit).

LOCAL TRANSPORT

Long-distance transport in China is good, but local transport is not so efficient.

The choice of local transport is diverse but vehicles can be slow and overburdened, and the network confusing for visitors. Hiring a car is often impractical, while hiring a bike can be inadequate. Unless the town is small, walking is often too tiring. On the plus side, local transport is cheap, and taxis are usually ubiquitous and affordable.

BUS

Bus services are extensive and fares inexpensive but vehicles are often packed; navigation is tricky for non-Chinese speakers as bus routes at bus stops are generally listed in Chinese, without Pinyin. Traffic can be slow. In Běijīng and Shànghǎi, stops will be announced in English.

Maps of Chinese cities and bus routes are available from hawkers outside train stations. Ascending a bus, point to your destination on the map and the conductor (seated near the door) will sell you the right ticket. They usually tell you where to disembark, provided they remember. Buses with snowflake motifs are air-conditioned.

METRO & LIGHT RAIL

Going underground is fast, efficient and cheap; most networks are either very new or relatively new and can be found in a rapidly growing number of cities.

TAXI

Taxis (出租汽车; chūzū qìchē) are cheap, plentiful and easy to find. Congregation points include train and long-distance bus stations.

Taxi drivers rarely speak any English so have your destination written down in characters.

To use the same driver again, ask for his card (名片; míngpiàn). Taxis can be hired for a single trip or on a daily basis.

Taxi rates per kilometre are clearly marked on a sticker on the rear side window of the taxi; flag fall varies from city to city, and also depends upon the size and quality of the vehicle.

Most taxis have meters but they may only be switched on in larger towns and cities. If the meter is not used (on an excursion out of town, for example), negotiate a price before you set off and write the fare down. If you want the meter used, ask for dǎbiǎo (打表). Ask for a receipt (发票; fāpiào); if you leave something in the taxi, the taxi number is printed on the receipt so it can be located.

To share a car or minibus (ie paying per seat), ask to pīnchē (拼车); if you want to pay for the whole car, it's bāochē (包车).

OTHER LOCAL TRANSPORT

An often bewildering variety of ramshackle transport options exists across China. **Motor tricycles** are enclosed three-wheeled vehicles that congregate outside train and bus stations. Pedal-powered **tricycles** also muster outside train and bus stations and cruise the streets.

Motorbike riders also offer lifts in some towns for what should be half the price of a regular taxi. You must wear a helmet – the driver will provide one.

For all of the above agree on a price in advance (preferably have it written down). Prices can compare with taxis, so check fares beforehand and bargain.

🚆 TRAIN

Trains are the best way to travel around China in reasonable speed and comfort, despite crowding. They are also adventurous, exciting, fun, practical and efficient and ticket prices are reasonable to boot. Colossal investment over recent years has put the rail network at the heart of China's rapid modernisation drive. You don't have to be a trainspotter to find China's railways an enthralling subculture – you also get to meet the Chinese people at their most sociable.

THE CHINESE TRAIN NETWORK

One of the world's most extensive rail networks, passenger railways cover every province in China, including the insular bastion of Hǎinán, finally breached in the closing months of 2010. In line with China's frantic economic development and the pressures of transporting 1.4 billion people across one of the world's largest nations, expansion of China's rail network over the past decade has been astonishing.

The railway to Lhasa in Tibet began running in 2006, despite scepticism that it could ever be laid, so now you can climb aboard a train in Běijīng or Shànghǎi and alight in Tibet's capital. Thousands of miles of track are laid every year across China and new express train series are being continuously launched to shrink China's vast distances. Brand new state-of-the-art train stations are also incessantly appearing, many to serve high-speed links.

With the simultaneous advent of high-speed D-, G-, Z- and C-class express trains, getting between major cities as a traveller is increasingly a breeze. An ultra-high-speed railway is being built between Běijīng and Shànghǎi, with trains due to begin running in 2011.

For international trains to China, see p409.

TRAVELLING BY TRAIN

Trains are generally highly punctual in China and also generally a safe way to travel, with few accidents. Train stations are often conveniently close to the centre of town. Travelling on sleeper berths at night often means you can frequently arrive at your destination first thing in the morning, saving a night's hotel accommodation.

Think ahead, get your tickets early and you can sleep your way around a lot of China. Don't leave it till the very last minute to board your train as queues outside the main train station entrance (进站口; jìnzhànkǒu) can be shocking. You are required to pass your bags through a security scanner at the train station entrance.

On long train trips, load up with snacks, food and drink for the journey. Trolleys of food and drink are wheeled along carriages during the trip, but prices are high and the selection is limited. For tea and noodles, flasks of hot water are provided in each sleeper compartment. You can also load up on mineral water and snacks at stations, where hawkers sell items from platform stalls. Long-distance trains should have a **canteen carriage** (餐厅车厢; cāntīng chēxiāng) where you can buy cooked food and beer from a limited menu; they are sometimes open through the night.

In each class of sleeper, linen is clean and changed for each journey; beds are generally bed bug free. Staff rarely speak English, except sometimes on the high-speed express trains.

On a non-sleeper, ask a member of staff or a fellow passenger to tell you when your station arrives.

If taking a sleeper train, you will be required to exchange your paper ticket for a plastic or metal card with your bunk number on it. The conductor then knows when you are due to disembark, so you can be woken in time and have your ticket returned to you. Hold on to your paper ticket as it may be inspected at the train station exit.

CATEGORY OF TRAIN

Chinese train numbers are usually prefixed by a letter, designating the category of train. The fastest, most luxurious and expensive intercity trains are the streamlined, high-speed 'C', 'D' and 'G' type trains, which rapidly shuttle between major cities, such as

Train Categories

CATEGORY	MEANING	TYPE
C	chéngjì gāosù	ultra-high-speed express
D	dòngchē, héxié hào	high-speed express
G	gāotiě	high-speed
K	kuàisù (快速)	fast train
T	tèkuài (特快)	express
Z	zhídá tèkuài (直达特快)	direct express (overnight)

Běijīng and Tiānjīn and Běijīng and Shànghǎi.

With their modern looks, 200km/h to 250km/h D-class trains are also referred to as 'harmonious class' ('harmony' is the Chinese Communist Party's latest fix-all word). The wide-bodied trains breathlessly glide around China at the apex of speed and comfort. Temperature-regulated first-class carriages have mobile and laptop chargers, seats are two-abreast with ample legroom and TV sets showing peaceful programs. Doors between carriages are opened with electric buttons.

C- and G-class trains are even faster, with the speediest expected to reach 380km/h; by 2012 G-class trains will convey passengers from Běijīng to Kūnmíng in 12 hours (instead of the current 47 hours). In 2011, G-class trains were set to start shuttling passengers from Běijīng to Shanghai in a mere four hours. Overnight Z-class trains are not as fast but are still express and very comfortable; rather down the pecking order are T- and K-class trains, which are older and more basic.

There are also numbered trains that do not commence with a letter; these are pǔkuài (普快) or pǔkè (普客) trains, the most unsophisticated.

TICKET TYPES

It is possible to **upgrade** (补票; bǔpiào) your ticket once aboard your train. If you have a standing ticket, for example, find the conductor and upgrade to a hard seat, soft seat, hard sleeper or soft sleeper (if there are any available).

SOFT SLEEPER

Soft sleepers (软卧; ruǎn wò) are very comfortable, with four air-conditioned bunks in a closed compartment. Soft-sleeper tickets cost much more than hard-sleeper tickets; however, soft sleepers often sell out, so book early. Soft sleepers vary between trains and the best are on the more recent D- and Z-class trains.

All Z-class trains are soft-sleeper trains, with very comfortable, up-to-date berths. A few T-class trains also offer two-berth compartments, with their own toilet. Tickets on upper berths are slightly cheaper than lower berths.

HARD SLEEPER

Hard sleepers (硬卧; yìng wò) are available on slower and less-modern T-, K- and N-class trains, as well as trains without a letter prefix. Carriages consist of doorless compartments with half a dozen bunks in three tiers; sheets, pillows and blankets are provided. It does very nicely as an overnight hotel. There is a small price difference between berths, with the lowest bunk (下铺; xiàpù) the most expensive and the highest bunk (上铺; shàngpù) the cheapest. The middle bunk (中铺; zhōngpù) is good, as all and sundry invade the lower berth to use it as a seat during the day, while the top one has little headroom and puts you near the speakers.

As with all other classes, smoking is prohibited. Lights and speakers go out at around 10pm. Each compartment is equipped with its own hot-water flask, filled by an attendant. Hard-sleeper tickets are the most difficult of all to buy; you almost always need to buy these a few days in advance.

SEATS

Soft-seat class (软座; ruǎn zuò) is more comfortable but not nearly as common as hard-seat class. First-class (一等; yīděng) and second-class (二等; èrděng) soft seats are available in D-, C- and G-class high-speed trains. First class comes with TVs, mobile phone and laptop charging points, and seats arranged two abreast.

Second-class soft seats are also very comfortable; staff are very courteous throughout. Overcrowding is not permitted. On older trains, soft-seat carriages are often double-decker, and are not as plush as the faster and more modern high-speed express trains.

Hard-seat class (硬座; *yìng zuò*) is not available on the faster and plusher C-, D- and G-class trains and is only found on T-, K- and N-class trains and trains without a number prefix; a handful of Z-class trains have hard seat. Hard-seat class generally has padded seats, but it's hard on your sanity; often unclean and noisy, and painful on the long haul. Since hard seat is the only class most locals can afford, it's packed to the gills.

You should get a ticket with an assigned seat number, but if seats have sold out, ask for a **standing ticket** (无座、站票; *wúzuò* or *zhànpiào*), which gets you on the train, where you may find a seat or can upgrade; otherwise you will have to stand in the carriage or between carriages (with the smokers). Hard-seat sections on newer trains are air-conditioned and less crowded.

TICKETING

BUYING TICKETS

The Achilles heel of China's overburdened rail system, buying tickets can be a real pain.

Never aim to get a hard-sleeper (or increasingly, soft-sleeper) ticket on the day of travel – plan ahead. Most tickets can be booked in advance between two and 10 days prior to your intended date of departure. Buying hard-seat tickets at short notice is usually no hassle, but it may be a standing ticket rather than a numbered seat. Tickets can only be purchased with cash.

Most tickets are one-way only, with prices calculated per kilometre and adjustments made depending on class of train, availability of air-con, type of sleeper and bunk positioning. If you want to buy tickets for a train between two destinations beyond the city you are buying your ticket in, it is often better to go to an independent ticket office that charges a commission.

Tickets for hard sleepers are usually obtainable in major cities, but are trickier to buy in quiet backwaters. As with air travel, buying tickets around the Chinese New Year and during the 1 May and 1 October holiday periods can be very hard, and prices increase on some routes.

Touts swarm around train stations selling black-market tickets; this can be a way of getting scarce tickets, but foreigners frequently get ripped off.

TICKET OFFICES

Ticket offices (售票厅; *shòupiàotīng*) at train stations are usually to one side of the main train station entrance. Ticket sales are automated on very few routes. There may be a window (look for the sign) manned by someone with basic English skills; otherwise join the queue at one of the other windows.

Try and get to the station early but always prepare to queue for up to half an hour to get your ticket; you may queue for 20 minutes and when you reach the window it may shut temporarily. Some stations are surprisingly well run, others are bedlam. Take

Railing Against Rail

The Chinese have travelled by train (火车; *huǒchē*; literally 'fire vehicle') for decades like absolute naturals, but it was far from love at first sight. Railways were strongly resisted in the 19th century for fear they disturbed ancestors' graves and obstructed feng shui; Běijīng was also anxious that railroads would accelerate the military domination of China by foreign powers. China's first railway (1875) ran from Shànghǎi to Wúsōng at the mouth of the Yangzi River, operating for a few brief years before encountering stiff local resistance, being torn up and being shipped to Taiwan.

Tickets can also be bought online at **China Trip Advisor** (www.chinatripadvisor.com) or **China Train Timetable** (www.china-train-ticket.com), but it's cheaper to buy your ticket at the station. For trains from Hong Kong to Shànghǎi, Guǎngzhōu or Běijīng, tickets can be ordered online at no mark up from **KCRC** (www.mtr.com.hk).

To get a **refund** (退票; *tuìpiào*) on an unused ticket, windows exist at large train stations where you can get 80% of the ticket value back.

your passport in case you are asked for it when buying a ticket.

Alternatively, independent train ticket offices usually exist elsewhere in town where tickets can be purchased without the same kind of queues, for a Y5 commission; such outlets are listed in towns and cities within destination chapters. Your hotel will also be able to rustle up a ticket for you for a commission, and so can a travel agent.

Telephone booking services exist, but operate only in Chinese.

TIMETABLES

Paperback train timetables for the entire country (Y7) are published every April and October, but are available in Chinese only. Even to Chinese readers, their Byzantine layout is taxing. You can download an annual English translation for a fee from www.chinatt.org. Online English-language time-tables include the following:

China Highlights (www.chinahighlights.com)

China Train Timetable (www.china-train-ticket.com)

China Travel Guide (www.chinatravelguide.com)

INTERNET RESOURCES

Seat 61 (www.seat61.com/China.htm)

Shike (www.shike.org.cn, in Chinese)

Tielu (www.tielu.org, in Chinese)

A-Z

Language

To enhance your trip with a phrasebook, visit **lonelyplanet.com**. Lonely Planet iPhone phrasebooks are available through the Apple App store.

MANDARIN

In this section we've provided Pinyin (the official system of writing Mandarin in the Roman alphabet) next to the Mandarin script. The tones are indicated by accent marks on vowels: high (ā), rising (á), falling-rising (ǎ) and falling (à). Keep in mind that 'ü' is pronounced like 'ee' with pursed lips; 'c' as the 'ts' in 'bits'; 'q' as the 'ch' in 'cheese'; 'x' as the 'sh' in 'ship'; 'z' as the 'ds' in 'suds'; and 'zh' as the 'j' in 'judge'.

BASICS

Hello./Goodbye.
你好。/再见。   Nǐhǎo./Zàijiàn.
Yes./No.
是。/不是。   Shì./Bùshì.
Excuse me.
劳驾。   Láojià.
Sorry.
对不起。   Duìbùqǐ.
Please ...
请……   Qǐng ...
Thank you.
谢谢你。   Xièxie nǐ.
You're welcome./That's fine.
不客气。   Bù kèqi.
How are you?
你好吗?   Nǐhǎo ma?
Fine. And you?
好。你呢?   Hǎo. Nǐ ne?
Do you speak English?
你会说英文吗?   Nǐ huìshuō Yīngwén ma?
I don't understand.
我不明白。   Wǒ bù míngbai.

How much is this?
多少钱?   Duōshǎo qián?

ACCOMMODATION

Do you have a single/double room?
有没有单人/   Yǒuméiyǒu dānrén/
套房?   tào fáng?
How much is it per night/person?
每天/人多少钱?   Měi tiān/rén duōshǎo qián?

EATING & DRINKING

I'd like ..., please.
我想吃……   Wǒ xiǎng chī ...
That was delicious.
真好吃。   Zhēn hǎochī.
The bill/check, please.
买单。   Mǎidān.
I'm allergic to (nuts).
我对(果仁)过敏。   Wǒ duì (guǒrén) guòmǐn.

I don't eat ...
我不吃……   Wǒ bùchī ...
   fish   鱼   yú
   poultry   家禽   jiāqín
   red meat   牛羊肉   niúyángròu

EMERGENCIES

I'm ill.
我生病了。   Wǒ shēngbìng le.
Help!
救命!   Jiùmìng!
Call a doctor!
请叫医生来!   Qǐng jiào yīshēng lái!
Call the police!
请叫警察!   Qǐng jiào jǐngchá!

DIRECTIONS

Where's a/the ...?
……在哪儿?   ... zài nǎr?
   bank
   银行   Yínháng
   market
   市场   Shìchǎng
   museum
   博物馆   Bówùguǎn
   post office
   邮局   Yóujú
   restaurant
   餐馆   Cānguǎn
   toilet
   厕所   Cèsuǒ
   tourist office
   旅行店   Lǚxíng diàn

CANTONESE

If you read our pronunciation guides, provided in this section next to the Cantonese script, as if they were English, you'll be understood fine. The tones are indicated by accent marks on 'n' and on vowels: high (à), high rising (á), low falling (à), low rising (á) and low (a). Note that 'au' is pronounced like the 'ou' in 'out'; 'eu' as the 'er' in 'fern'; 'ew' as in 'blew' (with tightened lips); 'iu' as the 'yu' in 'yuletide'; and 'ui' as the French word *oui* (or the English 'we'). Also, the 'ng' sound can appear at the start of a word, and the words ending with 'p', 't' and 'k' must be clipped in Cantonese. You can hear this in English as well – say 'pit' and 'tip' and listen to how much shorter the 'p' sound is in 'tip'.

BASICS

Hello./Goodbye.
哈佬 。/再見 。 hàa·ló/joy·gin

Yes./No.
係 。/不係 。 hai/ǹg·hai

Excuse me.
對唔住 。 deui·ǹg·jew

Sorry.
對唔住 。 deui·ǹg·jew

Please ...
唔該…… ǹg·gòy ...

Thank you.
多謝 。 dàw·je

You're welcome./That's fine.
唔駛客氣 。 ǹg·sái haak·hay

How are you?
你幾好啊嗎 ? láy gáy hó à maa

Fine. And you?
幾好 。你呢 ? gáy hó láy lè

Do you speak English?
你識唔識講 láy sìk·ǹg·sìk gáwng
英文啊 ? yìng·mán aa

I don't understand.
我唔明 。 ngáw ǹg mìng

How much is this?
幾多錢 ? gáy·dàw chín

ACCOMMODATION

Do you have a (single/double) room?
有冇 (單人/ yáu·mó (dàan·yàn/
雙人)房 ? sèung·yàn) fáwng

How much is it per (night/person)?
一 (晚/個人） yàt (máan/gaw yàn)
幾多錢 ? gáy·dàw chín

EATING & DRINKING

I'd like ..., please.
我想食…… ngáw séung sìk ...

That was delicious.
真好味 。 jàn hó·may

I'd like the bill/check, please.
唔該我要埋單 。 ǹg·gòy ngáw yiu màai·dàan

I'm allergic to (nuts).
我對 (果仁） ngáw deui (gwáw·yàn)
過敏 。 gaw·mán

I don't eat ...
我唔吃…… ngáw ǹg sìk ...

    fish 魚 yéw
    poultry 雞鴨鵝 gài ngaap ngàw
    red meat 牛羊肉 ngàu yèung yuk

EMERGENCIES

I'm ill.
我病咗 。 ngáw beng·jáw

Help!
救命 ! gau·meng

Call a doctor!
快啲叫醫生 ! faai·dì giu yì·sàng

Call the police!
快啲叫警察 ! faai·dì giu gíng·chaat

DIRECTIONS

Where's a/the ...?
……喺邊度 ? ... hái bìn·do

    bank
    銀行 ngàn·hàwng
    market
    街市 gàai·sí
    museum
    博物館 bawk·màt·gún
    post office
    郵局 yàu·gúk
    restaurant
    酒樓 jáu·làu
    toilet
    廁所 chi·sáw
    tourist office
    旅行社 léui·hàng·sé

Behind the Scenes

Author Thanks
DAMIAN HARPER

Thanks of course to the authors of the 12th edition of Lonely Planet *China*: without their work this guide would not have been possible. Thanks also to Emily K Wolman and the staff at Lonely Planet for helping put this guide together and pointing it in the right direction.

Acknowledgments

Climate map data adapted from Peel MC, Finlayson BL & McMahon TA (2007) 'Updated World Map of the Köppen-Geiger Climate Classification', *Hydrology and Earth System Sciences*, 11, 163344.

Cover photographs: Front: Black Dragon Pool and Yúlóng Xuěshān, Líjiāng, Jochen Schlenker/Photolibrary; Back: Terracotta warriors, Xī'ān, Juliet Coombe/Lonely Planet Images. Many of the images in this guide are available for licensing from Lonely Planet Images: www.lonelyplanetimages.com.

This Book

This 1st edition of *Discover China* was coordinated and written by Damian Harper and researched and written by Piera Chen, Chung Wah Chow, David Eimer, Daisy Harper, Shawn Low, Daniel McCrohan and Christopher Pitts. This guidebook was commissioned in Lonely Planet's Oakland office, and produced by the following:

Commissioning Editors Emily K Wolman, Catherine Craddock-Carrillo

Coordinating Editors Evan Jones, Sonya Mithen, Jeanette Wall

Coordinating Cartographer Diana Duggan

Coordinating Layout Designer Kerrianne Southway

Managing Editors Brigitte Ellemor, Liz Heynes

Managing Cartographers David Connolly, Amanda Sierp

Managing Layout Designers Jane Hart, Celia Wood

Assisting Editors Jackey Coyle, Barbara Delissen, Dianne Schallmeiner, Louisa Syme, Angela Tinson

Assisting Cartographer Valeska Cañas

Cover Research Naomi Parker

Internal Image Research Sabrina Dalbesio

Language Content Branislava Vladisavljevic

Thanks to Shahara Ahmed, Judith Bamber, Melanie Dankel, Janine Eberle, Ryan Evans, Joshua Geoghegan, Chris Girdler, Laura Jane, Yvonne Kirk, Nic Lehman, John Mazzocchi, Wayne Murphy, Piers Pickard, Malisa Plesa, Averil Robertson, Lachlan Ross, Mik Ruff, Laura Stansfeld, Juan Winata

SEND US YOUR FEEDBACK

We love to hear from travellers – your comments keep us on our toes and help make our books better. Our well-travelled team reads every word on what you loved or loathed about this book. Although we cannot reply individually to postal submissions, we always guarantee that your feedback goes straight to the appropriate authors, in time for the next edition. Each person who sends us information is thanked in the next edition, and the most useful submissions are rewarded with a free book.

Visit **lonelyplanet.com/contact** to submit your updates and suggestions or to ask for help. Our award-winning website also features inspirational travel stories, news and discussions.

Note: We may edit, reproduce and incorporate your comments in Lonely Planet products such as guidebooks, websites and digital products, so let us know if you don't want your comments reproduced or your name acknowledged. For a copy of our privacy policy visit lonelyplanet.com/privacy.

Index

A

accommodation 49, 390-4, *see also individual locations*
acrobatics 99
activities 394, *see also* hiking, martial arts, rock climbing
aesthetics 375
air travel
  airlines 405-6, 412
  airports 405
  to/from China 405-8
  within China 411-12
An Lushan 350
ancient settlements 146
animals, *see* giant pandas, wildlife
archaeology 13, 130, 146
architecture 14, 62, 191, 374-9
  Běijīng 58
  CCTV Building 58, 89
  colonial 258
  courtyard 27
  Hong Kong & the south 260
  Huīzhōu 244
  imperial 57
  Kāipíng 309
  Ming dynasty 28
  modern 379
  Mògānshān 235-7
  National Centre for the Performing Arts 57, 74
  National Stadium & National Aquatics Center 85

000 Map pages

Qing dynasty 28, 239
  Shànghǎi 203, 203-6
  town walls 145
  traditional 23
  villa 28
area codes 402
art galleries
  Běijīng 80-1, 90
  Hong Kong 280
  Shànghǎi 201, 202
  Xī'ān 144
arts 374-9, *see also* literature, music
  National Centre for the Performing Arts 57, 74
ATMs 48, 399

B

Bādáling 57
Bai people 30, 326
Báishuǐtái 333
beer 177
Běijīng 62-123, **64-5**
  accommodation 90-3
  activities 89-90
  Cháoyáng 92-3, 96, **82**, **86**
  Chóngwén 83-5
  courses 89-90
  Dōngchéng 63-81, 90-2, 93-5, **66-7**, **77**
  drinking 97-8
  entertainment 98-101
  Fēngtái 85-6
  food 93-7
  Haidiàn 86-90, 93
  history 62-3
  hútòng 27, 40, 54-5, 79, 80, 81
  internet access 103-4
  itineraries 33, 37, 60-1, 69
  medical services 104
  money 104
  museums 104
  post 104
  scams 106
  shopping 101-2

  sights 63-89
  tourist information 105
  travel to/from 105
  travel within 107-9
  visa extensions 104-5
  Xīchéng 92, 95
  Xuānwu 85-6, 92
Běijīng & the Great Wall 51-123, **53**
  architecture 58
  drinking 58
  food 58
  highlights 54-7
  itineraries 60-1
  planning 59
  resources 59
  safety 59
  shopping 59
  travel seasons 48
  travel within 59
  views 58
Běijīng Olympic Games 63, 85
Běijīng opera 83, 98-9
bicycle travel, *see* cycling
boat travel 413, *see also* cruises, ferries
books 47, 376
border crossings 408-10
Boxer Rebellion 352
Buddha statues 121
  Lantau 274
  Lèshān 336
  Lóngmén Caves 153-4
  Mògāo Caves 341
  Yúngāng Caves 165-8
Buddhism 30, 350, 380-1
Buddhist culture 132
budget 49
Bund 186-7, **198-9**
bus travel 413-14
business hours 394

C

canal towns 239
  Jiāngsū 28
  Lùzhí 239
  Mùdú 239

Nánxún 239
Tóngli 226-8
Wūzhèn 237
Zhéjiāng 28
car travel 48, 414
caves
    Lóngmén 153-5
    Mògāo 21, 341
    Yúngāng 29, 130, 165
CCTV building 58, 59
cell phones 48, 402
ceramics 375-6
Chairman Mao Memorial Hall 76
Cháng Jiāng 15, 189, 247-51
Chéngdé 119-23
Chéngdū 26, 334
Cheung Chau 284
Chiang Kaishek 194, 354-5
children, travel with 214, 358-9
Chinese Communist Party (CCP) 354-5, 362, 363
Chinnery, George 293
Chóngqìng 248, 251
Christianity 382
Chuāndìxià 110
churches
    Church of St Dominic 292, 295
    Church of St Paul, ruins of 258, 275
    Protestant Church 177
    St Joseph's Church (Běijīng) 79
    St Joseph's Seminary Church (Macau) 292
    St Michael's Catholic Church (Qīngdǎo) 177
    St Michael's Church (Běijīng) 76
city walls 75, 145, 147, 160
climate 48, 396
Coloane 294-5, **302**
communism 355
communists 63

Confucian temples
    Běijīng 79
    Píngyáo 155-6
    Qūfù 172
    Xī'ān 131
Confucianism 149, 350, 362, 381-2
Confucius 171-4, 348-9
costs 49
courses 89-90, 311
courtyard hotels 93
credit cards 48, 399
Crescent Moon Lake 341
crime 401-2
Crouching Tiger, Hidden Dragon 244
cruises
    Three Gorges 190
    Victoria Harbour 15
    Yangzi River 15, 247-51
Cuàndìxià 110
Cultural Revolution 68, 356
culture 372-9
currency 48
customs regulations 394-5
cycling 313, 412-13

D

dangers, see safety
Dàtóng 40, 133, 163-5
Déhāng 315
demographics 361
Deng Xiaoping 356-7
dengue 396
deserts 385
diāolóu 309
Dōngchéng 63-81, 90-2, 93-5, **66-7**, **77**
Dowager Empress Cixi 352
Dragon's Backbone Rice Terraces 19, 308-10
drinking 58
drinks 177
driving licences 414
driving, see car travel

E

economy 346-7, 387-8
electricity 395
email services 47, 48, 398
Éméi Shān 334-6
emergencies 419, 420
Emperor Wu 349
Emperor Yongle 351
endangered species 386-7
entertainment 17
environmental issues 387-8
    climate change & travel 405
    coal 388
    desertification 387
    endangered species 386-7
    energy 387-8
    pollution 387-8
Ěrhǎi Hú 326
ethnic minorities 30, 308-9, 360-5
    Bai people 30, 326
    Hakka people 20, 259, 324
    Hui people 140
    Hui villages 191, 243, 244
    Miao people 30
    Naxi people 16, 30
    Naxi villages 30
    Yao villages 309
ethnic relations 347
events, see festivals & events
exchange rates 49

F

Fènghuáng 24, 39, 259, 316-20, **317**
ferries 410
festivals & events 42-5
    Běijīng International Literary Festival 43
    Běijīng Music Festival 100
    Chinese New Year 42
    Dragon Boat Festival 43
    Festival of Sacrifice (Kurban Bairam) 45

festivals & events *continued*
Formula One 43
Great Wall marathon 43
Lantern Festival 42
Macau Formula 3 Grand Prix 45
Man Hong Kong International Literary Festival 43
Monlam Great Prayer Festival 42, 339-40
Moon Festival 44
Peony Festival 43
Qīngdǎo International Beer Festival 44
Shànghǎi International Literary Festival 43
Spring Festival 42
Third Moon Festival 43
Torch Festival 44
films 47, 376-7
food 13, 17, 58, 366-73
Běijīng 58, 93-7
Cantonese 368
eastern China 369-70
Hong Kong 281-3
Hong Kong & the south 260
northern China 367-8
ordering 371
Peking duck 367
Píngyáo 129
Shànghǎi 210-12
Shànghǎi & the Yangzi region 190
southern China 368
table manners 372-3
vegetarian travellers 96, 373
western China 368-9
Xī'ān 139-41
Xī'ān & the north 132
Forbidden City 12, 56, 58, 68-73, **70**
Four Modernisations 356-7
free speech 347
French Concession 188, 191, 201-2, **204-5**

G

Gang of Four 356
Gate of Heavenly Peace 73-5
gay travellers 395
General Zhang Xueliang 355
Genghis Khan 63, 351
geology 384-5
getaways 21, 190
Giant Panda Breeding Research Base 26, 39, 334
giant pandas 26, 387
Grand Canal 349
Great Leap Forward 355
Great Wall 11, 22, 57, 111-23
accomodation 112
Bādáling 113-14
Chéngdé 119-23
history 112
Huánghuā 116-18
Jiànkòu 116
Jiāyùguān Fort 19, 341
Jīnshānling 115
Mùtiányù 114
Sīmǎtái 114-15
Great Yu 247
green card 404
Guǎngxī 19, 20
Guǎngzhōu 304-5
Guanyin (Goddess of Mercy) 118, 121, 231, 238, 382
Guilín 39, 41, 305-8
Gǔlàng Yǔ 28, 258, 322-4

H

Hakka people 20, 259, 324
Hakka Tǔlóu 20, 259, 324
Han Chinese 360-5
Han dynasty 349
Hángzhōu 31, 35, 37, 189, 229-35, **228-9**
accommodation 232-3
food 233-4
drinking 234
history 230
sights 230-2
travel to/from 234-5
travel within 235
harmony 347
health 395-8
health advisories 398
hepatitis A 396
hepatitis B 396
hiking 115, 116, 394
Déhāng 315
Huà Shān 148-9
Huángshān 189, 243-5
Lí River 314
Tài Shān 131, 169-70
Tiger Leaping Gorge 330-2
Wǔtái Shān 159
history 25, 348-57
holidays 400-1
Hong Kong 264-91, **265, 278-9**
accommodation 275-81
Admiralty 267-8, **272**
Central 267-8, **272**
drinking 284
entertainment 284-5
food 281-3
history 264
internet access 287
itineraries 39, 41, 269
Kowloon 269-71, **266**
Lantau 274-5
medical services 288
money 288
New Territories (New Kowloon) 271, 274
Peak Tram 268
post 288
Sheung Wan 267-8, **272**
shopping 285-92
sights 267-71, 274
Star Ferry 257-60, 282
tourist information 288
tours 274-5
travel to/from 288-9
travel within 289-91
Hong Kong Island 268-9, **278-9**
Hong Kong & the south 253-324, **255**

accommodation 260
architecture 260
drinking 260
food 260
highlights 256-9
islands 294-5
itineraries 262-3
planning 261
resources 261
safety 261
travel seasons 48
travel within 261
Hóngcūn 244
Hongwu 351
hotpot 369
Hu Jintao 357
Huà Shān 148-50
Huángshān 18, 189, 240, 242-4, **243**
Hui people 140
Hui villages 191, 243, 244
Huīzhōu villages 247
hútòng 27, 54-5

I

immigration 404
insurance 398-401
internet access 47, 48, 398-401
internet resources 47, 133, 191, 261, 390, 418
Islam 382-3
itineraries 33-41
Běijīng 69
Běijīng to Chuāndǐxià 61
Běijīng to Dàtóng 33
Běijīng to Hángzhōu 36
Běijīng to the Great Wall 60
Hong Kong 269
Hong Kong & the south 262-3
Hong Kong to Xī'ān 38-9
Hong Kong to Yángshuò 262
Luòyáng to Qīngdǎo 135
Shànghǎi 195
Shànghǎi to Hangzhou 34-5, 192
Shànghǎi to Hong Kong 40-1
Shànghǎi to Huángshān 193
Xī'ān to Luòyáng 134
Yángshuò to Yongdìng 263

J

Japanese B encephalitis 396
Jade Dragon Snow Mountain 16, 330
Jiāngsū 28
Jiànkou 57
Jiāyùguān Fort 19, 341
Jiuzhàigōu National Park 337

K

Kāipíng 309
Kang Youwei 352
Kashgar 342
Kowloon 269-71, **266**
Kublai Khan 63, 81, 351
Kūnmíng Lake 87
Kuomintang 353, 354, 355

L

Lama Temple 78
Lamma 284
languages 48, 62, 419-20
Lantau 274-5
Lánzhōu 338
legal matters 398-401
lesbian travellers 395
Lèshān 336-7
Lí River 20, 314
Li Yuan 350
lifestyle 364-5
Lìjiāng 325, 328-30, **328**
literature 47, 376
Liǔ Bang 349
Liǔ Xiaobo 347
Long March 354-5
Luòyáng 37, 150-5

M

Macartney, Lord 119
Macau 258, 291-304, **293**, **296-7**
accommodation 295-9
casinos 303
Coloane 294-5, **302**
drinking 299-300
food 299
history
internet access 300
itineraries
libraries 300
medical services 301
money 301
post 301
shopping
Taipa 294, **301**
tourist information 302
travel to/from 302-3
travel within 303-4
Macau Peninsula 292-304, **296-7**
malaria 396-7
Manchu 63, 351-2
Mao Zedong 63, 68, 74, 76, 355, 356
Marco Polo 230
Marco Polo Bridge 111
markets
Běijīng 103
Dōnghuámén 95
Fènghuáng 319
jade market 271
Kāifēng 17
Livestock Market 342
Shànghǎi 215
Stanley 269
Sunday market 342
Temple Street Night Market 270
Xī'ān 140
martial arts 99
mausoleums & memorials 76, 111, *see also* tombs
May Fourth Movement 354

measures 395
medical services 396
middle class 364-5
Miao people 30
Ming dynasty 28, 63, 351, 375
Ming Tombs 109-11
mobile phones 48, 402
Mògànshān 191, 235-7
Mógāo Caves 21, 341
money 48, 49, 395, 399-401
moneychangers 399-400
Mongol occupation 62, 63, 351
Moon Hill 323
mosques 136, 342
motorcycle travel 414
mountains 384-5
mountains, sacred 153
   Éméi Shān 334-6
   Huà Shān 148-50
   Tài Shān 40, 131, 169-71
   Wùtái Shān 30, 131, 159-62, **162**
museums
   Běijīng Police Museum 76
   Capital Museum 85
   China Great Wall Museum 113
   China National Museum 76
   Confucius Mansions 172-3
   Hong Kong Museum of Art 270
   Hong Kong Museum of History 270
   Luòyáng Museum 151
   Macau Museum of Art 293
   Ming Tombs Museum 110
   Monte Fort & Macau Museum 292
   Poly Art Museum 84
   Rìshēngchāng Financial House Museum 155
   Rockbund Art Museum 200
   Shaanxi History Museum 137
   Shànghǎi Museum 209
   Shànghǎi Art Museum 200

Shànghǎi History Museum 203
Shànghǎi Museum 203
Site of the 1st National Congress of the CCP 202
Stelae Museum 144
Sūzhōu 191, 226
Sūzhōu Silk Museum 222
Terracotta Warriors 143-5
Xī'ān Museum 137
music 47, 57
   Běijīng Music Festival 100
   Běijīng opera 83, 98-9
   Flower Drum opera 237
   Hong Kong 285

N

Nánjīng Massacre 355
Nanluogu Xiang 80
National Centre for the Performing Arts 57, 74
Naxi people 16
Naxi villages 30
New Territorites (New Kowloon) 271, 274
newspapers 395
Ngagong Tsunde 339
Northern Expedition 354-5

O

one-child policy 363
opening hours 394

P

painting 374-5
palaces
   Forbidden City 12, 56, 58, 68-73, **70**
   Summer Palace 56, 58, 86-9, **88**
parks
   Běihǎi Park 81-2
   Garden of the Master of the Nets 221-2
   Humble Administrator's Garden 222

Jingshān Park 58, 82
Lou Lim Loc Garden 294
Temple of Heaven Park 83
Victoria Park 268
Wàngchéng Park 151
Workers Cultural Palace 76-9
Yuen Po St Bird Garden 271
Yùyuán Gardens & Bazaar 201
passports 400, 402-3
Peak Tram 268
people 360-5
People's Republic of China 355
phonecards 402
photography 26
Píngyáo 23, 128-9, 155-60, **156**
   itineraries 33, 41
plains 385
planning 48-9, see also individual regions
   budgeting 49
   calendar of events 42-5
   China basics 48-9
   China's regions 367, 408
   children 358-9
   internet resources 47, 133, 191, 261, 390, 418
   itineraries 33-41
   resources 47
   travel seasons 48
plants 386
population 360-5
postal services 394
public holidays 400-1
Pǔdōng New Area 203-6
Puning Temple 118
Pǔtuóshān 238-40

Q

Qianlong 119
Qīngdǎo 176-81, **178**
Qing dynasty 23, 28, 63, 351-2, 376
Qin Shi Huang 149, 349
Qūfù 131, 171-5, **173**

R

rabies 397
radio 395
Red Guards 356
religion 380-3
   Buddhism 30, 350, 380-1
   Christianity 382
   Islam 382-3
   Taoism 381
Republic of China 353-4
residence permits 404
Revolutionary League 352
rivers 385
rock climbing 311
ruins of the Church of St Paul 258, 295

S

safety 359, 393, 401, 411
   Běijīng & the Great Wall 59
   Hong Kong & the south 261
   Shànghǎi & the Yangzi region 191
   Xī'ān & the north 133
scams 59, 191, 401
scenery 133
schistosomiasis (bilharzia) 397
senior travellers 395
Shang dynasty 348-9
Shànghǎi 194-220, 221, **196-9, 210**
   accommodation 206-10
   Bund 186-7, 195-200, 201
   children 214
   drinking 212-13
   entertainment 213-15
   food 210-12
   French Concession 188, 191, 201-2, **204-5**
   history 194
   internet access 216
   itineraries 35, 37, 40, 195
   medical services 216
   money 217

Old Town 201
People's Square 200
post 217
Pudōng New Area 203-6, **208**
shopping 201-2, 215-16
sights 195-206
Sūzhōu 35, 221-3, **224**
tourist information 217-18
tours 206
travel to/from 218-19
travel within 219-20, 223
Zhūjiājiao 188, 220-1
Shànghǎi & the Yangzi region 183-251, **185**
   accommodation 190
   drinking 190
   food 190
   highlights 186-9
   itineraries 192-3
   planning 191
   resources 191
   safety 191
   travel seasons 48
   travel within 191
Shen Congwen 316
shopping 29
   Běijīng & the Great Wall 59
   Hángzhōu 232
   Hong Kong 285-92
   Shànghǎi 201, 202, 215-16
   Xī'ān 141, 201-2
Sìchuān 325, 334-7
Silk Road 19, 325, 338-43
Singing Sands Mountain & Crescent Moon Lake 341
Sino-Japanese War 352
society 347
Song dynasty 230, 244, 350-1
Spring & Autumn period (722-481 BC) 349
Star Ferry 257-60, 282
Su Dongpo 230
Sui Yangdi 349
Summer Palace 56, 58, 86-9, **88**
Sun Yatsen 352-3, 354
Sūzhōu 35, 221-3, **224**

T

Tài Shān 40, 131, 169-71
Tài'ān 166-8
Taipa 294, **301**
Taiping War 352-3
Taizong 350
Tang dynasty 244, 350
Tāngkou 245-6
Taoism 381
taxis 414
telephone services 48, 402
Temple of Heaven 57
temples & monasteries 18, 338-9, 381
   A-Ma Temple 293
   Ancestor Worshipping Temple 155
   Big Goose Pagoda 137
   Chi Lin Nunnery 271
   Confucian Temple (Píngyáo) 155-6
   Confucius Temple (Běijīng) 79
   Confucius Temple (Qūfù) 172
   Confucius Temple (Xī'ān) 131
   Dài Temple 166
   Famén Temple 150
   Fayu Temple 238
   Fóguāng Temple 162-3
   Guāndì Temple 120
   Hanging Monastery 166
   Huáyán Temple 163
   Jade Buddha Temple 202
   Jīndìng Temple 335
   Jìngcí Temple 231
   Kun Iam Temple 294
   Labrang Monastery 339
   Lama Temple 78
   Léifēng Pagoda 231
   Língyin Temple 231-2
   Man Mo Temple 267
   Miàoyīng Temple White Dagoba 83
   Nánchán Temple 163
   Nánpūtuó Temple 320
   North Temple Pagoda 222
   Puji Temple 238

temples & monasteries
continued
Pǔlè Temple 121
Pǔníng Temple 118
Pǔtuózōngchéng Temple
58, 120-1
Puyòu Temple 121
Shuānglín Temple 158
Sik Sik Yuen Wong Tai Sin
Temple 271
Tǎyuàn Temple 161
Temple of Sumeru,
Happiness & Longevity
121
Temple of the Eight
Immortals 137
Tin Hau Temple 268, 270
West Garden Temple 222
White Cloud Temple 86
Wutái Shān 30, 131,
159-63
Xiānfēng Temple 335
Xiǎntōng Temple 164
Xītiān Fànjìng 82
Yong'ān Temple 82
Terracotta Warriors 13, 130,
134, 143-5
theft 401
Three Gorges 15, 39, 189, 190,
247-51
Three Gorges Dam 247, 251
Tiān'ānmén Square 63-8
Tiānzhú Peak Route 171
Tibet-Qīnghai plateau 15
Tiger Leaping Gorge 330-3
time 402
timeline 348-57
tipping 48, 400
tombs
Imperial Tombs 146-7
Ming Tombs 109-11
Tomb of Confucius 174
Tomb of Emperor Jingdi
146
Tóngli 191, 226-7, 229

town walls 145
train travel
to/from China 409,
410-11
within China 414,
415-18
Trans-Mongolian Railway
410-11
transport 401, 414-15
Trans-Siberian Railway
410-11
travel to/from China 404-11
travel within China 49,
411-18
travellers cheques 400
Treaty of Nanking 264
trekking, *see* hiking
tulóu 20, 259, 324
Túnxī 240-2
Tuó River 24
TV 395
typhoid 397

V

vacations 400-1
vaccinations 397
vegetarian travellers 96,
373
Victoria Harbour 15
Victoria Peak 268
visas 48, 402-4
volunteering 404

W

walking, *see* hiking
Wan Chai & Causeway Bay
276
Wànzhōu 248-9
Warring States period (475-
221 BC) 349
weather 42-5, 48, 396, *see
also individual regions*
websites, *see* internet
resources
weights 395

Wen Jiabao 357
West Lake 31, 189, 230-1
West Sea Canyon 245
wi-fi 48
wildlife 385, *see also* animals
women in China 362-4
women travellers 401
work 403, 404
Wu, Emperor 349
Wu Zetian 350
Wutái Shān 30, 131, 159-62,
162
Wùyuán 25, 247
Wūzhèn 237

X

Xiàhé 338-40, **340**
Xiàmén 319-21, **321**
Xī'ān 136-48, **138**
accommodation 137-9
city walls 147
drinking 141
entertainment 141
food 139-41
itineraries 37, 39, 41
Muslim Quarter 140
shopping 141
sights 136
tours 147-8
travel to/from 141-2
travel within 143
Xī'ān & the north 125-81,
127
accommodation 132
food 132
highlights 128-31
itineraries 134-5
planning 133
resources 133
safety 133
travel seasons 48
travel within 133
Xīchéng 81-3
Xīdì 244
Xuanzong 350

Y

Yang Jian 349
Yángshuò 24, 259, 311-14, **312**
Yangzi dolphin 386
Yangzi River 15, 189, 247-51
Yao villages 309
Yíchāng 39, 248-9, 251

Yongle, Emperor 351
Yuan dynasty 351
Yuan Shikai 353
Yùlóng River 24, 315
Yúlóng Xuěshān 16, 330
Yúngāng Caves 29, 130, 165
Yúnnán 325, 326-43, **327**

Z

Zhang Xueliang, General 355
Zhéjiāng 28
Zhou people 349
Zhu Yuanzhang, Emperor 351
Zhuang villages 309
Zhūjiājiao 188, 220-1

How to Use This Book

These symbols will help you find the listings you want:

- ⊙ Sights
- ✪ Activities
- 🎓 Courses
- 🎯 Tours
- 🎪 Festivals & Events
- 🛏 Sleeping
- 🍴 Eating
- 🍷 Drinking
- 🎭 Entertainment
- 🛍 Shopping
- ℹ Information/Transport

Look out for these icons:

- **FREE** No payment required
- 🌿 A green or sustainable option

Our authors have nominated these places as demonstrating a strong commitment to sustainability – for example by supporting local communities and producers, operating in an environmentally friendly way, or supporting conservation projects.

These symbols give you the vital information for each listing:

- ☎ Telephone Numbers
- ⊙ Opening Hours
- ℗ Parking
- ⊖ Nonsmoking
- ❄ Air-Conditioning
- @ Internet Access
- 🛜 Wi-Fi Access
- 🏊 Swimming Pool
- 🌱 Vegetarian Selection
- 🍴 English-Language Menu
- 👪 Family-Friendly
- 🐾 Pet-Friendly
- 🚌 Bus
- ⛴ Ferry
- Ⓜ Metro
- Ⓢ Subway
- 🚇 London Tube
- 🚊 Tram
- 🚆 Train

Reviews are organised by author preference.

Map Legend

Sights
- 🏖 Beach
- ☸ Buddhist
- 🏰 Castle
- ✝ Christian
- 🕉 Hindu
- ☪ Islamic
- ✡ Jewish
- 🗿 Monument
- 🏛 Museum/Gallery
- Ⓡ Ruin
- 🍷 Winery/Vineyard
- 🦁 Zoo
- ⊙ Other Sight

Activities, Courses & Tours
- 🤿 Diving/Snorkelling
- 🛶 Canoeing/Kayaking
- ⛷ Skiing
- 🏄 Surfing
- 🏊 Swimming/Pool
- 🚶 Walking
- 🏄 Windsurfing
- • Other Activity/Course/Tour

Sleeping
- 🛏 Sleeping
- 🏕 Camping

Eating
- 🍴 Eating

Drinking
- ☕ Drinking
- ☕ Cafe

Entertainment
- 🎭 Entertainment

Shopping
- 🛍 Shopping

Information
- 🏦 Bank
- 🏛 Embassy/Consulate
- ✚ Hospital/Medical
- @ Internet
- 👮 Police
- ✉ Post Office
- ☎ Telephone
- 🚻 Toilet
- ℹ Tourist Information
- • Other Information

Transport
- ✈ Airport
- ⊗ Border Crossing
- 🚌 Bus
- Cable Car/Funicular
- Cycling
- Ferry
- Ⓜ Metro
- Monorail
- ℗ Parking
- ⛽ Petrol Station
- 🚕 Taxi
- Train/Railway
- Tram
- • Other Transport

Routes
- Tollway
- Freeway
- Primary
- Secondary
- Tertiary
- Lane
- Unsealed Road
- Plaza/Mall
- Steps
-)=(Tunnel
- Pedestrian Overpass
- Walking Tour
- Walking Tour Detour
- Path

Geographic
- 🏠 Hut/Shelter
- 🚨 Lighthouse
- 👁 Lookout
- ▲ Mountain/Volcano
- ⊙ Oasis
- 🌳 Park
-)(Pass
- 🏕 Picnic Area
- 💧 Waterfall

Population
- ◉ Capital (National)
- ◉ Capital (State/Province)
- ● City/Large Town
- ∘ Town/Village

Boundaries
- — — — International
- — — — State/Province
- — — Disputed
- Regional/Suburb
- Marine Park
- Cliff
- Wall

Hydrography
- River/Creek
- Intermittent River
- Swamp/Mangrove
- Reef
- Canal
- Water
- Dry/Salt/Intermittent Lake
- Glacier

Areas
- Beach/Desert
- Cemetery (Christian)
- Cemetery (Other)
- Park/Forest
- Sportsground
- Sight (Building)
- Top Sight (Building)

DAVID EIMER

Shaanxi (Shǎnxī), Húnán, Yúnnán David first came to China in 1988. Since then, he has travelled across the country, from the far west to the Russian and Korean borders in the northeast, through the south and southwest and along the eastern coast. After stints as a journalist in LA and London, he succumbed to his fascination with China in 2005 and moved to Běijīng. As well as contributing to newspapers and magazines, David worked on the last edition of *China* for Lonely Planet, has co-authored the *Beijing* and *Shanghai* city guides and wrote the most recent *Beijing Encounter*.

SHAWN LOW

Shāndōng, Jiāngsū, Fújiàn, Ānhuī Shawn left his Singapore home for Melbourne and made his way into Lonely Planet as a book editor. Since then, he's done a stint as a commissioning editor, authored guides to Singapore and Southeast Asia, and is now the Asia-Pacific Travel Editor for Lonely Planet. His fascination with China began after he was dispatched to Yúnnán to host an episode of National Geographic & Lonely Planet's *Roads Less Travelled*. Returning to China for authoring felt like an obvious thing to do – so he did.

DANIEL MCCROHAN

Sìchuān, Chóngqìng Daniel trained as journalist in the UK and worked for several years on newspapers before turning to travel writing. An Asia fanatic, he travelled extensively throughout the continent for more than 15 years before settling down in China in 2005. He now lives with his wife and their children in a courtyard home in one of Běijīng's *hútòng* alleyways. Daniel has worked on Lonely Planet guides to China, India, Shànghǎi and Tibet. He also worked as a presenter for the Lonely Planet TV series *Best in China*. Find him on danielmccrohan.com.

CHRISTOPHER PITTS

Shànghǎi A Philadelphia native, Chris started off his university years studying classical Chinese poetry before a week in 1990s Shànghǎi (en route to school in Kūnmíng) abruptly changed his focus to the idiosyncrasies of modern China. After spending several years in Asia memorising Chinese characters, he abruptly traded it all in and moved to Paris, where he currently lives with his family, Perrine, Elliot and Céleste. He works as a freelance writer, editor and translator for various publishers. Visit his website at www.christopherpitts.net.

Our Story

A beat-up old car, a few dollars in the pocket and a sense of adventure. In 1972 that's all Tony and Maureen Wheeler needed for the trip of a lifetime – across Europe and Asia overland to Australia. It took several months, and at the end – broke but inspired – they sat at their kitchen table writing and stapling together their first travel guide, *Across Asia on the Cheap*. Within a week they'd sold 1500 copies. Lonely Planet was born.

Today, Lonely Planet has offices in Melbourne, London and Oakland, with more than 600 staff and writers. We share Tony's belief that 'a great guidebook should do three things: inform, educate and amuse'.

Our Writers

DAMIAN HARPER

Coordinating author, Běijīng, the Great Wall, the Yangzi, Gānsù After graduating with a degree in Chinese (modern and classical) from London's School of Oriental and African Studies, Damian moved to pre-handover Hong Kong before embarking on an epic nine-province journey for the 6th edition of Lonely Planet *China*. Since then he has worked on five further editions and has worked in Shànghǎi and Běijīng (developing a Mandarin accent somewhere between the two), contributing to multiple editions of the Lonely Planet *Beijing* and *Shanghai* city guides.

PIERA CHEN

Hong Kong, Macau Piera has been travelling to Macau since she was six. Over the years, while working in Hong Kong, it was poetry readings, *fado* concerts, and a masterfully executed *pato de cabidela* (duck stewed in its own blood) that kept luring her back. For this book, she spoke to insiders of the casino industry, and scoured the streets for indie music dives, art spaces and other unpolished gems. Piera also co-authored the 14th Lonely Planet *Hong Kong & Macau* city guide.

CHUNG WAH CHOW

Guǎngdōng, Guǎngxī Chung Wah is a Hong Kong native who has travelled extensively in the mainland. The sheer diversity of China's languages has always fascinated her. Cantonese, Hakka, Tai, Uighur, Teochew and Hokkien – she loves them all. With an advanced degree in translation studies, a penchant for travel and discovering new sounds and words, Chung Wah merged her talents by becoming a travel writer. She contributed to the previous Lonely Planet edition of *China* and co-authored Lonely Planet's *Hong Kong & Macau* city guide.

DAISY HARPER

Zhèjiāng, Shānxī, Húběi Daisy grew up in the old town of balmy Qīngdǎo on the Shāndōng coast before studying for four years at Běijīng Normal University. She moved to London in the mid-1990s but her seaside roots see her holidaying occasionally in Brighton, Hastings, Margate and even Bournemouth. Daisy has also lived in Shànghǎi, Běijīng, Hong Kong and Singapore and returns to China frequently to visit family and friends and to journey across her homeland. Married with two children, she has worked on two editions of Lonely Planet's *China*.

 More Writers ....

Published by Lonely Planet Publications Pty Ltd
ABN 36 005 607 983
1st edition – July 2011
ISBN 978 1 74220 289 1
© Lonely Planet 2011   Photographs © as indicated 2011
10 9 8 7 6 5 4 3 2 1
Printed in Singapore

Although the authors and Lonely Planet have taken all reasonable care in preparing this book, we make no warranty about the accuracy or completeness of its content and, to the maximum extent permitted, disclaim all liability arising from its use.